The New Era of
Investment Banking

INDUSTRY

STRUCTURE,

TRENDS AND

PERFORMANCE

Raymond H. Rupert

Editor

PROBUS PUBLISHING COMPANY
Chicago, Illinois
Cambridge, England

Dedicated to Pearl Rupert

Table of Contents

Part IX: Trends in Structuring Complex Financings

Part X: The High Yield and Below Investment Grade Markets

Part XI: Financial Distress

Part XII: The Valuation Process

Acknowledgements

This book has been a valuable personal experience. I have many individuals to thank. First, I would like to thank Michael Jeffers of Probus Publishing Company for supporting this project. I would like to thank all of the team members at Probus for their professionalism and help in getting the job done. Included are my senior editor, Marlene Chamberlain; my production manager, Kevin Thornton; my copy editor, Maria Romano; and my production editor, Teresa A. Quick.

The contributors to the book have been very generous. They have demonstrated their expertise through their well-crafted contributions. I thank all of them as well as the institutions, companies and firms in which they work for allowing them to participate in this book. It has been good working with them.

In addition, I would like to thank Gordon Sharwood and Ken Cutts of Sharwood and Company for having generously welcomed me into the industry. I would like to thank Emile Van Nispen, Michael Gundy and Hugh Wilmer, principals of Gundy & Associates, for their support while I venture off into my publishing enterprises.

I owe special thanks to my wife, Bonnie Stern, for her encouragement and support, and to my children, Fara, Mark and Anna, for their frequent, welcome and friendly interruptions. Thanks also to Max Stern for his enjoyable, in-depth discussion of business, ethics and values.

To my secretary, Dale Colacci, and to my word processing consultant, Tony Koch of Pagecraft, I owe thanks for their diligent efforts in working on this project.

Introduction

The New Era of Investment Banking is an important new book that describes the current issues and key trends in the U.S. investment banking industry. In the post-Milken era, the investment banking industry has been defined by a global recession, a period of severe credit contraction, the previously "unthinkable" restructuring of many former industrial giants, a generational change in political leadership and a shift to a global capital markets orientation. In response to these influences, the investment banking industry—which is complex, tightly regulated and very competitive—has had to change. This book describes those significant changes.

Historically, the investment banking business had been based on relationships with customers. The shift to transaction-based investment banking was created by the relative effectiveness of highly competitive houses in getting the business, sourcing capital, underwriting new issues and completing mergers and acquisitions. As a result, the investment banking industry has shown that financial engineering can create jobs, finance infrastructure, facilitate employee ownership of companies, and build world-class competitors. However, these positive impacts are often overlooked. This book shows what the investment banking business can do for the U.S. economy and how investment bankers serve their customers.

From the outset, the objective has been to produce a high-quality, lucid text that would deliver an accurate snapshot of activities in each of the major segments of the investment banking industry ranging from mergers and acquisitions to valuations. Another objective has been to provide a forecast of where the U.S. investment banking industry is heading. The book has combined the collective knowledge of the "best and brightest" in the industry to draw meaningful conclusions. It is written in non-technical language and is organized to provide the reader with an in-depth understanding of industry structure, trends, performance, regulations, and products.

The contributors to *The New Era of Investment Banking* are bankers, advisors, analysts, academics, publishers, investors and intermediaries who form the "knowledge infrastructure" of the investment banking industry. The contributors have been very generous with their experience and expertise. They have reduced the complex legal, technical, strategic, structural and tax aspects of corporate finance into an easily understood format. This book has been written for the business person interested in learning more about structuring, analyzing, and financing transactions.

The book is organized into several logically integrated sections. The first section explores the current economic and financial environment. Included is a description of the economic overhangs from the 1980s and their impact on the 1990s. This is followed by discussions of capital adequacy and consolidation within the banking sector, the role of foreign banks in the domestic banking sector, and, ironically, the investment opportunities that currently exist in savings institutions.

In this new financial environment, institutional investors have lost their traditional exit from investments by not being able to exercise the "Wall Street walk," and have been forced into the role of relationship investors. In their new roles as activist shareholders, institutional investors are making an impact on boards of directors and management through the corporate governance process. This significant trend is highlighted in the book. In addition, the book describes how institutional investors have committed to both private equity and venture capital.

The book describes the amounts invested in these classes of alternative assets, the returns, and the current attitudes of the investors.

Another topic included in the book is the Securities and Exchange Commission ("SEC") regulation of the U.S. capital markets. This section provides a comprehensive outline of recent regulatory changes in topics ranging from "blank check offerings" to cross-border tender offers and American Depositary Receipts.

In response to financial uncertainty, the book describes how investment banking firms act to manage both operating and market risk. Investment banking firms can incur a crisis very quickly if they overextend themselves, misread the markets, or fail to comply with regulations. This section describes how investment banking firms operate within a complex network of financial institutions and attempt to profit from market inefficiencies. The book also describes the risks of legal liability that investment bankers face in performing their jobs. The expert contributors provide an approach to understanding legal liability in a mergers and acquisitions context.

In addition, the book targets several very important new areas of business, including trends in merchant banking in the 1990s, the financial restructuring of companies in distress, reversing leveraged buyouts, and the opportunities in privatizations. Another area that is examined is the management of strategic communications in initial public offerings and in bank mergers. The "spin doctors" have an important role in the successful management of communications involving investments and transactions.

It is recognized that success in winning the business and completing financings is often based on "smart" innovations. Accordingly, the book contains a section on the financial engineering of new financial instruments. It provides an outline of corporate securities innovation ranging from the development of liquid yield options notes (LYONs™) to the use of hybrid debt in managing corporate risk. Other complex financing such as asset backed securities, private placements and employee stock ownership plans (ESOPs) are also examined. Examples are provided to clearly illustrate these types of financings. In addition, a leading tax expert reviews cross-border federal tax issues that are important in developing innovative financings.

Another significant opportunity examined in the book is investment in distressed securities. This section describes how to separate the jewels from the junk (bonds) and how to profit from investing in the securities of distressed and bankrupt companies. It explores emerging trends in bankruptcy reorganization, and describes the historic rating drift and outcome of high-yield bonds.

Valuation is of great importance in any investment. The book describes the valuation process and recent trends in transaction activity. Furthermore, the real estate industry has been hard hit by oversupply and a realignment of values. A chapter is dedicated to describing trends in real estate values, changes in the appraisal process, and valuation techniques for soft markets. This section concludes with the valuation methodology for thinly traded fixed income securities.

Other areas of significant interest to investment bankers are the mergers and acquisitions ("M&A") and the buyouts markets. Both markets peaked in 1989 with about $244 billion in total dollar volume. However, this had slowed to about $98 billion in 1991. The book explores historic and forecast trends in mergers and acquisitions. One segment of the M&A field that is chosen for special emphasis is the middle market buyout. A leading investment banker summarizes the middle market buyout activity over the past five years, defines the unique characteristics of middle market deals and describes the opportunities that exist in working with this group of companies.

Another trend that is examined is the shift by corporate and financial buyers into crossborder deals as U.S. mergers and acquisitions activity slowed. The book describes how crossborder deals are different. Another chapter provides a detailed case study of a transaction led by a U.S. buyout group that purchased a mid-market multinational company in a very complicated, risky and legally expensive transaction. Happily, the same financial buyout group sold the company within two years, making over $100 million in the process.

The book concludes with a complete ranking of the top 25 U.S. investment banking firms.

About the Editor

Raymond H. Rupert

Raymond Rupert is an investment banker and business writer. He is Managing Director at BAMF Corporation (an investment banking firm in Toronto, Ontario). He is actively involved in corporate finance advisory work, crossborder mergers and acquisitions, crossborder private placements and project financings. He is a regular contributor to *Mergers and Acquisitions* in Canada and *The Treasury Management Review*. Dr. Rupert has lectured at the Business School at the University of Toronto and for the Ontario Institute of Chartered Accountants. He has graduate degrees from the University of Toronto in Medicine and Business Administration. Dr. Rupert's previous book is *The Canadian Investment Banking Review* (McGraw-Hill Ryerson 1992).

About the Contributors

Edward J. Abahoonie

Mr. Edward J. Abahoonie is a Partner with Coopers & Lybrand in New York City. Mr. Abahoonie specializes in corporate taxation, mergers and acquisitions and financial restructurings. He is a member of the American Institute of CPAs' Corporations and Shareholders Taxation Committee and chairs its troubled companies working group.

Edward I. Altman

Dr. Edward I. Altman is the Max L. Heine Professor of Finance at the Stern School of Business, New York University. Dr. Altman has an international reputation as an expert on corporate bankruptcy and credit analysis. Dr. Altman is Editor of the *Journal of Banking and Finance*. He is the current editor of the *Handbook of Corporate Finance* (1986) and the *Handbook of Financial Markets and Institutions* (1987). Dr. Altman's most recent books include: *Corporate Financial Distress, Recent Advances in Corporate Finance, Investing in Junk Bonds: Inside the High Debt Market, Default Risk, Mortality Rates and the Performance of Corporate Bonds* and *Distressed Securities: Analyzing and Evaluating Market Potential and Investment Risk.*

Mark E. Bachmann

Mr. Mark E. Bachmann is a Managing Director in the Debt Rating Services Division of Standard & Poor's Corporation. He has responsibility for fixed income ratings on all domestic securities firms, and is a member of both S&P's Rating Policy Board and the Financial Institutions Criteria Committee. Mr. Bachmann joined S&P in 1982 in the corporate finance department had various managerial and analytic responsibilities for ratings in the retailing, media, leisure and consumer products industries. He has also had extensive experience in the analysis of high-yield bonds. Mr. Bachmann is a Chartered Financial Analyst and has an M.B.A. in Finance from New York University.

George J. Benston

Dr. George J. Benston is the John H. Harland Professor of Finance, Accounting and Economics at the Emory Business School and Professor of Economics in the College of Emory University, Atlanta, GA. Dr. Benston serves as Area Coordinator for Finance and Accounting and was Associate Dean for Research and Faculty Development. His Ph.D. is from the University of Chicago (finance and economics); his M.B.A. from New York University (accounting); and his B.A. from Queens College (liberal arts and accounting). He is a CPA (North Carolina). Dr. Benston's most recent book is *The Separation of Commercial and Investment Banking: The Glass-Steagall Act Revisited and Reconsidered* (Oxford Press, 1990).

Robert E. Bostrom

Mr. Robert E. Bostrom is Executive Vice President Legal and Regulatory and General Counsel National Westminster Bancorp. Mr. Bostrom has experience in government and private practice in the bank regulatory area and advises clients, including foreign banks and their branches and agencies, on legislative and regulatory developments, strategic planning, powers and activities, bank mergers and acquisitions, and the formation of banks. He was formerly an attorney with the Federal Reserve Bank of New York and has been in private practice since 1982. He has a B.A. with honors from Franklin & Marshall College, an M.I.A. from the School of International Affairs, Columbia University, and a J.D., cum laude, from Boston College Law School.

Judy Brennan

Ms. Judy Brennan has practised corporate and financial communications for more than 10 years. She is a vice president at Ogilvy Adams & Rinehart, a leading full-service public relations agency. Her expertise lies in corporate positioning, public affairs, media and investor relations, and merger communications. Ms. Brennan holds a B.A. with honors in history from Hunter College.

Christopher Chase

Mr. Christopher Chase is a Vice President in the Mergers and Acquisitions Department at Salomon Brothers Inc. Mr. Chase has advised domestic and international clients in a variety of transactions including acquisitions, divestitures, mergers and privatizations. He recently completed an assignment for the Defense Ministry of Argentina regarding the privatization of the national steel company, Sociedad Mixta Siderurgia Argentina (SOMISA). Mr. Chase holds a B.A., magna cum laude, from Harvard College and an M.B.A. in Finance from Columbia Graduate School of Business.

Donald H. Chew, Jr.

Dr. Donald H. Chew is a founding partner of Stern Stewart & Co., a New York based corporate financial advisory firm specializing in valuation, restructuring and incentive compensation. Dr. Chew is founding Editor-in-Chief of the Continental Bank's *Journal of Applied Corporate Finance*. He holds a Ph.D. in English literature as well as an M.B.A. in Finance from the University of Rochester.

Emanuele Costa

Mr. Emanuele Costa, co-founder of Overseas Partners, is the Principal in charge of its North American Operations. Previously, Mr. Costa was co-owner and held various senior positions with the Costa Group, a large Italian company with interests in transportation, textiles, food, construction and real estate. Among other positions, Mr. Costa was President of Costa Cruise Lines, Inc., a U.S. subsidiary of the Costa Group. Mr. Costa holds a degree in business administration from the University of Genoa.

Neil D. Dabney

Mr. Neil D. Dabney is President and a co-founder of Dabney/Resnick and Wagner, Inc. (DRW). Mr. Dabney specializes in fixed income portfolio management for high net worth individuals and institutional investors. Previously, he was director of the private investor group and a senior vice president in the high-yield bond department at Drexel Burnham Lambert Mr. Dabney began his career in 1975 and spent his early years at E.F. Hutton and Oppenheimer. For the past ten years, he has focused on research and investment strategy for special situations and distressed debt securities. He received a B.A. in Economics and Psychology from Claremont Men's College in 1974. At DRW Mr. Dabney oversees investment selection and client relations.

Patrick F. Dolan

Mr. Patrick F. Dolan is a senior manager in the valuation and appraisal group in the New York office tax department of KPMG Peat Marwick, and is responsible for going concern valuations. He has performed or directed the valuation of approximately 300 companies in varying fields. Mr. Dolan values closely held companies or subsidiaries of public companies operating diverse businesses ranging from manufacturing to banking. The business valuations which Mr. Dolan performs assist clients in developing bidding price strategies, selling price strategies and recapitalization alternatives; he assists clients in negotiating the sale of minority or majority blocks of stock, establishing an employee stock ownership plan and estimating gift or estate tax liability. Mr. Dolan is a graduate of the London School of Accountancy and is a fellow of the Chartered Association of Certified Accountants (U.K.). He received an MBA in corporate finance from Columbia Business School.

Duncan O. Douglas

Mr. Duncan O. Douglas is Director of Research for the Real Estate Advisory Group. In addition to project management and appraisal of portfolios, he is responsible for monitoring investment criteria and trends in the real estate investment field. He designs and implements report format and computer assisted modelling techniques for appraising investment real estate. Mr. Dougalas has extensive experience appraising investment real estate and is involved in the valuation of over one billion dollars of real estate property annually. Mr. Douglas joined American Appraisal Associates in 1988, serving the Minneapolis Real Estate Valuation Group as a senior appraiser. Before joining the firm, he worked as a commercial appraiser for three years at a major midwest banking company. He also spent five years appraising commercial and investment property in south central Ontario.

Michael Druckman

Mr. Michael Druckman was Vice President, Chief Financial Officer of Wallace & Tiernan Group, Inc. from 1989–1992. From 1982–1989, Mr. Druckman was with Matrix Corporation, his last four years as Vice President and Chief Financial Officer. Matrix was a publicly held multinational manufacturer of electronic imaging equipment with sales in excess of $100 million when it was acquired in 1988. Prior to joining Matrix, Mr. Druckman was with Exxon Office Systems and the accounting firm of Coopers & Lybrand. Mr. Druckman graduated, magna cum laude, from Boston University in 1972.

Peter M. Faulkner

Mr. Peter M. Faulkner is the head of distressed securities at Alex. Brown & Sons. Mr. Faulkner has been trading and analyzing bankrupt situations since 1983. He joined Alex. Brown in 1992 from Herzog, Heine where he worked as head of bankruptcies from 1983 to 1992. He has been involved in every major bankruptcy beginning with Penn Central. Mr. Faulkner has a B.S.F.S. from Georgetown University.

John D. Finnerty

Dr. John D. Finnerty is a General Partner of McFarland Dewey & Co., an investment banking firm in New York City, and is a Professor of Finance at Fordham University. Dr. Finnerty received an M.A. in economics from Cambridge University, which he attended under a Marshall Scholarship, and a Ph.D. in operations research from the Naval Postgraduate School. He has worked for Morgan Stanley & Co., Lazard Freres & Co., and as Executive Vice President and Chief Financial Officer of College Savings Bank, of which he was also a Director. He is a past president of the Fixed Income Analysts Society.

Patrick J. Foye

Mr. Patrick J. Foye is a partner with the legal firm of Skadden, Arps, Slate, Meagher & Flom, where he has worked from 1989 to the present. He is a graduate of the J.D. Fordham Law School, 1981 (Associate Editor, *Fordham Law Review)*, and holds a B.A. from Fordham College (1978). His areas of expertise are mergers and acquisitions, privatizations and foreign investment. He has worked on the levereged buyouts of Electrolux Corp., The Grand Union Company and Amstar Corporation, the acquisition of General Foods by Philip Morris Companies; the privatization of Maley Hungarian Airlines and the sale of shares to Alitalla; the sale of Amstar Sugar Corporation to Tate & Lyle, plc.; the acquisition of Praxis Biologics, Inc., by American Cyanamid Com-

pany; and the acquisition of The Regina Company, which was in Chapter 11 bankruptcy.

Edward J. Frydl

Mr. Edward J. Frydl is vice president and an assistant director of research at the Federal Reserve Bank of New York. He is responsible for financial policy studies. Mr. Frydl joined the New York Fed in September 1973 as an economist in the foreign research division. Mr. Frydl was named an officer with the title of manager in the financial markets department in January 1981. In August 1983, he was appointed assistant vice president of the research and statistics area. He was named assistant director of research in January 1984, and appointed vice president in July 1985. He earned a bachelor of arts degree in economics from Boston College, Chestnut Hill, Massachussetts, in 1969 and pursued graduate studies in economics at the Massachusetts Institute of Technology between 1969 and 1973.

Steven P. Galante

Mr. Steven P. Galante is editor and publisher of *The Private Equity Analyst* newsletter,which covers the private equity asset class from the viewpoint of the institutional investor. Mr. Galante is also the founder and president of Asset Alternatives, Inc., the West Newton, Massachusetts, information and research company that publishes *The Private Equity Analyst.* Prior to establishing Asset Alternatives in 1991, Mr. Galante was Vice President of Publications and Conferences at Venture Economics, Inc., Needham, Massachusetts. Previously, Mr. Galante was an editor and reporter for nine years at *The Wall Street Journal* in New York, where he wrote a weekly column on small business. He holds an M.B.A. from New York University and a B.A. from Syracuse University.

Gary J. Gartner

Mr. Gary J. Gartner is Resident Counsel with Goodman Freeman Phillips & Vineberg (New York), a joint venture of Goodman and Goodman (Toronto), Phillips & Vineberg (Montreal), and Freeman & Company (Vancouver). He practices in the area of United States international income tax law and has written and lectured on the topic. Mr.Gartner is admitted to practice in both the United States and Canada and is chairman of the income tax subsection of the New York State Bar Association International Law and Practice Section.

Michael L. Geczi

Mr. Michael L. Geczi is a Managing Director at Ogilvy Adams & Rinehart, a corporate and financial public relations firm. He has experience in advising large corporations on their communications requirements, including communications for initial public offerings, mergers and acquisitions, financial services, special situations and investor relations. Prior to joining Adams & Rinehart in 1989, he was vice president of media relations at Merrill Lynch Capital Markets and director of corporate communications at Midlantic National Bank. Before entering the corporate communications field, Mr. Geczi was a financial journalist for 16 years.

Peter G. Gould

Peter G. Gould is a Principal of Overseas Partner, Inc., in New York. Previously he has been President and CEO of Exxel Container, Inc. and held several positions with the Burroughs Corporation, including Chairman and CEO of its Plasma Graphics Corporation subsidiary and Corporate Director of Strategic Planning. He served the U.S. Government in the 1970's as Deputy Assistant Secretary of Commerce for Export Development. Mr. Gould holds a degree in Economics from Swarthmore College.

David W. Halstead

Mr. David W. Halstead is a Managing Director at Continental Bank in Chicago. He is responsible for all of the bank's asset securitization, long-term finance and lease capital activities. Mr. Halstead has been directly involved in asset securitization since the formation of the bank's specialty unit in 1986 and is a frequent speaker on the topic. Mr. Halstead received his B.A. from Cortland College in 1976 and his M.B.A. from Cornell University in 1978.

Sara Hanks

Ms. Sara Hanks is a partner in the international law firm, Rogers & Wells, based in New York. Prior to joining Rogers & Wells, Ms. Hanks was Chief of the Office of International Corporate Finance of the Securities and Exchange Commission. Ms. Hanks' practice focuses on public and private capital-raising by U.S. and foreign companies, with an emphasis on crossborder corporate finance. Her clients include U.S. and domestic companies and investment banks. Ms. Hanks is a frequent writer and speaker on the subject of securities regulation. She is a graduate of Oxford University's School of Jurisprudence, a member of the District of Columbia Bar and a solicitor of the Supreme Court of England and Wales.

Robert H. Herz

Mr. Robert H. Herz is a Partner with Coopers & Lybrand in New York City. He is a member of the American Institute of CPAs, a fellow of the Institute of Chartered Accountants in England and Wales and serves on the Financial Accounting Standards Board financial instruments task force.

Jared Kaplan

Mr. Jared Kaplan is a senior partner in the Chicago office of the national law firm of Keck, Mahin & Cate and is a graduate of UCLA and the Harvard Law School. Mr. Kaplan has written and lectured extensively on Employee Stock Ownership Plans (ESOPs). He is a co-author of the Bureau of National Affairs Tax Portfolio on Employee Stock Ownership Plans and of the portfolio on Corporate Acquisition-Interest Deduction, and co-editor-in-chief of Callaghan's *Federal Tax Guide*. Mr. Kaplan is past Chairman of the Administrative Practice Committee of the American Bar Association. He currently serves on the Board of Advisors of the *Corporate Taxation* journal and on the Board of Editors of the National Center for Employee Ownership's *Journal of Employee Ownership Law and Finance*.

Scott H. Lang

Mr. Scott H. Lang is an executive vice president and head of investment banking at Rodman and Renshaw. Mr. Lang founded the Rodman and Renshaw investment banking department when he joined the firm in 1985. Mr. Lang is a member of the Board of Directors and the Executive Committee of Rodman and Renshaw. He was a partner in the Washington, D.C., law firm of Arnold and Porter, and prior to that he was Assistant General Counsel at the U.S. Department of Energy. Mr. Lang received his B.A. from Harvard College and his J.D. from Harvard Law School.

Harvey Mallement

Mr. Harvey Mallement is Senior Managing Partner of Harvest Ventures which he co-founded in 1980. Harvest Ventures, a private equity firm specializing in buyouts and expansion financings, is the General Partner of several limited partnerships with capital aggregating in excess of $100 million from major Western European financial institutions and industrial companies. Previously, Mr. Mallement was the Managing Partner of Masco Associates, a private investment banking and venture capital firm. He is a director of Corporate Development for Ward Foods, Inc., and a Certified Public Accountant who worked on the professional staff of Coopers &

Lybrand. Mr. Mallement is currently a member of the Board of Directors and Executive Committee of Symbol Technologies, Chairman of the Board of Industrial Ceramics and a Director of several other privately held companies.

Marsha Matthews

Ms. Marsha Matthews is an associate lawyer in the New York office of the national law firm of Keck, Mahin & Cate. She assisted Jared Kaplan, senior partner, in the preparation of the chapter on ESOP Advantage: Tax, Legal and Financial Issues. She is a graduate of the University of Virginia and received her J.D. from the College of William and Mary.

Diane R. Maurice

Ms. Diane R. Maurice is a Vice President of Generale Bank's New York corporate division, where she is responsible for structuring and placing syndicated credits and private placements. Ms. Maurice has considerable experience in advising corporations on their financing requirements and has been involved in asset securitization, leveraged buy-outs and project financing. Prior to working at Generale Bank, which is the largest bank in Belgium, Ms. Maurice was with Lloyds Bank and Standard and Poor's Corporation, holding positions in New York and abroad. Ms. Maurice holds two advanced degrees, including a Masters from the London School of Economics.

Penny Mavridis

Ms. Penny Mavridis is a tax associate with Goodman Freeman Phillips & Vineberg (New York). Ms. Mavridis practices in the area of United States international income tax law and has co-authored articles for *The Journal of Taxation, Corporate Taxation,* and *Tax Management International Journal.* Ms. Mavridis is a graduate of New York University (B.A., 1983), Boston University School of Law (J.D., 1986) and New York University of Law (L.L.M., 1991).

John J. McConnell

Dr. John J. McConnell is Emanuel T. Weiler Professor of Management and Director of Doctoral Programs and Research at the Krannert School of Management at Purdue University. Dr. McConnell has served as a member of the Board of Directors of the Federal Home Loan Bank of Indianapolis and the American Finance Association, and has served as a consultant in the valuation and analysis of mortgage-backed securities and other complex financial instruments. He is Associate Editor of the *Journal of Financial and Quantitative Analysis,* the *Journal of*

Empirical Finance, Financial Management, and the *Journal of Fixed Income.* He received his B.A. in economics from Denison University (1968) and his Ph.D. from Purdue University (1974).

Steven C. Miller

Mr. Steven C. Miller is a senior analyst at Loan Pricing Corporation (LPC), a New York-based research firm specializing in commercial lending. LPC produces databases, analytical and valuation tools, research reports, and matrix pricing models for banks and other lending institutions. LPC's published analysis covers the pricing, structuring, syndication, and trading of commercial loans, as well as default, repayment, and recovery patterns. Mr. Miller manages the market analysis group at LPC and frequently writes about commercial loan pricing and distressed securities trading. He holds an accounting degree from New York University.

Ira M. Millstein

Mr. Ira M. Millstein is the Lester Crown Visiting Faculty Fellow at the Yale School of Organization and Management, Chairman of the Board of Advisors of Columbia University School of Law's Institutional Investor Project, and Senior Partner at the law firm of Weil, Gotshal and Manges. In 1989, Mr. Millstein served as Chairman of the New York State Pension Investment Task Force. He recently served on the Project Advisory Committee of the Council on Competitiveness and as a member of The Corporate Governance and Financial Markets Subcouncil of the Competitiveness Policy Council, and the Cuomo Commission on Competitiveness.

Nell Minow

Ms. Nell Minow is a Principal of Lens, Inc., a company that works with institutional investors and corporations to enhance shareholder value. Ms. Minow served as General Counsel of Institutional Shareholder Services, Inc., from 1986–1990, as its President from 1990–1991 and as a member of its board of directors from 1991–1992. Ms. Minow is a graduate of Sarah Lawrence and the University of Chicago Law School. She has lectured and published widely on issues of corporate governance, government regulation, communications, and management. She served as the first Director of The Samuel and Ronnie Heyman Centre on Corporate Governance at the Benjamin N. Cardozo School of Law, Yeshiva University. Together with Robert A. G. Monks, she co-authored *Power and Accountability.*

Lawrence R. Nicholson

Mr. Lawrence R. Nicholson is managing director of the Real Estate Advisory Group and vice president of American Appraisal Associates, Inc. Mr. Nicholson is an investment real estate valuation specialist and is involved in valuating numerous real estate properties annually. Mr. Nicholson attended the University of Wisconsin, Madison, where he received his Master's degree in Real Estate Appraisal and Investment Analysis and his Bachelor of Business Administration degree in Finance and Real Estate. The Real Estate Advisory Group, an operating unit of American Appraisal Associates, provides national investment real estate research, consulting and valuation services to pension funds, advisors, lenders and real estate operations.

Thomas J. Parliment

Dr.Thomas J. Parliment is the president of Parliment Consulting Services Inc. He advises banks, thrift institutions, credit unions, brokerage and investment banking companies and Federal Home Loan Banks. Dr. Parliment serves on the faculties of the Savings and Community Bankers Graduate School at the University of Texas, the Graduate School of Banking at the University of Wisconsin, and the School of Credit Union Financial Management at the University of Colorado, as well as training federal and state regulators through the Treasury Department's Office of Thrift Supervision. Previously, he had served as Senior Economist and Director of Portfolio Management with several investment banking and securities brokerage firms. Formerly, Dr. Parliment was a Professor of Economics at the University of Wisconsin. He earned his B.A., M.A. and Ph.D. from the State University of New York.

Ronald G. Quintero

Mr. Ronald G. Quintero is a Principal of R.G. Quintero and Co., which provides accounting, crisis management and financial advisory services on behalf of financially troubled companies and their creditors. Previously, he was active in financial restructuring at Bear, Stearns & Co., Inc.; Zolfo, Cooper & Co.; and Peat Marwick Mitchell & Co. Mr. Quintero has an A.B. from Lafayette College, and M.S. and A.P.C. from New York University. He has earned several professional designations, including CPA, CFA, and CIRA. Mr. Quintero is the creator of the Quintero Index of Bankrupt Stocks. He is a member of the board of directors of the Turnaround Management Association.

David G. Schutt

Mr. David G. Schutt is the editor-in-chief of Venture Economics. Mr. Schutt joined Venture Economics in 1991 from the daily newspaper, the American Banker, where he was Financial Editor. Prior to that he was the founding editor and publisher of Mortgage Backed Securities Letter, a weekly newsletter, and first became involved in financial journalism at Institutional Investor, where he was an executive editor. He graduated with a B.A. in classical languages from Hamilton College in Clinton, New York.

Eduardo S. Schwartz

Dr. Eduardo S. Schwartz is the California Chair Professor in Real Estate and Professor of Finance at the Anderson Graduate School of Management at UCLA. He obtained his Bachelors of Engineering at the University of Chile in Santiago and his M.Sc. and Ph.D. in Business Administration (Finance) at the University of British Columbia. He has published over 60 papers in areas which include Valuation of Fixed Income Securities, Convertible Bonds, Warrants, Options, Rate of Return Regulation, Evaluation of Natural Resource Investments, Mortgage Pricing, Portfolio Insurance. Dr. Schwartz is associate editor of eleven journals in Finance and Real Estate. He has also been a consultant to Governmental Agencies, Banks, Investment Banks and Industrial Corporations.

Samuel D. Scruggs

Mr. Samuel D. Scruggs is an associate at Skadden, Arps, Slate, Meagher & Flom, law firm with headquarters in New York. He holds a J.D. from Columbia University (1987) and a B.A. from the University of Utah (1984). In his law practice, Mr. Scruggs concentrates on banking and institutional investing.

Martin Sikora

Mr. Martin Sikora is editor of the publication, Mergers and Acquisitions, which concentrates on major issues influencing mergers and acquisitions, including pricing, strategic planning, deal structuring, financing, and post-merger integration. Prior to jointing M&A in 1983, Mr. Sikora was a political reporter and bureau manager with United Press International, a business and financial reporter with the Philadelphia Inquirer, and the vice president of an economic research and forecasting firm. A 1956 graduate of New York University, Mr. Sikora is a lecturer on mergers and acquisitions at the Wharton School of the University of Pennsylvania.

Richard Y. Smith

Mr. Richard Y. Smith is a managing director in Chemical Bank's Mergers and Acquisitions unit. Since joining Chemical Bank in 1987, Mr. Smith has supervised a broad range of transactions, including acquisitions, tender offers, LBO's, private placements, valuations and options and investments by Chemical Bank as principal. Before joining Chemical, Mr. Smith was a Senior Vice President at Rothchild, Inc., where he was active in general corporate finance. From 1968 to 1970 he was with Blyth & Co. as a securities analyst specializing in leisure-time, beverage and service industries. Mr. Smith earned a B.A. in economics from Wesleyan University and an M.B.A. from Harvard Business School.

Charles W. Smithson

Dr. Charles W. Smithson is a Managing Director in the Global Risk Management sector of the Chase Manhattan Bank. Dr. Smithson taught for nine years at Texas A & M University. He was an AT&T Resident Management Fellow at the University of Rochester and directed the Ph.D. program in finance at the University of North Texas. Dr. Smithson was a Managing Director of the Continental Bank, where he served as Director of Research for Global Trading and Distribution. He served with both the Federal Trade Commission and the Consumer Products Safety Commission. He is the author of five books, including *Managing Financial Risk* and *The Handbook of Financial Engineering*. He received his Ph.D. in Economics from Tulane University.

John Spears

Mr. John Spears joined Kidder, Peabody, in 1988 as a Vice President, after a seven year career with Merrill, Lynch. Mr. Spears is a graduate of Texas Tech University. His area of expertise is in providing customized financial services to the mid-market, closely-held business.

Lindy Spears

Ms. Lindy Spears joined Kidder, Peabody, in 1989, following a fifteen-year career with Dun & Bradstreet, Inc., where she was a senior account representative. Ms. Spears is a graduate of Texas Tech University, with a Bachelor of Science in Economics. She focuses on privately-held, mid-size business transactions, with an emphasis on business continuation strategies.

Katherine M. Todd

Ms. Katherine M. Todd is a Partner at the Boston, Massachusetts, law firm of Testa, Hurwitz & Thibeault. Ms. Todd practices in the general corporate area, with a particular emphasis on venture capital and high technology. She has substantial experience in representing venture capital and alternative investment funds and institutional investors in such funds. Ms. Todd is a frequent speaker on representing venture capitalists and high-technology companies. She is a graduate of Smith College (A.B., magna cum laude, 1976) and Harvard Law School (J.D., cum laude, 1979).

Donald C. Wiss

Mr. Donald C. Wiss is the President of BondCalc Corporation. At BondCalc he has developed a PC-based program for the analysis of all fixed income investments. Previously, Mr. Wiss worked at Merrill Lynch developing and writing computer models for corporate finance and trading. His areas of expertise include zero coupon bonds, debt/equity swaps, Section 483 Notes, TIGRS, LYONs, high-yield bond pricing, and Equipment Trust Certificates. Mr. Wiss received his M.B.A. from New York University in 1980.

Part I:
The Economic and Financial Environment

Chapter 1

Overhangs and Hangovers:
Coping with the Imbalances of the 1980s*

Edward J. Frydl
Vice President and Assistant Director of Research
Federal Reserve Bank of New York

In the spring of 1991 economic activity appeared to be following a familiar cyclical pattern, recovering from a mild downturn that seemed clearly linked to concerns about the Gulf War and the related spike in oil prices. Indicators such as industrial production, durable goods orders, and housing starts appeared to be tracing out a pattern of recovery from their troughs that was broadly consistent with earlier cycles (Figure 1.1). By the fall, however, it was apparent that no sustained recovery had emerged, and consumer confidence, which had bounced back with the end of the war, was again plummeting.

This renewed flattening in economic activity focused attention on some peculiar features of this cycle. First, credit expansion, whose pronounced deceleration had begun in 1990, continued to slow in 1991 to its lowest rate of growth in the postwar period. Behind this slowdown were factors affecting both the demand for and supply of credit. Clearly, the further retrenchment in economic activity that began in the summer of 1991 was a prominent feature reducing business needs for credit. On the other side of the market some lenders continued or extended the restraints on their supply of credit that had begun in 1990. Banks, pressed to upgrade their capital positions, widened their spreads above funding costs on loans and became more selective in providing credit. The worsened credit quality of many classes of borrowers, particularly the commercial real estate sector, made all lenders, regardless of their capital condition, more cautious.

Slow credit growth, combined with complaints from businesses that credit availability was being withdrawn from them, led many observers to attribute the uneven economic performance of the U.S.

economy to a prolonged and intensifying "credit crunch." More specifically, restrictions on lending by banks were viewed as going over and above what was warranted by economic fundamentals.

U.S. banks did indeed tighten the terms and conditions under which they would supply credit, but sustained caution in lending was not unwarranted. In large part this caution represented a needed return to prudent standards of creditworthiness in assessing loans. A too-easy credit supply in much of the 1980s was a principal factor leading to damaging imbalances in investment, manifested principally as an unprecedented overhang of commercial real estate, and in the indebtedness of the household and business sectors. Unbalanced investment and overleveraging were combining to damage the economy by depressing construction, bankrupting enterprises, inhibiting lending, and feeding a pervasive financial and economic conservatism among businesses and consumers. Resolving these excesses in real estate and debt will take time and will exert a drag on economic performance during the period of adjustment.

The real estate and debt overhangs are not the only structural features that have created problems for the economy. U.S. businesses have had to cope with an environment of increased competition that has made it difficult to improve profit margins by boosting prices even when demand shows some pickup. This difficulty in restoring profitability was acute in 1991 and contributed to a second peculiarity of the current cycle: the failure of employment, unlike other indicators of business activity, to show even the beginnings of a normal recovery. Firms met any expansion in demand by working the existing

*Source: Federal Reserve Bank of New York. Annual report for year-ended December 31, 1991. Released April 30, 1992.

1

Figure 1.1   The Failure to Recover

Some indicators, such as industrial production, showed that apparently a typical recovery process began but was short in late summer. However, other cyclical measures, notably employment, indicated that a recovery never got started.

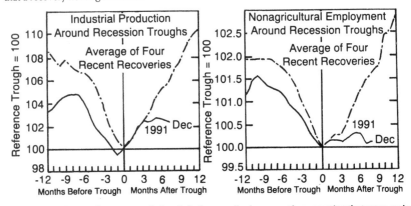

The recession began after an extended period of unusually slow growth, suggesting that some enduring factors—real estate and debt overhangs and intensified competitive pressures—were weighing against economic performance and inhibiting recovery.

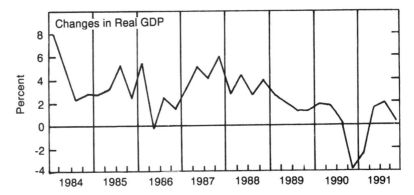

labor force longer and harder rather than by adding new jobs to payrolls. This lack of job growth was a drag on personal income and a key feature in the economy's stall in the final months of 1991.

Pressure on profit margins came in part from domestic factors such as deregulation in a number of industries or from new kinds of competition such as the commercial paper market's encroachment on traditional commercial and industrial bank loans. Another source of competitive pressure on the profitability of U.S. companies came from abroad. The world has moved toward a more open trading system at the same time that capital has become highly mobile internationally. In this environment, the pro-

ductivity of labor in low-wage countries is greatly enhanced by foreign investments that provide modern capital goods. The goods produced by this combination are very competitive in international markets and put pressure on profit margins and wage levels in high-wage industrial countries. A principal mechanism for coping with this competitive pressure, apart from exchange rate changes, has been for industrial countries to introduce new products or to improve production processes. For the United States, exports were strong in recent years, but import-competing industries still appeared to be suffering from a competitive disadvantage, even with a lower dollar, that showed up in part as difficulty in bouncing back from a recession.

The overhangs in commercial real estate and debt reflect excesses of the previous expansion, while the chronic international competitive pressures reflect a deficiency in productivity-enhancing investments. Still, both represent structural imbalances that have exerted a drag against the usual forces of recovery.

The Real Estate Overhang

In the 1980s an excess of commercial real estate arose, especially in sectors such as office space and retail space, that was unprecedented in the postwar period. By the middle of the decade many measures of capacity showed severe overbuilding (Figure 1.2). While downtown office building vacancy rates were only 4% early in the decade, they exceeded 16% by 1985 and have yet to drop below that level. Although the trend in suburban vacancies has been moderately downward in recent years, excess capacity in suburban office markets has been even worse than in downtown markets, with vacancy rates hovering above 20% from 1985 to 1991. Furthermore, the overbuilding of office space, typically a localized problem, became geographically pervasive in the past ten years. By 1991 only two of the 25 largest metropolitan regions had vacancy rates below 15%. Total returns on investments in office buildings had been in pronounced continuous decline throughout the 1980s; by 1991 returns were negative.

Despite these accumulating excesses, the value of commercial real estate put in place continued to expand into 1990. Net investment in structures began

---

Figure 1.2   The Commercial Real Estate Overhang

Continued large additions of commercial real estate...

In the face of extremely high vacancy rates...

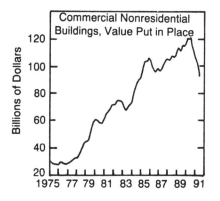

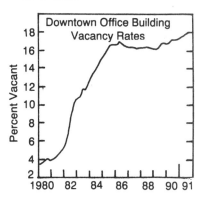

led to a massive overhang...

and diminished returns.

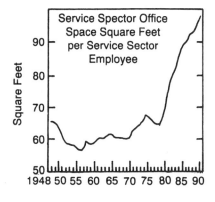

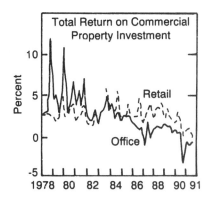

to slow by the mid-1980s but remained positive throughout the decade, even at the record high vacancy rates.

By 1991 the overhang in office space, measured as one estimate of square feet per service sector employee, had reached levels more than 60% higher than the relatively stable average for 1950-1980. Depending on assumptions about how intensively office space will be utilized, this overhang represents the equivalent of about ten years of service sector employment growth (at a growth rate of about 3% per year). Of course, as office rentals become cheap, space may find nontraditional uses to take up some of the slack. And old buildings that are fully depreciated may be razed at all accelerated pace, providing part of the needed adjustment.

On the demand side, however, demographic and labor market trends do not provide much support for rapid service sector growth in the years ahead. In fact, while the 1980s are popularly thought of as a decade of especially rapid services expansion, employment growth in that sector had slowed noticeably compared with growth during the preceding two decades (see table). Services did account for all of the net job creation in the 1980s, but the pace of overall services employment growth decelerated because of a slowdown in the growth of government services positions. Governments across the board are hard pressed by their fiscal problems and are unlikely to step up the pace of hiring. Even in the private services sector, sustaining the trend in employment growth will be difficult. The entry of the baby boom generation into the labor force has been exhausted. Also, the long trend of increasing female participation in the work force may have crested, ending a stimulus to the growth of both the supply of service sector workers and the demand for a wide variety of services to meet the needs of two-earner households. All in all, heavy investments were made in commercial structures that could have been supported only if service sector employment growth had accelerated, even as evidence of the opposite tendency was developing.

Table 1.1   Service Sector Employment Growth (Average Annual Growth Rates)

Years	Total	Private	Government
1949-1959	2.3	2.0	3.3
1959-1969	3.4	3.2	4.2
1969-1979	3.3	3.4	2.7
1979-1989	2.7	3.2	1.1

Several factors combined to create the overinvestment in commercial real estate. The 1981 Tax Act produced strong incentives for investments in

structures. Added to these incentives were powerful changes in the availability of finance. Deregulation of the thrift industry allowed savings and loan institutions to make direct investments in real estate projects. More important, savings institutions that had been damaged by the squeeze on their earnings from high interest rates in the early 1980s tried aggressively to grow their way back to a stronger financial position by pursuing new business.

Thrifts were not alone. Commercial banks were also rapidly expanding into commercial real estate lending. Banks had seen their shares erode in traditional markets (Figure 1.3). Nonbank issuers were cutting into the general credit card market. The securitization of credit card and auto loan receivables made institutional portfolio investors a growing source of credit to these borrowers. In the business credit markets, multinational and larger regional banks were put at a disadvantage by the expansion of the commercial paper market and by the slippage in their creditworthiness from the overhang of developing country debt carried on their balance sheets. To make up for these falling shares in consumer and business credit markets, banks moved aggressively to increase their presence in nonresidential mortgages.

These combined incentives were strongest in the first half of the 1980s. The pace of commercial nonresidential construction doubled between 1980 and 1985, and vacancy rates rose sharply. Although the 1986 Tax Act removed many of the fiscal incentives supporting the real estate boom, investment in the commercial sector continued to pile on to an already glutted market. Availability of finance based on optimistic assumptions for real estate prices supported this bubble for several years. By early 1990, however, the full dimensions of the real estate problem became clear. Estimates of the financing needs of the Resolution Trust Corporation, the vehicle for disposing of troubled thrift real estate exposures, had to be revised upward. In this environment, real estate lenders drastically altered their expectations and financial institutions curtailed real estate lending.

The Debt Overhang

Excess investment in commercial structures was not the only imbalance arising from heavy debt growth. The 1980s, in fact, witnessed a widespread leveraging of the U.S. economy. The traditional stable linkage between private sector debt and GDP broke down completely in the last decade, and by 1991 an extra $2 trillion of private sector debt had been created over and above what would have been

Figure 1.3   Trends in Banking Lending

As commercial banks lost market share
in their traditional business...

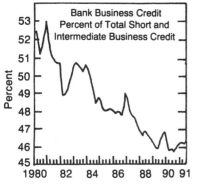

and consumer markets,...

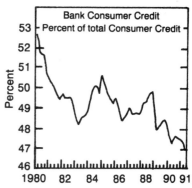

they sought to expand in the commercial real estate market.

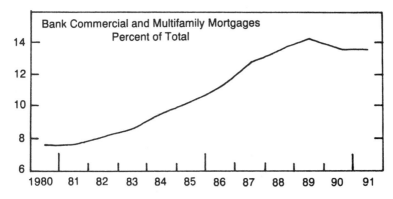

expected on the basis of the past relationship between private sector debt and GDP (Figure 1.4). Certainly, only part of this unusually rapid debt growth was generated by bad debts that were purely speculative. Most of the growth represented an economic use of financial and tax incentives for debt.

Corporate Leverage

Private sector debt has ballooned in both the business and household sectors. Corporate leveraging was driven by two processes: debt-financed acquisitions and stock repurchases, through which existing management reduced outstanding equity by buying stock from the public for the company's own account (Figure 1.5). The takeover boom of the 1980s differed crucially in the character of its financing from the previous merger wave of conglomerations in the 1960s. In the 1960s, acquiring companies often took over other enterprises in unrelated lines of business

through an exchange of stock, thereby avoiding the creation of debt. In the 1980s, acquisitions were typically effected through cash tenders financed by debt.

The leveraged buyout (LBO) of companies by their management or some other narrow set of individual buyers was an especially debt-reliant form of acquisition. Before the 1980s, LBOs had played a familiar but limited role in corporate finance, typified by the case of management at a particular plant buying out and taking the plant operations from the parent corporation private. In such a case, equity was put into the hands of knowledgeable production management. Because of the high debt burden created, the technique was usually limited to operations generating stable cash flows.

In the 1980s the riskiness of LBO deals increased for a number of reasons. Deal sizes grew larger to accommodate larger targets. Firms with more cyclical

Figure 1.4   The Debt Overhang

The relatively stable relationship between private debt and output broke down in the 1980s as businesses and households both increased their leverage.

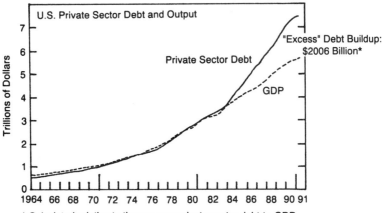

* Calculated relative to the average private sector debt-to-GDP
  ratio for 1964-84 (0.9569).

earnings streams became LBO candidates, and the paydown of high initial debt came to depend on sales of diverse corporate assets. These asset sales often consisted of the divestment of entire lines of business, in effect unwinding the conglomerates put together in the earlier merger wave. Buyers were willing for some time to pay premium prices for these assets, often because they were competitors in the same line of business and the purchases resulted in increases in market concentration. But leveraged buyouts were carried to the point where prospective asset sales, crucial to reducing the debt burden to manageable proportions, became speculative, relying more on a hoped-for general rise in asset values and less on the prospects of selling to specific buyers who had a clear business purpose behind their demands. In a nutshell, some highly leveraged acquisitions depended on the combined good fortune of no recession and no falloff in asset prices in order to service debt obligations without difficulty.

Both bank lending and bond issuance were important sources of debt finance for acquisitions. One particularly significant development was the emergence of original-issue junk bonds as a source of takeover finance, especially for hostile takeovers. This development, pioneered by the securities firm Drexel Burnham, increased the risk to firms of the hostile takeover event and prompted greater use of defensive leveraging. Potential targets may have reduced their attractiveness by acquiring other companies in a leveraged manner. Or they may have

repurchased their shares in the open market, usin available cash or even borrowing to do so. Of course not all share repurchases represented defensive lev eraging. Much of the activity was conducted by hug firms such as Exxon or IBM that were safely beyon any risk of takeover, even by the standards of th RJR-Nabisco acquisition.

The tax structure in the United States has alway favored corporate leverage because it allows th deduction from corporate tax liabilities of interes paid on debt but not of dividends paid on equity This incentive was not fully exploited, however, i earlier periods. The factors that changed busines attitudes toward indebtedness in the 1980s are no straightforward and easy to pin down. It is plausible however, that the readier availability of finance fo use in increasing leverage by way of acquisitions o otherwise helped to change attitudes among poten tial borrowers. In any case, the combination o debt-financed acquisitions, defensive leveraging stock buybacks to improve returns on equity, an increased availability of takeover finance created major leveraging of the corporate sector throug indebtedness and decapitalization. Between 198 and 1990, U.S. corporations borrowed some $40(billion from banks and other lenders and anothe $650 billion in the securities markets. This raised th aggregate corporate debt-to-assets ratio to a postwa record level of 32% (Figure 1.5). At the same time corporations retired $640 billion of equity throug acquisitions and stock repurchases.

Figure 1.5   Corporate Leverage

Leverage increased in the business sector...   as companies retired equity...

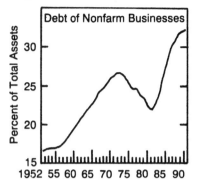
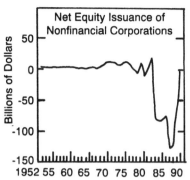

through both acquisitions and stock repurchases.

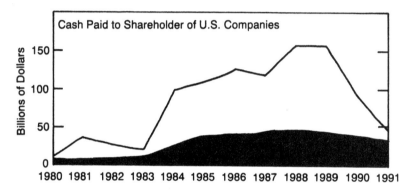

The Household Debt Buildup

Households, as well as corporations, boosted their reliance on debt in the 1980s (Figure 1.6). Most household debt is in the form of residential mortgages, which totaled $2.7 trillion in 1991, or 67% of total household debt. Likewise, most of the increase in household debt was explained by the $1.3 trillion rise in residential mortgages in 1981-1989, a period during which the ratio of mortgage debt to home values rose from 36% to 50%.

The factors behind this increased reliance on mortgage debt by households are not clear. High real interest rates, a hallmark of the 1980s, should themselves, of course, work to reduce the use of debt by increasing its cost. High rates should also encourage holders of low-rate mortgages to turn these over less frequently. A consequence of holding onto mortgages is that the housing stock should support a lower, not a higher, level of mortgage debt over time

as more of the original debt gets amortized. Yet in spite of incentives created by higher rates to reduce mortgage debt, the level of mortgage debt increased sharply relative to home values.

Most likely, the key to this anomalous behavior lies in the increased level and rate of change of house prices. As house prices rose, some new homeowners who otherwise would have preferred to take a higher initial equity than that required by mortgage lenders may have been forced into higher than desired leverage in order to buy a house. Also, homebuyers may have adapted their financial risk taking to the trend of rising house prices and may have counted on rising prices to support a more leveraged position. Such behavior, of course, can create a troubling financial condition if households have leveraged themselves beyond the ability of their other assets to support the mortgage debt in a weak housing market.

Supply-side factors may also have spurred greater leveraging through mortgages. The 1980s saw the

Figure 1.6   Household Leverage

Leverage increased in the household sector...   as homeowners borrowed against their equity...

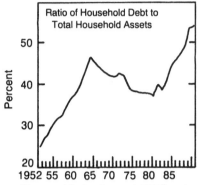

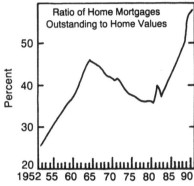

and increased their reliance on installment credit.

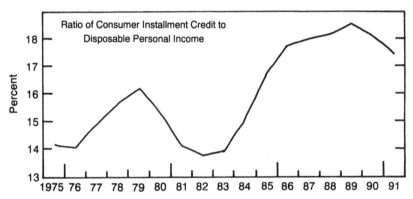

development of a deep, liquid market in mortgage-backed securities that allowed mortgage originators to pass off their exposures to a broader range of ultimate investors. Originators, then, may have adopted a more relaxed attitude on loan-to-value ratios, more readily accommodating demands for leveraging and indicating to borrowers a willingness to write large mortgages. The credit risk on the loan would quickly be passed through the mortgage pool to the guarantors or investors in the secondary market, making the originator less concerned about the degree of leverage on the loan.

Another supply-side innovation that may have contributed to the leveraging of the housing stock was the easy availability of home equity loan accounts. Home equity loan accounts offered homeowners a credit line backed by the equity interest in a house—in effect, a prearranged second mortgage. The accounts were fairly popular and substituted somewhat for other avenues of consumer borrow-

ing, partly because they retained tax deductibility for interest payments, a feature that other kinds of household debt lost through tax reform.

Nonmortgage debt also rose strongly relative to personal disposable income in the 1980s. Increased competitiveness among credit suppliers played a key role. Captive finance subsidiaries of automobile companies consistently resorted to subsidized financing terms as a competitive technique to sell cars. Also lenders on auto loans extended the maturity they offered; this practice reduced monthly cash payments, making the financing affordable to a broader range of car buyers.

In the revolving credit markets, the high profitability of the credit card business attracted new entrants into the market. Existing issuers became more aggressive in their marketing, seeking new customers among households previously regarded as of marginal creditworthiness. In consequence, the number of cards and credit card indebtedness surged.

Consequences of the Overhangs

The excesses in real estate and leveraging have left a legacy of weakened borrowers and lenders. In the corporate sector, the burden of debt service, as measured by the ratio of interest cost to cash flow for nonfinancial corporations, reached record post-war levels in 1991, higher even than at the trough of the 1981-1982 recession. This burden of debt has weighed heavily on businesses (Figure 1.7). The financial strains have shown up as a widespread increase in the downgradings of corporate debt, an increased default rate on corporate bonds, and a sharp increase in business failures, measured both by the number of failing firms and the value of failed liabilities.

Signs of financial strain have also been readily apparent in the household sector. Delinquency rates on broad classes of consumer credit, especially auto loans and credit card loans, were at unusually high levels in recent years. By 1991, mortgage delinquencies had moderated somewhat from the peak reached a few years earlier (although they have been turning up again recently), but they still averaged over the 1980-1991 period a higher rate than in the 1970s. The pace of mortgage foreclosures started—an indicator of extreme stress—has risen decidedly from 1981 to 1991. The number of personal bankruptcies also showed a dramatic surge after 1985.

With many real estate, corporate, and household borrowers in default, credit strains have been passed back to financial institutions (Figure 1.8). Loan loss rates at commercial banks have risen to levels last seen in the Depression, as all broad categories of bank loans have deteriorated. Still, commercial banks, large ones especially, have coped well with

---

Figure 1.7   The Debt Hangover: Weakened Borrowers

A legacy of the 1980s debt buildup has been a heavy burden on corporate cash flow...

and household incomes,...

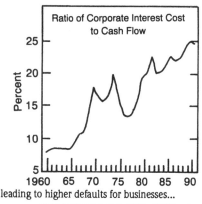

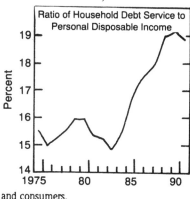

leading to higher defaults for businesses...

and consumers.

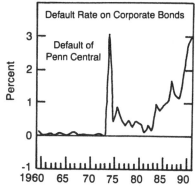

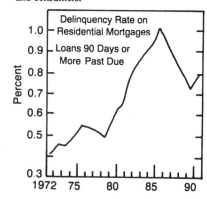

Figure 1.8   The Debt Hangover: Weakened Lenders

The aftermath of the debt binge shows damaged balance sheets at banks and other financial intermediaries.

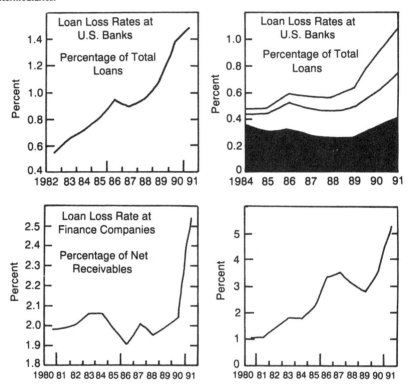

these difficulties and have managed to achieve impressive improvements in their capital positions. Nonbank lenders exposed to the commercial real estate sector, including finance and insurance companies, have also suffered a sharp rise in bad loans. The legacy of the overhangs of the 1980s is a hangover of damaged creditworthiness in the 1990s.

The Macroeconomic Consequences

The fallout of the real estate and debt overhangs has shown up in two principal features of the macroeconomic environment. First, corporate profitability has been depressed, second, credit growth has plummeted.

Corporate Profitability

The increased debt burden on the corporate sector and the associated servicing costs have been a major factor pushing down the profitability of business enterprises in the 1980s (Figure 1.9). Corporate profits, whether measured relative to GDP or to the net worth of corporations, did not recover after the 1981-1982 recession to levels that prevailed in the 1970s. If, however, the interest costs paid out by corporations are added to profits to provide a rough measure of income paid to capital in the corporate sector, then a rebound shows up after the recession of the early 1980s, although the measure still remains well short of its performance in the 1960s. This finding suggests that an important factor behind the continued downtrend in profitability in the 1980s, at least for the corporate sector, is the additional interest burden created by a higher level of

Figure 1.9   Pressure on Profits

The higher debt burden of the 1980s contributed to a squeeze on corporate profits that has prompted many firms to shrink and restructure, inhibiting a recovery in employment.

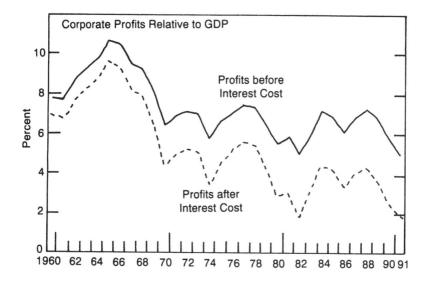

Note: Profits of nonfarm nonfinancial corporations before tax are adjusted for inventory valuation and capital consumption.

corporate indebtedness in an era of high real interest rates.

Strains on profitability have been a chronic problem of recent years, and they grew acute in the recessionary environment. What makes them especially troublesome in this cyclical episode, however, is their resistance to the typical and relatively quick resolution of cost reduction through inventory destocking. Inventories in general, and particularly in manufacturing, have been kept under tight control. Although retail inventories exclusive of autos are at higher than usual levels, overall the inventory cycle has been very muted in the recent recession. Firms, then, cannot easily lessen the pressures on profits from their heavy interest burden by cutting inventories.

An alternative remedy for the profit squeeze is to try to restore margins through price increases. Companies in many industries—including autos, airlines, and primary metals—attempted this approach on different occasions with a conspicuous lack of success. In many sectors, price increases could not be sustained or price cuts could not be avoided. Even if listed prices were maintained, discounting and incentives to purchase became a commonplace. Competitive pressures, whether from domestic or international sources, were too intense to allow price increases to get much ahead of costs. The recurrent faltering of attempts to recover from this persistent squeeze on profits must have made firms more reluctant to rehire workers to meet the resurgence of consumption demand after the Gulf War. The lack of recovery in hiring retarded personal income growth and colored the gloomy background of consumer confidence.

The inability of many firms to pass on cost increases, particularly those stemming from higher interest costs, arose in a number of ways. Deregulation in some domestic industries—airlines and banking are prime examples—led to intensified price competition that revealed substantial structural excess capacity.

On the international side, competitive pressures remained formidable, despite an improvement in the relative cost competitiveness of U.S. producers. Since 1985, the depreciation of the dollar has dominated all other factors influencing the production costs of U.S. goods relative to those of other countries. This improved cost competitiveness has contributed to a substantial reduction in the U.S. merchandise trade deficit from a peak value of nearly $160 billion in 1987 to an annual rate of less than

$75 billion in the first three quarters of 1991. This improvement has come principally by way of a rapid advance in U.S. exports. Competition in the American market from imports, however, has remained quite strong despite the weaker dollar. Import prices in dollars have risen more slowly than general price indicators in the United States, and import-to-income ratios have drifted up since 1985. In part, these developments may reflect especially vigorous efforts by the export industries of trade competitors to achieve productivity enhancements that offset the cost disadvantages of the weaker dollar. Or they may reflect a stubborn attempt to hold on to market share in the United States by tolerating lower profit margins here while trying to make up the difference in the domestic market or in other export markets. All in all, foreign sellers have remained determined competitors in the U.S. market.

The inability of U.S. businesses to raise prices aggressively in a competitive environment, and thereby restore profitability that had been eroded by debt costs, provoked a change in business behavior. Managers became more conservative in controlling costs and more reluctant to add labor. Many firms, in fact, committed to permanent staff reductions and were willing to take sizable special charges against earnings to carry out these steps.

These attempts to control costs through shrinkage by eliminating staff jobs and selectively closing plants, offices, or outlets are an important element of a total restructuring. They represent a shift to a more efficient scale of operation under existing cost structures. Equally important, however, if not more important, are efforts to shift the entire cost structure through productivity-enhancing investment.

Investment requires financing, either out of retained earnings or through equity issuance or borrowing. Building up retained earnings depends on the slow process of restoring profitability. While the equity markets have indeed come alive in recent months as a source of new funding for corporations after eight years of massive net equity retirement, only a small part of these funds are going directly to finance new investment. The majority are being used to restructure balance sheets and a good part are simply going to cover losses. Borrowing in securities markets has been extremely heavy recently, but again most of these funds are being directed to balance sheet restructuring, especially the refinancing of old high-rate debt. Borrowing from banks is depressed by both low demand and the apparent reluctance of some depository institutions to lend. The full benefits of restructuring await the revival of investment. Firms now are directing their efforts toward balance sheet restructuring to reduce the burden of heavy leverage built up in the 1980s. Net

credit demands are likely to be subdued until this balance sheet restructuring has gone farther. This process has contributed to the second major macroeconomic feature of the current cycle: a precipitous slowdown in credit growth.

Slow Credit Growth

Last year saw a continuation of the sharp deceleration in the growth of credit to the private sector that began early in 1990. Private credit expansion had been slowing since 1985, but growth rates had stayed within a familiar range of fluctuation until 1990. By then it was clear that a significant deceleration was under way (Figure 1.10). This development coincided with a rise in complaints from businesses that commercial banks had restricted credit—the emergence of a credit crunch.

The term "credit crunch" usually connotes some restriction, or rationing, of the supply of credit. It can be equated with conditions in which the market supply of credit to a particular borrower or class of borrowers reaches a maximum regardless of the interest rate that the borrower is willing to pay, leaving the borrower with some frustrated demand for credit. Typically, these conditions emerge because of new concerns about the underlying creditworthiness of the borrower. The borrower wants to get a bigger loan at the prevailing rate of interest than lenders are prepared to give. The borrower may even be willing to pay a premium, but offering to pay above-market rates does not induce more supply. In this regard the credit markets differ from other markets: in a credit crunch environment, higher bids only create greater lender uncertainty about the financial condition of the borrower.

Some commentators have applied the credit crunch designation to what can better be described as increases in the costs of financial intermediation. As banking system loan losses have risen, credit rating agencies have downgraded the standing of many banks, raising their cost of capital. At the same time, banks have faced a need to improve their capitalization to satisfy stock market desires for a stronger capital ratio and to gain leeway for regulatory approval of expanded powers. Motivated by both higher costs of raising capital in the markets and the desire to improve their capital ratios, banks have increased their lending margins and tightened terms and conditions to borrowers. These measures may have elicited complaints from borrowers because even when credit was available, the costs were higher and the conditions tighter than what borrowers anticipated on the basis of the funding costs to banks.

Restrictions on credit supplies have probably played a role in this cyclical episode (Figure 1.11).

Figure 1.10   The Slide in Credit Growth

By 1991, credit growth had decelerated to the lowest rates in postwar experience.

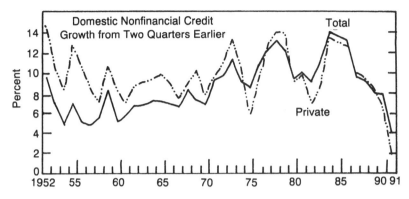

The sharp slowdown occurred in both business and household credit.

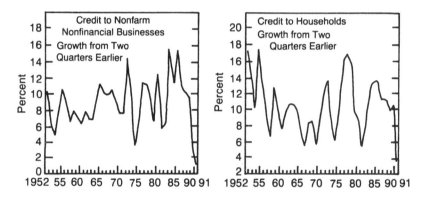

To some extent restricted credit is always a characteristic of downturns, since the ability of some borrowers to service debt is damaged by recessions. The present cycle is no exception. In fact, for overextended sectors such as commercial real estate and heavily indebted companies, the damage to creditworthiness from the recession has been so bad that creditor caution is entirely justified.

Concerns about a credit crunch, however, do not focus on credit restrictions that are a consequence of a weak economy but rather on restrictions that are unusual in the cyclical context and that may have worked to bring about a downturn.

A variety of surveys provided evidence that lenders in 1990-1991 did restrict the availability of lending, not only for commercial real estate and highly leveraged acquisitions, but also for nonmerger commercial and industrial loans. Furthermore, for

several reasons lenders desired to improve their capital ratios and were reluctant to expand their assets. This feature of the 1990-1991 cyclical episode was generally not evident in earlier downturns.

By and large, reductions in credit supply were warranted. The overhangs in real estate and debt were partly brought about by a too-easy supply of credit based on optimistic assumptions of borrower performance and a highly competitive financial environment. The restoration of prudent lending standards by depository institutions required a slowdown in credit growth.

Improvements in bank capital positions have been encouraged (and in some cases required) by regulators, rating agencies, and even the stock market. Strengthened capitalization of the banking system is a structural improvement that will protect the Bank Insurance Fund and the creditors of banks and

Figure 1.11   A Bank Credit Crunch?

Much of the slowdown in bank-provided credit has been warranted. The deceleration in lending was fastest at banks...

in weaker economic regions...

or with higher capital needs...

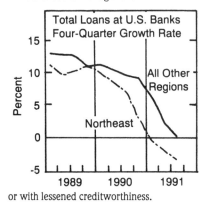

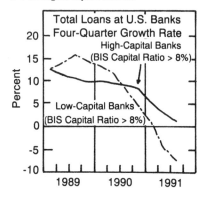

or with lessened creditworthiness.

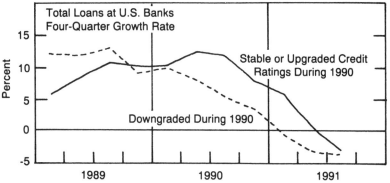

give bank management leeway to pursue a wider range of potentially profitable business. The broad support for this long-term policy of seeking a stronger capital base for banking warrants carrying out the policy independent of cyclical business conditions.

Borrowers have sometimes charged that the restrictions on credit supply that prevailed in 1990-1991 were not justified by fundamental economic and financial factors. Rather, they saw these restrictions as brought about by overzealous regulators determined not to repeat with banks the delays experienced in dealing with thrift problems. The frustrations of borrowers are understandable and incidents of a heavy regulatory hand may have occurred. As we have seen, however, the overhangs of real estate and debt, together with the need to improve bank capital positions, provide a sufficient

fundamental explanation for the recent restrictions on credit supply.

Finally, measured credit has also been growing slowly because of a fundamental reason that has been underemphasized in analyses of the recent credit cycle: declining demand. Whatever factors may have touched off the economic recession, since mid-1990 the dynamics of the down phase of the cycle have become the compelling determinant of credit growth. Of course, the relative effects of demand versus supply declines have varied over time and across regions, an observation that may help explain why bankers and businessmen view the causes of the credit slowdown so differently. Demand-side and supply-side effects have been further muddied by the emergence of discouraged borrowers, some businesses may not have bothered to seek new credit, knowing that their lenders had become more restrictive. To bankers, however, this reluctance to seek credit would appear as a falloff in credit demands. Still, the persistently sluggish behavior of spending since the onset of the recession accounts for much of the weakness in credit growth.

Implications for the Future

The overhangs that are the legacy of financial excesses in the 1980s have exerted a drag on the overall economy. But adjustment is advancing in many sectors. Households have been paying down their installment debt, reducing the burden on their personal incomes. Businesses have begun a vigorous balance sheet restructuring that is reducing the degree of leverage and the cost of debt service. These steps are contributing importantly to lowering the interest burden on corporate cash flow. Companies have also aggressively sought to control noninterest costs through the elimination of excess capacity and the reduction of overhead staff levels. Financial institutions, banks especially, have faced up to the damage on their loan portfolios, increasing their loss reserves and strengthening their capital base.

All of these actions are part of the process of adjustment and recovery that will restore financial health to the economy and prepare the way for an economic upswing. Central bank policy has aided this process of restoration and can continue to do so. It is important, however, to clarify what central banking actions are appropriate and helpful. Occasionally, commentators have called for a relaxation of supervisory criteria on capital, asset quality, and other features of bank performance. These rules have been put in place to promote a long-run improvement in the financial strength of the banking system. Some, such as the Basle Accord capital standards,

have been negotiated in an international context to ensure fairness. An abrupt reversal of the commitment to these rules and standards would undercut the credibility of efforts for a structural improvement in banking and would risk undermining confidence in the banking system. Nor is it clear that easier prudential standards would be much help now in starting a recovery, since the downward dynamics of the cycle have likely made weakness in demand the chief drag on business activity.

As usual, monetary policy is the principal vehicle for dealing with the economic cycle even in this period of burdensome overhangs. Some aspects of the current environment improve the potency of the stimulus that comes from lower interest rates. Lower rates, of course, alleviate the squeeze on profitability that has been a major block to recovery in hiring. The adoption by business of a more conservative attitude toward capital structures in 1990-1991 will hasten this process as firms take advantage of opportunities to refinance, recapitalize, and deleverage. And as banks succeed in strengthening their capital positions, they will be more forthcoming as providers of credit to finance recovery.

The lingering effects of the real estate and debt overhangs can be expected to create pressures to use monetary policy as the remedy to ease the strains on specific sectors. But a monetary policy stance that packs enough stimulus to resuscitate the commercial real estate sector quickly or to cut short the restructuring of balance sheets will almost certainly carry the risk of renewed high inflation. That temptation must be resisted. The appropriate pitch for policy is to complement and facilitate the process of economic and balance sheet restructuring in a context of stable financial conditions. That process is now under way.

Part II:
The Financial Institutions

Chapter 2

The Purpose of Capital for Institutions with Government-Insured Deposits

George J. Benston[*]
John H. Harland Professor of Finance, Accounting, and Economics
Emory University, Atlanta, GA

Capital has two basic meanings that are not inter-changeable, which gives rise to much confusion. Capital can refer to assets, such as plant and equipment. It also refers to the other side of the balance sheet, to claims over the assets. In banking, "capital adequacy" usually refers to stockholders' equity, although for purposes of deposit insurance, debt claims that are not guaranteed, de jure or de facto, by a federal government agency also should be considered. Indeed, as is shown below, such debt claims are superior in several important ways to equity capital.

When people say that "banks are overcapitalized" or "there is too much capital in the banking industry," they could be referring to the asset or the liability side of the balance sheet.[1] If their concern is with the asset side, they would be calling for mergers of banks that would reduce physical plant, loans, and investments. If they mean the equity and nongovernment insured debt portion of the liability side, they would be claiming that the federal deposit insurance agency (hereafter, the FDIC [2]) is not sufficiently subject to risk, either from the point of view of the owners of banks or for social purposes (e.g., to offset externalities from bank runs or to optimize the quantity of bank money and financial intermediation). If "capital" is used to describe the equity portion of the liability side of the balance sheet, it could mean that the bank should hold more debt that is de facto as well as de jure uninsured (usually called subordinated debentures) in the same sense that nonbanks are said to have suboptimal

debt/equity ratios.[3] One reason that the two concepts might be confused is that they are related, as the assets in which a bank invests and regulatory restraints on these investments are important determinants of the cost of debt and equity capital. For example, laws and regulations that prevent banks from diversifying their assets efficiently increase risk and the cost of equity capital. Underpriced federal deposit insurance gives rise to an intangible asset, the deposit insurance put option. This linkage might be the source of some confusion.

The balance of the chapter first considers capital as assets and then capital as equity and uninsured debt. Capital here and throughout the chapter is assumed to reflect economic market values. As presently reported, capital is an accounting construct that often badly measures market or current values of assets and liabilities. Although a thorough discussion of market-value accounting for banks is beyond the scope of this chapter, it should be clear that public policy is poorly served when the supervisory authorities are concerned with numbers that inadequately report banks' present economic conditions. Following the descriptions and analyses of the alternative definitions of capital, some concerns about the limitations and advantages of equity and debt capital to protect the FDIC are discussed. The chapter then delineates and critiques four methods of getting banks to hold the optimal level of capital and proposes a procedure to get banks and the authorities to act in an effective and timely way. A summary and conclusions follow.

[*]Mr. Benston gratefully acknowledges helpful suggestions from Larry Wall, George Kaufman, and Larry Mote. An earlier version of this paper was presented at a conference sponsored by Arthur Andersen, Freddie Mac, and Salomon Brothers, "Capitalizing for the 90s," held in Washington, DC, on March 21, 1991.
Source: Journal of Financial Services Research 1992.

Capital as Assets Used for the Production of Goods and Services

Definition

A bank's asset capital is its buildings, computers, check processing machinery, furniture and fixtures, and so forth. These also are referred to as "fixed assets." Capital also refers to such assets as loans and investments that are used to produce income for a bank. These often are called "monetary assets." A bank also holds intangible capital in the form of personnel training, operating procedures, computer programs, and customer recognition and satisfaction (i.e., goodwill). These intangible assets usually are written off (charged against stockholders' equity) as they are incurred, and hence do not appear on a bank's books as assets.

Over- and Suboptimal Asset Capitalization

A bank would be overcapitalized if it held more assets than were optimal. This would occur if the marginal return on the assets used by the bank were less than those assets could earn if used in some other way (in present value terms). Such a situation might result from restrictions on asset sales imposed by the supervisory authorities or from decisions made by bank managers that were contrary to the interests of shareholders. For example, a bank might be prevented by the supervisory authorities from closing branches that serve a politically powerful constituency, even though the bank could sell or otherwise dispose of the assets invested in the branches and use the proceeds to earn more than the branches generate (again, on a present value basis). Or, bank officers who supported developing branches designed to serve "upscale" clients may keep these branches open even when the decision turns out to have been a mistake.

A reduction in the demand for loans might result in overcapitalization if banks invest the funds that become available in securities that yield less than their cost of funds (including the returns that stockholders could earn if the funds were distributed to them). This situation could occur if the bank's managers valued maximizing bank size over maximizing stockholder wealth, and the managers could not be displaced because laws (such as the Bank Holding Company Act) make takeovers prohibitively expensive. However, the bank would not be overcapitalized if the managers determined that the loan demand situation was temporary and stockholders were best served by retaining the funds in the bank rather than subjecting the bank to the higher cost of obtaining additional funds when the situation changed.[4]

A bank might hold a suboptimal portfolio of assets, and hence be overcapitalized with respect to some assets and overcapitalized with respect to others. For example, the National Banking Act and state bank chartering acts prevent banks from holding equity securities. If other assets were not sufficient substitutes for equities (perhaps because they did not offer the same covariance of cash flows), the bank would have to hold assets that yield less or imposed more risk than is optimal. The bank might be able to cure this situation by scaling down its asset size. But, if the supervisory authorities required that the bank be financed with an amount of equity capital that exceeds a preferred lower amount (given the restrictions on the assets a bank may hold), the bank would be forced to be overcapitalized with respect to its holding more assets of the kind permitted than is optimal.

Another example of overcapitalization is where banks must hold assets that generate lower returns or impose higher risks because of a legislative mandate, such as the Community Reinvestment Act. This act requires that banks demonstrate that they serve their local communities. Threatened lawsuits by community activists and bank examiners' criticisms may compel some banks to invest in mortgages and business loans that do not meet optimal underwriting requirements.

Finally, the banking industry may be asset overcapitalized because economies of scale and scope cannot be realized as a result of antibranching and anticombination legislation that prevents them from merging with or being acquired by banks in other states and nonbanks. For example, banks in adjacent states might be able to effect economies in computer operations, advertising, lending administration, and specialized services if they could merge and become a single bank rather than units of a bank holding company. Banks in different regions (such as the West and East Coasts, and the Midwest and South) could reduce geographic risk by merging into a nationwide bank. Economies of scope might be obtained by the merger of commercial banks and securities firms or by the operation of securities departments within commercial banks. It should be emphasized that this source of overcapitalization depends on legislative constraints. Thus, the charge that there are too many loan officers at too many banks chasing after too few loans cannot be supported by reference to presumed economies of scale in lending, because banks are not legally prevented from lending nationwide and worldwide. Their failure to lend at optimal operating cost levels must be due to offsetting diseconomies (such as presumed greater risk as a result of poorer control over a larger scale of operations), to legislatively imposed constraints (such as branching restrictions that prevent economies of scope of lending and depositing from being achieved), or to managers not operating in the interest of shareholders.

Overcapitalization with respect to assets, then, is a result of legislation that 1) prevents banks from holding an optimal portfolio of assets (most notably the bank chartering acts and prohibitions against banks' involvement with activities defined as nonfinancially congeneric); 2) requires banks to invest in lower yielding and riskier assets (for example, the Community Reinvestment Act); and 3) restricts economies of scale and economies of scope from being realized (most notably antibranching laws, asset prohibitions, and bank ownership restraints that keep managers who do not operate banks in the interest of shareholders from being displaced).

Apparent Overcapitalization

The "real" asset overcapitalization just discussed should be distinguished from apparent overcapitalization that results from past mistakes or changed conditions, the effects of which are not recorded in a bank's financial reports. For example, a bank might have invested in branches as a means of attracting deposits when the Regulation Q ceilings on deposit interest payments were binding. When the ceilings are removed or reduced (or market rates of interest decline below the ceilings), the branch might become a more expensive means of obtaining funds than floating certificates of deposit (CDs) in the market. The economic value of the branch is the present value of the now reduced cash flows expected from the branch.[5] However, the amount for which the branch and its equipment could be sold might be less than this present value; hence, the branch would be kept and the bank would have incurred a capital loss equal to the difference between its book and present values. However, this write down of book value and recording of a capital loss rarely is done, and the bank's balance sheet would continue to report the original cost of the branch less accumulated depreciation. Consequently, the branch would appear to be unprofitable and the bank would appear to have an overinvestment in fixed assets.

Real overcapitalization also should be distinguished from reductions in asset values (and, hence, in stockholders' equity capital) resulting from the imposition of costs on banks but not on alternative suppliers of bank products. In particular, regulations and supervision that impose costly record keeping requirements and constrain banks from optimally serving their customers increase banks' costs,

thereby reducing the value of bank-specific assets, such as employee training, specialized equipment, and charter value. Hence, deposit insurance premiums might be increased beyond the value of the insurance to a bank. In these situations, the bank may appear to be overcapitalized because its recorded assets are not written down, with an equivalent charge made to stockholders' equity.

The regulatory authorities may impose additional costs on banks by requiring them to hold higher levels of stockholder equity capital than are optimal (assuming deposit insurance is fairly priced), given the tax laws. At present, debt subordinated to the claims of the FDIC is not fully counted as meeting capital requirements. As a result, banks may pay higher income taxes because factor payments to debtholders, not to equity holders, are counted as deductible business expenses. The result, though, is not overcapitalization but a reduction in the value of assets and of stockholders' claims over assets (which is reflected in the price of bank shares).

The reduction in restrictions on banks' competitors, such as increased entry into banks' market made possible by improved technology and changes in laws that restricted alternative suppliers, may result in some banks no longer being able to earn competitive returns on assets. These banks then are faced with three choices: liquidate, merge with another firm, or exploit deposit insurance to increase expected returns. Bank regulators have helped managers avoid the first choice, and managers might use the protections afforded by the Bank Holding Company Act to avoid the second option. Only a few banks have used the third option.

The imposition of higher costs on banks than on alternative suppliers of banking products does not result in a shortage of new capital to existing banks as long as the present shareholders' previously invested capital is sufficient to absorb these costs. For example, assume that a bank has 100,000 common shares outstanding that trade at $100 a share, for a total market capitalization of $10,000,000. Deposit insurance premiums and supervisory costs are then expected to increase. If the present value of these previously unanticipated costs were $4,000,000 for this bank, the market value of its equity would be reduced to $6,000,000. Consequently, the 100,000 shares would decrease in price to $60 a share. Assume now that the authorities required the bank to increase its stockholders' equity by $6,000,000. If potential investors assume that the regulatory costs imposed on the bank would not change as a result of the bank obtaining more stockholder-generated funds and that the bank could earn the same return on the new funds as is currently earned, they would invest about $60 a share and the market value of the current shares would not decline.[6] However, if the regulatory costs (particularly deposit insurance premiums that are greater than the value of the insurance to a depository institution) were imposed on new investment, the current share prices would decline as the present shareholders would have to absorb those additional costs. As long as the share price remains positive after regulatory costs are factored in, additional capital can be raised. There is no shortage of capital, although present shareholders bear capital losses. Regulatory costs, though, could be sufficiently high to make equity values negative, at which point the current owners would abandon their investments and new capital could not be raised.

Undercapitalization

However, even when current bank equity values are not totally destroyed, the imposition of regulatory costs can cause a shortage of capital to the banking industry. New banks will not be started because the present value of these costs cannot be imposed on prospective shareholders. Alternative suppliers of bank products will expand instead. The consequence could be socially desirable or not, depending on the effect on externalities. For example, expensive field examinations and intrusive supervision could reduce failures that impose costs on third parties or prevent invidious discrimination against individuals. However, a socially undesirable outcome would result if the regulatory costs exceeded the value of these benefits. An unambiguously socially desirable outcome would be the removal of a deposit insurance subsidy that encouraged banks to take risks that they would not take if they bore the full cost of as well as the benefits from such risk taking.

Capital as Debt and Equity Holders' Claims Over Assets

Definition

In terms of both accounting and economics, the sum of debt plus equity (liabilities) is equal to and represents contractual and residual claims over assets. Debt and equity thus represent alternative ways of financing investments in assets. In a market without federal deposit insurance, the distinction between debt and equity is important only with respect to income taxation (interest payments are deductible expenses while dividends are not), bankruptcy costs, and monitoring costs. As the proportion of the assets of a firm that is financed increases with debt that is not government insured, the risk to the debt holders

increases and the interest rate that they demand increases accordingly. Thus, the market determines the optimal proportions of debt and equity.

The situation is different for banks because of the presence of federal deposit insurance that is not priced explicitly according to the risk borne by the FDIC. Consequently, debt holders' claims should be classified into two distinct groups. One is deposits, defined as debt claims that are guaranteed, *de jure* or *de facto,* by the FDIC. Short-term liabilities, such as banks' accounts and notes payable, probably are *de facto* insured, as they either will be covered should the FDIC take over an insolvent bank, or they will have been paid out or collateralized before the bank is taken over. The second group is uninsured debt—subordinated debentures.

Purposes of Capital for Banks

For banks, capital should be defined as the sum of equity and debt that is not insured by the FDIC. Capital, so defined, serves two important purposes. One is to absorb losses incurred by a bank. Thus, capital protects the deposit insurance fund. An important attribute of capital for banks with insured deposits (from the perspective of the FDIC) is that a bank experiencing financial difficulties should be prevented from distributing funds to capital holders before the authorities can act to close or otherwise reorganize the bank. (This is not generally a problem for other enterprises experiencing financial difficulties, because they can obtain funds only at an increasingly higher cost, unlike banks that can get FDIC-insured deposits at close to the riskless rate.) For the FDIC, then, subordinated debentures are as much capital as are equity claims, as long as the subordinated debenture holders cannot be repaid, directly or indirectly, within a period of one to two years.

The second purpose of capital is as an incentive to nongovernment agents to monitor a deposit-insured bank's risk taking and other activities. Deposit insurance removes this incentive from depositors, at least to the extent that they expect to have unrestricted access to the full amount of their funds whether or not their bank fails.

Equity Capital

Equity capital absorbs losses first, thereby protecting debtors (including the FDIC). The amount of capital required depends on the extent to which losses might occur. Because equity capital can be removed in the form of cash dividends, repurchases of stock, and payments such as bonuses and transfers to controlled entities for "services" priced above the market, debt holders often insist on covenants that restrict such asset drains when capital declines below some specified amount or ratio. Government-insured depositors have no such concern; hence, the deposit insurance agency should act to restrict asset drains before the probability is more than trivial that a loss might exceed a bank's capital.

Although equity holders clearly have incentives to monitor bank performance, they can benefit from a high degree of risk taking because they get all the returns from successful outcomes but absorb losses only to the extent of their investments in the bank. In effect, equity holders have a "put option" on the bank, with the exercise price being the amount owed to depositors.[7] Although the holders of equity in any limited liability corporation have this put option, the debt holders usually demand sufficiently high interest and protections (such as covenants and collateral) to reduce the *ex ante* value of the option to zero. However, the option usually has value to bank equity owners because, unlike most other creditors, the FDIC does not price its deposit insurance to account sufficiently for the risks taken by banks.

The value of the "deposit insurance put option" increases with variance of returns and the time through which the authorities take over the bank. As a bank's capital declines towards zero, the value of this put option increases because the equity holders have less to lose. Hence, once the value of the equity goes below the point where the option might be exercised, equity holders have incentives to increase its value. They can do this by increasing the riskiness of the bank's investments and operations, withdrawing funds from the bank, and delaying actions by the FDIC to displace them.

The authorities have attempted to limit risk taking by banks with legislative and regulatory restraints on the assets in which banks can invest and activities that they can undertake. Examples include the Glass-Steagall Act's separation of commercial and investment banking (assuming that this is the purpose of the separation[8]) and prohibitions against direct investments and insurance products. But these restraints rarely are effective because too many options remain within the set that is permitted to banks. For example, banks can accept exceptionally risky loans, invest in undiversified asset portfolios, and hold duration-unbalanced portfolios of assets and liabilities that subject banks to interest-rate risk or buy and sell interest rate options and futures for the same purpose. Furthermore, the restraints tend to increase risk as they limit the extent to which banks can diversify their portfolios and operations.[9]

Banks can delay being taken over by the authorities with at least two procedures. One is to employ the options available under generally accepted ac-counting principles (GAAP) to appear solvent when they really are not. For example, they can classify securities that have gone down in value since they were purchased as long-term investments; consequently, they do not have to record the capital losses. Securities that have gone up in value can be sold or classified as current investments, which allows the gains to be recorded. Similarly, loans on which unrecorded interest-rate-change losses have been incurred can be kept rather than sold. The other procedure is to convince the authorities to forbear from enforcing capital requirements. For example, banks in farm areas have used political influence to get Congress to grant them special exemptions. The authorities have allowed accountants to forbear from writing down loans to less developed countries despite strong evidence that these countries cannot repay their debt as contracted. The Federal Home Loan Bank Board adopted "regulatory accounting principles" that permitted savings and loans to defer losses on mortgage loan sales over the original maturities of the loans. As Edward J. Kane (1988) points out, government regulators have considerable incentives to put off taking prompt actions that force the reorganization or closure of capital-deficient banks.

Debt Capital—Deposits

Although deposits are debt to a bank, deposit insurance generally shifts the risk (and concerns about bank failures) from depositors to the FDIC. Time depositors can protect their funds from loss by limiting their investments to the insurance limit of $100,000 per account or per bank. Demand depositors with balances above $100,000 are protected if the FDIC follows a policy of having other banks purchase and assume the liabilities of failed banks or if the depositors can remove their funds before the authorities act to freeze uninsured deposit accounts. Depositors in banks deemed by the authorities to be "too large to fail" also are protected from loss. For most depositors, then, the cost of a bank's failing is, at most, disruption in the services they obtain should a bank fail—which is of minor importance, given the existence of many banks. Consequently, few depositors have incentives to monitor banks' activities. Demand depositors with large accounts need only be concerned with a bank's being closed before they can wire out their funds.

Debt Subordinated to the Depositors' and the FDIC's Claims

Subordinated debt serves to absorb losses, as does equity capital. As is the situation for equity capital, it can serve this purpose only if it cannot be redeemed, directly or indirectly, before the authorities can act to reorganize or close a bank. Hence, subordinated debt ought to have a maturity of at least a year or two and the bank or its subsidiaries should not be permitted to purchase it at any time. Because holders of subordinated debt cannot expect to be reimbursed by the FDIC, they should serve well as monitors over banks' activities.

Subordinated debt has several important advantages over equity capital. First, it promises an asymmetric payoff. Should a bank do well, debt holders collect only the interest promised. Should a bank do badly, the debt holders will absorb losses that exceed the equity holders' investment. Second, the interest on subordinated debt serves as a risk-adjusted deposit insurance premium, because the debt holders stand to lose should a bank engage in risky activities; hence, they will have to be reimbursed for this risk or they will not purchase the debentures. Third, when subordinated debt is publicly traded, the authorities are provided with an early warning signal in the form of the interest rate demanded on the debt and the difficulty for a bank in replacing maturing debt. Fourth, subordinated debt probably can be sold by closely held banks more inexpensively than the cost of their obtaining additional equity. Owners of such banks may not want to invest more of their personal wealth (thereby subjecting themselves to undiversified portfolios, particularly when they also work for these banks); outside investors rarely are interested in being minority shareholders. Closely held banks and banks with rarely traded securities, however, can sell subordinated debentures to the public or to institutional investors, such as pension funds and other banks, who are capable of monitoring the banks' activities. Fifth, interest on subordinated debt is a deductible expense; hence, it is no more costly (with respect to taxes) to a bank than are deposits. Indeed, subordinated debt differs from time deposits only in that the debentures are explicitly and implicitly not government insured.

Note that should losses wipe out a bank's equity capital, subordinated debt holders become equity holders. As equity holders, they now have incentives to increase the put option value of deposit insurance by increasing risks. Hence, unless the bank supervisors reorganize or close a bank before this occurs, an important advantage of subordinated debentures will be lost.

The Optimal Level of Debt and Equity Capital

The amount and type of capital used to finance the assets and operations of financial and nonfinancial corporations that do not have deposits (or other debt) guaranteed by a government agency is determined

by the marketplace of investors. The FDIC is the principal investor in banks, as it stands in place of insured depositors. Consequently, the FDIC (or other supervisory agencies or the Congress) should specify the conditions under which, at the least, the marginal and total losses that might result from a bank's failing equal the amount it pays for deposit insurance. If there are externalities from such failures, the amount paid for deposit insurance should be greater than the private costs of a bank's failure.

Four methods of reducing the cost of bank failure to the optimal amount are now described and critiqued. One is for the FDIC to charge premiums that equal the risks imposed on it by individual banks. The second is to require banks to hold capital in amounts that reflect and offset the risks of its assets; Third, a bank might be required to collateralize its deposits or restrict its assets to marketable securities. Fourth, a "high" level of capital could be required. Finally, a set of "capital triggers" is proposed to deal with the disincentives of banks and the authorities to replenish depleted capital.

Risk-Adjusted Deposit Insurance Premiums

Similar to many other debt holders or guarantors, the FDIC could rely on the price it charged for its guarantee to reimburse it for expected losses and to restrain banks from taking excessive losses. However, risk-adjusted deposit insurance premiums are not likely to be operational or effective, for several reasons. Thus far, despite substantial efforts by academics and others, no one has been able to determine what the appropriate charge should be. At most, estimates have been made of the risk of holding individual assets and liabilities, although it is (or should be) clear that risk is a function of the portfolio of assets and liabilities held by a bank. Assuming a price that adequately reflects risk could be determined, it is doubtful that it could be implemented without political interference that seeks to channel investments towards or away from specific assets and activities.

But, even if an unbiased but not instantaneously priced risk-adjusted premium were charged, banks with levels of capital below the amount at which the put option is "in the money" still would have considerable incentives to increase risk taking. Absent a change in the present regulatory situation (other than risk-adjusted deposit insurance premiums), banks with low capital levels could count on the authorities failing to act to prevent the bank from taking additional risks before the bank either won or lost its gamble. The FDIC could discourage this behavior if it could take away a bank's profits from successful risk taking with an after-the-fact extra premium. However, it is doubtful that the agency could separate these gains from gains a bank might have gotten as a result of exogenous events (including dumb luck) or superior skills.

The situation facing the FDIC differs from that of other guarantors not only because the FDIC is a government agency (and, hence, is likely to be ineffectively run), but because banks hold capital at levels that are much lower than almost any other kind of corporation. Borrowers and insurees who operate in nongovernment markets usually find this form of coinsurance to be considerably less expensive than selling no or low equity obligations (assuming that these could be sold). Thus, lenders and guarantors other than the FDIC rely on their customers having substantial amounts of their own capital at risk rather than on price alone as a means of discouraging opportunistic behavior (the moral hazard problem). For this reason and the reasons just outlined, this discussion now focuses on capital requirements.

Risk-Adjusted Capital

Under the sponsorship of the Bank for International Settlements, the bank regulatory agencies of the 12 major commercial countries (including the United States), adopted risk-based capital requirements in 1989 (the Basle Agreement).[10] These requirements specify two tiers of capital and four asset risk classes. It is applied to banks on a consolidated basis that includes subsidiaries undertaking banking and financial business. "Core capital" essentially is common equity stock, noncumulative perpetual preferred stock, and post-tax retained earnings less goodwill and investments in subsidiaries engaged in banking and financial activities that are not consolidated in national systems. "Supplementary capital" includes subordinated debentures with an original term to maturity of over five years, preferred stock, perpetual debt instruments, mandatory convertible debt instruments, and general and undisclosed (secret) loan loss reserves (later phased out). Core capital must be at least 4% of assets weighted according to risk, and total capital must be at least 8% of risk-weighted assets.

The first asset "risk" category, against which no capital is required (a weight of zero is applied) includes cash and claims collateralized by cash, claims on OECD central governments and central banks, and claims on central governments and central banks denominated in the national currency and funded in that currency. At national discretion, claims on and loans guaranteed by domestic public-sector entities can be zero weighted. The second category carries a 20% weight. It includes claims on multilateral development banks, claims on banks incorporated in the OECD and loans guaranteed by them, short-term (less than one-year maturity) claims on and loans guaranteed by other banks, claims on and loans guaranteed by nondomestic OECD public-sector entities, and cash items in the process of collection. The third category, 50% weight, consists only of mortgage loans on borrower-owned or rented residential property. All other assets fall into the fourth category, which is fully (100%) weighted. Off-balance-sheet exposures must be added to the amounts in the four assets categories to which they relate, after weighting by "credit conversion factors."

The Basle risk-related capital standards suffer from several serious shortcomings. First, interest-rate risk, which is largely responsible for the $150 billion or so savings and loan debacle, is not included. Nor is foreign exchange risk. The U.S. banking authorities are "working" on this problem; however, as Wall, Pringle, and McNulty (1990) demonstrate, measuring the effect of interest rate and foreign exchange risk hedges is complicated and is likely to be expensive to effect and monitor. Second, the presumed risk of individual broad classes of assets provides a poor measure of the total risk of a bank, which depends on the covariances of cash flows from individual assets and liabilities in addition to the variance of the cash flows from individual assets. Third, subordinated debentures, which have properties that are preferable to equity capital for the purpose of protecting the deposit insurance fund (as previously discussed), are relegated to secondary importance. Fourth, the actions the authorities must take should a bank fail to meet the capital requirements are not specified. Even if the shortcomings of the Basle standards could be corrected, it still is the case that risk-related capital standards, in general, share many of the shortcomings of risk-adjusted deposit insurance premiums. The capital level specified of 8% of risk-weighted capital is not sufficient to absorb losses that are likely to occur, at least for some banks. Hence, some banks still will have incentives to "bet the bank." In addition, the risk categories are so broad that banks easily can increase risk without affecting the capital required. In particular, loans to all commercial customers and countries are equally weighted—a loan to General Motors is deemed to be as risky as a loan to Chrysler and a loan to Belgium as risky as a loan to Bulgaria.

Collateralized Deposits or the "Narrow Bank" Proposal[11]

Banks could be required to hold assets that are valued at no more than the price they command if sold at very short notice (say, a day) as collateral against insured deposits. These assets would have to exceed the deposit amounts sufficiently to absorb losses in market value that could occur under all except extremely abnormal circumstances (such as a major depression or massive destruction of lives and property). The capital required would be the difference between this asset amount and the deposits that are insured. Alternatively, a bank could be organized as a separately incorporated holding company subsidiary holding only such assets; all other activities (such as lending) would be carried on in other subsidiaries of the holding company.

Were this proposal adopted, losses to the deposit insurance fund would be slight. They would be limited to those resulting from fraud and possibly to misestimation of the losses that could be taken on the assets securing the deposits, assuming that the authorities act sufficiently quickly and effectively to get a holding company to invest additional assets should its bank subsidiary's assets decline in value. Furthermore, the FDIC could reduce the scope and cost of field examinations. Thus, banks would directly save on FDIC premiums and would indirectly benefit from the cost of intrusive government supervision. An important shortcoming of this proposal is that banks that are separately organized would lose economies of scope because they could not engage in both deposit and lending operations and offer customer-related services, such as securities underwriting and trading. The cost of reorganizing banks or of creating the legal documentation to collateralizing deposits also might be considerable.

"High" Required Capital

Banks with insured deposits could be required to hold capital that is sufficient to absorb almost all losses that might be incurred. A problem with this "solution" is that, unlike the collateralized deposits proposal, the market value of the assets in which banks could invest would not be as accurately measured. Indeed, loans to other than very well known companies or in aggregates with well-estimated properties (such as residential mortgages and consumer loans) are not liquid and cannot be readily priced by reference to market transactions. This problem, though, can be dealt with by current value accounting that records the present value of assets and by requiring banks to hold capital amounts that are sufficient to cover measurement errors as well as losses. As with the collateralized deposits or narrow bank proposal, then, the result would be very low losses to the deposit insurance fund.

One possible shortcoming of the "high" required capital solution is the cost to banks of having to hold the capital. However, if subordinated debentures were counted fully as capital, the only cost to banks would be loss of a deposit insurance subsidy. In effect, all that is required is that banks hold time deposits that are explicitly and definitely not insured by the FDIC. The interest rates that a bank would have to pay on these obligations would reflect the actual risk incurred; in effect, the interest paid on subordinated debentures would be a market-determined risk-adjusted deposit insurance premium. Banks also would have to pay subordinated debt lenders for the cost of assessing and monitoring risk. But savings from the lesser amount of examinations and supervision that the FDIC would have to require would largely offset these now private costs. Indeed there might be a net savings to the extent that the private market risk assessors and monitors were more efficient than their government counterparts.

A shortcoming of this and the previously discussed "solutions" is the likelihood that the government agencies would not act quickly and decisively to require banks with inadequate capital to correct the situation before the put option incentives to take higher risks became operative. The "capital trigger" proposal discusses how this can be dealt with.

The "Capital Trigger" Proposal[12]

The essence of this proposal is that as a bank's capital ratios decline, the regulatory authorities first may and then must take specified actions to correct the situation. If a bank were *adequately capitalized,* say when its capital is above 15% of its assets[13], the banking authorities would only have to supervise it generally to be sure that the bank's risks were not excessively concentrated and potentially so large as to use up the capital, that correct reports were being filed, and that the bank was not being run fraudulently or otherwise contrary to law. In this regard the authorities could rely largely on audits by certified public accountants, particularly if GAAP were changed to include market values, as the Financial Accounting Standards Board has proposed. The *first level of supervisory concern* would occur when a bank's capital declined below 15% to perhaps 8% of assets. Should this occur, the bank would be subject to increased regulatory supervision and more frequent monitoring of its activities. This wide range should give the authorities room to get a bank back to adequate capitalization or to merge with another institution. At their discretion, the supervisory authorities could restrict the bank's growth, require it to sell especially risky assets and possibly shrink in size, allow transfers of funds within a holding company system only with the authorities' approval, and not permit dividends to be paid until the capital ratio had been brought back to 15% of assets.

The *second level of supervisory concern,* when the capital/asset ratio declines below 8%, triggers mandatory actions by the authorities. In addition to being subject to intense regulatory supervision and monitoring, the authorities must suspend dividend and interest payments on equity and subordinated debt serving as capital and approve all transfers of funds within a holding company system. Should this occur, it is likely that the suspension of interest on subordinated debt would trigger covenants that would result in the displacement of some or all of the board of directors. Because these actions are mandatory, bankers would have very great incentives to keep their banks' capital from declining below 8% of assets.

Should the capital/asset ratio decline below, for example, 5%, *mandatory recapitalization and reorganization* would be triggered. The bank would be taken over by the authorities and put into a conservatorship. Any amounts remaining after the institution is reorganized, sold, or liquidated would be returned to the debt and equity holders. This step should not be interpreted as a taking of assets by a government agency, for two reasons. First, if the equity capital had positive value, the stock and subordinated debt holders would recapitalize, merge, or liquidate the bank rather than allow it to be taken. Second, the possibility that the bank might be taken over prematurely should be considered a cost of deposit insurance; this cost can be avoided by a bank's either holding sufficiently high levels of capital or forbearing from investing in assets that might decline precipitously and considerably in value.

Conclusion

Banks may be over- or undercapitalized with respect to assets as a result of government-imposed restrictions and management that is not in the interests of shareholders. Overcapitalization could result from banks not being permitted to close branches or withdraw services that no longer were profitable. Legislation, such as the Glass-Steagall Act, prevents banks from holding optimal portfolios of assets and engaging in a preferred set of activities. Requirements that banks make loans to favored borrowers also causes overcapitalization in these assets. Restrictions on branching and mergers (including acquisitions of banks by nonbanks) may prevent banks from achieving economies of scale and scope. In addition, overcapitalization could be due to managers who can maximize bank size rather than stockholder wealth or who are incompetent, but who cannot be displaced because of legislative restrictions on bank takeovers. These situations should be distinguished from apparent (but not real) overcapitalization that results from banks not writing down assets that have lower present values when the decline in values

occurred. Undercapitalization could result from inefficient bank regulation that lowers returns to banks, thereby reducing entry into the industry.

The solution to asset over- and undercapitalization is removal of restrictive legislation and elimination of inefficient regulation (which is best achieved by less regulation). Aside from the costs to competitors, there are few (if any) externalities that might result should restrictive legislation be repealed.[14] Furthermore, if banks were required to hold adequate levels of capital and the requirement was enforced, little intrusive supervision or restrictions on assets and activities would be required.

Capital defined as explicitly not deposit insured debt and equity holders' claims over assets serves to absorb losses and give nongovernment agents incentives to manage banks effectively so that banks rarely become insolvent. Equity capital serves this purpose but has several important shortcomings. Dividends are not deductible expenses for purposes of computing tax liability, and deposit insurance gives equity holders incentives to "bet the bank" when their investments decline sufficiently. Debt subordinated to the claims of the FDIC also absorbs losses, is not subject to the shortcomings of equity, and offers other advantages.

This chapter presented four ways for the optimal level of capital to be achieved: risk-adjusted deposit insurance premiums, risk-adjusted capital, collateralized deposits or the "narrow bank" proposal, and "high" required capital. Each of these has faults, with the exception of "high" required capital. When subordinated debentures are included fully in capital, virtually the only cost to banks of holding high ratios of capital to assets is loss of a subsidy from underpriced deposit insurance. This is because subordinated debentures have exactly the same properties as time deposits, except that there is no doubt that they are not *de facto* insured by the FDIC. Finally, a means for overcoming bankers and the authorities' incentives to delay recapitalizing or reorganizing capital-depleted banks before they became insolvent is proposed. If adopted, this "capital trigger" proposal would be effective and easy to implement.[15]

Endnotes

1. The term "banks" encompasses all institutions with government-insured deposits, including commercial banks, savings banks, savings and loan associations, and credit unions.

2. The FDIC and the U.S. Treasury guarantee deposits in commercial banks, savings banks, and savings and loan associations and the National Credit Union Share Insurance Fund guarantees

deposits in credit unions up to $100,000 per account. In practice, almost all deposits are guaranteed at banks and there is usually assumed to be an implicit Treasury guaranty of the debt of government-sponsored enterprises.

3. For example, Bryan (1988) discusses "overcapacity" at some length, but he is not clear about what he means by capital. His text implies that he refers to assets (e.g., he says that other industries' response to overcapacity "is to disaggregate and restructure integrated suppliers, usually through spin-offs, mergers, joint ventures, or shared production"). But he describes "overcapacity" in banking with a chart showing equity capital.

4. Shareholders who would not have sold their shares also would save taxes on the funds that would have been distributed via dividends.

5. If this number is less than the amount that could be obtained and saved from selling or closing the branch, the branch should have been sold or closed, in which event the loss would have been recorded.

6. Unlike the situation for corporations without government-insured debt, the share price of banks' stock would not decrease when new shares were issued because there would not be a transfer of wealth to debt holders as a result of their risk having been reduced. However, if some bank debt holders (such as those with deposits over $100,000 and subordinated debt holders) believed that they are at risk, the share prices of banks issuing equity probably would decrease somewhat.

7. For perhaps the first formal analysis of this way of viewing deposit insurance, see Robert C. Merton (1977). This model has been applied by Marcus and Shaked (1984), Ronn and Verma (1986), Pennacchi (1987), and others.

8. See Benston (1990, Chapter 6) for arguments and evidence that supports the view that the purpose and effect of the Glass-Steagall Act is to restrict competition between banks and securities firms rather than reduce bank risk.

9. See Benston (1989) for a review and analysis of the risk and returns from combining commercial and investment banking.

10. See Benston (1991) for a more complete description and critique.

11. See Benston, et. al (1989), proposal 2 for details.

12. See Benston and Kaufman (1988) for the earliest version of this proposal, and Benston, et al. (1989) and Shadow Financial Regulatory Committee (1989) for similar versions.

13. The original proposal used 10% as the base percentage. This percentage has been increased (along with some others) to reduce the possibility that the deposit insurance fund would be used. In addition, I have come to believe even more strongly that a high capital requirement that includes subordinated debentures being counted fully as capital would impose costs only on poorly run banks. The optimal percentages, though, should be based on research findings.

14. See Benston (1983) for an analysis on which this assertion is based.

15. The "capital triggers" concept was adopted by Congress and the President in the Federal Deposit Insurance Improvement Act of 1991. Unfortunately, the regulatory agencies have set the "trigger" levels so low as to negate largely the intent of the Act.

References

Benston, George J., 1983, "Federal Regulation of Banking," *Journal of Bank Research.* 13 (Winter): 216-44. Updated versions are published as "Federal Regulation of Banking: Historical Overview," in George G. Kaufman and Roger C. Kormendi, eds., *Deregulating Financial Services: Public Policy in Flux,* Ballinger Publishing Company, Cambridge, MA, 1986, 1–47, and "Why Continue to Regulate Banks?: An Historical Assessment of Federal Banking Regulation," *Midland Corporate Finance Journal,* 5 (Fall): 1987, 67–82.

Benston, George J., 1989, "The Federal 'Safety Net' and the Repeal of the Glass-Steagall Act's Separation of Commercial and Investment Banking," *Journal of Financial Services Research,* 2: 287–305.

Benston, George J., 1990, *The Separation of Commercial and Investment Banking: The Glass-Steagall Act Revisited and Reconsidered,* Oxford University Press, New York.

Benston, George J., "International Bank Capital Standards," in *Emerging Challenges for the International Financial Services Industry,* James R. Barth and Phillip F. Bartholomew, eds., Greenwich, CT: JAI Press (an earlier version was presented at the Joint Universities Conference on Regulating Commercial Banks: Australian Experience in Perspective,

Canberra, Australia, August 1989), 1991, forthcoming.

Benston, George J., R. Dan Brumbaugh, Jr., Jack M. Guttentag, Richard J. Herring, George G. Kaufman, Robert E. Litan, and Kenneth E. Scott, 1989, *Blueprint for Restructuring America's Financial Institutions: Report of a Task Force,* The Brookings Institution, Washington, D.C.

Benston, George J. and George G. Kaufman, 1988, *Risk and Solvency Regulation of Depository Institutions: Past Policies and Current Options,* Monograph Series in Finance and Economics, Salomon Center, New York University Graduate School of Business Administration, Monograph 1988 -1; a shorter version appears as "Regulating Bank Safety and Performance," in *Restructuring Banking & Financial Services in America,* William S. Haraf and Rose Marie Kushmeider, eds., American Enterprise Institute for Public Policy Research, Washington, D.C.: 63–99.

Bryan, Lowell C., 1988, *Breaking Up the Bank,* Dow Jones Irwin, New York, N.Y.

Kane, Edward J., 1988, "How Market Forces Influence the Structure of Financial Regulation," in *Restructuring Banking & Financial Services in America,* William S. Haraf and Rose Marie Kushmeider,

eds., American Enterprise Institute for Public Policy Research, Washington, D.C.: 343–82.

Marcus, Alan and Israel Shaked, 1984, "The Valuation of FDIC Deposit Insurance Using Option-Pricing Estimates," *Journal of Money, Credit and Banking,* 16: 446–59.

Merton, Robert C., 1977, "An Analytic Derivation of the Cost of Deposit Insurance and Loan Guarantees: An Application of Modern Option Pricing Theory," *Journal of Banking and Finance,* 1: 439–52.

Pennacchi, George G., 1987, "A Reexamination of the Over- (or Under-) Pricing of Deposit Insurance," *Journal of Money, Credit and Banking,* 19: 340–360.

Ronn, Ehud I. and Avinash K. Verma, 1986, "Pricing Risk-Adjusted Deposit Insurance: An Option-Based Model," *Journal of Finance,* 41: 871–95.

Shadow Financial Regulatory Committee, 1989, *An Outline of a Program for Deposit Insurance Regulatory Reform,* Statement No. 41, February 13. Reprinted in Wall, Larry D., John J. Pringle, and James E. McNulty, 1990, "Capital Requirements for Interest-Rate and Foreign-Exchange Hedges," *Economic Review* (Federal Reserve Bank of Atlanta), LXXV (May/June): 14–28.

Chapter 3

Mergers and Acquisitions: The Banking Industry
When Will Foreign Banks Step Up?
Is Now the Time or Is it Too Late?

Robert Everett Bostrom
Executive Vice President, Legal and Regulatory and General Counsel
National Westminster Bancorp, New York, NY

In the midst of the high level of domestic bank merger and consolidation activity, the question arises as to why foreign banks have not been more active. There are a number of reasons that explain the lack of activity. Several new legal considerations in the United States will also impact considerably upon future decisions by foreign banks to move forward in the domestic bank acquisition market.

The absence of significant acquisitions of domestic banks by foreign banks at present contrasts with the 1980s which were marked by a number of such acquisitions. These transactions were cash purchases and were typically for a high premium over book value.

Foreign Bank Acquisitions

Foreign bank acquisitions of domestic banks in the late 1970s and 1980s included the following acquisitions.

♦ Bank of Ireland of First NH Banks Inc. in 1988.

♦ Citizens Financial Group in Rhode Island by The Royal Bank of Scotland in 1989.

♦ First Maryland Bancorp by Allied Irish Banks in 1983.

♦ National Bank of North America by National Westminster Bank in 1979 and subsequent acquisitions of First Jersey Corp. and Ultra Bancorporation in 1987 and 1989.

♦ Banco Commercial de Mayaguez by Banco Bilbao-Vizcaya in 1988.

♦ Algemene Bank Nederland ("ABN") of LaSalle National Bank and subsequent acquisitions of banks in Illinois in 1987 and in 1988.

♦ European American Bank by Amro Bank in 1989.

♦ Commerce Bank by Banco Mercantile.

♦ J. Henry Schroeder Bank and Trust Company by Industrial Bank of Japan in 1986.

♦ Harris Bancorp by Bank of Montreal in 1984.

♦ Crocker National Bank by Midland Bank in 1981.

♦ Marine Midland Bank by Hongkong and Shanghai Banking Corporation in 1979.

♦ Western Diversified Bancorp in 1984 by Canadian Commercial Bank.

♦ Tri-state Bank Corporation by Mitsubishi Bank in 1984.

♦ Union Bank by The Bank of Tokyo in 1988.

In addition, a number of *de novo* banks were established by foreign banks during this period. However, the 1990s have been marked by a virtual cessation in major bank acquisition activity by foreign banks in the United States. The window of opportunity that existed with low bank stock prices in the early 1990s was missed by most foreign banks that were struggling with the same kinds of problems that U.S. banks were experiencing, including declining capital, increased capital requirements, declining margins, and increasing amounts of nonperforming

29

HLT and real estate loans. In addition, multinational and cross-industry acquisitions in other countries, such as the merger of the NMB Postbank Group and Nationale-Nederlanden and the acquisition of Midland Bank PLC by the parent of Hongkong and Shanghai Banking Corporation, have diverted the energy and resources of foreign banks away from the United States.

New Domestic Transactions

Recently announced transactions are evidence that the consolidation of the banking industry in the United States is continuing. Some of these include BancOne's agreement to acquire Valley National Corporation in a $1.2 billion exchange of stock; Key Corp.'s agreement to purchase 100% of Puget Sound Bancorp for $760,000,000 in stock; and National Bank of Detroit's $853,000,000 transaction with INB Financial Corp. In addition, a number of banks in the United States are currently poised to continue major acquisition efforts. The number of potential targets is large, and they include a number of less than healthy institutions, such as First City Bancorp, MNC Corp., Hibernia, Riggs, and others which have been identified in published reports. The First Union Corporation acquisition of Southeast Bank in 1991 may prove to be a model for similar types of assisted situations. In addition, the emergence of Kohlberg, Kravis, Roberts & Company as a partner in the Fleet Financial Group purchase of the Bank of New England and the recent announcement that it may be involved in a similar transaction involving First Interstate is yet another approach in this area.

The situation in New England is uncertain and the future of Shawmut, Bay Banks, and Bank of Boston is not clear. In the Southeast, a merger of Sun Trust and Barnett Banks would create another substantial regional bank and further reduce the number of possible major acquisition targets in the Southeast. In the western United States, no one is quite certain what will happen to Wells Fargo and First Interstate. A number of major healthy thrifts, including H.F. Ahmanson, Great Western and Golden West, could be major players going forward. In the Midwest, First Chicago and Continental may be candidates for consolidation.

The institutions emerging as potential acquirors in the future include Bank of New York, Key Corp., Fleet, CoreStates, BancOne, and NationsBank. In addition, institutions which appear well-positioned and have thus far approached acquisitions cautiously, include Wachovia Corp., First Union Corporation, Fifth Third Bancorp, Sun Trust Banks, and PNC Financial Corp. Other strong regional institutions that have emerged in the marketplace as potential

acquirors include NBD Bancorp, Marshall & Ilsley Corp., Firstar Corp., First Alabama Bancshares, First Virginia Banks, and Mercantile Bankshares.

With the exception of the acquisition in 1991 of the York Bank and Trust Company from Midlantic by First Maryland Bancorp, a wholly owned subsidiary of Allied Irish Banks, in a transaction valued at approximately $130,000,000, the acquisition by Banco de Santander of a 24.9% interest in First Fidelity Bancorp in 1991, and the acquisition of Talman Savings and Loan Association by ABN AMRO in 1992, foreign banks have been noticeably quiet. It is important to question why foreign banks have remained inactive considering the industry-wide consolidation that is occurring, the number of healthy institutions that are poised for acquisition, and the number of institutions that are unhealthy and that will, ultimately, be subject to an acquisition at a favorable price.

Economic, Legal, and Regulatory Issues

Current developments in the U.S. economy, the global economy, and in the legal and bank regulatory arena in the United States suggest that foreign banks will not be making major acquisitions in the United States in the near future. With the price of domestic bank stocks up 65% from their historic lows before the recent sell-off and with the level of domestic bank merger activity accelerating, the cost of entry has increased as a function of high stock prices and higher acquisition premiums. The ability to pay the higher prices is a function of stock-for-stock deals the use of favorable accounting treatment, economies of scale from in-market mergers, and sufficient knowledge of the domestic market to turn around troubled institutions. These factors were all present in BancOne's recent acquisition of Valley National Corporation. Foreign banks that do not already own a bank in the United States cannot easily benefit from these advantages. As consolidation continues, there will be fewer acquisition targets and the price of entry will become higher. In addition, many banks especially foreign banks, are reluctant to make acquisitions of unhealthy institutions which limits one category of opportunities. The experience of Midland Bank, Hongkong and Shanghai Banking Corporation, and others has not been lost on foreign banks considering expansion by acquisition in the United States.

The current legal and regulatory climate in the United States for a major acquisition by a foreign bank is also not favorable. Provisions of the Federal Deposit Insurance Corporation Improvement Act of

1991 (FDICIA) not only have heightened the regulation and supervision of foreign banks in the United States, but also have significantly raised the level of scrutiny and analysis to which a foreign bank will be subject in seeking approval of the Federal Reserve Board to acquire a bank in the United States. This will affect foreign bank acquisitions in the United States in the near future.

In considering making an investment in a bank in the United States, foreign banks have a number of different options. They include the following:

1. A strategic alliance which does not necessarily involve any share or ownership interest;

2. A less than 5% investment;

3. A less than controlling investment between 5% and 25%;

4. A controlling investment in excess of 25%; or

5. A merger of equals approach which would involve the creation of a new bank with a new host country charter and the issuance of new stock in the new host country.

Any of the alternatives which the exception of a less than 5% investment will be subject to substantially new burdens and application criteria under the Bank Holding Company Act as a result of FDICIA.

Foreign banks must also consider the impact of restrictive state statutes which may prohibit the acquisition of banks chartered under state law and interstate banking statutes that may have an unintended impact on acquisitions by foreign (non-U.S.) banks. These obstacles were faced and overcome by Allied Irish Banks, National Westminster Bank and, more recently, ABN AMRO. In addition, state regional reciprocity statutes may inadvertently preclude foreign (non-U.S.) banks from making acquisitions in the region by virtue of anti-leap frog provisions which require that a bank holding company seeking to expand within the region have some required percentage of their deposits within the region.

One possible strategy is to acquire a small institution and then expand by purchasing assets and deposits from the RTC and the FDIC and other smaller opportunities. However, this requires a high level of U.S. management. At a time when profits from traditional banking activities are declining, when nonbank competitors, such as credit card and consumer finance operations, are taking away traditional banking business and customers, and when regulation of banks is becoming more restrictive, one alternative for a foreign bank to expand in the United States is to acquire permissible nonbanking activities that are complementary with a foreign bank's operations.

As U.S. banks sell their leasing companies, finance companies, credit card companies, mortgage banking operations, and other nonbanking subsidiaries to raise capital, an alternative opportunity to bank acquisitions exists. However, such acquisitions require prior approval and it is anticipated that foreign banks will face heightened scrutiny even in connection with expansion into these areas. In addition, as U.S. banks sell commercial and industrial loan assets, significant opportunities will arise to expand in these areas by asset purchases.

Case Studies of Foreign Buyers

The few recent investments and acquisitions by foreign banks have raised many issues and have been quite diverse in structure and approach. The Banco de Santander and the ABN AMRO applications are examples of how complicated the reach of the International Banking Act and state interstate banking statutes can be for foreign banks with diverse interests in the United States and outside the United States. Such applications will be more difficult as a result of FDICIA.

The Banco de Santander transaction involved a substantial noncontrolling investment, presumably to provide First Fidelity with the additional capital necessary to support a strategic plan that would be profitable for shareholders. This acquisition involved substantial analysis of various interstate banking provisions. It was further complicated by the fact that Banco de Santander had originally selected Florida as its home state but changed its home state to Rhode Island pursuant to the provisions of Regulation K which permit a one-time change of home state. Because First Fidelity had subsidiary banking organizations located in New Jersey and Pennsylvania, it was necessary to review the interstate banking laws of those statutes to determine whether those states authorized the acquisition of a bank on a reciprocal basis by a New Jersey bank holding company. Such determinations were reached by the various state banking authorities.

In addition, incident to the transaction, Banco de Santander, (which also owns 9.89% of the voting shares of The Royal Bank of Scotland which owns Citizens Financial Group, a Rhode Island bank holding company), applied for the Federal Reserve Board's approval to retain those voting shares of The Royal Bank of Scotland and thereby to retain the interest in Citizens Financial Group.

AMRO and ABN faced a host of similar issues in connection with AMRO's acquisition of 100% of the voting shares of European American Bancorp and the subsequent merger of ABN and AMRO. The merger of ABN and AMRO involved a determination under state interstate banking statutes and the prior approval of the New York Superintendent of Banks. In granting approvals in such situations, the Superintendent is generally required to find that the laws of the state where the out-of-state holding company is located permit the acquisition of banks in that state by New York bank holding companies on a reciprocal basis. The application was filed in early 1990, before the Illinois nationwide trigger date of December 1, 1990. Thus, the New York and Illinois interstate banking statutes were not reciprocal at the time. However, the New York Banking Law provides that the Banking Board may vary or waive any requirement of the New York Banking Law. The Banking Board waived the reciprocity requirement normally required by the Superintendent because of the predominately foreign nature of the proposed transaction, the fact that Illinois had enacted in a law providing for reciprocal banking acquisitions with New York that would become effective in December 1990, and the potential adverse effects on Algemene and AMRO of delaying the consummation of the proposed transaction until December 1990.

Prior to the Foreign Bank Supervision Enhancement Act (FBSEA), in addition to the problems that domestic banks encounter in satisfying the criteria under Section 3 of the Bank Holding Company Act, foreign banks have had difficulty in satisfying the Federal Reserve Board requirement that the foreign bank has the ability to be a source of financial and managerial strength and support to the U.S. subsidiary bank. In some cases, the Federal Reserve Board has required commitments to maintain a specified capital level in the bank or bank holding company that is acquired as a condition for approval of the aquisition. The Federal Reserve Board has always analyzed the financial condition of the foreign organization and required sufficient information to permit an assessment of the financial strength and operating performance of the foreign organization. Although this is not any different than the criteria applied to domestic banks, the application of the criteria to foreign banks has been more troublesome and more difficult. In addition, when assessing the capital of foreign banks, it is difficult to determine the extent to which capital guidelines as adopted in the home country are consistent with those in the United States and the extent to which the parent country regulator applies those standards.

Future applications will be more difficult as a result of FBSEA which is Subtitle A of Title II of FDICIA. The Congressional reaction to the domestic banking crisis and the BCCI and Banca Nazionale del Lavoro affairs in the United States resulted in the passage of FBSEA which imposed new requirements on foreign banks in the United States and increased the level of scrutiny and supervision of foreign banks in the United States.

Several provisions of FBSEA will impact upon foreign banks seeking to make an investment in or acquire a bank in the United States. First, Section 3 of the Bank Holding Company Act now applies to foreign banks even if the foreign bank does not already own a domestic bank. Thus, a foreign bank must obtain prior Federal Reserve Board approval before acquiring directly or indirectly more than 5% of the voting shares of any U.S. bank as if the foreign bank was a domestic bank holding company. Under prior law, unless a foreign bank already owned 25% or more of the voting shares or otherwise controlled a U.S. bank, an application was not necessary. Although, this change could require Federal Reserve Board approval for any two foreign banks with branches or agencies in the United States to merge in their home countries, staff of the Federal Reserve Board has recently indicated that a full application would probably not be required in such a situation.

More importantly, FBSEA expands the criteria which the Federal Reserve Board applies in considering applications to acquire shares of a bank or bank holding company by a foreign bank. In particular, a foreign bank seeking to acquire a domestic bank must satisfy the Federal Reserve Board that it can and will make available to the Federal Reserve Board sufficient information on the activities of its operations and those of its affiliates as required by the Federal Reserve Board in order to determine compliance with the Bank Holding Company Act and other applicable laws. This involves disclosure and analysis of the existence and applicability of bank secrecy laws in those jurisdictions in which the foreign bank operates. In addition, a foreign bank will be required to satisfy the "comprehensive consolidated supervision and oversight" standard. This means that the foreign bank must be subject to comprehensive supervision or regulation on a consolidated basis by the appropriate authorities in its home country. Recent interim regulations promulgated by the Federal Reserve Board ("Interim Regulations") have provided guidance as to what it will assess in making that determination. The Interim Regulations provide that the Federal Reserve Board will assess the extent to which the home country supervisor does the following:

♦ ensures that the foreign bank has adequate procedures for monitoring and controlling its worldwide operations;

♦ receives information on the condition of the foreign bank and its subsidiaries or offices, whether through examination, audit reports, or otherwise;

♦ obtains information on the dealings and relationship between the foreign bank and its affiliates;

♦ obtains financial reports that permit analysis of the consolidated, worldwide condition of the foreign bank;

♦ evaluates prudential standards on a worldwide basis.

Further, the Federal Reserve Board will also consider whether the foreign bank has provided the Board with adequate assurances that it will make available such information on the operations or activities of the foreign bank or any of its affiliates that the Federal Reserve Board deems necessary to determine and enforce compliance with law.

At this time, it appears that satisfying the information disclosure requirement and the comprehensive supervision requirement will require significant time and attention by a foreign bank. There are a number of other aspects of FBSEA that will affect the processing of foreign bank applications, such as new concerns for shareholder identity and the competence, experience, and integrity of the officers, directors, and principal shareholders and their record of compliance with applicable law and the record of the foreign bank in fulfilling commitments to, and conditions imposed by the Federal Reserve Board in prior applications, and others.

Finally, although not relevant to the actual application process, under new capital restoration provisions in FDICIA, a person who controls an undercapital-ized institution is required to guaranty any capital restoration plan which is submitted to the appropriate Federal banking agency. This guaranty remains effective until the institution has been adequately capitalized on an average during each of four consecutive calendar quarters. These requirements should not be overlooked by any foreign bank considering an acquisition in the United States.

The most likely candidates for expansion in the United States at present include the Canadian banks and other European banks who view their own home markets as being unable to provide sufficient opportunity for expansion. Unique circumstances may force some banks to act, notwithstanding the unfavorable climate. For example, the Canadian banks may believe they have to act as a result of the free trade agreement which may encourage U.S. expansion as a defensive measure to protect their position in an expanding North American market. Foreign banks with a presence may be compelled to act to defend current market shares in an era of consolidation. Although foreign banks continue to be interested in bank acquisitions in the United States, as evidenced by public announcements and reports about Credit Lyonais, Westpac Banking Corporation, Royal Bank of Canada, Bank of Montreal, and Canadian Imperial Bank of Commerce, acquisitions will be increasingly difficult in view of high stock prices, increasing premiums over book value, the intense competition for potential targets, and the unfavorable regulatory climate for foreign banks.

Chapter 4

Savings Institutions:
The Salvaged Star of Equities?

David W. Giesen
Advisor, Financial Institutions Group
Kemper Securities, Inc., Chicago, IL

Thomas J. Parliment
President
Parliment Consulting Service, Inc., Delavan, WI

Not long ago, investment managers reviewing the fleets of their portfolios consigned savings institution equities to scrap yards behind the brackish marsh of Wall Street.

With good reason, many swore that they would walk on water before sailing any equity ship backed by a savings institution. These equities, most acknowledged, struck an iceberg in the late 1980s, sinking many portfolios, causing others to list badly and generally inflicting seasickness.

But the Titanic of 1989 has become the posh cruise ship of 1992. From the depths of 1991, savings institution equities have been so well salvaged that many investors have posted one-year returns of between 50% and 100%, or more. Multiyear investors have benefitted from a consumer franchise that is increasingly becoming the talk of the equity seas.

What happened? Nothing short of one of the biggest top-to-bottom makeovers in history. Beginning with a dramatic change in regulation and supervision in 1989, today's healthy thrifts have benefitted from an improved economic climate, elimination of government-controlled (and backed) competitors, and a resurgence in demand for mortgage lending products.

Perhaps surprisingly, most of the big beneficiaries on this stock in recent years have been relatively small investors whose preferred investment vehicle generally has been on Main Street rather than Wall Street. Indeed, some of these depositor-owners bought shares of their institution in 1991 for $10 a share and, in a matter of weeks, saw their investment value double. Few have seen less than a 20% rise.

Moreover, with most savings institutions trading at a percentage of rather than a multiple of book value, most of these institutions are getting second, very positive looks from portfolio managers and shrewd investors.

Fundamental Changes

After the Keating debacle, many professional investors completely avoided savings institutions on the grounds that

1. the institutions' managers were ill-equipped to control the investments in their portfolio;

2. regulators were unsure and unstable; and

3. perhaps, most importantly, the holy grail of accounting that reported on this industry was flawed to the core.

Many thought the accounting of the times was nothing more than paint hiding deep gashes on the hull of most institutions.

But in the past year, savings institution equities have been refloated due to their relatively inexpensive pricing. As investor demand improved, price-to-book ratios, on average, rose from between 30% and 40% to between 60% and 80%. Similar improvements were encountered in price-earnings ratios, although like price-to-book ratios, these performance measures are significantly under comparables for banks. Table 4.1 illustrates the significant financial changes in performance of savings institutions from 1987 to 1992.

Legislative Clean-up

Much of today's fundamental strength in savings institution stocks can be traced directly to the passage of the Financial Institutions Reform, Recovery & Enforcement Act of 1989 (FIRREA). Universally decried by most savings institutions, FIRREA's objective was to clean up the mess of the 1980s and to

toughen the capital standards that form the basic strength of savings institutions.

From a capital markets standpoint, FIRREA laid a foundation for a more stable earnings base by moderating the laws and regulations that gave rise to the excesses of the 1980s. FIRREA prohibited investments in junk bonds, which most institutions were ill-equipped to underwrite and manage, effectively stopped direct investment in real estate developments,

---

Table 4.1   Selected Savings Institutions Financial Data National Aggregates (Dollars in Millions)

	March 31, 1992	At December 31, 1991	1990	1989	1988	1987
Assets	910,916	946,333	1,114,868	1,290,064	1,392,268	1,298,655
Investments	123,725	124,273	150,236	170,751	192,984	175,576
Loans	587,338	612,761	705,960	821,617	848,284	787,813
One-to-four family mtgs.	418,757	431,124	483,777	545,644	552,502	509,359
Real Estate Owned	18,330	20,413	27,270	27,866	25,530	19,924
Real Estate for Inv.	1,738	2,026	3,387	6,022	6,988	7,452
Service Corp. Inv.	10,717	11,059	15,816	21,631	24,455	23,423
Deposits	725,975	753,201	860,013	974,659	1,003,043	963,391
Capital	52,737	49,502	32,447	27,267	49,294	38,405
One-to-four family mtgs/Total Assets	45.97%	45.56%	43.39%	42.30%	39.68%	39.22%
Loans/Assets	64.48%	64.75%	63.32%	63.69%	60.93%	60.66%
REO/Total Assets	2.01%	2.16%	2.45%	2.16%	1.83%	1.53%
REO & REI/Assets	2.20%	2.37%	2.75%	2.63%	2.34%	2.11%
Service Corporation/Assets	1.18%	1.17%	1.42%	1.68%	1.76%	1.80%
Capital/Assets	**5.79%**	**5.23%**	**2.91%**	**2.11%**	**3.45%**	**2.96%**

	1992[1]	For the 12 Months Ended December 31, 1991	1990	1989	1988	1987
Interest Margin	24,108	21,245	18,335	16,043	18,269	20,098
Other Income	6,516	7,101	5,721	8,296	8,119	8,054
Gains on Sale	1,736	1,897	(45)	998	2,389	2,727
Other Expenses	19,696	23,248	27,680	28,834	25,419	26,598
Income Before Taxes	6,596	(294)	(12,164)	(18,065)	(8,953)	(2,744)
Taxes	2,636	2,411	1,111	872	2,175	2,877
Net Income[2]	3,960	(2,705)	(13,275)	(18,937)	(11,128)	(5,621)
Return on Avg Assets[3]	0.43%	−0.26%	−1.10%	−1.41%	−0.83%	−0.87%
Return on Avg Equity	NA	−6.60%	−44.46%	−49.47%	−25.38	−29.27%

[1] 1992 totals are annualized based on March 31, 1992 results.
[2] Before extraordinary items.
[3] Estimated 1992 full-year results.

Notes: Savings institution income finally began to turn the corner in 1991 as the RTC became more successful in liquidation problem savings institutions and as interest rates decreased. As a result of fewer problem institutions and higher percentages of interest bearing assets to costing liabilities, margins improved consistently during the 5.25 year timeframe. Further, FIRREA's effects are most most evident in the significantly reduced services corporation investment, which reflects FIRREA's significant restrictions on real estate development.

Source: Sheshunoff Information Services, Inc.

oughened capital standards, and set in motion the mechanism to resolve problem institutions that were sapping healthy institution's earnings.

Through the late 1980s, many thinly-capitalized institutions had been bidding up the cost of deposits to cover their ongoing losses. As losses mounted for some, institutions paid through lost earnings because deposits were needed to replace lost or nonexistent capital. To acquire the deposits, problem institutions bid up deposit costs. The former Federal Savings and Loan Insurance Corporation's inability to react (due to lack of funds) compounded the problem and ultimately led to FIRREA.

Because of FIRREA, many marginal thrifts with embedded franchise value were acquired or merged into stronger thrifts or, for the first time on an "official" basis were merged into banks. Alternatively, some institutions went to the capital markets, raised needed equity, and returned to financial viability.

The second step in restoring earnings stability was creation of the Resolution Trust Corporation (RTC) and, in subsequent years, providing the funding necessary for the RTC to close problem institutions. While the RTC was not without its problems, its effect has been to terminate many weak savings institutions bereft of capital and sapping earnings from the healthy.

Atop these changes, the regulatory environment for savings institutions improved dramatically. Supervisors and examiners became more experienced and more aggressive at identifying and stopping problems before they reached crisis proportion. FIRREA further enhanced this ability by providing broader supervisory authority to stop practices perceived as "unsafe and unsound" and to level civil money penalties against managers and directors that failed to abide by regulation and regulatory directives.

Savings institutions stocks declined dramatically in the months following the passage of the Financial Institutions Reform, Recovery and Enforcement Act. Using August 1, 1989 as a base, savings institution stocks have fallen deeper and have yet to recover as strongly as either the S&P 500 or the Dow Jones Industrial Average (Figure 4.1).

Environmental Changes

The provisions in FIRREA that lifted restrictions on bank ownership of savings institutions came amid a fundamental restructuring of the financial system that changed the overall attractiveness of thrifts to other financial intermediaries. Simply, thrifts have the asset products and experience that many community bankers are seeking.

The reason is that for many smaller banks commercial credits have been harder to come by. The rise of Wal-Mart in the Midwest in the late 1980s (and, more recently, in New England), for example, forced many small businesses to close and reduced the number of small commercial credits. Many banks in smaller communities have turned to consumer credit to replace these customers.

In looking at banks of between $100 million and $500 million in assets, this convergence becomes quite apparent. In both 1989 and 1990, these "community banks" had more than half their loans in mortgages. If their liquidity was factored in, most could qualify as thrifts for tax purposes and, prior to 1989, for regulatory purposes.

Moreover, the emphasis on mortgages has led many community banks to join the Federal Home Loan Bank System, the central credit facility for housing lenders. It is as if the time-honored war of cultures between thrifts and banks is over—*the thrifts won!*

Savings institutions are suddenly desired because they have the single largest concentration of core relationship drivers of any set of financial institutions—mortgage loans. From this relationship, which brings about prolonged, monthly contact with customers, also comes consumer lending products, investment vehicles, and deposit services that enhance a financial institution's stable of low-cost deposits.

Many savings institutions have been slow or hard-pressed to utilize the tangible impact of this intangible asset in cross-selling efforts. By contrast, banks recognize the value of mortgage servicing but have had a disadvantage similar to what savings institutions face in building core deposits. Most banks are fairly recent entrants in the mortgage market and have limited experience in originating and managing mortgage-related assets.

Banks also view savings institutions as an inexpensive means to enter new markets. Buying a bank might mean, for example, paying a multiple in excess of two times book value, whereas a savings institution can often be had for between book value and 1.5 times book value.

Figures 4.2–4.5 describe the dollar volume and number of thrift IPO by year and by region.

Portfolio Considerations

The questions for portfolio managers often are:

♦ How big is the remaining opportunity?

♦ How does one differentiate the "winners" from the "losers"?

Figure 4.1   Thrift Stock Performance from FIRREA to Present

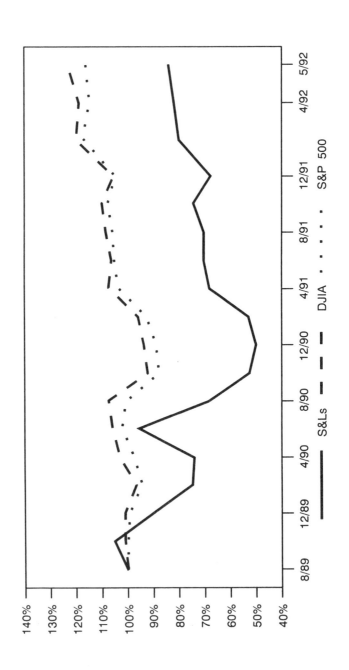

Note: August 1989 = 100

Figure 4.2   Thrift IPOs: Total Dollar Amount by Years

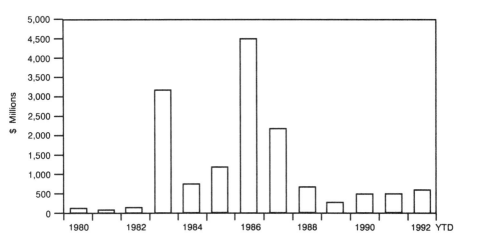

Source: Sheshunoff Information Services, Inc.

♦ What factors will drive the price of savings institution stock skyward?

♦ How does one take advantage of the opportunity available in the marketplace?

The most obvious question is, "How much opportunity remains?" The simplest answer is to review the number of savings institutions and the number of mutual institutions remaining. The former defines the universe of acquisition opportunities and the latter presents the potential that exists for initial public offerings of stock during the next decade.

In general, like the financial institution business, the sheer number of savings institutions has declined markedly in the past decade. From more than 4,000 institutions in 1980, the total number of operating savings institutions declined to approximately 2,000 in 1992 and is expected to decrease even further in the next five years. Consolidation brought about by mergers with larger institutions is expected to bring this number to about 1,500 or less by 1997.

For the investment community, two means exist to capitalize on this change. The first is to invest directly in the 1,000 or so publicly traded savings institutions' stock. The second, as an individual, is to place a deposit in a mutually chartered institution and hope it completes an initial public offering process known as conversion. Upon conversion, an eligible depositor receives nontransferable "subscription rights" to acquire at a set price an amount of shares less than or equal to a preset maximum, usually 5% or less of an institution's offering. It is expected that by 1997, more than half of the remaining mutuals will convert to public ownership.

But not all institutions considering a public offering, whether already public or mutual, are worthy investment candidates. The key, is to review an institution's stability of earnings. For the savings institution of today, this stability is a function of consistent net interest margin, minimal dependence on gains from sale of assets, good development of noninterest income, and tight cost control.

Figure 4.3   Thrift IPOs: Deal Volume by Year

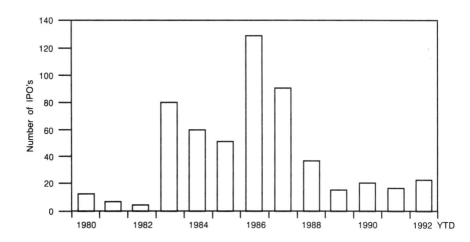

Source: Sheshunoff Information Services, Inc.

Most investors who consider savings institution equities as a potential investment begin by looking at interest margins. One sign of stable margins is an institution's one-year gap to asset ratios. Savings institutions, because their assets are primarily longer-term mortgages funded by short-and-intermediate-term deposits, generally have negative one-year gaps or more liabilities than assets that reprice in a year or less. The more negatively gapped an institution, the higher the probability that interest expense increases in a rising rate environment will exceed improvements in interest income.

Savings institutions have made strong strides in reducing negative gaps in recent years. The authorization of adjustable rate mortgages (ARMs) in the early 1980s, and the subsequent consumer confidence in this instrument (caused by its growing awareness and caps limiting annual and lifetime loan payment increases) have made ARMs an easier sell.

Likewise, a cautious diversification into consumer loan products, such as automobile, home equity, and unsecured personal purpose loans, also has brought shorter-term assets to many institutions' books. As a result, many well-run institutions have stated gap-to-asset ratios of between -5% and -15%. Many of the "outliers" are institutions with strong capital and those capable of withstanding a significant change in market interest rates.

Alternatively, a few institutions will use core deposits, notably passbooks, to stabilize interest margins. Chicago-area savings institutions, for example, have frequently benefitted from large bases of passbook savings from ethnic savers of Hispanic and Eastern European origin. Passbooks at some of these institutions often exceed 30% of total deposits and move within a relatively narrow range of interest rates. The comparably higher values that have arisen among Chicago institutions during 1992 (initial offerings are, in some cases, priced at more than 50% of pro forma book value) were due to a large extent to the stabilizing influence of these deposits.

Figure 4.4   Thrift IPOs: Volume of Deals by Region

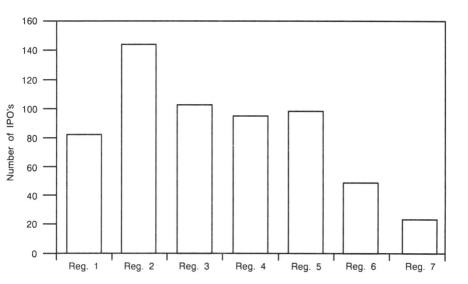

Source: Sheshunoff Information Services, Inc.

Most savings institutions, however, haven't had quite the advantage of Chicago-based institutions. That is the reason for the use of ARMs.

Ultimately, the basis for measuring the contribution of an institution's margin to overall profitability is to divide net interest income after provisions for loan loss by operating expenses. If the ratio is less than 1.0, the association either had better be a strong mortgage banker (which has high operating expenses offset by higher than average fee income) or else have a consistent and strongly profitable service corporation. The higher the margin divided by operating expenses during each of the past three to five years, the more likely it becomes that a thrift will remain consistently profitable.

An additional factor affecting net interest income stability is the ratio of interest-earning assets to interest-bearing liabilities (IBA/IBL). Most of today's strong investment opportunities have IBA/IBL ratios in excess of 100%, a function of relatively modest facilities and equipment investment and, perhaps

more importantly, strong asset quality. The difference between today's strong market and that of the mid-1980s is that despite the temptations of the early 1980s, most of the surviving publicly traded and mutual institutions stuck to their knittings and generally avoided large concentrations of commercial and multifamily real estate mortgages in far-away communities.

Noninterest Income

While a negative gap in the interest rate environment that prevailed in 1992 was feared by many as an indicator of a problem that foretold diminishing spreads, many institutions simply avoided this problem by selling fixed-rate mortgages, servicing retained. Such a move provided servicing income that ranged from 0.25% to 0.40% of the face value of the underlying mortgage. This revenue offsets part of the costs of maintaining a mortgage servicing department

Figure 4.5   Thrift IPOs: Total Dollar Amount by Region

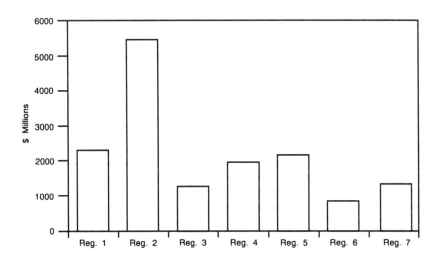

Source: Sheshunoff Information Services, Inc.

and, if originated by an institution, is a completely off-balance sheet asset.

More importantly, mortgage servicing is a strong hedge against rising interest rates. As rates increase, prepayments on sold mortgages slow and cash flows to an institution do not diminish. Plus, the lower the average yield on a portfolio, the more valuable and more stable an institution's servicing revenue.

By contrast, the mid-to-late 1980s saw many institutions that showed net income actually posting losses on an operating basis. Their income was bloated by accelerated mortgage loan fees, today considered adjustments to yield, large gains on sales of mortgages, and a propensity by managements to sell assets that could be liquidated at a profit while burying assets with imbedded losses in portfolio as "held for investment" assets that were carried at historical cost.

Again, under the aegis of FIRREA and with prompting from the Securities & Exchange Commission and the Financial Accounting Standards Board, regulators put the brakes on so-called "gains trading" that grossly inflated savings institution earnings in the mid-to-late 1980s.

Conversions

One of the most effective means of investing in healthy savings institutions is to be a "ground-floor" investor. Such investors are generally depositors in savings institutions and are granted preference rights to acquire shares in a newly public savings institution.

Savings institution initial public offerings, or conversions, occur when the Board of Directors of a mutually chartered institution elects to change to a stock charter. In a mutual, depositors technically own the retained earnings through their ownership rights. But these rights are subordinated to the interests of the Federal Deposit Insurance Corporation (FDIC).

In a conversion, a savings institution sells stock in a prescribed order that guarantees a "tax-free reorganization." Specifically, stock is first sold to depositors of the institution at a given date (called an "eligibility record date"), then to other depositors, other customers (borrowers), residents of a local community or market area and finally, to any other interested investors.

Recognizing the value of these subscription rights, many professional investors rushed during 1991 and 1992 to place deposits in mutual institutions that were healthy and appeared "convertible." In some cases, investors even attempted to illegally buy subscription rights from existing eligible depositors.

Why was the market so hot? Very simply, savings institution stock was so unattractive to the market in 1990 and 1991 that converting institutions were priced at 28% to 35% of pro forma book value.

Two healthy Chicago institutions, Cragin Financial and NS Bancorp, hit the market at about this time. For about 28% to 30% of pro forma book value, Cragin was priced initially at approximately 30% of pro forma book value, or $10 per share. Within hours after trading started, Cragin was trading $15 a share and has since continued a rise to $22 a share. In the course of slightly more than a year, Cragin investors doubled their investment.

More recently, deep discounts on savings institution stock have moderated. The reason is a general increase in the market pricing ratios of savings institution stocks and the increased demand for these issues by more savvy investors. In mid-1992, initial issue savings institution stocks were generally priced at between 40% and 50% of pro forma book value, with a few high-quality Chicago savings institutions converting in the mid-to-upper 50% range.

The irony for many recent investor/depositors seeking new issue savings institution stock is that management of many smaller mutual institutions has been more interested in maintaining local ownership than in building a wide stock distribution. As such, eligibility record dates are set for 18 months to two years or more before an institution elects to convert, thus freezing out newcomer depositors and last-minute investors. As depositors get attuned to the investment opportunities in converting institutions, most initial public issues of savings institution stock sell out before an institution works through its long-time depositor list. Often allocations that diminish ownership concentration are a by-product of this effort.

Acquisition Opportunities

There remain considerable opportunities for tapping into the returns of converting mutual institutions. One is to "get the institution before it converts." In this scenario, called a "merger-conversion," another publicly traded entity, such as a bank, agrees to acquire a mutual. This mechanism is deceptively simple. A mutually chartered institution converts to a stock charter and issues all of its equity to the publicly traded entity. The latter then sells its stock to the depositors, customers, residents, and other investors who would normally have priority rights in a standard conversion.

Two examples of recent merger conversions are Northern States Financial of Waukegan, Illinois acquiring First Federal Savings of Waukegan and First Northern Financial, Green Bay, Wisconsin, acquiring New London (Wisconsin) Savings and Loan. In the former, the savings institution was operated separately, while in the latter, First Northern and New London were merged.

The biggest players in the merger-conversion market are both banks and well-capitalized savings institutions. The reason for this is that mutuals in this transaction are acquired at newly converted institution values. Assuming a 45% of pro forma book value, the surviving public entity acquires $1 in capital for 45 cents. The merger-conversion enhances the public entity's capital without shareholder dilution and provides a broader market base. One consequence is that an expansion-minded institution picks up fuel for its acquisition efforts.

From the public entity's shareholder standpoint, merger conversions are a godsend. The initial issue discount that accrues to a converting institution's shareholders (the biggest reason for the value pop in Cragin, for example), accrues to the shareholders of the public entity.

For the acquired institution, a merger-conversion often offers the benefits of an economy of scale and, in some cases, the opportunity to provide investors with a more liquid stock with a longer history as a publicly traded company. Depending on the size of an institution, a merger-conversion may also be a more efficient means of becoming public since the costs of underwriting and selling stock are borne by a larger capital base.

Nonetheless, very few merger conversions have been completed in recent years. In balancing the pros and cons of conversion options, managers usually opt for the standard conversion, followed by a sale. The reason is that most standard conversions offer the same benefits as a merger-conversion. Moreover, a shareholder profits twice: once with the recovery of the initial issue discount and twice if the savings institution is sold.

Other Opportunities and Future Potential

Regardless of conversion method, savvy investors have been targeting institutions that appear most likely to be consolidated into larger institutions in the decade ahead. This consolidation is believed by many to be behind a wave of 1,1 conversions in 1991 and 1992, in the Chicago area. Most of these institutions fit the profile of an acquisition candidate. This profile includes the following:

◆ Good net worth;

◆ Mature franchises with relatively modest cost of savings;

◆ Limited lending opportunities as exhibited by higher than average levels of out-of-area loans, MBS's, or shrinkage;

◆ No clear management succession, and;

◆ Senior management that was between 55 and 60 years of age and a Board that is near or has reached retirement.

Simply put, many of these franchises are positioning themselves for acquisition. A preview of this trend also occurred in 1992 when Dakota Bancorp, Inc., a 1991 convert to a stock charter, announced in August that it was seeking a buyer. Dakota converted at 28 percent of pro forma book value and, if the company nets book value from an acquiror, the initial investors in the company will receive a return equal to nearly 4.0 times their initial investment.

Dakota represents an example of a well-capitalized institution that, while reasonably profitable, could not generate a return from its local market that exceeded the potential return to shareholders from a sale of the company. In many similar cases, including the Chicago-based institutions, strong capitalization, lack of any significant leverage strategies, and a low purchase price for initial investors almost assures that a sale of an association in today's environment exceeds the return from an ongoing operation.

Amid the good news of 1991 and 1992, the doubting portfolio manager still legitimately can ask whether the current favorable trends in savings institution stock will continue. The answer is, inevitably, "maybe." While the fundamental performance of the business is good, as problem assets have decreased and earnings are significantly improved,

two major trends are combining to create a low pressure that ultimately may be another hurricane.

The first trend is the low interest rate environment that prevailed in 1992. Interest rates on 30-year, fixed-rate mortgages in some markets decreased to below 8.0% during the third quarter of 1992. This deep and virtually unparalleled decrease triggered a massive wave of refinancing that unwound many institutions' restructuring efforts and put perilously low yielding fixed-rate mortgages in portfolio.

If this weren't enough, many Treasury-indexed ARMs were designed with interest rate caps but no floors. As a result, these mortgages often repriced to 2.5% above the one-year Treasury index, which decreased to approximately 3.5% in the third quarter of 1992. A 6.0% ARM, no matter how flexible, hardly covered the all-inclusive costs of savings at most institutions.

Moreover, many ARMs originated at today's "teased" rates pose a problem of their own—imbedded interest rate risk. While admittedly few ARMs are taken today, those that are often have interest rates below 5.5%. Assuming even this rate, the maximum interest rate on this instrument, given a standard 6% cap on the loan's lifetime interest rate, is 11.5%, far beneath the performance of ARMs originated as recently as 1989.

Combined with a flood of certificates moving to passbook savings accounts, the effect of this trend will be to make one-year gaps deceptively small. As rates rise, the "new" passbooks move back to certificates of deposit and prepayment speeds slow, these gaps will balloon dramatically. The ultimate bottomline impact: less stable margins and more erratic earnings.

The second storm front is a push by financial accounting standards setters to require asset values to be recorded at the lower of cost or market, or some other form of market value. Such a push has the strong potential of injecting far more volatility into savings institution income statements as managers recognize asset and/or liabilities value changes in an institution's income statement.

Finally, while FIRREA created a more determined and better equipped regulatory force, it by no means ended the uncertainty in the regulatory arena governing savings institutions. For the past 18 months, Washington has been filled with rumors regarding the consolidation of thrift and banking regulators and the insurance fund. Bureaucratic lifespans being what they are, this hasn't happened yet. However, for all its faults, the Office of Thrift Supervision (OTS) has a far broader and better grasp of savings institution balance sheets and mortgage lending risks than do its counterparts.

While out of sheer spite, many thrift managers would like nothing better than to terminate OTS, its cure may be worse than the problem. From a capital markets standpoint, an untested "bank" regulator cutting his or her teeth on the savings institution business may pose many of the same problems to earnings stability that the paralysis of the Federal Home Loan Bank Board did between 1987 and 1989.

In effect, while the business has reduced its exposure to income changes caused by sharp changes in interest rates in recent years, the basic nature of savings institutions core assets and liabilities—mortgages and certificates of deposit—force the business to effectively be an interest rate play. So long as the business is a mortgage lender, it can mitigate but not eliminate the threat of prepayment changes and certificate "shifting" in fluctuating interest rate environments. Too much of the business in recent years has failed to fully grasp this reality and has "overinsured" its portfolio against rate sensitivity.

Consolidation

Ultimately, however, banking policy in the United States has favored consolidation of financial intermediaries. Well-capitalized, well-run savings institutions are poised to benefit from this consolidation as many have the expertise and experience to be effective mortgage lenders. Shareholders of these institutions, to the extent that the institutions seek acquisition opportunities (either as an acquiror or an acquiree), usually will benefit handsomely unless they are part of a distressed situation.

For many banks, savings institutions offer significant stakeout or consolidation opportunities in new markets. Savings institutions enhance many banks' ability to build core deposits using the savings institution's basic franchise—mortgage lending. So long as this trend exists, savings institutions will continue to be attractive targets. Getting in on the party means knowing how to select and invest in the right targets.

Part III:
Corporate Governance

Chapter 5

The Evolving Role of Institutional Investors in Corporate Governance*

Ira M. Millstein
Senior Partner
Weil, Gotshal and Manges, New York, NY

With institutional investors' significant growth in corporate ownership, an evolution in corporate governance is occurring; institutions are replacing individuals as the predominant owners of corporate securities. The re-emergence of concentrated ownership in the third leg of the corporate triad—the shareholders—represents the return of the "owner" from abstraction to reality. To some observers, it signals a new opportunity to improve the efficiency and competitiveness of U.S. corporations, without the excesses of the market for corporate control. Those observers believe institutional investors are now uniquely positioned to improve corporate performance by taking longer-term equity positions (thereby removing some of the short-term pressure that many managers attribute to the capital markets) and by selectively but actively engaging in the corporate governance process.[1] These investors can, if they wish, supplement transactional investing with relationship investing.[2] However, others question whether institutional investors' investment and fiduciary concerns, and cultural bent for displacing responsibility, are inherently in conflict with Graham & Dodd, relationship investing;[3] and whether these shareholders will become motivated to obtain the information and expertise necessary to play a meaningful role in corporate governance. The ensuing debate over what role institutional investors can or should play in the financial markets and in corporate governance is complicated by the diversity represented in the institutional universe and the varied legal and cultural constraints that surround institutions.

This chapter takes the view that institutional owners can complement the market for corporate control and transactional investing with some forms of relationship investing, and thus assist the corporations, which are the core of our enterprise economy, to be more efficient competitive wealth producers in a global economy. At the very least, relationship attitudes and knowledge about the corporations they own will enable institutions intelligently to participate in the corporate governance process.

The limitations and impediments to effective institutional governance action are not insubstantial. Nevertheless, they can be overcome with a little effort and primarily by modifying, to a degree, the culture that permeates the governance paradigm and the investor universe. The most important modifications necessary are not ones that need be mandated by the Securities Exchange Commission (SEC) or legislated by Congress. The key modification is in culture—a broader acceptance of the view that good corporate governance requires knowledge and diligence by both shareholders and boards; that knowledge and diligence are essential to intelligent oversight, and that intelligent oversight will—over time—produce managers best able to maximize the enterprise's wealth-producing capacity. In short, good director is one who, based on sufficient knowledge, regularly questions management; and a good shareholder is one who, based on sufficient knowledge, prods boards where necessary to do their jobs. This modification in culture must involve institutional owners who come to recognize that shareholders,

*This chapter is based on a paper prepared for the American Bar Association Panel on *Institutional Investors: Monolithic or Diverse? Implications for Corporate Governance* (8/10/92). Copyrighted 1992, Ira Millstein.

boards, and managers have one common goal—maximizing the enterprise's wealth-producing capacity—and who then undertake their respective responsibility to achieve that goal. As noted, being a relationship owner (having knowledge and being diligent) requires few, if any, new laws or regulations, but simply motivation. The motivation is obvious—the well-being of corporations that are our core wealth producers.

Within this context, the prescription for an institutional owner seeking to play its role is to be sufficiently informed and diligent to participate intelligently in selecting and monitoring the boards of directors of the corporations it owns. Institutions have the means to do so to a degree now. Where new means are needed, they can be developed without rocket science artistry. Although the empirical evidence may be equivocal, it is intuitive that a corporation's wealth-producing capacity simply by ensuring that the accountability mechanism provided in the structure of the governance system works. The certain knowledge of being subject to scrutiny improves responsibility and performance at every level of an organization. Therefore, the most important role for institutional investors as owners is to ensure that the body charged with management oversight in the governance paradigm—the board of directors—functions appropriately. The simplest, most straightforward and appropriate means by which institutions can improve corporate performance is by paying attention to the boards who should actively and independently monitor management.

Relationship investing provides a straight line between shareholders and boards, and there are alternatives available. The balance of this chapter will expand on these concepts.

Concentration of Shareholder Ownership

In the recent past history of corporate ownership, most large corporations were owned directly by masses of individuals, none of whom had the commitment or the power to oversee the board or management of the corporation. As described by Berle and Means[4] in their seminal treatise, this fragmented ownership left effective control of the corporation with management rather than with its nominal owners. Although shareholders formally elected the directors charged with overseeing management, it was usually the management itself that chose the only slate of board nominees—allegedly most frequently colleagues of or persons acceptable to the then CEO. Therefore, although under a duty

to the shareholders, many directors might have owed a personal allegiance to the CEO that was difficult to overcome. With little power to promote change if unhappy with the performance of the corporation, the widely held belief was that the shareholders' principal recourse was to sell their interest in the enterprise—the "Wall Street Walk." The Wall Street Walk was easy; fragmented owners sold shares in a "perfectly" fluid market, which provided no problems or ripples (or waves). Theoretically, if enough shareholders sold, the stock price dropped, management got the signal, and management undertook change. That was the "system," and it worked at least as well, if not far better than, other systems all operating within essentially locked geographical and political borders.

But even within that system there was some concern that public constraints were needed. Mechanisms were sought to hold managers more directly accountable to shareholders, including both state and federal laws and regulations devised to protect shareholders from management self-interest.[5] With concerns about corporate responsibility in the 1960s and 1970s, and the emergence of tough Japanese and German global competitors (in many of whom ownership and control appear closely tied) in the late 1970s and early 1980s, calls for additional means of management discipline became more pointed. In the 1970s, emphasis was placed on director liability, shareholder derivative actions, outside directors, and new board committee structures.[6] And in the 1980s, for a short but frenzied period, discipline by the capital markets (the market for corporate control) in the form of hostile takeovers and LBOs was viewed by some as an effective management discipline.[7] Hostile takeovers might have been the ultimate form of the Wall Street Walk!

The growing inability to raise financing for this admittedly severe form of management discipline[8] coincides with at least some evolving economic movement away from total reliance on the "value-free black box of the marketplace" as the final arbiter for capital allocation and corporate governance decisions.[9] In hindsight, the perceived weakening of U.S. corporations' competitive position may be evidence of the inappropriateness of granting exclusivity to the stock market as the major governing tool of management discipline.

In the late 1980s, and now the 1990s, with the rise of more concentrated corporate ownership—largely in the form of ownership by one form or another of institution,[10] some of whom are unable or unwilling to simply trade shares in response to stock market performance—the focus has moved from stock market discipline and shifted to the existing governance structure. Concentration of ownership makes more possible a real, as distinguished from theoretical, model of corporate governance. A few owners of significant shareholdings in a single corporation can, in fact, have an impact on governance. Fragmented ownership doesn't lend itself to the organization necessary for action (there are too many agency costs and free riders), but concentrated ownership does. Thus it is theorized that, in contrast to the 1980s, when the fear of takeover exerted a form of discipline, in the 1990s a less expensive, less disruptive[11] means of oversight will evolve—driven by more concentrated ownership—as to governance of a corporation (including the makeup and functioning of its board).[12] This shift from a "financial" approach to corporate control to what is termed a "political" approach is argued to be inherently more effective because it directly addresses corporate performance problems in the "marketplace of ideas."[13]

The revitalization of shareholder interest in corporate governance and its potential impact attests to the fact that, as the statistics gathered by Dr. Carolyn Brancato for the Institutional Investor Project indicate,[14] the Berle and Means model of corporate ownership—small individual shareholders lacking the commitment and power to impact on the corporation—no longer applies. Ownership and control are once again merging, although not quite in the form they were joined in the late nineteenth and early twentieth centuries. With the explosive growth of the assets under their control, institutional investors have both the power—and increasingly, on the part of some of them, the inclination—to influence the corporation.

The institutions' emerging inclination to improve corporate performance stems from both a recognition of their own power and their inability easily to exit from under-performing investments due to their size. The more active institutional investors— mainly public pension funds—are now seeking, with increasing sophistication, to augment the value of the companies in which they invest. Yet the vast majority of institutions—of a variety of types—have not been heard from on issues of corporate governance. Whether they will become more active participants remains to be seen and, as discussed later, may never happen absent changes in cultural and other impediments to more active participation in corporate governance.

It is by no means a certainty that concentration in ownership will result in the activism advocated by public pension funds, academics, and others, unless there develops a wider acceptance of the responsible role which knowledgeable and diligent ownership (relationship investing) can play in causing corporations to better maximize their wealth-producing capacity in the global economy.

Moreover, because we all fear concentrated power—too few owners of too much wealth-producing capacity—the concentration of ownership may yet be circumscribed by public policy, especially if these powers are irresponsibly exercised.

The Wall Street Walk (or Race) will never disappear as a discipline, nor should it. The degree to which it should and will be complemented by a concentrated ownership/corporate governance paradigm is what is at issue.

Impediments to a New Concentrated Ownership/ Corporate Governance Paradigm

Corporate Resistance and Indexing

Many corporate managers resist the notion that institutional investors have an important role to play in corporate governance. Citing the upheaval of the 1980s' market for corporate control, they argue that institutional investors have an inherent short-term focus on immediate profit.[15] They assert that, as a result, corporate managers are unduly pressured to focus on quarterly or yearly performance rather than on the longer-term horizons that are necessary for developing strategies for growth and research and product development.[16] They also contend that the institutions do not understand the individual corporation's products, markets, and competitive pressures, or management's long-term strategies. They question whether institutional investors, with their increasing reliance on indexing and hence with vast numbers of corporations in their portfolios, can ever become informed on a company-specific basis.[17] And they question whether active involvement by institutional shareholders really improves corporate performance.

There is undoubtedly truth in these observations. The need for institutional investors to diversify, and the growth of indexing (whereby investors own a bundle of stocks designed to reflect the performance of an index representing the market) as a means of achieving that end, are impediments to the development of knowledgeable institutional investors who can actively monitor all the corporations represented in their equity portfolios. The more diverse the portfolio, the more daunting the task of compiling and analyzing the information necessary for institutions intelligently to engage in the corporate governance process. Nevertheless, as discussed later in this chapter under "Overcoming Barriers," means of marshalling the necessary data and selectively monitoring an investment's progress can be, and are being, created.

At first glance, it may appear that a more active shareholder role for institutional investors is antithetical to the concept of indexing. Indeed, many investors are drawn to indexed funds as a means of reducing the time and money they expend to monitor their portfolios. As a result, an investor's holdings of equity in an index typically are not based on any consideration or analysis of each corporation's individual performance, but solely on the corporations' inclusion in the index. Thus, some of the benefits of indexing in saving time and energy (and money) may be lost if the institutions must become knowledgeable about every corporation in their indexed portfolios. On the other hand, indexing may make attention to individual corporate governance and performance even more important.[18] Because an institution is in essence locked in to the corporations in its indexed portfolio, the only way it can influence the value of that portfolio is to push for improved performance by the corporations represented in the index. Moreover, as an investment strategy, indexing may make institutions perforce longer-term holders because indexed investors are not readily able to sell large blocks of the stock included in the index without negatively affecting the stock's price or upsetting the very concept of index investing.

In light of these developments, rather than resisting institutional investors' emerging interest in corporate governance, management might well consider how to inform and assist them in adapting to their new role. Properly informed, institutional investors—even if heavily indexed—may be the long-term owners that managements say they need.

It is certainly true that most institutional investors do not have the entrepreneurial acumen of the early owner/managers of this nation's industries. Nonetheless, they now own a concentrated piece of most major publicly traded corporations—a fact that management cannot ignore. For example, it is predicted that by the year 2000, just 30 institutional investors will control as much as 28% of the ten largest U.S. corporations.[19]

In formulating a role for institutional investors in corporate governance, it must be recognized that, as corporate owners, institutions are very different from shareholders of the past. Articulating an appropriate role for institutions in corporate governance is hindered by attempting to view the relationship through the lens of older concepts of ownership. Institutions are not traditional "owners" such as the Fords, Duponts, or Rockefellers, whose personal fortunes depended on the entrepreneurial skill and acumen they brought to the enterprises they "owned." But not unlike those entrepreneurs, the institutions cannot prosper unless the enterprises they invest in

improve their performance. The institutional investors' ownership role should be viewed through a competitive-enhancing lens whose focus is the alignment of the interests—both risks and rewards—of managements and shareholders in their common undertaking. Their interests are aligned in the one overriding objective of the corporate triad: to "maximize the wealth-producing capacity of the enterprise."[20]

Whether or not active involvement by shareholders improves corporate performance is subject to debate. Measuring the value of institutional activism is a difficult task. California Public Employees' Retirement System (CalPERS) recently reported that a Wilshire Associates study estimates its proposals have increased the fund's value by as much as $137 million from expenditures of only $500,000.[21] Richard Schlefer, Investment Officer of College Retirement Equities Fund (CREF) has stated that, "Surveys have shown that poison pills reduce the market value of shares by an average of 1%, which would amount to $75 million in CREF's holdings. CREF's anti-poison pill campaign in 1987 involved total costs in time and communications of less than $10,000—about .1% of CREF's stake in the outcome of the campaign."[22]

Such isolated examples may not give an accurate picture of the value of institutional activism. Professor Bernard Black's recent review of the existing empirical evidence on the impact of institutional investor ownership cites evidence that the presence of a majority shareholder results in a significant rise in share price.[23] Similarly, owner-controlled firms assertedly generate higher operating profit margins and higher earnings growth rates.[24] However, acquisition of a significant block of stock by shareholders without significant ties to the corporation yields inconclusive results. It is uncertain whether large outside blockholders add value by opposing antitakeover amendments and by waging proxy contests, or whether such gains simply reflect investors' anticipation of an impending takeover.[25] On balance, there is a dearth of information with respect to the value of institutional investor activity, but since this activity is only in its infancy, an equivocal result is not surprising. Before a more empirical conclusion on the value of institutional monitoring can be reached, more research is required.[26] The importance of determining whether institutions actually add value through their activities should not be underestimated. Once institutional investors (other than the public pension funds) are convinced of the value of shareholder activism, they may have the motivation to take a greater interest in the governance of corporations in their portfolios. And if the empirical evidence is substantial, management may find it in their own best interest to become more attuned to the institutions.

But do we need to await empirical proof of the value of informed owners—especially in an era of growing concentrated ownership? Can our corporate system risk uninformed concentrated ownership? At least intuitively, and from a policy standpoint, it would appear that owners becoming motivated and informed is preferable to their not exercising any ownership responsibilities at all, or exerting an ownership role without knowledge. Subjecting boards—and derivatively, managements—to greater scrutiny by stockholders may have at least a minimum beneficial effect in causing boards and managements to look over their shoulders. And from boards' and managements' standpoint (with, for example, 30 or fewer institutions owning enough shares to really make a difference), are not such institutions, if aligned with boards' and managements' goals, capable of being allies in global competition?

Motivational Barriers

As noted earlier, I believe the better view is that maximizing the corporation's wealth-producing capacity requires that there be some mechanisms, in addition to the Wall Street Walk, to monitor the corporation's performance and results.[27] To play a meaningful role in corporate governance, institutions must be motivated and informed. Intelligent monitoring is not without costs, but the increased costs will hopefully be offset by improved corporate performance.[28]

The search for a workable model for institutional investors as owners of the corporations whose securities they hold (generally as fiduciaries for others)—and the debate whether acting as owners is even appropriate—is complicated because the institutions are not monolithic. Institutional investors are a very diverse group, and generalities about their universe are therefore difficult to make. Ranked in descending order of ownership of the total equity market, they include public, private, and union pension funds (with 28.2% of the total equity market), bank trusts (with 9.2%), investment companies/mutual funds (with 7.2%), life, property and casualty insurance companies (with 6.9%), and foundations/endowments (with 1.8%).[29] This institutional investor universe is complicated by the existence of employee stock ownership plans, many of which are included in the categories listed above, particularly in private pension plans and bank trusts. Unfortunately, there is no readily available source for separately determining their percentage ownership of the total equity market.[30] While employee ownership plans are estimated to account for only 2.9% of the market value

of all public companies,[31] unlike the other holdings listed above—which are large but somewhat dispersed by individual institutions among corporations—the employee stock ownership holdings of an individual plan are significantly concentrated in a single corporation.

Diverse institutional investors have shared characteristics as well as important differences: although they all invest the money of others for the benefit of others, they function under different objectives, performance needs, fiduciary obligations, cultural norms, governance paradigms, compensation schemes, and legislative and regulatory constraints. The extent and nature of institutional investors' participation in corporate governance is most likely influenced by the various political, economic, regulatory, and cultural pressures they face.[32] For many types of institutions, legal and cultural disincentives may prevent their activity, and few incentives may exist that encourage active involvement in issues of corporate governance.

For example, Glass-Steagall limits the amount of stock a bank may hold in a given company. Banks retain their last link to stock ownership through their trust departments and have the voting power for nearly 14% of the shares on the New York Stock Exchange.[33] Bank trust beneficiaries often have conservative goals and seek stable performance, consistent with taking an interest in improving fundamental competitiveness of the corporations in their portfolios.[34] However, extensive business dealings with particular companies may restrain their enthusiasm to oppose management on critical issues.[35] Many such trustees may prefer to avoid the potential conflicts as well as the costs of monitoring, and incentives may be necessary to involve them in corporate governance. Many contend that improved corporate—and hence portfolio and loan—performance is not sufficient motivation to overcome the apparent disincentives.

Mutual funds' investments may be more subject to short-term pressures than some other types of institutional investors, such as pension funds.[36] Because open-ended mutual funds are generally required to redeem investors' shares upon demand, liquidity is of paramount importance. To preserve their access to cash, they may avoid committing significant funds to the kind of long-term stock positions that are consistent with investor activism. Additional short-term pressure stems from competition from other mutual funds; quarterly evaluations are quite common.[37] To attract new investors and retain the ones they already have, mutual fund managers are under pressure to post impressive quarterly gains and may be more likely to seek short-term market gains.[38] The competitive nature of the industry, the need for liquidity, unrecoverable costs, and uncertainty about the value of activism, would seem to make mutual funds reluctant participants in corporate governance. At the same time however, the restraints on mutual funds' willingness to become active in corporate governance are somewhat less pronounced than for other institutions. For the most part, mutual funds' income is not as dependent on corporate accounts; therefore, unlike banks and corporate pension funds, they have less to lose by opposing managers. And if mutual funds begin to sense that results are cost-justified, they may be willing to follow others' lead.[39]

Some mutual funds appear to be gaining interest in corporate governance. In a departure from industry practice, America's largest mutual fund company, Fidelity, has amended the fundamental investment policies of many of its mutual funds to allow for more active participation in proxy contests.[40] Recently, John Bogle, CEO of the Vanguard Group of funds, the second largest in the United States, stated: "[F]und companies aren't going to be quiet shareholders anymore."[41] His comments were echoed by the CEO of a mid-sized mutual fund group: "It used to be if you can't support management, don't own the stock. That's not the case anymore."[42]

Private pension funds sponsored by corporations are subject to regulation by ERISA, which requires the fund trustee to act for the sole benefit of the fund's beneficiaries.[43] While there is no specific prohibition on the size of an investment, risk reduction through diversification is generally viewed as prudent. Therefore private funds (some of whose portfolio managers argue they are not paid to monitor) have to date generally elected to invest smaller amounts and remain largely silent.[44] It is contended that some of the private funds' reluctance to become more involved in corporate governance may stem from portfolio managers' fear of offending the fund sponsor.[45] Corporations commonly delegate their pension funds to outside asset managers who also control the voting of proxies. Private fund managers may believe that they are expected to vote with management except in extraordinary circumstances.[46] While such perceived pressure may have lessened since the Department of Labor's 1988 "Avon" letter describing proxy voting as a fiduciary duty,[47] corporations' influence on pension fund managers may nevertheless be a significant restraint.[48]

It must be noted, however, that there is a lack of empirical evidence on the touchy subject of why banks, mutual funds, and private pension funds do not take a more active role in corporate governance. A review of the literature indicates only an intuitive belief that the reluctance is cultural/pragmatic—an unwillingness to become involved in what could be considered contentious corporate meddling.

To date, the most active institutional investors in corporate governance have been public pension funds, although they hold only 11.6% of all institutional investor assets and only 30.5% of all pension fund assets.[49] While public pension funds are also subject to fiduciary duties, their activities are largely unhampered by close ongoing business relations with corporate managers and may even be driven by other concerns, including political pressures. Unlike banks and private pension funds, public pension funds do not have separate business relationships with corporate managers; thus they may be less concerned about offending them. But public fund trustees are often appointed or elected, and as participants in the political arena they may be subject to political pressure, including calls to help balance budgets[50] or to aid the local economy.[51] While politics and fear of publicity may silence some funds,[52] these same factors may spur others to action.[53] With little countervailing activity, the inertia of other institutions may serve to strengthen the perception of public funds' initiatives. That is, by default, the public funds are often viewed as representing "the" institutional investor viewpoint, and because of their "political" birth and control, that viewpoint is perceived to be tainted by "nonbusiness" motivations.

Employee stock ownership plans, which were in part created by management as a means to create a large, stable, patient block of long-term shareholders as a hedge against market discipline, may eventually position employees to have a greater voice in corporate governance. At present, employees own an average of 12.2% (the median is 9.8%) of the equity in the top 1000 corporations on all stock exchanges as measured by employee ownership.[54] Because employee ownership stakes are significantly concentrated in the employees' corporation, it is therefore no surprise that employees are the largest shareholders in over 41% of these corporations, and in a much larger percentage of companies, employees are included among the largest three shareholders.[55] By the year 2000, it is estimated that more than one quarter of the companies traded on the major U.S. exchanges will be more than 15% owned by their employees.[56]

Notwithstanding this concentration of ownership in employees, and perhaps because the plans have been set up by corporate management and are managed within the corporate structure with little employee involvement, to date the majority of these plans have not been actively involved in corporate governance. Even though, in order to be viewed by a court as independent of management in a takeover battle or a proxy fight,[57] many plans engage in pass-through voting—whereby each beneficiary/employee votes his own proxy, and the non-allocated shares mirror that vote. Unless the issue is one of corporate control, it is unlikely that individual beneficiaries/employees are sufficiently motivated, knowledgeable, and coordinated to vote their shares as a block on an issue. Yet these "inside" institutional investors represent the type of patient, long-term, and knowledgeable shareholders that may best be positioned to participate in governance as "relationship investors."[58] They are not subject to the limitations of indexing nor can it be said that they do not understand the corporation's products, markets, and competitive pressures.

Creating Motivation

To the extent that existing laws and regulations actually impede some institutions from becoming relationship investors—holding larger stakes as knowledgeable owners—changes should be considered.[59] Aside from removing legal disincentives, it is also necessary to address the factors that may contribute to institutions' inertia in actively becoming relationship investors. Some institutions need to wean themselves away from overwhelmingly reflexive indexing and move toward more direct investment in fewer companies, or at least toward obtaining sufficient knowledge about some of the companies represented in an institution's indexed portfolio to enable intelligent appraisals of their boards and managements. This approach would create a more knowledgeable class of owners. To accomplish this requires the cultural shift discussed earlier—developing a consensus that oversight can lead directly to "better" performance. That debate and discussion is underway.[60]

Additional motivation might come from subjecting institutional investors to increased scrutiny by both their beneficiaries and the public at large.[61] Aside from CalPERS, the New York State Common Retirement Fund, and a few other public pension funds that regularly disclose their governance activities, it is difficult to assess how or to what extent institutions are in fact exercising their ownership rights. By-and-large, institutions make their ownership decisions outside of public view, with no articulation of their rationales or goals. Even for those who don't think it wise to encourage institutional governance activities, scrutiny would provide information as to what is happening in the institutional world.

In the end, however, institutions probably will not buy into significant relationship investing unless and until they are motivated to do so by a developing policy consensus on the oversight/"better" performance paradigm.

Overcoming Barriers

Once motivated to engage in governance, institutions will need to determine how, where, and on what issues to focus their attention. The focus of their monitoring efforts will be on both the individual corporations and specific issues that are likely to result in improved corporate performance. Obviously, where an institution acquires a major ownership position in a corporation, either directly or through an intermediary, monitoring can be anticipated as a matter of care and prudence.

As to lesser investments, either through indexing or otherwise, the board and its processes should be the key concern for shareholders. If a corporation is performing well, it may not be a wise use of resources to expend any energy on that corporation. To conserve resources, institutions will likely focus primarily on those corporations with "substandard" performance, beginning with those whose performance is most problematic. This is not as easy as it sounds—nor as trouble-free. Defining "substandard" and "problematic" performance requires a great deal of further elaboration.

Monitoring Methods

Various methodologies for institutional monitoring (principally of corporations included in an indexed investment of one type or another) have been suggested,[62] but none overcomes wholly the limitations of time, expense, information, expertise, and specificity. The least costly, time-consuming, and knowledge-intensive monitoring model is the utilization of screening mechanisms to locate underperformers based on stock performance and other measures.[63] Such screening mechanisms require expertise in determining what "poor" performance is and, when found, from what it stems. Screens assume that once underperformers are identified, an investor can somehow act to improve performance or replace management. For example, the New York State Common Retirement Fund uses a computerized screening system to identify consistent underperformers, based on measures such as stock returns, valuation ratios, accounting data, and capital spending over both single and five-year periods. Once underperformers are identified, outside experts assist in determining whether to support or oppose the current board of directors in an election.[64]

Attempts at constructing such screening devices for identifying underperformers, however, raise significant questions:

1. Different classes of institutions may seek different performance standards in the corporations in which they invest;

2. Uniform screening criteria even within classes of institutions may ignore the unique qualities of individual corporations and undervalue long-term management strategies;

3. Most institutions do not currently possess the expertise nor the manpower necessary to analyze further the "underperformers" targeted by such systems;

4. Screening services shared among institutional investors may implicate collective action problems; and,

5. The use of simplistic screening methods may create perverse incentives for management to operate so as to avoid the "radar screens."

Communicating Concerns

Assuming, however, some devices for identifying "underperformers," there remains the issue of communicating shareholders' concerns to boards and managements. To date, institutional investors primarily have relied upon shareholder proposals submitted for inclusion in managements' proxy materials as their forum for communicating their concerns to boards and managements; less frequently, they have engaged in informal dialogues with boards and managements. As a result, the proxy process is emerging as an extremely important forum for the "political debate" model of management discipline.[65] In the existing world of concentrated institutional share ownership, narrowly-focused proxy initiatives are viewed increasingly as a way to voice concerns, affect corporate policies, replace specific directors or managers, or propose long-term strategies—efforts that do not require the change in ownership inherent in a hostile takeover.[66] However, although institutional investors have employed the proxy process to influence corporate governance with some success,[67] until recently it has been difficult to amass the votes necessary to succeed with a shareholder proposal in face of opposition from management.[68] Although sizable votes in favor of shareholder proposals are becoming more common and, in and of themselves, send strong messages to management, the prime power of the proxy vote remains its ability to put pressure on management in a public forum.[69]

Institutional investors are not relying on the proxy process as their sole forum for influencing corporate governance of underperforming companies—nor should they. They should communicate their concerns about corporate performance to boards and managers in less formal and more discreet forums whenever possible. It is only after continued poor performance and an unwillingness of the board to change management or strategy or both, that more extreme—and public—corrective measures such as proxy contests should be required. And except in extraordinary circumstances, communicating with management on narrow business issues is not likely to be particularly productive. Considering institutions' limited resources and lack of industry-specific expertise, they simply don't have the knowledge to debate a management team immersed in the day-to-day running of the business.

CalPERS has had limited success with addressing its concerns privately to "underperformers" in its recent "quiet diplomacy" campaign. In that initiative, which began in October of 1991, CalPERS targeted a dozen corporations that it determined were under performing on a long-term basis.[70] CalPERS then sought a private dialogue with each corporation on one of three issues: the independence of directors, executive compensation, or shareholder advisory committees. However, dissatisfied with some responses from a few of the more uncooperative corporate managements, CalPERS eventually went public with the identity of its targets in an effort to pressure the more recalcitrant to take its concerns seriously.[71]

Longer-Term Approaches; Developing a Relationship

To date, institutions' submissions of proxy resolutions and engagement in dialogues with boards and managements have represented short-term approaches to issues of corporate governance. It has been proposed that institutional investors engage in longer-term ongoing private dialogues with a corporation's board and management much like the Japanese and British experience.[72] Such a monitoring strategy could provide a means for shareholders to analyze performance but presumes a cooperative management, no legal impediments to sharing significant information with special groups of shareholders and, again, a certain level of expertise and a substantial commitment of time and money. Proposals to create shareholder advisory committees[73] represent an effort to create forums for long-term ongoing dialogue. However, shareholder advisory committees pose a number of troubling issues, including problems of collective action and of creating a special class of shareholders who are more privy to board and management attention than other share-holders.[74]

The strategy that would likely be most company-specific and provide institutions with both the information necessary and expertise required to constructively critique corporate performance would also involve the most expense: Institutional investors hire highly specialized professionals with expertise in the subject corporation's industry to closely monitor management's decisions.[75] However, this would require either hiring scores of advisors or taking much larger-equity positions in a handful of industries. It also presumes that the hired monitor has as much or more experience and knowledge as management, with access to superior information or with less bias in evaluating information. Yet senior management in a given industry is likely to be more knowledgeable than any available monitor, and the cost to institutional investors to hire superior monitors and obtain superior information seems prohibitive.

Short of this—and far more practical—an institution could focus exclusively on the boards of "underperformers." Institutional investors can improve corporate performance within the existing structure of the corporate governance paradigm—and with a minimum of effort, information and expertise—simply by focusing their governance efforts on the board of directors and its processes.[76]

Where there is a "problem" company, an institution can ask for meetings with the board, pose the problem, and determine whether the board is dealing with it or ignoring it. If the institution was uncertain as to how to evaluate the board and sought help, such help would surely be available.[77] In evaluating a board's response to a problem, its attentiveness and diligence is more appropriate for a shareholder than devising new management strategies. In our system, if the shareholder satisfies itself that the board is knowledgeable, diligent, aware of the problems and attempting to deal with them, generally this should suffice. The shareholder ordinarily doesn't know enough to second-guess a diligent board—and it shouldn't.

The foregoing discussion relates essentially to corporations held by an institution in one form or other in an indexed investment, but in any event to a corporation in which there is less than a major investment. There are a number of other investment approaches—although involving significant monitoring costs—which are accessible to institutional investors and which will result in the sought after long-term relationship between institutional investors and boards of the corporations in which they invest. For example:

1. A portion of an institution's portfolio could be actively managed by specialists in a particular industry;

2. An institution could invest in actively managed funds: (for example, Lazard Freres' Corporate Partners fund; Alliance Capital's fund; the funds that American Industrial Partners and Dillon Read & Co. are attempting, independently, to start); or,

3. An institution could buy larger stakes, presumably in many fewer companies, a la Warren Buffett; hire professional monitors to work with management; and agree not to sell out so as to facilitate a close working relationship with management.[78]

These "relationship" investing proposals all to some degree or another borrow from our competitors abroad.

Although substantially different in structure, German and Japanese corporations seem to benefit from the presence of large, stable, long-term owners.[79] In Germany, banks serve as lenders and own substantial blocks of stock; typically the banker/owner sits on the supervisory board. Three banks directly control more than 40% of all shares in industrial corporations.[80] Deutsche Bank alone holds 28% of Daimler-Benz, the largest industrial corporation in Germany and was instrumental in fostering recent diversification efforts.[81]

About 60% of the common stock listed on Japan's stock exchanges is controlled by banks and other corporations.[82] Japanese banks function as both lenders and owners; other corporations in the bank's network (keiretsu) own stock in one another and maintain strong commercial relationships among themselves. They are well qualified to render strategic advice. Their involvement with the corporation, often as suppliers or customers, gives them the expertise and the incentive to be effective monitors. These institutions remain largely silent when the corporation is functioning smoothly but are not reluctant to exercise their "voice" when performance falters.[83] However, just the possibility of their becoming involved causes most managers to remain vigilant; they don't want to be embarrassed by forcing keiretsu members to usurp their authority.[84]

With appropriate cultural modifications, adopting selected elements of these systems may help position institutional investors to become more credible and beneficial in their governance actions by replacing passive indexing with a more active and direct involvement in fewer corporations.[85] Movement toward such relationship investing should lead to the creation of a more knowledgeable and committed class of investors. However, more product needs to be developed. Not only pension funds, but some corporate managers as well are expressing interest in the creation of investment vehicles that could facilitate the implementation of some of the suggestions previously noted. Recognizing that institutional investors are a fact of corporate life, some thoughtful corporate managers are apparently interested in fostering well-informed, large, long-term owners who might support them in turning away from the short-term pressures that are perceived to emanate from the capital markets, thereby allowing for more effective long-term corporate strategies.

Conclusion

It is undeniable that there is and will be more concentrated ownership of major U.S. corporations, as is the fact that such concentrated ownership is capable of a significant impact on the governance of these corporations. If one believes that the Wall Street Walk and transactional investing will and should remain a monitor of corporate performance and that some complimentary means can help, then those complimentary means should be encouraged.

One complimentary means is greater relationship investing by the institutions (including employee owners) who comprise the concentrated owners. Relationship investing refers to holding long-term positions in blocks of stock sufficient to motivate the shareholder to monitor corporate performance knowledgeably and to be prepared to influence—knowledgeably—corporate strategy and governance. Relationship investing can include a variety of means, such as direct investment in corporations, investment in financial intermediaries that directly invest in corporations, and even indexing, *provided* the investor becomes knowledgeable about the corporation invested in and about which governance prerogatives are to be exercised. To the extent that institutions come to emphasize direct investment or support relationship investing through financial intermediaries, they also serve to free up capital that many see as underproductive when predominantly indexed.

This chapter describes how institutions can, if motivated to do so, become relationship investors and how, as relationship investors, they can best exercise their abilities to influence corporate governance. The question which remains is how to motivate institutions, including the public pension funds, to become relationship investors as here defined, i.e., knowledgeable and diligent.

Motivation should not be directed or legislated; our corporate universe is too vast and varied to fit cookie-mold solutions. Motivation can best come about through at least some consensus that knowledgeable and diligent ownership by the new, large owners will be of benefit in making more productive use of a vast pool of capital as well as bringing about better corporate performance. This is, to a degree, a modification in the culture of corporate governance. This conclusion is intuitively obvious. When and if enough of the interested community agrees, the motivation will be there.

Endnotes

1. See Robert Teitelman, *The Revolt Against Free Market Finance*, Institutional Investor, June 1992: 37, 38–39.

2. For purposes of this chapter, relationship investing is defined as investing in substantial long-term positions in blocks of stock sufficient to motivate the shareholder to monitor corporate performance knowledgeably and to be prepared to influence corporate strategy and governance based on a perception of performance. In contrast, transactional investing implies a shorter-term strategy that focuses more on the present value of the stock as measured by the securities market and on market trends, rather than the underlying fundamental value of the particular business, and hence places less emphasis on monitoring corporate performance. A third relevant type of investing, which has become popular in recent years especially among institutional investors, is index investing. Index investing is a "passive" strategy whereby all the stocks included in an index are purchased in proportion to their index weighting and are held for the long term, without any fundamental analysis, in an effort to generate the same return as the index (no better; no worse). It can be argued that, with regard to corporate governance, index investing has something in common with relationship investing. (See the discussion later in the chapter under, "Impediments to a New Concentrated Ownership/Corporate Governance Paradigm.")

3. Benjamin Graham and David Dodd, proponents of value investing, authored Graham and Dodd's *Security Analysis*, first published in 1934.

4. Adolf A. Berle and Gardiner C. Means, *The Modern Corporation and Private Property* (1933).

5. *See, e.g.,* Del. Code Ann. tit. 8, §144 (1991) (requiring officers to disclose material facts as to relationship or interest in contract or transaction of corporation); Ga. Code Ann. §14-2-842 (Michie 1989)(requiring officers to act in good faith and in the best interests of the corporation); Iowa Code §490.842 (1991) (same); Miss. Code Ann. §79-4-8.42 (1988)(same); 15 U.S.C.A. 78p (b) (1981) (prohibiting officers from short-swing trading); Rule 10b-5, 17 C.F.R. §240 10b-5 (1989) (prohibiting fraudulent or deceptive behavior in connection with sale of securities).

6. *See, e.g.,* The Business Roundtable, *The Role and Composition of the Board of Directors of Publicly Owned Corporations,* 33 Bus. Law. 2087 (1978); Committee on Corporate Laws, Section of Corp., Banking and Business Law, American Bar Association, *Corporate Directors Guidebook,* 33 Bus. Law. 1595, 1619-28 (1978); The Conference Board, Corporate Directorship Practices: Role, Selection and Legal Status of the Board 135 (1973).

7. *See, e.g.,* Michael C. Jensen, *Eclipse of the Public Corporation,* Harv. Bus. Rev., Sept. - Oct. 1989, at 61, 64 ("The idea that outside directors with little or no equity stake in the company could effectively monitor and discipline the managers who selected them as proven hollow at best. In practice, only the capitol markets have played much of a control function—and for a long time they were hampered by legal constraints."); Daniel R. Fischel, *The Corporate Governance Movement,* 35 Vand. L. Rev. 1259, 1264 (1982) ("The operation of the market for corporate control simultaneously gives managers of all firms who wish to avoid a takeover an incentive to operate efficiently and to keep share prices high and provides a mechanism for displacing inefficient managers."); Frank H. Easterbrook and Daniel R. Fischel, *The Proper Role of a Target's Management in Responding to a Tender Offer,* 94 Harv. L. Rev. 1161, 1165-68 (1981) ("[S]hareholders benefit even if their corporation never is the subject of a tender offer. The process of monitoring by outsiders poses a continuous threat of takeover if performance lags.").

8. *See, e.g.,* Louis Lowenstein, *What's Wrong With Wall Street* 127 (1988); Gail Appelson, *Bleak Future in Store at Nation's Bankruptcy Courts,* The Reuter Business Report, Feb. 4, 1991, available in LEXIS, Nexis Library, Busrpt File.

9. *See generally* Teitelman, *supra* note 1.

10. *See, e.g.,* William Power, *Small Investor Continues to Give Up Control of Stocks,* Wall St. J., May 11, 1992, at C1 (reporting that direct stock holdings by individuals dropped from 84.1% of the market in 1965 to 53.5% of the market in 1991).
Research supported by the Institutional Investor Project underscores the high level of concentrated ownership among institutions. The study shows that for the last five years at least, the identity of the 20 largest pension funds has remained virtually the same and includes public funds (California Public Employee Retirement System (CalPERS) Cal Teachers, New York City, New York State, New Jersey, Michigan, and Wisconsin), as well as private funds (AT&T, IBM, GE, GM, EXXON, DuPont). Carolyn K. Brancato, *Institutional Investors and Capital Markets: 1991 Update* [hereinafter Brancato, *1991 Update].*
When the 20 largest pension funds are combined with the ten largest money managers— which include Alliance, Capitol Guardian, Wells Fargo, and Batterymarch—but with no double counting, these 30 shareholders alone owned almost 12% of the equity of our ten largest corporations in 1985, and, by 1989, owned almost 16% of the equity of our ten largest corporations. The Institutional Investor Project speculates that by the year 2000 these 30 shareholders will own somewhere between 22% and 29% of the ten largest corporations. Carolyn K. Brancato, Institutional Investor Project, Columbia University School of Law, *Concentration of Equity Holdings in the Top 10 Corporations by the Largest Pension Funds and Money Managers: 1985 to 1989, with Projections to the Year 2000 (1990)* [hereinafter Brancato, *Projects to the Year 2000].* Thus, a small group of shareholders own concentrated shares in a number of significant American companies.

11. *See, e.g.,* Jonathan P. Charkham, Panel Paper No. 25, Bank of England II ("Takeovers . . . are expensive and founded on a monstrous illogicality—that a change in ownership is necessary in order to change management.").

12. John Pound, *Beyond Takeovers: Politics Comes to Corporate Control,* Harv. Bus. Rev., (Mar.-April 1992): at 83.

13. *Id.*

14. Research funded by Columbia Law School's Institutional Investor Project reveals that institutional investors' total assets have more than tripled from $2.1 trillion in 1981 to $6.5 trillion in 1990. Institutional investors now hold approximately 53.3% of outstanding equities. Together they hold 54.8% of the shares of *Business Week*'s top 100 corporations, and it is estimated that just five institutions own between 10% and 11% of the largest 25 corporations (valued by shares outstanding). As these statistics indicate, institutional investors have the power to substantially impact the corporations in which they invest. The magnitude of that potential is dramatic when individual corporations are considered. For example, just five institutions now own over 21% of Coca Cola. Brancato, *1991 Update, supra* note 10.

15. John M. Conley & William O'Barr, *The Culture of Capital: An Anthropological Investigation of Institutional Investment,* 70 N.C.L. Rev. 823, 839 (1992) [hereinafter Conley & O'Barr, *The Culture of Capital*] (quoting Andres Sigler, CEO of Champion International., "[W]e have money managers, at the direction of plan sponsors, working like mad to make short-term money that puts pressure on corporations . . . .); Terrence P. Pare, *Two Cheers for Pushy Investors,* Fortune, July 30, 1990 at 95 (noting the common complaint by CEOs that "fund managers push too hard for short-term results making long-range planning difficult if not impossible.")."

16. Pare, *supra* note 15.

17. H.B. Atwater, Jr., *The Governance System is Sound,* Directors & Boards, Spring 1991: 17, 19.

18. Letter from Dale Hanson, CEO CalPERS, to Linda Quinn, Director, Division of Corporate Finance, Securities and Exchange Commission 3 (Oct. 12, 1990). ("While the decision to buy a company's stock may initially be based upon objective index criteria, this does not mean we stop caring about how that company performs. To the contrary, the fact that CalPERS' initial investment relates to index criteria means that we look to improve performance as a further

opportunity to enhance the value of our assets. Given our index strategy, we are all the more interested in systemic improvements in corporate governance.")

19. Brancato, *Projections to the Year 2000, supra* note 10.

20. See Peter F. Drucker, *Reckoning with the Pension Fund Revolution,* Harv. Bus. Rev., (March-April 1991): 106, 112.

21. CalPERS' Press Release on Wilshire Assoc. Study (February 13, 1992).

22. Alfred F. Conrad, *Beyond Managerialism,* 22 U. Mich. J. L. Ref. 117, 145 n.94 (1988).

23. Bernard S. Black, *The Value of Institutional Investor Monitoring: The Empirical Evidence,* 39 UCLA L. Rev. 895, 919 (1992) [hereinafter Black, *Value of Institutional Investor Monitoring*] (citing Holderness & Sheehan, *The Role of Majority Shareholders in the Publicly Held Corporation,* 20 J. Fin Econ. 317 (1988)("[P]urchase of a majority block, without announced plans for a complete takeover, produces 9.4% stock price gains over a 30 day window period."); Rosenstein & Rush, *The Return Performance of Corporations that Are Partially Owned by Other Corporations,* 13 J. Fin Res. 39 (1990)("[P]ositive stock price returns, but their sample is tiny (11 firms), and abnormal returns based on a characteristic that was known at the beginning of the sample period are in tension with market efficiency."))

24. Black, *Value of Institutional Investor Monitoring, supra* note 23, at 920 (citing Bothwell, *Profitability, Risk and the Separation of Ownership from Control,* 28 J. Indus. Econ. (1989): 303, 308–09; Stano, *Monopoly Power, Ownership Control, and Corporate Performance,* 7 Bell J. Econ. (1976): 672).

25. *Id:* 923.

26. *Id:* 927.

27. *See* Drucker, *supra* note 20: 118.

28. Although becoming knowledgeable about all the companies in their portfolio, as a practical matter, may be difficult if not impossible to achieve (depending on the diversity of the portfolio), there is a wealth of information publicly available in corporations' annual reports and 10-Ks, quarterly 10-Qs and other periodic filings.

In addition, financial analysts and other experts regularly provide reports concerning the performance of many of the most widely-held portfolio companies. Once obtained, however, the available information must be analyzed to determine how well the corporation is performing for both the long and short-term objectives of the institution. Admittedly, the analysis, which should go well beyond the short-term stock, prices, is complex. Some institutions may have the staffing to analyze the information in-house, and others may rely on outside experts. If the analysis is done in-house, larger staff with more financial analysts may be necessary. If institutions elect to rely on outside analysis, it is likely that more organizations, representing varying viewpoints, will merge to provide institutions with information and analysis, but all of this will involve additional costs, which must be perceived as somehow value enhancing.

29. Brancato, *1991 Update, supra* note 10.

30. *See* Joseph R. Blasi & Douglas L. Kruse, *The New Owners: The Mass Emergence of Employee Ownership in Public Companies and What it Means to American Business* 6 (1991) [hereinafter Blasi & Kruse, *The New Owners*]; Conversation between Holly J. Gregory, Associate at Weil, Gotshal & Manges, and Joseph R. Blasi, Professor at the Institute of Management and Labor Relations, Rutgers University, in New York, N.Y. (June 17, 1992)[hereinafter Conversation between Gregory and Blasi]. The New York Stock Exchange has reported that in 1990 approximately 34% of new shareholders entered the market through employee ownership plans. New York Stock exchange, *Shareownership 1990* 24.

A special thanks is owed to Joseph R. Blasi, coauthor of *The New Owners: The Mass Emergence of Employee Ownership in Public Companies and What it Means to American Business,* for his insights concerning employee ownership plans.

31. Blasi & Kruse, *The New Owners, supra* note 30, at 11. The figure of 2.9% cited by Joseph Blasi and Douglas Kruse has been updated to 4% based on new employee ownership plans since 1991 and an estimate of equity in employee share purchase plans. *See Joe Sixpack's Grip on Corporate America,* Business Week, July 15, 1991, at 108; Conversation between Gregory & Blasi, *supra* note 30.

32. The failure of institutional investors to purchase large stakes in individual corporations, to form voting blocks, and to engage in collective action has been attributed in part to the legal limits, risks, and costs faced by institutional investors in taking such action, see Bernard S. Black, *Shareholder Passivity Reexamined,* 89 Mich. L. Rev. 520, 533-564 (1990) [hereinafter Black, *Shareholder Passivity Reexamined*]; Mark J. Roe, *A Political Theory of the Corporation,* 91 Column. L. Rev. 10, 31–53 (1991), and to the institutions' "culture." *See* William M. O'Barr & John M. Conley, *Fortune and Folly: The Wealth and Power of Institutional Investing* (forthcoming 1992) (manuscript at 74–93, 225–236).

33. New York Stock Exchange, *Institutional Investor Fact Book 1990* App. A1-A6, B (1990).

34. Black, *Shareholder Passivity Reexamined, supra* note 32: 600.

35. It is asserted that financing the long- and short-term capital needs of large public companies is a core source of banks' revenue and they may be wary of losing commercial loan opportunities by taking a public stance against prospective clients. In addition, as managers of corporate pension funds, it is alleged that many banks may fear they will upset sponsor management and lose business if they take a public anti-management position. *Id.* Despite the fact that the trust and commercial loan departments of a bank may be totally separate, some are concerned that signals may be sent discouraging trustees from opposing corporate management. *Id.* at 601 (citing J. Heard & H. Sherman, Conflicts of Interest in the Proxy Voting system 50 (1987)). Hard evidence is simply not available, however.

36. Jayne W. Barnard, Institutional Investors and the New Corporate Governance, 69 N.C.L. Rev. 1135, 1142 (1991).

37. Roe, *supra* note 32: 19–20.

38. Barnard, *supra* note 36, at 1142. Although its potential to influence investment managers' behavior is difficult to measure, mutual funds often benefit from the "soft" information generated at corporations' meetings with analysts; to preserve these informal contacts, mutual funds may be reluctant to oppose corporate management through proxy voting. Black, *Shareholder Passivity Reexamined, supra* note 32, at 602. Also,

the prevailing compensation structure of mutual funds is based on a set percentage of the assets under management, so monitoring costs generally come out of the management fee. Barnard, *supra* note 36: 1142.

39. Black, *Shareholder Passivity Reexamined, supra* note 32: 602–603.

40. *Fund Managers: Education is Key,* USA Today, May 22, 1992: B6.

41. *Id.*

42. *Id.*

43. As applied to corporate pension funds, the obligations of a fiduciary consist of (1) a duty of undivided loyalty to participants and their beneficiaries with respect to the corporate pension fund, (2) a duty to act for the exclusive purpose of providing benefits to participants and beneficiaries, (3) a duty to act prudently, (4) a duty to diversify investments to avoid large losses, and (5) a duty to comply with plan documents to the extent consistent with ERISA. Employee Retirement Income Security Act, §404, 29 U.S.C. §1104 (1990).

44. *See* Conley & O'Barr, *The Culture of Capital, supra* note 15: 842–843.

45. *See* Roe, *supra* note 32, at 23–24; Black, *Shareholder Passivity Reexamined, supra* note 32: 596–597.

46. Some assert that corporate managers instruct portfolio managers to back away from a significant role in corporate governance., Conley & O'Barr, *The Culture of Capital, supra* note 15: 842–843 (Some commentators have even speculated about the existence of an unspoken covenant among corporations: "you keep your pension funds off our backs and we'll do the same for you."). And approximately half of the corporate managers surveyed stated that it was "appropriate" to advise pension money managers on how to vote their shares. Black, *Shareholder Passivity Reexamined, supra* note 32: 597 (*citing Institutional Investor,* December 1987: 101).

47. *See,* Letter from Alan Lebowitz, Deputy Assistant Secretary of Labor, to Helmuth Fandl, Avon Products, Inc., 15 Pens. Rep (BNA) 391 (February 23, 1988) ("[I]t is the Department's position that the decision as to how proxies should be voted . . . are fiduciary acts of plan asset management . . .").

48. *See, e.g.,* Brett D. Fromson, *The Big Owners Roar,* Fortune, July 30, 1990: 67.

49. Brancato, *1991 Update, supra* note 10.

50. *See, e.g.,* Joyce Terhaar, Wilson Seeks Sway Over PERS, Sacramento Free Press, June 14, 1991, at D1; Stephen E. Clark, *Are Public Funds Mortgaging Their Future,* Institutional Investor, July 1991: 59.

51. As of 1989, 41 retirement systems reported making nearly $7.3 billion in economically targeted investment ("ETIs") including home loans, commercial mortgages, venture capital, small business loans, privately placed loans to medium size companies, and other programs. Institute for Fiduciary Education, *Economically Targeted Investments* (1989). Although public funds should be wary of political pressure to invest in risky projects or those with sub-optimal returns (the Kansas Public Employees Retirement System lost about $200 million in a poorly executed instate investment program, Fran Hawthorne, *Who's In Charge Here Anyway?,* Institutional Investor, February 1992, at 58), if properly structured, local economies and the funds' beneficiaries can benefit from such investment opportunities. Early in 1991, Philadelphia's municipal workers' fund and the state teachers' fund provided the city with emergency financing by purchasing about $75 million dollars worth of municipal bonds, but at a rate of return commensurate with the risk. Clark, *supra* note 50: 61. Michigan's ETI program has invested more than $700 million in venture capital projects, creating an estimated 3,500 jobs and prompting private investors to commit an additional $200 million to Michigan businesses. Steven Bartlett, *States Weigh Use of Pension Funds,* N.Y. Times, (January 26, 1990): D2.

In keeping with the practice of seeking competitive investments while also promoting the local economy, New York State has set up the Excelsior Capital Corporation to facilitate ETIs. Excersior helps design and locate investment opportunities that can provide competitive returns in relation to their risks for pension funds and other institutional investors while also providing collateral economic benefits. It relies on outside professional managers to evaluate and manage the investments on a nonconcessionary basis.

52. *E.g.*, Black, *Shareholder Passivity Reexamined, supra* note 32: 559. (citing Steven Bartlett, *Life in the Executive Suite After Drexel*, N.Y. Times, February 18, 1990 §3, at 1 (political pressure caused Massachusetts public funds not to invest in the RJR Nabisco leveraged buyout).

53. *See* Conley & O'Barr, *The Culture of Capital, supra* note 15: 843 ("The extensive and largely favorable press coverage enhances the attractiveness of an active approach to governance.").

54. Blasi & Kruse, *The New Owners, supra* note 30: 12.

55. *Id.*: 11.

56. *Id.*: 3.

57. *See e.g.*, *Shamrock Holdings, Inc.* v. *Polaroid Corp.*, 559 A. 2d 257 (Del. Ch. 1989); *Shamrock Holdings* v. *Polaroid Corp.*, 559 A. 2d 278 (Del. Ch. 1989).

58. For a detailed discussion of corporate governance participation by employee ownership plans, see Blasi & Kruse, *The New Owners, supra* note 30: 217–238.

59. For example, Robert A. G. Monks has, as least since 1984 when he served as Administrator of the Office of Pension & Welfare Benefits, U.S. Department of Labor, asserted that given the size of current pension funds, the capital needs of the U.S. cannot be met under the existing 'prudent man' investment standard as it is currently interpreted and applied: "The objective is to remove obstacles for creativity and to enable investment capital to flow into areas where opportunity and need combine to suggest a potential for profit." Robert A. G. Monks, Remarks at the Florida Labor/Management Council 5 (December 7, 1984); *see also* Robert A. G. Monks, *Reckless "Prudence": Investment of Pension Fund Assets in the United States of America*, Social Science Inst., University of Tokyo, (forthcoming September 4, 1992) manuscript at 1 [hereinafter *Reckless "Prudence": Investment of Pension Fund Assets in the USA]* ("America has taken the largest single accumulation of capital in the country—indeed the world—and squeezed it into a suffocatingly narrow range on the investment spectrum, designed by traditional notions of 'prudence.'");

John C. Coffee Jr., Liquidity Versus Control: The Institutional Investor as Corporate Monitor, 91 Colum. L. Rev. 1277, 1355 (1991) ("[R]estrict portfolio diversification including indexing, to a level consistent with the institution's ability to monitor."); Bernard S. Black, *Agents Watching Agents: The Promise of Institutional Investor Voice*, 39 UCLA L. Rev. 811, 846 (1992) ("Labor Department and IRS clarification that cross-investments [corporate pension plans holding blocks of each others sponsor's stock] through pension plans can be prudent and won't be subject to unrelated business taxation might encourage such investment."). Clearly, the factors that may deter institutions from relationship investing deserve greater attention, but the scope of this article does not permit it.

60. *See generally* Teitelman, *supra* note 1.

61. For example, institutions might be required to publicly state their ownership policies and objectives. Such statements are likely to be general and aspirational. Nonetheless, the exercise of formulating and articulating these statements would at least cause institutions to think about what their role as owners is and should be. Further, institutions could be asked to report, at appropriate intervals, on how they have exercised their ownership responsibilities with respect to their portfolio corporations and how such exercise is consistent with their stated policies and objectives. For example, if an institution votes in favor of (or against) a corporation's director nominees or an executive compensation package, or meets with management concerning environmental policy, it would so state and explain why.

Such required disclosure might encourage boards to act more thoughtfully in addressing specific issues. Perhaps fewer incumbent directors of consistent poor performers would be re-elected, fewer excessive compensation packages would be approved, and a more constructive dialogue would flow between owners and corporations.

62. *See e.g.*, William Taylor, *Can Big Owners Make a Big Difference?*, Harv. Bus., September-October 1990, at 70; Roe, *supra* note 32: 55–56.

63. Roe, *supra* note 32: 67–68.

64. Edward V. Regan, *A New Way to Discipline Badly Run Companies*, Wall St. J., June 5, 1992: A10.

65. *See* Pound, *supra* note 12.

66. *See* Ronald J. Gilson, Lilli A. Gordon and John Pound, *How the Proxy Rules Discourage Constructive Engagement: Regulatory Barriers to Electing a Minority of Directors*, Corp. Voting Res. Project (February 1992).

67. A recent Business Roundtable study indicates that between 1984 and 1990 dissident shareholders made "impressive gains" in election contests: 1) by winning the vote in 28% of the election contests for control of the Board of Directors, while incumbents did so in 40% of the contests; 2) by gaining control of the company through other means shortly after the vote or obtaining minority board representation, in 50% of such control contests; and 3) by acheiving some or all of their objectives in a total of 74% of the control contests. Dissident shareholders also made similar gains in opposing management proposals or in sponsoring shareholder proposals: 1) in 50% of the cases in which shareholders solicited against management proposals, the proposals were not adopted; and 2) in 25% of the cases in which shareholders initiated proposals, shareholders won or later negotiated a compromise. Letter from The Business Roundtable to Linda C. Quinn, Director of the SEC Division of Corporate Finance, 6–8 (December 17,1990) [hereinafter Business Roundtable Letter] (*citing* Georgeson Company Inc., Proxy Contest Study: October 1984- September 1990 (December 14, 1990)).

68. *See* Letter from the California Public Employees' Retirement System to Linda C. Quinn, Director of the SEC Division of Corporation Finance, 9 (Nov. 1989) [hereinafter CalPERS Letter 1989] (restrictions on solicitation activities by institutional shareholders must be lessened "to redress, carefully and deliberately, the imbalance between owners and managers."). In October 1992, in response largely to requests from CalPERS and other institutional shareholders, the SEC adopted comprehensive amendments to the proxy rules intended to facilitate increased participation by shareholders in the proxy process. *Regulation of Communications Among Shareholders*, SEC Exch. Act

Rel. No. 31, 326 (Oct. 16, 1992), 57 Fed. Reg. 48, 276 (Oct. 22, 1992).

69. *See* Pound, *supra* note 12, at 85 (describing instances where proxy vote was not able to defeat management on an issue but nonetheless caused management to change position).

70. *See* Richard W. Stevenson, *Huge Fund Turns Up Proxy Heat*, N.Y. Times, (March 21, 1992): L37.

71. *Id.*

72. Taylor, *supra* note 62: 78–82; Roe, *supra* note 32: 66–67.

73. *See Looking Over the Shoulder—Sears, Avon the Target of Fund's Governance Efforts*, Pensions & Investment Age, (November 26, 1990): 3.

74. Shareholder advisory committees have the potential to represent the viewpoint of a powerful but narrow group of shareholders—certain institutions—at the expense of other shareholders. The best interests of the corporation require that the board weigh all viewpoints, not just the selected views of a single constituency. Shareholders should either trust the board they elected, or seek to change its membership. Additionally, both the creation and functioning of shareholder advisory committees pose significant practical problems:

1. How should committee representatives be selected, and by whom? If investment size is a determining criteria, what would happen to the representative who sells, or the non-representative who buys a significant portion of stock? If long-term ownership is determinant, would that requirement undermine, for example, a pension fund's fiduciary duty to its beneficiaries? *See* Employee Retirement Income Security Act of 1974 §1104, 29 U.S.C. §1104 (1990).

2. What information would the committee have access to? If it is material, nonpublic information, the representatives would be prohibited from trading. *See* Securities Exchange Act of 1934 §10b, 15 U.S.C. §78j(b) (1990); SEC Rule 10b-5, 17 C.F.R. 240.10b-5 (1990). How would that impact on fiduciary duties and who would be willing to serve with that limitation?

75. Taylor, *supra* note 62: 81–82; Drucker, *supra* note 20: 113–114.

76. *See* The Working Group on Corporate Governance, *A New Compact for Owners and Directors*, Harv. Bus. Rev., July-August 1991, at 141, 143–44 (the appropriate concern of shareholders in "maximizing the wealth producing capacity" of the corporation should be positioning the board to actively and independently monitor management). Focus by institutional investors on board process is of critical importance in overcoming the inherent power of the CEO that tends to define the culture of the corporation. Corporate leaders may be surrounded by intermediaries who may be hesitant to tell them discomforting news and are "monitored" by boards that may be inclined to accept the CEO's strategies and explanations when things go wrong, a situation that has been analogized to the fable of The Emperor's New Clothes. Arnold Brown, *The Naked Emperors,* Across the Board, June 1992, at 13. Boards should encourage energetic, competent managements who are capable of planning for, and obtaining, profitable growth. Specifically, boards must be willing to replace failing managers when necessary; design appropriate management incentives; assist management to find the highest value use for assets; limit management's expansion strategies to those with credible potential to create value; and, return cash to shareholders when value-creating strategies are not available. Most importantly, when necessary, boards must be able to give corporate managers the honest but unwelcome news, in the private confines of the board room, that "you don't have any clothes on." *Id.*

77. Although suggestions for improving boards abound, and range from convening commissions to study boards, *see* Philip R. Lochner, *A Commission On Corporate Boards?*, The Corporate Board, Jan.-Feb. 1991, at 1, to adding several full-time "professional directors" to each board, *see* Ronald J. Gilson & Reinier Kraakman, *Reinventing the Outside Director: An Agenda for Institutional Investors*, 43 Stan. L. Rev. 863 (1991), to requiring quinquennial terms for directors and related performance reports, Martin Lipton & Steven A. Rosenblum, *A Proposal For A New System of Corporate Governance: The Quinquennial Election of Directors*, 58 U. Chi. L. Rev. 187 (1991), elaborate reforms are un-

necessary. The generic formula is simple: Ensure 1) that the independent directors' role is distinct from the CEO; 2) that outside directors meet regularly, by themselves, to evaluate the CEO and senior management's performance, the corporation's long-term strategy and the board's own effectiveness; and 3) that a leader is openly designated to call the outsiders together when necessary. *See generally,* Working Group on Corporate Governance, *supra* note 76. Finally, nominating committees should develop model profiles for their directors reflecting the corporation's unique needs, share that information with shareholders, and create some means for providing shareholder access to the process of nominating director candidates. Shareholders should be able to at least informally suggest candidates to the board's nominating committee, and boards should listen. Participation by institutional shareholders would enhance the credibility of the nominating process (but shareholders should avoid attempting to create "constituent directors" or advisory boards).

78. Taylor, *supra* note 62: 82.

79. *See, e.g.,* Lester Thurow, *Let's Learn From the Japanese*, Fortune, Nov. 18, 1991, at 183; Anton Peisl, *Can a Keiretsu Work in America?*, Harv. Bus. Rev., September-October 1990: 180; Howard D. Sherman, *Governance Lessons From Abroad*, Directors & Boards, Spring 1991: 24.

80. Hermann H. Kallfass, *The American Corporation And The Institutional Investor: Are There Lessons To Be Learned from Abroad,* 3 Colum. Bus. Rev. 775, 783 (1988).

81. *The Banker Behind the Shakeup at Daimler-Benz,* Bus. Wk., (July 27, 1987): 36.

82. Barnard, *supra* note 36: 1148.

83. Black, *Value of Institutional Investor Monitoring, supra* note 23: 928.

84. Erik Berglof, "Capital Structure as a Mechanism of Control: A Comparison of Financial Systems," in *The Firm as a Nexus of Treaties* 237 (M. Aoki, B. Gustaafsson and O. Williamson eds., 1990).

85. *See* Monks, *Reckless "Prudence": Investment of Pension Fund Assets in the USA, supra* note 59, at 10-11; Tim W. Ferguson, *Pension Funds as Yeast for Rising Companies,* Wall St. J., (April

21, 1992): A17 (citing the need for developing investment vehicles through which pension funds can provide capitalization for mid-market companies); Felix G. Rohatyn, *Looking at Busi-* *ness in 1991*, Directorship, (January 1991): 1 (predicting a shortage of capital for infrastructure investment).

Chapter 6

The Impact of Institutional Investors on Corporate Governance*

Nell Minow
Principal
LENS, Inc., Washington, D.C.

The most important development in corporate governance this century has been the rise of the institutional investors and their impact on corporate structure and direction. Exercising ownership rights that were almost vestigial, institutional investors have begun to bring new vitality to corporate democracy. While shareholder activism has many of its roots in social issues like investment in South Africa, it is increasingly framed in terms that are strictly financial, another kind of fundamental analysis. Empirical data shows that companies with strong monitoring shareholders outperform those that do not. For instance, shareholders can add value if they persuade management to adopt more performance-based compensation plans (or vote down those that are badly designed). A 1992 study by Wilshire Associates concluded that the shareholder initiatives sponsored by the California Public Employees' Retirement System had a net gain of $137 million, a rate of return very competitive with any other investment. More important, every one of the initiatives added value, even when they did not get a majority vote.

Background

The rise in shareholder activism results from the collision of two enormous changes in the 1980s. The first was the takeover era, which presented shareholders with great opportunities and great risks in their role as *owners*. Both raiders and managers engaged in abusive tactics and shareholders paid the price.

The second change was in the character of the shareholders themselves. Before the 1980s, most stock was held by individuals. But the development of increasingly attractive investments in mutual funds and other institutions and the strong incentives for employers to establish pension funds after the passage of the Employee Retirement Income Security Act (ERISA) in 1972 transformed the markets. Within 20 years, the majority of stock was held by large institutional shareholders, on behalf of individual pension beneficiaries and other investors.

Who the Institutional Investors Are

The largest groups of institutional shareholders had the equity holdings (in billions of dollars) in 1990 shown below. Their holdings were skewed towards the larger capitalization companies with the result that by 1989, institutional ownership of the top 50 corporations had reached 50%. Clearly, concerns of institutional investors should be of the utmost importance to corporate management.

Private pension funds	– $679.3
State/local pension funds	– $282.5
Open-end investment companies	– $245.8
Life insurance companies	– $140.8
Other insurance companies	– $ 94.9
Bank trusts	– $431.7
Foundations/endowments	– $ 61.7[1]

*This material is adapted from *Power and Accountability* by Robert A.G. Monks and Nell Minow. Copyright (c) 1991 by Harper Collins Publishers, Inc. All Rights reserved. Reprinted by permission of Harper Business, a division of Harper Collins Publishers. Thanks to Robert A. G. Monks for allowing me to adapt the material from our book, and to Kit Bingham for his assistance in research and updating it.

65

These institutions have one very significant thing in common. All are subject to the highest standard of care and prudence our legal system has developed, the fiduciary standard. In Justice Benjamin Cardozo's classic terms, they must be "above the morals of the marketplace." Beyond this guiding standard, however, the groups of institutions have little in common with each other. As one observer noted, "institutional investors are by no means a monolithic group."[2]

Private Pension Funds

The largest category of institutional investors are pension funds managed for the benefit of employees of private companies. ERISA, the law that governs private pension funds, was intended to encourage private companies to create pension plans and to protect the money in those plans once they were created. The statute was designed to resolve questions of conflicts of interest and liability that had left the private pension system uncertain, even chaotic. ERISA funds are most often handled by outside money managers who range from one extreme to the other in their focus on proxy voting. A recent trend, endorsed by the Business Roundtable, is for plan sponsors to leave other aspects of the fund management outside but to take the proxy voting in-house. This can be expected to result in more consistently promanagement votes.

ERISA funds face the same problem of collective choice that all shareholders do: can it be prudent for them to expend resources, knowing that without the ability to communicate with other shareholders any positive results are unlikely? Even if the results are positive, any returns to the active shareholder will only be proportionate to its holdings, all of the other shareholders getting a free ride. Furthermore, to the extent that a company's pension department adopts an activist posture with respect to portfolio companies, it risks retribution: retaliation in the marketplace and invitation to other pension professionals to take an equally aggressive view of their own functioning. From the point of view of all institutions, then, it is simplest to do nothing, to try to maximize value by trading, despite the fact that all evidence indicates that the majority of those who do so fail to outperform the market.

ERISA imposes obligations beyond those of traditional trust law, which the legislative history explicitly incorporates. But it also permits a "nonneutral fiduciary,"[3] which would not be allowed under the common law of trusts, in recognition of the fact that in pension plans, unlike traditional trusts, employers and employees are both settlors and beneficiaries. This is also acknowledgement that the plan sponsor is the party at risk if the plan is poorly run. ERISA requires that a "named fiduciary"[4] with responsibility for the plan be designated by the company, called a "plan sponsor."[5] Typically, a major corporation designates a committee of the Board of Directors as the "named fiduciary." ERISA recognizes that these people are too busy and important to watch over the pension fund money, so it permits them to delegate authority (and responsibility and potential liability) to an investment manager. So long as the selection of the investment manager is prudent, and the plan sponsor monitors its performance, the plan sponsor company will not be liable for the investment manager's mistakes. The standard is utterly process oriented. As long as there is a reasonable process, and it is followed, the Labor Department will not second-guess the results. This applies to all investment decisions, whether buy-sell decisions or decisions on the exercise of proxy voting and other governance rights.

For two reasons, the emphasis has been overly narrow. First, the issues on proxies are remote from whatever goods or services the plan sponsor company produces, so it is easier to file the pension fund away under "human resources."[6] Second, meaningful exercise of the ownership rights of the pension assets is thankless. No investment manager, in-house or outside, ever got paid extra for voting proxies well, because that would mean a number of votes against management recommendations. For that reason, the ERISA funds have been among the least visible of institutional shareholders.

While generally taking a promanagement line, the ERISA funds sharply distinguished themselves from at least some traditional management positions in the letter to the SEC from the Committee on Investment of Employee Benefit Assets (CIEBA).[7] CIEBA's 39 members are corporate benefit plan sponsors, representing $350 billion in collective assets managed on behalf of 8 million plan participants.

Bank Trusts

Another large category of institutional investors is the banks, which act as trustees for everyone from pension plans to private estates. Trust administration is dominated by the complexities of federal income, gift, and estate taxes. Like other institutions, trusts have different classes of beneficiaries who have different kinds of interests.

In most instances, the trust is irrevocable, and, unless there is fraud, which is almost impossible to discover or prove, the bank can expect to continue to serve and collect fees as trustee, regardless of its investment performance. The security of the trust business may well be the reason for the traditional poor investment performance by banks. After all, in quite literal terms, they—unlike the beneficiaries—

have nothing to lose. The trust contains "other people's money." What does that mean for the way that the bank trustee votes proxies?

Banks generally get the most profitable, and certainly the most interesting, portion of their business from prominent local corporations. The smaller the community in which the bank is located, the more completely its tone is apt to be dominated by the locally based businesses. Banks, especially trust departments, do not encourage innovation, especially positions that are contrary to corporate management's recommendations on proxies.

One rare lawsuit exposed the conflicts of interest that can occur in these situations. In the late 1980s, Karla Scherer watched her husband, as CEO, ruin the R.P. Scherer Corporation, the company her father founded. As a major shareholder and board member, Ms. Scherer soon realized that the inefficiently run company was more valuable to shareholders if it was sold. However, the board repeatedly refused to consider this option, forcing her to take the matter to shareholders in the form of a proxy fight for board seats. She filed a lawsuit, challenging the way her trust shares were being voted.

Scherer recalls the most devastating blow to the ultimately successful campaign to force a sale was when she had to deal with her own trustees. "Manufacturers National Bank, the trustee of two trusts created by my father for my brother and me, indicated it would vote all 470,400 shares for management, in direct opposition to our wishes. Remember the bank's chairman sat on our board and collected director's fees as well as more than half a million dollars in interest on loans to Scherer. During the trial, the then-head of the bank's trust department admitted under oath that he did not know what the prudent man' rule was. He also stated that he had arrived at his decision to vote the stock for management in less than 10 minutes, without conferring with us and after affording management an opportunity to plead its case over lunch in a private dining room at the Detroit Club." The court initially ordered the appointment of an independent voting trustee, but the ruling was reversed.

Mutual Funds

Mutual funds are trusts, according to the terms of the Investment Company Act of 1940, which governs them. Otherwise, they bear little resemblance to the other institutional investors because of one important difference: they are designed for total liquidity. The "one-night stands" of institutional investment, they are designed for investors who come in and out on a daily basis, or at least those who want the flexibility to do so.

The investors are entitled to take their money out at any time, at whatever the price is that day. The investment manager has no control over what he or she will have to pay out or when he or she will be forced to liquidate a holding. The fund manager, thus, has to view his or her investments as collateral to the promise to shareholders to redeem their shares at any time. This is not the kind of relationship to encourage a long-term attitude towards any particular company the fund happens to invest in, and if there is a tender offer at any premium over the trading price, they have to grab it.

In the face of the real need to attract new money and to retain the investors he or she has in a world of perpetual and precise competition, the mutual fund manager cannot be concerned with the long term, because his or her investors may all show up today, and he or she has to be prepared to deliver.

Insurance Companies

Insurance is the only major industry that has successfully avoided any significant Federal regulation, although "special accounts" and subsidiary manager investments are subject to ERISA and other Federal rules. Life and casualty insurance companies prefer to deal with state legislatures, with whom they have historically had a close relationship.

State law has until most recent times severely circumscribed the extent to which insurers are allowed to invest their own funds in equities. Even today, only 14% of insurance fund assets are invested in common stocks. The current limit on stock is 20% of a life insurer's assets, or one-half of its surplus. But insurers still cannot take influential blocks; life insurers cannot put more than 2% of the insurance company's assets into the stock of any single insurer; and property and casualty insurers cannot control a noninsurance company.[8]

The insurance companies, perhaps more than any other class of institutional investor, have a symbiosis with the companies in which they invest. First, they are usually holders of debt securities of any company in which they have an equity investment; debt instruments are very compatible with their needs because they have a reliable, set payout. Second, they either have a commercial relationship with the company by selling it insurance against a variety of risks, or they would like to. Third, they certainly want to sell the company an insured product to meet its pension obligations. Finally, like most other institutional shareholders, they are under no obligation to report to their customers on their proxy voting (but the companies whose proxies they vote—and with whom they do business—do know), and, like all other shareholders, the collective choice problem makes any form of activism uneconomic. Therefore, it is not surprising that the insurance industry consistently votes with management, regardless of the impact on share value.

Universities and Foundations

Universities and foundations are institutional shareholders because they are funded through endowments. People contribute to a fund, and the interest that fund generates is used for whatever charitable or educational purpose the endowment permits. The J. Paul Getty Trust has $3.98 billion. The Ford Foundation has $5.83 billion, and the MacArthur Foundation (the one that gives out the "genius grants") has $3.13 billion. This money is put into widely diversified investments, including common stock. Nonprofits are as rigorous in making sure that their investments produce high returns as any other investor. But they have not been rigorous about exercise of ownership rights.

Foundations and universities are no less subject to commercial pressures than banks and insurance companies. After all, their money comes from alumni, who are often business executives and from businesses themselves. One study reported that in 1985 corporate contributions to American universities and colleges "surpassed donations from alumni for the first time."[9] Indeed, nonprofits are "selling" a much less tangible product, so they must be extra diplomatic. Foundation and university trustees are usually drawn from the business community. The trustees of the Ford Foundation, Harvard, any museum, symphony, or the New York Public Library are drawn from the same list as the directors of the S&P 500. Many corporate boards include members of the academic community whose programs and schools receive large contributions from the grateful companies. One dean served as head of the compensation committee of the company headed by his Chairman of the Board and large contributor. So conflicts of interest, real or apparent, are found in the ivory tower as well as the financial community.

Public Pension Plans

In direct contrast to the above groups of institutions are the public pension funds, the most visible of the institutional investors with regard to governance issues. They are all organized differently. Some are directed by bureaucrats, some by politically appointed officials, and some by elected officials. The California Public Employees' Retirement System, for example, is overseen by trustees who are intimately involved, whereas the New York State employee's fund is overseen by a single trustee, Edward Regan, one of only four statewide elected officials.

Public pension plans differ in their perspectives, policies, and politics. But they are all fiduciaries, obligated by law to protect the interests of their plan beneficiaries, the public employees. And they all have more independence than other categories of institutional investors, which makes it possible for them to become involved in governance issues. Many public funds, as well as many union funds, belong to the Council of Institutional Investors which, under the direction of Sarah Teslik, acts as a resource for its members, holding conferences, providing information and acting as a clearinghouse, occasionally issuing policy papers.

But public institutions have relationships too, and like their private counterparts, those relationships can affect proxy votes and other governance activity. When the Wisconsin state pension fund wanted to object to General Motors' $742.8 million of greenmail to Ross Perot, it was stopped by the governor, who was trying to get General Motors to build some plants in his state. In 1991, California governor Pete Wilson initiated what some observers called a "hostile takeover" of the state's pension funds to reduce the budget deficit and gain more control over the trustees. And a number of states, including New York, are experimenting with "social investing" (sometimes called "economically targeted investments"), the investment of state pension funds in local companies, programs, or securities which may not meet traditional standards for risk and return.

The Rise of Shareholder Activism

The 1980s saw new threats to the rights of shareholders, the most significant since the securities legislation passed after the stock market crash of 1929. But these threats were posed not to the disparate and ineffectual individual investors all but disregarded since the days of Berle and Means, but to a limited number of sophisticated investors with significant holdings. They were smart enough to understand what was being done to them and big enough to object in a meaningful way. Furthermore, as regulators made increasingly clear, if they could limit the abuses of the takeover era in a cost-effective manner, as fiduciaries, they were obligated to do so. This does not just mean responding by casting a proxy vote; it can also mean submission of shareholder resolutions or even a proxy contest.

The traditional way to object was, of course, the "Wall Street Rule"—vote with management or sell your shares. But this alternative was either not effective or not available to address the concerns of the institutional shareholders during the takeover era. First, the institutions were just too big. If they did decide to sell out, the sale itself could depress the market. Second, many of the institutions were indexed, that is, their investments replicated the market as a whole and involved no active trading, so they did not have the option to sell out. Third, many of the abuses were so widespread that selling out of the stock of all the companies involved would have left investors with virtually nowhere else to go. More than 1000 companies adopted "poison pills"[10] without shareholder approval, including virtually every major company in America. An investor could not sell out of all of them.

Moreover, the Wall Street Rule was plain ineffective in addressing shareholder concerns. As Edward Jay Epstein points out, "just the exchange of one powerless shareholder for another in a corporation, while it may lessen the market price of shares, will not dislodge management—or even threaten it. On the contrary, if dissident shareholders leave, it may even bring about the further entrenchment of management—especially if management can pass new bylaws in the interim."[11]

But if selling out of a company was ineffective, the alternatives left to shareholders were not much better. The right to file a lawsuit, either a class action or a derivative action ("deriving" the right to sue the officers and directors from the corporation itself) has all but been turned over to the "Delaware regulars." The majority of shareholder lawsuits are brought by a small group of people, who hold a small group of shares, working with a small group of Delaware law firms, and the conclusions are generally favorable only to them. For example, in the settlement of a shareholder lawsuit against CBS, the plaintiff, who held 12 shares, received $15,000 or $1,250 per share. His attorneys got $1.5 million. The rest of the shareholders got nothing. To make things worse, corporations welcome these suits, because they can be settled quickly and cheaply, extinguishing the claims of all shareholders. Buying off the "Delaware regulars" is a small price for directors to pay to protect themselves from a serious lawsuit. Even if they do not think so, their insurers do. One disadvantage of indemnifying directors is that decisions like these are then made by the insurance companies.

The last of the rights of ownership is proxy voting. The right to vote proxies, while the theoretical justification for the legitimacy of corporate action, was more myth than reality. The process for sending out and collecting proxy cards was byzantine. The rules allowed broker votes on "routine" issues. Management nominated the candidates for the board, who ran unopposed, and management counted the votes. With some notable exceptions in the establishment of the right to have shareholder

proposals included in the corporate proxy, the rules imposed extraordinary, all but insurmountable obstacles to effective action through proxy voting by shareholders. Beyond that, there were the commercial pressures. A money manager hoping for business has a hard time voting against management knowing that management will know how he or she votes but his or her beneficial holders never will.

For a variety of reasons, including the collective choice problem and the risks of commercial retaliation, institutional investors have not been as active as they can be. But this is changing, as proxy voting is considered another aspect of asset management, both by the market and by the government agencies with responsibility for enforcing the fiduciary standard for institutional investors.

Shareholder Proxy Proposals on Governance Issues

The evidence of the impact of institutional shareholders can be seen in the number of shareholder proposals and the number of votes in favor of them. For many years such proposals were the exclusive province of legendary corporate gadflies like the Gilbert brothers and Evelyn Davis, but now dozens are submitted by public pension funds and are supported by institutional investors in every category. Even though virtually all shareholder resolutions are precatory only, as discussed below, companies are increasingly responding to them, often negotiating with proponents so that the proposals are not voted on at the annual meeting.

Since 1932, the Gilbert brothers and others have been submitting shareholder resolutions on corporate governance topics like executive compensation, cumulative voting, and the location of the annual meeting. Over the last 20 years, public pension funds, union pension funds, and church groups have sponsored shareholder resolutions on "social policy" issues like investment in South Africa or the sale of infant formula. The votes of less than 3% for Ralph Nader's 1970 "Campaign GM" shareholder proposals was an unprecedented level of support.

But that was before large institutional investors met large-scale abuses. A little more than 20 years later, shareholder resolutions routinely get votes ranging from 20% to 40%, and occasionally even get majority support. In 1987, the first corporate governance resolutions from institutional investors (mostly relating to poison pills) were submitted at 34 companies, with votes in favor ranging from approximately 20% to 30%. In 1988, a year later, two of these resolutions got majority votes, one concerning a poison pill, one prohibiting payment of green mail.

Both were at companies where proxy contests for control provided a good deal of visibility (and engendered a good deal of shareholder support).

The more significant development that year, though, was the "Avon letter," issued by the Department of Labor on February 23, 1988. As described in greater detail below, it was the first formal ruling by the agency with jurisdiction over the ERISA funds that the right to vote proxies was a "plan asset." Money managers across the country began to establish procedures and policies for voting proxies.

But the following year, in 1989, there was the first (and so far the only) proxy contest that was not over director candidates but over corporate governance. A large individual shareholder of Honeywell joined with two public pension funds and Institutional Shareholder Services, Inc. to prevent management from adopting two of management's proposed changes.[12] The company wanted to stagger the election of directors and to eliminate the right of the shareholders to act by written consent, instead of waiting for the annual meeting. The ad hoc coalition circulated their own proxy card and was successful at preventing management from getting the necessary level of support. Over the three-month period of the initiative, Honeywell common stock rose 22%, with each state of the contest sparking a favorable market reaction. While takeover rumors played a role, the market clearly recognized the value of active shareholder involvement in an underperforming company. The individual investor who paid the costs of the solicitation got a substantial return on his investment in activism—as did the other Honeywell shareholders.

In 1990, shareholder resolutions on governance, mostly from public pension funds, continued to receive growing support. Two resolutions got majority votes, the first majority votes without a formal proxy solicitation. But the most important corporate governance issue of the year was the battle over Pennsylvania's controversial new antitakeover law. Like most states, Pennsylvania adopted new laws to protect companies incorporated there from takeovers. But it went further, with a second set of amendments, when local company Armstrong World became a takeover target. The 1990 amendment was objected to so strongly by shareholders that nearly one-third of the state's companies (including over 60% of the Fortune 500 companies located in the state) opted out of at least one of its provisions.

The following year, 1991, saw an unprecedented level of cooperation and negotiation between shareholders and managements. Many of the shareholder resolutions submitted by institutional investors were withdrawn, following discussions with management

and agreed-upon changes. Representatives of the shareholder and corporate community negotiated a "Compact Between Owners and Directors" that was published in the *Harvard Business Review*. It provided that 1) the outside directors evaluate the CEO; 2) the outside directors meet alone at least once a year; and 3) the directors establish qualifications for board members and communicate those qualifications to shareholders and that they also screen board candidates. The end result was that the shareholders: 1) evaluate directors; 2) don't get involved in day to day management; and 3) recognize that "the only goal common to all shareholders is the ongoing prosperity of the company."

Significant as the "Compact Between Owners and Directors" was, however, the 1991 proxy season demonstrated that managements and investors had not become instant bedfellows. One of the top governance stories of the year was Robert A.G. Monks's proxy contest for one board seat at Sears, Roebuck. Monks's quixotic campaign won 13% of the vote but not before the troubled retailer had budgeted $5.6 million to oppose his candidacy, sued to prevent his access to the shareholder list, and axed five members from the board in order to increase the number of votes he needed to win. "If you want a demonstration of entrenched management" said Monks "this is it."

And in the same year, for the first time, a corporate governance issue leapt from the business pages to the front pages to the editorial pages to the comic pages, of course, executive compensation.

Even the business press used terms like "obscene" and "out of control" in describing executive compensation. The only thing that got more press than President Bush's flu on his trip to Japan was the salaries of the auto executives he took with him. Politicians and the mass media made it a central issue. And shareholders came full circle, with shareholder proposals reminiscent of the proposals by the Gilbert brothers, half a century ago. In 1991, the poster boy for outrageous executive pay was ITT's Rand Aroskog, whose pay increased by 103% to more than 11 million dollars, in a year when ITT's shareholders watched the value of their stock decline 18%. Pressure from shareholder groups led the company to overhaul its compensation scheme for the top 500 employees, with very positive effects on the stock price. Also in 1991, the SEC reversed its long-term policy and allowed shareholder resolutions about pay. Ten resolutions submitted by individual shareholders were approved.

They were presented at annual meetings in the spring of 1992, with one getting 44% of the vote. Overall, though, the volume of shareholder proposals was down, largely because both shareholders and management were more interested in trying to find common ground through less confrontational methods. The $68 billion California Public Employees' Retirement System, long at the vanguard of institutional shareholder activism, announced itself "kinder and gentler," and did not submit any shareholder resolutions. Instead it targeted a dozen underperforming companies, many with compensation schemes that had several of their widely distributed list of "danger signals." Many of the companies were willing to meet and negotiate. Others did not even return their calls (until their failure to respond was reported in the press). Many other institutional investors withdrew their proposals after successful negotiations.

Focus on the Board

The watershed in 1992 was when the outside directors of General Motors, Robert Stempel, resigned following intense media speculation that he had lost the confidence. This is the most recent—and the most visible—evidence of a seismic shift in the role of the independent director. General Motors, after all, is the company that forcibly greenmailed Ross Perot. After putting him on the board with much fanfare about the new perspective he would bring, management quickly decided the perspective was a little too new, and they bought him out for over $1 billion, a premium of more than $6 a share, with an additional $7.5 million for agreeing not to say anything publicly about the company. Despite reactions from the shareholder community ranging from concern to outrage, and despite Perot's efforts to continue to work with the company, he was pushed out. The loss to the company was critical, in both senses of the word. Evidence that GM's board is at last beginning to exercise some independent judgment is the best news for GM shareholders since the Corvette.

Large institutional shareholders, legislators, and even the corporate community are beginning to look to boards to provide a more independent review of corporate performance, direction, and strategy. From the shareholder perspective, the "Just Vote No" strategy became an increasingly important mechanism for sending a vote of no confidence. The 1% "withhold" vote at ITT in 1991 was overtaken in 1992 by 2% withhold votes at Dial and GM, 3% withhold votes at American Express, 4% at Westinghouse, Unisys, Occidental Petroleum, 6% at Sears and Travelers, and a stunning 9% at Champion.

Further concerns about the board were reflected in shareholder resolutions calling for separate individuals to serve as Chairman and CEO, compensa-

tion and nominating committees to be entirely made up of independent outside directors, and an overall majority of independent outside directors on the board as a whole.

New York State Comptroller Edward Regan circulated a proposal to permit large shareholders access to the company's proxy statement for brief evaluations of the performance of the board. Robert A.G. Monks submitted a shareholder proposal at Exxon which would permit the creation of a Shareholder Advisory Committee, a group of shareholders, elected by shareholders, to meet (at company expense). As with Regan's proposal, this group would be permitted to include its comments on the company in the corporate proxy statement. The California Public Employees' Retirement System negotiated the creation of such a committee with Ryder and is currently discussing similar committees with other companies.

SEC's Proxy Reform Proposals

But the most significant development of 1992 was the SEC's issuance of new rules governing shareholder communication. The initial reform proposals in 1991 elicited an avalanche of comments. Nearly every representative of management objected; nearly every representative of shareholders supported them. The SEC accepted comments on these proposals, including the Regan model described above, and on proposed revision to the rules governing disclosure of executive compensation.

The new rules will make it easier for shareholders who are not seeking control of a company to communicate with each other. The old rules required any shareholder who wanted to communicate with more than 10 other shareholders to have his or her comments approved by the SEC before they could be circulated. The new rules eliminate the SEC's role as editor/censor of this material and require only that it be filed. Other aspects of the rules make it easier for shareholders to get their material to each other, and substantially revise the rules for reporting on executive compensation. They will make possible more effective shareholder oversight. But managers, directors, and shareholders must keep in mind that as shareholders' liability is limited, so is their agenda. Shareholders do not have the expertise, the resources, or the right to get involved in matters of day-to-day management and should not become involved in second-guessing "ordinary business." Indeed, such involvement is currently prohibited by sections of the proxy rules that are not under consideration for change.

But as Graham and Dodd argued, over a half century ago, shareholders do have the right and responsibility to focus their attention on matters where "the interest of the officers and the stockholders may be in conflict," including executive compensation. Developments since the time of Graham and Dodd have shown that shareholders must also be vigilant about preserving the full integrity—and value—of their stock ownership rights. For example, the right to vote may be diluted by a classified board or by dual class capitalization, and the right to transfer the stock to a willing buyer at a mutually agreeable price may be abrogated by the adoption of a "poison pill." These kinds of issues present conflicts of interest not contemplated at the time of Graham and Dodd's first edition, as shareholders are interested in accountability and officers and directors are interested in protecting themselves. It isn't that poison pills are bad—on the contrary—it is just that they should be submitted to a shareholder vote, because there is a conflict of interests between shareholders and management in the design and timing of a poison pill.

Of course, the shareholders' most important function as monitors concerns their election of the directors. As noted above, the "just vote no" strategy is an increasingly important way for shareholders to send a message of concern about the performance of the company or the board. Company proxy statements reveal information about whether individual directors attend 75% of the meetings, how much stock they own, which committees they serve on, and about transactions with the company. Shareholders can withhold votes for directors who do not attend meetings, who hold no stock, who serve on committees that approve bad compensation schemes, or who have conflicts of interest. While even a majority of "withhold" votes cannot keep an unopposed director candidate off the board, it can send an effective message to the board, management, and maybe even to members of the financial community who may be considering running a dissident slate.

It is not only the shareholder community that has changed in the last decade. The corporate community has also changed, in response to the increased ownership focus of shareholders. John Wilcox of Georgeson, one of the leading proxy solicitation firms, reports that many of his clients decide not to make certain changes that would require shareholder approval, after Georgeson advises them that they would have trouble getting a majority vote.

And many companies are responding to governance concerns raised by the shareholder, financial, and legal communities. SpencerStuart's annual Board Index (analyzing board trends and practices at 100 major companies) shows some dramatic shifts. Over the past five years, there has been a net loss of 91 inside directorships and a net gain of two outside directorships. The median ratio of outsiders to insiders is now 3 to 1, and more than a quarter of the boards in the study had a ratio of 5 to 1 or greater. Only seven of the boards in the survey had a majority of inside directors. A study by the National Association of Corporate Directors revealed unanimous support for "small, proactive, informed and truly independent boards." When shareholders submitted resolutions asking for a majority of independent directors on the board, some companies agreed to the terms of the proposals, so they never went to a vote.

Institutional investors are transforming the world of corporate governance. The issues they must consider in voting proxies are more complicated and diverse, with economic and fiduciary consequences to consider and evaluate. The priorities of the institutional investor community are evolving quickly, past the secondary issues of poison pills, and toward the central concerns of board composition, independence, and effectiveness. The "New Compact Between Owners and Directors" drafted by a committee of shareholder and management representatives, shows the commitment by both parties to better board oversight.

The process is evolving as well. The SEC's comprehensive review of the proxy rules reflects technological and ownership changes of the last decade. Amendments to those rules may turn the myths of director "election" and accountability to owners into reality. Finally, the relationship between shareholders and management is developing into a continuing and constructive dialogue. Ultimately, the annual meeting will be simply one small aspect of a long-term, committed partnership.

Endnotes

1. Brancato, Carolyn Kay and Gaughan, Patrick, Columbia Institutional Investor Project, as cited in William M. Barr and John M. Conley, *Fortune and Folly: The Wealth and Power of Institutional Investing* (Homewood, Illinois: Business One Irwin) 1992, 34.

2. Brancato, Carolyn Kay, "Breakdown of Total Assets by Type of Institutional Investor, 1989," Riverside Economic Research, February 21, 1991.

3. *See* Fischel, Daniel and Langbein, John H. "ERISA's Fundamental Contradiction: The Exclusive Benefit Rule" University of Chicago Law Review, 55(4), September 1988: 1105–1160.

4. Employment Retirement Income Security Act of 1974, See 402(a)(2).

5. Id., See 3(16)(B).

6. The government seemed to agree—administration of ERISA was given to the Labor Department, not to the Treasury Department.

7. Letter from J. Grills, Chairman of CIEBA, to Linda Cane, Director of the Division of Corporate Finance, SEC, February 25, 1991. CIEBA is a committee of the Financial Executives Institute, a professional association of 13,500 senior financial executives.

8. Roe, Mark J. "Legal Restraints on Ownership and Control of Public Companies," Paper presented at the Conference on the Structure and Governance of Enterprise, Harvard Business School, March 29–31: 8.

9. Rohter, Larry "Corporations Pass Alumni in Donations to Colleges," New York Times, April 29, 1986: A-16.

10. Poison pills, or shareholder rights plans, are a device that make hostile takeovers all but impossible. They take the form of rights or warrants issued to shareholders that are worthless unless triggered by a hostile acquisition attempt. If triggered, pills give shareholders the ability to purchase shares from or sell shares back to the target company (the "flip-in" pill) and/or the potential acquirer (the "flip-over" pill) at a price far out of line with the fair market value. The basic function of pills is to confront a hostile purchaser with an immediate and unacceptable dilution of the value of his or her investment.

11. Epstein, Edward J. Who Owns the Corporation? Management versus Shareholders, Priority Press, New York: 1986: 24–25.

12. The author was, at that time, General Counsel of Institutional Shareholder Services, Inc.

Part IV:
Regulation of the Capital Markets

Chapter 7

SEC Regulation of the Capital Markets

Sara Hanks
Partner
Rogers & Wells, New York, NY

The Securities and Exchange Commission (SEC) regulation did not, in general, have as much effect on the conduct of investment banking business in 1991–1992 as it did in the preceding two-year period. In 1990 the SEC adopted Rule 144A and Regulation S and reproposed the multijurisdictional disclosure system. During 1991–1992 the SEC adopted the multijurisdictional disclosure system, addressed matters of U.S. investor access to rights offerings and tender offers made overseas and the regulation of American Depositary Receipts and, on the domestic side, adopted rule changes to make it easier for small businesses to raise capital and to increase investor protection in "blank check" offerings. Rule 144A continued to have a substantial impact on the U.S. markets, although only minor regulatory initiatives were taken in this area.

All of these matters reflect in one way or another the SEC's continuing concern to balance the protection of investors and the reputation of the U.S. markets and the access of U.S. investors to investment opportunities and the access of issuers (whether large or small U.S. issuers or foreign issuers) to the U.S. markets.

Domestic Markets

Private Placements

The distinction between public offerings and private placements was blurred to some extent by the 1990 adoption by the SEC of Rule 144A, although the rule's principal effect has been in the area of offerings in the United States by foreign companies (discussed below).

Rule 144A under the Securities Act of 1933 (the "Securities Act") was adopted in order to clarify the circumstances in which privately placed ("restricted") securities could be resold without registration and without waiting the two- to three-year period before such sales can be made pursuant to Rule 144. It permits unlimited resales to "qualified institutional buyers"—institutions that the SEC deems able to fend for themselves in the purchase of unregistered securities.

The conditions of the rule are simple. In order to resell securities under the rule the following conditions must be met:

♦ The securities cannot be "fungible" with (the same class as) securities listed on a U.S. securities exchange or quoted on the National Association of Securities Dealers Automated Quotation System (NASDAQ), or the securities of an investment company required to register as such in the United States.

♦ Sellers must offer and sell the securities only to entities they reasonably believe to be "qualified institutional buyers" (QIBs).

♦ Information about the issuer must be available. This requirement is met if 1) the issuer files periodic reports with the SEC under the Securities Exchange Act of 1934 (the "Exchange Act"), 2) the issuer is a foreign entity that has established the exemption from reporting under Rule 12g3-2(b) under the Exchange Act; or 3) the issuer agrees to provide investors and prospective investors with two years of financial statements.

♦ The seller must take "reasonable steps" to ensure that the buyer is aware that it is buying unregistered securities from the seller in reliance on the rule.

QIBs are institutions, such as banks, insurance companies, securities firms, pension plans, corporations and partnerships, but excluding individuals that in the aggregate own and invest on a discretionary basis at least $100 million worth of securities of an unaffiliated entity. Bank deposit notes and certificates of deposit, swaps and repurchase agreements, and securities subject to repurchase agreements are excluded from this test. Broker-dealers need only own and invest $10 million of securities. To be QIBs, banks and savings and loan associations must also have a net worth of at least $25 million.

In October 1992, the SEC expanded the QIB definition to include collective trust funds, which combine the pension funds of several employers, and master trusts, which combine funds of employee benefit plans that are under the common sponsorship of a single employer (or its affiliates) into a single administrative arrangement.

It is important to bear in mind that Rule 144A permits unregistered *resales* of securities to qualified buyers. It does not apply to primary sales by issuers. Issuers generally take advantage of the rule by making a primary sale to one or more buyers (typically investment banks), relying on the exemption from registration provided to issuers by Section 4(2) of the Securities Act. Resales by such intermediary and end investors then take place pursuant to the rule. SEC staff have reminded practitioners several times during the course of the year that offerings of securities that are intended to trade pursuant to Rule 144A must be made in accordance with the requirements of Section 4(2). Thus, the protections traditionally used to ensure that an issuer has the benefit of Section 4(2) (such as legending the securities issued, requiring representations to be made by buyers of the securities, and creating procedures monitoring the manner of subsequent resales) may still be appropriate or necessary in many cases. Which protections are required depends on the circumstances of the offering, including the likelihood of an unregistered "distribution" of securities resulting.

The rule has proved to be the basis for the development of "quasi-public" debt offerings by U.S. issuers. Thus, for example, when an issuer seeks to issue debt with relatively straightforward terms with liquidity in the secondary market but chooses not to register the offering for public sale, the rule has been used. In an increasing number of offerings, investment bankers that in a regular private placement would normally act as placement agents act instead as "underwriters" (in the practical rather than the

legal sense). In addition to the normal benefits of underwriting, negotiation between issuer and investor is largely precluded and the deal can be closed within a short time. In such cases, the terms of the securities are generally straightforward and no complex financial covenants are involved. Rule 144A offerings on such terms have even appealed to issuers that already report to the SEC and for whom the registration of a new offering is not generally a painful event. When favorable financing opportunities are perceived in the capital markets, the ability to take advantage of them without waiting for SEC review (or even the taking of a "no review" position) is invaluable. For such "quasi-public" treatment, the securities offered should generally be rated as "investment grade"; U.S. broker-dealers are then subject to more favorable treatment under the "haircut" provisions of the net capital rules.

Rule 144A does not yet seem to have been used a great deal for domestic equity offerings.

Capital-Raising by Small Businesses

In July 1992, the SEC adopted revisions to rules and forms under the Securities Act, the Exchange Act, and the Trust Indenture Act of 1939 (the "Trust Indenture Act") in order to facilitate capital-raising by small businesses and reduce the compliance burdens placed on these companies by the federal securities laws. The revisions expand the availability of small issues exemptions under Regulation A and Rule 504 of the Securities Act and simplify registration and reporting disclosure requirements for "small business issuers."

The revisions are intended to improve the access of small businesses to financing markets and to lower the costs for small businesses that undertake offerings of either equity or debt securities. According to the SEC, "small businesses are the cornerstone of the U.S. economy," since they produce half the gross domestic product and frequently develop new technology, patents, products, and services. Start-up and developing companies that want to raise capital, however, have faced an array of regulatory barriers. Smaller businesses have been disproportionately affected by the complexities of registration and disclosure requirements, and the availability and number of small business financings have declined dramatically in recent years. Recognizing that "a critical factor in the viability of these small business ventures is access to capital and debt financings," the SEC's new rules are intended to eliminate impediments to small business financing without compromising the basic goal of investor protection.

Regulation A permits the unregistered public offering of securities under specified conditions. Previously, a U.S. or Canadian issuer could use the exemption to offer up to $1.5 million of securities in any 12-month period. The changes raise that dollar ceiling and introduce a "test the waters" provision, while at the same time limiting availability of the exemption.

Only U.S. and Canadian issuers not subject to Exchange Act reporting requirements are eligible for a Regulation A exemption. The revisions allow unregistered offerings of up to $5 million in any 12-month period for issuer sales, including no more than $1.5 million in secondary offerings. A Regulation A offering will not be integrated with any previously completed or registered offering, or any subsequent offering made under Regulation S, Rule 701, an employee benefit plan or more than six months later.

The "test the waters" provision should reduce the risk for companies preparing an offering of securities without any knowledge of potential investor interest. The provision allows eligible issuers to send solicitation material to prospective investors or publish it in the print media prior to filing an offering statement. The issuer will thus be better able to gauge investor receptiveness to a possible offering and determine whether to incur the expense of proceeding with a Regulation A offering. The solicitation material has to be filed with the SEC and can include only factual information. A coupon to be returned by interested purchasers can be included. The provision also allows oral communications between the issuer and prospective investors after solicitation materials are filed. A 20-day "cooling off" period is required between the last use of the solicitation document and any sale of securities.

The Regulation A exemption still requires the issuer to file an offering statement with the SEC which must be "qualified" by the SEC. The form and content of the offering circular has been revised to allow companies to use a "user friendly" question and answer format, which the SEC believes should reduce costs but will continue to maintain investor protection.

Previously, Regulation A imposed a 10 business day qualification period between filing of the offering statement and actual offers and sales. Pursuant to the revisions, oral offers and written offers through a preliminary offering circular may be made as soon as the offering statement is filed. Actual sales, however, have to wait until after a 20 calendar day qualification period.

While Regulation A is for offerings by small businesses that file an offering statement with the SEC, Rule 504 under the Securities Act permits unregistered offerings by a nonreporting company of up to $1 million in a 12-month period to be made without an offering statement if the issuer furnishes

material information to the purchaser at a reasonable time prior to the sale of securities. Limitations on general solicitation pursuant to a Rule 504 offering have been dropped, and securities purchased pursuant to such offerings will be freely transferrable and not "restricted."

Rules relating to trust indentures, which must generally be "qualified" with the SEC in the case of a public offering, with certain exemptions, have been amended to increase the dollar ceilings of such exemptions to permit unqualified indentures to be used in connection with offerings under the new initiatives.

The SEC also adopted an integrated disclosure system for small business issuers so that small businesses may register offerings under the Securities Act and file reports under the Exchange Act pursuant to more straightforward disclosure requirements.

Commissioner Fleischman (who has since resigned) issued a separate statement on the proposals and the initiatives. He argued that the objective of the SEC's new rules should be to "eliminate those regulations that impose costs on small business exceeding their benefits to investors." To that end, the Commissioner requested comment on his own proposals, which would have, inter alia, relaxed materiality and liability rules for small business issuers and broker-dealers and permit more exemptions from registration.

Since adoption, there has been some concern expressed by state securities regulators with respect to facilitating the sale of these, the riskiest kind of securities. The fact that offerings are subject to both state and federal regulation means that, without the concurrence of state regulators, the value of the SEC's reforms could be limited.

Blank Check Offerings

In April 1992, the SEC adopted amendments and new rules under the Securities Act requiring a "blank check company" that sells penny stocks to disclose additional information prior to and after the effectiveness of its registration statement. A blank check company is defined as a company that 1) is devoting substantially all of its efforts to establishing a new business in which planned principal operations have not yet commenced; 2) is issuing "penny stock"; and 3) either has no business plan or purpose or has indicated its business plan is to engage in a merger or acquisition with an unspecified business entity.

Under former rules, investors in blank check offerings were told only the industry in which their funds would be invested but not the specific entity or property. The SEC expressed its hope that by assuring adequate disclosure in blank check offerings, the potential for fraud and manipulation in the market for securities issued in such offerings would be restricted.

Rule 419 requires funds received and securities issued in an offering of penny stock from a blank check company to be placed in an escrow account maintained by an insured depository institution or in a separate bank account maintained at a bank with a registered broker-dealer acting as trustee. Funds and securities in a Rule 419 account, including dividends and interest, must be held for the sole benefit of the purchaser. These funds may only be invested in specified safe investments.

Underwriters' commissions and expenses and dealer allowances for underwriters and dealers unaffiliated with the registrant need not be deposited.

Once a blank check company agrees to an acquisition or acquisitions that meets certain criteria (including the requirement that the acquisition represent at least 80% of the offering proceeds), a post-effective amendment to the blank check company's registration statement must be filed, disclosing details of the acquisition. Funds may be released to the company from a Rule 419 account upon effectiveness of this amendment.

The new rules require that purchasers be informed of their right to withdraw funds and receive a refund. Within five business days of the effective date of the post-effective amendment, the issuer is required to furnish each purchaser with a prospectus describing the acquisition. Upon receipt of this prospectus, purchasers have the opportunity to have their deposited funds (less certain withdrawals) returned. A purchaser would have no less than 20 and no more than 45 business days to either confirm an intent to invest or request a refund. If the purchaser does not respond, the funds are returned to the purchaser within five business days after the 45th business day after the effective date of the post-effective amendment. Additionally, if the conditions set out in the initial offering (i.e. an acquisition) are not met within 18 months from the effective date of the initial registration statement, the funds would be required to be returned to the purchasers.

International Markets

The Partial Success of Rule 144A

Rule 144A, the provisions of which were discussed previously, was adopted in 1990. It was, among other things, intended to encourage foreign issuers to access the U.S. private placement markets by increasing the liquidity and efficiency of the market for privately placed securities. Foreign issuers had long been discouraged from making public offerings in the United States by the SEC's registration and disclosure requirements. Private placements were also unattractive to foreign issuers because of the "illiquidity premium" demanded by U.S. investors as a result of the difficulty in reselling restricted securities. The rule has so far proved successful in achieving at least part of the SEC's aims.

Primary Offerings. Although a large principal amount of debt securities has been offered by foreign issuers pursuant to the rule, the rule's impact has been more noticeable in the equity markets than in the debt markets. Foreign issuers that would not otherwise have made offerings in the United States have made U.S. offerings or extended Euro-offerings to encompass the U.S. markets. Especially noticeable has been the number of companies from emerging markets making equity offerings in the United States, with issuers from Latin America (primarily Mexico) being the most numerous.

Many Rule 144A offerings of debt securities by foreign issuers are offered in the United States only. Tax issues have had some impact on the attractiveness of debt 144A offerings to foreign issuers. The IRS requires that withholding tax be imposed on bearer debt securities (or securities convertible into bearer form) issued in the United States. Since foreign offerings of debt, especially in Europe, tend to be in bearer form (although registered form securities are gaining more acceptance), the issuers' ability to make a global offering of debt securities in the same form in Europe and the United States, with liquidity between the two markets, is limited.

Equity offerings pursuant to the rule have generally received more attention than have debt offerings and for good reason. Most such offerings have been made by non-U.S. issuers that have never before accessed the U.S. markets and that probably would not have extended offerings into the United States had the rule not existed. A typical recent Rule 144A equity offering would appear to involve a Latin American or Asian company making a "Euroequity" offering with about a quarter of the total offering in the United States. Some additional paperwork is necessary to extend such offers into the United States. While the question of the extent to which disclosure in selling documents prepared for the non-U.S. markets needs to be expanded or amended has been the subject of debate in the legal community, the disclosure is generally less than would be required for public offerings, and financial statements prepared according to U.S. generally accepted accounting principles (GAAP) are not necessary.

Secondary Trading. Because most of the equity offerings made so far have been by foreign issuers who have an active market for their securities in their home jurisdiction, it is too early to pass judgment on whether some of the SEC's intentions in this area have yet been met. Certainly, foreign issuers have been attracted to the U.S. private markets. But where an active secondary market for their shares exists elsewhere, there has been no real need for a secondary market to develop in the United States. In this respect, Regulation S, which the SEC adopted at the same time as Rule 144A, has been a crucial element in encouraging U.S. investors to buy the shares of non-U.S. issuers, because Regulation S permits them to resell such securities easily overseas. It is possible, however, that the regulation is a double-edged sword, as the very ease with which such securities can be resold outside the United States discourages the development of an active U.S. market and the permanent diversification of a non-U.S. issuer's shareholder base.

In addition to affecting the "flowback" of foreign securities, issues relating to secondary trading will greatly affect the way in which the Rule 144A market develops in the next year or two. In the case of some debt securities, there is no need for a great deal of additional liquidity because holders do not wish to trade. But in the case of "quasi-public" debt and equity securities, the lack of an efficient trading mechanism could diminish the attractiveness of the market. The National Association of Securities Dealers' PORTAL system has thus far proved too restrictive, and for that reason proposed amendments to the system are currently before the SEC (and have been for some time). If PORTAL and its future competitors are permitted to function as efficient quotation and trading systems, with a minimum of regulation, the market's true potential may be realized.

The Multijurisdictional Disclosure System

In June 1991, the SEC and Canadian securities regulators led by the Ontario and Quebec commissions adopted the Multijurisdictional Disclosure System (MJDS). The MJDS's initial application is for use in the United States by Canadian companies (and vice versa), but it has the potential to be extended to other countries. On the U.S. side, the MJDS permits Canadian issuers to comply with SEC disclosure requirements for public offerings and ongoing reporting requirements by filing their home-jurisdiction disclosure documents with the SEC. The purpose of the MJDS is to encourage Canadian issuers to extend rights offers and tender offers to U.S. shareholders, rather than having to have them "cashed out" in order to avoid U.S. registration (which actually tends to happen more often with European than with Canadian issuers), and generally to encourage transnational capital formation.

The SEC had requested comment in 1985 on two alternative approaches to facilitating multinational securities offerings. While some commenters felt that the first alternative—the development of a common prospectus—was attractive, it was generally felt that a system of mutual recognition of prospectus disclosure was more workable. The MJDS is based on the latter theory, although it is sometimes referred to as a hybrid of the two approaches because Canadian disclosure requirements are already similar to those of the United States. The MJDS was first proposed in 1989. In 1990, a reproposal of the MJDS was made that modified and extended the system; the adoption of the MJDS in 1991 was made with limited changes from the reproposal.

The MJDS does not alter a company's registration and reporting obligations under the Securities Act or the Exchange Act, but it allows those obligations to be met by the filing of documents prepared in accordance with Canadian requirements. Such documents are deemed to have met U.S. disclosure standards, although issuers remain liable for misleading statements or omissions. Some commenters had expressed concern that documents that complied with Canadian requirements but failed to make the disclosure of information required in the United States would lead to potential liabilities in the United States. In response, the SEC pointed out that SEC forms have different levels of disclosure for different types of offerings and that the MJDS was not unusual in this respect. The effect of the system, the SEC stated, was as if Canadian disclosure requirements were set forth in the applicable SEC MJDS form. The SEC will not generally review Canadian documents filed pursuant to the system.

In order to use the system to register rights offerings the following conditions must be met:

1. Issuers must have been reporting to a Canadian securities commission for 36 months and must be listed on the Toronto or Montreal stock exchanges or the Senior Board of the Vancouver Stock Exchange for the most recent 12 months prior to the offering.

2. The rights must be granted to U.S. shareholders on the same terms as to shareholders in the issuer's home jurisdiction.

3. The rights may not be transferable except outside the United States, pursuant to Regulation S, although the securities obtainable upon exercise of the rights may be transferable in the United States.

With respect to registering exchange offers the following conditions must be met:

1. Issuers must have been reporting to a Canadian securities commission for 36 months and must have been listed on the Montreal or Toronto stock exchanges or the Senior Board of the Vancouver Stock Exchange for the most recent 12 months prior to the offering.

2. Issuers must have a market float (aggregate market value of equity securities held by non-affiliates) of $75 million (Cdn).

3. The securities must be offered to U.S. residents on the same terms as to Canadian residents.

4. Less than 40% of the class of securities to be exchanged must be held of record by U.S. holders (including affiliates of the issuer).

The registration forms for exchange offers can also be used for business combinations on similar terms, provided that each participant in the combination is organized or incorporated in Canada.

With respect to registration of other capital-raising transactions, the following conditions must be met for investment grade debt or preferred securities:

1. Issuers must have a 36-month reporting history with a Canadian securities commission (12 months in the case of crown corporations) and currently be in compliance with such requirements.

2. The aggregate market value of the issuer's outstanding equity shares is at least $180 million (Cdn) and the market value of such securities held by nonaffiliates is at least $75 million (Cdn).

3. The securities are rated in one of the four highest categories by a nationally recognized statistical rating organization.

4. The securities are not convertible for a period of one year from the date of issuance.

5. The securities are convertible only into another class of the issuer's securities. Where the securities are not convertible at all, the market-value and public float tests do not apply.

Canadian issuers can sell other securities publicly in the United States if:

1. They have a 36-month reporting history with a Canadian securities commission (and are currently in compliance with such requirements).

2. Their equity shares have an aggregate market value of at least $360 million (Cdn), $75 million (Cdn) of which must be held by non-affiliates.

In contrast to the other offerings previously described, disclosure supplemental to Canadian documentation would be required. Reconciliation of accounts to U.S. GAAP as specified in Item 18 of Form 20-F is required but only for a period of two years (through July 1, 1993), unless this requirement is extended by the SEC.

The MJDS expressly permits "U.S. only" offerings to be made by Canadian issuers, despite the fact that the system was originally adopted to facilitate multijurisdictional offerings. Since the SEC would not generally undertake a substantive review of the filings, use of the MJDS in these circumstances requires that filing also be made with one of the participating Canadian securities commissions.

The MJDS can also be used to comply with the SEC's requirements regarding the conduct of tender offers. Tender offers in the United States must be made in accordance with the requirements of the Williams Act (the portion of the Exchange Act dealing with tender offers). Eligible issuers may comply with the Williams Act by complying with Canadian tender offer regulations. To qualify for this treatment, less than 40% of the securities subject to the tender offer must be held by U.S. holders (including affiliates of the issuer).

The MJDS may additionally be used for registration and reporting under the Exchange Act. Most Canadian issuers required to register with the SEC (whether because they have made public offerings in the United States or are listed on a stock exchange or have a certain number of shareholders) will be able to register and file annual reports with the SEC by using Canadian disclosure documents.

The SEC requires that financial statements included in a prospectus used pursuant to the MJDS be audited in accordance with U.S. concepts of "auditor independence." While the SEC's original proposal required financials to have been so audited for the last three fiscal years, as adopted this requirement applies only for the most recent financial year included in the registration statement filed with the SEC (this requirement would, of course, apply to all subsequent financial years). Canadian auditor-independence rules do not exactly mirror those of the United States, so Canadian companies considering taking advantage of the MJDS still have to determine whether the nonaudit services provided by their auditors or their relationships with those auditors satisfy the U.S. rules and, if not, whether to make some changes in their auditing system to take advantage of the MJDS in future years.

Each U.S. state requires that securities offerings into that state be registered with the state authorities or be made pursuant to an exemption from registration. The North American Securities Administrators Association endorsed the system and formed a task force to recommend changes to state securities laws to accommodate the MJDS. Substantial progress has been made in the states' adopting exemptions for offerings using the MJDS.

Initial experience with the MJDS suggests steady rather than heavy usage. The possibility of expansion of the MJDS to other countries has been raised; indeed, when the idea was originally floated, the United Kingdom was cited as a potential partner in the system. Since no such expansion has yet been proposed, however, the utility of the MJDS remains limited to Canadian/U.S. offerings.

The Challenges of Foreign Accounting Systems

During the course of the last few years, the SEC has been asked with increasing frequency to reconsider its requirement that the financial statements of foreign issuers registering securities or offerings with the SEC be reconciled to U.S. GAAP. Certain European and Japanese companies especially have expressed reluctance to access the U.S. markets under current rules. Institutions such as the New York Stock Exchange have encouraged the SEC to consider accepting foreign financial statements, in order to protect the competitiveness of U.S. capital markets.

The SEC under Chairman Breeden, however, has shown resistance to acceptance of foreign accounting standards (other than in the form of the MJDS previously discussed). The SEC's principal concerns in this area appear to be 1) the maintenance of investor protection and 2) the continuance of a "level playing field" wherein U.S. companies are not forced to compete for capital with foreign companies that disclose financial information in a different, possibly less complete manner. Despite the SEC's intransigence on these matters, pressure is continuing to mount from both foreign and domestic sources. The SEC may in the near future have to react in some way to demands that it afford a measure of flexibility to established foreign companies seeking to list or offer their securities in the United States, if only in the interests of U.S. investors' ability to invest in such securities.

Cross-Border Tender Offers, Exchange Offers and Rights Offerings

In June 1991, the SEC voted to propose for public comment new rules and forms designed to make it easier for foreign companies to make rights offerings into the United States, and for any person (U.S. or foreign) to extend into the United States tender offers or exchange offers that are made primarily outside the United States. The SEC proposed these changes in response to the fact that when, as is usual, U.S. investors are excluded from such offers, they are unable to receive the full economic benefit of their investments.

The proposals would do the following:

1. Permit tender offers to be made for the securities of a foreign issuer when less than 10% of the target class of securities is held by U.S. holders by complying with the requirements of the target company's home country tender offer regulations instead of those of the United States.

2. Grant blanket relief from certain U.S. tender offer regulations (regardless of the percentage of U.S. offerees) to tender offers for securities of a U.K. company made in accordance with the City Code of the United Kingdom.

3. Permit exchange offers and rights offerings for less than $5 million to be made without registration under the Securities Act of 1933.

4. Permit other exchange offers and rights offerings to be made by means of an easy (and immediately effective) registration process whereby disclosure documents prepared in accordance with the standards of a foreign jurisdiction are used to fulfill the SEC's disclosure requirements.

As discussed above, tender offers in the United States must be made in accordance with the provisions of the Williams Act. Foreign offerors have often found it difficult to comply with the SEC's requirements in this area. Sometimes it is impossible; for example, where the requirements of the offeror's home country relating to tender offers are directly in conflict with the requirements of the SEC. Moreover, compliance often involves additional time and expense in the preparation of disclosure materials, and many foreign offerors have felt that this has not been worth the effort in order to extend offers to a limited number of U.S. persons. Foreign offerors in a number of instances have attempted to avoid jurisdiction by excluding security holders resident in the United States from their offers. U.S. investors have thus not been able to take advantage of the terms of tender offers and have frequently been reduced to selling into the secondary market at a less advantageous price or forced to become minority shareholders.

Until now, the SEC has done two things in this area. First, it has asserted its extraterritorial jurisdiction with regard to tender offers as broadly as possible. Having asserted this position, however, the SEC has also attempted to be accommodating, and has waived some of its requirements in order for foreign tender offers to be extended to U.S. persons.

The SEC proposes that tender offers for the securities of foreign issuers may be made (by both U.S. and foreign persons) in accordance with the tender offer regulations of the target company's home jurisdiction, provided the following:

1. No more than 10 percent of the target class of securities is held by U.S. holders (any single holder of more than 10 percent of the target class would be excluded from this calculation).

2. U.S. holders are able to participate in the offering on terms no less favorable than those available to any other holders.

3. All information is disseminated to U.S. holders in English on the same basis as it is disseminated to holders in the target's home jurisdiction (by publication in a U.S. newspaper if any publication is required).

4. All offering materials (with certain exceptions) are "furnished" (not officially "filed") in English to the SEC.

In the case of tender offers that would have a "going private" effect, the issuer and any affiliated bidder would be required to comply with the Exchange Act's "going private" requirements, which involves enhanced disclosure beyond what may be required in the target company's home jurisdiction.

The SEC proposed a blanket order exempting from certain provisions of the SEC's tender offer rules all tender offers for the securities of companies incorporated in the United Kingdom made in accordance with the City Code on Take-Overs and Mergers. The SEC identified several areas where the U.S. and U.K. regulations conflict and proposes relief from the U.S. requirements in such cases to permit offers to be made in compliance with both the U.S. and U.K. regulations. No limit would be imposed on the percentage of U.S. holders. The proposed order would also provide that offering materials prepared in accordance with the City Code met the disclosure requirements of the Williams Act and could be filed with the SEC under cover of the applicable SEC schedule.

Exchange offers are not only tender offers but also involve public offerings of securities in the United States. They must therefore not only comply with the Williams Act but must also be registered under the Securities Act. Having to comply with the dual requirements of the Securities Act and the Exchange Act has made offerors even more reluctant to extend exchange offers to limited numbers of U.S. security holders.

The SEC would divide such offerings into those that can be made without registration and those that can be made pursuant to a simplified registration process, depending upon whether the value of the securities offered for exchange in the United States exceeds $5 million.

Proposed Rule 802 would exempt from registration under the Securities Act exchange offers where the market value of the securities offered to U.S. holders pursuant to the exchange offer does not exceed $5 million, provided:

1. The offer is extended to U.S. holders (except where the offer cannot be made in a particular state due to state law) on no less favorable terms than those offered to any other persons.

2. U.S. holders are provided with the same documents or other information provided to holders in the target's home jurisdiction. Any offering materials used must bear legends with respect to the different disclosure requirements that apply, the enforcement of remedies overseas, and the possibility of the offeror trading in the securities overseas (thus affecting their price).

Proposed Form F-12 would be made available to register exchange offers, mergers, arrangements, or similar business combinations in excess of $5 million, provided the following:

1. Less than 5% of the target class of securities prior to the exchange are held by U.S. holders (other than any single holder of more than 10% of the target class).

2. The issuer of the securities to be offered is a foreign private (i.e., nongovernmental) issuer.

3. The issuer files periodic reports with the SEC under the Exchange Act, or is exempt from reporting pursuant to the "information-furnishing" exemption provided by Rule 12g3-2(b) under the Exchange Act.

4. The issuer *either* has had a class of its securities listed for three years on a "designated offshore securities market" (such exchanges are defined in Regulation S) and is in compliance with such listing requirements, *or* has

securities so listed, is in compliance with such listing requirements, has been in operation for three years, and has a public float of $75 million.

5. The offer is extended to U.S. holders on terms no less favorable than those offered to any other holder.

Disclosure to be made on Form F-12 would consist of whatever disclosure is made in accordance with the target company's home country requirements. Form F-12 itself is just a "wraparound," with brief information about the offering and legends warning investors as to the fact that non-U.S. accounting and auditing standards have been applied and the possible difficulty of enforcing remedies against foreign persons.

Filing of a registration statement on Form F-12 would, unlike most other SEC registration forms, give rise to no ongoing reporting obligations under the Exchange Act.

Rights offerings (more accurately, the *exercise* of rights distributed in a rights offering) are treated by the SEC as public offerings, despite the fact that they are limited to existing holders of the issuer's securities. They must, therefore, be registered under the Securities Act or be made pursuant to an exemption from registration. Although occasionally rights offerings have been made on a nonpublic basis in the United States, in general, structuring such offerings has been more trouble than foreign issuers have believed it was worth. U.S. investors have therefore been "cashed out" of rights offerings (i.e., rights have been sold on their behalf overseas, with the proceeds of sale being transmitted to the holders), or alternatively they have been excluded altogether.

Again, the SEC proposes to divide rights offerings according to their size, exempting rights offerings below $5 million and providing a simplified registration process for the others. The following conditions would apply to securities offered pursuant to rights offerings in both exempt and registered transactions:

1. The securities issued must be equity securities of foreign issuers of the same class as those held by the offerees in the United States and must be offered on a pro rata basis.

2. The issuer must be either a) a reporting issuer or b) exempt from reporting pursuant to Rule 12g3-2(b), have a class of equity securities listed or quoted on a "designated offshore securities market" (and be in compliance with the listing or quoting obligations), and *either* have been so listed or quoted for three years *or* have a public float of at least $75 million.

(This protects against use of the exemption by start-up companies.)

3. The rights must be offered to U.S. persons on terms no less favorable than they are offered to persons elsewhere.

4. The rights (but not the securities available on exercise of the rights) may not be transferrable within the United States (although they may be sold outside the United States in reliance on Regulation S).

5. The consideration for exercise of the rights must be cash.

Rule 801 would provide an exemption for rights offerings made in the United States where the value of the securities offered to U.S. holders upon exercise of the rights in reliance on Rule 801 is less than $5 million, provided U.S. holders are provided the same information (in English) as those in the issuer's home country (by advertisement in a U.S. newspaper, if necessary).

Form F-11 would permit registration of the rights offering on the basis of home country disclosure provided the following:

1. The foreign offering document is delivered to U.S. holders and is supplemented by legends advising U.S. holders that the investment may have foreign tax consequences, U.S. holders may have to pursue legal remedies in a foreign jurisdiction, and that financial statements were prepared in accordance with foreign accounting and auditing standards.

2. The offering document, together with exhibits and the supplemental legends, is filed with the SEC under cover of Form F-11.

Form F-11, like Form F-12, gives rise to no ongoing Exchange Act obligations, and therefore does not affect the issuer's 12g3-2(b) exemption. Like Form F-12, it is effective immediately upon filing and will not be reviewed by the SEC.

The SEC's proposed actions in this area are an example of the SEC's great flexibility in this area. Although the SEC's "dual" approach to the question of rights offers and exchange offers (exempting small offers and permitting streamlined registration for larger offers) may initially seem strange, this is because the SEC is statutorily unable to grant exemptions for offerings that involve more than $5 million. The streamlined registration process provided is as close as the SEC could come to a blanket exemption.

American Depositary Receipts

In May 1991, the Securities and Exchange Commission issued a "concept release" on the subject of American Depositary Receipts (ADRs). ADRs are a convenient format for offering foreign securities in the United States. They represent the right to receive foreign securities held by the depositary (usually a bank) which issues the ADRs. The depositary converts all dividends received on the deposited securities into dollars, and ADRs settle and clear in the same way as U.S. securities. Thus, ADRs are often more attractive than holding the underlying securities. The SEC has become increasingly interested in the regulation of ADRs and the functioning of the ADR market over the last few years. In particular, the SEC appears to be investigating whether the deposit agreements that govern the terms upon which ADRs are issued disclose adequate information to the holder of ADRs about the nature of the security that he or she holds and the rights that relate to it.

The SEC has asked whether changes are necessary with respect to the process of registration under the Securities Act and the information elicited by that process. In particular, the SEC asks whether more information should be disclosed in the Form F-6 (a short form upon which the ADRs, but not the underlying securities, are registered, and which describes the terms of deposit, but not the issuer or the securities) about the issuer of the deposited securities and the securities themselves.

The SEC also asks, in effect, whether some kind of merit regulation should be imposed, in that ADRs could only be registered when certain rights were granted to ADR holders. Other requests for comments cover the information provided by depositaries and their qualification to act as such and the information currently provided about the terms upon which ADRs are issued.

Part V:
Managing the Investment Banking Firm

Chapter 8

Managing Risk in Investment Banking

Mark E. Bachmann
Managing Director
Standard & Poor's Ratings Group, New York, NY

The securities industry is undergoing a dynamic evolution which is both a reflection of its vitality and one source of its problems. Analysis of the industry must factor in the enormous potential enjoyed by firms that are well-positioned for the future, while at the same time recognizing the speed with which these same firms can incur a crisis if they overextend themselves or misread the direction of the fast-paced markets they serve. Standard & Poor's presently has fixed-income ratings on 12 securities firms, primarily among the large investment banks and national brokers. The following discussion covers mainly that tier of the industry, although many of the dynamics considered here have implications for regional brokers as well and other financial institutions participating in the securities markets.

History of the Past Decade

The history of the past decade demonstrates both the heady successes and the turbulence to which the industry is prone. The spectacular rise and fall of Drexel Burnham was one of the most explosive boom-bust stories in the history of American business. However, several other securities firms with long histories and well-established franchises, such as First Boston and Shearson Lehman, also endured serious financial crises, in some cases shortly following periods of what had appeared to be successful expansion. More recently, the government bond trading scandal which engulfed Salomon Brothers in August of 1991, interrupting one of the most profitable years in the firm's history, demonstrated once again the speed with which success in this industry can be derailed.

The events of the past decade were driven by unique historical circumstances. More importantly for this discussion, however, the events also developed in response to pressures that are inherent in the business that securities firms do, and they are therefore instructive for understanding risks that affect the industry now and in the future. While there were many trends that shaped the financial markets during the 1980s, probably the two most visible were the evolution of the so-called "junk" bond market and the powerful bull market in equities, which underwent a sudden and destabilizing contraction in October of 1987. In fact, the courses of these two markets were interconnected and reflected many of the same underlying forces.

Junk Bonds

At the beginning of the decade, the term "junk bonds" was applied primarily to securities which had been issued at ratings of "BBB" or higher and subsequently downgraded, usually because of operating problems on the part of the obligor. Junk bonds had a stigma attached to them and investors tended to avoid them. However, traders and investors who specialized in this sector of the market found themselves on fertile ground because there were many securities whose obligors, while weakened, nonetheless generated cash flows that were strong enough to justify values for their bonds well in excess of prevailing market prices. In short, junk bonds offered a classic case of market inefficiency and, therefore, of profit opportunities for knowledgeable investors.

As generally happens, however, the success of these junk bond pioneers did not go unnoticed by other market participants. As the decade moved on, junk bonds lost their stigma and securities firms, with Drexel Burnham in the lead, began to channel a powerful flow of institutional and private money into what was now generally referred to as the "high-yield" bond market, a term more befitting its new respectability. The growing perception that high yields could be achieved while incurring only limited risk fueled growth in the market, and soon demand for high-yield bonds was outstripping supply. The next stage in the market's evolution was probably inevitable. Finding that speculative-grade credit ratings no longer blocked their access to large pools of capital, many industrial companies began leveraging their balance sheets and issuing large amounts of debt to finance recapitalizations, buyouts of their own stock, and leveraged takeovers of other companies. For their part, securities firms participating in the high-yield bond business profited from all stages of the process: underwriting new issues, trading in the secondary markets, and providing advice to companies contemplating or targeted by leveraged takeovers. Wary of the risks, many securities firms were initially reluctant to commit their resources to this business. However, incentives increased at the same time risk assessments became more favorable, and by late in the decade virtually all major securities firms were participating in the market to one degree or another.

What too few people were willing to acknowledge was that the market inefficiencies which had facilitated the junk bond boom were mostly gone by the latter part of the decade. Most new junk bonds were being issued to finance the purchase of stock in one form or another, and as equity prices rose, junk bond obligors were incurring more and more balance sheet leverage. In short, junk bonds entering the market late in the 1980s were qualitatively different and, in the aggregate, were of lesser quality than the small universe of "fallen angels" that had offered such attractive trading opportunities several years earlier.

The market began to show signs of weakness late in the decade and, finally, in 1990 junk bond prices underwent a dramatic contraction and the new issue market largely disappeared. While regulatory actions and other factors influenced the timing and extent of the downturn, an implosion at some point could hardly have been avoided. Securities firms benefitted from several dimensions of the junk bond boom, and were now hit with a spectrum of problems, the write-down of high-yield inventories being only the most obvious. Underwriting, distribution, trading, and advisory revenues slumped, and companies had to begin paring back costly infrastructures which had been built up to support these activities. One partic-

ularly dangerous problem for some firms stemmed from "bridge loans" advanced generally as temporary acquisition or buyout funding to be repaid from the proceeds of subsequent bond issues. When the new issue market disappeared in 1990, many such loans turned into longer-term subordinated stakes in what proved to be troubled companies. In the cases of First Boston and Shearson Lehman, bridge loans were substantial enough that, coinciding with other problems for the firms, the economic loss would have jeopardized their very viability had it not been for affiliation with strong parent companies.

The story of the junk bond market is well-known and it is not being repeated here for its own sake. Rather, this history highlights a key dynamic that tends to be characteristic of the securities industry. The distribution of securities is a low-margin business, and in order to maintain an adequate return on their own equity, securities firms must continuously seek out market inefficiencies and unexplored business opportunities. When such opportunities are found, firms generally must build human and organizational infrastructures to exploit them. The problem is that the securities industry is highly competitive and pockets of high-margin business rarely remain secrets for very long. Competing securities firms, as well as some other types of financial institutions, move into the field and margins fall at the same time risks increase. The services provided by the securities industry, by their very nature, over time tend towards commoditization and over-supply, and wrenching cycles are necessary to bring costs into line when markets mature.

Equities

Coinciding with the junk bond drama that unfolded during the 1980s was a more conventional but nonetheless drastic cycle that drove the stock market. The S&P 500 Index moved from 122 at the beginning of 1982 to nearly 330 early in October of 1987. This simple statistic is symbolic of a massive shift that occurred in the financial markets during the middle years of the decade and that had major financial and organizational implications for securities firms.

The rise in stock prices was only one aspect of a general surge in asset values that affected nearly everything from homes to art to baseball cards, and it both reflected and influenced a powerful expansion in the general economy. The bullish market psychology that accompanied all this, affecting institutional and retail investors alike, resulted in an upsurge in the volume of financial transactions throughout the financial markets. Again, the increase in NYSE reported share volume from 12 to 47 billion shares between 1981 and 1987 was only symbolic of a more general phenomenon. Since the volume of financial transactions is the most important driver of brokerage profits, securities firms in general were highly profitable and expanded rapidly. Total employment within the industry increased by more than 50% and approximately doubled between 1981 and 1987 at the large investment banks. The added infrastructure was needed to support equity activity, in addition to junk bonds, traditional fixed income, merger and acquisition, and all the other aspects of the securities business that were contributing to its success during the middle years of the decade.

Then suddenly on a single day in October of 1987, the stock market lost around 20% of its value. This collapse actually exceeded the 1929 crash in percentage terms and seemed to constitute the kind of debacle that most business school students for years had been taught could never happen again. Even though the 1987 crash did not even fully erase the enormous gains that were achieved earlier in the same year, and even though the S&P 500 resumed its upward trajectory afterwards, the damage to investor confidence had been done. For the first time in more than at least a decade, reported share volume on the NYSE was actually down in 1988, and it was down by around 15%. The infrastructures that had been built to handle portfolios of bull-market businesses were suddenly too costly for securities firms to support. The end of 1987 was so bad for the industry that aggregate pretax return on equity fell to under 5%, down from 29% the year before and from an average 30% for the preceding six years.

End of the Decade

The years 1988 and 1989 were years of adjustment for the industry. Having increased continuously and sharply throughout the decade, industrywide employment was cut back by 8% in 1988 and another 5% in 1989. Profitability overall was still fairly weak, even though comparisons across companies were uneven and some of the large investment banks turned a relatively strong performance. Despite the aftermath of the stock market crash, new junk bond issuance and the related merger and acquisition activity held relatively steady at high levels and helped boost the earnings of those firms active in this market. Then suddenly in 1990, the junk bond market echoed what had happened in the stock market three years previously. Because there is no truly objective measure of aggregate junk bond prices, the steepness of the drop is difficult to quantify. Perhaps the most useful statistic, however, is the volume of junk bond underwriting, which had been averaging around $30 billion annually since 1985 and which fell abruptly to less than $3 billion in

1990. This volume in real terms was less than it had been in 1982 and left those securities firms with large junk bond and related operations trying to support bull-market costs with revenue streams that were suddenly inadequate.

What caused the collapse of the junk bond market is a hotly-debated and politicized issue. It is the impact, however, and not the cause of the crash that is important for this discussion. Coming at a time when the industry was still recovering from the stock market disaster, and in the midst of growing concerns about the general economy, the fall-off in high-yield and M&A activity contributed in 1990 to one of the worst years the securities industry has had in recent history. Aggregate return on equity for the industry turned negative after having surged up until 1987 and then limping along at under 10% for the last three years. Again, performance across companies was uneven, and several of the large investment banks, although affected by the slump, continued to show reasonably solid level of earnings. Nevertheless, the failure of Drexel Burnham and the severe problems being experienced by First Boston, Shearson Lehman, and some other firms contributed to the sense of growing uneasiness about the future of the industry.

Then, in yet another of the dramatic twists that seem more the rule than the exception for this industry, 1991 emerged as a year of powerful recovery. As is usually the case, there were multiple factors at work and they affected various tiers of the industry and individual companies in different ways. For one thing, the stock market, having slumped again in 1990, recovered its upward momentum and reached towards new heights during the year. The favorable impact on transaction volume and underwriting activity boosted earnings, and a return to greater optimism stabilized the junk bond market as well. Of even greater importance for some firms, however, were highly favorable conditions in the traditional fixed-income markets that boosted both trading and underwriting results. The fixed-income business benefited from a downward movement in interest rates, together with a degree of interest rate volatility, which tends to help trading results and other factors. Salomon Brothers, for example, in spite of the devastating upheaval in its business following the government bond scandal that erupted in August 1991, ended the year with a reasonably strong 24% pretax return on equity, largely on the strength of its powerful fixed-income trading and distribution business.

The favorable trend for the industry that emerged during 1991 has continued. The specific conditions giving rise to the strong results will not continue indefinitely, although this is not to say necessarily that another sharp contraction is looming. The future market trends that will drive the industry during the 1990s are as unpredictable now as they have been at other points in history. From the vantage point of 1982, not many observers could have imagined the radical evolution that today's hindsight shows us lay ahead at the time. Any forward look from 1992 suffers from the same deficiency. Analysis of the industry, therefore, cannot be soundly based on any concrete forecast of trends but rather on a careful examination of individual firms in terms of their franchise value, human infrastructure, business strategies, risk control methods, and other variables that determine the ability of each firm to cope with opportunity, uncertainty, and change.

Risk Control Challenges

The history of the securities industry is well-publicized and widely known. Because of its importance and because of the drama and excitement that often characterize the dealings of its participants, the securities industry attracts a great deal of press attention and popular commentary. As a result, the industry tends to be vulnerable to exaggerations and misconceptions, which are compounded by complexities that defy easy analysis by anyone attempting to look behind the headlines. Two mistakes are commonly made: 1) overstating the risks confronted by the industry, and 2) painting all firms with the same brush. When considering the last decade, it is important to recognize than many firms were able to avoid serious instability and emerged from the 1980s and from 1990 in sound financial condition with competitive strengths that position them well for the years ahead. Credit analysis has to begin with a sober acknowledgment of the hazards inherent in the business, but the credit rating of any individual firm is a function of how effectively it minimizes those risks while pursuing its opportunities. There are a number of very specific risk variables that confront every firm in the industry. It is the control of these factors that determines the financial stability of a securities firm.

Funding Risk

Financial institutions by their nature are asset intensive and securities firms are particularly so. Securities distribution and trading operations require the maintenance of sizeable inventories in order to service customer needs and facilitate the enormous volume of transactions that characterize the business. At the beginning of 1991, for example, Salomon Brothers had assets of $110 billion and grew to around $150 billion by August 1991. This enormous balance sheet was necessary to generate revenues that by the end of 1991 totaled $3.5 billion. While among domestic securities firms, Salomon Brothers has typically carried the largest balance sheet, the extremely high ratio of assets to revenues is typical of all firms in the industry and is inherent in the nature of the business.

The problem that asset intensity poses is that these huge positions have to be continuously funded. Complicating the problem further is the rapid turnover rate typical of most brokerage assets; the average shelf-life of security inventories is often measured in days or even hours. Since one of the keys to balance sheet management in any industry is an appropriate matching of assets and liabilities, most of the funding has to be short-term in nature. This places a burden on all firms to maintain diversified sources of funding that can be relied upon under all market conditions and through good times and bad. This challenge combines with the sometimes explosive nature of the securities markets to create a particularly vexing risk.

The crisis that hit Salomon Brothers in August of 1991 demonstrated both the enormous danger that can be posed by this risk and the appropriate methods for defusing the danger when it does materialize. When Salomon Brothers announced that certain individuals had repeatedly violated rules governing treasury bond auctions, the firm in a matter of days jumped from one of the most successful and profitable periods of its history into what some people at the time considered to be a life-threatening crisis. The rule violations, together with the threat of government sanctions, sharply undercut the market's confidence in the firm. While this damaged Salomon Brothers' core underwriting and trading operations, the crisis actually stemmed from the immediate threat to its funding. With around $150 billion in assets mostly short-funded, the threat of even a part of this funding being withdrawn was potentially devastating. As is typical for the industry, most of the funding was in the form of repurchase agreements, short sales, and other secured vehicles. However, the firm also had a substantial amount of unsecured funding outstanding, including around $9 billion in commercial paper, a notoriously "hot" funding vehicle in times of crisis. However, while Salomon Brothers had aggressively expanded its balance sheet during the year, it had also carefully managed the relationship between its assets and liabilities. The financial managers were able to reduce the size of the balance sheet and draw on a substantial pool of unencumbered liquid assets to repay maturing obligations. Salomon Brothers was successful in maintaining the majority of its funding, and the rest, including nearly all of its commercial paper, was paid down without any serious risk of default.

One of the lessons to be learned from the Salomon Brothers experience is that when a funding crisis occurs in this business, it comes suddenly. The other more optimistic lesson, however, is that a firm which manages its balance sheet with this risk continuously in mind can minimize the dangers involved.

Systemic Risk

Related to funding risk but incorporating other potential problems as well is the whole issue of systemic interdependence. The liabilities of any business operation, to the extent they have to be rolled over, create a dependency on external parties. However, in the case of financial institutions, the left-hand side of the balance sheet is also dependent on the performance of other parties, constituted as it is mainly of securities, receivables, and other financial assets. This risk, again, is aggravated in the case of securities firms because of the high velocity of both assets and liabilities, which requires not only that counterparties perform but that they do so quickly and repeatedly within the context of the web of institutional interrelationships that make up the financial marketplace.

As a simplistic illustration, if Institution A enters into repurchase agreement with Institution B, Institution B may cover its obligation by matching it with a mirror transaction entered into with Institution C, which may continue the chain with Institution D, and so forth. If any one party in the chain fails to perform, its counterparty must find another cover for its obligation or else itself default and thereby spread the damage. The nature of securities firms is such that many of their assets and liabilities consist of instruments that are theoretically vulnerable to this sort of chain phenomenon. Systemic risk then arises from the danger of a major financial institution failing at some point and defaulting on obligations that are large enough to trigger default by other small or weak institutions, which in the aggregate are enough to destabilize still others until even healthy firms are in jeopardy.

Speculation about this kind of doomsday scenario tends to be easily exaggerated. For one thing, many financial markets, the "repo" market being the most important, are based largely on secured transactions. If a financial institution fails, in most cases the large majority of its repo counterparties will already have possession of the collateral necessary to cover any matching transactions, thus insulating the market from the individual failure. Borrowed securities, broker and customer receivables, and other instruments that make up much of a security firm's

balance sheet tend to result from secured transactions, thus serving to limit systemic risk. Furthermore, the fact that the financial markets have operated as long as they have without systemic meltdown is strong evidence that controls, both private and regulatory, are functioning effectively to isolate and contain problems when they occur. Nonetheless, it is one of the paradoxes of the financial markets that systemic risk is limited only because financial institutions and regulators respect it enough to protect against it. The biggest risk to the markets tend to come from surges of optimism about financial instruments which are growing rapidly and are too young to be fully understood or controlled.

At the present time, there is much speculation regarding the potential risks of "derivative" securities, i.e., swaps, options, futures, and all their various permutations. While these instruments are certainly not new, they have in recent years grown enormously in both complexity and volume. In general the major financial institutions that dominate these markets are presently demonstrating a healthy regard for the risk characteristics of derivatives and are developing a variety of techniques to control them. Nevertheless, as people become increasingly comfortable with derivatives in the future, it is possible that the risks may, paradoxically, increase. Comfort can be a dangerous state of mind in the financial markets to the extent it encourages players to relax their judgment and overextend themselves. How much discipline securities firms and other financial institutions exercise in developing the markets for derivative securities will be an important determinant of their financial stability in the years ahead.

Asset Risk

Securities firms utilize relatively narrow wedges of equity used to support their massive assets positions. Morgan Stanley, for example, at the end of 1991 was carrying $64 billion in assets on $3 billion in equity capital, giving a gross assets to equity ratio of 21x. This ratio was actually more conservative than most other rated securities firm. High leverage is possible and, from a credit risk standpoint, generally acceptable because of the high quality that tends to characterize the large majority of a security firm's assets. The "quality" of a financial asset is a function primarily of 1) the stability of its value and 2) its liquidity. Usually these two characteristics are related.

Among the major securities firms, government and liquid corporate securities, reverse repos, and various types of generally short-term secured receivables constitute much of the asset base. The mix of assets varies among companies, but short maturities, liquid markets, collateralization, limited credit risk, and hedging are among the factors which, in various combinations, support the quality of brokerage assets. Asset risk, however, remains a serious consideration because of the thin margin for error permitted by the relatively small amounts of equity. Miscalculations can be made sometimes regarding both the price volatility of specific assets and the liquidity of the markets in which they trade. Once again, crisis that overtook the high-yield bond market at the end of the 1980s came about in part because many institutions underestimated the downside volatility of high-yield bonds and also failed to recognize the illiquidity that would develop in the market once prices began to fall.

Operating Risk

One of the more conventional risks confronted by securities firms stems from the combination of cyclical markets and relatively high fixed and semi-fixed costs. This is a problem similar to that confronted by competitors in any cyclical industry, where weak market conditions periodically cause revenues to drop more sharply than costs. Securities markets by their nature ebb and flow, and the fluctuating volume of transactions drives the revenue stream of securities firms up and down. As in any industry, there is a tendency to build both staff and physical infrastructure to maximize profit potential during an upcycle, thus leveraging the drop in profits that occurs when the inevitable downcycle sets in. While there were a number of unusual determinants for the industry's poor results in 1990, one major problem was that many firms had to cope with a downdrift in revenues while saddled with cost structures built up during one of the most bullish and sustained upcycles the industry had ever experienced. While much credit analysis of securities firms tends to focus on balance sheet risk, it is a serious mistake to make judgments solely on the basis of the balance sheet. Operating losses can erode the equity base of a securities firm as surely as the writedown of a troubled asset, and operating discipline is as much a key to financial stability over time as is balance sheet risk control.

Keys to Financial Stability

Given the multitude of risks confronted by securities firms, popular commentators sometimes seem to suggest that disaster must be lurking around the corner for just about any of them. While it is true that even well-established firms have exhibited instability at times, it is neither a miracle nor an accident that many firms not only prospered during the 1980s but emerged from the aftermath in sound condition and well-positioned for the next decade.

It is the task of credit analysis to identify the factors that determine long-range success and to evaluate individual firms within that context. Solid prospects for long-range success provide momentum likely to overcome any short-term crisis that may result from temporary market instability or misjudgments.

Franchise

The term "franchise" is hard to define and is often used with vague meaning. However, there is no better word to describe a characteristic of any business that provides the foundation for its long-range staying power. It refers to both a firm's position in its markets and the reputation that allows the firm to maintain and enhance that position over time. The franchise of any securities firm resides in the attitudes of its customers and counterparties, whose willingness to do business is determined by their confidence in a firm's ability to deliver service and meet its obligations. Names like Goldman Sachs, Merrill Lynch, Morgan Stanley, and others carry a weight in the financial markets that both facilitates business opportunities and protects these companies in times of crisis or market instability. Powerful franchises like these reflect many years of constructive evolution that is unlikely to come to a sudden halt because of a temporary upheaval. The fact that Salomon Brothers survived its government bond trading scandal is, as much as anything, a testimony to the power of its franchise. As destabilizing as the crisis was, the majority of the firm's customers, creditors, and counterparties derived enough value from their relationships with Salomon Brothers to continue doing business, thereby carrying the firm through its difficulties. Had a relatively unknown firm or one whose business rested on shallow relationships with clients undergone the same adversity, the outcome would likely have been different.

Risk Discipline

No securities firm, any more than competitors in other industries, can prosper or even survive very long by avoiding risk. Securities markets are complex and rapidly changing, and any securities firm that becomes overly cautious will find itself unable to meet the needs of its customers and irrelevant to the marketplace. Successful firms, therefore, welcome risk but never without measuring and managing its impact.

Understanding risk is the first stage of risk control and is often the most difficult, particularly when evaluating new business ventures or expansion into markets that have relatively short histories. New areas of opportunity inevitably engender enthusiasm, and firms incur trouble when they allow that enthusiasm to cloud their risk evaluation. Once risk is understood, protection against it requires adequate allocation of equity capital to cover losses that may be incurred. For mature markets, this process involves a reasonably scientific study of market volatility and quantification of possible losses under various scenarios. For less mature markets, the process is more subjective. The hallmark of healthy risk discipline in a securities firm is a careful weighing of new business opportunities in light of the tradeoff between projected profits and the real cost of the risk-adjusted equity needed to support them. Disciplined management will always study this equation and pass up opportunities when it is unfavorable.

Liquidity Management

A securities firm's first line of defense is liquidity. Although its markets are volatile and its financial leverage high, the typical firm in this industry enjoys as liquid a balance sheet as any business operation can have. Upon encountering adversity, a securities firm can quickly turn assets into cash to satisfy maturing obligations. However, this safety valve does not operate automatically in a crisis and requires careful management at all times if it is to be available when it is needed. The problem is that unless structured properly, the liabilities of a securities firm can consume liquidity even more quickly than the assets provide it. Liquidity management requires careful assessment of the speed with which various assets could be sold or monetized in a crisis environment and a conservative matching of this schedule against the structure of maturing liabilities.

It was this technique that allowed Salomon Brothers to maintain its liquidity throughout the fall and winter of 1991 and into the spring of the following year. The key to the firm's success, however, was that its liquidity discipline was in place prior to the advent of the crisis. Liquidity management must be taken seriously in good times if its benefit is to be available in the unforeseen circumstances that could make it a life-or-death requirement.

Cost Control

The inherent cyclicality of the securities markets makes cost control a critical discipline. Securities distribution is a people-intensive business, and the high profits that can be earned during upcycles encourage headcount expansion, which is easily justified in the short term but becomes burdensome when markets turn down. Once again, the discipline of bypassing peak profit potential in order to mitigate earnings cyclicality is key to the long-range financial stability of a securities firm.

Effective compensation systems stabilize earnings by establishing a close relationship between profit performance and compensation. However, designing a performance-oriented compensation system provides only a starting point for the effective control of compensation costs. Success depends not so much on the mechanics of the system, as on the skill with which it is implemented and managed. The objective of any compensation program is to minimize costs while at the same time maximizing the creative power and cohesiveness of the organization. Integrating the system with the culture of a firm is a subtle and difficult management challenge. Any crude system can cut payroll dollars in a downturn, but if it does so at the cost of serious morale problems, defections of key people, and organizational instability, these losses are likely to exceed the value of any dollars saved. One of the challenges faced by Salomon Brothers in the aftermath of its 1991 to 1992 crisis will be adapting to the revised compensation system implemented by the new management of the firm.

Beyond the issue of cyclical cost control, managing the ongoing fixed costs of a securities distribution operation is an increasingly important variable. To the extent underwriting, brokerage, and other services become more commoditized over time, the ability to deliver those services more cheaply than a competitor becomes a key competitive advantage. An effective securities distribution network is a complex and costly system involving people, technology, and physical infrastructure. Cost effectiveness requires both economies of scale and careful control of expenses in good times and bad.

Diversification

Finally, firms with strong positions in a variety of markets are going to be better positioned to withstand market instability than those with a more narrow focus. Mistakes made by the firm, or disruptions in any particular market, are less threatening if the firm has other operations that are unaffected. Merrill Lynch, for example, which enjoys the most powerful retail franchise in the industry, also is the largest security underwriter in the business and benefits from major institutional and other operations as well. While these operations are certainly not independent of one another, they constitute a breadth of operation that tends to provide both mass and institutional momentum likely to help the firm survive turbulence when it occurs. The bankruptcy of Drexel Burnham occurred in part because of its overwhelming dependence on the high-yield bond market, giving the firm little to fall back on when that market began to contract. Other major firms, Merrill Lynch included, also had major exposures to the high yield market but in relatively smaller proportions to the bread-and-butter securities operations on which their franchises were based. In a business that virtually requires major firms to participate in new and experimental markets as they evolve, long-range stability depends on having a relatively diverse base of business to shelter the firm against inevitable failures and disruptions that will occur as new opportunities are explored.

Future Trends

The economic role of the securities industry is to facilitate the movement of capital. It is a role of enormous importance for the economy and one which gives the industry both a powerful influence over and a vulnerability to economic developments. The economic boom of the 1980s could never have happened to the extent it did without the extraordinary funding capabilities provided by the securities industry, whose own heady growth and relative instability during the period in turn were influenced by parallel currents in the general economy.

Few industries have undergone such radical transformation in short periods of time. The securities industry has been both the beneficiary and one of the instigators of a major shift that has been underway for some time now in the capital intermediation function performed by all financial institutions. Traditional relationships between borrowers and lenders have steadily given ground to the impersonal and often anonymous relationship that exists between a security holder and an issuer. Progressively, traditional lending risks are being commoditized and securitized. The explosive growth of the markets for structured securities, derivatives, commercial paper, and other instruments are all indicative of this trend. Lending and investment decisions increasingly are being made in the context of the trading culture that dominates the financial marketplace and which tends to assume that any risk can be quantified and, when desired, quickly traded or "laid off" onto the markets with minimal friction. In the case of derivative securities, the very essence of risk itself is converted into a commodity and traded independently of the instruments giving rise to it. Securities firms have been both the facilitators and the beneficiaries of this broad trend towards the commoditization of risk.

The importance of technology in this evolution is often commented on but can hardly be exaggerated. The complex nature of modern trading strategies, as well as that of many of the securities themselves, could never have evolved without the power and flexibility afforded by computers. Furthermore, advances in telecommunications have made possible the rapid transmission of prices, orders, and other essential trading data upon which the modern financial markets are being built. As is usually the case with technology, it is difficult to see ahead to what future evolution may hold. However, one thing that can be predicted is that rapid change in the financial markets will have to continue just to catch up with technology that already exists. Globalization of the financial markets, another phenomenon much remarked upon, has only just begun. With the political and economic upheavals currently underway around the world, it is probably no exaggeration to say that future generations of investment bankers and traders will still be coming to grips with "globalization."

Hence, the securities industry today must be seen as riding a powerful and somewhat uncontrollable wave into the future. As is always the case, rapid change involves opportunities and risks in equal proportion. In the context of the macro trends underway over the past decade, the boom-bust cycles of the stock and the junk bond markets come into perspective as phenomena that were neither accidental nor unrelated to one another. Both reflected the exuberance of the trading culture which was just then beginning to come fully into its own and exert more power over the markets than it was able fully to understand or control. Fast and massive movements of capital into any market can create the illusion of strong liquidity, aggravating the instability that occurs when the capital flows out again and the liquidity is interrupted. Sudden illiquidity in any financial market is what the popular press likes to refer to as a crash, because it results in a precipitous drop in market prices.

It is sometimes said that securities firms are moving too fast to ever learn from their mistakes. This is not true. Major securities firms studied both the causes and the aftermath of the Drexel bankruptcy more closely than many outside observers realize. It is in fact the lessons learned from that crisis that prompted Salomon Brothers to establish liquidity management procedures that allowed that firm to navigate safely through its own crisis that occurred two years later. The experience of both these companies, as well as that of other firms who have encountered difficulties, have provided insights for the entire industry, instigating a general improvement in the risk control and liquidity management practices in place today.

The problem is not that securities firms fail to learn from the past, but rather that the industry is changing too rapidly for the past ever to be a fully reliable guide for the future. Neither the junk bond roller coaster nor the stock market crash nor any other historical event will ever replay itself. However, given the explosive secular trends that remain underway in the financial markets, dislocations of an unknown nature but similar magnitude are certainly possible and, arguably, even probable over the course of the next decade. Securities firms have a job to do which requires confronting the risk of periodic market instability. The major firms which dominate the business today have not achieved their positions without understanding this. The opportunities for profitable growth in the years and decades ahead are highly attractive for any firm that possesses the franchise and the infrastructure necessary to participate in future evolution of global financial markets. Careful attention to risk discipline, liquidity, and costs will be the defining characteristics of those who ultimately reap the rewards.

Chapter 9

Investment Banker Liability in Mergers and Acquisitions

Patrick J. Foye
Partner
Samuel D. Scruggs
Associate
Skadden, Arps, Slate, Meagher & Flom, Brussels and New York

The directors of a company involved in a change in corporate control transaction generally rely on a variety of professional advisors to evaluate alternatives and implement the plan chosen. Investment bankers, of course, play a significant role in such transactions, advising both targets and bidders. The increase in the number and the value of such transactions during the 1980s led to a bonanza of fees for investment banking firms and other corporate advisors. The scale of the transactions and fees, the importance of the work performed by investment bankers, and the reliance placed by clients on fairness opinions and financial advice have exposed investment bankers to the possibility of significant liability.

Improper or negligent execution of any of the functions performed by investment bankers can result in liability. For example, in August 1988, a Florida state court jury awarded over $20 million against a leading investment banking firm based on allegedly negligent client advice. In 1985, privately-held Rawson Food Stores Inc. acquired 43 supermarkets from Pantry Pride Enterprises Inc. for approximately $40 million based, in part, on the advice it received from its investment banker. Shortly thereafter, Rawson filed for bankruptcy reorganization and sued the banker, alleging that the purchased stores were worth substantially less than Rawson had been told. The jury found for Rawson, awarding owner John V. Rawson, Jr. $2 million and the company $21.6 million in compensatory and punitive damages. The investment banking firm disputed this judgment but reportedly settled for an undisclosed amount before the case was appealed.

In another case, investors in the 1986 leveraged buyout of Revco D.S. Inc., a drugstore chain operating in the East coast of the United States, reportedly received nearly $30 million in settlement of federal securities claims against the investment banking firm which had acted as principal underwriter for Revco's securities. Revco sold more than $800 million in subordinated high-yield bonds and preferred stock to finance the $1.5 billion transaction before filing for bankruptcy court protection in 1988.

The securities purchasers claimed that the investment banking firm knew that the leveraged buyout was flawed and that the management and financial condition of Revco were in poorer condition than was disclosed. The banking firm is reported to have previously agreed to pay over $9 million to Revco's estate in settlement of a fraudulent conveyance suit arising out of the transaction.

This chapter focuses on the significant possible liability arising out of mergers and acquisitions especially from the issuance of "fairness opinions" not only to the client company but possibly, based on recent case law, to the shareholders of the target company.

Fairness Opinions

A fairness opinion is a written statement of an investment banker as to the fairness from a financial point of view of the financial terms of an offer for the equity securities or assets of a company. Typically, such opinions are addressed to the board of directors or to a special committee of the board and not to the shareholders of the company. Fairness opinions usually conclude that an offer is either "fair from a financial point of view to the stockholders of the company" or "is inadequate from a financial point of view." Fairness opinions are usually explicitly limited to the appropriateness of the monetary value of

95

the offer made by the potential acquiror. Delivery of a written fairness opinion is typically preceded by one or more detailed oral presentations to the board of directors at which detailed supporting material is distributed setting forth the basis on which the fairness opinion is given.

Why Fairness Opinions Are Sought

Changes in corporate control transactions are often the most significant transactions a company will undergo and fundamentally affect the equity value of the acquired enterprise. Boards of directors involved in such transactions are confronted with issues often outside their normal business experience. Therefore, boards of directors nearly universally seek the advice and support of outside professionals, including investment bankers. However, boards of directors have reasons for soliciting such advice other than the need for specialized advice: to protect their members from liability to disgruntled shareholders.

Current American corporate law makes the board of directors the overseers of the corporation's business and affairs.[1] While day-to-day management responsibility is vested in the officers of the corporation, a board of directors assumes a more critical role in the corporation's decision making during a change of corporate control transaction.

A director is a fiduciary. As such, directors are guardians of the shareholders' property and, like other trustees, they take on special duties and responsibilities by virtue of this relationship. However, applicable state law generally allows directors to rely on the advice of outside professionals (within the area of such professionals' expertise) in the course of the performance of their responsibilities to the shareholders.[2] Investment bankers have been recognized by courts as having such expertise in mergers and acquisitions transactions.

Boards of directors of companies involved in potential change in corporate control transactions are required to act on behalf of the interests of the shareholders. Shareholders have often challenged board decision-making in change of corporate control transactions, regularly alleging that because of some action (or lack thereof) on the part of the board the shareholders received too little for their interest in the company. In order to make an informed decision and to minimize their exposure in these shareholder suits, boards of directors involved in these transactions generally follow a more or less prescribed series of steps which, it is hoped, permit them to fulfill and to document that they have fulfilled their obligations to the company's shareholders. Obtaining fairness opinions from a third-party investment banker is one of the methods used

by boards of directors or special committees of board to discharge these obligations in an accepted an readily provable manner.

The fiduciary duties of directors to shareholder have been subdivided into areas known as "the dut of loyalty," "the duty of candor" and "the duty c care." The duty of loyalty may be summarized as th duty to act in good faith in a manner which th directors reasonably believe to be in the best interes of the corporation.[3] This duty is probably not ac dressed by fairness opinions. The duty of candc compels a board of directors seeking shareholde action to disclose fully and fairly pertinent informa tion within the board's control.[4] The duty of candc usually compels the board of directors, which ha obtained a fairness opinion, to disclose it to share holders.

The universal use of fairness opinions is bes explained by the requirements of the duty of care The duty of care requires the board of directors t act in an informed and considered manner. Th Delaware Supreme Court has stated that "director have a duty to inform themselves, prior to making business decision, of all material information reasol ably available to them. Having become so informec they must then act with requisite care in the di: charge of their duties."[5]

In the much publicized case of *Smith v. Va Gorkom*,[6] the Delaware Supreme Court ruled tha the directors of Trans Union breached their fiduciar duties to the company's shareholders in approving cash-out merger which had been negotiated by th company's chief executive officer. The court se verely criticized several aspects of the director performance, including the failure of the directors t make meaningful inquiries into the circumstance that led to the negotiated transaction, the failure of the directors to question senior management regarc ing the value of the company, the board's approva of the transaction after only two hours deliberatior and the unavailability of any written documentatior including a summary of the terms of the transactior at the time of the board's determination.

Finally, the court noted that the board of dire tors failed to seek a fairness opinion from an inde pendent financial adviser, even though the compan had an established relationship with an investmer banker. The Delaware Supreme Court considere such failure in its determination that the Trans Unio board was insufficiently informed to rely on th "business judgment rule" and that the board ha been grossly negligent. While the Delaware St preme Court specifically stated that no general rul requires boards of companies involved in change i corporate control transactions to seek fairness opi ions, the decision reinforced in a high profile mann the value of fairness opinions in the eyes of corporate directors and counsel.

It is possible to overstate the importance of fairness opinions in protecting boards of directors. A board which has sought and obtained a favorable fairness opinion has not completely fulfilled its obligations to its shareholders in a change in corporate control transaction. Corporate law permits board of directors to rely on expert advice in fulfilling their duties to shareholders and the company, not to delegate those duties to the outside experts. In determining whether directors have discharged their duties of care and loyalty, courts have applied the "business judgment rule" which affords a presumption of propriety to the business decisions of directors made in good faith and for rational business reasons. This rule has been articulated by the Delaware Supreme Court as follows:

> It is a presumption that in making a business decision the directors of a corporation acted on an informed basis, in good faith and in the honest belief that the action taken was in the best interests of the company . . . The burden is on the party challenging the decision to establish facts rebutting the presumption.[7]

In essence, a court will not substitute its own judgment for that of a board of directors whose action can be attributed to a "rational business purpose."[8]

This presumption can be rebutted only if it can be proved that directors did not act 1) on an informed basis, 2) in good faith or 3) in a manner they reasonably believed to be in the best interests of shareholders.[9] It is widely accepted that a board of directors which reasonably relies on a fairness opinion offered by investment bankers regarding adequacy of an offer for the shares of a company may use the existence of such a letter (together with other appropriate actions) to invoke the business judgment rule and defend its members against charges that the negligence of the board resulted in the sale of the shares for an insufficient price.

While the board of directors may, in part, rely on the fairness opinion of an investment banker for its individual analysis of an offer for a company, this does not necessarily mean that the investment bankers offering up such a fairness opinion assume the directors' obligations and potential liabilities to shareholders.

Privity of Contract

Directors are fiduciaries of shareholders; investment banking firms are providers of services on a contrac-

tual basis and the bankers' contract is not with the shareholders. Based on a truly hoary English common law tenet of "privity of contract," until recently it was generally assumed that shareholders could not bring an action against an investment banking firm which negligently prepared a fairness opinion because of the lack of a contractual relationship between the investment bankers and the shareholders.

In cases where the damaged party suffered monetary damage alone, the "privity of contract" doctrine has regularly continued to be observed, though subject to certain revisions. Fifty years ago the New York Court of Appeals, New York's highest court, stated in *Ultramares Corporation v. Touche*[10] that accountants, and by implication other professionals, are liable for their negligence to third parties only if the relationship between the negligent professional and the injured party was "so close as to approach that of privity."

In 1985, the New York Court of Appeals held in the case of *Credit Alliance Corp. v. Arthur Andersen & Co.*,[11] that a lender had a right of action against a borrower's accountant if: 1) the accountant was aware that the reports it prepared were to be used for one or more specific purposes; 2) that such a purpose requires that a known party rely on the reports; and 3) the relying party had some link to the accountant which can provide evidence of the party's reliance. In applying these standards, the court held that a bank which had not been in direct contact with the accountant did not have a valid claim of action. Conversely, an accountant that knew that its report was to be reviewed by a bank in its credit decision and which was in direct contact with such bank could be liable to the bank for its negligence in preparing the audit report.

The *Ultramares* standard has generally been accepted as the appropriate measure of professional liability to third parties for negligence. In applying this standard to disputes between an investment banking firm and shareholders arising from fairness opinions, the investment banking firm, which has typically not addressed itself to or otherwise directly communicated with shareholders, often argues that because 1) its contract is with the company and the fairness opinion and advice are rendered directly to the board of directors or a special committee of the board; and 2) the injury suffered by shareholders is monetary alone, lack of privity of contract with shareholders bars shareholder recovery.

Privity and Fairness Opinions

Recently, however, several courts have decided that this apparent lack of privity should not prohibit recovery by shareholders from investment banking firms for negligently prepared fairness opinions. These cases question whether the doctrine of contractual privity has any significance in a shareholder suit against an investment banker for a negligently prepared fairness opinion. This result can be traced, at least in part, to the uses to which fairness opinions are known to be put. One significant distinction between an accountant's audit reports and financial fairness opinions is that an auditor's opinion is delivered to and relied upon by possibly countless people and enterprises, none of whom are known to the accountant, for a variety of purposes. The investment banker knows its opinion will be relied upon by a known, if large and possibly litigious, group only for purposes of assessing a known transaction.

The boards of directors of public companies involved in change of corporate control transactions are required to include all material information on which they relied in reaching their decision to accept or reject an offer for the company in the proxy materials filed with the Securities and Exchange Commission and distributed to the shareholders. The proxy rules require that this information should include the full text of any fairness opinion delivered to the board and a detailed description of the opinion. Furthermore, federal securities law requires extensive disclosure of fairness opinions (and their underlying analysis) in "going private transactions"[12] and the staff of the SEC has in practice extended this requirement to nonaffiliate transactions. The board of directors' recommendation to the shareholders whether or not to accept the offer, or to vote for the proposed merger, is usually made in explicit reliance, in part, on the fairness opinion. It may be expected that a fairness opinion coming from respected and experienced professionals will be given substantial weight by shareholders considering the sale of the company.

Investment Banker Liability

Fairness opinions rendered by investment bankers have regularly been subject to attack by shareholder plaintiffs. Courts have, for instance, compelled investment bankers to make additional disclosure, including the factors known or assumed and the methodology utilized in computing the valuation of the company. In 1984, Royal Dutch Petroleum Company made a tender offer for all of the publicly held shares of Shell Oil Company, approximately 70% of which were already owned by Royal Dutch. A group of minority shareholders sought to enjoin this tender offer in a suit brought before the Delaware Chancery Court. In *Joseph v. Shell Oil Company*,[13] the Chancery Court ordered that the tender offer be held in abeyance until, among other things,

additional information was disclosed to the minority shareholders.

The shareholders alleged that Royal Dutch, through one of its subsidiaries, was offering an insufficient price for their shares. Royal Dutch's offer was supported by, among other things, a fairness opinion provided by an investment banking firm retained by Royal Dutch. In reviewing the significance of this valuation the *Joseph* court stated: "Obviously, a primary purpose of the fairness opinion . . . was to convince the stockholders . . . that the price offered was fair. To believe otherwise is unrealistic."[14]

Royal Dutch's failure to provide the investment bankers with the opportunity to review nonpublic information regarding Shell's "probable" oil and gas reserves "falls short of the fiduciary duty owed to the stockholders of Shell by the maker of the tender offer" and this shortfall could not be cured by a statement that the investment banker "based its opinion of value on publicly disclosed information."[15] The court stated that such a limited statement fell "far short of the full and complete disclosure with absolute candor required by Delaware law." The *Joseph* court implicitly criticized the basis of the valuation for not including a valuation of a recently announced significant oil discovery by Shell and the brief time, eight days, in which it was prepared.

One of the bases on which shareholders challenge the fairness opinions of investment bankers is that investment banking firms often render fairness opinions, and consequently earn their fee, only if the transaction is not aborted at an earlier stage. Thus, banking firms have an obvious economic interest in the completion of the transaction. Such fee arrangements make some sense from a business perspective, as they lower the cost of abandoned transactions and can be argued not to have any legal significance in the absence of evidence that the judgment of the investment bankers was affected by the prospect of earning a fee. Nonetheless, many feel that self-interest on the part of investment bankers raises concerns of actual or potential conflicts of interest about the impartiality of their fairness opinions.

Recently, fairness opinions have been challenged in the context of leveraged buyouts. These recent court cases have raised the possibility that investment bankers can be liable directly to shareholders for negligently prepared fairness opinions. In *Wells v. Shearson Lehman/American Express*,[16] the court ruled that investment bankers owed shareholders a duty of care and could be held liable for negligently or improperly prepared fairness opinions.

In 1984, the principal officers of Metromedia acquired all of the company's publicly held shares for approximately $1.1 billion. Prior to the completion of this acquisition, certain shareholders of Metromedia brought a suit alleging that the management buy-out group was not offering an adequate price. Following this suit, the board of directors of Metromedia created a special committee of its members to evaluate the fairness of the management offer. This special committee hired two investment banking firms to render fairness opinions. The investment bankers opined that the assets of Metromedia were worth an aggregate of $1.114 billion. This fairness opinion was included in the proxy material distributed to shareholders who approved the acquisition. Subsequently, Metromedia sold its assets in a series of transactions for an aggregate of approximately $4.5 billion.

The *Wells* court, whose jurisdiction includes New York City, found "untenable" the defense of a lack of contractual privity between the shareholders and the investment bankers. The court stated that the special committee of the board of directors was formed to, "Serve the shareholders by determining the fairness of the buyout. The committee hired [the investment bankers]. Anybody hired by the committee ... was actually retained to advise the shareholders ... [A]ssuming [the investment bankers] were aware (as they must have been) that their opinion would be used to help shareholders decide on the fairness of Metromedia's stock offer, they can be liable to the shareholders."[17]

Similar issues arose in the aftermath of the RJR Nabisco, Inc. leveraged buyout, the largest and one of the most discussed transactions of the 1980s. After an initial offer was made by a management group led by the then-chief executive officer of RJR Nabisco, F. Ross Johnson, a vigorous bidding war developed between the management group and Kohlberg, Kravis, Roberts & Co., one of the leading leveraged buyout firms. The winning offer by KKR contained less cash than the final offer by the management group. This offer was attacked by shareholders not only because of the smaller cash component and the alleged over-valuation of the securities it contained, but also because certain shareholders believed that the auction was terminated prematurely.

Initially, the shareholders brought suit in Delaware against the directors of the company. The Delaware court, in applying a business judgment rule standard, upheld the board's decision to favor the bid with the somewhat lower cash amount, noting among other things that the accepted bid had a larger package of securities and included different future business plans for the company. The court also focused on the fact that the special committee, in deciding to accept one of the two bids, had reason to believe that the bids were in the upper range of fairness and also were presented with the possibility

that if they did not act decisively, one or both of the bidders might have withdrawn. The court emphasized that in closing an auction, directors who have acted independently, in good faith, and with due care will be given wide latitude to determine the circumstances under which to end the auction.

In *Schneider v. Lazard Freres & Co.*,[18] the former shareholders of RJR Nabisco brought suit against the investment banking firms retained to advise the special committee of the directors of RJR Nabisco in the auction. The shareholders again alleged that the auction of the RJR Nabisco shares was unfairly conducted, resulting in a lower purchase price than would have been obtained by a fair auction. The shareholders further alleged that the auction was prematurely terminated as a result of faulty advice given by the investment bankers.

In *Schneider*, the investment bankers moved for an order dismissing the complaint for failure to state a cause of action on a number of grounds, including that their advice was given to the special committee of the directors of RJR Nabisco, not the shareholders, and therefore they did not owe a duty to the shareholders.

The investment banking firms relied, in part, on the traditional defense that they were not in contractual "privity" with the shareholders. The *Schneider* court did not dispute the investment bankers' argument that, unlike in *Wells*, the shareholders never saw the fairness opinion comparing the competing offers for RJR Nabisco. The *Schneider* court noted that the shareholders did not claim to have met the *Ultramares* standard of a relationship with the investment banking firms that "approached privity," as restated in the three part test of *Credit Alliance*. The court noted that the shareholders could not have relied on, or could have been expected to rely on the fairness opinion because "it was the expectation of all concerned that the shareholders were not to do anything other than passively follow the recommendation of the Special Committee."[19]

The *Schneider* court decided that this passivity on the part of shareholders, and the unique relationship between the special committee administering an auction and the shareholders, permitted the relationship to be viewed as that of principal and agent. "In this 'buyout' context, if something less than the highest possible price was obtained, the loss was sustained by the shareholders, not the corporation and, for that reason, we are of the view that relationship between the shareholders and the Special Committee was essentially that of principal and agent on which principles of corporate law should not be superimposed."[20] Having reached this conclusion, the *Schneider* court seemingly felt free, unlike the *Wells* court, to ignore the requirements of *Credit Alliance.* "We do not think it a startling proposition that a principal is in privity with his agent's agent, or with anyone else his agent deals with on his behalf, so that a negligent statement made by a third person to an agent and relied on by the agent to the principal's detriment is actionable by the principal."[21] Accordingly, the shareholders could have a cause of action against the investment banking firm for a negligently prepared fairness opinion delivered to the board of directors.

Similarly, in *Dowling v. Narragansett Capital Corporation,*[22] the court denied an investment banker's motion to dismiss a claim against it for its role in the sale of a company for what was allegedly a "grossly" unfair price. The investment banker had delivered a fairness opinion to the board of the company that the proposed purchase price fairly reflected the value of the company's stock. The court determined that the investment banking firm "was hired to guide shareholders in deciding whether to approve the sale. Consequently, [the investment banker's] duty to exercise reasonable care in preparing its assessment was extended to [the company's] shareholders."

In a case arising out of the Nutri-System leveraged buy-out, the Third Circuit Court of Appeals held that there was a jury question whether investment banking firm had acted reasonably in delivering an opinion. In its opinion, the banker had assumed that Nutri-System's income would continue to be taxed for the next five years at the then-existing rate of 46%. An expert witness testified for the shareholders that it was inappropriate in delivering a fairness opinion in July 1986 to assume a 46% effective tax rate over five years in light of the then-prevailing belief that tax reform legislation pending before Congress would be enacted, and as a result tax rates would decline. The Third Circuit held that recovery should be permitted "when an expert, in making a projection, adopts an assumption which the factfinder concludes was objectively unreasonable in the circumstances."

The Nutri-System case indicates one peril awaiting investment bankers. The investment banking firm was paid $75,000 (a modest amount by industry standards) for the opinion which was included in a proxy statement which itself indicated that the tax law and rates might change. The litigation arising out of the leveraged buy-out has been to the United States Supreme Court and back.

These recent court cases do not include an award of damages against an investment banking firm for a negligently prepared fairness opinion. Nevertheless, they create a framework for such judgments and should be of concern to the investment banking community. The *Schneider* case would extend liability in corporate auctions to fairness opinions which the shareholders never had the opportunity to see and which they could not possibly have relied upon. The cumulative effect of these cases shows that investment banking firms can no longer rely on protection from shareholder suits on fairness opinions based on the doctrine of contractual privity.

Preventive Steps

The authors believe it is likely that courts generally will continue to expand their inquiry of fairness opinions and their underlying analyses. Accordingly, investment banking firms should continue to practice "defensive banking." Banking firms should assume that their fairness opinions will be challenged in litigation and should ensure that their internal files reflect accurately the work and analyses that have gone into the opinion. While each financial advisory engagement is unique and each fairness opinion must reflect and be based on the specifics of the particular transaction, several suggestions are presented below designed to limit investment banker liability in mergers and acquisitions.

Step 1: Description of Materials Reviewed

The fairness opinion should state which documents the investment bankers have reviewed, to what extent the investment bankers have relied on reports or interviews with management which have not been independently confirmed, and a statement as to any special time pressures or other constraints which limited the ability of the investment bankers to perform a complete review. In light of *Shell Oil,* the opinion should specifically refer to any material information not received or considered by the investment banker.

Step 2: Material Assumptions

Investment bankers should carefully consider those material assumptions inherent in fairness opinions and consider stating them in the text of the opinion. In the *Herskowitz* case, the Third Circuit failed to give the banking firm the benefit of possible tax law change disclosure set forth in the proxy statement but not in the opinion itself. In light of this view that the opinion had "independent significance to shareholders," banking firms should carefully review their own internal analyses and the proxy statement for material assumptions and protective disclosure which should be expressly incorporated in the text of the opinion.

Step 3: Narrow Purpose for the Fairness Opinion

Although the privity defense is clearly being eroded, fairness opinions should be addressed to the board of directors of the company or to the special committee of the board. The fairness opinion should include a statement that the fairness opinion is delivered for a specific purpose, for example to assist the board of directors in the analysis of competing bids, and it should not be used for any other purpose.

Engagement Letter Provisions

Investment banking firms uniformly require the inclusion of indemnification, contribution, and other protective provisions in their engagement letters. In light of recent cases, bankers should review their form of engagement letter.

Contingent Fees

Investment banking firms can avoid the suggestion that their opinions are affected by the financial incentives of their fee arrangements if their fees for fairness opinions are not contingent, in whole or in part, on the successful conclusion of the underlying transaction. The *Wells* court noted the existence of such an arrangement in its conclusion that investment bankers may be liable to shareholders for negligently prepared fairness opinions. The engagement letter, if at all possible, should not provide for disparate fees depending on whether or not the opinion is favorable. In addition, the engagement letter should not compensate the banker differently depending on whether one bidder or another prevails.

Indemnification

An indemnification provision provides the most direct way for an investment banker to protect itself against monetary loss resulting from shareholder litigation.

In an indemnification provision, the company agrees to hold the investment banking firm harmless against judgments, awards, costs, and expenses (typically including reasonable legal costs) arising out of any action stemming from its engagement with certain specified exceptions. An appropriate provision would make the investment banker whole, including against any judgment against it, unless a final court judgment finds that the liability primarily resulted from the banking firm's recklessness, bad faith, or gross negligence. Because it is difficult to prove recklessness or bad faith, shareholders have tended to challenge fairness opinions by alleging

negligence by the investment bankers in their preparation, as was the case in *Wells* and *Schneider*.

While indemnification provisions are critical, they are not a panacea for investment banking liability. Indemnification provisions themselves are subject to enforcement by courts which may be unwilling to provide the contractual protection to bankers whom the court believes have failed to perform to industry standards. It is fairly easy for a plaintiff to argue on grounds of public policy that indemnification should not be made available because the banker was negligent or grossly negligent. A subsequent bankruptcy by the company (or the successor company) could make the indemnification provision practically unenforceable. This is of special concern in leveraged buyout transactions which leave the acquired company encumbered with significant debt.

Settlement

Investment bankers should consider a provision in their engagement agreement that requires the board of directors to obtain a written release for the investment bankers in any settlement arrangement reached by the board of directors with suing shareholders. The decision of the New York Court of Appeals in reversing the decision of the *Wells* court indicates that in New York investment banking firms may benefit from a general release executed by shareholders.[23] Nonetheless, prudence requires that investment bankers insist that such releases specifically state that they are for the benefit of the named investment banking firm. Such a release signed by the shareholders should effectively bar them from bringing any claim against the investment banking firm.

The company may respond to the request for such a provision by saying that settling shareholder litigation is difficult enough without the additional complication of securing releases for agents who may or may not even be parties to the litigation.

Choice of Law/Choice of Venue

It is not clear that all state courts will follow the cases permitting investment banking firm liability to shareholders for negligently prepared fairness opinions. Investment bankers should consider including a two part provision in their engagement letter: first, that the engagement letter will be construed under Delaware law; and second, that any action brought against the investment banker arising out of the engagement must be brought in the Chancery Court of New Castle County, Delaware.

Such a provision would bring the action into a jurisdiction which has, to date, not followed the reasoning of the *Wells* and *Schneider* cases, and which is generally considered to be liberal and forward-looking in the protection it provides to corporate managers and advisors.

This provision would bind the company in any action which it may bring against the investment banking firm. It is possible that a court would not be willing to enforce such a provision against the shareholders of the company. However, the investment bankers could argue that the directors, as agents for the shareholders, have the right to bind the shareholders. In any event, companies, especially Delaware corporations, normally agree to such a provision in the engagement letter; at worst it will simply not be effective.

Agreement Not to Claim/Contribution

A variation of the indemnification agreement is an undertaking by the client company not to sue the investment banking firm based on its engagement, including the fairness opinion, unless the investment bankers were reckless or acted in bad faith. Such a provision should be binding against the client, but as previously mentioned it may not be enforceable against a shareholder plaintiff.

In the event that indemnification is not available to the investment bankers, a contribution provision could achieve a similar (if somewhat less satisfactory) end. Pursuant to such a provision, any loss suffered by the investment banker would be shared by the investment banker and the company according to a formula. This formula usually provides that the investment banking firm is liable for such costs up to an amount equal to the compensation it received for its services in the transaction. All additional liabilities and costs would be borne by the company.

Waiver of Trial by Jury

Counsel representing investment banking firms have begun to include a provision in the engagement letter which waives the right of the board of directors, the company, and its shareholders to a jury trial of any claim arising from the engagement letter, including any advice given by the investment banker. The value of such provisions rests in the belief that merger and acquisition transactions are complex and require a high degree of sophistication and that the jury system today contains a significant element of random chance. A judgment rendered by a judge is likely to be more reasoned and well-developed. As discussed earlier, such a provision may not be enforceable against the shareholders of the company who have themselves not agreed to it.

Endnotes

1. Delaware General Corporation Law (the "DGCL") §141 (a).

2. DGCL §141 (e); New York Business Corporation Law §717.

3. *Aronson v. Lewis*, 473 A.2d 805, 814, 815 (Del 1984).

4. *Stroud v. Milliker Enterprises, Inc.*, 552A.2d 476, 480 (Del. 1989): 480 (citing *Lacos Land Co. v. Arden Group, Inc.*, 517 A.2d 271, 279 (Del. Ch 1986)).

5. *Aronson:* 812.

6. 488 A.2d 858 (Del. 1985).

7. *Aronson: 812.*

8. *Sinclair Oil Corp. v. Levien,* 280 A.2d 717, 720 (Del. 1971).

9. *Unocal Corp. v. Mesa Petroleum Co.,* 493 A.2d 946, 958 (Del. 1985). See also, *Grobow v. Perot,* 539 A.2d 180 (Del. 1988).

10. 255 N.Y. 170 (1931).

11. 65 N.Y.2d 536, 493 N.Y.S.2d 435, 483 N.E.2d 110 (1985).

12. Securities Exchange Act of 1934 Rule 13e-3.

13. 482 A.2d 335 (Del. Ch. 1984).

14. *Joseph:* 341.

15. *Id.*

16. 127 A.D.2.d 200, 514 N.Y.S.2d 1 (1st Dep't Apr. 9, 1987), rev'd on other grounds, 72 N.Y.2d 11, 526 N.E.2d 8, 530 N.Y.S.2d 517 (1988).

17. *Wells* at 2.

18. 552 N.Y.S.2d 571, 159 A.D.2d 291 (A.D. 1 Dept. 1990).

19. *Schneider:* 574.

20. *Schneider:* 575.

21. Id.

22. 735 F. Supp. 1105 (RI 1990).

23. *Wells v. Shearson Lehman,* 72 N.Y.2d 11 (1988).

Part VI:
Managing Communications in Investment Banking Transactions

Chapter 10

Managing Initial Public Offering Communications

Michael L. Geczi
Senior Managing Director
Ogilvy Adams & Rinehart, New York, NY

In 1992, the boom in initial public offerings continued, enabling a record number of corporate issuers
to raise needed capital and pay attractive returns
both to original investors and those who benefitted
from strong aftermarket performance. Indeed, an
offering's success or failure almost always is judged
by the investment performance that is achieved.
From the standpoint of corporate issuers, however,
and the managers and advisors who direct the offering process, every successful IPO is the result of
effective management of one crucial area: communications. From road shows and press conferences
announcing the offering to the prospectus itself,
every phase of the offering depends on some type of
communications vehicle aimed at potential investors
and the financial media. Just as products and services
must be "positioned" to consumers, customers, and
clients to highlight their benefits, the strengths and
growth potential of a company considering an IPO
must be presented properly to key audiences if the
offering is to be successful and the company is to
maximize shareholder value.

A successful communications program for an
initial public offering will:

♦ help create demand for the company's stock
when it is offered;

♦ support the pricing established by the
company's investment banking advisors;

♦ communicate and establish a favorable corporate image to encourage long-term investment in the company; and

♦ ensure that there are no problems with SEC
compliance.

Managing the communications program also will
establish a structure for responding—within SEC
guidelines—to inquiries during the IPO. By doing so
in a controlled way, in conjunction with legal and
investment banking advisors, the company can ensure the best possible reception for the issue.

If the corporate issuer does not take the initiative
in managing the flow of information about the offering, investors and the press will get their information
from sources who may be ill-informed or even negative about the offering. Clearly, if the prospectus is
not prepared in accordance with SEC regulations,
the offering may not be allowed to proceed. But the
SEC may also intervene if other communications
with investors do not meet their guidelines. In the
case of American Express Company's spin-off of First
Data Corporation, Alex. Brown & Sons was removed
from the underwriting syndicate for the offering after
one of the firm's securities analysts made earnings
projections for First Data available to the media, in
spite of SEC restrictions.

Most offerings that have come to market in the
recent boom were well-received. The 10 best-per-
forming IPOs of 1991, for example, saw their stock
prices increase an average of 162% in the first 12
months of trading. Others, however, proved disap-
pointing, when demand for the offering failed to
materialize, or investor expectations of the stock's
financial performance were not met.

In their first year of trading, investors in 1991's
10 worst-performing IPOs saw the value of their
investment decline an average of 66%. With the
success of the offering and the company's financial
health at stake, leaving investor perceptions of the
company and the offering to chance is certainly too
great a risk to take.

103

Through carefully managed communications, a company can demonstrate its strengths and foster an understanding of its business in the financial community and the media far enough in advance of the planned public offering to support demand for the company's stock. In addition, the program will support the company's overall corporate communications and marketing efforts by influencing other important audiences, including lenders, prospective clients, and employees.

A public offering (or other entry into the capital markets) isn't an isolated event. Much like any other business endeavor, a public offering is the product of a long and carefully managed process that should be approached with the same care a company uses to manage the rest of its business. Successful management of the long, complex offering process involves close coordination of investment banking counsel and senior management, effective legal advice, and having a clear overall business objective behind the offering.

In addition, offerings can be affected by industry issues and market trends beyond the issuing company's control. But all of these other factors are influenced by communications—one element that the issuer can and must manage.

Planning and implementing the right outreach program may seem a daunting task at first. However, by the time the decision is made to proceed with an IPO, the hardest work is over.

The key element of IPO communications is successfully articulating to the financial community the rationale behind the offering. Remember: If it makes sense to the issuer from a business perspective, if it supports the company's business plan and provides new opportunities for growth, it should make sense to prospective investors. If the issuer has done the necessary preparation in planning the offering, the foundation for a successful communications program—and a successful offering—already has been established.

Figure 10.1 is a timeline for IPO communications. It details the timing and activity from 18 months prior to an initial public offering, to ongoing communications for a newly public company.

The private companies that choose to enter the financial marketplace for the first time with a stock offering confront significant communications challenges but also significant opportunities. This chapter will discuss elements of IPO-related communications, from positioning of private companies long before the IPO occurs through post-offering investor relations. With planning, forethought, and effective coordination of communications, there is no reason why an offering that makes economic sense to the corporate issuer should not be favorably received by the financial community, to the benefit of issuer and investors alike.

Before undertaking a financial communications program, it is important to address a few considerations in advance: SEC regulations concerning financial communications; some communications challenges specific to private companies; and the concerns of the financial community.

SEC Regulations

Any communications program designed to support a stock must comply with SEC regulations. Any violation of SEC regulations, whether a mere oversight or a blatant disregard for the rules, can seriously impede an IPO's success, cause delay of trading of a new issue on the day of the offering, or even result in cancellation. To ensure safe compliance, a company should clear all intended press releases or public statements with attorneys and investment bankers in advance.

The underlying motivation of the SEC is to ensure that prospective investors receive accurate and objective information about any planned offering. To this end, the SEC demands that all communications concerning the issuing company and the offering itself during the filing process for the IPO be reviewed and approved prior to distribution.

The SEC requires that the following communications guidelines be adhered to by a company planning an IPO: quiet period, preliminary prospectus, offering, and post-offering communications.

Quiet Period

From a communications standpoint, the greatest risk occurs during an offering's "quiet period." That is because the 1933 SEC Act prohibits a company from "offering" securities from the time a managing underwriter is chosen (typically about three months before the offering date) until 25 days after the offering becomes effective. During this time, the SEC restricts communications other than the prospectus which can be interpreted as discussing the securities for sale. It is important to remember, therefore, that the prospectus is not only a key legal document, but also an issuing company's most important public relations tool. Once filed, the prospectus will become the primary marketing document for the offering.

Although this period of time is known as the "quiet period," some communication with external audiences beyond the prospectus still is permitted. The broad SEC definition for these communications includes "the publication of information and statements, and publicity efforts, made in advance of a

Figure 10.1   Timeline for IPO Communications

TIMING	ACTIVITY
18 Months Prior	Identify (target) key financial media, analysts and conduct audit.
	Develop communications messages.
	Begin development of collateral materials, company brochure, and marketing materials.
16 Months Prior	Begin introductions to financial media and analysts.
	Coordinate employee communications, community and government relations with media, and financial communications program.
One Year Prior	Evaluate communications program to date; refine and retune messages.
	Begin investor targeting; target regional media.
	Begin to set up investor relations program.
100 Days Prior	Choose underwriter.
	First all-hands meeting with company executives, attorneys, underwriter, accountants and public relations counsel.
	Develop offering-related themes; agree on communications activities and procedures.
85 Days Prior	Begin drafting registration statement/prospectus.
	Begin drafting road show materials and analyst presentation.
	Begin drafting press materials for offering day, including press release, Q and As, management bios, and fact sheets.
	Begin drafting analyst materials for offering day.
45 Days Prior	Revise registration statement; complete signature page.
	Rehearse road show.
30 Days Prior	File registration statement with the SEC; "quiet period" begins.
	Issue press release announcing intent for an IPO.
	Road show and selling effort begins.
	Continue normal ongoing disclosures of factual and financial information about the company.
	Do not begin any new publicity efforts, advertising campaigns, or project revenues, income or earnings per share.
	Evaluate press and analyst response; finetune themes and outreach efforts.
5 Days Prior	Receive SEC comment letter.
	Respond to SEC letter, revise red herring, and request acceleration of offering day.
	Approve offering day press materials and analyst materials.
	Begin rehearsing for press conference and response to analyst questions.
1 Day Prior	File pricing amendment.
	Assemble press kits and analyst kits.
Offering Day	Selling begins.
	Distribute press release, press kits, and analyst kits.
	Run tombstone ad.
	Conduct series of media interviews and press conferences for financial media.
	Begin investor relations program.
1 Day After	Evaluate press and analyst response; finetune themes.
7 Days After	Closing day, underwriters are paid, and private owners receive proceeds of offering.
25 Days After	"Quiet period" ends.
90 Days After	First quarterly earnings announcement.
	Conduct analyst breakfast or lunch.
Ongoing	Regular reports to the SEC (8K, 10Q, 10K, . . .).
	Investor relations program up and running.
	Press relations program up and running.

proposed financing which have the effect of conditioning the public mind or arousing public interest in the issuer or in its securities." New publicity efforts, advertising, or forecasts and projections of revenues, income, or earnings per share are prohibited.

Usual ongoing disclosures of factual information about the company are permitted, however. In fact, the SEC recommends and encourages companies to continue advertising campaigns and press announcements on factual and financial developments, so that prospective investors will have the opportunity to evaluate the company's daily operations.

Additionally, the SEC requires that once a managing underwriter is chosen, communications can only proceed at the level that was in effect before preparations for the offering began. Therefore, it is in the company's interest to have established a fairly high level of outreach activity well in advance of the offering.

Preliminary Prospectus

After the registration statement for the offering is filed, SEC regulations prohibit the distribution of any written sales literature about the offering other than the preliminary prospectus (called a "red herring" because red ink is used to denote its preliminary status on the cover) and "tombstone ads," so called for their stark appearance and sparse text.

A news release may be distributed stating only limited information about the issuer and the size of the offering and must clearly indicate that securities may only be offered by the prospectus.

The issuing company is allowed to use the red herring in outreach to prospective investors, typically through road shows where the company's senior management presents information about operations and the offering in cities where likely investor groups are located.

Until the quiet period is over, written commentary by research analysts and hard copies of slides used in road show presentations to investor groups may not be distributed to other audiences. In addition, the cooperation by the company or its underwriters in the preparation of news stories on the pending offering is not permitted. No communications activities are allowed to project earnings growth or geographic or operational expansion.

Offering

Once the SEC has commented on the initial filing, the issuer has responded, and the SEC in turn has expressed its final satisfaction, the prospectus becomes final, and the last stage of preparation for the offering begins.

At this point, another news release may be distributed, with a bit more specific information about the offering than was previously allowed. The issuer's attorneys then request an acceleration of the effective date, and investment banking counsel determines final pricing. When the SEC grants permission for the offering to become effective, the underwriters determine the offering price, and the attorneys file a pricing amendment with the commission. The pricing information is also added to the prospectus, which is then printed for distribution by the underwriters.

On the day when the offering becomes effective, the SEC allows for outreach to the press and investors through news releases, press conferences, tombstone ads, and one-on-one meetings. However, the quiet period will remain in effect for another 25 days, and so the content of these communications must conform with the information contained in the prospectus.

Post-Offering Communications

After the offering is closed, the issuer has become a public company and must conform to all SEC requirements for filing of quarterly and annual financial reports. The issuer must also provide timely disclosure of any information about the company that would affect the investment decisions of a reasonable investor.

Communications Challenges for Private Companies

Private companies making an initial public offering face unique challenges in communicating to the financial press, analyst, and investor communities for the first time.

Unlike public companies, which are required by law to disclose financial information, private companies are not used to publicly announcing information about their business. And the financial community usually has little interest in companies whose stock is not publicly traded, so their level of knowledge of private companies is generally quite low.

Often a private company's owners and senior management have little knowledge of the disclosure requirement applied by the SEC to public companies, and frequently no one person is assigned the responsibility of outreach to the financial community or the media. It can be difficult for these managers to get used to the idea of a diminished amount of privacy surrounding their business practices and results.

A company planning an IPO must work closely throughout the entire planning process with its underwriters, attorneys, accountants, and public/financial relations counsel in order to coordinate all of the required materials and present a unified message to the financial community and other important audiences.

Many private companies do not already have relationships with these types of professionals, and the first step in preparing for an offering is to assemble the "working group" that will bring the issue to market. Some back-tracking may be necessary as well. For example, it is generally required that corporate issuers provide audited financial statements for the prior three years. If these reports do not already exist, the company must enlist the assistance of an accounting firm without delay and have the financial statements prepared. Of course, it is easier and less costly to produce these reports in advance.

In order to ensure that there is sufficient demand in the market for an offering of its stock, the issuing company must establish relationships with the financial community, create a base of public knowledge about its operations, and differentiate itself from its competitors. For most private companies, this entails significantly raising the current level of communications activity.

At most private companies, personal relationships do not yet exist between senior management and the financial press and securities analysts who influence investor perceptions. Members of the financial community would have had little reason or opportunity to learn about the average private company.

Once the preliminary "quiet period" of an IPO begins, the company will be prohibited from conducting introductory meetings. Unless the company had strategically approached reporters and analysts well in advance of the preliminary filing, it will have to wait until after the offering is underway. If this happens, the company loses the advantage in establishing its key messages with this important audience.

Without personal contacts, reporters will depend on their own research, which may be incomplete or include erroneous information, to cover the offering. By beginning its outreach to the financial media early and generating consistent coverage of its business, the issuer can create background material and a database of articles about the company's operations and management for financial reporters to use in covering the offering.

In addition, it is important for private companies to begin to cultivate relationships with key sell- and buy-side securities analysts. Analysts, like reporters, generally will have little or no knowledge about the company or its prospects.

It is beneficial for private companies to begin to disclose selected financial information before going public in order to generate interest among analysts and to provide them with historical financial information to use when they evaluate the offering.

Perceptions of the issuer also are affected by how little or how much is understood about its industry as a whole. If the issuing company is in an industry that generally is composed of other private companies, most analysts and media will have little or no background knowledge to work from. They will need to receive a significant amount of very fundamental information in order to begin to understand the company's operations and how its financial performance should be evaluated. Although this can entail a major commitment of time and effort for the private company's management, it also presents an opportunity for the issuer to develop its own positioning statement for its industry and its own benchmarks and criteria by which to be judged.

However, if the issuer has some public companies among its peers, the business press and investment community will be predisposed to evaluate the offering company in terms of its public competitors. Although the issuer will not be able to take an immediate leadership role in positioning its industry with this audience, reporters, analysts and investors will be more knowledgeable about the operations and earnings dynamics in the industry if they have had the opportunity to follow public companies within that segment.

Undertaking an initial public offering without advance support—increasing the visibility of the company's executives, the distribution of marketing and other corporate materials, and the proper positioning of the company—would mean that this important audience would start at ground-zero in its knowledge of the company at the time of the offering.

By beginning to build the level of communications about 18 months prior to the planned IPO, a company will be able to establish definitively its messages with the financial community, to communicate its fundamentals, and to comment on current industry perceptions and the state of the IPO market to the media, analysts, and investors before the restrictions of the "quiet period" take effect.

Financial Community Concerns

All communication with the media and analysts is directed ultimately at addressing, whether explicitly or implicitly, the concerns of prospective investors. It is important to remember that the financial community's concerns surrounding an IPO are the same as they would be about any company doing anything new—an acquisition, a change in management, or the sale of debt.

However, these issues are especially important in IPO communications because investors have not yet heard them addressed by the company making the offering, so they will be receiving this information for the first time.

An effective IPO communications program should encompass the following general areas:

♦ Management competence. Demonstrate the strength of the management team: their personal and professional backgrounds, technical skills, competence in financial management, and business planning.

♦ Financial Strength. Demonstrate the company's financial strength: successful operations, growing revenues, effective management of earnings and assets, and successful financings.

♦ Use of Proceeds. The rationale for an offering or what the company's business goals are and how greater access to capital would help achieve them.

♦ Growth Prospects. Both short- and long-term growth potential must be emphasized, including information about market growth and projections on operational and sales strength, new products, and customers in the pipeline.

♦ Competitive Position. What is the potential for market leadership? Data should be provided on the company's share of current and proposed markets, customer demand for products or services, and information on customer response to product quality.

♦ Commitment to Shareholder Value. Although this is probably the most nebulous area for a private company to address, it is possible, nevertheless, for senior management to convey their sensitivity to investor concerns and the dynamics of public ownership—rather than to give the impression of owners/managers who would undertake an offering for self-profit.

How these issues are actually addressed in financial communications activities will depend on the company's specific situation at the time preparation for the offering begins. It will also take into account overall industry conditions, the current condition of the IPO market, and the concerns of the company's targeted financial reporters, analysts, and investors as identified through outreach to those audiences.

Private Company Positioning

Corporate Positioning Statement

Central to any financial communications program is the creation of a corporate positioning statement. The financial positioning should be closely coordinated with any messages and vehicles developed for an overall corporate communications program to ensure that a consistent positioning of the company is transmitted to all audiences both internal and external, and to provide for the leveraging of corporate communications activities with the financial audience and vice versa.

Creating a corporate image is a time-consuming task, one that requires a significant time commitment. Management can not expect to create a corporate image the week before offering day; it must be established long before IPO preparations begin. Fortunately, the process of creating an image is already underway for the majority of companies considering an IPO. The necessary information is already available as a result of the company's ongoing marketing effort. It is then necessary to leverage the company's strengths with the financial community in a way that will enhance the corporate image and encourage investment.

There are often a number of industries that the company could conceivably fit into, and a number of different companies that could be considered competitors. Thus, choosing the industry categorization that will be the most beneficial to the company in terms of attracting investors is extremely important. If the company does not fit clearly into a defined industry, it may have a unique opportunity to define its own market and industry. For the purposes of strategic communications, no situation could be better. The task of market definition must be considered seriously, as the company's image will be affected by the industry of which it is considered a part.

Internal Audit

In developing a positioning statement, it is necessary first to use internal resources to determine the desired perception of the company within the financial community. This will provide the overall goal for the financial communications program and will involve internal fact-finding to address the following issues:

♦ What are the company's strengths and weaknesses?

♦ What are its future prospects? Where is it going?

♦ Who are the competitors? What are their strengths and weaknesses?

♦ What industry does it fit into?

♦ What is the desired result from the communications program?

Answering these questions will provide the initial information needed to determine the image it makes sense for the company to project to the financial community.

External Audit

Once a preliminary internal assessment is complete, the next step in developing a corporate positioning message is the performance of a confidential audit of targeted journalists and analysts to identify their level of knowledge about the company, its competition, and its industry.

About half the time, audits serve to confirm the company's sense of its audience's most important concerns. In these cases, the research serves as a cheap insurance policy. However, the other half of financial community audits reveal misperceptions and problems which cannot be identified by any other means.

Understanding what these key audiences think about the company's specific strengths and weaknesses will enable the company to develop messages to address the financial community's particular concerns and interests and to reinforce or change existing perceptions. These messages should fit strategically into a company's overall corporate communications program.

Audience Targeting

The essential element of any communications program is audience targeting. The most sophisticated communications program will have no impact on a company's business if it is aimed at the wrong people. Before developing specific messages to communicate the company's positioning statement and address the strengths and vulnerabilities identified in the audit, it is necessary to identify the audiences to be reached through the company's financial communications program and to consider their various concerns and levels of knowledge about the company.

There are several groups of audiences to target in an IPO communications plan—financial media, trade media, buy- and sell-side analysts, and potential investors—and all are important. A brief discussion of each audience follows.

Media. A thorough review of national and regional financial media is the first step in targeting key audiences. Targeting publications begins with considering what newspapers and magazines are read by key financial audiences (primarily analysts and

investors) and the geographic regions in which the company currently operates and has the largest potential for growth. The company should begin to compile a list of national, regional, and trade publications and key reporters that cover the IPO market, finance, investing, management, and the company's industry and competition as early as possible.

Analysts. Next, the company must identify key buy- and sell-side analysts who follow companies in the industry within which the company would be most advantageously positioned. Because not every SIC code has an analyst assigned to cover it, there may be an opportunity for the company to define its own coverage. If the company's primary competitors are all private companies, identifying which analysts to target will be difficult.

Should this be the case, the management team will have to work a little harder at defining its industry and persuading analysts who might cover a similar one to expand their scope and begin writing reports on the company after it goes public.

Prospective Investors. When the final decision to proceed with an IPO is made (about one year before the offering), it is time to begin to target prospective investors. First, the company must work with investment bankers to determine what types of investors the company can and wishes to attract.

Institutional investors have the most available capital and often are viewed as the "ideal" investor. However, the company must consider whether it is more beneficial to have several institutions who own a large part of the company or many individual investors who each own small parts. Since some institutional investors have particular requirements about how the company is run or predetermined sell prices, the management team may be more comfortable with a significant proportion of smaller, individual investors.

Institutional Investors. Much information on the investing activities of institutional investors, such as employee pension funds and private money managers, is publicly available. Investors owning more than 5% of any public company's stock are required to disclose their holdings, and competitors' shareholder lists will indicate what institutions may be likely prospective investors for the issuing company. It is also important to note where the ideal institutional targets are located, in case other large institutions in those cities might be interested in investing in the company's IPO.

A typical analysis of institutional investors also involves researching other public information, such as: buying and selling decisions; the criteria that different institutional investors use in making those decisions; their historical investing patterns; their stability and loyalty, and even their cost bases. It is helpful to examine investing trends that appear in the industry to identify the institutions that seem to be "dumping" or accumulating stock.

Individual Investors. Targeting individual investors is conducted differently, because these individuals are usually investing much smaller amounts for their own account and thus are not required to disclose their equity holdings. Although as many as 48 million men and women in the U.S. own publicly issued securities, collectively they own only about 20% of all securities. Many IPOs are marketed to individual investors through retail brokers. Investment bankers will coordinate outreach to the appropriate institutional and individual investors once the offering is underway.

Figures 10.2 and 10.3 illustrate financing vehicles for 1990 and 1991, respectively.

Message Development

Once internal and external audits and audience targeting have been completed, the company can begin to develop messages that will communicate its business strengths and investment potential to key audiences. As mentioned earlier, the key to developing effective messages is to carefully examine the reasons behind the decision to undertake an IPO and to look for a way to communicate those reasons to target audiences. It will save a considerable amount of time and effort to leverage the data that has been developed during the intense IPO planning process for use in the IPO communications program.

The company's key messages must also address the overriding concerns of investors in initial public offerings. Therefore, specific messages should be geared toward the company's management competence, financial strength, use of proceeds, growth prospects, competitive position, and commitment to shareholder value.

Operations/Results Positioning

Introductions to the previously targeted financial media and analysts should begin as soon as possible after the communications messages have been developed. Media tours and analyst meetings are key ways to get a company's name out.

Media Tours. The management team should conduct regional media tours to start building contacts with key journalists, especially in the areas where there are a large number of prospective investors. In these meetings, the management team should begin to articulate—within the framework of the key messages—the company's business accomplishments, operations, and results.

Because private companies are not required to disclose financial information, and because they do not have shares listed on a stock exchange, they tend to be covered less in newspapers and financial publications than public companies. Thus, in order to get the company's name in print, creative thinking is required. Ideas for trend stories based on proprietary data are usually welcomed, but they must be pertinent to the publication's focus and readership.

However, because financial information about private companies is not readily available, reporters are more likely to write a story about a private company when provided with such information.

Months before an IPO, a company's financial performance can be promoted through the use of some statistics. Some of these include research and development expenditures, marketing initiatives, or selected use of financial results expressed in terms of percentages rather than absolute numbers, so that the company's performance dynamics can be shown without divulging actual revenues or expenses. New developments in corporate strategy should be announced as well.

Analyst Meetings. In addition to meeting key reporters and journalists, senior management, especially the CEO and CFO, must make contacts with key analysts. Although it may be more difficult to arrange to speak to analysts before the company is public, it is possible. Analyst societies scattered across the country are always looking for outside speakers for their regular meetings. Often they will ask a CEO or CFO of a private company to speak to the group about a topic of interest—such as market trends, business dynamics, or regulatory issues—at one of their luncheons. This is an excellent way for a private company to get its name out to the financial community and position its experts as smart, knowledgeable business people.

These regional analyst meetings should be coordinated with the company's regional media tour. Ideally, the local paper will print a trend piece or management story about the company during the week its executives are meeting with analysts, thereby reinforcing the company's name with its entire audience.

Executive Positioning

As mentioned earlier, the perceived competence and stature of the company's management team is a critical determinant in the success or failure of an IPO.

During the 18-month period before an IPO, a major component of the communications plan should be aimed at establishing and enhancing the profile of the CEO and other senior management with the financial community. This can be accomplished by the following:

- conducting background meetings with key journalists and analysts;

- distributing source letters and bylined articles to the financial media positioning managers as expert sources of comment on industry-related issues; and

- arranging appearances at industry-related financial forums sponsored by media groups, analyst societies, and underwriters.

Announcing the IPO

Creation of Materials

When the planning for an IPO begins, the pace of financial communications activity accelerates to support the announcement of the offering. Ideally, the company and its senior executives will have been positioning the company over the previous year with the financial community. If executives have already been introduced to key journalists and analysts by the time the actual financial planning begins, announcing the IPO will be much easier.

Planning for an IPO is a hectic endeavor. Prospectuses and road show materials must be created within a short timeframe, and often many drafts must be written before one is agreed upon by all parties involved. At the first all-hands meeting—with the company's executives, underwriter, attorney, accountants, and public and financial relations counsel—the assignments to be completed over the next three months are determined and responsibility is assigned.

Next, the writing begins. The underwriter, accountants, and attorneys draft the preliminary prospectus. The underwriter and public and financial relations counsel draft the road show materials, press releases and press and analyst kits. The company's executives try to balance their time between preparing for the IPO and running the company.

Filing the Preliminary Prospectus

When the preliminary prospectus is filed with the SEC, companies are permitted to distribute a press release announcing their intention to issue an IPO. It is important to take advantage of this opportunity. Although a company is not permitted to say anything in the release that is not in the preliminary prospectus, the chance to inform the public of the company's offering should not be missed. The prospectus itself is the company's most important public relations tool. It should include a description of the company, its executives, and its financial performance in a way

that supports the key messages communicated over the previous 18 months.

Road Show Presentation

Once the preliminary prospectus is filed, the selling begins. For about a two-week period, the company's management team and its underwriters go on a "road show" to visit prospective investors and securities analysts in various cities to build interest in the stock and encourage investment in the company. As mentioned, the SEC prohibits the distribution of any materials other than the "red herring" at these meetings, but the road show offers the company the opportunity to present its management team and explain its long-term business plan.

The road show is the company's only opportunity to actively sell and market its new offering, therefore, the presentation must be carefully scripted. The messages developed for the IPO communications program should be incorporated into the presentation to ensure consistent outreach to the financial community. If core messages are changed or appear radically different at this point, potential investors will be confused about the company's objectives and discouraged from investing in the offering.

It is important, of course, to keep in mind the concerns that analysts have expressed in the past about the industry, the company, or the competition. If these issues can be effectively addressed and alleviated during the road show, the company may be able to interest a few more investors than if these issues had been ignored. Prospective investors will be more interested, however, in the financial future of the company. While forecasting revenues and earnings is prohibited by the SEC, the company may discuss historical numbers and how its business plan going forward will allow the company to improve on the past.

Media and Analyst Outreach

Once the offering day arrives, the company will receive considerably more attention from the financial community and the media. However, the "quiet period" does not end until 25 days after closing day. It is imperative, therefore, that the company understands that restrictions are still in effect.

On the first morning of trading, it is useful to hold a press conference and a series of media interviews with key financial journalists. The company will probably be able to attract more media interest on offering day than any other and this is a good time to expand its corporate positioning activities.

Preparations for interviews and a press conference must be made several weeks in advance of the

Figure 10.2   Financing Vehicles–1991

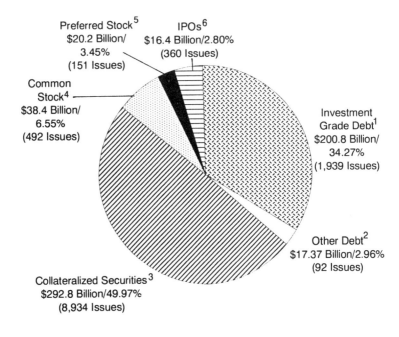

Preferred Stock[5]
$20.2 Billion/
3.45%
(151 Issues)

IPOs[6]
$16.4 Billion/2.80%
(360 Issues)

Common Stock[4]
$38.4 Billion/
6.55%
(492 Issues)

Investment Grade Debt[1]
$200.8 Billion/
34.27%
(1,939 Issues)

Other Debt[2]
$17.37 Billion/2.96%
(92 Issues)

Collateralized Securities[3]
$292.8 Billion/49.97%
(8,934 Issues)

All Domestic Issues $585.97 Billion/100%(11,968 Issues)

[1] Excludes mortgage-backed securities, asset-backed securities, convertible bonds and junk bonds.
[2] Junk bonds and convertible bonds.
[3] Mortgage-backed securities and asset-backed securities.
[4] Secondary issues.
[5] Non-convertible and convertible.
[6] Excluding closed-end funds.
Source: Securities Data Corporation

offering day to ensure adequate attendance and coverage of the offering. Again, SEC regulations will continue to prohibit speaking to any issues beyond what is available in the prospectus or from making any financial projections. Therefore, all intended speeches and answers to questions must be cleared with attorneys.

All the news coverage of the offering must be carefully monitored from offering day (preferably months earlier) and going forward. Knowing what types of articles are being written about the company, and what issues and concerns are being expressed by analysts quoted in them, will enable the company to modify its messages to address these audiences' concerns. In addition, seeing news coverage from across the country on the day it is published allows the working group to quickly correct errors of fact that could materially affect the success of the offering.

Communications as a Public Company

Once public, a company's requirements for communications are significantly greater than they were when it was private. It is now important that the same messages be communicated to investors as well

Figure 10.3 Financing Vehicles–1992

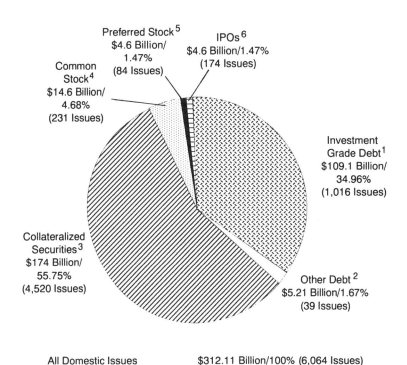

Preferred Stock[5]
$4.6 Billion/
1.47%
(84 Issues)

Common
Stock[4]
$14.6 Billion/
4.68%
(231 Issues)

IPOs[6]
$4.6 Billion/1.47%
(174 Issues)

Investment
Grade Debt[1]
$109.1 Billion/
34.96%
(1,016 Issues)

Collateralized
Securities[3]
$174 Billion/
55.75%
(4,520 Issues)

Other Debt[2]
$5.21 Billion/1.67%
(39 Issues)

All Domestic Issues $312.11 Billion/100% (6,064 Issues)

[1] Excludes mortgage-backed securities, asset-backed securities, convertible bonds and junk bonds.
[2] Junk bonds and convertible bonds.
[3] Mortgage-backed securities and asset-backed securities.
[4] Secondary issues.
[5] Non-convertible and convertible.
[6] Excluding closed-end funds.
Source: Securities Data Corporation

as the media and analysts and that all audiences have the same access to information about the company.

Public Relations

The public company must develop a long-term financial communications program similar to that conducted in the pre-IPO period. Outreach to key reporters at national, business, and trade publications is just as important now, and a substantial commitment must be made to actively communicate with reporters to ensure that the company will not be forgotten. Regular press releases on new business developments, new products and financial results,

speeches or presentations to journalist groups, press conferences, media mailings, and interviews will be part of the company's daily routine.

It is imperative to maintain personal contacts with key journalists and to be aware of who is covering the company's industry. Leverage business trips by meeting with key media representatives in the cities senior executives are visiting. Even if there is no news to tell, dropping by for a half-hour meeting with the editor of a trade or business publication will help senior management of the company remain top of mind with reporters.

Investor Relations

Subsequent to the offering day, the now-public company must communicate with investors and disclose financial information quarterly. There is a big difference in accountability for the managers of public versus privately owned companies, and management must come to terms with this new fiduciary responsibility to shareholders. Management must demonstrate their commitment to the interests of the new investors by must maintaining open, two-way communications with investors, soliciting feedback, and reconciling investors' short- and long-term goals and concerns with management's business plan.

A comprehensive investor relations program must be developed at least six months before the planned IPO. Senior management must appoint an investor relations manager whose job will be to communicate with investors, analysts, and financial journalists and to set up an investor relations department where inquiries on the company's finances will be handled. The IR manager will be responsible for maintaining contact with the company's key audiences, noting their concerns, and targeting prospective investors. Regular contact between all interested parties requires a full-time commitment. Analysts, investors, and journalists need to have a senior professional at the company with whom they feel comfortable talking.

Once public, the company will have to deal directly with requests for financial information from investors, analysts, and journalists. The system for handling such requests must be efficient and timely, for these audiences want current information as soon as they ask for it. In addition, quarterly and annual earnings announcements must be made now that the company is public.

Ongoing research is important in an investor relations program as well. The newly public company should research its competitors' IR activities, attitudes of both buy- and sell-side analysts, and investor holdings of peer stocks as an aid to identifying and reaching out to potential "ideal" investors.

Like the public relations program, the investor relations program has objectives, strategies, messages, and tactics. Its messages will typically be more financial in nature but they should fit strategically into the company's overall communications messages. Senior management will have to maintain their visibility with key analysts and investors by participating in buy- and sell-side analyst meetings and analyst presentations.

Leverage Corporate and Financial Communication

With proper leveraging and coordination, many tactics for communicating with the fiancial community can be used to further the overall corporate communications program, and vice versa. It is important to build on corporate communications activities by distributing materials developed for one audience to others as appropriate. For example, selected marketing materials should be sent to journalists to provide background information on operations and market outreach. Similarly, reprints of media coverage and byliners should be sent to analysts when it makes sense.

Develop Collaterals

Corporate brochures and other marketing materials will be necessary for a complete financial community outreach effort. Materials should be developed about 16 months before the planned IPO and distributed to all key audiences. A simple but comprehensive corporate brochure should be the first marketing piece developed. It should include a description of the business and the market, and highlight the company's strengths.

After the brochure is completed, the company should examine the possibility of creating a more complete collateral piece, a fact book, for distribution to prospective institutional investors, sell-side analysts, and key journalists. The format of the book should allow for easy updating (at least every six months). Ideally, the book would include detailed descriptions of key lines of businesses, revenue data (if possible), case studies, profiles of senior management, excerpts from noteworthy recent news coverage and analyst reports, and a rolodex card listing key executive contacts. Regular updates of all materials should be prepared and distributed on a quarterly basis.

Disclosure Requirements

A public company will be confronted with the SEC's legal reporting requirements, including quarterly and annual reports to shareholders, 10Q and 10K filings with the SEC, and regular financial audits. Disclosure requirements for public companies will mean that information that had previously been kept confidential, such as business plans, market data, and financial results, must be made publicly available for all to see. Officers and directors must keep inside information confidential until it is properly disclosed to the public.

Conclusion

By developing a managed communications program well in advance of an IPO, a company can ensure that the offering is received positively by the financial community, and to the benefit of the company's new shareholders, employees, and customers. The better the company is positioned among its key journalists, analysts, and prospective investors, the better it will be perceived by the financial community when it offers stock for the first time. The company has much to gain if it undertakes to carefully manage the communications surrounding an important event such as an initial stock offering, and much to lose if it does not.

Chapter 11

Communications:
A Critical Factor in Bank Mergers

Judy Brennan
Vice President
Ogilvy Adams & Rinehart, New York, NY

Take a last look at the banking industry as it exists today—quickly. In 1980, 14 out of the 100 largest banks in the world were U.S.-based, down from 24 in 1970. By 1990, this figure had shrunk to eight, with no American banks ranking in the top ten.

Banking is an industry that is changing fast. From regulatory reforms to technological innovation, from globalization to increased competition, the environment in which banks do business is changing on all fronts. The most recent and, in many ways, the most significant of these changes is the merger mania that has taken the banking industry by storm.

From 1980 to 1990, the number of bank holding companies in the United States decreased from 12,700 to 9,700. By the year 2010, the Federal Reserve expects that number to shrink even further to 5,500. According to these figures, the number of players in the banking industry will shrink by nearly two-thirds over a 30-year period. Mergers are taking on all sorts of shapes and sizes—from in-market to intrastate and even transnational unions. All sectors of the industry are joining the trend: small community banks, superregionals, and money center banks alike.

To date, over 30 states already have unlimited nationwide or national reciprocal banking laws. These relaxations of interstate branching restrictions are providing many opportunities for banks to expand their operations without having to establish different accounting systems, boards of directors, and other operational mechanisms. And federally sanctioned nationwide banking, if instituted, would allow even more companies to expand in the same cost-effective manner.

The year 1991 saw three of the biggest bank mergers in history—Bank of America/Security Pacific, NCBN/C&S Sovran, and Chemical/Manufacturers Hanover—along with a spate of smaller mergers and acquisitions among regional institutions that sought to expand certain businesses, product lines, or market positionings. Driven by the factors outlined, extensive consolidation is likely to characterize the U.S. banking industry over the next two decades as competitive and economic pressures create an unprecedented impetus for banking mergers and acquisitions both at home and abroad, facilitated by regulators' favorable attitudes toward consolidation of the industry.

Forces Behind the Banking Merger Wave

In recent years, rising loan problems, a slowing economy, and the crisis in commercial real estate, in particular, have created considerable incentives for banking organizations to merge. Merging two banks provides opportunities to improve profit margins by cutting costs and maximizing operating efficiencies while building capital.

What Makes a Bank Merger Successful?

The gains that banks achieve through merging—improved operating efficiency, strengthened balance sheets, and increased capitalization—along with the sheer increase in size catapults the newly merged institution into an entirely new peer group. While the new institution is built from the components of

117

each of its founders, it is an entirely new entity—the whole being greater than the sum of its parts.

Support of all the banks' constituencies is key to creating a successful new institution. To achieve this, a strong communications effort must be launched. Providing these groups with news of the merger and conveying the character of the new bank in a clear, positive fashion on a timely basis is essential to winning and sustaining their approval and support.

This chapter provides a blueprint for a communications plan covering the process from the announcement to the implementation of a bank merger. It is based on firsthand experience in communicating several bank mergers that began in the second half of 1991: in New York, the merger of Chemical and Manufacturers Hanover to create the new Chemical, an institution with $135 billion in assets; in California, the merger of Bank of America and Security Pacific to create the new Bank of America, an institution with $190 billion in assets; and in Michigan, the merger of Comerica and Manufacturers National to create the new Comerica, an institution with $27 billion in assets. All were mergers of equals; each of them distinctive in its own way. Chemical was the first in-market merger of major money center banks. Bank of America is the largest merger to date. Comerica is a union of two strong and healthy institutions.

Every merger is different. Each has its own set of peculiarities. What follows are some general principles incorporated from the three milestone bank mergers that can be adapted for any merger communications effort. As a rule of thumb, communicating a bank merger falls into three separate phases: premerger planning; merger announcement day; and merger implementation.

Premerger Communications Planning

Maximizing Confidentiality

There are four steps critical to maximizing confidentiality. Each is described below:

1. **As soon as you are notified about the decision to merge, retain outside public relations counsel familiar with the merger process and the banks involved, if possible.** As a stabilizing force in an often chaotic situation, an outside firm can provide several of the following benefits:

♦ An experienced staff of counselors who can provide sound guidelines to follow and anticipate developments throughout the process.

♦ A management team to coordinate all the moving parts of the announcement.

♦ A team of professionals to handle the monumental logistical effort required for the announcement of the merger.

2. **Designate an off-site workplace for the communications team to meet and draft materials during the period prior to the announcement.** Working off-site, away from each bank's headquarters, maximizes confidentiality and provides a neutral territory from which both sides can operate. If possible, the worksite should be fully equipped with word processors, fax machines, phones, etc. In New York, a "war room" was set up at Ogilvy Adams & Rinehart (OA&R); in San Francisco, part of the time was spent in the office of one of the bank's investment bankers and in a hotel conference room; in Detroit, work was operated from a hotel conference room and the office of one of the bank's local public relations firms. All sites were near each bank's headquarters so bank executives could leave their offices and confer without raising too much suspicion from their staff members not involved in the effort.

In New York, the bank executives involved in the merger took "impromptu" vacations and settled in at OA&R for the two weeks leading up to the merger. In Detroit, executives carried on a business-as-usual schedule as much as possible. They showed up at their offices every day but scheduled a lot of meetings outside the office during this period.

3. **Involve staff—both internal and external—in the process on a need-to-know basis only.** The fewer people who know about the transaction before it is announced, the smaller the potential for leaks. Brief employees about the transaction only when their role in the communications process becomes critical. For instance, in Detroit, the graphic designer of the employee newsletter was brought in two days before announcement day to format and produce the announcement in the company's newsletter style.

In New York, the heads of each bank's communications departments brought in their staffs two days before the day of the announcement to draft texts for various customer materials. To further ensure confidentiality, all arrangements with outside vendors (copying, messengers, hotels, audio-visual, and satellite communications) were made by the bank's public relations firm, and all outside vendors were required to sign confidentiality agreements.

4. **Assign code names to each institution and use them to identify the merger parties.** Never, never refer to the merging institutions by their proper names in conversation or in writing at

any time leading up to the announcement. Use the code names assigned by the investment bankers or devise your own. Using real names could compromise confidentiality and could result in leaks that jeopardize the entire effort. In New York, Chemical Bank was "Symphony" and Manufacturers Hanover was "Vanguard"; the merger effort was dubbed "Concert." In Detroit, Comerica was "Curley," Manufacturers National was "Moe," and the project was "MOE" (for "Merger of Equals"). In San Francisco, Bank of America was "Bear" and Security Pacific was "Sunshine"; the merger effort was called "Project Sunshine." While the code names should have some relevance to the players, they should not be obvious to outsiders.

Getting—and Staying—Up to Speed

1. **Coordinate your efforts with the core merger team—each of the bank's senior officers and outside lawyers and investment bankers.** Regular meetings should be scheduled for briefings on the merger process and reviewing communications strategies and draft documents with key players from both sides, including the point people for investor relations, human resources, government relations, and community affairs. They all will have input that will assist preparation of materials.

2. **Develop a 24-hour communications system among all merger transaction players.** Frequent communication is critical. Every member of the merger team—communicators, investment bankers, lawyers, and bank principals—should be "reachable" 24 hours a day. A working group directory should be developed that provides the information necessary to reach each member of the group during and after working hours. Home and weekend phone and fax numbers and addresses should be included. A merger situation is fluid, and team members must be kept apprised of all developments that concern their role on a real-time basis. In fact, on the announcement day of some of the mergers, the situation changed so quickly that each member of the communications team used cellular phones to adapt as needed.

Managing the Process

1. **Identify all key constituent groups to be notified of the merger and develop a coordinated strategy on how to reach each of them.** Before the drafting of communications materials can begin, the team must determine who needs to be reached and when, how, and what news should be communicated to each audience. This process is more complex than it may seem at first, and it requires lead time for careful groundwork and logis-

tical planning to ensure successful implementation. Each audience has subgroups; each subgroup requires different documents and, in some instances, different forums. However, the news is usually communicated through channels that each bank already has in place.

Each bank's internal audience can serve as an example. This group usually comprises senior officers, branch managers, loan officers, data systems executives and employees, and rank-and-file employees at both bank headquarter locations and all other sites, including branches located in- and out-of-state. The announcement press release is the only common document distributed to all of these groups. All other communications materials and vehicles for each group vary considerably. The question-and-answer documents address different issues; the chairmen's letters often use different language and have different tones. Some groups require documents that others do not. Documents that are optional usually include annual reports of the "other bank," fact sheets about the new institution, bios of the new institution's key management, instructions on conveying information to other employee and customer groups, customer notification form letters, and phone scripts. The communications vehicles can range from broadcast satellite to E-mail systems to truck delivery of printed materials to small roundtable discussion meetings to big gatherings. To ensure all constituencies are contacted according to plan, a grid outlining the audiences and documents to be prepared and sent to each group should be prepared and updated throughout the process. Figure 11.1 is a sample documents and projects schedule. Figure 11.2 is a sample of announcement materials.

2. **Create a tracking system to coordinate the myriad facets of the merger announcement process.** There are a number of working parts integral to reaching each audience in a coordinated, timely fashion. These include the following:

♦ production of large quantities of many different documents

♦ logistics for staging three or four meetings in one day, often in different cities (travel arrangements, invitation by phone and fax, meeting site details, audio-visual and satellite broadcast arrangements, on-site management, catering)

♦ logistics for simultaneous delivery of materials (messengers, faxes, trucks) to each audience

♦ videotaping of analyst, press, and employee meetings

Figure 11.1 Confidential Documents and Projects Schedule

Document	Responsibility	Due Date	Submitted	Status
Rollout Schedule				
Themes				
Release				
Fact Sheets:				
Combined Entity				
CRA Commitment				
Ad Copy				
Questions and Answers				
Master				
Employees				
Government/Community Leaders				
Customers				
Retail				
Middle Market				
Corporate/Institutional				
Letters				
Employees				
Retail Customers				
Corporate Clients				
Branch Managers				
Government/Community Leaders				
VIPs				
Announcement Materials Grid				
Bios				
Presentation Remarks				
Analysts				
Media				
Senior Officers				
Presentation Slide Copy				
Invitation Phone Scripts				
Analysts				
Press (Media Alert)				
Senior Officers				
Lists				
Media				
Analysts				
Government/Community				

Figure 11.1   Confidential Documents and Projects Schedule (continued)

Project	Responsibility	Due Date	Status
Ad Outlets Identification			
Ad Reservations			
Ad Placement			
Announcement Materials Production			
Research			
Media Tracking			
Graphics			
Stationary			
Signage			
Labels			
Release Distribution			
Material Assemblage			
Analysts			
Media			
All Employees			
Branches			
Senior Officers			
Government/Community			
VIPs			
Staffing			
Material Production			
Kit Assembly			
Announcement Meetings			
Release/Alert Distribution			
Analyst Invitations			
Media Tracking			
Analyst Meeting Locations			
Press Conference			
Senior Officers Meetings			
E-mail Input			
Interviews with:			
Media			
Analysts			
Government/Community			
Photographer			
Transcription			
Reproduction of Photos of Key Management			
Identify and Prioritize			
Audience Members			
Analyst Meeting			
Press Conference			
Senior Officers			
Meeting I			
Meeting II			
Audiolink			
Satellite Broadcast			
Analyst Meeting			
Senior Officer Meeting			
Travel/Hotel Arrangements			

Figure 11.2 Announcement of Materials

	Employees	Senior Officers	Media	Analysts	Government/Community	Customers	VIPs*
Release	X	X	X	X	X		X
Bios	X	X	X	X	X		X
Combo Fact Sheet	X	X	X	X			X
CRA Commitment Sheet			X				X
Slide Copy				X			
Employee Letter	X	X					
Retail Customer Letter						X	
Corporate Client Letter		X					
Branch Manager Letter	X						
Government/Community Letter					X		
VIP Letter							X
Master Q & A		X					
Employee Q & A	X	X					
Retail Customer Q & A	X						
Government/Community Q & A					X		
Mid-Market Customer Q & A	X						
Corporate/Institutional Customer Q & A		X					
Photos			X				
Analysts Invitation				X			
Seniort Officers Invitation		X					
Media Alert			X				
Annuals			X	X			

♦ invitations to each event

♦ creation of member lists of each audience

♦ arranging press interviews and handling analyst and press calls

♦ developing and executing VIP phone calling programs for each bank's selected executives

♦ drafting and approving of documents

♦ drafting ad copy and arranging media placement for the ad

♦ production of slides for each meeting and drafting copy for them

♦ rehearsing the chairmen for their presentations and interviews

♦ arranging photograph sessions

♦ hiring and working with vendors on a confidential basis

♦ establishing customer and employee phone hotlines

♦ answering requests for information on a real-time basis throughout announcement day and days following the event

Each of these activities requires diligent attention to detail. Careful record keeping is essential. Therefore, for every merger OA&R has been involved in, a set of loose-leaf binders was prepared for each member of the merger communications team in which documents, schedules, grids, and lists are included, divided by tabs into separate sections.

3. **Create a flexible system that can respond to an ever-changing, fast-paced situation.** Every facet of the merger communications process is a moving part, subject to change at a moment's notice. To manage the process, all scheduling of the various components of the merger communications effort should be laid out on a timetable keyed to the expected date of the merger announcement. (However, even the date scheduled for the announcement can change, depending on negotiations, the due diligence process, and even resolution of the members of the new bank's senior management team.) The drafting of materials is a constant, ongoing process that often requires hours of discussion with key merger decisionmakers until final agreement is reached. As a result, all communications team members, particularly the vendors, must be adaptable to fluid schedules and deadlines. They must be on standby, ready to act quickly at a moment's notice once decisions are finalized. In most cases, details are not finalized until the very last hours before the

announcement, and hundreds of thousands of documents must be produced overnight, ready for delivery early the next morning when the merger is announced.

4. **One executive should be appointed project manager to oversee the entire coordination of the communications process.** This position should be held by a third-party member from outside the bank's public relations team. The project manager is responsible for ensuring that the entire announcement effort is implemented successfully. He or she coordinates all logistics, all drafting of documents, and all production as well as keeping all parties informed of pertinent developments. Staff members come under his or her direction to carry out assignments. In effect, the project manager is the point person where all communications team members can get reliable information.

Carrying the Message

1. **Learn the facts and issues immediately and prepare a set of core messages that convey the merger in succinct and positive terms.** These messages should capsulize the essence of the merger and its significance. They should outline the reasoning underlying the merger; characterize the size and rank of the new institution and the significance of this bigger bank; and underscore the benefits of the merger for the constituent groups of both banks. The core messages will be used consistently in communicating with each constituent group. Themes should be developed and approved by all decisionmakers early in the process, with the understanding that they could change as the merger announcement nears.

2. **Draft a set of documents that communicate the merger announcement in terms relevant to the interests and concerns of each of the bank's constituent groups.** In addition to the core messages and the press release announcing the merger, a host of documents needs to be drafted and reviewed for approval. These include a financial fact sheet on the combined entity, a chairman's letter for each bank's employees, the new institution's CRA policy, ad copy, questions and answers for all audiences, bios of the principal members of the new bank's management team, slide copy for each presentation, and invitation phone scripts for the announcement meetings. While all of them should convey the core messages about the merger, they should be tailored to each audience.

3. **Create a merger announcement ad to appear in key print media the day(s) following the announcement.** Once the themes of the merger have been approved, work should begin at once on drafting text for a corporate ad announcing

the merger. Running an ad after announcement day accomplishes several objectives: it ensures the key messages of the merger are accurately conveyed; it fuels the momentum of follow-up media coverage of the merger announcement for several key audiences; and it can serve to counter possible negative coverage which can accompany a merger transaction, usually in follow-up reporting.

4. **Rehearse, rehearse, and rehearse the presentation of senior management on announcement day.** On the eve of the merger announcement, it is imperative that each bank's chairman and other senior management go through a full-dress rehearsal of the presentation of the merger announcement. Senior public relations counsel—both from the bank and the outside firm—should be present to critique the entire presentation, from the delivery of the remarks, to the look of the slides, to the speakers' handling of tough (and easy) questions from the audience. No detail is too small. Nerves are frayed, tempers are uneven, and emotions are intense as announcement day looms. The groundwork has been laid for a successful rollout of the announcement. But without a smooth presentation, all of the hard work could be for naught. The attention of the bank's constituents—reporters, analysts, employees, and community leaders—is focused on the people who intend to lead this new institution. The significance of the new institution relative to their interests and the interaction of the two former competitors are of particular interest to them. The messages and their delivery in this presentation can have a lasting effect on the new institution's relations with its constituencies.

Announcement Day Communications

1. **A merger should be announced on a "good" news day.** The optimal day for announcing a merger is Monday. Since the two days preceding the announcement are not workdays, the likelihood of keeping the news of the merger quiet until it is official is stronger. In addition, with capital markets closed on weekends, each bank's stock prices are less likely to be affected by the rumors and information leaks that could escalate as more and more people are brought into the announcement process. From a media standpoint, an announcement early in the week enables reporters to do follow-up stories and analysis throughout the rest of the week.

2. **Delivering the news.** The news release announcing the merger is distributed to the newswires before the market opens. The stock exchange that the banks trade on is notified of the transaction and faxed a copy of the release. All of the bank's key audiences—analysts and shareholders, the media, employees, community leaders, and other VIPs—need to be informed of the merger on the same day. The sequence in which they are contacted varies according to each merger situation. In some instances, securities analysts are approached first because of the role they play in affecting the stock price of each bank and the quotes they provide reporters in the media coverage of the merger.

In those cases, a press conference is usually held after the analyst meeting, usually in each bank's headquarter city. Joint interviews with key reporters of major business press and local media are arranged around the press conference for both chairmen. Analysts and reporters located in remote sites are linked via two-way audio/video hook up. Keep in mind that the timing of these events is arranged according to what best suits each merger situation. There are no rights or wrongs.

Each bank's internal audiences, if they haven't heard the news on their way to work, should learn about the merger at the start of the work day. Written communications, usually the news release and the chairman's letter, are distributed to employees at all levels. Senior level officers and managers are called to early morning briefing sessions to be given more information and to get instruction on how to convey additional news about the merger to their direct reports and how to answer their questions. Senior officers are addressed by their respective chairman either jointly or separately, depending on the cultures of the institutions. In New York, for example, a joint senior officers meeting was held at the end of announcement day, followed by a celebration party. In Detroit, senior officers meetings were held separately the day after the initial announcement.

Key government and community leaders are usually contacted by phone by the appropriate bank senior executives as soon as the announcement crosses the newswires. In fact, because their official blessing is so key to the bank's future community relations, in several instances the bank chairmen have contacted government officials on the eve of the announcement, requesting confidentiality, to assure them of the new institution's commitment to its communities.

Other priority groups, such as key bank customers, board members, and key shareholders, are notified by the banks' chairmen and other appropriate members of senior management by phone throughout the day. A VIP calling program should be designed so that phone calls can be made easily between meetings throughout the day. The calls are followed by letters signed by appropriate bank executives and sent on the same day.

3. **Develop a rollout schedule covering all the events of announcement day.** By the time announcement day arrives, each and every element of the merger communications process should have been anticipated and addressed. All details ranging from the logistics to the staffing of each initiative have been worked out. The single purpose of this day is to implement all of the events without a hitch. Scheduling can be extremely tight, especially if the announcement events necessitate traveling to different cities. Each professional responsible for some part of the announcement process should have in hand a master schedule outlining a minute-by-minute unfolding of the day's events. Contained in this two- to three-page document is a listing of all the key activities—from the signing of the merger agreement to an evaluation of events by the merger communications team at the day's end. This document clarifies the roles and interaction of all participants within the context of the rhythm and flow of the day's initiatives.

Merger Implementation Communications

After the euphoria and excitement of the merger announcement, the "real work" begins. The transition period in which the two banks become one is often arduous, marked by communications challenges on every front. These challenges must be addressed directly with strong, positive messages communicated quickly to all bank constituents.

While it is nearly impossible to generalize about merger communications, there are two basic communications goals in every merger implementation. Near term, it is essential to convey merger-related developments to all key audiences quickly, clearly, fully, and in a context relevant to each group's concerns and interest. Long term, it is necessary to establish and communicate a strong corporate positioning for the new institution based on a mission statement that resonates with each of the key audiences.

Initiatives to be undertaken during this transition period to become a fully integrated institution comprise a broad spectrum of communications activities. The following is a brief outline of some of the program elements aimed at each audience during this critical period.

1. **Develop a schedule of merger activities, emphasizing milestone events, and communications initiatives to support them.** Similar to the

announcement, merger activities require communications support and logistical planning in nearly every sector of the bank's operations. At the corporate level, they include special shareholder meetings to approve the merger and the proxy statements mailed to shareholders prior to those meetings, regulatory approval of the merger by federal and state bodies, announcements of the mergers of the holding companies and the lead banks, and possibly an equity offering and a roadshow presentation. In the retail sector, they include announcement of branch consolidations, notification of changes in products, pricing, and services, and possibly accommodation banking. In the human resources arena, they can include the announcement of an early retirement plan and senior level management appointments as well as changes in employee benefits.

Any merger announcement that provides a cause for celebration—such as the merger of the corporate entities or the lead banks—can be the occasion for a special event that involves all appropriate bank constituencies, especially employees.

2. **Survey each of the bank's constituents to learn their reactions to the merger and the new institution and, based on the findings, develop fresh messages about the new bank, tailored for each group.** Research is key to defining the issues that the bank needs to address for each audience. Key members of each group should be surveyed periodically throughout the merger process to stay informed on any changes in views and attitudes.

In the case of the new Chemical Bank, a major concern in the investment community was management's ability to meet the cost-cutting targets laid out in the initial announcement of the transaction. This concern was specifically addressed, first in a securities analyst meeting and then in a roadshow presentation for the equity offering six months after the merger was announced. As a result, analyst and shareholder concerns were alleviated. Their change in attitude was reflected in positive media coverage and a very successful equity offering—the largest of any U.S. financial institution. Concurrently, the rating agencies raised the bank's debt ratings.

3. **Create a strong identity for the new bank.** It is imperative to position the new bank effectively to each of its audiences from the outset. Determining that identity is a task that merits participation of senior management in a way that brings concentrated involvement on their part with minimal demands on their time. Once the identity is crafted and approved by senior management, it should be communicated through the following vehicles:

♦ A corporate mission statement that embodies the corporation's culture and philosophies, announces its priorities in the marketplace, and captures its goals and strategies in one clear, concise description.

♦ A corporate advertising campaign developing each of the concepts in the mission statement. If possible, the bank's new identity should be unveiled with the launch of its corporate advertising campaign and coordinated public relations activities on the day of the official merger of the corporate entities.

♦ A corporate public relations campaign based on a set of corporate messages derived from the mission statement and incorporated in all media materials.

♦ A corporate brochure portraying the new bank, beginning with the mission statement and providing a detailed outline of the management structure of the new institution.

4. Step up investor relations activities during this period. The interest of the investment community in the new entity will undoubtedly heighten at this time. Given the increased size of the institution, analyst coverage could rise significantly. A regular schedule of meetings with securities analysts, portfolio managers, and key shareholders should be developed, supplemented by frequent phone updates on pertinent developments at the bank. This effort is particularly important in the event the bank is considering raising new capital. Once the merger of the corporate entities has been completed, consideration should be given to publishing a financial fact book that outlines all pertinent financial data on the new bank in detail for analysts and money managers.

5. Provide customers with a steady flow of information about the merger process and the new bank through a range of standard and innovative communications channels. Customer attrition is a strong possibility during this transition period. While corporate customers may recognize the benefits of a stronger bank, retail customers have a tendency to mistrust the "bigger is better" theory. They can perceive the new bank as a monolithic institution that intends to raise prices, cut services, and lay off the bank employees who know their accounts. Customer communications should be geared to allaying these fears and emphasizing the benefits customers will gain through the merger. Some communications initiatives to consider include the following:

♦ A direct mail campaign in which a steady flow of information is directed to each custome group, keyed to specific merger events and developments, particularly those that affect a customer's day-to-day banking, such as service and pricing issues. In all direct mai materials, the merger messages developed fo customers should be sounded again and again.

♦ Interesting, low-cost videos in which top management addresses customer issues and concerns directly, in which customer mes sages are powerfully conveyed. The video would be played in branch locations and other public areas throughout the bank. They could also be sent to key customers as well a to members of other bank audiences.

6. Reassure and motivate employees with constant progress reports on the merger and affirmative news about their new employer Fear of job loss and domination by the "other" bank as well as a host of other uncertainties about the future can contribute to low morale among employee groups at all levels. Much of this can be alleviated through effective communications that address employee concerns upfront. Some initiatives to consider include interactive communications using media, and establishing a new employee news letter.

Interactive Communications. Communication between different levels of employees and between the staffs of each bank should be frequent to encour age open dialogue at both banks. This can be accomplished by scheduling regular senior office meetings, after which senior officers report back to their staffs and the news cascades down through the organization. Another technique is establishing an Employee Communications Council comprising a representative from each bank department to discuss merger developments and the concerns of their peers.

Media. Augment existing internal communications systems by producing videos adapted from customer videos on merger topics for use in interna meetings; and by ensuring all bank departments are linked to an E-mail system for real-time delivery o information; and by using teleconferences to reach key audiences expeditiously. Important merger news should also be conveyed by hotline phone services.

Newsletter. Develop a new bank employee publication to convey the spirit of the new institution. The newsletter can serve as a platform for answering tough employee questions, running controversia letters to the editor, and keeping employees up to date on positive merger news by highlighting custo-mer success stories and examples of excellent em-ployee performance. The inaugural issue, distributed on the first day of the corporate merger, should include an outline of the structure of the new bank, articles describing each department, a welcome let-ter from the new top officers, and an editorial ex-plaining what the new newsletter is designed to communicate.

7. **Determine the full spectrum of the new bank's community relations program and make it public as soon as possible.** Community groups will be anxious to discuss the bank's plans for com-munity support. Appropriate bank representatives should resolve the variety of community action pro-grams appropriate for the new bank's sponsorship and participation. The criteria for these programs include: answering a real community need, using the bank's expertise when possible, and heightening the bank's visibility. The initiative should also support the bank's mission statement. Establishing commu-nity initiatives that position the new institution as an involved corporate entity responsive to the needs of the communities and neighborhoods it serves would be extremely beneficial to the new bank.

Conclusion

A merger is one of the more dramatic events that an institution will ever experience in the course of its corporate life. Well-coordinated, thoughtful, and ef-fective communications can play a major role in achieving the merger's objectives.

The blueprint outlined in this chapter provides an overview of the kinds of challenges a communi-cations team will face during the process and sug-gests some responses to those challenges that have proved effective in past mergers.

Part VII:
Trends in Investment Banking Services

Chapter 12

Merchant Banking in the 1990s

Richard Y. Smith
Managing Director, Banking and Corporate Finance Group
Chemical Bank, New York, NY

"Merchant Banking" is a somewhat vague term that came into popular use in the United States in the 1980s but seems to be almost forgotten in the 1990s. In the public perception, merchant banking activity is somehow linked to leveraged buyouts (LBOs) and management buyouts (MBOs), and everyone knows these transactions are now out of style. This chapter attempts to clarify what is meant by the term "merchant banking"; argues that merchant banking is alive and well in the 1990s; suggests that, among other changes from the 1980s, merchant banking firms will work more closely with corporate partners in this decade, and, finally, briefly reviews the merchant banking process including the principal financial and other characteristics of 1990s-style merchant banking transactions.

What Is Merchant Banking?

The term "merchant banking" originated in the 19th century to describe European banking groups or families such as the Barings or Rothschilds who pioneered various aspects of trade finance and foreign exchange for the rapidly emerging industrial concerns of the era. The vagueness of the term is not new since 19th century "merchant [bankers] moved in and out of commissions banking, issues, foreign exchange, arbitrage, insurance, and other related activities according to changing circumstances and the dispositions of the senior partners."[1] Credit exposure, underwriting, and agency services were an integral part of most of these activities, and the survival of these firms frequently depended on the financial health of the industries in which a given merchant banking firm specialized. Today, London's

"merchant bankers," several bearing the names of 19th-century forebears, are largely engaged in activities that would be called investment banking in the United States, although several have the appropriate licenses to make loans and collect deposits.

In the United States, both state and federal laws including the Glass-Steagall Act enforced a sharp separation between institutions collecting deposits and making loans and institutions or entities permitted to own equity interests or offer underwriting services to their clients. For legal and other reasons, the U. S. financial services industry grew up with distinct groups of financial firms extending credit, making equity investments, and performing underwriting or similar agency services. Commercial banks fulfilled the deposit gathering and senior debt roles; investment banks fulfilled the underwriting and advisory roles; and individuals and institutional investors such as insurance companies, pension fund managers, mutual fund managers, and others made most of the equity investment decisions. During the past decade, some firms have begun to recombine several of these capabilities in certain transactions, thus bringing "merchant banking" to the United States.

A form of merchant banking emerged in this country in the early 1970s when certain investment and investment banking firms, Laird & Co., for example, began assembling financial groups to acquire established manufacturers—usually small, privately held companies or subsidiaries of larger companies. These investment groups often installed new management teams comprised of executives with proven track records at large public companies. The executives were willing to trade size and current income for meaningful equity stakes in the companies they

129

managed. Acquisitions were financed with debt from banks and with equity from deep family pockets and a few pools of privately managed capital. The investment banks leading these deals would sign a letter of intent with a seller, subject to financing and other conditions, and would then take several months to arrange the required financing, frequently providing some of the equity capital themselves from firm or partner pockets. Some of these deals, including Bairnco Corp. and Lydall, Inc., survive and prosper today.

As the 1970s turned into the 1980s, this concept grew. Pension funds, insurance companies, and other financial institutions entrusted a portion of their assets to funds managed by partnerships such as Kohlberg Kravis Roberts and Company. These partnerships sought out underdeveloped or underperforming situations that, with the help of substantial financial leverage and new or refocused management, could provide substantial equity returns. The acquisition process and financing requirements for these "LBO" transactions, however, were meaningfully different from those of the Laird-type deals. These transactions were substantially larger— $100-$200 million being a minimum size, frequently involved public companies, were often initiated through a high pressure auction process (public or private), and increasingly required *committed* capital even to get into the auction. Spotting a golden opportunity, investment banks and some commercial banks rushed to work with LBO firms and management groups both as acquisition advisors and as arrangers of financing to supplement the equity capital provided by LBO funds. Initially, the investment banking firms attempted to maintain their role as agents or intermediaries. The best example of this effort was Drexel Burnham Lambert's "Highly Confident" letters which effectively risked none of Drexel's capital. For a fee, Drexel (and other investment banking firms) simply said in writing that the firm was "highly confident" that the necessary financing for a transaction could be arranged. Drexel's financing track record in the mid-80's was good enough that its "highly confident" letters were, for a time, considered by sellers to be *almost* as good as committed capital.

The combined advisory and financing fees available to investment banking firms in these transactions were substantial, sometimes reaching 2-4% or more of the total value of the transaction—compared with 1% or less for purely advisory services—and competition among intermediaries to obtain these assignments was intense. Since, *committed* capital is, by definition, better than *almost committed* capital, a number of investment banks either raised their own equity and subordinated debt funds for investment

and/or began to invest firm capital in these transactions. Similarly, as commercial banks expanded into investment banking, they also became active as providers of senior debt, subordinated or bridge debt, and equity as well as advisory services.

One example of 1980s-style merchant banking was Merrill Lynch's role in the 1988 acquisition of Insilco. Insilco Corporation was a New York Stock Exchange listed company with revenues of almost $640 million from a broad range of products for the electronics/communications, metal parts, paint, and publishing/office products markets. On August 4, 1988, Insilco announced that it had signed a definitive merger agreement with a newly organized holding company formed by affiliates of First Boston Corporation and certain members of Insilco's senior management. Under this agreement, Insilco shares would be acquired for $29 per share in cash for a total transaction value of about $900 million. On the day of Insilco's public announcement, Merrill Lynch contacted Wagner & Brown, a Texas-based investment company, regarding its interest in making a competing bid for Insilco. Less than three weeks later, on August 24, 1988, a corporation newly formed by Messrs. Wagner and Brown proposed a fully financed acquisition of Insilco for $31.75 per share. Their proposal was accepted by Insilco's Board, a merger agreement with Wagner and Brown's holding company was signed, and the holding company commenced a tender offer on August 31, 1988.

To initiate, research, negotiate, finance, and document a $1 billion acquisition in 27 days, including the commencement of a tender offer, could only have been accomplished with Merrill's merchant banking capability. To finance the transaction, including the refinancing of certain existing Insilco debt, the purchaser estimated it would require $1.009 billion, of which about $880 million (including expenses) was required to complete the cash tender offer. Merrill Lynch delivered a commitment letter to Wagner & Brown on August 24 under which Merrill Lynch agreed to provide up to $780 million of debt financing, effectively providing a bridge loan for *both* the senior and subordinated debt portions of the acquiror's capital structure.

In return, Merrill received a 1% commitment fee for its $780 million bridge loan and a 1% fee for any amounts actually funded under the bridge loan. Merrill also 1) acted as financial advisor to the holding company for the acquisition of Insilco for an upfront fee of $1.5 million and a contingent fee of $5.5 million; 2) committed to underwrite the high-yield debt expected to take out its bridge loan for underwriting fees of 3-4%; 3) committed to underwrite a $50 million public equity offering for the purchaser; and 4) retained rights of first refusal on any investment banking services required by the purchaser for a two-year period. From the Insilco purchase alone, Merrill could have earned over $25 million of advisory and financing fees or about 2.5% of the total value of the transaction. For Wagner & Brown, however, Merrill's ability to initiate the acquisition, advise Wagner & Brown during the negotiations, and commit senior and subordinated bridge financing to complete the transaction on an extremely tight timetable represented value-added available from only a limited number of integrated merchant banking firms.

Although there are exceptions, acting as both principal and agent in a single transaction is a generally accepted definition of merchant banking in the United States. The "agent" half of the merchant banking equation can take many forms including: 1) acquisition advisory services on behalf of the acquiror as in the Merrill Lynch/Wagner & Brown/Insilco transaction; 2) divestiture advisory services on behalf of the seller; 3) agency services to arrange debt or equity for the transaction; or 4) other functions not requiring the commitment of firm capital. In some cases, particularly with LBO fund managers, the advisory role may be a *de facto* one in which the LBO firm effectively assumes responsibility for putting a transaction together and receives a contingent fee from the newly formed company for its efforts.

The "principal" half of merchant banking involves the commitment of capital, from either the firm itself or the funds under its management as a fiduciary. Whether the capital commitment is intended to be temporary, as in bridge financing, or permanent, as in purchasing a portion of the equity securities in the transaction, is irrelevant. In either case, the institution puts its own capital at risk to help complete a transaction in which it will earn significant agency compensation only if the transaction closes.

Is the Merchant Banking Party Over?

According to *Mergers & Acquisitions*, the dollar value of LBOs/MBOs in the United States dropped from $67 billion in 1989 to $5.5 billion in 1991. The sudden decline of large, highly leveraged transactions in this country, however, did not mark the end of the trend toward merchant banking, although it did reveal some of the pitfalls. (Insilco, for example, was one of several late 1980s LBOs that have filed for protection under Chapter 11 of the bankruptcy code.) The fundamental logic of combining the ability

to act as both principal and agent to help complete a client's transaction is still very valid.

In fact, *Buyouts* magazine estimates that about $4 billion of new funds were committed to merchant banking or similar firms during 1991 including $1.5 billion each to Kohlberg Kravis Roberts and Forstmann Little. During the first six months of 1992, *Buyouts* reports that another $2.6 billion was committed to about 13 managers, including $1 billion to Goldman Sach's GS Capital Partners, L.P. In addition to these new flows, *The Wall Street Journal* estimated that at least $10 billion of uninvested subordinated debt and equity capital remained under the management of merchant banking firms in the United States at the end of the 1980s. While only a part of these funds will be used in transactions involving both principal and agency roles for a single firm, capital for merchant banking activities in the 1990s is clearly available.

Who Are the 1990s Merchant Bankers?

Today, firms offering merchant banking capabilities fall into three categories: investment banks, commercial banks, and LBO funds.

Investment Banks. Although less active as bridge lenders than in the 1980s, several large investment banking firms have set aside or manage funds that can be temporarily or permanently invested in transactions where the firm is providing other services as well. Donaldson, Lufkin & Jenrette manages a substantial pool of its own funds and funds provided by others for investment in merchant banking transactions, including $500 million recently committed to its DLJ Merchant Banking Partners, L.P. fund. Morgan Stanley was an early entrant into the field, initially investing its own funds, which were then supplemented by Morgan Stanley Leveraged Equity Fund I and II. These two merchant banking funds were raised from institutional investors including banks, pension funds, insurance companies, and others.

Shearson Lehman Brothers, Inc. makes mezzanine and equity investments with its own funds and with the funds of four merchant banking partnerships under its management. Merrill Lynch has made equity and mezzanine investments through two entities: Merrill Lynch Capital Partners, which tends to do larger deals, and Merrill Lynch Interfunding, which has typically provided mezzanine and equity financing for smaller transactions. As previously noted, Goldman Sachs recently raised $1 billion for its GS Capital Partners fund. Dillon Read's Saratoga Partners I and II and Lazard Freres & Company's

Corporate Partners fund are also examples of merchant banking funds affiliated with major investment banks. Depending on the firm, these funds may be invested in situations where the investment bank is acting in fee-paying advisory roles. They may also be invested in situations that have no other connection with the investment bank.

Commercial Banks. As commercial banks and investment banks offer increasingly similar services, some commercial banks have established merchant banking capabilities. Theoretically, commercial banks' ability to provide senior debt coupled with their affiliated venture capital or merchant banking arms could make them powerhouses among merchant bankers. Several large commercial banks have established successful investment banking advisory capabilities that enable them to compete with the investment banks for acquisition, divestiture, restructuring, or other forms of advice. Examples include Chemical Banking Corp. which also manages about $750 million of funds designated for equity or subordinated debt investments. Citicorp, Banker's Trust, Bank of Boston, and Bank of America all have active principal investing capabilities.

The equity investing activities of most commercial banks are governed by Federal Reserve regulations that limit the percentage of voting securities and total capital these institutions can own in a nonbanking company. In response, most of these institutions have developed working relationships with a broad range of equity and mezzanine debt providers that permit them to quickly syndicate and commit financing. Commercial banks may invest mezzanine and equity funds in transactions organized by their investment banking arms, in transactions where the bank is leading the senior debt syndication effort, or in situations where the bank is playing no other role.

LBO Funds. The 1992 edition of the *Directory of Buyout Financing Sources* lists approximately 400 firms managing mezzanine and equity funds designated for LBO/MBO transactions. The partners of most LBO management firms are active investors who not only make investment decisions but also actively seek transactions, design acceptable capital structures, and arrange for any portion of the senior debt, mezzanine, and/or equity financing not provided from funds under their management. For such services, some firms charge a "transaction fee" that is effectively paid out of the financing arranged for the LBO transaction. These groups are specialists, and their firms typically do not provide advisory or other services to unaffiliated clients.

Merchant Banking Transaction Trends

While the industry is alive and well funded, merchant banking in the 1990s may be more like that of the 1970s than that of the late 1980s. Specifically, transactions will be smaller, less leveraged, and completed in a longer timeframe. A new trend in the 1990s will be the increasing use of merchant banking firms and techniques by U.S. corporations to help achieve corporate accounting, tax, financial, or risk goals. Such opportunities may arise, for example, in the course of corporate divestitures where the seller has decided it can obtain maximum value by spinning off a subsidiary to its management, perhaps retaining a partial ownership interest. While many of the 1980s merchant banking deals involved independent, publicly traded companies, *Buyouts* reports that over 60% of the LBO/MBO transactions in 1991 and the first six months of 1992 have involved corporate divestitures. Similarly, a corporate acquisition may only make sense if a transaction can be developed that does not result in complete financial consolidation of the target with the acquiror. Limiting the amount of debt or goodwill on corporate balance sheets; providing unique incentive arrangements for management; raising additional equity for a new acquisition without directly diluting a corporation's existing equity base; and entering into joint ventures with other corporate entities are all valid corporate reasons for using an acquisition or divestiture structure that includes a financial partner.

One example of corporate partner/merchant banker cooperation is The Blackstone Group's 1991 purchase of 35% of Six Flags, Inc., an amusement park operator, in partnership with Time Warner, Inc. Time Warner owned 20% of Six Flags, which had been taken private in a 1987 LBO led by Wesray. Six Flags did not perform at forecast levels and, by 1991, needed additional equity. Wesray was, by then, out of the equity investing business. Time Warner, although probably capable of providing the $130 million of new equity needed, had recently completed a rights offering to deleverage its balance sheet. Blackstone developed a structure that would keep Six Flags' $500 million of debt off Time Warner's balance sheet and minimize Time Warner's investment while permitting the giant media company to put into place its development plans for the amusement park company.

Similarly, in the fall of 1991, Cablevision Systems Corp., a large and highly leveraged cable TV firm, wished to acquire the Newark cable TV properties of Gilbert Media. Cablevision called on Warburg, Pincus, a leading U. S. merchant banking firm which was also a major participant in the refinancing of another Cablevision subsidiary, to acquire 75% of the equity of the acquisition vehicle. Cablevision thus avoided consolidation of the $60 million of new debt used to fund the acquisition with Cablevision's already substantial and carefully structured existing debt.

For different reasons, New Line Cinema, a publicly traded independent film producer and distributor (*Teenage Mutant Ninja Turtles*, among others), purchased a 50% stake in RHI Entertainment, Inc., a highly regarded producer of high-quality made-for-television movies, to help finance RHI's acquisition of a library of TV films. In this situation, Chemical Bank's merchant banking group arranged a transaction in which Chemical made an equity investment and sought out New Line as an equity partner. This structure met the needs of RHI's founders who wished to make a substantial acquisition while retaining their autonomy; of New Line which was able to enter an attractive business with top quality producers who could not be "acquired"; and of Chemical which gained, in New Line, a very knowledgeable industry partner.

During the past few years, there have been many other examples of partnerships that permit each partner to achieve complementary goals. As corporate CFOs become more comfortable with merchant banking techniques and capital structures, they will more actively utilize the principal investing capabilities of large financial services firms as well as their advisory, underwriting, lending, and other more traditional functions.

Structuring a Merchant Banking Transaction—Engagement

As bankers work more closely with corporate clients in merchant banking roles, the inherent conflicts of interest that arise in these transactions must be addressed. Given the multiple roles an institution plays as a merchant banker, the structure of the merchant banking engagement and the procedural choices involved in carrying out the assignment must be carefully developed. Conflicts will arise not only between the banking firm and its advisory client but also within the corporation and within the banking institution. For example, a long-time client of a commercial or investment bank may ask the bank to advise it regarding the sale of a subsidiary. It may also ask the bank to determine, as part of its assignment, the feasibility of a divestiture transaction in which the

subsidiary's management will acquire the subsidiary with financial backing arranged or provided by the banking firm. A request of this nature would raise most of the conflicts inherent in merchant banking transactions:

Merchant Banker versus Client. The banking firm is effectively advising the seller regarding a transaction in which it might be a principal on the other side of the transaction.

Parent versus Subsidiary. The subsidiary management's cooperation and judgment is often critical to a purchaser's perception of the subsidiary's possible future success and, therefore, to its present value. Yet, this management may also be part of a prospective acquiror group. Expecting completely independent judgments from this group regarding the subsidiary's future presumes a level of saintliness that may not be obtainable by mere mortals.

Merchant Banker versus Subsidiary Management. The merchant banker, acting as a provider of debt and/or equity, would like to provide financing for the transaction on terms acceptable or favorable to it. Where one merchant banking firm has an exclusive right to arrange the buyout transaction, it may be difficult for the subsidiary's management to "shop" for better financing or equity participation terms elsewhere.

Merchant Banker versus Itself. The banking firm will incur internal conflicts among 1) those groups responsible for advising the parent or maintaining a strong, long-term relationship with the parent who would like to see the highest possible sale price for the subsidiary; 2) those groups providing advice or financing services, who are only paid if a transaction is completed; and 3) those groups who are responsible for making creditworthy loans or sound equity investments in merchant banking transactions, who wish to pay the lowest possible purchase price.

None of these issues automatically prevents completion of a sound transaction, profitable for all parties. However, the engagement of the banking firm and the execution of the project should be structured to ensure, as far as is practicable, that all phases of the transaction will have direct or indirect market input. For example, the above transaction could proceed in the following manner:

♦ The corporation hires the banking firm's Mergers and Acquisitions Group to advise it regarding the possible sale of Subsidiary X. This group should be able to estimate the approximate purchase price financial buyers and strategic buyers could offer. If the divestiture is either time-critical or disclosure-sensitive to the seller and if the estimated purchase price range is acceptable, the seller may elect to authorize the banking firm to contact the banking firm's affiliated principal investing group to seek a formal offer. Alternatively, the banking firm can be instructed to pursue the broader marketing program outlined below.

♦ The banking firm prepares an information memorandum describing Subsidiary X and contacts all logical strategic and financial buyers. Prospective buyers may include the bank's own principal investing group if fully disclosed to and approved by the seller. So-called "Chinese Walls" at the banking firm should be erected to ensure that the same information flows to all prospective bidders.

♦ Subsidiary X's management is expressly prohibited from committing to or working exclusively with any prospective purchaser.

♦ The corporation requires all buyers to disclose and negotiate all aspects of their offers, including management equity or compensation packages, only with the parent or its advisors.

♦ Should the banking firm's principal investment group become one of the final bidders, an open auction format can be adopted to rule out charges of favoritism from losing bidders.

This procedure ensures 1) that the banking firm's principal responsibility is to the seller; 2) that independent third parties will help determine a "fair market value"; 3) that management is treated fairly and that its conflicts are minimized; and 4) that the seller receives the highest possible price.

Transactions in which a corporate client has asked a banker to both advise it regarding an acquisition and invest in the acquisition as a financial partner present fewer conflicts. In these situations, the bank's responsibility both as M&A advisor and as investor is to negotiate the lowest possible purchase price for the acquisition. Once an acceptable price is negotiated, the primary conflict will be the economic and other terms on which the corporate and financial partners will make their investment. To help ensure fair economic terms, third party "market" feedback, once again, is helpful. Although the banking firm may insist on an exclusive M&A advisory role, the corporate partner should be free to seek debt and/or equity financing for the joint venture from any source. Alternatively, the banking firm, as part of its advisory assignment, can be asked to solicit financing proposals from unaffiliated funders as well as from its own inhouse financing sources. As part of this negotiation, the parties will need to agree on the economic value of any indirect benefits, such as

off-balance-sheet accounting treatment, that will accrue to the corporate partner.

Other terms of a corporate partner/financial partner joint venture will include provisions for management ownership and compensation, corporate governance, return of capital, sale of stock or assets, and the rights and duties of the partners if the venture encounters financial difficulty. As discussed in the following section, the relative rights of the partners do not have to be directly proportional to their economic interests.

Structuring a Merchant Banking Transaction—Non-Financial Issues

For corporate CFOs and operating managements, one of the greatest attractions of merchant banking transactions is the structuring flexibility available from providers of private equity. A merchant banker's primary concerns are its rate of return on investment and its ability to realize that rate of return in a three- to seven-year timeframe through contractual "exit" provisions. While private equity investors may be active in the board level management of a company, their fundamental corporate governance concern is their ability to take definitive action, such as replacing management or selling part or all of the company, if they believe the value of their investment is or may become impaired.

On the other hand, a corporate partner 1) is frequently very interested in controlling day-to-day management; 2) has a longer investment horizon; 3) usually plans to eventually be the 100% owner of a joint venture transaction; and 4) while concerned about return on investment, may realize financial and other benefits—accounting, tax, or credit ratings, for example—at the corporate level that do not flow directly through the joint venture's financial statements.

A third party in most merchant banking or joint venture deals is operating management, which is concerned about its autonomy, its financial reward for assuming the very heavy burden of successfully operating a leveraged company, and the time horizon within which it must demonstrate results.

To address these issues, a very useful part of many merchant banking deals is a Shareholders' Agreement among the equity holders, including management. This agreement specifies the relative rights of the various parties for a defined period of time and under a defined set of circumstances. These provisions can ignore the actual equity ownership of a company in order to accomplish other goals. For example, a board made up of an equal number of directors nominated by the corporate partner and operating management plus one nominee by the financial partner can provide board-level input for all parties and avoid "control" for GAAP or other purposes of the dominant equity holder. Shareholders' Agreements may also provide for supermajority voting to approve major corporate events such as asset sales, liquidations or dividends to protect minority holders. Coupled with management contracts, these agreements can formalize management's performance goals, performance horizons, and financial rewards. The agreements can automatically terminate in certain events such as initial public offerings, sale of one partner's shares, material shortfalls from forecast cash flows, and/or material defaults under debt or other agreements.

Shareholders' Agreements can also be useful to ensure the ultimate ownership structure of the venture and assure the financial investor of an "exit" from its investment within its investment horizon. Such provisions may include rights to require the joint venture company to register its shares for a public offering, put and call options among the corporate partner, the financial partner and the joint venture company, and rights of first refusal on proposed stock sales to insure orderly changes in the joint ventures ownership structure.

These are only a few examples of the many ways Shareholders' Agreements or other nonfinancial structuring techniques can be used to meet the differing needs and concerns of various equity investors, including accounting, tax and other needs of corporate partners, in ways that may not directly reflect the ownership percentage of each group.

Structuring a Merchant Banking Transaction—Financial Issues

A major advantage offered by firms with merchant banking capabilities is their ability to quickly commit most or all of the necessary funding to complete a transaction. Some merchant banking firms will provide 100% of the permanent financing for a transaction. Others will provide initial financing or financing commitments that permit the transaction to be completed; then they will arrange the subsequent public or private distribution of a substantial portion of their commitment. These firms may begin to syndicate the permanent financing after providing a commitment, but prior to the closing of a transaction.

Clearly, the type and availability of funds available for merchant banking transactions today is quite different from what was available in the late 1980s.

Nevertheless, the same fundamental capital structuring rules still apply. Equity funds continue to be the most expensive, so designers of capital structures still start by determining the amount of debt—senior, subordinated or "creative"—a transaction can support. A brief review of the principal sources, types, current availability, and current (mid-1992) cost of debt and equity financing for merchant banking or LBO/MBO transactions follows.

Senior Debt

Still largely the domain of commercial banks, senior debt for merchant banking transactions is available, but the necessary credit quality and upfront cost is substantially higher than a few years ago. Transactions in mid-1992 must have a ratio of operating cash flow less "normal" capital expenditures to total interest of approximately 2:1 based on historical results, compared with ratios of 1.25:1 or less based on projected earnings that prevailed in the 1980s. Senior lenders for merchant banking-type transactions may require up to a 4% upfront fee which will be paid to other banks in the syndicate group and to the agent bank as an arranging fee. Two percent was the 1980s norm. Interest rates are still typically 1.25%-1.75% over prime, but prime has declined from a peak of 11.5% in February 1989 to 6% in September 1992. Since the late 1980s, many commercial banks, as a matter of policy, syndicate all but 5% or 10% of the principal amount of any loan they underwrite. As a result, the market for senior debt for leveraged transactions has become much more uniform in terms of credit quality and pricing, and knowledgeable financial structuring advice has become crucial. Although the "HLT" or Highly Leveraged Transaction designation (for certain borrowers with Total Liabilities equal to 75% or more of Total Assets) has been phased out for Federal Reserve reporting purposes, banks must still report their "HLT" levels in SEC filings and publicly disseminated financial reports. This regulation will undoubtedly restrict the availability of such financing and make it more expensive in the foreseeable future.

Other providers of senior debt include finance companies such as Congress Financial and Heller Finance, General Electric Capital Corp., and a few insurance companies, such as Teachers' Insurance and Massachusetts Mutual. Finally, at least two LBO fund managers have raised senior debt funds from institutional investors to complement their mezzanine and equity funds.

Subordinated Debt

In the late 1970s and early 1980s, the primary providers of subordinated debt, with and without equity "kickers," were the major insurance companies. As the LBO boom got rolling, more participants, including the investing public entered the market, and many of the insurance companies stopped making loans for what they (accurately) felt were inadequate reward/risk ratios. To partially fill the gap, the major investment banks, making their initial efforts as merchant bankers, provided "bridge" loans to buyout groups and others that were intended to be refinanced with public offerings of subordinated debt within a month or two of the initial closing. In the fall of 1989, the public market for subordinated debt abruptly dried up as well, effectively halting the LBO boom of the preceding decade.

In mid-1992, permanent subordinated debt remains in short supply, and, as a result, bridge financing is also limited. Interestingly, the public market for high-yield debt has revived somewhat. According to *Investment Dealers' Digest* about $18.6 billion of new "junk" debt was issued during the first half of 1992 (compared with $2.6 billion in the first half of 1991)—much of it to refinance old bridge loans or restructured loans generated in the late 1980s. The private markets for subordinated debt are also reviving, but the insurance companies are generally still out of the market. To fill the gap, there has been a surge in the number of fund management firms (including insurance companies) in the market seeking money for mezzanine funds—about $1.4 billion at the end of 1992's first quarter according to *Buyouts*.

The all-in cost (including equity kickers) of subordinated debt has not changed greatly in absolute terms. It is still in the late teens and low 20% range, although the spread over the yield on "riskless" U.S. Treasury securities of comparable maturities has widened considerably. Some of the major LBO firms, Forstmann Little for example, have raised subordinated debt funds along with their equity funds and have been less affected by the shortage of subordinated debt.

Merchant bankers and others have also turned to creative methods to obtain this crucial slice of the capital structure. Seller financing has become popular again as divesting corporations effectively decide to complete transactions at prices below targets while retaining an ongoing financial interest. Similarly, some of the merchant banking deals involving companies in Chapter 11 reorganizations have retained subordinated debt in the capital structure by including new subordinated debt securities as part of the reorganization package offered to holders of the bankrupt company's pre-petition senior and subordinated debt.

Equity

Equity for merchant banking transactions is, comparatively, the financing commodity in greatest supply. As previously noted, an estimated $10 billion of uninvested capital remained under management of merchant banking or similar firms in the United States at the end of the 1980s, and several groups are currently raising additional funds. Furthermore, the availability of the market for initial public offerings in early 1992 has helped return some of the investment equity locked up in 1980s transactions to fund managers for reinvestment. Today, however, most transactions require 30-40% of the capital structure to be in the form of equity, compared with 15-25% a few years ago. Hurdle rates of return for equity investments have declined from the 30-40% range to the 25-35% range. Part of this reduction reflects the inherently lower risk that accompanies today's less leveraged capital structures, but some of the reduction in hurdle rates also reflects a surplus of equity seeking high quality transactions that can be leveraged with the comparatively limited supplies of senior and subordinated debt.

Conclusion

In the 1990s, merchant banking will continue to be an important part of the financial landscape. Although applied differently by various investors/managers of merchant banking funds, merchant banking firms represent transaction expertise backed by substantial principal investing capabilities. Properly structured and executed, joint merchant banking transactions can benefit both corporate and financial investors, and merchant banking techniques are likely to play a larger role in the corporate finance activities of major U.S companies during this decade.

Endnotes

1. Chapman, Stanley. The Rise of Merchant Banking. London, England: George Allen and Unwin Publishers Ltd., 1984: 57.

Chapter 13

Financial Restructuring

Ronald G. Quintero
Principal
R. G. Quintero & Co., New York, NY

The creative financings and multitiered capital structures of the 1980s have planted the seeds for the bumper crop of financial restructurings of the 1990s. As architects of many of the capital structures-gone-awry, investment bankers are logical choices for redesigning companies' balance sheets to make them suitable for the economic conditions and the state of the capital markets that will prevail during the 1990s. This chapter describes the key activities of investment bankers as catalysts for reengineering the balance sheets of companies that have gone astray.

Background

A leading cause of financial distress is an inability to adapt to change. The environment in which a company operates changes, yet the company is unable to adapt to the change. Many companies were lured by corporate America's love affair with debt during the 1980s. But circumstances changed: 1) capital that fueled the junk bond financings was no longer available from institutional investors and savings & loan associations; 2) commercial banks restricted their lending policies; 3) the unprecedented economic prosperity of the 1980s gave way to economic malaise upon the dawning of the new decade; 4) pricing declined on sales and divestitures that were often vital to enabling companies to service debt; and 5) the kingpin of the junk bond market, Drexel Burnham, went bankrupt and out of business.

The impact of the demise of high-wire finance is most clearly manifested in the proliferation of large bankruptcies as the 1980s wound down and gave way to the 1990s. The total assets of publicly held companies that filed for bankruptcy protection to-

taled only $5.8 billion as recently as 1985 (see Figure 13.1). By 1990, this figure had grown to $82.8 billion. More than three-quarters of the largest bankruptcies in U.S. history were filed between 1988 and 1991. Bankruptcies were getting bigger and more numerous. The growth in the number of bankruptcies in recent years is shown in Figure 13.2.

Besides the burgeoning of financially troubled companies seeking Chapter 11 protection, many more have teetered on the edge of insolvency. An analysis of *Standard & Poor's Stock Guide* (Summer 1992) revealed that more than 25% of the 5,000+ companies listed lost money during the preceding 12-month period. Moreover, many additional companies were marginally profitable. Those companies that chose to file for bankruptcy protection are only the tip of the iceberg in terms of companies that may require financial restructuring.

Anatomy of a Financially Troubled Company

The flavor of the unique operating and financial environment is provided in Table 13.1, which lists key symptoms of financial distress. It is an environment in which rapid deterioration can take place if there is not timely and effective intervention by qualified professionals. Key attributes of the environment faced by a financially troubled company include the following:

♦ Management has lost credibility.

♦ Reluctant to extend additional credit, banks are closely monitoring their loans, and possibly, reducing loan availability.

137

Figure 13.1 Total Assets of Publicly Held Companies That Filed Chapter 11

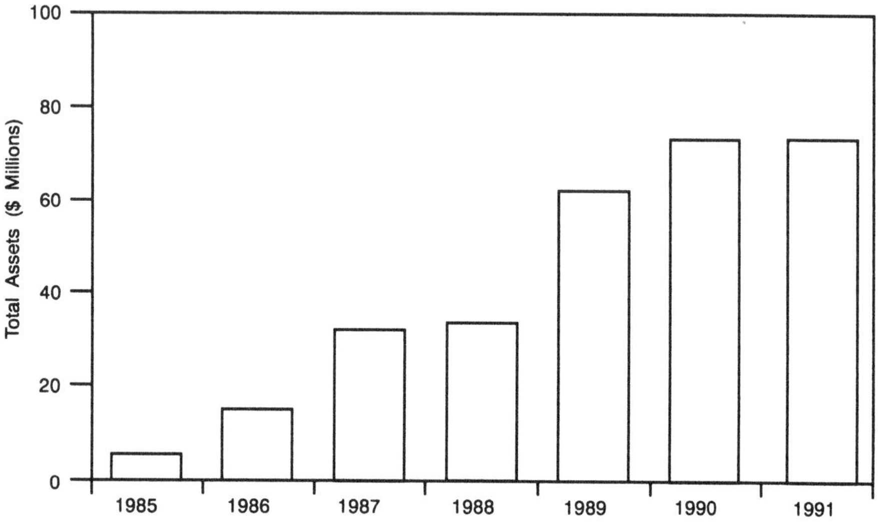

Source: The 1992 Bankruptcy Yearbook and Almanac

♦ Trade creditors are reluctant to provide goods and services on terms.

♦ Banks, bondholders, and/or trade creditors are organizing to take a more aggressive position with the company.

♦ Conventional financing sources are unavailable.

♦ Customers are becoming uneasy about the ability of the company to deliver quality goods and services on a timely basis.

♦ Key employees are in danger of defecting due to the company's financial instability.

In summary, the company is rapidly approaching a waterfall without a paddle. Management and its advisors—investment bankers, legal counsel, insolvency accountants, crisis managers, and professionals serving other parties to the insolvency—constitute the strong oarsmen who, through intense, prompt intervention can avert disaster and remove the boat from turbulent waters.

Few financially troubled companies have problems that are confined to excessive leverage. Sometimes excessive debt levels are partly attributable to funding losses or deteriorating operating performance. In some instances mushrooming debt has hampered the company's ability to reinvest in innovation and in its plant, which in turn has led to operational difficulties. Resolving financial distress requires finding a cure to the company's financial and operational problems. The financial remedy is the workout; the operational fix is the turnaround. The two activities are generally interdependent. Creditors are unlikely to support a workout if they see no evidence of a potential turnaround. The ability to launch a turnaround often depends upon the willingness of creditors and other stakeholders to participate in a workout. A key activity of the investment banker is often to orchestrate the workout in order to buy time for the company to pursue a turnaround. Workouts or financial restructurings may be achieved out-of-court on a consensual basis, or via a bankruptcy proceeding.

Role of the Investment Banker in Financial Restructurings

The financial restructuring process is graphically depicted in Figure 13.3. The figure shows that the prefinancial crisis company has a capital structure that is in equilibrium with the nonlevered value of

Figure 13.2   Bankruptcy Filings, 1980–1991

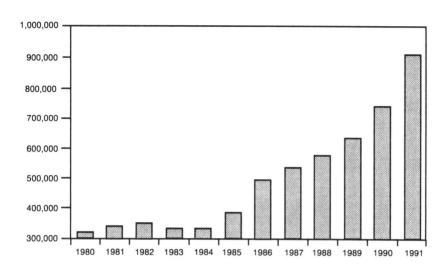

Source: The 1992 Bankruptcy Yearbook and Almanac

the company. The nonlevered value of the company reflects its value, irrespective of the capital structure employed. If the company's nonlevered value declines more rapidly than the amount of debt outstanding, or if indebtedness increases more rapidly than the nonlevered value of the company, it can precipitate a financial crisis. Financial restructuring is all about modifying the capital structure of the company so that it is in equilibrium with the nonlevered value of the company. If new capital is required, that equilibrium also takes into account the portion of the nonlevered value of the company which must be provided to the sources of new capital.

Services rendered by investment bankers in financial restructurings constitute the tools used to accomplish the restructuring goal. They require a combination of hard skills and soft skills. These services may be categorized in terms of advisory services, functional tasks, and transactional services. Advisory services include advising on the financial implications of alternative sources of action or interfacing with key parties in interest. Functional tasks may include fairness opinions or evaluating the debt capacity of the company. Examples of transactional services include raising capital or renegotiating debt. The investment banker's client may be the company,

secured lender(s), unsecured creditors, bondholders, equity holders, prospective investors, or any other party which may have a potential interest in the company. A summary of the key services rendered by investment bankers on behalf of various classes of clients is provided in Table 13.2. The successful implementation of these services is often heavily dependent upon soft skills such as interpersonal skills, as well as a willingness to commit the appropriate professional resources on a timely basis.

The Negotiating Matrix

Each of the services that the investment banker renders must be considered within the context of the endgame strategy: to restructure the company's balance sheet so that there is equilibrium between the nonlevered value of the company and its total capitalization. The restructured balance sheet should provide adequate capital for the company to meet its operating requirements, and should provide an adequate return on capital employed. The means by which the investment banker achieves a financial restructuring is by building consensus among the stakeholders. A company's stakeholders may include its employees, lenders, unsecured creditors, bondholders, and equity holders. Financial restructurings

Table 13.1   Symptoms of Financial Distress

External Symptoms

♦ Competitors are known to be experiencing financial difficulties.

♦ Industry unit sales volume has declined.

♦ Industry price structure has deteriorated.

♦ Industry cost structure has increased.

♦ Industry has surplus capacity.

♦ Customers are suffering from a downturn or industry slowdown.

♦ Legislative or regulatory developments threaten key products or may significantly increase the cost structure.

♦ Competition from new competitors or substitute products and services is being felt.

♦ Fluctuations in the value of the dollar are encouraging foreign competition or discouraging foreign purchases.

♦ Technological changes requiring significant product innovations or capitol expenditures are necessary.

♦ Capital markets are restricting access to debt or equity funding.

Operational Symptoms

♦ Turnover of senior management has occurred.

♦ Members of the board of directors have resigned.

♦ Board members insist on improved directors' liability insurance coverage.

♦ Management information system fails to provide management information which is accurate, timely, and meaningful.

♦ Company has an inadequate planning process; business plans are not developed, meaningful, or executed.

♦ Management lacks credibility in the eyes of employees, customers, creditors, or vendors.

♦ The scope or scale of the business has changed as a result of rapid growth, acquisitions, new products, entry into new markets, or adoption of new production methods.

♦ Staff reductions, wage freezes, spending cuts, asset sales, product line eliminations, and other downsizing measures have been imposed.

♦ Labor unrest impedes productivity.

♦ Excessive overtime has been paid.

♦ Prices have been reduced to generate additional sales.

♦ Shipments are consistently late.

♦ A major customer has been lost.

♦ Company uses an unusually large number of vendors, perhaps to elicit additional credit, or because of poor vendor relations.

♦ Vendors demand C.O.D., payments in advance, deposits, cash payments, or simply refuse to ship under any terms.

♦ Creditors which are also customers are increasing purchases, possibly to offset outstanding balances due from the company.

♦ Key elements of the cost structure have increased significantly, or are excessive in comparison to the level of revenues.

Financial Symptoms

♦ Company lacks certified financial statements.

♦ Auditor is late in completing the annual audit.

♦ Auditor has expanded scope of audit due to concerns over risk or the financial condition of the company.

Table 13.1   Symptoms of Financial Distress (continued)

Financial Symptoms (continued)

♦ Auditor is unknown, poorly regarded, or inexperienced in the company's industry.

♦ A change of auditors has occured, perhaps as a result of disputes over accounting or auditing issues.

♦ Accounting methods which maximuze earnings are employed.

♦ Nontraditional financing methods, such as off-balance-sheet financing or offering unusual incentives for prompt payment are being used.

♦ Indebtedness has increased.

♦ Company is shopping for new leaders or other sources of capital.

♦ Debt has been renegotiated at terms which are more onerous than those which were previously in place.

♦ Lenders have requested additional collateral, pledging of assets, equity infusions, and/or personal guarantees to keep loan in force.

♦ Bank is reluctant to engage in a candid conversation about the company due to fear of lender liability.

♦ Company's financial projections are consistently inaccurate.

♦ Owners have transferred funds or other assets out of the company.

♦ Personal guarantors have transferred personal assets to become judgment proof.

♦ Average days outstanding of accounts receivable have grown, suggesting possible customer dissatisfaction with products or services, or the failure of the company to recognize a writeoff.

♦ Returns and allowances have increased, suggesting a relaxing of quality control standards to generate sales more quickly or to reduce costs.

♦ Inventory turnover has slowed, suggesting a possible accumulation of slow-moving or unsalable goods.

♦ Inventory levels have declined below seasonal norms because company is unable to obtain sufficient trade credit.

♦ Accounts payable are being "stretched."

♦ Trade credit is insufficient to meet the company's needs.

♦ Trade creditors are being asked to extend the term or reduce the amount of indebtedness.

♦ Security interests in assets are being granted to certain key creditors.

♦ Deposits in trust funds such as payroll taxes are deliquent.

♦ Discretionary expenditures, such as capital expenditures, product development, advertising, and maintenance, have been reduced.

♦ Dividends have been reduced or eliminated.

♦ Shareholders have made loans to the company or provided capital infusions.

♦ Legal costs have increased due to lawsuits or the cost of contesting creditor actions.

♦ Uneconomical purchase commitments have been made.

♦ Long-term sale agreements are below current market prices.

♦ Company has a large unfunded pension liability.

♦ Company is liable for significant retiree medical costs.

Miscellaneous Symptoms

♦ Stock price and/or value of publicly traded bonds have deteriorated.

♦ Publicly traded stock has a heavy "short" interest

♦ Insiders are selling stock.

♦ Brokerage reports, published articles, and other media information is adverse.

♦ Company is being "shopped" to several potential investors.

Table 13.1   Symptoms of Financial Distress (continued)

Miscellaneous Symptoms (continued)

♦ Company representatives express a sense of urgency to close a transaction.

♦ Company representatives resist information requests or a thorough due diligence review.

♦ Judgements have been awarded against the company.

♦ Bank is reluctant to engage in a candid conversation about the company due to fear of lender liability lawsuit.

♦ Lender has transferred the loan to the workout department.

♦ Factors are unwilling to advance against receivables from the company.

♦ Trade creditors are organizing to more closely scrutinize the company.

♦ Financial fraud has occurred.

♦ Company has significant legal exposure as a result of environmental contamination, defective products, or other asserted or unasserted claims.

♦ Insurance coverage is insufficient to meet potential liabilities from pending litigation and unasserted claims.

♦ Company has engaged bankruptcy counsel and/or other insolvency professionals.

---

are achieved by fashioning a plan that is fair and meets the objectives of each of the stakeholders. These plans usually require an equitable "sharing of the pain."

Financial restructurings are generally multilateral negotiations in which each stakeholder must be induced to embrace the restructuring plan for its own self-serving reasons. A good test of a proposed financial restructuring is the "WIFM test"—*i.e.*, what's in it for me. A proposed financial restructuring must seem fair to each stakeholder and meet its needs, subject to the financial constraints of the company. Factors that will impact any financial restructuring include:

♦ the viability of the business;

♦ credibility of management;

♦ interpersonal skills and relationships of key parties and their advisors;

♦ economic climate;

♦ quality of advisors;

♦ creditor sophistication; and

♦ the existence of previous financial restructurings that have failed.

The negotiating matrix can be quantified to reveal the relative financial strength of the bargaining positions of each stakeholder. Each of the various business scenarios must be considered. Table 13.3 quantifies the negotiating matrix for a company with two main lines of business. It considers liquidation value, appraised asset value, the various permuta-

tions of selling either or both lines of business, and the potential impact of turning around the company and the resultant value two years hence. The relative legal claims of the stakeholders to the value of the company are based on their respective treatment under the Bankruptcy Code. A simplified version of this hierarchy of claims, as it relates to this example is as follows:

1. Secured creditors, up to the value of their collateral (which can be a matter of dispute);

2. Post-petition creditors (if the company is in bankruptcy);

3. Unsecured creditors (including any deficiency claims of secured creditors for deficiencies in the value of their collateral below the amount of their claims);

4. Subordinate creditors—usually the legal status of junk bondholders;

5. Preferred stock; and

6. Common stock.

The absolute priority doctrine of the Bankruptcy Code states that a class of claimants cannot receive any payment unless all classes of senior claimants have been paid or otherwise satisfied in full. However, negotiating latitude exists because of the possibility of:

♦ divergent opinions regarding the value of collateral;

♦ alternative business and economic scenarios;

Figure 13.3   Graphic Example of Financial Restructuring

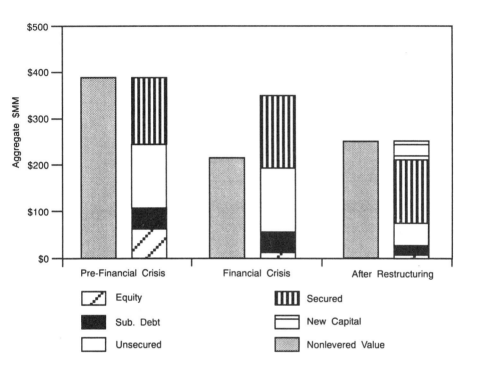

♦ the impact of timing on the value realized by each stakeholder;

♦ the value attributed to financial instruments issued in a financial restructuring; and

♦ the willingness of senior classes of creditors to make concessions in order to facilitate a financial restructuring.

In the example shown on Table 13.3, the secured creditors seem to be highly secure. In each of the scenarios, the secured creditors' interest in cash realized and the unrealized value of the company's assets seem to be approximately equal to the full amount of their claims. Unsecured creditors seem to have asset value and asset coverage to support much of their claim, although there is a shortfall at the valuation date. There seems to be no value that would be realized by bondholders or equity holders in any current transaction. On the other hand, ev-

erybody, including equity holders, would be able to realize a full payout if the company were turned around and sold in two years, based on the projected value of the company in two years.

Factors that would impact financial restructuring negotiations at the valuation date include: 1) the willingness of secured creditors and unsecured creditors to wait two years to realize value; 2) confidence in the prospective value of the company; and 3) the willingness of secured creditors and unsecured creditors to transfer some of the value of their claims to bondholders and possibly, to equity holders, in order to obtain their consent to a particular restructuring transaction or a sale. Lacking concessions by senior creditors and unsecured creditors, bondholders and equity holders have no motive to support any transaction which involves a sale of the company's assets or a restructuring which does not recognize their interest in the prospective value of the company.

Table 13.2 Examples of Activities of the Investment Banker in Financial Restructuring

Activity	Investment Banker's Client					
	Company	Secured Lender(s)	Unsecured Creditors	Bond Holders	Equity Holders	Prospective Investors
Advisory						
Develop/evaluate financial restructuring alternatives	X	X	X	X	X	
Interface with parties in interest	X	X	X	X	X	X
Evaluate financial implications of proposed company actions		X	X	X	X	
Anticipate actions of company		X	X	X		
Anticipate negotiating positions of other parties in interest	X	X	X	X	X	X
Functional Tasks						
Prepare/review business plan	X	X	X	X	X	X
Prepare/review financial projections	X	X	X	X	X	X
Fairness opinion/valuation analysis	X	X	X	X	X	X
Viability analysis/due diligence	X	X	X	X	X	X
Evaluate debt capacity	X	X	X	X	X	X
Evaluate feasibility of proposed reorganization plan	X	X	X	X	X	X
Expert testimony	X	X	X	X	X	X
Transactional						
Negotiate financial restructuring plan	X	X	X	X	X	
Business or asset sales and divestitures	X					
Acquisitions						X
Exchange offer	X					
Raise capital	X					X

Table 13.3   A & B Corporation: Example of Allocation of Recovery and Unrealized Value Alternative Scenarios Estimated at Bankruptcy Filing Date ($000)

Description	Net Book Value	Liquidation Value	Appraised Asset Value	Sell A& B Corp.	Sell Co. A/Keep Co. B	Sell Co. B/Keep Co. A	Sell A & B in Two Years
Total							
Net cash realized		275,000		300,000	200,000	100,000	
Unrealized value	460,000		375,000		100,000	200,000	600,000
	$460,000	275,000	375,000	300,000	300,000	300,000	600,000
Claims							
Post–petition creditors	0	0	0	0	0	0	50,000
Secured creditors	225,000	225,000	225,000	225,000	225,000	225,000	225,000
Unsecured creditors	175,000	175,000	175,000	175,000	175,000	175,000	175,000
Subordinated debentures	50,000	50,000	50,000	50,000	50,000	50,000	50,000
Equity	10,000	10,000	10,000	10,000	10,000	10,000	10,000
	$460,000	460,000	460,000	460,000	460,000	460,000	510,000
Allocation of Net Cash Realized[1]							
Post–petition creditors	0	0	0	0	0	0	0
Secured creditors	0	215,000	0	215,000	160,000	90,000	0
Unsecured creditors	0	60,000	0	85,000	40,000	10,000	0
Subordinated debentures	0	0	0	0	0	0	0
Equity	0	0	0	0	0	0	0
	$0	275,000	0	300,000	200,000	100,000	0
Allocation of Unrealized Value[1]							
Post–petition creditors	0	0	0	0	0	0	50,000
Secured creditors	225,000	0	225,000	0	55,000	125,000	225,000
Unsecured creditors	175,000	0	150,000	0	45,000	75,000	175,000
Subordinated debentures	50,000	0	0	0	0	0	50,000
Equity	10,000	0	0	0	0	0	100,000
	$460,000	0	375,000	0	100,000	200,000	600,000
Total Recovery and Unrealized Value [2]							
Post–petition creditors	0	0	0	0	0	0	50,000
Secured creditors	225,000	215,000	225,000	215,000	215,000	215,000	225,000
Unsecured creditors	175,000	60,000	150,000	85,000	85,000	85,000	175,000
Subordinated debentures	50,000	0	0	0	0	0	50,000
Equity	10,000	0	0	0	0	0	100,000
	$460,000	275,000	375,000	300,000	300,000	300,000	600,000
Recovery and Unrealized Value as Percentage of Claim							
Post–petition creditors	0.0%	0.0%	0.0%	0.0%	0.0%	0.0%	100.0%
Secured creditors	100.0%	95.6%	100.0%	95.6%	95.6%	95.6%	100.0%
Unsecured creditors	100.0%	34.3%	85.7%	48.6%	48.6%	48.6%	100.0%
Subordinated debentures	100.0%	0.0%	0.0%	0.0%	0.0%	0.0%	100.0%
Equity	100.0%	0.0%	0.0%	0.0%	0.0%	0.0%	1000.0%
	100.0%	59.8%	81.5%	65.2%	65.2%	65.2%	117.6%

[1] Based on absolute priority doctrine.
[2] Sum of net cash realized and unrealized value.

Tools of Financial Restructuring

Key goals of financial restructuring are to increase liquidity and to extend the due dates of obligations. The primary means by which these goals are accomplished include: selling or liquidating assets, restructuring existing debt, raising additional capital, and selling the company.

The effect of asset sales and liquidations can be accomplished by numerous means. A simple downsizing of the business can have the effect of an asset sale. A smaller sales volume requires less of an investment in receivables and inventory. The one-time cash flow from the reduction in receivables and inventory can be used to reduce the debt burden.

Other actions that can achieve the equivalent of an asset sale include: securitizing inventory or receivables, a sale/leaseback transaction, joint venture, licensing or royalty agreement, franchising, or a sale with a buyback option.

In considering any form of a sale, it is necessary to determine whether the transaction contributes to alleviating the company's problems. Often only the crown jewels are saleable, and the remaining company is nonviable. In such an instance, any sale should be on an all-or-nothing basis. It is important to anticipate that any transaction accompanied by a sense of necessity is likely to result in lowball offers. The buyers are often referred to as vulture capitalists, bottom fishers, or grave dancers. Needless to say, they are not seeking to pay highest and best price. To the extent that the company acquiesces to such a sale to appease its lenders, it should seek to extract a concession in return for selling assets at an inopportune time.

Debt restructurings are often engineered differently, depending upon whether the debt is a loan, trade debt, or bonds. Features of loan workouts include:

♦ the extension of additional borrowings;

♦ deferral of principal or interest;

♦ concessions or increases in interest or fees;

♦ conversion of debt into equity;

♦ debt forgiveness;

♦ providing additional collateral or personal guarantees; and

♦ imposition of hair-trigger default provisions.

Lenders are often the most formidable party that the company has to negotiate with. They usually have a concentration of the largest amount of the company's debt, have key corporate assets as collateral, and may be the most ready source of cash. A general practice of lenders is that they don't give something up unless they get something in return. For example, they will not gratuitously forgive debt. Forgiveness is usually accompanied by accelerated debt repayment. In most cases, the company's equity has limited appeal to lenders. Concern over lender liability in the event that they own equity in the company, have board membership, or are active in management causes lenders to avoid equity in most cases. Furthermore, in most workouts they deem the equity to be worthless. Principal reasons that lenders may accept equity or equity kickers include having the opportunity to recover any losses from loan writeoffs in the event that the company's equity appreciates in value, and being able to use the equity as a carrot to return to the company if it can achieve predetermined goals.

Lenders do not generally like to increase their exposure to a financially troubled company unless it is in their interest to do so, because the value of their collateral would otherwise diminish rapidly in value without their intervention. Lenders generally want to see that there is an equitable "sharing of the pain" before they agree to be a party to a restructuring. This "sharing of the pain" can include the company's developing a reasonable business plan, management and employees agreeing to compensation reductions, and trade creditors making certain concessions.

Restructuring appeals to lenders in the current economic climate need to focus on two factors: bankers' desire for job security and the need for banks to spruce up their loans for regulatory reporting purposes. The emphasis on job security is hardly unique to bankers, but it is a more pressing concern. The United States does not need 12,000 banks and all the bankers they employ. The number of banks and bankers is diminishing every day. There is less career risk in saying "no" and doing nothing than in agreeing to a restructuring. Accordingly, bankers have to be persuaded and provided with documentation in order to justify the rationale for a restructuring.

Regulatory issues have also become of paramount importance as banks face more pressure as a result of loan losses and possible takeovers by the FDIC or the RTC. Loan restructurings are often designed to convert a loan from 100% nonperforming to one that limits the "bad loan" to as small a portion of the loan as can be justified to regulators and restructures that balance so that it can be classified as a performing loan. Surprisingly, the banker may be motivated to charge a low rate of interest and to reduce fees in order to maximize the size of the "good loan."

Trade creditors constitute the majority of the unsecured creditors of most companies. Outside of bankruptcy, debt is normally restructured with trade creditors by extending payment terms. Occasionally, certain large trade creditors accept liens against their inventory (provided that the company's secured lender agrees) or modify the terms of sale to a consignment basis.

Many companies attempt to restructure trade debt on a piecemeal basis, by offering each trade creditor the best deal that can be negotiated. This approach may be problematic because trade creditors often talk among themselves and may be offended if they learn that they did not get as good a deal as somebody else. Moreover, a piecemeal approach with a few vendors often provides insufficient relief. An alternative to a piecemeal restructuring and to bankruptcy is a composition agreement.

Under the terms of a composition agreement, creditors agree to modify the amount and/or the due date of their outstanding claims. A typical composition agreement will provide for a significant (at least 10%) payment, upon gaining adequate creditor consent, and a specified repayment schedule for the remaining balance due. If the company has access to the cash, it may offer to repay all debt subject to the composition agreement at a discount. A composition agreement may be offered to one or all classes of creditors. Provided that adequate acceptance (usually at least 80%) is obtained and that the company performs as promised, a composition agreement is a legally binding contract that enjoins creditors from suing for delinquencies under the terms of the original obligations to them. If proper disclosure is provided to creditors, their vote in favor of a composition agreement may be used for purposes of approving a prepackaged bankruptcy reorganization plan. Most composition agreements require supermajority acceptance to provide adequate relief. On the other hand, the Bankruptcy Code deems a class of creditors to have approved a plan of reorganization if the majority of those voting constitute two-thirds of the dollar amount of claims held by those who vote to accept the plan. Voting is on a use-it-or-lose-it basis. As a consequence, dissenters may be bound by the will of the majority in bankruptcy.

A vehicle for restructuring bonds outside of bankruptcy is the exchange offer. Exchange offers may be on a debt-for-debt basis; or they may be accomplished by deleveraging the company and converting some or all of the bond debt into equity. Modifications of the timing and amount of principal and interest payments are key features of exchange offers. They also may include warrants or other forms of "equity kickers."

Equity may be restructured outside of bankruptcy via a deferral of preferred stock payments, or through a dilution of common equity to accommodate any equity or equity equivalents issued as part of debt restructurings. In closely held companies, controlling equity holders may be incentivized to dilute their equity positions by being relieved in part or in full of personal guarantees provided to lenders.

Refinancing seems to be the "El Dorado" of every financially troubled company. More often than not, substantial time and money are wasted pursuing this elusive crisis capital. A general precept is that lenders do not intentionally bail each other out of problem loans. (However, they do so by accident with sufficient frequency as to not rule out this possibility altogether.) Refinancing a financially troubled company generally depends upon being able to locate an asset-based lender who will provide additional availability above that which is provided by the company's existing lender. The quest is often an exercise in futility. The company has usually already pledged all of its existing collateral. The ability to refinance with a new lender often depends upon the willingness of the existing lender to forgive debt or relinquish collateral.

Money from the public markets is generally not a viable option. The cost, time delay, SEC hurdles, and lack of investor appeal of issuances of troubled debt or equity instruments precludes this market for most companies.

Equity capital is not available to most financially troubled companies. The risk that funds invested in a financially troubled company will quickly be dissipated and accorded a junior status in a bankruptcy proceeding causes investors to be reluctant to invest in equity unless: 1) they obtain operating and ownership control; and 2) they believe that their equity investment will be protected as a result of creditor support and the ability to solve the company's problems outside of bankruptcy. "Vulture capitalists," who do invest in financially troubled companies, frequently structure their investments as convertible debt instruments or debt with warrants that provide the upside of equity, but the more senior position of debt. Equity capital is a more realistic option as a means of funding a reorganization plan of a bankrupt company which has achieved an operational turnaround.

Parties to bankruptcy proceedings frequently settle for a greater array of financial instruments than in out-of-court restructurings. Reorganization plans are more likely to include longer-term payouts for unsecured creditors, and to offer equity or equity equivalents to settle debt.

A key constraint impacting the term and structure of the financial instruments to be used in a financial restructuring plan is the debt capacity of the company. Debt capacity depends upon the company's assets and its future cash flow. A detailed analysis of the company's balance sheet, a conservative and well-contemplated business plan, and cash flow projections which quantify the business plan are key ingredients of a financial restructuring plan. The plan must be based on the company's projected cash flow and tailored to meet the requirements of parties in interest.

Table 13.4 provides an example of how a financial restructuring can be used to alleviate a company's financial problems. Through a series of actions, the company can raise cash, extend the term of debt payments, and improve its equity position, which will enable management to shift its attention from dealing with creditor and cash problems to managing and rehabilitating the business.

Financial Restructuring in Bankruptcy

At times, as a result of a voluntary action by the debtor or the collective action of three or more creditors, a company may wind up using the Bankruptcy Court as a means to resolve financial distress. Bankruptcy is not a solution to a company's financial ills; it merely gives the company time to restructure its financial affairs. Companies which successfully reorganize typically require two to three years to emerge from Chapter 11. The key milestones of the bankruptcy process are shown in Figure 13.4.

The involvement of the investment banker begins when a retention order is approved by the Bankruptcy Court. The investment banker is at risk that compensation and expenses incurred for postpetition services rendered prior to the effective date of the retention order will not be authorized by the court for payment, unless a *nunc pro tunc* order is issued. The constituencies that the investment banker can serve may include any party in interest to the bankruptcy proceeding that is authorized by the court to engage professionals. These parties may include: secured creditors, one or more classes of unsecured creditors, bondholders, creditors with unliquidated claims (*e.g.*, parties to litigation), and equity holders.

The investment banker is generally part of a team which may include a law firm, an accounting firm, and other such professionals as the constituency the investment banker represents is authorized by the Bankruptcy Court to engage. The nature of professional services that the investment banker renders may include many of those services listed in Table 13.1. The precise nature and depth of services rendered depends upon: 1) what is required; 2) what has been authorized by the Bankruptcy Court; and 3) fee constraints.

There is an important distinction between the roles of the investment banker serving the debtor-in-possession (the bankrupt company) and the investment banker serving the other parties to the bankruptcy proceeding. The investment banker serving the debtor-in-possession is duty-bound to seek the reorganization of the company or, if that becomes unfeasible or less desirable, to sell the company or its assets for the highest possible value. The investment banker serving the company does not represent incumbent management or the shareholders, who are sometimes required to engage their own professionals to avoid inherent conflicts. The role of the investment banker serving secured lenders or a committee is to maximize his client's recovery in terms of cash and/or an interest in the reorganized entity.

During the initial months after the commencement of a typical bankruptcy proceeding the focus of the investment banker's attention is generally on developing an understanding of the business of the debtor-in-possession and the needs and wants that must be considered in the previously described negotiating matrix. The debtor has a period of exclusivity for the first 120 days after the filing of the bankruptcy petition, during which time the debtor has the exclusive right to file a proposed plan of reorganization with the court. Typically, this period of exclusivity is extended upon the request of the debtor, unless creditors have vehement objections that the bankruptcy judge finds persuasive.

The endgame strategy for entering into bankruptcy should be to reorganize. Despite this, there are many obstacles to reorganization. A study released in 1989 by the Administrative Office of the United States Courts reported that more than 50% of companies with assets in excess of $100 million had reorganization plans that were confirmed.[1] This same study indicated that the success rate for plan confirmation declined precipitously for companies below $100 million in assets. The events that enable a company to emerge from Chapter 11 usually require one or more of the following:

♦ the recovery of the debtor's business;

♦ new financing;

♦ the willingness of creditors to accept a payout over an extended period of time;

♦ the willingness of creditors to compromise the amount of debt owed to them;

Table 13.4   SOS LTD:
Example of *Pro Forma* Impact of Restructuring as of and for
the Year Ended December 31, 19XX ($000)

Description	Beginning	#1	#2	#3	#4	#5	#6	#7	Pro Forma
Balance Sheet									
Assets									
Cash	$ 500	3,000	27,000	3,700	(23,000)	(2,500)	(5,000)	(500)	3,200
Accounts receivable	50,000	(500)	(15,000)	(2,500)					32,000
Inventory	45,000	(400)	(13,000)	(1,600)					30,000
	95,500	2,100	(1,000)	(400)	(23,000)	(2,500)	(5,000)	(500)	65,200
Fixed assets	35,000	(3,000)	(9,000)	(500)					22,500
	$130,000	(900)	(10,000)	(900)	(23,000)	(2,500)	(5,000)	(500)	87,700
Liabilities and Stockholders' Equity									
LTD–current	$ 10,000					(5,000)	(5,000)		0
Revolving line of credit	60,000				(25,000)				35,000
Payables and accruals	18,000		(5,000)	(1,000)				(1,500)	10,500
	88,000	0	(5,000)	(1,000)	(25,000)	(5,000)	(5,000)	(1,500)	45,500
Term loan	10,000					2,500			12,500
Debentures	25,000						(5,000)		20,000
Note payable	0							1,000	1,000
	123,000	0	(5,000)	(1,000)	(25,000)	(2,500)	(10,000)	(500)	79,000
Stockholders' equity	7,500	(900)	(5,000)	100	2,000		5,000		8,700
	$130,500	(900)	(10,000)	(900)	(23,000)	(2,500)	(5,000)	(500)	87,700
Income Statement									
Sales	$200,000	(2,000)	(60,000)	(3,000)					135,000
Cost of goods sold	(150,000)	1,700	51,000	5,500					(91,800)
Gross profit	50,000	(300)	(9,000)	2,500	0	0	0	0	43,200
Selling, gen. & admin.	(55,000)	1,200	19,000	2,500					(32,200)
Operating income	(5,000)	900	10,000	5,000	0	0	0	0	10,900
Interest	(11,700)				2,950	550	2,100	(90)	(6,190)
Income before taxes	($16,700)	900	10,000	5,000	2,950	550	2,100	(90)	4,710

Restructuring Actions
#1 Close down uneconomical production facility; liquidate assets.
#2 Sell money—losing division to synergistic buyer.
#3 *Pro forma* impact of turnaround activities.
#4 $2MM in debt forgiveness and reduction in interest rate obtained in exchange for major paydown.
#5 Interest rate relief and deferral of principal repayment schedule obtained in exchange for $2.5MM payment.
#6 Exchange offer in which debenture holders received a $5MM payment in exchange for reduction of $5MM in indebtedness, interest rate relief, adjustment of amortization schedule, and conversion of $5MM of debentures into equity.
#7 Payment of $500M to key vendor to reduce payable and in exchange for willingness to convert $1MM trade payable into a note payable.

Figure 13.4   Examples of Key Chapter 11 Milestones Affecting Activities of Investment Bankers

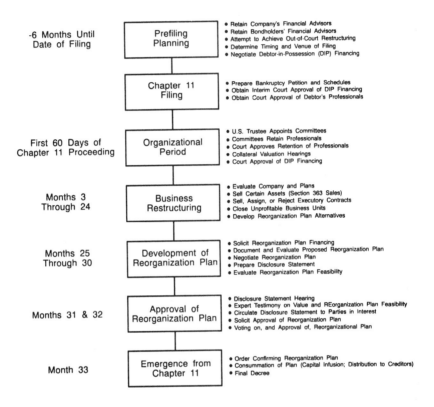

♦ the willingness of creditors to accept equity or other financial instruments in lieu of debt; and

♦ the sale of some or all of the assets of the company.

A plan of reorganization can be either a liquidating Chapter 11 (if all the assets are sold), or a reorganization in which the company will emerge from Chapter 11 in its reorganized form. The amount of time required to reorganize can range from a few months in a prepackaged Chapter 11 in which creditors are supportive of the company, to several years. The average interval from filing until confirmation for companies with assets in excess of $100 million is approximately three years.[2]

The momentum for filing a plan of reorganization may come from creditors rather than from the debtor. Creditors can be active in seeking a sale or liquidation if they believe that the company is deteriorating to their detriment, or if a sale at an attractive price is imminently possible. Also, deficiencies in the value of the company relative to debt can cause creditors to effectively become the equity holders of the company. Many plans of reorganization settle the claims of unsecured creditors or bondholders by giving them a large share of the equity of the reorganized company. Acquiring control of a bankrupt company can sometimes be inexpensively achieved by acquiring the claims of unsecured creditors or bondholders at a discount, and then promoting a plan of reorganization which provides control to the class of claims that was acquired. Some of the more celebrated recent cases in which this approach has been successfully implemented include Allegheny International and Interco. Deciding which class is the "swing" class, which has the potential to receive equity, and estimating the prospects for being able to successfully sponsor a plan of reorganization require careful teamwork between the investment banker and legal counsel.

The time commitment of the investment banker during the course of a Chapter 11 proceeding can be sporadic. It is often weighted toward the beginning and the end of the case. At the early stage, the investment banker can spend considerable time evaluating the company and the negotiating positions of the various parties in interest, and responding to various initial issues such as debtor-in-possession financing and the value of collateral. The intensity of the investment banker's activities during the intermediate phase of a bankruptcy is often dependent upon how much operational rehabilitation the company requires in order to be in condition to reorganize.

Many months or even years may be required to rehabilitate the business, sell off certain assets, close down operations, and resolve litigation or disputed claims. Sometimes the passage of time works to the advantage of proponents of a plan of reorganization, as creditors eventually have diminished expectations and become more open to any reasonable plan that provides some prospect of a meaningful recovery. As reorganization plan discussions become more imminent, the investment banker's role can become more crucial. The investment banker can be a key player in: 1) crafting the plan of reorganization; 2) obtaining financing; 3) developing key documentation for the disclosure statement; 4) selling the plan to creditors; 5) evaluating the plan on behalf of creditors or other parties in interest; and 6) delivering expert testimony in the bankruptcy court.

The Bankruptcy Code allows professionals to be paid no more frequently than once every 120 days, subject to approval by the Bankruptcy Court. Applications for payment must be accompanied by a detailed accounting of time and expenses. Increasingly, the Bankruptcy Courts are requiring investment bankers to conform to the compensation standards applied to other professionals, and are basing compensation on hours expended (the "lodestar" principal). Many jurisdictions require time records to be detailed to the nearest tenth of an hour. It is not unusual for fees to be reduced by holdbacks or by judicial determinations that hours and/or billing rates are excessive in relation to what was accomplished. The increasing scrutiny that is applied to all professional fees and the obligation to conform to the lodestar principal have caused a few leading investment banks to withdraw from the bankruptcy advisory arena.

Conclusion

An increasing number of companies in the United States face financial distress. Those in bankruptcy represent just the tip of the iceberg. The skills of the investment banker can be vital in alleviating financial distress in or outside of bankruptcy through: 1) raising capital; 2) selling assets; 3) balance sheet restructuring; and 4) financial advisory services.

Endnotes

1. Ed Flynn, *Statistical Analysis of Chapter 11*, (Washington: Administrative Office of the United States Courts, 1989: 34.

2. *Ibid.*: 26.

Chapter 14

The Deleveraging Bubble and Reverse Leveraged Buyout (LBO) Pricing*

Steven C. Miller
Senior Analyst
Loan Pricing Corporation, New York, NY

Reverse LBO lending has been the hottest area of the syndicated loan market over the past year. During the first quarter of 1992 alone, $6.5 billion of reverse LBO transactions were syndicated.

Reverse LBOs are a compelling concept. They bring together improved balance sheet strength with rich pricing. The reverse LBO loans have generally been well received at the underwriting stage due to strong agency and top tier syndicate fees and wide spreads. However, banks' lenders must contend with higher exposures as a percentage of borrower capitalization and the presence of *pari passu* senior notes in many reverse LBO transactions.

This chapter reviews the pricing, structuring, and risks involved in reverse LBO lending. The appendix discusses the relative value of structural seniority of reverse LBO term loans to borrowers with *pari passu* senior notes.

Reverse LBO Pricing

Pricing of reverse LBOs that remain noninvestment grade is tiered, a pattern observed in the original LBO market. Deals for Burlington Industries, Coltec Industries, and CNW Corp. have featured spreads of about 275 bps over LIBOR, with upfront fees as high as 300 bps at the $75 million commitment level and 150 bps at the $25 million level.

This pricing is even richer than that of their predecessors. This reflects the fact that loan pricing has increased over the past several years. It also reflects the risks that these credits continue to pres-

ent, as they still have tight fixed-charge coverage. Table 14.1 lists *pro forma* financial projections of recent reverse LBO transactions. Table 14.2 lists the pricing and structuring of the loan packages.

The steep pricing was intended to create momentum in the loan syndications market which could carry over into the IPO market. It is interesting to note that three recent reverse LBO credits were structured with tranches designed for institutional investors. York International and Burlington Industries each had term loans with richer spreads and longer maturities. CNW Corp.'s $700 million loan was reduced with the proceeds of *pari passu* notes. The notes were privately placed with institutional investors.

Raising the Stakes

For banks that already have exposure to a reverse LBO when that credit comes to market, the numbers are compelling. The cash flow coverage of the borrower almost always improves significantly, to 1.5 to 2.0 times *pro forma* interest expense. Leverage ratios also improve markedly, from negative net worth to as little as 80%. Most of the reverse LBO transactions involve the repayment of expensive subordinated debt with bank debt and equity. Further, the bank debt is often contingent on success of the IPO, meaning that banks are not left holding the bag if the equity offering is successful.

One major setback for banks is that the new loans account for a large portion of a company's improved capital structure. Table 14.1 shows the before-and-

*This chapter is based on reporting and published analysis in GoldSheets. Mary McNamara contributed to the pricing analysis presented in this chapter. Tim Cross provided invaluable editing and feedback. Mike Sepesi was instrumental in auditing the data presented and maintaining the integrity of the data.

153

Table 14.1 The New Class of Reverse LBOs: Balance Sheet Strength ($ millions)

	Burlington Industries		CNW Corporation		Coltec Industries		Foodmaker Inc.	
	Historical	Pro Forma	Historical	Pro Forma	Historical	Pro Forma	Historical	Pro Forma
Projection								
Timeframe	12 months	12 months	9 months	9 months	9 months	9 months	12 months	12 months
Period Ended	9/28/91	9/28/91	9/30/91	9/30/91	9/29/91	9/29/91	1/9/92	1/9/92
Bank Loans as a Percent of Capitalization								
Total Bank Debt	$807.20	$840.60	$275.54	$590.00	$0.00	$515.50	$119.60	$154.39
Other Senior Secured Debt			368.18	108.18	418.40	350.00	184.93	209.93
Subordinated Debt	731.00				497.10	141.60	334.17	159.17
Total Debt	1,756.60	858.30	1,222.83	1,323.19	1,633.50	1,312.50	668.32	553.11
Stockholders' Equity	−253.10	519.80	−5.61	112.51	−1,192.40	−827.60	52.95	164.65
Total Capitalization	1,502.80	1,277.00	1,373.57	1,355.03	440.00	458.80	690.06	686.55
Percentage of Bank Debt to Total Debt	46.0%	97.9%	22.5%	44.6%	0.0%	39.3%	17.9%	27.9%
Percentage of Bank Debt to Total Capitalization	53.7%	65.8%	20.1%	43.5%	0.0%	112.4%	26.1%	22.4%
Borrower Leverage								
Short-Term Debt	$60.70	$101.10	$42.24	$80.67	$1.10	$26.10	$31.21	$31.21
Long-Term Debt	1,695.90	757.20	1,180.59	1,242.52	1,632.40	1,286.40	637.11	521.90
Redeemable Preferred Stock			198.59	0.00				
Stockholders' Equity	−253.10	519.80	−5.61	112.51	−1,192.40	−827.60	52.95	164.65
Total Capitalization	1,502.80	1,277.00	1,373.57	1,355.03	441.10	484.90	690.06	686.55
Ratio of Long-Term Debt to Equity	—	1.46	—	11.04	—	−1.55	12.03	3.17
Ratio of Total Debt to Equity	—	1.65	—	11.76	—	−1.59	12.62	3.36
Leverage Ratio (Total Debt/Total Capitalization)	—	0.67	—	0.98	—	—	0.97	0.81
Cash Flow Coverage								
EBIT	$156.80	$156.80	$137.83	$151.78	$173.40	$173.80	$99.85	$99.85
Interest Expenses	251.70	112.70	119.40	98.88	151.40	89.80	93.57	61.70
EBIT Net of Interest	−94.90	44.10	18.43	52.90	22.00	84.00	6.28	38.15
Ratio of EBIT to Interest Expenses	0.62	1.39	1.15	1.54	1.15	1.94	1.07	1.62

Table 14.2 Reverse LBO Databank

	Arrow Electronics	Burlington Industries	CNW Corporation	Coltec Industries	Warnaco Group
Active Date	9/27/91	2/1/92	2/15/92	1/15/92	4/19/91
Term (months)	60	66	84	84	59
Size (millions)	$225	$1,025	$700	$685	$120
Pricing (bps)					
Prime	150	275	275	275	150
LIBOR	275	300	300	300	250
Upfront Fees	200	—	—		285.71
Annual Agent Fee	—				7.14
Commitment Fee	50	50	50	50	50
Performance Pricing	Tied to borrowing base				Leverage Ratio
Initial Fixed-Charge Coverage	2	1.1	—	—	—
Initial Cash Flow Coverage		—	—	—	—
Pricing for Bullet Term Loan		350			
Agents	Bankers Trust MHT First Chicago	Bankers Trust Chemical NationsBank Bank of Nova Scotia	Chemical Bank of America Bank of Montreal Banque Paribas Chase Manhattan Bank Continental Bank First Chicago LTCB	Bankers Trust Barclays MHT Credit Lyonnais	GECC Bank of Nova Scotia Union Bank of Switzerland

	Joy Technologies	York International	Kroger Co.	Payless Cashways
Active Date	11/12/91	7/29/91	1/21/92	2/20/92
Term (months)	73	50	72	75
Size (millions)	$325	$625	$1,455.8	$450
Pricing (bps)				
Prime	212.5	150	25	175
LIBOR	—	250	125	275
Upfront Fees	—	—	50	300
Annual Agent Fee	—	—	—	—
Commitment Fee	50	50	37.5	50
Performance Pricing	Fixed Charges & Outstandings	HLT Delisting	Cash Flow Coverage	Funded Debt Ratio
Initial Fixed-Charge Coverage	1.2	2	1.1	—
Initial Cash Flow Coverage	—	—	1.8	—
Pricing for Bullet Term Loan	262.5	—	—	—
Agents	Bankers Trust Chase Manhattan Bank	Chemical Canadian Imperial	Citibank Chemical First Chicago IBJ	Canadian Imperial Bank of America Westpac Chase Manhattan NationsBank

after financial profiles of four recent reverse LBO candidates, based on *pro forma* projections. In every case the balance sheet is strengthened by the transaction, while the bank loans, as a percentage of overall debt, increased.

Another concern is the level of fixed-charge coverage, or the ability of the company to meet interest expenses, principal repayments, and capital expenditures from cash flow. Thin fixed-charge coverage is often the result of term loan repayment schedules. Most of reverse LBOs call for term loan repayments during the first year of the terms.

Burlington Industries is a model reverse LBO. The slightly distressed textile producer used the IPO market to revitalize its balance sheet. Though the company's leverage ratio improved, bank debt as a percentage of debt plus equity increased from 54% to 66%. Further, bank debt as a percentage of total debt increased from 46% to 98%. Though the ratio of *pro forma* cash flow coverage (earnings before interest and taxes (EBIT) to interest expenses) improved from 0.98:1 to 2.20:1 because of the credit, fixed-charge coverage is far slimmer. Burlington's credit agreement calls for a fixed-charge coverage ratio of 1:1 in the first year of the term and 1.1:1 thereafter. This implies that the transaction leaves the company little flexibility if earnings are not in line with expectations.

The improved cash flow coverage of the new transactions suggests a lower probability of default. At the same time, banks' exposure in the case of default may be higher because their loans account for a larger percentage of the total capital structure.

Tiered Pricing and Market Reception

Clearly, the stories presented by these cases are different. However, like the LBO buyout cycle of 1987–1989, pricing of these credits appear to be tiered at 275 bps over LIBOR. Upfront fees are consistent, at 300 bps for co-agents, with lead banks reportedly receiving between 100–200 bps extra for their roles. The similar pricing for vastly different stories is reflected in the market reception.

Burlington and CNW have both been well received at the underwriting level market. Burlington, which is in a highly cyclical industry and will continue to have tight fixed charge coverage, has had more difficulty in the general syndication. Also, Burlington, with a total commitment of $1.05 billion, is the largest reverse LBO. Coltec, which remains in a negative net worth position despite the recapitalization, had difficulty at both the underwrit-

ing and syndication level until the company's over allotment option was exercised.

Agent Allocations and Fees

Dr. Pepper/Seven-Up Company's equity offering disclosure statement provides some insight into the fee income currently being offered on reverse LBO credits and the elements that have made the credit a "blow-out." Dr. Pepper/Seven-Up paid a total of $22.5 million, or 300 bps, in syndication fees for its $750 million reverse LBO package, which was underwritten by a group of six banks led by Bankers Trust. The credit was syndicated in April and May of 1992. Given the subsequent syndication of the credit, agents received upfront fees of 450–650 bps as a percentage of final allocations. The transaction was later cancelled due to a soft IPO market in mid-1992.

Allocations

With 11 co-agents stepping up for commitments of $50 million each at fees of 150 bps on allocation, the underwriting agents made substantially higher than 300 bps on their final allocation. According to bankers, co-agent commitments were used first to reduce Bankers Trust from an initial commitment of $150 million to $100 million and the five managing agents from initial commitments of $120 million to $75 million. The balance was reported to be applied to all lenders on a *pro rata* basis. This would mean that final allocations prior to general syndication would be:

	($Million)
Bankers Trust	75.00
Managing Agents	52.50
Co-agents	37.50

Fees

For purposes of this discussion, Loan Pricing Corporation (LPC) will assume that Bankers Trust received a premium of 100 bps over the other managing agents, which is a standard rule for these types of large leverage deals. Under this scenario Bankers Trust would have received underwriting fees of 380 bps, while the other underwriters would have received fees of 280 bps. Given the allocation scenario described above and the 150 bps fee level paid to co-agents, Bankers Trust would have realized fees of 659 bps on allocation prior to general syndication, while the co-agents would have received fees of 485 bps.

Most traders and loan investors expect an active general syndication and secondary selldown with lenders receiving upfront fees of 50–100 bps for commitments of $10–25 million. Subsequent sell-down at these levels, of course, would increase the fees of agents and co-agents as a percentage of allocation.

Underwriting

Bankers Trust, in addition to earning the lucrative fees associated with syndicating Dr. Pepper, is one of five domestic managing underwriters for the company's related 23.8 million share IPO. Stock underwriting, of course, is a lucrative business which has been sought after by Bankers Trust, Citibank, J.P. Morgan & Co., and other large banks with Section 20 underwriting powers. Morgan, in fact, is reported to have declined at least one agency position (for Payless Cashways) because the company did not tap the bank's securities unit to lead the company's IPO. If the stock offering is completed, Bankers Trust will retain 0.83% of Dr. Pepper's common stock. It had a 1.2% stake in the company prior to the recapitalization.

Dr. Pepper Background

Dr. Pepper has been an acknowledged blow-out. Bankers Trust, along with the five managing agents, has received 11 co-agent commitments of $50 million, making the loan 173% oversubscribed prior to general syndication. The loan is full secured by materially all assets of the company and capital stock in operating units.

The credit is priced at the standard reverse LBO level of LIBOR plus 275 bps with a 50 bps commitment fee on undrawn amounts. The underwriting fees, at 3% of total commitment, is lower than the levels reported on Burlington Industries and Coltec Inc.'s reverse LBOs, which were rumored to be 400–450 bps at the underwriting level. However, Dr. Pepper is considered less cyclical credit and it has reported steady improvements in cash flow since its 1988 LBO. Table 14.1 shows that on a pro forma basis, the company's 1991 interest coverage ratio (EBITDA to post-recapitalization interest expense) is a comfortable 2.3:1. The loan also clearly has momentum, riding the crest of improved market liquidity and the overall reverse LBO trend.

Risks

Dr. Pepper mirrors the risk associated with reverse LBOs outlined above. Banks are being paid wide margins and high fees on Dr. Pepper for: 1) relatively thin fixed-coverage ratio; 2) high leverage ratio; and 3) high bank loan total debt ratio. The company's ratio of EBITDA to total *pro forma* debt servicing costs in year one (including term loan repayments) would be 1.1:1. The company notes in its disclosure statement that capital expenditures are nominal. Therefore, EBITDA-to-total debt servicing can be used to approximate a fixed coverage ratio.

The company plans to improve its shareholder's deficit from $657.1 million to $193.7 million as a result of the recapitalization. It will remain a highly leveraged borrower with a leverage ratio (long-term debt to long-term debt plus equity) of 137%. Further, the company expects to have $640 million outstanding under the credit agreement. This is equal to 89% of total debt and 96% of total capitalization (total debt less shareholder's deficiency).

Conclusion

Many bankers attribute the relatively strong reception of these deals in the syndicated market to a return of liquidity to the commercial lending market and a strong desire for banks to replace the overall decline in performing HLT holdings with new wide-margin product. A review of the numbers shows that the reverse LBO deals are fairly ambitious transactions from the perspective of fixed-charge coverage. They clearly indicate that the liquidity crunch at the lower credit quality end of the credit spectrum is beginning to ease. This is also evident in the bond market where Merrill Lynch & Co. has reported a decline in the market spread of BB and B bonds (as quoted over Treasuries) of 86 bps and 100 bps, respectively, during the first five months of 1992. The lack of high-yield bonds has pushed many traditional junk bond investors into the equity and private placement market. In addition, some insurance companies and other nonbank investors have again begun to explore wide-margin opportunities in the syndicated loan market.

Appendix 14

The Value of Structural "Seniority"

Several recent reverse LBO and recapitalization transactions have been structured with senior notes which rank *pari passu* to bank loans. Some bank lenders are uncomfortable with sharing the senior secured creditor class with another investor group without a layer of subordinated debt. Syndicators have argued that the notes are, in fact, "structurally" subordinated to the loans due to their longer repayment schedule. Estimating the value of structural seniority is difficult. The leveraged transactions of the late 1980s were generally structured with unsecured subordinated bonds which clearly stood behind the banks in collateral protection. *Pari passu* senior notes, by contrast, have an equal claim on collateral and are repaid with asset sales and excess cash flow on a *pro rata* basis with the bank loans.

Primary Differences

A review of three large note and bank loan placements used in leveraged transactions, Del Monte Corp., CNW Corp, and Specialty Coatings Group, show that the notes and loans share substantially similar collateral security and covenant protection. Principal repayments on the notes begin about the time that the loans are repaid. The notes also have makewhole provisions which require the companies to pay a penalty on optional prepayments if the discount rate (generally set at Treasuries plus 50–150 bps) is lower than coupon of the note. Bank loans, of course, rarely have prepayment penalties because they are floating rate instruments. Therefore, the assumption is that banks can generally reinvest at a similar rate. Table 14.3 compares the pricing and terms of CNW Corp. and Specialty Coatings Group, and Time-Warner Inc.'s bank loans and *pari passu* notes.

Estimating the Value of Structural Subordination

In order to estimate the value of structural seniority it is necessary to review two factors: the loan repayment schedules and default incidence by year. For purposes of this review, Loan Pricing Corporation (LPC) has used the ten-year corporate bond default incidence for noninvestment grade borrowers (reported by Standard & Poor's Corp. in a supplement to *CreditWeek* dated September 13, 1991) as a proxy for default probability. The report shows default incidence by the borrower's senior debt rating. LPC used the average repayment rate of four reverse LBO term loans (Table 14.4) as a proxy for term loan paydowns. The loans were all part of a transaction that also included a senior note tranche or a separate term loan tranche aimed at institutional investors.

Figure 14.1 shows a comparison between the scheduled term loan repayments and the noninvestment grade bond default incidence. Table 14.4 shows that the maximum incidence of default occurs during years three through six, with the greatest incidence in year four. The incremental default incidence and the average term loan repayments suggest an average repayment prior to default of 47%, based on stated repayments. Therefore, from a bank's perspective, the value of structural seniority would be the probable repayment of 47% of claims—excluding prepayments shared between banks and senior noteholders—prior to default.

Expected Losses

Taking this a step further, an estimated repayment of 47% prior to default and the 17.43% default incidence reported by S&P suggest a default rate—or the amount of loan portfolio that defaults as a percentage of initial commitments—of 9.32% for noninvestment grade loans. Table 14.4 shows that based on this default estimate and recovery assumptions of 70–85%, banks may see losses of 140–280 bps for noninvestment grade loans. LPC studies have estimated recoveries for senior secured HLT loans at 80–85%. Given the upfront fees associated with reverse LBO loans, which have run as high as 300 bps for co-agents and 150 bps for participants, this loss estimate appears to be manageable from a portfolio perspective.

Clearly, the improved cash flow and leverage position of the reverse LBOs should reduce the probability of default for these transactions, compared to the original crop of HLT loans. However, the recovery levels for loans that do default may be lower than those originally observed by LPC in its

159

Table 14–A.1 Term Loans versus Notes

	Type	Amount	Active Date	Term (mos.)	Average Life (yrs.)	Pricing Spread (bps)	Coupon	Upfront Fees Commit. Amount ($mils.)	Amount (bps)	Sched. Repay. Year	Amount ($mils.)	Prepayments Asset Sales	Excess Cash Flow	Init. Fin. Ratio Min. Fixed Charge (x:1)	Max. Leverage (x:1)
CNW Corp.	TL	$315M	3/28/96	72	3.30	L+250		100	300	1	30.00	100%	100%	1.50	13.5
								75	250	2	40.00				
								25	150	3	55.00				
								15	100	4	65.00				
										5	65.00				
										6	60.00				
	Note	$465M	3/28/96	117	8.30	T+270	9.92%			6	116.25	100%	100%	1.50	13.5
										7	116.25				
										8	116.25				
										9	116.25				
Specialty Coatings Group	TL	$40M	5/1/95	84	4.76	L+250		NA		1	2.25	100%	NA	1.64	1.05
										2	3.75				
										3	5.50				
										4	7.50				
										5	8.75				
										6	9.75				
										7	2.50				
	Note	$130M	5/1/95	120	8.51	T+275	10.75%			7	32.50	100%	NA	1.64	1.05
										8	32.50				
										9	32.50				
										10	32.50				
Time Warner	TL	$2,000M	NA	90	NA	L+125[1]		225	158		NA		NA		NA
	Note	$500M	NA	120	NA	T+207		200	150						

[1] Tied to a performance grid based on borrower's rating.

Table 14–A.2 Default Incidence and Expected Outstandings

Default Incidence by Year	Year 1	Year 2	Year 3	Year 4	Year 5	Year 6	Year 7	Cumulative
BB Borrowers	0.61%	1.26%	2.50%	4.08%	4.30%	2.95%	1.14%	16.84%
B Borrowers	1.03	2.82	4.01	3.67	3.17	3.31	0.00	18.01
Average	*0.82*	*2.04*	*3.26*	*3.88*	*3.74*	*3.13*	*0.57*	*17.43*
Default Incidence as a Percentage of all Defaults	4.71%	11.71%	18.68%	22.24%	21.43%	17.96%	3.27%	100.0%
Average TL Outstandings Each Year[1]	100.0%	94.0%	81.1%	58.8%	32.0%	14.6%	1.6%	

Estimated Outstandings at Default 53.47%
(Based on the sum of Default Incidence and Average Outstandings)

Expected Default Rate 9.32%
Expected Default Rate = Cumulative Default Incidence * Estimated Outstandings at Default

Expected Losses
If recovery estimates of 70–85% are assumed, a 9.32% default rate would suggest the following expected losses where:
Expected Loss = Default Incidence * (1 – Repayments Prior to Default) * (1 – Recoveries Following Default)

Recovery Estimate	Loss Expectation
85%	1.40%
80	1.86
75	2.33
70	2.80

[1] Based on the stated repayment schedule of CNW Corp., Burlington Industries, Specialty Coatings and Del Monte Corp.
Source: Standard & Poor's Corp., Loan Pricing Corp.

Figure 14–A.1 Outstandings Under Term Loans versus Noninvestment Grade Bond Default Incidence by Year

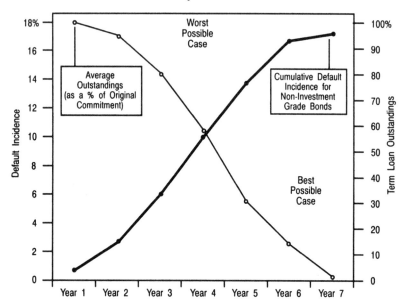

Source: Loan Pricing Corporation, Standard & Poor's Corp.

study of HLT recovery rates. This is because: 1) the HLT loans had a layer of subordinated debt rather than *pari passu* notes; and 2) the percentage of overall capitalization in bank loans is higher in the reverse LBOs than in the original HLT transactions. These two factors could reduce the recovery levels of the banks in a default situation.

Chapter 15

Privatizations

Christopher Chase
Vice President
Salomon Brothers Inc, New York, NY

The global privatization movement is in full swing. Although the first modern privatization program is thought by some to have occurred over 60 years ago in Queensland, Australia, a convergence of economic and political events brought over $200 billion worth of state enterprises into the private sector during the 1980s. For each of the past three years, analysts estimate the annual rate of privatization to have been from $25 to $30 billion. New programs in Eastern Europe, Latin America, Asia, and other regions suggest that the privatization boom will extend well into the 1990s.

The current wave of privatizations was kicked off in earnest with the sale of British Aerospace in 1981. Since then, the United Kingdom has probably been the world's leading privatizer, receiving over $30 billion for dozens of enterprises during the past decade. Elsewhere in Western Europe, Spain has sold shares in its national oil company, electricity company, and other enterprises. Portugal, Austria, Greece and the Netherlands have each privatized on a smaller scale; and even France, which has historically resisted privatization on ideological grounds, is beginning to contemplate the private distribution of some of the shares of its state enterprises.

With the collapse of Communism, Eastern Europe is engaged in the herculean task of privatizing entire economies. Many believe that Eastern Germany has made the most progress under the auspices of the Treuhandanstalt, a 3,000 person state agency dominated by human and financial resources provided by Western Germany. Poland, Hungary, and Czechoslovakia are battling political instability and macroeconomic hardships to make progress in privatizations, and all three have found international investors to be more reluctant to invest new capital than they had hoped.

Latin America has been another focus of privatization activity, as the ideological climate has become more hospitable to private enterprise and states recognize that mobilizing state assets can provide a means of reducing large public sector borrowings. Mexico followed the $4 billion sale of its telephone system with the privatization of its banking system for more than $10 billion. Venezuela and Argentina have realized billions through the sales of nationalized airlines, telecommunications, and industrial enterprises. Brazil has not moved quite as quickly as these three, but has closed significant transactions such as the sale of Suitings, the state-owned steel company last year.

In Asia, privatization activity has not been quite as intense as in other parts of the world. One reason is that national budgets are not so strapped that privatization is perceived to be such a vital means of balancing the budget. Another reason is that many Asian state enterprises are profitable and well-run. The most significant regional privatization was New Zealand's massive sale of its telecommunications company. Nevertheless, analysts see a solid flow of privatizations in the region during the next decade.

Privatization in the United States has had a slightly different flavor than in the rest of the world. Here, many of the traditionally state-owned sectors such as telecommunications, railroads, power generation and various heavy industries, are already private. Much recent privatization activity in the United States has been at the state and local level as cash-strained states and municipalities have turned to private providers of services such as sanitation, corrections, and automobile towing.

163

The broadest definition of privatization encompasses a wide range of approaches. These approaches differ as much as each enterprise differs in terms of its unique attributes and environment. Nevertheless, there is now a large body of experience from which a participant in a given privatization can draw to devise and execute an effective privatization strategy.

Simply organized, the particular approach that a government may choose in order to privatize an enterprise is driven by the government's objectives, external constraints imposed by the political and economic characteristics of the region, and by the financial and organizational characteristics of the enterprise.

Privatization Objectives

The principal objective in many privatization programs is to raise money which can be used by the government to reduce the federal deficit or to fund other programs. For example, in Latin America, privatizations have played an important part in producing hard currency to balance budgets and retire foreign debt. Argentina has sold its telephone monopoly, national airline, and petrochemical company for more than $2 billion. Mexico is estimated to have raised over $10 billion so far through privatization of its telephone and banking system; and Brazil and Venezuela have programs in place to raise similar multibillion dollar figures.

Some countries, in fact, have encouraged buyers of state enterprises to more directly assist the government in reducing their deficits by offering sovereign debt as a portion of the consideration for the businesses. Although buyers and sellers are each well aware that these debt instruments are worth less than their face value, these debt-for-equity exchanges can provide a useful medium for governments to relieve themselves of obligations and the buyers to use discounted currency. For example, Salomon Brothers' client, the Defense Ministry of Argentina, gave potential bidders for the state-owned steel company, Somisa, specific instructions regarding the portion of the consideration that could be paid in sovereign debt as part of the bidding package for the privatization.

There are examples, however, of revenue-driven privatization programs that backfired because the enterprises did not prove viable over the long term. Chile privatized a number of enterprises in the 1970s which floundered during the economic crisis of the early 1980s. Many of these were financial institutions that the state was forced to renationalize and then finally reprivatize later in the 1980s. One lesson in these cases is that revenue maximization

must be balanced by a number of other factors, including macroeconomic conditions as well as the fiscal health of the enterprise and the purchaser.

An often complementary objective of privatization programs is to improve receipts by ridding the government of loss-making bureaucracies and replacing them with profitable enterprises that generate tax receipts. Perhaps the most celebrated example of this phenomenon is the British privatization program initiated by the Thatcher government in 1979. A former British minister estimated that state-owned enterprises that cost U.K. taxpayers £3 billion a year in 1979, were adding £2 billion in revenue through taxes and fees by 1990. This was in addition to the £34 billion that he estimated the British government realized in the sales themselves.[1]

Another objective of privatizations is to improve economic efficiency on the theory that private organizations are by their nature more efficient than state-owned enterprises. One critique of state-owned enterprises is that, because they are ultimately administered by politicians, the managers of these enterprises pursue political goals rather than economic goals. For example, in 1982, the Chairman of then-public British Steel proposed the closure of the Ravenscraig Steelworks in Scotland. This plant was one of the company's five major integrated operations, but with the decline of the Scottish manufacturing base, it was the furthest from major markets. The proposal met a firestorm of opposition and was withdrawn. In 1990, a privatized British Steel revived the shut-down plan. By this time, the political and economic landscape had changed and even union leaders admitted, "the case for the hot strip mill and for Ravenscraig as a whole must be fought and determined on commercial grounds, and on those grounds alone."[2] The plant was ultimately closed.

Although the anecdotal case for economic efficiency of privatizations is compelling, the empirical case is less clear. Academic studies have not identified a significant correlation between economic growth measures and the degree of ownership by the private sector, particularly in developing countries.[3] On a macroeconomic level, it appears that other factors such as education, infrastructure, and market development must play as important a role as the degree of public ownership.

Two other interrelated goals of privatization are to widen ownership of assets and to strengthen local capital markets. Here again, Britain is often cited as a paradigm of "taking capitalism to the people" through broad distribution of shares. The sale of British Telecom in 1984 was several times the size of the largest prior public offering in history and placed over £4 billion worth of shares in the hands of two million people. In this offering, the state offered a special inducement to small investors in the form of a 10% bonus that was remitted to shareholders who held shares longer than three years. When the offering was oversubscribed, the issuers allocated shares to the smallest orders first, standing underwriting tradition on its head by ensuring that the offering received the broadest distribution possible.

The record is rich with counterexamples of instances in which the goal of shareholder democracy fell flat. It is not broadly remembered that West Germany attempted to introduce popular privatization back in the 1960s in a program that anticipated many of the features of the U.K. program of the 1980s. After a successful placement of DM 400 worth of the shares of Volkswagon, the Federal Republic turned to the mining, chemical, and electricity holding company, VEBA. The offering gave strict preference to lower income shareholders and employees.

The offering of VEBA was initially quite successful, but the disclosure of operating problems at the company drove the share price down sharply during the first few months after the placement. The government was forced into the market to support the shares, and the episode left the public with a diminished appetite for people's capitalism. The privatization movement in Germany languished for more than a decade until the late 1980s when the Kohl government gingerly returned to the privatization market.

External Constraints

A number of external constraints hinder the accomplishment of the state's objectives in a privatization. The first is ideology. The triumph of state enterprise has been so profound during the past decade that it is sometimes difficult to recall some of the very logical arguments that were made on behalf of state enterprises in the first place. Ideological resistance to privatization has persisted in many parts of the world to this day, in spite of the overwhelming success of many programs.

In 1988, President Mitterand of France articulated a *"ni-ni"* policy of neither further nationalization nor privatization of the government's large industrial holdings. Although this policy is beginning to break down, it reflects a deeply rooted socialist tradition and a comparatively efficient state industrial sector. In developing countries, the ideological argument against privatization mingles with nationalism and class consciousness. In many of these countries, the public flotation of shares is constrained by illiquid capital markets; and many opponents share the legitimate fear that state assets will

be scooped up by foreign interests and local private oligopolies.

Even when the state is committed to privatization, ideology shapes the methods by which the state implements the privatization. One of the most important political considerations in the privatization process is "transparency"; that is, the government's obligation to demonstrate that it is selling public assets in a fair and open process and that the state is receiving a fair price. Transparency is best assured, of course, in a public offering of shares into a liquid equity market. One critical reason for the broad acceptance of "people's privatization" in the United Kingdom was that the state's assets were being distributed widely among the public.

When the enterprise is not appropriate or the capital markets are not liquid enough for an equity placement, the state is obliged to sell an enterprise to a private party. Many governments go to great lengths through formal bidding procedures to assure transparency. In more than one case, the sealed bids for privatizations were actually opened on national television so that the public could be convinced of the integrity of the process.

Another enemy of privatization that often cloaks itself in ideology is the bureaucracy of the state-owned enterprise. Although the bureaucracy will be overwhelmed by a full-scale political mandate for change, it can certainly offer plenty of resistance in the process. The legal infrastructure may also pose a forbidding obstacle to privatization. Most privatizations are preceded by elaborate legislation and detailed legal groundwork to create viable public entities. Particularly in the case of utilities and other government monopolies, privatization usually requires the careful substitution of a regulatory framework for a bureaucracy.

Also, competing ownership claims may also pose a legal obstacle to privatization. In West Germany, the first attempt to privatize Volkswagon in 1957 was derailed when the province of lower Saxony asserted an ownership claim in the company. In that case, the privatization proceeded after the province received a significant equity stake in the company.

Regional economic and market conditions also have a powerful influence on privatizations. As mentioned above, Chile's initial privatization program crashed on the rocks of the Latin American debt crisis of the 1980s. The current global recession helped swamp the privatization of Indonesia's cement company, Semin Gresik, in which the shares of the company fell 20% below the offering price during the first day of trading. Although balanced by a desire to enter emerging markets, many of the international companies that could be strong buyers for state enterprises are focused on preserving their core businesses rather than seeking new external investments.

The most imposing external economic and market conditions are confronted by countries that barely have markets, such as Eastern Europe and the former Soviet Union. With a crumbling infrastructure, massive pollution, hyperinflation, and markets distorted by decades of state intervention, it is difficult to imagine where these states should begin to introduce private investment.

Eastern Germany is perhaps the best developed example of privatization in a market vacuum. There, the process has been managed by the Treuhandanstalt, a ministry dominated by financial and human resources provided by western Germany. After an expectedly rocky start, the agency evolved into a decentralized structure with 15 national branches that now total more than 3,000 people. About one-third of the staff is western, as are most of the senior appointments.

The Treuhand's approach has been a kind of "industrial triage," in which subject enterprises are quickly separated into groups of: attractive marketable firms; companies that could improve with management attention and capital; and enterprises for which there is no solution but closure. The Treuhand has chosen in many cases to balance the overall proceeds of divestment with promises on the part of buyers to invest in plants and retain labor. The agency gave away a chemical plant in Dresden, for example, in exchange for a commitment on the part of the buyer to invest DM 500 million there.

In its haste to quickly dispatch the thousands of enterprises in its portfolio, the Treuhand has sacrificed some of the elaborately arranged transparency that other governments have scrupulously attempted to maintain. On the other hand, some critics argue that the airline Interflug might have survived relatively intact had the agency quickly sold it to Lufthansa rather than shopping for a higher bid from other international carriers.

Enterprise Constraints

Labor issues are usually critical in each privatization. A persuasive argument can be made that the primary economic benefit of privatization arises from the fact that state-owned enterprises are often dominated by employment concerns at the expense of efficiency and profit. State enterprises haven't the will to cut personnel and "the brutal truth about privatization is that, in the case of loss-making companies, it works mainly through job redundancies."[4]

In Salomon Brothers' experience with Somisa, the Argentine steel company, the level of overstaffing was so vast that the Ministry made the judgment that

no new buyer would incur the liability of attempting to restructure the workforce on its own. The Ministry believed it had no choice but to offer severance packages to approximately 10,000 of the steel mill's 15,000 workers, at a cost well over $100 million. In this dramatic case, the state chose to completely restructure the workforce prior to the sale to shield the buyer from potential liabilities. In other cases the state might share the burden of workforce reductions or, conversely, accept a lower sale price in exchange for employment guarantees on the part of the buyer.

Another important characteristic of an enterprise is its market position, particularly whether or not the enterprise is a national or regional monopoly. The state must appreciate that even efficient private enterprises are created to serve shareholders, not public policy. Competition is the best guarantee that the privatized enterprise will price products fairly and deliver high quality services. In the case of monopolies such as utilities and telephones, a carefully designed regulatory structure must replace state control. In other cases, such as energy and transportation, the state may rely on global competitors and free trade to protect local consumers. The privatization of a national steel company, oil company, or airline will not create a license for monopoly profits as long as imports are available to local consumers at competitive prices.

The market position of an enterprise is also important in evaluating the potential acquiror of an enterprise. For example Eastern European enterprise may lack the cost structure or technology of their western competitors, but they frequently offer access to millions of new consumers. Privatizations offer companies unique opportunities to penetrate markets instantly rather than having to spend decades painstakingly building a presence in a new region. Moreover, as in the case of our many telecommunications clients, successfully winning a privatization means that competitors face a large disadvantage in entering the local market in the future.

The most important characteristic of an enterprise is its financial condition. First, many states turn to privatization as a means of injecting capital into cash-deprived operations. In the past, governments used trade barriers to protect undercapitalized, inefficient industries at the expense of domestic consumers. In developing countries in particular, the debt crisis has created pressure from international agencies such as the World Bank as well as international lenders to lower these restrictions. Forced to compete with better-capitalized companies, these countries have had no choice but to solicit private investment.

Financial viability is the essential variable in determining the appropriate privatization methodology.

Profitable, efficient operations are best suited for the placement of equity in the public markets as independent enterprises. In some cases, it is possible to transform financially weak or unprofitable enterprises into more viable companies in anticipation of privatization. In these cases, the state may assume liabilities accumulated through years of state management, write down assets, and otherwise create a clean company that can then be offered to the public or a private investor. The government may also offer post-privatization support through tax or regulatory benefits to help ensure that the enterprise will prosper as an independent entity.

Privatization Methodologies

Although each privatization is by its nature unique, there are two basic techniques of privatization, each with a virtually limitless number of variations. The first is the distribution of all or a portion of the shares of an enterprise to the public. Although this is usually done in the familiar form of an underwriting of shares in exchange for cash, there has been a great deal of consideration lately, particularly with respect to Eastern Europe, of other novel techniques in the absence of liquid capital markets.

The other basic methodology is the sale of shares or assets of an enterprise to a private buyer or group of buyers. In this methodology especially, there has been a tremendous variation in approaches and structures to achieve transactions.

Public Distribution

As noted above, public distribution is often the preferred privatization technique because it offers the state a means of accomplishing virtually all of its privatization objectives. The process is by its nature relatively transparent and can take advantage of existing securities laws regarding disclosure to assure transparency. It provides the state an opportunity to offer ownership broadly and it can also be used as a means of creating or expanding local equity markets. The Telefonos de Mexico offering, for example, not only brought $4 billion into the treasury, but it created an important new vehicle for attracting international equity capital into the economy.

There is some genuine debate whether public offerings realize the best valuation for the state seller. First, it has been observed that state offerings tend to be underpriced, even relative to traditional initial public offerings of private companies.[5] It appears that the state's eagerness to launch a successful placement typically outweighs its desire to maximize

returns and the result is to "leave something on the table" for the public investor.

Another valuation critique is that corporate investors should value businesses more highly than the public because of their ability to extract additional value from the enterprise through management and strategic redeployment. This argument was most powerful during the mergers and acquisitions heyday of the late 1980s when corporate acquirors often paid 50–100% premiums to acquire publicly held companies. The M&A market has since cooled and the equity market has improved. As a consequence, the strategic premium has narrowed and in some cases vanished.

The criteria for a public offering are often too demanding for a given enterprise to be taken public. Most fundamentally, an enterprise must be a viable independent entity. Certainly, the state has the latitude to shape and focus an enterprise to meet this criterion. Nevertheless, many enterprises are not at their core viable enough to stand alone as a private enterprise.

Another key element of a public offering is that there must be a public equity market capable of receiving the offering. If the U.K. stock market, one of the world's oldest and most highly evolved, was initially considered to be too small for British Telecom, one can imagine the difficulty of placing stock in much less developed markets. Relatively recent advances in technology and the emergence of truly international securities firms have opened the markets immeasurably for equity that in an earlier era would have swamped local markets. Nevertheless, countries with less developed equity markets still face a meaningful limitation in their ability to employ this privatization technique.

In Eastern Europe in particular, people are now considering fascinating new techniques for public distribution of state-owned enterprises. These include vouchers, citizens' shares, citizen-owned mutual funds, and spontaneous privatizations. All of these plans wrestle with the enormous task of democratically redistributing ownership of assets in economies devoid of the most basic market mechanisms.[6]

Private Sale

In a situation in which the public offering is unworkable or the state perceives the private market valuation to be superior, the state will typically turn to some form of private market disposition. The private sale is not only the preferred alternative for enterprises with weak financial performance, but it also provides the government more flexibility in allocating liabilities and influencing the post-closing operation of the enterprise.

In some cases, governments have chosen to combine the benefits of a private and public sale by selling a significant interest to strategic investors prior to a public offering. This combination of techniques has been a preferred approach in telecommunications privatizations, in which strategic investors provide critical access to technology and management expertise to create a viable company that can be owned in part by public investors. By retaining a stake that it can offer to the public, the state also captures some of the valuation "upside" that is created by private investment in the enterprise.

Politically, a private sale challenges the state to ensure that the enterprise is sold in a transparent process at a fair price. Often, the government will employ a highly formalized process with a rigid set of bidding and negotiating procedures. The state may also employ internationally recognized financial and legal advisors to provide further assurances that the sale is being handled in a professional manner.

For the bidder in a private sale of a state enterprise, the process can be quite frustrating. Financial information may be sparse and/or unintelligible; the operating environment may be highly volatile; and the formalized process may be inhospitable to the give-and-take of typical negotiations. For international bidders, it may prove essential to work with a local partner who is familiar with the characteristics of the enterprise and the environment. The process itself will typically proceed in fits and starts, with long delays punctuated by spurts of intense activity. Nevertheless, the rewards of winning a stake in newly privatized companies are so great that international companies continue to subject themselves to the indignities and uncertainties of the privatization process. Particularly in industries that are maturing back at home, privatizations offer opportunities that are too great to ignore.

The most successful bidders in privatizations typically are the most appreciative of the local climate. Most often, this is because the purchaser is a local or regional firm. In Eastern Germany, for example, the *Economist* estimated that out of 3,000 transactions, only 115 had gone to foreign buyers. Foreign acquirors often have long business or cultural links with the privatizing country, such as Iberia Airlines' involvement in the Argentine and Venezuelan airlines privatizations.

An international acquiror certainly faces a disadvantage in assessing the private value of a public enterprise in an often chaotic environment with which the acquiror may be completely unfamiliar. In fact, this is why many of our clients hire us at Salomon Brothers for buy-side assignments. Experienced financial advisors can often be quite helpful in navigating the terrain, identifying local partners, analyzing risk, performing complicated valuations, and negotiating transactions.

Conclusion

This chapter was intended to be a reasonably concise overview of a topical subject matter about which there is a large body of theoretical and practical knowledge. There is absolutely no reason for any government or business person to participate in a privatization without being fully informed about this rich experience. Each enterprise may certainly be unique, but an awareness of the key economic, political and industrial issues, as well as the experience of prior privatizations, will help sellers and buyers of privatized assets formulate and implement the appropriate strategy.

Endnotes

1. John Moore, "British Privatization, Taking Capitalism to the People," *Harvard Business Review*, (January-February 1992): 115.

2. Anthony Ferner and Trevor Colling, "Privatization, Regulation and Industrial Relations," *British Journal of Industrial Relations*, (September 1991): 391.

3. Richard A. Yoder, Phillip L. Borkholder and Brian D. Friesen, "Privatization and Development: The Empirical Evidence," *The Journal of Developing Areas* (April, 1991): 425–434.

4. Matthew Montagu-Pollock, "Privatization: What Went Wrong," *Asian Business*, (August 1990): 34.

5. Kojo Menyah, Krishna N. Paudyal and Charles G. Inyangete, "The Pricing of Initial Offerings of Privatised Companies on the London Stock Exchange," *Accounting and Business Research*, Vol. 21, No. 81: 50–56.

6. Eduardo Borensztein and Manmohan S. Kumar, "Proposals for Privatization in Eastern Europe," *IMF Staff Papers*, Vol. 38, June, 1991: 300–325.

7. "Privatizing East Germany," *The Economist*, (September 14, 1991): 22.

Part VIII:
Financial Engineering of
New Financial Products

Chapter 16

An Overview of Corporate Securities Innovation*

John D. Finnerty
Professor of Finance
Fordham University, New York, NY
General Partner
McFarland Dewey & Co., New York, NY

The rapid pace of securities innovation over the past two decades has brought about revolutionary changes in the array of financial instruments available to corporate treasurers and investors. A variety of factors have stimulated the process of securities innovation. Among the most important are increased interest rate volatility and the frequency of tax and regulatory changes. Also, the deregulation of the financial services industry and increased competition within investment banking worldwide have placed greater emphasis on being able to "engineer" new securities.

The purpose of securities innovation is to develop new financial instruments that increase investor wealth and, ultimately, of course, general economic growth. To achieve this end, the new security must enable issuers and investors to accomplish something they could not achieve with existing securities. For investors, this means higher after-tax returns for bearing a given level of risk, greater liquidity, or perhaps just a more desirable *pattern* of payoffs. For issuers, securities innovation holds out the possibility of reducing the corporate cost of capital, thus expanding the range of investments companies should be willing to undertake. The challenge facing corporate treasurers is to determine whether issuing a new type of security will benefit the company and its shareholders or just enrich the investment bankers who designed and sold it.

When Is an Innovative Security Significant?

Some securities innovations are designed primarily to circumvent provisions of the tax or regulatory code. Indeed, Merton Miller has likened the role of regulation in stimulating innovation to that of the grain of sand in the oyster.[1] And since few things in this world are as mutable as the current tax code or set of regulations, securities intended to overcome such obstacles are likely to disappear along with the tax or regulatory quirk that gave rise to them.

Significant securities innovations, by contrast, are those that endure because they provide a new way of meeting *fundamental* economic demands of issuers or investors. For example, financial futures have enjoyed an ever-expanding role in corporate finance since their start in the early 1970s.[2] But some securities innovations developed within the past two decades, such as zero-coupon bonds, were issued in large volume for a time but have since been issued only infrequently, because changes in tax law eliminated their advantages or because more recent innovations superseded them. Other innovations, such as extendible notes, medium-term notes, and collateralized mortgage obligations, have had a more lasting impact. Still others, such as indexed currency option notes, variable duration notes, and certain commodity-linked bonds, disappeared quickly, in some cases after just a single issue. And many others, such as unbundled stock units, failed to catch on at all.

*This article is a revised and updated version of my earlier article, "Financial Engineering in Corporate Finance: An Overview," *Financial Management* (Winter 1988): 14-33 and also appeared in Continental Bank *Journal of Applied Corporate Finance* Vol. 4, No.4 (Winter 1992): 23–39. New issue data were provided by Securities Data Company, Inc.

This chapter describes a variety of innovative corporate securities and attempts to identify the sources of value added by each of them. In some cases, my assessments of value added can be interpreted as carrying my forecast of the security's "staying-power." Although many of the new securities defy categorization, the following discussion is organized by assigning them all into one of the following four categories: 1) new debt instruments; 2) new types of preferred stock; 3) new forms of convertible securities; and 4) new types of common equity instruments. Besides discussing innovations in each of these four categories, this chapter also provides four tables listing some 60 distinct new securities I have been able to identify. For each security, the tables provide a brief description of its distinctive features, probable sources of value-added, the date of first issue, and an estimate of the number of issues and total new issue volume for each security through year-end 1991.[3]

Debt Innovations

Innovative debt securities and the process of securities innovation generally can add value in the following ways:

♦ Reallocates some form of risk from issuers or investors to other market participants more willing to bear them.

♦ Increases liquidity; that is, the ability of investors to sell without lowering the price or incurring high transactions costs.

♦ Reduces the "agency costs" that arise from conflicts of interest among management, shareholders, and creditors.

♦ Reduces issuers' underwriting fees and other transaction costs.

♦ Reduces the combined taxes of issuer and investors.

♦ Circumvents regulatory restrictions or other constraints on investors or issuers.

Risk Reallocation

Most of the debt innovations (see Table 16.1) involve some form of risk reallocation as compared to conventional debt instruments. Risk reallocation, as mentioned, adds value by transferring risks away from issuers or investors to others better able to bear them. Risk reallocation may also be beneficial if a

company can design a security that better suits the risk-return preferences of a particular class of investors. Investors with a comparative advantage in bearing certain risks will pay more—or, alternatively, require a lower yield premium—for innovative securities that allow them to specialize in bearing such risks.

For example, an oil producer could design an "oil-indexed" debt issue with interest payments that rise and fall with the level of oil prices, and investors might be willing to charge significantly lower yields for two reasons: 1) the company's after-interest cash flows will be more stable than in the case of a straight, fixed-rate debt issue, thereby reducing default risk; and 2) some investors may be seeking a "play" on oil prices not otherwise available in the commodity futures or options market. In this latter sense, many securities innovations that reallocate risk also add value by "completing the market."

That investors are willing to pay more for such "scarce securities" is clear from a different process of securities innovation. Financial intermediaries have made considerable profits by simply buying outstanding securities, repackaging the cash flows from those securities into two or more new securities, and then selling the new securities.[4] The success of stripped U.S. Treasury securities (created by "stripping" the coupon payments from bearer U.S. Treasury bonds) and stripped municipal securities illustrates that the sum of the parts can exceed the whole when a particular debt service stream is subdivided and its constituent parts sold separately. As another example, investment banks purchased portfolios of mortgages from originating institutions, placed them in trusts or special purpose corporations, and then used those new entities to issue new securities called *mortgage pass-through certificates.* The debt payments to the mortgage certificate holders are serviced with the cash flows from the purchased mortgage portfolios; and the investment banker pockets the difference (with an important exception to be noted later) between the payments it receives from the individual mortgages and the coupon it pays on the pass-through securities.

Like mortgage pass-through certificates, *credit card receivable-backed securities* and *loan-backed certificates* also represent undivided ownership interests in portfolios of credit card receivables and other consumer loans, respectively. Such securities enable the financial institutions that originated the individual loans to transfer the interest rate risk as well as the default risk (or at least a portion of it)[5] of those loans to other investors. Investors, in turn, are willing to accept lower yields on the securitized assets because of the diversification provided by the pooling process.

Table 16.1   Selected Debt Innovations

■ Security	■ Year Issued	■ No. of Issues	■ Aggregate Proceeds ($B)
□ Distinguishing Characteristics	□ Risk Reallocation		
● Enhanced Liquidity	● Reduction in Agency Costs		
○ Reduction in Transaction Costs	○ Tax and Other Benefits		
■ Adjustable Rate Notes and Floating Rate Notes	■ 01/21/75	■ 2,372	■ 385.0
□ Coupon rate floats with some index, such as the 91-day Treasury bill rate.	□ Issuer exposed to floating interest rate risk but initial rate is lower than for fixed-rate issue.		
● Price remains closer to par than price of fixed-rate note of same maturity.			
■ Bonds Linked to Commodity Price or Commodity Price Index	■ 04/10/80	■ 34	■ 1.9
□ Interest and/or principal linked to a specified commodity price or commodity price index.	□ Issuer assumes commodity price risk in return for lower (minimum) coupon. Serves as a hedge if the issuer produces the commodity.		
	○ Attractive to investors who would like to speculate in commodity options but cannot, for regulatory reasons, purchase them directly.		
■ Collateralized Mortgage Obligations (CMOs) and Real Estate Mortgage Investment Conduits (REMICs)	■ 04/23/81	■ 3,548	■ 701.0
□ Mortgage payment stream is divided into several classes which are prioritized in terms of their right to receive principal payments.	□ Reduction in prepayment risk to classes with prepayment priority. Appeals to different classes of investors; sum of parts can exceed whole.		
● More liquid than individual mortgages.			
■ Commercial Real Estate-Backed Bonds	■ 03/14/84	■ 53	■ 8.4
□ Nonrecourse bonds backed by specified piece (or portfolio) of real estate.	□ Reduced yield due to greater liquidity.		
● More liquid than individual mortgages.	○ Appeals to investors who like to lend against real estate properties.		
.redit Card Receivable-Backed Securities	■ 01/16/87	■ 151	■ 66.9
□ Investor buys an undivided interest in a pool of credit card receivables.	□ Supplemental credit support in the form of a letter of credit, surety bond, limited guarantee, over-collateralization, or senior/subordinated structure.		
● More liquid than individual receivables.			
○ Investors could not achieve the same diversification as cheaply on own.			
■ Credit Sensitive Notes	■ 12/6/89	■ 4	■ 1.0
□ Coupon rate increases (decreases) if the issuer's credit rating deteriorates (improves).	□ Protects the investor against deterioration in the issuer's credit quality because coupon increases when rating declines.		
■ Deferred Interest Debentures	■ 09/17/82	■ 6	■ 0.5
□ Debentures that accrue—and do not pay in cash—interest for a period.	□ Reduces bankruptcy risk during the interest deferral period.		
■ Dollar BILS	■ 08/22/88	■ 1	■ 0.1
□ Floating rate zero coupon note with effective interest rate determined retrospectively based on value of a specified corporate bond index.	□ Issuer assumes reinvestment risk. Useful for hedging and immunization purposes because Dollar BILS have a zero duration when duration is measured with respect to the specified index.		
■ Dual Coupon Bonds/Fixed-Floating Rate Bonds	■ 11/25/85	■ 12	■ 1.4
□ Interest is calculated on a fixed-rate basis during the early life of the bond and on an inverse-floating-rate basis for the bond's remaining life.	□ Issuer exposed to the risk that interest rates may decrease during the inverse-floating-rate period because the coupon will increase if the specified market benchmark interest rate decreases.		
	○ Useful for hedging and immunization purposes because of very long duration.		
■ Dual Currency Bonds	■ 01/21/83	■ 291	■ 22.7
□ Interest payable in US dollars but principal payable in a currency other than US dollars.	□ Issuer has foreign currency risk with respect to principal repayment obligation. Currency swap can hedge this risk and lead, in some cases, to yield reduction.		
	○ Euroyen-dollar dual currency bonds popular with Japanese investors subject to regulatory restrictions and desiring income in dollars without principal risk.		

Table 16.1 Selected Debt Innovations (continued)

■ **Euronotes and Euro-commercial Paper**	■ N/A	■ N/A	■ N/A
□ Euro-commercial paper is similar to US commercial paper.	O Elimination of intermediary brings savings lender and borrower can share.		
O Corporations invest in each other's paper directly rather than through an intermediary.			
■ **Extendible Notes**	■ 03/09/82	■ 332	■ 42.8
□ Interest rate adjusts every 2-3 years to a new interest rate the issuer establishes, at which time note holder also has option to put notes back.	□ Coupon based on 2-3 year put date, not on final maturity.		
O Lower transaction costs than issuing 2 or 3-year notes and rolling them over.	● Investor has a put option, which provides protection against deterioration in credit quality or below-market coupon rate.		
■ **Floating Rate, Rating Sensitive Notes**	■ 06/28/88	■ 9	■ 1.6
□ Coupon rate resets quarterly based on a spread over LIBOR. Spread increases if the issuer's debt rating declines.	□ Issuer exposed to floating interest rate risk but initial rate is lower than for fixed-rate issue.		
● Price remains closer to par than the price of a fixed-rate note of the same maturity.	● Investor protected against deterioration in the issuer's credit quality because of increase in coupon rate when rating declines.		
■ **Global Bonds**	■ 06/14/89	■ 60	■ 31.1
□ Debt issue structured so as to qualify for simultaneous issuance and subsequent trading in U.S., European, and Japanese bond markets.			
● Structure facilitates a relatively large issue. Simultaneous trading in U.S., Europe and Japan coupled with large size enhance liquidity.			
■ **Increasing Rate Notes**	■ 04/12/88	■ 8	■ 1.3
□ Coupon rate increases by specified amounts at specified intervals.	□ Defers portion of interest expense to later years, which increases duration.		
	● When issued with bridge financing, step-up in coupon rate compensates investors for the issuer's failure to redeem the notes on schedule.		
■ **Indexed Currency Option Notes**	■ 10/24/85	■ 1	■ 0.2
□ Issuer pays reduced principal at maturity if specified foreign currency appreciates sufficiently relative to the US dollar.	□ Investor assumes foreign currency risk by effectively selling the issuer a call option denominated in the foreign currency.		
	O For investors who would like to speculate in foreign currencies but cannot purchase currency options directly.		
■ **Indexed Sinking Fund Debentures**	■ 07/12/88	■ 6	■ 3.7
□ The amount of each sinking fund payment is indexed to a specified interest rate index (typically the 10-year constant maturity Treasury yield).	□ The security's duration and convexity are closer to those of a fixed-rate mortgage than a conventional fixed-rate bond ; so it is useful to financial institutions that invest in mortgages for duration-matching purposes.		
■ **Interest Rate Reset Notes**	■ 12/06/84	■ 41	■ 6.0
□ Interest rate is reset 3 years after issuance to the greater of (i) the initial rate and (ii) a rate sufficient to give the notes a market value equal to 101% of their face amount.	● Reduced (initial) yield due to the reduction in agency costs.		
	O Investor is compensated for a deterioration in the issuer's credit standing within 3 years of issuance.		
■ **Loan-Backed Certificates**	■ 03/07/85	■ 456	■ 103.2
□ Investor buys an undivided interest in a pool of automobile, manufactured housing, residential second-lien, or other consumer loans.	□ Supplemental credit support in the form of letter of credit, limited guarantee, surety bond, over-collateralization, or senior/subordinated structure. Provider of credit support bears residual default risk. Reduced yield due to the benefit to the investor of credit support, diversification, and greater liquidity.		
● More liquid than individual loans.			
O Investors could not achieve same diversification as cheaply on their own.	O Can be structured as sale of assets to remove loans from balance sheet.		
■ **Medium-Term Notes**	■ 04/17/73	■ 1,426	■ 690.2
□ Notes are sold in varying amounts and in varying maturities on an agency basis.	□ Issuer bears market price risk during the marketing process.		
O Agents' commissions are lower than underwriting spreads.			

Table 16.1   Selected Debt Innovations (continued)

■ **Mortgage-Backed Bonds**	■ 11/14/73	■ 38	■ 7.1
❑ Bonds issued by financial institutions (or other borrowers) that are collateralized by a specified pool of mortgages.	❑ Collateral provides added security to the investors making possible a lower interest rate than an unsecured issue of like maturity.		
■ **Mortgage Pass-Through Certificates**	■ 09/21/77	■ 1,400	■ 336.4
❑ Investor buys an undivided interest in a pool of mortgages.	❑ Supplemental credit support in the form of a letter of credit, surety bond, limited guarantee, senior/subordinated structure, insurance or a reserve fund. Provider of credit support bears residual default risk. Reduced yield due to the benefit to the investor of credit support, diversification, and greater liquidity.		
● More liquid than individual mortgages.			
○ Investors could not achieve same diversification as cheaply on their own.	○ Can be structured as sale of assets to remove loans from balance sheet.		
■ **Negotiable Certificates of Deposit**	■ 07/10/79	■ 118	•■ 5.2
❑ Certificates of deposit are registered and sold to public on an agency basis.	❑ Issuer bears market price risk during the marketing process.		
● More liquid than non-negotiable CDs.			
○ Agents' commissions are lower than underwriting spreads.			
■ **Pay-in-Kind Debentures/Variable Duration Notes**	■ 09/18/87	■ 4	■ 1.4
❑ Debentures on which the interest payments can be made in cash or additional debentures, at the option of the issuer. Variable duration notes give the issuer this option throughout the life of the security.	❑ Defers the risk that the issuer will not be able to make timely debt service payments. Reduces bankruptcy risk during the pay-in-kind period.		
■ **Principal Exchange Rate Linked Securities**	■ 03/12/87	■ 20	■ 1.4
❑ Principal repayment is linked to a specified foreign exchange rate. Amount of repayment in U.S. dollars increases (decreases) as the specified foreign currency appreciates (depreciates) relative to the dollar.	❑ Investor has effectively purchased a call option on the specified foreign currency and sold a put option on the same currency.		
	○ Attractive to investors who would like to speculate in foreign currencies but cannot purchase currency options directly.		
■ **Puttable Bonds**	■ 08/16/73	■ 822	■ 107.5
❑ Bond redeemable at holder's option, or in case of "poison put" bonds, if a certain specified "event" occurs.	❑ Option to redeem benefits holders if interest rates rise.		
	● Put option provides protection against deterioration in issuer's credit standing.		
■ **Real Yield Securities**	■ 1/20/88	■ 3	■ 0.4
❑ Coupon rate resets quarterly to the greater of (i) change in consumer price index plus the "Real Yield Spread" (3.0% in the first such issue) and (ii) the Real Yield Spread, in each case on a semi-annual-equivalent basis.	❑ Issuer exposed to inflation risk, which may be hedged in the CPI futures market. Real yield securities have a longer duration than alternative inflation hedging instruments.		
● Real yield securities could become more liquid than CPI futures, which tend to trade in significant volume only around the monthly CPI announcement date.			
○ Investors obtain a long-dated inflation hedging instrument that they could not create as cheaply on their own.			
■ **Remarketed Reset Notes**	■ 12/15/87	■ 3	■ 1.4
❑ Interest rate reset at end of each interest period to a rate remarketing agent determines will make notes worth par. If issuer and remarketing agent can not agree on rate, then the coupon rate is determined by formula which dictates a higher rate the lower the issuer's credit standing.	❑ Coupon based on length of interest period, not on final maturity.		
● Designed to trade closer to par value than a floating-rate note with a fixed interest rate formula.	● Investors have a put option, which protects against issuer and remarketing agent agreeing to set a below-market coupon rate; flexible interest rate formula protects investors against deterioration in issuer's credit standing.		
○ Intended to have lower transaction costs than auction rate notes and debentures, which require periodic Dutch auctions.			
■ **Reverse Principal Exchange Rate Linked Securities**	■ 10/03/88	■ 6	■ 0.5
❑ Principal repayment is linked to a specified foreign exchange rate. Amount of repayment in U.S. dollars increases (decreases) as the dollar appreciates ·preciates) relative to the specified foreign currency.	❑ Issuer has effectively purchased a call option on the specified foreign currency and sold a put option on the same currency.		
	○ For investors who would like to speculate in foreign currencies but cannot purchase currency options directly.		

Table 16.1   Selected Debt Innovations (continued)

■ **Spread-Adjusted Notes**	■ 05/08/91	■ 1	■ 0.2
□ The interest rate spread off a specified Treasury benchmark yield is reset on each interest payment date through a Dutch auction.	□ Investor protected against credit risk but, unlike conventional auction rate debt, is still exposed to interest rate risk.		
	● Interest rate spread off Treasury benchmark yield will increase if issuer's credit standing deteriorates—whether or not issuer's credit rating changes.		
■ **Spread Protected Debt Securities**	■ 01/15/87	■ 1	■ 0.1
□ The notes can be redeemed on a specified date (in one case, 2 years after issuance) prior to maturity, at the option of the holders, at a price equal to the present value of the remaining debt service stream calculated on the exercise date by discounting the future debt service payments at a rate equal to a specified Treasury benchmark yield plus a fixed spread.	□ Investor protected against credit risk up until the put date but is not protected against interest rate risk.		
	● Investor has a put option, which provides protection against deterioration in the issuer's credit standing prior to the put date.		
■ **Standard & Poor's 500 Index Notes (SPINs)/Stock Index Growth Notes (SIGNs)/Equity-Indexed Notes**	■ 11/30/89	■ 304	■ 12.0
□ Zero coupon note, principal payment on which is linked to appreciation in value of specified share price above a specified threshold.	□ Equivalent to a package consisting of a zero coupon bond and a long-dated call option on a specified share price index.		
○ Cheaper than buying a combination of a zero coupon note and rolling over a series of shorter-term options.			
■ **Step-Down Floating Rate Notes**	■ 07/11/88	■ 14	■ 3.1
□ Floating rate notes on which the interest margin over the specified benchmark (e.g., 30-day high-grade commercial paper rate) steps down to a smaller margin on a specified date during the life of the instrument.	□ Designed to reduce interest rate margin to reflect direct dependence of required margin on remaining maturity of notes.		
■ **Stripped Mortgage-Backed Securities**	■ 01/14/88	■ 136	■ 38.3
□ Mortgage payment stream subdivided into two classes: one with below-market coupon and the other with above-market coupon, or one receiving interest only and the other receiving principal only from mortgage pools.	□ Securities have unique option characteristics that make them useful for hedging purposes. Designed to appeal to different classes of investors; sum of the parts can exceed the whole.		
■ **Super Premium Notes**	■ 11/18/87	■ 5	■ 0.9
□ Intermediate-term U.S. agency debt instrument (typically maturing in between 1 and 3 years) that carries a coupon rate well above current market rates (and therefore sells at significant premium to its face amount).	○ Attractive to government bond funds that would like to report very high-coupon debt in their portfolios and do not have to amortize the premium over the life of the instrument (or in some cases, money market mutual funds that do not have to show a capital loss even at redemption). As a result, Super Premium Notes provide a lower cost of funds than conventional U.S. agency notes of like maturity.		
■ **Variable Coupon Renewable Notes**	■ 03/16/88	■ 4	■ 1.2
□ Coupon rate varies weekly and equals a fixed spread over the 91-day T-bill rate. Each 91 days the maturity extends another 91 days. If put option exercised, spread is reduced.	□ Coupon based on 1-year termination date, not on final maturity.		
○ Lower transaction costs than issuing 1-year note and rolling it over.	○ Designed to appeal to money market mutual funds, which face tight investment restrictions, and to discourage put to issuer.		
■ **Variable Rate Renewable Notes**	■ 02/02/88	■ 24	■ 5.0
□ Coupon rate varies monthly and equals a fixed spread over the 1-month commercial paper rate. Each quarter the maturity automatically extends an additional quarter unless the investor elects to terminate the extension.	□ Coupon based on 1-year termination date, not on final maturity.		
○ Lower transaction costs than issuing 1-year note and rolling it over.	○ Designed to appeal to money market mutual funds, which face tight investment restrictions.		
■ **Yield Curve Notes/Maximum Rate Notes/Inverse Floating Rate Notes**	■ 11/18/85	■ 48	■ 4.3
□ Interest rate equals a specified rate minus LIBOR.	□ Issuer exposed to the risk that interest rates may decrease, which would raise the coupon. Can reduce yield relative to conventional debt when coupled with an interest rate swap against LIBOR.		
	○ Useful for hedging and immunization purposes because of long duration.		
■ **Zero Coupon Bonds (sometimes issued in series)**	■ 04/22/81	■ 452	■ 38.0
□ Non-interest-bearing. Payment in one lump sum at maturity.	□ Issuer assumes reinvestment risk. Issues sold in Japan carried below-taxable-market yields reflecting tax advantage over conventional debt.		
	○ Straight-line amortization of original issue discount pre-TEFRA. Japanese investors realize significant tax savings.		

Managing Reinvestment Risk. Pension funds are concerned about the "reinvestment risk" they face when attempting to reinvest interest payments received on standard debt securities. *Zero coupon bonds* were designed in part to appeal to such investors by eliminating the need to reinvest interest payments. With zeros, interest is effectively reinvested and compounded over the life of the debt issue at the yield to maturity at which the investor purchased the bond. When PepsiCo sold the first issue of zero coupon bonds in 1982, the yield to maturity was almost four percentage points lower than the yield on U.S. Treasury securities of the same maturity!

Managing Prepayment Risk. Both *collateralized mortgage obligations* (CMOs) and *stripped mortgage-backed securities* address a somewhat different kind of "reinvestment risk"—one that investors in mortgage pass-through certificates find troublesome.[6] Most mortgages are prepayable at par at the option of the mortgagor after some brief period. The fact that many mortgages will be paid off if interest rates decline creates a significant prepayment risk for lenders; that is, if their principal is returned prematurely, they will be forced to reinvest at lower rates.

To address this "prepayment" risk, CMOs repackage the mortgage payment stream from a portfolio of mortgages into several series—sometimes more than two dozen—of debt instruments that are prioritized in terms of their right to receive principal payments. In the simplest form of CMO, each series must be repaid in full before any principal payments can be made to the holders of the next series. By so doing, such a CMO effectively shifts most of the mortgage prepayment risk to the lower priority class(es), and away from the higher priority class(es), which benefit from a significant reduction in the uncertainty as to when the debt obligation will be fully repaid.

With the same motive, *stripped mortgage-backed securities* divide the mortgage payment stream into two separate streams of claims. In their most extreme form, such securities offer one set of claims on interest payments exclusively (IOs) and another on just principal repayments (POs).[7]

Other New Vehicles for Managing Interest Rate Risk. *Adjustable rate notes* and *floating rate notes* are among the many other innovative securities developed in response to rising and increasingly volatile interest rates. By adjusting interest payments to correspond to changes in market interest rates, such floating-rate securities reduce the lender's principal risk by transferring interest rate risk to the borrower. Of course, such a transfer exposes the issuer to floating interest rate risk. But such a reallo-

cation of interest rate risk can be of mutual benefit to issuers with assets whose values are directly correlated with interest rate changes. For this reason, banks and credit card companies are prominent among issuers of these securities.

Inverse Floaters. A recently introduced mechanism for transferring interest rate risk goes by two different names because it has two different sponsoring securities firms. *Yield curve notes* and *maximum rate notes,* known collectively as "inverse floaters," carry an interest rate that decreases as interest rates rise (and vice versa).[8] Investors with long horizons find inverse floaters useful for immunization purposes because of their very long duration.

Managing Price and Exchange Rate Risks.[9] Commodity-linked bonds were developed in response to rising and increasingly volatile prices. The principal repayment and, in some cases, the coupon payments of a commodity-indexed bond are tied to the price of a particular commodity, such as the price of oil, or the price of silver, or a specified commodity price index. As mentioned earlier, such bonds are often structured to enable the producer of a commodity to hedge its exposure to a sharp decline in commodity prices and thus in its revenues. And, to the extent interest or principal payments rise and fall with the company's revenues, the new security will reduce the volatility of the company's after-interest cash flow. Such securities effectively increase a company's debt capacity by shifting the debt service burden from times when the commodity producer is least able to pay to periods when it is most able to do so.

Dual currency bonds, indexed currency option notes, principal exchange rate linked securities (PERLs), and *reverse principal exchange rate linked securities* (Reverse PERLs) illustrate different forms of currency risk reallocation. They are attractive to institutions that would like to speculate in foreign currencies but cannot, for regulatory or other reasons, purchase currency options directly.

Enhanced Liquidity

If a company can securitize a loan so it becomes publicly traded, lenders will require a lower yield to reflect their ability to sell the security without lowering the price or incurring high transactions costs. Examples of such securitization are CMOs, credit card receivable-backed securities, stripped mortgage-backed securities, and loan-backed certificates. They are all publicly registered securities that, because of their liquidity, have yields significantly lower than those on the underlying assets.[10] For example, when General Motors Acceptance Corporation began issuing automobile loan-backed securities, it noted that its cost of funds was significantly lower than the cost of factoring receivables. Interestingly, the Resolution Trust Corporation recently announced that it intends to issue securities backed by commercial mortgages and that its issues will increase the amount of such securities outstanding by about 25%.

Reductions in Agency Costs

A new security can increase shareholder value by reducing the agency costs that arise out of inherent conflicts of interest among professional corporate managers, stockholders, and bondholders. For example, managers in some cases may increase shareholder value at the expense of bondholders by leveraging up the firm. *Interest rate reset notes* address this problem by adjusting the coupon to a current market rate on a future date, providing bondholders with protection against a drop in the issuer's credit standing prior to that date.[11] Similarly, *credit sensitive notes* and *floating rate, rating sensitive notes* bear a coupon rate that varies inversely with the issuer's credit standing.[12]

Puttable bonds provide a series of put options that also protect bondholders against deterioration in the issuer's credit standing. Certain puttable bonds reduce agency costs by giving investors the right to put the bonds back to the issuer if there is a change in control of the corporation or if the corporation increases its leverage above some stated threshold through a recapitalization. Such "poison put" options protect bondholders against "event risk."[13]

Increasing rate notes, when used in connection with a bridge financing, provide an incentive for the issuer to redeem the notes (using the proceeds of a "more permanent" financing) on schedule. Unfortunately, as many issuers have discovered, if the increasing rate notes cannot be refinanced as quickly as originally planned, the increasing coupon rate acts like a ticking time bomb that threatens to damage the issuer's credit standing by continually eroding the issuer's interest coverage.

Reductions in Transaction Costs

A number of innovative debt securities increase stockholder value by reducing the underwriting commissions and other transaction costs associated with raising capital. *Extendible notes, variable coupon renewable notes, puttable bonds, remarketed reset notes,* and *euronotes and eurocommercial*

paper are all designed to reduce issuance expenses and other forms of transaction costs by giving the issuer or investor the option to extend the security's maturity. For example, extendible notes typically provide for an interest rate adjustment every two or three years, and thus represent an alternative to rolling over two- or three-year note issues that does not incur additional issuance expenses. Refinements of the extendible note concept, such as certain puttable bonds and remarketed reset notes, give the issuer greater flexibility in resetting the terms of the security.

Euronotes and eurocommercial paper represent the extension of commercial paper to the euromarket.[14] Transaction cost savings result from the use of commercial paper because corporations invest directly in one another's securities rather than through a financial intermediary.

Reducing Investor Transaction Costs. By issuing securities backed by a diversified portfolio of assets, some companies may benefit by providing investors with a degree of diversification that could be significantly more expensive to accomplish on their own. This, in turn, could also lead to a reduction in investors' required yields. As mentioned earlier, mortgage pass-through certificates, credit card receivable-backed securities, and loan-backed certificates may all lead to a reduction in issuers' overall cost of capital for this reason.[15]

Reductions in Taxes

Corporate issuers can increase stockholder value by designing securities that reduce the total amount of taxes payable by the company and its investors. Such "tax arbitrage" takes place whenever a corporation issues debt to investors with a marginal tax rate on interest income that is lower than the corporation's marginal income tax rate.

Zero-coupon bonds, which do not make interim interest payments but instead pay all debt service in a single lump sum at maturity, represent a good example of such arbitrage activity. Prior to passage of the Tax Equity and Fiscal Responsibility Act of 1982 (TEFRA), the U.S. tax code allowed an issuer of zero-coupon bonds to amortize the original issue discount (the difference between the face amount of the bonds and their issue price) on a straight-line basis for tax purposes. Being able to deduct interest expense for tax purposes faster than interest on the bonds implicitly compounded produced significant tax savings for corporate issuers. The size of such tax savings, moreover, was a direct function of the level of interest rates: the higher the yield on the issue, and thus the greater the discount to be amortized, ie larger the savings. When interest rates rose narply in 1981 and 1982, there was a flood of low ɔupon bonds and zero-coupon bonds, sold primar- y to tax exempt pension funds, to exploit this tax ophole. Since that period of high interest rates (and change in the tax law), however, they have all but sappeared (except in convertible form).

Circumvention of Regulatory Restrictions or Other Constraints

ank regulations specifying the requirements for ebt instruments to qualify as "primary capital" have nanged several times in recent years. Banks and eir financial advisors have responded predictably ith new debt securities designed primarily to meet ıch requirements. Examples include *equity con- act notes,* which obligate holders contractually to ɔnvert the notes into common stock of the bank (or s holding company); *equity commitment notes,* hich the issuer (or its parent) commits to refinance y issuing securities that qualify as capital; and sink- ıg fund debentures that pay sinking fund amounts ı common stock rather than cash.

Variable coupon renewable notes represent a finement of the extendible note concept. The aturity of the notes automatically extends 91 days : the end of each quarter, unless the holder elects ɔ terminate the automatic extension, in which case ıe interest rate spread decreases. A holder wishing ɔ terminate the investment would avoid the reduc- ɔn in spread by selling the notes in the marketplace. hese features were designed to meet regulatory vestment restrictions then faced by money market ıtual funds.[16]

Commodity-linked bonds are attractive to insti- ations that would like to speculate in commodity ɔtions, or invest in them as an inflation hedge, but ıat cannot for regulatory or other reasons purchase ɔmmodity options directly. Similarly, bonds with terest or principal payments tied to a specified reign exchange rate or denominated in a foreign ırrency are attractive to institutions that would like speculate in foreign currencies but cannot make ıch investments directly. Many of the securities eveloped in the 1980s and since contain embedded ɔmmodity options or currency options of various rms and were motivated by a desire to circumvent gulatory investment restrictions.

Preferred Stock Innovations

eferred stock offers a tax advantage over debt to ɔrporate investors in the United States. Because

U.S. corporations are permitted to deduct from their taxable income 70% of the dividends they receive from unaffiliated corporations, corporate cash man- agers have a tax incentive to purchase preferred stock rather than commercial paper or other short- term debt instruments, the interest on which is fully taxable. Nontaxable corporate issuers find preferred stock cheaper than debt because corporate investors are willing to pass back part of the value of the tax arbitrage by accepting a lower dividend rate.

Managing Interest Rate Risk with Preferreds

Purchasing long-term, fixed-dividend-rate preferred stock, however, exposes the purchaser to the risk that rising interest rates could lead to a fall in the price of the preferred stock that would more than offset the tax saving. A variety of preferred stock instruments (see Table 16.2) have been designed to deal: with this problem.

Adjustable rate preferred stock was designed to lessen the investor's principal risk by having the dividend rate adjust as interest rates change. The dividend rate adjusts according to a formula specify- ing a fixed spread over Treasuries. But, at times the spread investors have required to value the securities at par has differed significantly from the fixed spread specified in the formula, causing the value of the security to deviate significantly from its face amount.[17]

Convertible adjustable preferred stock (CAPS) was designed to eliminate this deficiency by making the security convertible on each dividend payment date into enough shares to make the security worth its par value. But, although CAPS have traded closer to their respective face amounts than adjustable rate preferred stocks, there have only been 13 CAPS issues. Issuer reluctance may have stemmed from the security's conversion feature, which could force the issuer to issue common stock or raise a large amount of cash on short notice.

Auction rate preferred stock carried the evolu- tionary process a step further. The dividend rate is reset by Dutch auction every 49 days, which repre- sents just enough weeks to meet the 46-day holding period required to qualify for the 70% dividends-re- ceived deduction. There are various versions of auc- tion-rate preferred stock that are sold under different acronyms (MMP, Money Market Preferred; AMPS, Auction Market Preferred Stock; DARTS, Dutch Auction Rate Transferable Securities; STAR, Short- Term Auction Rate; etc.) coined by the different securities firms that offer the product. Although the names may differ, the securities are the same.[17]

In an effort to refine the adjustable rate preferred stock concept further, there have been at least two

Table 16.2   Selected Preferred Stock Innovations

■ Security	■ Year Issued	■ No. of Issues	■ Aggregate Proceeds ($)
□ Distinguishing Characteristics	□ Risk Reallocation		
● Enhanced Liquidity	● Reduction in Agency Costs		
○ Reduction in Transaction Costs	○ Tax and Other Benefits: SEE NOTE		
■ **Adjustable Rate Preferred Stock**	■ 05/11/82	■ 140	■ 11.0
□ Dividend rate reset each quarter based on maximum of 3-month T-bill, 10-year, or 20-year Treasury rates plus or minus a specified spread.	□ Issuer bears more interest rate risk than a fixed-rate preferred would involve. Lower yield than commercial paper.		
● Security is designed to trade near its par value.			
■ **Auction Rate Preferred Stock (MMP/DARTS/ AMPS/STAR)**	■ 08/27/84	■ 381	■ 25.2
□ Dividend rate reset by Dutch auction every 49 days. Dividend is paid at the end of each dividend period.	□ Issuer bears more interest rate risk than a fixed-rate preferred would involve. Lower yield than commercial paper.		
● Security is designed to provide greater liquidity than convertible adjustable preferred stock.	● Dividend rate each period is determined in the marketplace, which provides protection against deterioration in issuer's credit standing .		
■ **Convertible Adjustable Preferred Stock**	■ 09/15/83	■ 13	■ 0.5
□ Issue convertible on dividend payment dates into number of issuer's common shares, subject to cap, equal in value to par value of preferred.	□ Issuer bears more interest rate risk than a fixed-rate preferred would involve. Lower yield than commercial paper.		
● Security is designed to provide greater liquidity than adjustable rate preferred stock (due to the conversion feature).			
■ **Fixed Rate/Adjustable Rate or Auction Rate Preferred**	■ 11/16/84	■ 6	■ 0.4
□ Fixed-dividend-rate preferred stock that automatically becomes adjustable rate or auction rate preferred after a specified length of time.	□ Once the adjustment or auction period begins, issuer bears more interest rate risk than a fixed-rate preferred would involve.		
● Security is designed to trade near its par value once the adjustment or auction period begins.			
■ **Indexed Floating Rate Preferred Stock**	■ 10/01/85	■ 3	■ 0.2
□ Dividend rate resets quarterly as a specified percentage of 3-month LIBOR.	□ Issuer bears more interest rate risk than a fixed-rate preferred would involve. Lower yield than commercial paper.		
● Security is designed to trade closer to its par value than a fixed-dividend-rate preferred.			
■ **Remarketed Preferred Stock (SABRES)**	■ 06/27/85	■ 77	■ 4.5
□ Perpetual preferred stock with a dividend rate that resets at the end of each dividend period to a rate the remarketing agent determines will make the preferred stock worth par. Dividend periods may be of any length, even 1 day. Different shares of a single issue may have different periods and different dividend rates.	□ Issuer bears more interest rate risk than a fixed-rate preferred would involve. Lower yield than commercial paper.		
● Security is designed to trade near its par value.	○ Remarketed preferred stock offers greater flexibility in setting the terms the issue than auction rate preferred stock, which requires a Dutch auction for potentially the entire issue once every 49 days.		
■ **Single Point Adjustable Rate Stock**	■ 12/13/85	■ 2	■ 0.2
□ Dividend rate reset every 49 days as a specified percentage of the high-grade commercial paper rate.	□ Issuer bears more interest rate risk than a fixed-rate preferred would involve. Lower yield than commercial paper.		
● Security is designed to trade near its par value.			
○ Security is designed to save on recurring transaction costs associated with auction rate preferred stock.			
■ **Variable Cumulative Preferred Stock**	■ 07/07/88	■ 8	■ 0.5
□ At start of dividend period issuer can select between auction method and remarketing method to reset dividend rate at beginning of next period.	□ Issuer bears more interest rate risk than a fixed-rate preferred would involve. Lower yield than commercial paper.		
● Security is designed to trade near its par value.	● The maximum permitted dividend rate increases according to a specified schedule if the preferred stock's credit rating falls.		
○ Saves on transaction costs the issuer would otherwise incur if it wanted to change from auction reset to remarketing reset or vice versa.	○ Security is designed to give the issuer the flexibility to alter the method rate reset.		

NOTE: All preferred stock innovations are designed to enable short-term corporate investors to take advantage of the 70% dividends received deduction.

attempts to design a superior security, but only one was successful. *Single point adjustable rate stock* (SPARS) has a dividend rate that adjusts automatically every 49 days to a specified percentage of the 60-day high-grade commercial paper rate. The security is designed so as to afford the same degree of liquidity as auction-rate preferred stock, but with lower transaction costs since no auction need be held. The problem with SPARS, however, is that the fixed dividend rate formula involves a potential agency cost that auction-rate preferred stock does not. Because the dividend formula is fixed, investors will suffer a loss if the issuer's credit standing falls. Primarily for this reason, there have been only two SPARS issues.

Remarketed preferred stock, by contrast, pays a dividend that is reset at the end of each dividend period to a dividend rate that a specified remarketing agent determines will make the preferred stock worth par. Such issues permit the issuer considerable flexibility in selecting the length of the dividend period (it can be as short as one day). Remarketed preferred also offers greater flexibility in selecting the other terms of the issue. In fact, each share of an issue could have a different maturity, dividend rate, or other terms, provided the issuer and holders so agree. Remarketed preferred has not proven as popular with issuers as auction-rate preferred stock, but that could change due to the greater flexibility remarketed preferred affords.

Variable cumulative preferred stock was born out of the controversy over whether auction-rate preferred stock or remarketed preferred stock results in more equitable pricing. This variation effectively allows the issuer to decide at the beginning of each dividend period which of the two reset methods will determine the dividend rate at the beginning of the next dividend period.

Convertible Debt/Preferred Stock Innovations

Convertible bonds (see Table 16.3) reduce agency costs arising from possible conflicts of interest between bondholders and stockholders. The conflict is this: once a company issues significant amounts of debt, its managers can take actions, subject only to the restrictions imposed by the bond indenture, that increase shareholder value at the expense of bondholders. For example, when a highly leveraged company approaches insolvency, managers have an incentive to take on riskier projects—even those with negative expected net present values—as long as they offer the possibility of extraordinarily high returns. Financial economists refer to this as the

"asset substitution problem." Convertible bonds control this incentive, and thus reduce the potential conflict, by allowing the bondholders to share in the higher returns that riskier projects might provide.[18]

Convertible Reset Debentures. These provide for a coupon adjustment to a current market rate on a specified future date, which protects bondholders against deterioration in the issuer's credit standing prior to the reset date. Such deterioration could result from actions managers take to increase stockholder value. Certain *puttable convertible bonds* reduce agency costs by giving bondholders the right to put the bonds back to the issuer if there is a change in control of the corporation, or if the corporation increases its leverage above some stated threshold through a recapitalization.

Convertibles and Taxes. Many of the convertible debt innovations involve a form of tax arbitrage because 80–90% of convertible bond investors are tax-exempt.[19] The tax motive is especially clear in the case of *convertible exchangeable preferred stock.* This security starts out as convertible perpetual preferred stock, but the issuer has the option to exchange the preferred for an issue of convertible subordinated debt with the same conversion terms and with an interest rate that equals the dividend rate on the convertible preferred. The exchange feature enables the issuer to reissue the convertible preferred as convertible debt, should it become taxable in the future, but without having to pay additional underwriting commissions. Not surprisingly, a large volume of such securities have been issued by companies that were not currently taxpayers for federal income tax purposes. Similarly, *exchangeable auction rate preferred stock* permits the issuer to exchange auction rate notes for auction rate preferred stock on any dividend payment date.

Adjustable Rate Convertible Debt. This was a very thinly disguised attempt to package equity as debt. The coupon rate varied directly with the dividend rate on the underlying common stock, and there was no conversion premium at the time the debt was issued. After just three issues, the IRS ruled that the security is equity for tax purposes, thereby denying the interest deductions. And the security, not surprisingly, has not been issued since that ruling.

Zero-coupon convertible debt, which includes *Liquid Yield Option Notes* (LYONs)[20] and *ABC Securities,* represents a variation on the same theme. If the issue is converted, both interest and principal are converted to common equity, in which case the issuer will have effectively sold common equity with a tax deductibility feature.

Table 16.3 Selected Convertible Debt/Preferred Stock Innovations

■ Security	■ Year Issued	■ No. of Issues	■ Aggregate Proceeds ($B)
□ Distinguishing Characteristics	□ Risk Reallocation		
● Enhanced Liquidity	● Reduction in Agency Costs		
○ Reduction in Transaction Costs	○ Tax and Other Benefits		

■ ABC Securities	■ 02/06/91	■ 2	■ 0.4
□ Non-interest-bearing convertible debt issue on which the dividends on the underlying common stock are passed through to bondholders if the common stock price rises by more than a specified percentage (typically around 30%) from the date of issuance.	○ If issue converts, the issuer will have sold, in effect, tax deductible common equity. If holders convert, entire debt service stream is converted to common equity.		

■ Adjustable Rate Convertible Debt	■ 04/18/84	■ 3	■ 0.4
□ Debt the interest rate on which varies directly with the dividend rate on the underlying common stock. No conversion premium at issuance.	○ Effectively, tax deductible common equity. Security has since been ruled equity by the IRS. Portion of each bond recorded as equity on the issuer's balance sheet.		

■ Cash Redeemable LYONs	■ 06/20/90	■ 1	■ 0.9
□ Non-interest-bearing convertible debt issue that is redeemable in cash for the value of the underlying common stock, at issuer's option.	○ If issue converts, the issuer will have sold, in effect, tax deductible common equity. Issuer does not have to have its equity ownership interest diluted through conversion.		

■ Convertible Exchangeable Preferred Stock	■ 12/15/82	■ 129	■ 10.1
□ Convertible preferred stock that is exchangeable, at the issuer's option, for convertible debt with identical rate and identical conversion terms.	○ Issuer can exchange debt for the preferred when it becomes taxable with interest rate the same as the preferred and without any change in conversion features. Appears as equity on the issuer's balance sheet until it is exchanged for convertible debt.		
○ No need to reissue convertible security as debt—just exchange it—when the issuer becomes a taxpayer.			

■ Convertible Reset Debentures	■ 10/13/83	■ 8	■ 0.6
□ Convertible bond the interest rate on which must be adjusted upward, if necessary, 2 years after issuance by an amount sufficient to give the debentures a market value equal to their face amount.	● Investor is protected against a deterioration in the issuer's credit quality or financial prospects within 2 years of issuance.		

■ Debt with Mandatory Common Stock Purchase Contracts	■ N/A	■ N/A	■ N/A
□ Notes with contracts that obligate note purchasers to buy sufficient common stock from the issuer to retire the issue in full by its scheduled maturity date.	○ Notes provide a stream of interest tax shields, which (true) equity does not. Commercial bank holding companies have issued it because it counted as "primary capital" for regulatory purposes.		

■ Exchangeable Auction Rate Preferred Stock/Remarketed Preferred Stock	■ 11/20/86	■ 5	■ 0.1
□ Auction rate preferred stock or remarketed preferred stock that is exchangeable on any dividend payment date, at the option of the issuer, for auction rate notes, the interest rate on which is reset by Dutch auction every 35 days.	□ Issuer bears more interest rate risk than a fixed-rate instrument would involve.		
● Security is designed to trade near its par value.			
○ Issuance of auction rate notes involves no underwriting commissions.	○ Issuer can exchange notes for the preferred when it becomes taxable. Appears as equity on the issuer's balance sheet until it is exchanged for auction rate notes.		

■ Liquid Yield Option Notes (LYONs)/Zero Coupon Convertible Debt	■ 12/18/70	■ 124	■ 17.0
□ Non-interest-bearing convertible debt issue.	○ If issue converts, the issuer will have sold, in effect, tax deductible equity. If holders convert, entire debt service stream converts to common equity.		

■ Preferred Equity Redemption Cumulative Stock (PERCS)/ Mandatory Conversion Premium Dividend Preferred Stock	■ 08/16/91	■ 7	■ 4.7
□ Preferred stock that pays a cash dividend significantly above that on the underlying common stock in exchange for a conversion option that has a capped share value.	□ Investor trades off a portion of the underlying common stock's capital appreciation potential in return for an enhanced dividend rate.		

■ Puttable Convertible Bonds	■ 07/21/82	■ 667	■ 44.8
□ Convertible bond that can be redeemed prior to maturity, at the option of the holder, on certain specified dates at specified prices.	● Issuer is exposed to risk that the bonds will be redeemed early if interest rates rise sufficiently and common stock price falls sufficiently. Investor has one or more put options, which provide protection against deterioration in credit quality.		

Debt and warrants exercisable into the issuer's common stock can be combined into a unit to create synthetic convertible debt, the features of which mirror the features of conventional convertible debt.[21] Synthetic convertible bonds enjoy a tax advantage relative to a comparable convertible debt issue because, in effect, the warrant proceeds are deductible for tax purposes over the life of the debt issue.

Meeting Regulatory Restrictions. Banks have issued *capital notes* because they can be substituted for equity (subject to certain restrictions) for regulatory purposes while still generating the normal interest tax shields provided by debt. For example, prior to the passage of FIRREA, banks issued interest deductible *debt with mandatory common stock purchase contracts* (which qualified as primary capital for regulatory purposes because conversion was mandatory).[22]

Common Equity Innovations

Five of the common equity innovations listed in Table 16.4 serve to reallocate risk: the Americus Trust, callable common stock, puttable common stock, SuperShares, and unbundled stock units.

The first Americus Trust was offered to owners of AT&T common stock on October 25, 1983. Since then, more than two dozen other Americus Trusts have been formed. An Americus Trust offers the common stockholders of a company the opportunity to strip each of their common shares into a PRIME component, which carries full dividend and voting rights and limited capital appreciation rights, and a SCORE component, which carries full capital appreciation rights above a threshold price. PRIMES and SCORES appear to expand the range of securities available for inclusion in investment portfolios, thus helping make the capital markets more complete.[23] Unfortunately, a recent change in tax law made the separation of a share of common stock into a PRIME and a SCORE a taxable event, and no new Americus Trusts have been formed since that change in law took effect.

Callable common stock consists of common stock, typically issued by a subsidiary company, that is sold by the parent company subject to a stock purchase option agreement. The option agreement provides for periodic step-ups in the call price and may require the parent company to exercise all the outstanding purchase options if any are exercised. The option agreement gives the parent company the right to reacquire the subsidiary's shares at a prespecified price, which limits the shareholder's capital appreciation potential.

Puttable common stock involves the sale of put options along with a new issue of common stock.[24] By giving investors the right to put their shares back to the firm at a price no less than the price they paid, the put option reduces the information "asymmetry" associated with a new share issue.[25] The assurance provided investors by this put option may be especially valuable in the case of initial public offerings, where investor uncertainty is particularly great and investment bankers are accordingly forced to underprice IPOs.

SuperShares are intended to divide the stream of annual total returns on the S&P 500 portfolio of common stocks into two components that are similar to the two components created by the Americus Trust: 1) Priority SuperShares that pay the dividends on the S&P 500 stocks and provide limited capital appreciation and 2) Appreciation SuperShares that provide capital appreciation above the Priority SuperShares' capital appreciation ceiling. The new securities are issued by a trust that contains a portfolio of common stocks that mirrors the performance of the S&P 500 Index and a portfolio of Treasury bills. The trust also issues two other classes of securities, one of which (Protection SuperShares) functions like portfolio insurance.

Unbundled stock units (USUs) were intended to divide the stream of annual total returns on a share of common stock into three components: 1) a 30-year "base yield" bond that would pay interest at a rate equal to the dividend rate on the issuer's common stock (thereby recharacterizing the "base" dividend stream into an interest stream); 2) a preferred share that would pay dividends equal to the excess, if any, of the dividend rate on the issuer's common stock above the "base" dividend rate; and 3) a 30-year warrant that would pay the excess, if any, of the issuer's share price 30 years hence above the redemption value of the base yield bond. Despite extensive marketing efforts, the USU concept failed to gain wide investor support and encountered regulatory obstacles that led to its withdrawal from the marketplace before a single issue could be completed.[26] Like the Americus Trust and SuperShares, USUs were designed to give shareholders more flexibility in choosing among the different components of the total returns from common stock; each of these new forms would effectively allow shareholders to tailor the corporation's dividend policy to suit their own preferences.

Table 16.4   Selected Common Equity Innovations

■ Security	■ Year Issued	■ No. of Issues	■ Aggregate Proceeds ($B)
□ Distinguishing Characteristics	□ Risk Reallocation		
● Enhanced Liquidity	● Reduction in Agency Costs		
○ Reduction in Transaction Costs	○ Tax and Other Benefits		
■ **Americus Trust**	■ N/A	■ N/A	■ N/A
□ Outstanding shares of a particular company's common stock are contributed to five-year unit investment trust. Units may be separated into PRIME component, which embodies full dividend and voting rights in the underlying share and permits limited capital appreciation, and SCORE component, which provides full capital appreciation above stated price.	□ Stream of annual total returns on a share of stock is separated into a dividend stream (with limited capital appreciation) and a residual capital appreciation stream.		
	○ PRIME component would appeal to corporate investors who can take advantage of the 70% dividends received deduction. SCORE component would appeal to capital-gain-oriented individual investors.		
	○ PRIME component resembles participating preferred stock if the issuer's common stock dividend rate is stable. SCORE component is a longer-dated call option than the ones customarily traded in the options market.		
■ **Callable Common Stock**	■ 05/23/91	■ 2	■ 0.1
□ Common stock of a subsidiary sold by the parent subject to a stock purchase option scheme. Exercise prices step up overtime. Callable common stock often issued with warrants to purchase common stock of the parent company.	□ Call option causes holders of the callable common stock to forgo capital appreciation in excess of the strike price (unless the callable common stock was sold in units that include warrants to buy the parent company's common stock).		
	● Warrant to purchase parent company's shares enables holders of callable common stock to share in the upside if the common stock is called away.		
	○ Issuer retains the right to regain 100% ownership of the subsidiary's common stock.		
■ **Master Limited Partnership**	■ 11/29/82	■ 114	■ 9.1
□ A business is given the legal form of a partnership but is otherwise structured, and is traded publicly, like a corporation.	○ Eliminates a layer of taxation because partnerships are not taxable entities.		
■ **Paired Common Stock**	■ 08/20/86	■ 4	■ 0.3
□ Common shares of two related companies are paired and trade as a unit. Can be used when a company has a real estate-related business that can be organized as a real estate investment trust (REIT) but wishes to conduct other operations that a REIT is not permitted to engage in.	○ A REIT is not subject to federal income taxation on the income it distributes to its shareholders (except for certain specified classes of income).		
■ **Puttable Common Stock**	■ 11/84	■ 3	■ 0.1
□ Issuer sells a new issue of common stock along with rights to put the stock back to the issuer on a specified date at a specified price.	□ Issuer sells investors a put option, which investors will exercise if the company's share price decreases.		
	● The put option reduces agency costs associated with a new share issue that are brought on by informational asymmetries.		
	○ Equivalent under certain conditions to convertible bonds but can be recorded as equity on the balance sheet so long as the company's payment obligation under the put option can be settled in common stock.		
■ **SuperShares**	■ None Issued	■ N/A	■ N/A
□ A trust is formed to hold a portfolio of common stocks that comprise the S&P 500 and a portfolio of Treasury bills. The trust sells four hybrid securities: (1) Priority SuperShares paying dividends on the S&P 500 and providing limited capital appreciation, (2) Appreciation SuperShares providing appreciation above the Priority SuperShares' appreciation ceiling, (3) Protection SuperShares providing the value of any decline in the S&P 500 below some specified level, and (4) Money Market Income SuperShares paying proceeds from the Treasury bill portfolio after Protection SuperShares have been paid.	□ Shareholders can hold the components of total return in any proportions they choose, and Protection SuperShares function like portfolio insurance.		
■ **Unbundled Stock Units**	■ None Issued	■ N/A	■ N/A
□ The total return stream from a share of common stock would be divided into three components: (1) a 30-year base yield bond (BYB) paying an interest rate equal to the dividend rate on the underlying common stock at the time the trust was formed plus limited capital appreciation, (2) a 30-year preferred stock instrument paying a dividend rate equal to the excess, if any, of the common dividend rate above the base rate, and (3) a 30-year warrant providing capital appreciation above the BYB's redemption value.	□ Shareholders could hold the components of a common share's total return in any proportions they choose.		

How to Make Securities Innovation Work to Your Company's Advantage

Prospective issuers of securities are often bombarded with new securities ideas. How can a company decide whether a new security is more advantageous than existing alternatives? A new security may be different, but is it really better for the issuer's shareholders?

The following is a checklist of important considerations for corporate treasurers in evaluating the issuance of new securities:

♦ How do the new security's features differ from the features of the most closely comparable conventional securities?

♦ How will interest (or dividend) payments and principal payments vary under different interest rate conditions? If the interest (or dividend) or principal payments depend on exchange rates, commodity prices, or some other general economic variable, how do the debt service requirements vary under different scenarios?

♦ Under what circumstances might the holders be able to force redemption to their advantage and to the issuer's disadvantage? Will the issuer be adequately compensated for bearing this early redemption risk?

♦ Under what circumstances might the issuer be able to force redemption to its advantage and to investors' disadvantage? Is such a call option worth more to the issuer than the "call premium" investors will build into the interest rate? Alternatively, will the new security limit the issuer's optional redemption flexibility more than conventional securities—and if so, will the issuer receive compensation for reduced flexibility in the form of a lower interest rate?

♦ Are there any unusual covenant or other restrictions on the issuer's operating or financial flexibility relative to conventional securities? If so, will the issuer be fully compensated through a reduced interest rate?

♦ Does the new security entail any sort of risk-shifting when compared to conventional securities? If so, does this risk-shifting work to the issuer's advantage? For example, does it appreciably reduce the risk of financial distress, and if so, are investors charging a lower interest rate to reflect this reduced risk?

♦ Does the new security enhance investors' liquidity by making it publicly marketable or by broadening the base of investors? And, if so, does the reduction in interest costs resulting from greater liquidity outweigh the expected cost of the resulting reduction in the company's ability to reorganize its more dispersed claims in the event of financial distress?

♦ How do the underwriting spread and other issuance costs compare to the cost of issuing conventional securities?

♦ Does the new security confer tax benefits or impose tax liabilities on either the issuer or investors as compared to conventional securities of the same type? If there is a significant net tax advantage, does it involve significant risk that the IRS will disallow the intended tax treatment?

♦ Are there significant regulatory benefits?

♦ Are there accounting benefits? Will these benefits enhance shareholder value?

♦ On balance, will issuing the new security add sufficiently more to shareholder value than the available alternatives to justify the risk inherent in issuing an unfamiliar security? Or, can comparable benefits be obtained just by using a simpler, more conventional securities structure?

Conclusion

Securities innovation increases the efficiency with which capital markets perform their central role of channeling savings into corporate investment. Innovative securities that offer more cost-effective means of transferring risks, increasing liquidity, and reducing transaction and agency costs all act to reduce market frictions that otherwise reduce efficiency.

Securities innovations are a profit-driven response to changes in the economic, tax, and regulatory environment. One of the more important questions concerning the process of securities innovation is whether that process has reached the point of diminishing returns. If the tax regime remains static, interest rates stabilize, and the regulatory landscape solidifies, diminishing returns to securities innovation are bound to set in eventually. But, to the extent that securities innovation occurs in response to unexpected economic, tax, and regulatory "shocks," a steady stream of such abrupt shifts can keep the process of securities innovation going indefinitely. And, together with a continuously changing economic and regulatory climate, further consolidation within the financial services industry will continue to intensify competition and drive market participants to seek better securities designs and more efficient ways of conducting securities transactions.

For a corporate treasurer or chief financial officer, the opportunity to issue a new security, and to become part of the process of securities innovation, is a tempting prospect. Those companies that innovate successfully can increase shareholder value (along with "reputational capital"). But the process is not costless (or riskless), as the failed experiment with unbundled stock units so clearly demonstrates. A company should decide to issue a new security only after it has determined that the new security is truly innovative and that issuing it will increase shareholder value.

Endnotes

1. "Financial Innovation: The Last Twenty Years and the Next," *Journal of Financial and Quantitative Analysis* (December 1986): 459–471.

2. Cited by Merton Miller as perhaps the most significant financial innovation in the past 25 years. See Miller, 1986, cited above.

3. The year the security was first issued and the number of issues and aggregate proceeds raised through year-end 1991 were provided by Securities Data Company, Inc.

4. This aspect of financial innovation is emphasized by Stephen Ross in "Institutional Markets, Financial Marketing, and Financial Innovation," *Journal of Finance* (July 1989): 541–556.

5. The securities are often issued in a senior-subordinated structure. The senior class of securities, which is sold to investors, has a prior claim to the cash flows from the underlying collateral pool. The issuer typically retains the subordinated interest in the collateral pool, although in many cases in recent years the subordinated class has also been sold to investors. The relative sizes of the senior and subordinated classes determine how the default risk is allocated between the two classes.

6. See Frank J. Fabozzi (ed.), *The Handbook of Mortgage-Backed Securities,* Chicago, Probus, 1985; also F.J. Fabozzi (ed.), *Advances & Inno-*

vations in the Bond and Mortgage Market, Chicago, Probus, 1989.

7. The introduction of these securities also enhanced market completeness because of their duration and convexity characteristics. The apparent failure to understand fully the riskiness of these securities led to a substantial and highly publicized financial loss in 1987 by a major brokerage house. For an account, see Sterngold, "Anatomy of a Staggering Loss," *New York Times* (May 11, 1987): D1ff.

8. Typically, the incentive in issuing an inverse floater is to fix the coupon by entering into an interest rate swap agreement. The two transactions together benefit the issuer when they result in a lower cost of funds than a conventional fixed-rate issue. For a discussion of inverse floaters, see L.S. Goodman and J.B. Yawitz, "Innovation in the U.S. Bond Market," *Institutional Investor Money Management Forum* (December 1987): 102–104.

9. For a more detailed consideration of hybrid debt securities designed to manage commodity and exchange rate risks, see the article by Charles Smithson, "The Uses of Hybrid Debt in Managing Corporate Risk," in Chapter 18.

10. The issuer often retains a subordinated interest in the underlying collateral pool so that a large portion of the actual yield reduction results from the investors' senior position with respect to mortgage or receivable pool cash flows. Such lower yields, moreover, do not necessarily imply a lower overall cost of capital for the issuing firm. Asset securitization, in a sense, involves carving out a company's highest quality assets and selling them on a stand alone basis. To be certain that there is an overall reduction in the issuer's cost of capital, one has to examine the effect on the firm's other liabilities, including the risk of the firm's equity.

11. A variant of reset notes, known as "remarketed" reset notes, includes a put option that protects investors against the possibility of the issuer and the remarketing agent conspiring to set a below-market coupon rate. It also provides a flexible interest rate formula in the event the issuer and the remarketing agent cannot agree on a rate that provides for a higher interest rate, should the issuer's credit standing decline.

12. These securities, however, have a potentially serious flaw: The interest rate adjustment mechanism will tend to increase the issuer's debt service burden just when it can least afford it—when its credit rating has fallen, presumably as a result of diminished operating cash flow.

13. Bondholders began to demand such protection in high-grade debt issues in the wake of the LBO of RJR Nabisco. The announcement of that transaction triggered decreases of between 15% and 20% in the market value of publicly traded RJR Nabisco debt.

14. See *Recent Innovations in International Banking*, Bank for International Settlements, April 1986.

15. See the important qualification noted in footnote 10.

16. Variable coupon renewable notes were given a nominal maturity of one year, which was the maximum maturity permitted money market mutual fund investments. Also, because of the weekly rate reset, variable coupon renewable notes were permitted to count as seven-day assets in meeting the 120-day upper limit on a money market mutual fund's dollar-weighted average portfolio maturity.

17. This result increases the volatility of the security's rate of return. One study documents the high volatility of adjustable rate preferred stock holding-period returns relative to those of alternative money market instruments. See B.J. Winger, C.R. Chen, J.D. Martin, J.W. Petty, and S.C. Hayden, "Adjustable Rate Preferred Stock," *Financial Management* (Spring 1986): 48–57.

18. At least one study has documented the tax arbitrage that auction rate preferred stock affords under current tax law. See M.J. Alderson, K.C. Brown, and S.L. Lummer, "Dutch Auction Rate Preferred Stock," *Financial Management* (Summer 1987): 68–73.

19. For a more detailed examination of these sources of shareholder-debtholder conflict, see Clifford W. Smith and Jerold B. Warner, "On Financial Contracting: An Analysis of Bond Covenants," *Journal of Financial Economics*, 7 (1979): 117–161. See also Chapter 9 of Douglas Emery's and my book, *Principles of Finance with Corporate Applications*, (West, St. Paul, 1991).

20. See J.D. Finnerty, "The Case for Issuing Synthetic Convertible Bonds," *Midland Corporate Finance Journal* (Fall 1986): 73–82.

21. See John McConnell and Eduardo Schwartz's account of "The Origin and Evolution of the LYON" in this issue of the *JACF*. For a more technical analysis, see also McConnell and Schwartz, "LYON Taming," *Journal of Finance* (July 1986): 561–576.

22. See Finnerty (1986), cited above, and E.P. Jones and S.P. Mason, "Equity-Linked Debt," *Midland Corporate Finance Journal* (Winter 1986): 47–58.

23. The Financial Institutions Reform, Recovery and Enforcement Act of 1989 (FIRREA) established new minimum capital standards for financial institutions. Prior to the passage of FIRREA, banks could include mandatory convertible debt in primary capital up to 20% of the sum of the other elements of primary capital. FIRREA excludes mandatory convertible debt from "core capital," which is the new definition of what was formerly called primary capital.

24. The AT&T Americus Trust was formed prior to the breakup of AT&T. The trust therefore provided an opportunity for investors to acquire units representing shares in pre-reorganization AT&T (i.e., proportionate interests in post-reorganization AT&T and in the seven regional holding companies AT&T spun off) perhaps more cheaply than they could by accumulating the shares of the different entities on their own.

25. As discussed by Chen and Kensinger, such a package of securities is comparable to a convertible bond. A.H. Chen and J.W. Kensinger, "Puttable Stock: A New Innovation in Equity Financing," *Financial Management* (Spring 1988): 27–37.

26. Puttable common stock issues often provide a schedule of increasing put prices in order to ensure a minimum positive holding period rate of return.

27. Victor Borun and I analyze USUs and explain how negative tax attributes and investors' liquidity concerns apparently outweighed the benefits of USUs. J.D. Finnerty and V.M. Borun, "An Analysis of Unbundled Stock Units," *Global Finance Journal* (Fall 1989): 47–69.

Chapter 17

The Origin of LYONs™:
A Case Study in Financial Innovation*

John J. McConnell
Emanuel T. Weiler Professor of Management,
Krannert Graduate School of Management
Purdue University, Lafayette, IN
Eduardo S. Schwartz
California Professor of Real Estate and Professor of Finance,
Anderson Graduate School of Management
University of California, Los Angeles, CA

Viewed at a distance and with scholarly detachment, financial innovation is a simple process. Some kind of "shock"—for instance, a sudden increase in interest rate volatility or a significant regulatory change—is introduced into the economic system. The shock alters the preferences of either investors or issuers in such a way that there then exists no financial instrument capable of satisfying a newly created demand. Observing the unsatisfied demand, an entrepreneur moves quickly to seize the opportunity by creating a new financial instrument. In the process, the entrepreneur reaps an economic reward for his efforts; investors and issuers are better served; and the entire economic system is improved.

On closer inspection, however, the actual process of financial innovation turns out, like most other human endeavors, to be a lot less tidy than economists' models would have it. In this article, we provide an "up-close" view of the origin and evolution of one financial instrument, the Liquid Yield Option Note (LYON™).

The LYON™ is a highly successful financial product introduced by Merrill Lynch in 1985. Between April 1985 and December 1991, Merrill Lynch served as the underwriter for 43 separate LYON™ issues, which raised a total of $11.7 billion for corporate clients. LYON™ issuers include such well-known firms as American Airlines, Eastman Kodak, Marriott Corporation, and Motorola. In 1989, other underwriters entered the market and have since brought an additional 13 LYON™-like issues to market. In the words of a recent *Wall Street Journal* article, the LYON™ is "one of Wall Street's hottest and most lucrative corporate finance products."[1]

As academics examining a new security, we begin by posing some questions. What does the LYON™ provide that was not available previously? Does the LYON™ really increase the welfare of investors and issuers? Or is it simply a "neutral mutation," that is, a now-accepted practice that serves no enduring economic purpose, but is sufficiently harmless to avoid being extinguished by competitive forces.[2]

In the spirit of full disclosure, however, we must admit that we are not entirely disinterested observers. Our association with the LYON™ is longstanding. When the early LYON™ issues were being brought to market in April 1985, questions arose about LYON™ pricing. We were hired by Merrill Lynch to develop a model for analyzing and pricing this new financial instrument. A by-product of this assignment was the opportunity to learn about the train of events that led to the creation of the LYON™, and we have since followed the evolution of this market with interest. In the pages that follow, we relate what we have observed, thought, and contributed during the development of this new security.

What Is a LYON™?

The LYON™ is a complex security. It is a *zero-coupon, convertible, callable, and puttable* bond. None of these four features is new; it is only their combination that makes the LYON™ an innovation. These general features of the instrument are perhaps best illustrated by considering a specific issue. Because it

*Source: Previously appeared in the Continental Bank Journal of Applied Corporate Finance Vol. 4, No. 4 (Winter 1992): 40–47. It is reprinted here with the permission of the publisher, Stern Stewart and Co.

was the first one, we consider the LYON™ issued by Waste Management, Inc., on April 12, 1985.

According to the indenture agreement, each Waste Management LYON™ has a face value of $1,000 and matures on January 21, 2001. There are, by definition, no coupon interest payments. If the security is not called, converted, or redeemed (i.e., put to the issuer) prior to that date, and if the issuer does not default, the investor will receive $1,000 per bond. If this turns out to be the case, based on an initial offering price of $250 per bond, the investor will receive an effective yield-to-maturity of 9%.

The Investor's Conversion Option. At any time prior to or on the maturity date, the investor may convert the bond into 4.36 shares of Waste Management common stock. Given a stock price of about $52 at the time of issue, this conversion ratio would appear to indicate an initial conversion "premium" of about 10% ($250/4.36 = $57.34). But, because the LYON™ is a *zero-coupon* convertible and thus issued at a large discount from par value, the conversion "premium" is not fixed. That is, as we discuss in more detail later, the minimum share price at which holders would willingly exchange their bonds for 4.36 shares effectively increases throughout most of the life of the bond.

The Investor's Put Option. Although not entirely new, the most unfamiliar feature of the LYON™ is the right it gives investors to put the bond to Waste Management beginning on June 30, 1988, and on each subsequent anniversary date, at predetermined exercise prices that increase through time, as shown in Table 17.1.

Based on the issue price of $250.00 per bond, this schedule of put exercise prices provides investors with a minimum 6% rate of return at the date of first exercise, rising in three 1% increments to a level of 9% over the next three years.

The Issuer's Call Option. Finally, Waste Management has the right to call the LYON at exercise prices that also increase through time. Although the issuer may call the LYON™ immediately after issuance, the investor does receive some call protection because Waste Management may not call the bond prior to June 30, 1987, unless the price of the Waste Management common stock rises above $86.01. The schedule of call prices is shown in Table 17.2.[3]

As in the case of convertibles generally, investors may respond to the call by choosing either to accept redemption payment from the issuer or to convert their bonds into stock.

As mentioned earlier, although the LYON™ is a complex security, it is not entirely new. Callable convertible bonds certainly existed prior to the LYON, as did zero coupon bonds. And so did put and call options on a wide array of common stocks. What demand, then, did the LYON™ fulfill that was not being adequately met by an already existing financial instrument?

Table 17.1 Put Pricing and Implied Yield with LYONs™

Date	Put Price	Implied Yield	Date	Put Price	Implied Yield
6/30/88	$301.87	6%	6/30/95	$613.04	9%
6/30/89	$331.51	7%	6/30/96	$669.45	9%
6/30/90	$375.58	8%	6/30/97	$731.06	9%
6/30/91	$431.08	9%	6/30/98	$798.34	9%
6/30/92	$470.75	9%	6/30/99	$871.80	9%
6/30/93	$514.07	9%	6/30/00	$952.03	9%
6/30/94	$561.38	9%			

Table 17.2 Schedule of Call Prices

Date	Call Price	Date	Call Price
Issuance	$272.50	6/30/94	$ 563.63
6/30/86	$297.83	6/30/95	$ 613.04
6/30/87	$321.13	6/30/96	$ 669.45
6/30/88	$346.77	6/30/97	$ 731.06
6/30/89	$374.99	6/30/98	$ 798.34
6/30/90	$406.00	6/30/99	$ 871.80
6/30/91	$440.08	6/30/00	$ 952.03
6/30/92	$477.50	Maturity	$1,000.00
6/30/93	$518.57		

The Seeds of the Idea

To address that question, it is useful to trace the history of the LYON™. This history begins with Merrill Lynch and Mr. Lee Cole. During the mid-1980s, Merrill Lynch was the largest broker of equity options for retail (that is, noninstitutional) investors. During that period, owing to the success of its Cash Management Accounts (CMAs), Merrill Lynch was also the largest manager of individual money market accounts. Individuals had over $200 billion invested in CMAs. CMAs are funds invested essentially in short-term government securities and, for this reason, are subject to little interest rate risk and virtually no default risk.

During 1983, Lee Cole was Options Marketing Manager at Merrill Lynch. Cole discerned (or, more aptly, divined) a pattern in the transactions of individual retail customers. As Options Marketing Manager, Cole observed that individuals' primary activity in the options market was to buy calls on common stocks. The most active calls had a maximum term to maturity of 90 days and often expired unexercised. Viewed in isolation, this strategy appeared to be very risky.

In reviewing customers' consolidated accounts, however, Cole observed that many options customers also maintained large balances in their CMA accounts while making few direct equity investments. From these observations, Cole deduced a portfolio strategy: some individuals were willing to risk a fraction of their funds in highly volatile options as long as the bulk of their funds were largely safe from risk in their CMA accounts. These individuals also avoided direct equity investment. He leaped to the further inference that funds used to buy options came largely from the interest earned on CMA accounts. In short, individuals were willing to risk all or a fraction of the interest income from their CMAs in the options market as long as their CMA principal remained intact.

With these observations and deductions in hand, Cole drafted a memorandum describing in general terms a corporate security that would appeal to this segment of the retail customer market. Cole's intent was to design a security that would allow corporations to tap a sector of the retail market whose funds were currently invested in government securities and options. The security described in Cole's memo eventually turned into the LYON™. Because it is convertible into the stock of the issuer, the LYON™ effectively incorporates the call option component of the portfolio strategy perceived by Cole. Because of the put option, the investor is assured his principal can be recovered by putting the bond back to the issuer at prespecified exercise prices. The LYON™ thus approximates the features of the trading strategy as perceived by Cole.

If Cole's theory were correct, the LYON™ would be a desirable security for individual investors and would give corporate issuers access to an untapped sector of the retail market. As with most theories, however, Cole's rested upon a number of unproven assumptions. The ultimate question, of course, was whether the security would pass the market test.

The Search for the Ideal Issuer

It takes two sides to make a market. And while Cole had identified what he perceived to be a demand by investors, that demand could not be satisfied by every issuer. The ideal issuer would have to satisfy at least two, perhaps three, criteria: first, because of the put feature and the downside protection desired by investors, issuers would have to have an investment-grade bond rating. At the same time, however, the issuer's equity would have to exhibit substantial volatility; otherwise the security would not provide the "play" desired by option investors. These two features were critical. Because the initial target market for the security was to be individuals, a third, highly desirable characteristic of the issuer would be broad name recognition.

Beginning in mid-1984, the investment banking department of Merrill Lynch began the challenging search for the first LYON™ issuer. First, the population of candidates was obviously limited to those firms that needed to raise funds. Second, every issuer, even those issuing already tried and true securities, was anxious about the possibility that an issue might "fail." That anxiety was compounded by the newness and complexity of the LYON™. Third, because investment grade credit ratings tend to be assigned to firms with less volatile earnings (and, presumably, less volatile stock prices), the subset of companies with investment grade ratings and volatile stock prices is a fairly small one.

After repeated presentations to and rejections from a variety of potential issuers, Waste Management, Inc. expressed an interest in the security and authorized Merrill Lynch representatives Chuck Lewis and Thomas Patrick to move forward with a proposal. Furthermore, Waste Management exhibited most (perhaps all) of the requisite characteristics of the ideal issuer. Its debt was rated Aa. In terms of volatility, the annual variance of its common stock of 30% placed it in the top half of all NYSE stocks. The only question was whether Waste Management had sufficient name recognition to attract Merrill Lynch's retail customers.

Its stock was traded on the NYSE and it operated in communities throughout the country. It specialized in the disposal of industrial and household waste; but it was not necessarily a well-known consumer product. The Waste Management name was by then a familiar one, however, to the extensive Merrill Lynch brokerage network. Between 1972 and 1985, Merrill Lynch had managed four separate new equity issues for Waste Management, a number of secondary equity issues, and nine issues of industrial revenue bonds. All of these raised the broker and customer awareness of the company.

Over the same 1972–1985 time period, Merrill Lynch had also arranged a private placement of $50 million in debt for Waste Management and had represented the company in two hostile takeovers. This working relationship may have been the key factor necessary to overcome "first-issuer anxiety."

In any event, Merrill Lynch finally brought the first LYON™ to market in April 1985, roughly two years after Lee Cole drafted his outline memorandum. The issue sold out quickly and Cole turned out to be at least partly right. In the case of a traditional convertible bond issue, roughly 90% of the issue is purchased by institutional investors with only a tiny fraction taken by retail investors. Approximately 40% of the first LYONs™ were purchased by individual investors. Apparently, Merrill Lynch had designed a corporate convertible that appealed to an otherwise untapped sector of the market.

And the appeal of the LYON™ to the retail sector of the market has persisted. For example, Euro Disney raised $965 million with a LYON™ issue in June 1990. Of that issue, 60% were purchased by individual investors and 40% by institutions. Individuals accounted for over 45,000 separate orders. Over time, the fraction of LYONs™ purchased by retail customers has varied from issue to issue, but has averaged roughly 50% of the total. Furthermore, the zero coupon puttable, convertible bond apparently has staying power. Roughly half the total proceeds raised through convertible bonds during 1991 were zero coupon, puttable convertibles.

Moreover, Merrill Lynch, the entrepreneurial source of this successful innovation, has profited handsomely from the LYON™. In the case of the typical convertible bond, the underwriter's spread is about 1.7% of the dollar amount of funds raised. For the earliest LYONs™, the spread was 3% and, at the present time, continues to be about 2.5% of the amount of funds raised. Merrill Lynch was able to "corner" the market for almost five years before other investment bankers brought LYON™-like securities to market. According to the *Wall Street Journal* article cited earlier, Merrill Lynch has earned some $248 million from sale of LYONs™ since 1985.

The Case for Convertibles (Or Financing Synergies from Combining Debt with Call Options)

This brings us to the obvious question about the LYON™: What was the source of the gains to issuers and investors that would allow Merrill Lynch to earn such large rewards?

Because the LYON™ is a variant of the convertible, let's begin by revisiting the "case for convertibles" made by Michael Brennan and Eduardo Schwartz in an article published in 1981.[4] The popular argument for convertible bonds is that they provide "cheap debt" (that is, they carry coupon rates below those on straight debt) and allow companies to sell stock "at a premium" relative to the current market price. But, as Brennan and Schwartz demonstrate, this reasoning conceals a logical sleight of hand: it effectively compares convertibles with a debt issue under one set of circumstances (when the firm's stock price does not rise and the issue does not convert) and with a stock issue under another (the stock price rises and the issue converts). What it fails to point out is that the convertible issuer would have been better off issuing stock in the first set of circumstances and straight debt in the second. In short, convertibles do not provide the average issuer with a financing "bargain."

After exposing this popular fallacy, Brennan and Schwartz go on to argue that the real source of convertibles' effectiveness is *that their value is relatively insensitive to the risk of the issuing company*. Increases in company risk reduce the value of the bond portion of a convertible, but at the same time increase the value of the built-in option (by increasing the volatility of the stock price). Because of this risk-neutralizing effect, convertibles are useful in resolving disagreements (arising from what academics refer to as "information asymmetries") between management and would-be investors about the risk of a company's operations. And it is largely for this reason that the use of convertibles tends to be concentrated among relatively smaller, high-growth companies with volatile earnings—the kind of companies that ordinary fixed-income investors shy away from. Convertibles are also well suited to such issuers because the lower current interest payments reduce the risk of financial distress, which is likely to be especially disruptive for companies on a high-growth track.

Convertibles are also effective in cases where management has significant opportunity to increase the risk of the firm's activities. When such risk-shifting is a real possibility, the firm will be required to pay an especially high premium to issue straight debt, far more than management believes is warranted given its true intentions for the company. Convertible debt, because it can be exchanged for common stock, provides the bondholder with built-in insurance against such risk-shifting behavior.

But what has all this to do with the LYON™, which, after all, is intended for investment grade companies? To the extent the equity values of LYON™ issuers are more volatile than those of other investment grade issuers, LYON™ issuers also presumably benefit from this risk-neutralizing effect that comes from combining debt with options.

To have succeeded in the manner it has, the LYON™ must also provide benefits that go well beyond those of conventional convertibles. The success of the LYON™, as suggested earlier, has much to do with Merrill Lynch's ability to design a convertible that would appeal to individual investors.

Retailing Convertibles (Or the Value of the Put Option)

Lee Cole was apparently correct in his assessment that there was a latent demand among retail investors for a convertible-like payoff structure—one combining, in the case of the LYON™, a *zero-coupon*, fixed-income component with an equity call option. By offering what amounts to a continuous option position, such a convertible would have the added appeal to investors of potentially large transaction cost savings. Recall that, under the call-option-*cum*-CMA strategy perceived by Cole, purchasing a series of calls that expire at 90-day (or shorter) intervals, thereby incurring commission costs at least four times a year.[5] By buying and holding a newly issued LYON™, the retail investor could maintain continuous ownership of an option position over the life of the bond without paying any brokerage fees.

But, to allow retail investors to take advantage of these long-dated, low-transaction-cost options, Cole realized the new security would have to be designed to overcome retail investors' normal resistance to convertibles. This could be accomplished, in part, by choosing only issuers with name-recognition and investment grade bond ratings. But, to reduce the principal risk to levels acceptable to retail investors, the new security would also have to include a stronger, contractual assurance.

Hence, the put option. By giving investors the right to put the notes back to the company after three years (and at one-year intervals thereafter), the Waste Management LYON™ greatly reduced the exposure of investors' principal to a sharp increase in interest rates or to a drop in the issuer's credit standing. In so doing, it dramatically increased the value of the security. (As we show later, the put option accounted for almost 20% of the value of the Waste Management LYON™ at the time of issue).

Of course, granting investors such an option could turn out to be costly to the LYON™ issuer. A jump in rates or fall in operating cash flows could force the company to retire the bonds at the worst possible time. For this reason, LYON™ issuers are likely to "self-select" in the following sense: among companies with sufficient market volatility to provide LYON™ investors with the desired option "play," LYON™ issuers will also tend to be those with greatest confidence in the ability of their operations to weather either a sharp rate increase or the need to raise new capital under those conditions.

In short, ideal LYON™ issuers are companies for which the benefit of granting the put option (and thereby gaining a retail following) most outweighs the expected cost of having to deliver on that option.

A Retail Clientele Effect?

This brings us back to the alleged benefits of appealing to a retail clientele. Generally speaking, the "modern theory" of finance has offered little encouragement to explanations of securities designed for specific kinds of investors. But there are notable exceptions. Robert Merton, in his 1987 Presidential Address to the American Finance Association, developed a model of asset pricing in which the size of the firm's investor base is an important determinant of the price of the firm's securities.[6] Starting from the assumption that investors invest only in a limited set of securities about which they have information, Merton's proposed model suggests that securities markets may effectively be "segmented," that is, companies lacking retail investors may be selling at a sharp "information discount" relative to their retail-owned counterparts. To the extent such segmentation exists—and this is still a matter of sharp contention—management actions that expand the firm's investor base would increase the firm's value.

Moreover, a recent study by Greg Kadlec and John McConnell provides empirical support for the predictions of Merton's model.[7] Their study reports that the prices of stocks newly listed on the NYSE during the 1980s increased in value by 5% to 6% at the time of listing. This increase in value is significantly correlated with the increase in the *number of investors* in the firm's stock from the year before to the year after listing. If we extend Merton's argument and this supporting evidence to the case of the LYON™, it is plausible that the LYON™'s extension of convertibles to a previously untapped sector of the market could be providing significant value for issuers.

The Appeal to Institutional Investors

But what about institutional investors? Why would they "pay up" for a convertible with a put option relative to an otherwise identical convertible bond without one? To this question, our answer is again tentative and follows from the form of potential payoffs under the LYON™.

During the mid-1980s, portfolio insurance began to flourish as a popular tool for portfolio managers. The general objective of portfolio insurance is to provide upside potential while limiting downside risk. That is essentially the payoff pattern presented by the LYON™. If the underlying stock price increases, the value of the LYON™ increases accordingly. If the stock price falls or interest rates increase, the LYON™ holder is protected by the floor provided by the put exercise price.

To the extent some institutional investors are willing to "pay" for portfolio insurance, then those investors might also be willing to pay a slight premium for the "insurance" provided by the LYON™. Over time, however, as more LYON™-like securities are brought to market, and as more investment bankers produce competing products, the spread commanded by underwriters should decline. In the meantime, Merrill would have earned its "reward."

Enter the Model Builders

It was only after the Waste Management LYON™ had been brought to market successfully that Merrill Lynch asked us to build a model to value the security. Why the need for a model? The answer has as much to do with marketing as with the need of traders and issuers to analyze and price the security. The answer is also reassuring to those like us who view modern finance theory as a powerful and practical scientific discipline with important implications for corporate managers and investors.[8]

Following the issuance of the Waste Management LYON™, Merrill Lynch intensified its effort to bring additional issues to market, both to increase the liquidity of the market for the security and to demonstrate that the security was not just a passing curiosity.[9] Following the success of the first LYON™, other potential issuers showed more interest, but also asked more questions.

Three questions typically came up: first, what was a "fair" price for a specific LYON™ given the characteristics of the company and security in question?[10] Second, how would the security react under different market conditions? Third, under what conditions would investors elect to convert the security to common stock? This last question was asked by managers concerned about the dilutive effect of conversion on the company's EPS.

Pricing the LYON™

The model we developed to answer those questions is based on the Brennan-Schwartz (1977) model for analyzing convertible bonds—which is based in turn upon the classic Black-Scholes (1973) option pricing model.[11] Interestingly, with some minor modifications, this model is still used by Merrill Lynch to analyze LYONs™ today.

Given the similarity between a LYON™ and a call-option-cum-CMA strategy, the great temptation in developing a model to analyze this security is simply to sum the value of the components—to add the values of the put and call options to that of a zero coupon (callable) bond issued by the same firm. The problem with such an approach, however, is that it ignores the *interactions* between these values. For example, both the issuer's call option and the investor's conversion rights reduce the value of the put option by reducing the expected maturity of the put. The value of the conversion option is similarly reduced by the issuer's call option, and the put option, both of which reduce the probability of eventual conversion. Because of these interactions, the value of the LYON™ depends both on the conversion and redemption strategies followed by the investor and on the call strategy followed by the issuer.

Our model makes the by-now standard assumptions of the option pricing literature: that the investor follows conversion and redemption strategies that maximize the value of the security, while the issuer adheres to a call strategy that minimizes the security's value.[12] These assumptions, coupled with the assumptions that the value of the LYON™ depends upon the issuer's stock price and that securities are all priced to eliminate arbitrage profits, yield a fairly complicated differential equation for valuing and analyzing the LYON™. Despite its complicated appearance, the equation can be solved numerically on a personal computer in a few minutes.

The "intuition" underlying the model is this: the higher the general level of interest rates, the lower the value of the LYON™; the higher the volatility and the level of the issuer's stock price, the greater the value of the LYON™; the lower the LYON™ call price and the sooner the call can be exercised, the lower the value of the LYON™; the higher dividend on the issuer's stock, the lower the value of the LYON™ (since higher dividends imply less stock price appreciation and less chance of conversion); and, the higher the put exercise prices, the higher the value of the LYON™.

For purposes of illustration, consider the Waste Management LYON™ described earlier. Table 17.3 presents the basic market characteristics, the characteristics of the firm, and the features of the bond as of the issue date. Given these characteristics our model predicted that the market value of the bond as of the issue date should be $262.70. In fact, at the close of the first day of trading, the bond's price was $258.75. We tracked the bond over the next 31 days and determined that the model's predicted prices closely tracked the actual closing prices, but were typically slightly above the closing price. Apparently, the model has a slight upward bias in valuing the LYON.

Sensitivity Analysis

Table 17.4 shows the effects of changes in market conditions, the issuing company and features of the security, on the value of Waste Management's LYON™. There are a number of interesting insights from this "sensitivity analysis." The value of the Waste Management LYON™ is highly insensitive to interest rate changes (a 200 basis point increase in yields would cause less than a 4% decline in value of the LYON™). But this insensitivity to rates is caused by the put option, which our analysis indicates accounts for almost 20% of the security's value. That is, *without* the put option, the LYON™'s value would be reduced from roughly $260 to under $215 per bond. At the same time, however, the

issuer's call option reduces the value of the LYON™ by roughly $20 per bond (or 8% of its total value). It does so, as mentioned, by reducing both the probability of the investor exercising his conversion rights and the likely length of time that option is allowed to remain outstanding.

The Question of Conversion

As noted, one question of frequent concern to LYON™ issuers is the stock price at which investors will choose to convert the bond to stock. In deciding whether to convert, the investor weighs the value of dividends forgone by holding the LYON™ against the downside protection provided by the put. Thus, if the dividend yield is relatively low, the benefits of conversion (to obtain the dividend) are also relatively low. But, even for low-dividend paying stocks, if the stock price rises high enough, it will be so far above the put price that the protection provided by the investor's put option becomes negligible.

Our model assumes the critical conversion stock price is the price at which the investor becomes indifferent between holding the LYON™ versus converting to common stock. As illustrated in Table 17.5, the critical conversion stock price for the Waste Management LYON™ changes throughout its life, increasing steadily throughout the first 13 years, and declining sharply thereafter. There are two opposite effects driving these changes: one that is present in all convertibles and one that is unique

---

Table 17.3   Characteristics of the Waste Management LYON™

Interest rate of intermediate term bond	11.21%
Stock price	$52.25
Stock price volatility	30.0%
Dividend yield	1.6%
LYON maturity	15 years
Face value	$1,000/bond
Conversion ratio	4.36 shares/bond
Call prices	In text
Put prices	In text

Table 17.4   Waste Management's LYON™: A Sensitivity Analysis

	Bond Value	Effect of Change on Bond Value
Basic features	$262.70	
Stock price to $56.00	271.68	+8.98
Stock price volatility to 40.00%	271.89	+9.19
Dividend yield to 3.0%	260.78	−1.92
Interest rate to 13.21%	252.38	−10.32
Without call	283.29	20.59
Without put	215.04	−47.66

for the LYON™. As in the case of a conventional, current-coupon convertible, the optimal conversion price of the LYON™ is reduced because the value of the conversion option is shrinking along with the remaining time to maturity. But, unlike conventional convertibles, the conversion price of the LYON™ is also *increased* through time by the fact that the redemption price increases while the conversion ratio remains constant (4.36 shares per bond)—which, of course, reduces the value of conversion option. In all but the last two years, the latter effect dominates the former.

Conclusion

Although the Liquid Yield Option Note is just one of many successful financial innovations of the 1980s the case history of the LYON™ does illustrate that successful financial innovation requires ingenuity, perseverance, and, perhaps, a measure of good fortune. It also illustrates the potential practical power of modern financial theory in assisting in the development of new financial products and strategies. As practitioners of the science of modern finance, we were fortunate enough to be present at the creation of what now appears to be a successful financial innovation.

Endnotes

1. Randall Smith, "Tax Status of LYONs™, One of Street's Hottest Products, Gets IRS Challenge," (December 17, 1991): Cl.

2. Merton H. Miller introduced this Darwinian metaphor in "Debt and Taxes," *Journal of Finance* (May 1977): 273.

3. The imputed interest is computed by increasing the call prices at a rate of 9.0% per year compounded semiannually. If the LYON™ is called between the dates shown above, the call price is adjusted to reflect the "interest" accrued since the immediately preceding call date shown in the schedule.

4. Michael Brennan and Eduardo Schwartz, "The Case for Convertibles," *Chase Financial Quarterly*, Vol. 1 No. 3 (Fall 1981). Reprinted in *Journal of Applied Corporate Finance*, Vol. 1 No. 2 (Summer 1988). This article extends insights about the role of convertibles formulated earlier by Michael C. Jensen and William H. Meckling, "Theory of the Firm: Managerial Behavior, Agency Costs, and Capital Structure," *Journal of Financial Economics* (1976): 305-360. See also Clifford W. Smith and Jerold B. Warner, "On Financial Contracting: An Analysis of Bond Covenants," *Journal of Financial Economics*, 7 (1979): 117-161.

5. Traded equity options are available with maturities as long as 270 days, but such options are much less liquid than their 90-day counterparts.

6. See Robert Merton, "A Simple Model of Capital Market Equilibrium with Incomplete Information," *Journal of Finance*, Vol. 42 (July 1987).

7. Greg Kadlec and John J. McConnell, "The Effect of Market Segmentation and Illiquidity on Asset Prices: Evidence from Exchange Listings," unpublished manuscript, Krannert School of Management, Purdue University (1992).

8. The model can also be used to determine the appropriate LYON™ hedge ratio.

9. It goes without saying that generating a fee for bringing the security to market was also an important consideration, but to continue generating fees from LYON™ issues it was necessary to demonstrate the continued viability of the security.

Table 17.5   Waste Management LYON™ Stock Conversion Price

Date	Conversion Stock Price	Date	Conversion Stock Price
Issue	$129.50	6/30/93	$273.00
6/30/85	$132.00	6/30/94	$287.00
6/30/86	$145.50	6/30/95	$301.50
6/30/87	$158.50	6/30/96	$316.00
6/30/88	$173.50	6/30/97	$329.50
6/30/89	$194.50	6/30/98	$339.00
6/30/90	$217.00	6/30/99	$340.00
6/30/91	$238.50	6/30/00	$317.50
6/30/92	$257.00	1/21/01	$229.36

10. Interest in this question was motivated, at least in part, by critics who used a crude option pricing model to argue (to potential issuers) that the Waste Management LYON™ was underpriced by roughly 30%. The likely cause of such underpricing, as this article goes on to explain, was its failure to take account of the interaction of the values of the various components of the LYON™.

11. For the formulation of the Black-Scholes option pricing model, see Fischer Black and Myron Scholes, "The Pricing Options and Corporate Liabilities," *Journal of Political Economy,* Vol. 81, No. 3 (May-June 1973). For the extension of that model to the valuation of convertible bonds, see Michael Brennan and Eduardo Schwartz, "Convertible Bonds: Valuation and Optimal Strategies for Call and Conversion," *Journal of Finance,* Vol. 32, No. 5 (December 1977).

12. This discussion draws heavily on our article, "LYON™ Taming," *Journal of Finance* (July 1986). Whether investors and issuers follow these strategies is an issue of some contention. For a discussion of this controversy see Michael Brennan and Eduardo Schwartz, "Convertible Securities," *Palgrave Dictionary of Accounting and Finance* (MacMillan, 1992).

Chapter 18

The Uses of Hybrid Debt in Managing Corporate Risk*

Charles W. Smithson
Managing Director, Global Risk Management
Chase Manhattan Bank, New York, NY
Donald H. Chew, Jr.
Founding Partner
Stern Stewart and Co., New York, NY

The corporate use of hybrid debt securities—those that combine a conventional debt issue with a "derivative" such as a forward, swap, or option—increased significantly during the 1980s. And, while many of the more esoteric or tax-driven securities introduced in the last decade have disappeared, corporate hybrids now seem to be flourishing. In so doing, they are helping U.S. companies raise capital despite the restrictive financing climate of the 1990s.

Hybrid debt is not a new concept. Convertible bonds, first issued by the Erie Railroad in the 1850s, are hybrid securities that combine straight debt and options on the value of the issuer's equity.[1] What is distinctive about the hybrid debt instruments of the 1980s is that their payoffs, instead of being tied to the issuing company's stock price, are linked to a growing variety of *general* economic variables. Figure 18.1 shows corporate hybrids that index investor returns to exchange rates, interest rates, stock market indices, and the prices of commodities such as oil, copper, and natural gas.

The recent wave of corporate hybrids began in 1973, when PEMEX, the state-owned Mexican oil producer, issued bonds that incorporated a *forward contract* on a commodity, in this case, oil. In 1980, Sunshine Mining Co. went a step further by issuing bonds incorporating a commodity *option* (on silver). In 1988, Magma Copper made yet another advance by issuing a bond giving investors a *series of commodity options* (on copper)—in effect, one for every coupon payment.

Other new hybrids, as mentioned, have had their payoffs tied to interest rates, foreign exchange rates, and the behavior of the stock market. In 1981,

Oppenheimer & Co., a securities brokerage firm, issued a security whose principal repayment is indexed to the volume of trading on the New York Stock Exchange. Notes indexed to the value of equity indexes appeared in 1986, and inflation-indexed notes (tied to the CPI) were introduced in 1988.

The 1980s also saw new hybrids with payoffs that, like those of convertibles, are tied to company-specific performance. For example, the Rating Sensitive Notes issued by Manufacturer's Hanover in 1988 provide for increased payments to investors if Manny Hanny's creditworthiness declines. And the LYON™ (LYON™ is a trademark of Merrill Lynch and Co.) pioneered and underwritten by Merrill Lynch in 1985 grants investors not only the option to convert the debt into equity, but also the right to "put" the security back to the firm.

The pace of hybrid innovation peaked around 1987. But hybrids are now staging a comeback. As the title of a recent *Wall Street Journal* article put it, 1991 was "A Boom Year for Newfangled Trading Vehicles."[2] The past year witnessed the introduction of notes indexed to a subset of a general equity index, Goldman Sachs' notes indexed to a commodity index, private placements incorporating options on commodities, and a boom in convertible debt.

Why do companies issue, and investors buy, such complex securities? Before the development of derivative products in the 1970s, investors may have been attracted by the prospect of purchasing a "bundle" of securities, for instance, debt plus warrants, that they could not duplicate themselves by purchasing both of the components separately. And this

Source: This article was first published in the Continental Bank *Journal of Applied Corporate Finance* Vol. 4, No. 4 (Winter 1992): 79–89. It is printed here with the permission of the publisher, Stern Stewart and Co.

Figure 18.1   Development of Hybrid Securities: 1973–1991

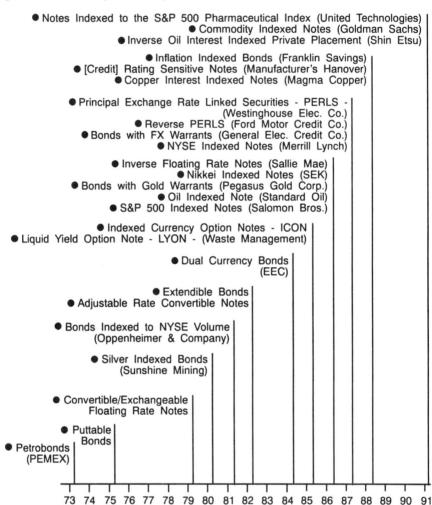

● Notes Indexed to the S&P 500 Pharmaceutical Index (United Technologies)
● Commodity Indexed Notes (Goldman Sachs)
● Inverse Oil Interest Indexed Private Placement (Shin Etsu)

● Inflation Indexed Bonds (Franklin Savings)
● [Credit] Rating Sensitive Notes (Manufacturer's Hanover)
● Copper Interest Indexed Notes (Magma Copper)

● Principal Exchange Rate Linked Securities - PERLS -
(Westinghouse Elec. Co.)
● Reverse PERLS (Ford Motor Credit Co.)
● Bonds with FX Warrants (General Elec. Credit Co.)
● NYSE Indexed Notes (Merrill Lynch)

● Inverse Floating Rate Notes (Sallie Mae)
● Nikkei Indexed Notes (SEK)
● Bonds with Gold Warrants (Pegasus Gold Corp.)
● Oil Indexed Note (Standard Oil)
● S&P 500 Indexed Notes (Salomon Bros.)

● Indexed Currency Option Notes - ICON
● Liquid Yield Option Note - LYON - (Waste Management)

● Dual Currency Bonds
(EEC)

● Extendible Bonds
● Adjustable Rate Convertible Notes

● Bonds Indexed to NYSE Volume
(Oppenheimer & Company)

● Silver Indexed Bonds
(Sunshine Mining)

● Convertible/Exchangeable
Floating Rate Notes

● Puttable
Bonds
● Petrobonds
(PEMEX)

73 74 75 76 77 78 79 80 81 82 83 84 85 86 87 88 89 90 91

Source: *Journal of Applied Corporate Finance*, Stern Stewart Management Services.

"scarce security" or "market completion" argument also holds for some of today's debt hybrids (especially those that provide longer-dated forwards and options than those available on organized exchanges).

But, because active exchanges now provide low-cost futures and options with payoffs tied to a variety of interest rates, exchange rates, and commodity prices, markets are becoming increasingly "complete," if you will. Given the existence of well-functioning, low-cost markets for many of the components making up the hybrid debt instruments, we have to ask the following question: is there any reason investors should be willing to pay more for these securities sold *in combination* rather than separately?

In this article, we argue that hybrid debt offers corporate treasurers an efficient means of managing a variety of financial and operating risks—risks that, in many cases, cannot be managed if the firm issues straight debt and then purchases derivatives. By hedging such risks and thereby increasing the expected stability of corporate cash flows, hybrids may lower the issuer's overall funding costs.[3] At the same time, though, part of the present corporate preference for managing price risks with hybrids rather than with derivative products stems from current restrictions on the use of hedge accounting for derivatives, as well as on tax and regulatory arbitrage opportunities afforded by hybrids.

Price Volatility: The Necessary Condition for Hybrids

The stability of the economic and financial environment is a key determinant of the kinds of debt instruments that dominate the marketplace. When prices are stable and predictable, investors will demand—and the capital markets will produce—relatively simple instruments.

In the late 1800s, for example, the dominant financial instrument in Great Britain was the *consol*, a bond with a fixed interest rate and no maturity—it lasted forever. Investors were content to hold infinite-lived British government bonds because British sovereign credit was good and because inflation was virtually unknown. General confidence in price level stability led to stable interest rates, which in turn dictated the use of long-lived, fixed-rate bonds.

But consider what happens to financing practices when confidence is replaced by turbulence and uncertainty. In 1863 the Confederate States of America issued a 20-year bond denominated not in Confederate dollars, but in French Francs and Pounds Sterling. To allay the concern of its overseas investors that the Confederacy would not be around to service its debt with hard currency, the issue was also convertible at the option of the holder into cotton at the rate of six pence per pound. In the parlance of today's investment banker, the Confederate States issued a *dual-currency, cotton-indexed* bond.[4]

The Breakdown of Bretton Woods and the New Era of Volatility

Throughout the 1950s and most of the 1960s, economic and price stability prevailed in the United States, and in the developed nations generally. Investment grade U.S. corporations responded predictably by raising capital in the form of 30-year, fixed-rate bonds (yielding around 3-4%). But, toward the end of the 1960s, rates of inflation in the United

States and United Kingdom began to increase. There was also considerable divergence among developed countries in monetary and fiscal policy, and thus in rates of inflation. Such pressures led inevitably to the abandonment, in 1973, of the Bretton Woods agreement to maintain relatively fixed exchanged rates. And, during the early 1970s and thereafter, the general economic environment saw higher and more volatile rates of inflation along with unprecedented volatility in exchange rates, interest rates, and commodity prices. (For evidence of such general price volatility, see Figure 18.2.)

In response to this heightened price volatility, capital markets created new financial instruments to help investors and issuers manage their exposures. Indeed, the last 20 years has seen the introduction of 1) futures on foreign exchange, interest rates, metals, and oil; 2) currency, interest rate, and commodity swaps; 3) options on exchange rates, interest rates, and oil; and 4) options on the above futures and options. Flourishing markets for these products in turn helped give rise to corporate hybrid debt securities that effectively incorporate these derivative products.

Using Hybrids to Manage Commodity Risk

Unlike foreign exchange and interest rates, which were relatively stable until the 1970s, commodity prices have a long history of volatility. Thus, it is no surprise that hybrid securities designed to hedge commodity price risks came well before hybrids with embedded currency and interest rate derivatives.

As mentioned earlier, the Confederacy issued a debt instrument convertible into cotton in 1863. By the 1920s, commodity-linked hybrids were available in U.S. capital markets. A case in point is the gold-indexed bond issued by Irving Fisher's Rand Kardex Corporation in 1925. Similar to the PEMEX issue described earlier, the principal repayment of this gold-indexed bond was tied directly to gold prices.[5] Fisher realized that he could significantly lower his firm's funding costs by furnishing a scarce security desired by investors, in this case, a long-dated forward on gold prices. And Fisher's successful innovation was imitated by a number of other U.S. companies during the 1920s.

Like so many of the financial innovations of the 1920s, however, that wave of hybrid debt financings was ended by the regulatory reaction that set in during the 1930s.[6] Specifically, the "Gold Clause" Joint Congressional Resolution of June 5, 1933 virtually eliminated indexed debt by prohibiting "a lender to require of a borrower a different quantity or number of dollars from that loaned." And it was not until October, 1977, when Congress passed the Helms Amendment, that the legal basis for commodity-indexed debt was restored.

Hybrids with Option Features

The hybrids issued by Rand Kardex and PEMEX represent combinations of debt securities with forward contracts, that is, the promised principal repayments were designed to rise or fall directly with changes in the prices of gold and oil, respectively. In the case of PEMEX, moreover, this forward-like feature reduced the risk to investors that the issuer wouldn't be able to repay principal; it did so by making the *amount* of the principal vary as directly as possible with the company's oil revenues.

Unlike the PEMEX and Rand Kardex issues, Sunshine Mining's 15-year silver-linked bond issued in 1980 combined a debt issue with a *European option*[7] on silver prices. In this case, the promised principal repayment could not fall below a certain level (the face value), but would increase proportion-

ally with increases in the price of silver price above $20 per ounce at maturity.[8] Because most of the commodity-linked hybrids that followed the Sunshine Mining issue in the 1980s contain embedded options rather than forwards, let's consider briefly how the embedding of options within debt issues manages risk and lowers the issuer's cost of capital.

How Hybrids with Options Manage Risk. Corporate bondholders bear "downside" risk while typically being limited to a fixed interest rate as their reward. (In the jargon of options, the bondholder is "short a put" on the value of the firm's assets). Because of this limited upside, they charge a higher "risk premium" when asked to fund companies with more volatile earnings streams. Like the forward contract embedded in the PEMEX issue, options also provide bondholders with an equity-like, "upside" participation. In return for this upside participation, bondholders will reduce the risk premium they charge. Indeed, the greater the expected volatility of the commodity price in question, the more valuable is that embedded option to the bondholders.[9]

Figure 18.2 General Price Volatility

Panel A
Percent Change in Yen/
U.S. Dollar Exchange Rate

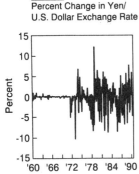

Panel B
First Difference in
U.S. Treasury Yield
(5-Year Constant Maturity)

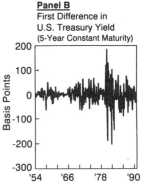

Panel C
Percent Change in
U.S. Crude Oil Price
(Average Refiner's Acquisition Cost)

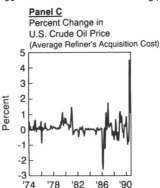

Source: *Journal of Applied Corporate Finance,* Stern Stewart Management Services

Unlike hybrids with forwards, hybrids with embedded options provide investors with a "floor," that is, a minimum principal repayment or set of coupons. And, though options effect a less complete transfer of risk than in the case of forwards (in the sense that the firm's financing costs don't fall below the floor in the event of an extreme decline in commodity prices), investors should be willing to pay for the floor in the form of a reduced base rate of interest. To the extent they lower the rate of interest, option-like hybrids reduce the probability of default, thus reassuring bondholders and the rating agencies.

A good example of corporate risk management with options was a 1986 issue of Eurobonds with detachable gold warrants by Pegasus Gold Corporation, a Canadian gold mining firm. In effect, this issue gave investors two separable claims: 1) a straight debt issue with a series of fixed-interest payments and a fixed-principal repayment; and 2) European options on the price of gold. By giving bondholders a participation in the firm's gold revenues, the inclusion of such warrants reduced the coupon rate on the bond, which in turn lowered the issuer's financial risk.

Probably the most newsworthy hybrid in 1986, however, was Standard Oil's *Oil-Indexed Note.* This hybrid combines a zero-coupon bond with a European option on oil with the same maturity. The issue not only aroused the interest of the IRS, but also succeeded in rekindling regulatory concerns about the potential for "speculative abuse" built into hybrid securities.[10]

Commodity Interest-Indexed Bonds. The commodity hybrids mentioned thus far are all combinations of debt with forwards or options with a single maturity. In effect, they link only the principal repayment to commodity prices, but not the interim interest payments. But, in recent years, hybrids have also emerged that combine debt with a *series of options* of different maturities—maturities that are typically designed to correspond to the coupon dates of the underlying bond.

In 1988, for example, MAGMA Copper Company issued *Copper Interest-Indexed Senior Subordinated Notes.* This 10-year debenture has embedded within it 40 option positions on the price of copper—one maturing in three months, one in six months, . . ., and one in 10 years. The effect of this series of embedded option positions is to make the company's quarterly interest payments vary with the prevailing price of copper, as shown in Table 18.1.

In 1989, Presidio Oil Company issued an oil-indexed note with a similar structure, but with coupons linked to the price of natural gas. And, in 1991, Shin Etsu, a Japanese chemical manufacturer, issued a hybrid with a similar structure; however, the issue was a private placement and the coupon payment floated *inversely* with the price of oil.

The Case of Forest Oil: The Consequences of Not Managing Risk

It was Forest Oil, however, and not Presidio, that first considered issuing natural gas-linked debt. But Forest's management was confident that natural gas prices would go higher in the near future and thus decided that the price of the natural gas-linked debt would turn out to be too high. Unfortunately, the company's bet on natural gas prices went against them. Since the issue was contemplated, natural gas prices have fallen dramatically, and the company has been squeezed between high current interest costs and reduced revenues. Indeed, the squeeze has been so tight that Forest has been forced to restructure its debt.

Using Hybrids to Manage Foreign Exchange Risk

As Figure 18.2 suggests, exchange rates became more volatile following the abandonment of the Bretton Woods agreement in 1973. As a result, many companies have experienced foreign exchange risk

Table 18.1   The Pricing of Copper Interest–Indexed Senior Subordinated Notes

Average Copper Price	Indexed Interest Rate
$2.00 or above	21%
1.80	20
1.60	19
1.40	18
1.30	17
1.20	16
1.10	15
1.00	14
0.90	13
0.80 or below	12

arising from transaction, translation, and economic exposures.

The simplest way to manage an exposure to foreign exchange risk is by using a forward foreign exchange contract. If the firm is long foreign currency, it can cover this exposure by selling forward contracts. Or if it has a short position, it can buy forwards.

Dual Currency Bonds. Similar to PEMEX's oil-indexed issue, the simplest FX hybrid debt structure is a *Dual Currency Bond.* Such a bond combines a fixed-rate "bullet" (that is, single) repayment bond and a long-dated forward contract on foreign exchange. For example, in 1985, Philip Morris Credit issued a dual-currency bond in which coupon payments are made in Swiss Francs while principal will be repaid U.S. Dollars.

PERLs. A variant of the dual currency structure is the *Principal Exchange Rate Linked Security.* In 1987, Westinghouse Electric Company issued *PERLs* wherein the bondholder received at maturity the principal the USD value of 70.13 million New Zealand dollars. The issuer's motive in this case was likely to reduce its funding costs by taking advantage of an unusual investor demand for long-dated currency forwards. Earlier in the same year, and presumably with similar motive, Ford Motor Credit Company issued *Reverse PERLs.* In this case, the principal repayment varied inversely with the value of the yen.[11]

Creating a Hybrid By Adding Options

As in the case of commodity-linked hybrids, forward-like FX hybrids seemed to have given way to structures containing warrants or other option-like features. In 1987, for example, General Electric Credit Corporation made a public offering made up of debt and yen-USD currency exchange warrants.

Bonds with Principal Indexed (Convertible) to FX. Like bonds with warrants, convertible bonds are made up of bonds and equity options. But there is one important difference: in the case of bonds with warrants, the bondholder can exercise the option embodied in a warrant and still keep the underlying bond. With convertibles, the holder must surrender the bond to exercise the option. Sunshine Mining's Silver-Indexed Bonds and Standard Oil's Oil Indexed Notes are similar constructions. The bondholder can receive either the value of the bond or the value of the option, but not both.

When this debt structure appeared with an embedded foreign currency option, the hybrid was called an *Indexed Currency Option Note* (or *ICON*). This security, which was first underwritten by First Boston in 1985, combines a fixed rate, bullet repayment bond and a European option on foreign exchange.[12]

Using Hybrids to Manage Interest Rate Risk

Some companies have significant exposures to interest rates. Take the case of firms that supply inputs to the housing market. When interest rates rise, the revenues of such firms tend to fall. The use of standard, floating-rate bank debt in such cases would likely increase the probability of default.

Creating a Hybrid with Embedded Swaps

To manage interest rate risk, such companies may be best served by a debt instrument wherein the coupon payment actually declines when interest rates rise. Such an *Inverse Floating Rate Note*—or a *Yield-Curve Note,* as it was called when first issued by the Student Loan Marketing Association (Sallie Mae) in the public debt market in 1986—can be decomposed into a floating-rate, bullet repayment note and a plain vanilla interest rate swap for twice the principal of the loan.

Creating a Hybrid By Adding Options

Just as bondholders can be provided options to exchange their bonds for a specified amount of a commodity or foreign currency, hybrid securities have been issued that give bondholders the option to exchange a bond (typically at maturity) for another bond (typically with the same coupon and maturity).

Convertible/Exchangeable Floating Rate Notes. These hybrids, which give the holder the right to convert to (or exchange for) a fixed-rate bond at a prespecified interest rate, first appeared in 1979. Such notes contain embedded "put" options on interest rates; that is, investors are likely to exercise their conversion or exchange rights only if interest rates fall below a certain level.

Extendible Notes. The same, moreover, is true of extendible notes, which give the holder the right to exchange the underlying bond for a bond of longer maturity. Such bonds first appeared in 1982.

Using Hybrids to Reduce Conflicts between Bondholders and Shareholders

In "normal" circumstances, that is, when operations are profitable and the firm can comfortably meet its debt service payments and investment schedule, the interests of bondholders and shareholders are united. Both groups of investors benefit from managerial decisions that increase the total value of the firm.

In certain cases, however, corporate managements find themselves in the position of being able to increase shareholder value *at the expense of bondholders*.[13] For example, as happened in a number of leveraged recapitalizations, management could reduce the value of outstanding bonds by increasing debt or adding debt senior to that in question. (In professional circles, this is known as *event risk;* in academic parlance it is the *claims dilution problem*.) Or, if the firm were in danger of insolvency, management could choose, as did some S&L executives, to invest in ever riskier projects in desperate attempts to save the firm (the *asset substitution problem*). Finally, a management squeezed between falling revenues and high interest payments could choose to pass up value-adding projects such as R&D or, if things are bad enough, basic maintenance and safety procedures (the *underinvestment problem*).[14]

Corporate debtholders are well aware that such problems can arise, and they accordingly protect themselves by lowering the price they are willing to pay for the debt. For corporate management, such lower prices translate into higher interest payments, which in turn further raise the probability of financial trouble.

Hybrids reduce these shareholder-bondholder conflicts by reducing current interest rates, shifting debt service payments to periods when firms are better able to pay, stabilizing cash flow, and thereby reducing the likelihood of financial distress. In so doing, they also raise the price of the corporate debt to investors and lower the overall corporate cost of capital.

Using Hybrids to Reduce the Claims Dilution Problem (or Protect Against Event Risk)

Puttable Bonds. Introduced in 1976, these bonds give their holders the option to "put" the bond back to the issuer. Such an option would be exercised only if interest rates rise or the issuer's credit standing falls. In this sense, puttable bonds give bondholders both a call option on interest rates and an option on the credit spread of the issuer.[15] Such put options thus protect bondholders not only against increases in interest rates, but also against the possibility of losses from deteriorating operating performance or leveraged recapitalizations. In the wake of the widely publicized bondholder losses accompanying the KKR buyout of RJR Nabisco in 1989, the use of put options to protect against such event risk enjoyed a new vogue.

Floating Rate, Rating Sensitive Notes. These notes, issued by Manufacturer Hanover in 1988, contain explicit options on the issuer's credit standing. In this security, Manufacturer's Hanover agreed to pay investors a spread above LIBOR that increased with each incremental decline in the bank's senior debt rating.

From the standpoint of risk management, however, there is an obvious flaw in the design of this security. Although it may partially compensate investors for increases in risk, it actually increases the probability of default instead of reducing it. The security increases the corporate debt service burden precisely when the issuing firm can least afford it—when its credit rating has fallen and, presumably, its operating cash flow declined.

A hybrid structure designed to overcome this problem was a syndication of oil-indexed bonds created by Chase Manhattan for Sonatrach (the state hydrocarbons company of Algeria) in 1990. As illustrated in Figure 18.3, the transaction was structured so that Chase accepted two-year call options on oil from Sonatrach and then transformed those two-year calls into seven-year calls and puts that were passed on to the syndicate members. Investors were compensated for a below-market interest by a payoff structure that would provide them with higher payoffs in the event of significantly *higher or lower* oil prices.

For the issuer, however, the security requires higher payments to Chase *only in the event of higher oil prices*. If the price of oil declines, although the syndicate members receive a higher yield, the increase comes from Chase, not Sonatrach.

Using Hybrids to Reduce the Asset Substitution and Underinvestment Problems

Convertibles. At the outset, we noted that convertible bonds contain embedded options on the company's equity. By providing bondholders with the right to convert their claims into equity, management provides bondholders with the assurance that

Figure 18.3   Oil–Linked Credit–Sensitive Syndicate

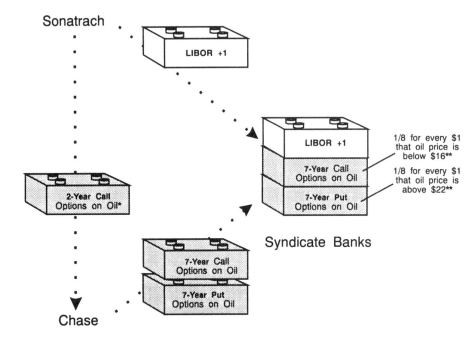

*During the first two years, if the price of oil exceeds $23, Sonatrach will pay a supplemental coupon to Chase.
**In the first year, the syndicate receives additional interest if the price of oil falls outside the range of $16–$22. In year 2 the range widens to $15–$23, then to $14–$24 in year 3, and to $13–$25 in years 4 through 7.
Source: *Journal of Applied Corporate Finance,* Stern Stewart Management Services

they will participate in any increase in shareholder value that results from increasing the risk of the company's activities, whether by leveraging up or undertaking riskier investments. By lowering current interest rates and thus reducing the likelihood of financial trouble, convertibles also reduce the probability that financially strapped companies will be forced to forgo valuable investment opportunities.[16]

Convertibles, (and debt with warrants, their close substitutes,) are also potentially useful in resolving disagreements between bondholders and shareholders about just how risky the firm's activities are. The value of convertibles are risk-neutral in the following sense: unexpected increases in company risk reduce the value of the bond portion of a convertible, but at the same time increase the value of the embedded option (by increasing volatility). It is largely because of this risk-neutralizing effect—and for their role in reducing the "underinvestment problem" mentioned below—that convertible issu-

ers tend to be smaller, newer, riskier firms characterized by high growth and earnings volatility.[17]

The Case of LYONs™

While a number of bonds are puttable or convertible, the Liquid Yield Option Note (LYON™) introduced by Merrill Lynch in 1985 is both puttable and convertible. The combination of the put and conversion features are especially useful in controlling the asset substitution, or risk-shifting, problem just described.[18] For this reason, the LYONs structure should be particularly attractive to issuers with substantial capital investment opportunities and a wide range of alternative investment projects (with varying degrees of risk).

It is thus interesting to note that the LYON™ structure was first used to fund companies where the asset substitution problem was acute. Take the case of Waste Management, the first issuer of LYONs™. Although Waste Management is today a household name among even small investors, in 1985 the company could best be viewed as a collection of "growth options." As such it posed considerable uncertainty for investors.

The Economic Rationale for Issuing a Hybrid Security

This still leaves a fundamental question: Given the well-functioning, low-cost markets for derivative products available today, why should a corporate issuer ever prefer the "bundled" hybrid to simply issuing standard debt and buying or selling the derivatives? We now discuss the following three reasons why corporate management might choose hybrids:

1. If the firm issuing the hybrid can provide investors with a "play" not available otherwise, that is, a derivative instrument not available in the traded derivatives markets, the issuing firm will consequently be paid a premium for "completing the market."

2. The hybrid may enable the issuer to take advantage of tax or regulatory arbitrages that would lower the cost of borrowing.

3. By embedding a risk management product into a hybrid, the issuer may be able to obtain hedge accounting treatment, which may not be allowed if the derivative was bought or sold separately.

Using Hybrids to Provide Investors with a "Play"

The most straightforward reason for issuing a hybrid is to provide investors with a means of taking a position on a financial price. If the issuer provides a "play" not otherwise available, the investor will be willing to pay a premium, thereby reducing the issuer's cost of funding. (And, if the hybrid provides investors with a "scarce security" not otherwise obtainable, it may also provide corporate issuers with a hedge they can't duplicate with derivative products.)

The "play" can be in the form of a forward contract. Perhaps the best example of this is dual currency bonds, which provide investors with foreign exchange forward contracts with longer maturities than those available in the standard market. The forward contracts embedded in dual currency bonds have maturities running to 10 years, whereas liquidity in the standard foreign exchange forward market declines for maturities greater than one year, and falls very significantly beyond five years.

The "play," however, has more commonly been in the form of an option embedded in the bond—generally an option of longer maturity than those available in the standard option market. Sunshine Mining's Silver Indexed Bond fits this category, as do Standard Oil's Oil-Indexed Note and the gold warrants issued by Pegasus Gold Corporation. In 1986, long-dated options on stock market indices were introduced with the development of hybrid debt in which the principal was indexed to an equity index. While the first such debt issues were indexed to the Nikkei, Salomon Brothers' "S&P 500 Index Subordinated Notes (SPINs)" have probably received more public attention. A SPIN is convertible into the value of the S&P 500 Index, rather than into an individual equity. Since then, debt has been issued that is indexed to other equity indices (for example, the NYSE index) or subsets of indices. For example, in 1991, United Technologies issued a zero-coupon bond indexed to the S&P Pharmaceutical Index.

Using Hybrids to "Arbitrage" Tax and/or Regulatory Authorities

Hybrid debt has also been used to take advantage of asymmetries in tax treatment or regulations in different countries or markets. One classic example is a case of "arbitrage" reported in *Business Week* under the provocative title, "A Way for U.S. Firms to Make 'Free Money'." The "free money" came from two sources:

1. A difference in tax treatment between the United States and Japan—the Japanese tax authorities ruled that income earned from holding a zero-coupon bond would be treated as a capital gain, thereby making interest income on the zero non-taxable for Japanese investors. In contrast, U.S. tax authorities permitted any U.S. firm issuing a zero-coupon bond to deduct from current income the imputed interest payments.

2. A regulatory arbitrage—the Ministry of Finance limited Japanese pension funds' investments in non-yen-dominated bonds issued by foreign corporations to at most, 10% of their portfolios. The Ministry of Finance also ruled that dual currency bonds qualified as a yen issue, thus allowing dual currency bonds to command a premium from Japanese investors.

Consequently, U.S. firms issued zero-coupon yen bonds (to realize the interest rate savings from the tax arbitrage), and then issued a dual currency bond to hedge the residual yen exposure from the yen zero, while realizing a further interest savings from the regulatory arbitrage.

Tax-Deductible Equity. Perhaps the most thinly disguised attempt to issue tax-deductible equity was the *Adjustable Rate Convertible Debt* introduced in 1982.[19] Such convertibles paid a coupon determined by the dividend rate on the firm's common stock moreover, the debt could be converted to common stock at the current price at any time (i.e., there was no conversion premium). Not surprisingly, once the IRS ruled that this was equity for tax purposes, this structure disappeared.

On a less aggressive level, hybrid structures like Merrill Lynch's LYON™ take advantage of the treatment of zero-coupon instruments by U.S. tax authorities, that is, zero-coupon bonds allow the issuer to deduct deferred interest payments from current income (although the holder of the bond must declare them as income). Given the impact of the IRS ruling on adjustable rate convertible debt, it is not surprising that a great deal of attention has been given to the tax status of the LYON™.

Using Hybrids to Obtain Accrual Accounting Treatment for Risk Management

If a U.S. company uses a forward, futures, swap, or option to hedge a specific transaction (for example, a loan or a purchase or a receipt), it is relatively simple to obtain accrual accounting treatment for the hedge. (Changes in the market value of the hedging instrument offset changes in the value of the asset being hedged, so there is no need to mark the hedging instrument to market.)

If, however, the firm wishes to use one of the risk management instruments to hedge expected net income or an even longer-term economic exposure, the current position of the accounting profession is that the hedge position must be marked to market. Some companies have been reluctant to use derivatives to manage such risks because this accounting treatment would increase the volatility of their reported income—even while such a risk management strategy would stabilize their longer-run operating cash flow.

With the use of hybrids, by contrast, which contain embedded derivatives, the firm may be able to obtain accrual accounting treatment for the entire package. Accountants are accustomed to valuing convertible debt at historical cost; and, given this precedent, they can extend the same treatment to hybrids.[20]

Conclusion

Beginning in 1980 with Sunshine Mining's issue of silver-linked bonds, U.S. corporations have increasingly chosen to raise debt capital by embedding derivatives such as forwards or options into their notes and bonds. In the early 1980s, such hybrids typically provided investors with payoffs (at first only principal, but later interest payments as well) indexed to commodity prices, interest rates, and exchange rates. But, in recent years, companies have begun to issue debt indexed to general stock market indices and even subsets of such indices.

Critics of such newfangled securities view them as the offspring of "supply-driven" fads. According to this view, profit-hungry investment banks set their highly paid "rocket scientists" to designing new securities that can then be foisted on unsuspecting corporate treasurers and investors.

As economists, however, we begin with the assumption that capital market innovations succeed only to the extent they do a better job than existing products in meeting the demands of issuers and investors. The evidence presented in these pages, albeit anecdotal, suggests that hybrid debt is a capital market response to corporate treasurers' desire to manage pricing risks and otherwise tailor their securities to investor demands. In some cases, especially those in which hybrids feature long-dated forwards or options, hybrids are furnishing investors with securities they cannot obtain elsewhere.

Like the remarkable growth of futures, swaps, and options markets beginning in the late 1970s, the proliferation of corporate hybrids during the 1980s is a fundamental attempt to cope with increased price volatility. The sharp increase in the volatility of exchange rates, interest rates, and oil prices, to name just the most important, during the 1970s provided the "necessary condition" for the rise of hybrids.

But another important stimulant to hybrids has come from other constraints on companies' ability to raise debt. In the early 1980s, for example, when interest rates were high, hybrid debt was used by riskier firms to reduce their interest costs to manageable levels. Given the current level of interest rates today, most companies would likely choose to borrow as much straight debt as possible. But except for the highest-rated companies, many firms also now face *non-price* credit restrictions that have greatly enlarged credit spreads. In some such cases, companies are using hybrid debt to lower their risk profile and thus avoid the higher funding costs now associated with being a riskier corporate borrower. In other cases, hybrids are providing access to debt capital that would otherwise be denied on any terms.

Endnotes

1. The date for the introduction of convertible bonds is reported by Peter Tufano in "Financial Innovation and First-Mover Advantages," *Journal of Financial Economics*, 25: 213–240.

2. December 26, 1991, p. Cl. The *Wall Street Journal* article dealt more with exchange-traded products than with hybrids.

3. For preliminary evidence of the impact of issuing hybrid debt on the firm's cost of capital, see Charles Smithson and Leah Schraudenbach, "Reflection of Financial Price Risk in the Firm's Share Price," Chase Manhattan Bank, 1992.

4. Waite Rawls and Charles Smithson, "The Evolution of Risk Management Products," *Journal of Applied Corporate Finance*, Vol. 1 No. 4 (1989).

5. See J. Huston McCulloch, "The Ban on Indexed Bonds," *American Economic Review* 70 (December 1980): 1018–21.

6. Merton Miller, "Financial Innovation: Acheivements and Prospects" *The Continental Bank Journal of Applied Corporate Finance* Vol. 4, No. 4, (Winter 1992): 4–11.

7. European options can be exercised only at maturity, as distinguished from American options, which can be exercised any time before expiration.

8. From the perspective of 1991, during which the silver price has averaged $4.00 per ounce, this exercise price of $20 per ounce may seem bizarre. But keep in mind that this bond was issued in early 1980. During the period October 1979–January 1980, the price of silver averaged $23 per ounce.

9. For a discussion of how the equity option embedded in convertibles could make convertible bondholders indifferent to increases in the volatility of corporate cash flow, see Michael Brennan and Eduardo Schwartz, "The Case for Convertibles," *Chase Financial Quarterly* (Fall 1981). Reprinted in *Journal of Applied Corporate Finance* (Summer 1988).

10. See James Jordan, Robert Mackay, and Eugene Moriarty, "The New Regulation of Hybrid Debt Instruments," *Journal of Applied Corporate Finance*, Vol. 2 No. 4 (Winter 1990).

11. See Michael G. Capatides, *A Guide to the Capital Markets Activities of Banks and Bank Holding Companies*, (Browne & Co.), 1988: 132.

12. In his article in this issue, "Securities Innovation: An Overview," John Finnerty notes that ICONs "were introduced and disappeared quickly."

13. For the seminal discussion of the effect of conflicts between shareholders and debtholders (and between management and shareholders as well) on the behavior of the firm, see Michael C. Jensen and William H. Meckling, "Theory of the Firm: Managerial Behavior, Agency Costs, and Capital Structure," *Journal of Financial Economics* (1976): 305–360.

14. For an account of the underinvestment problem, see Stewart Myers, "The Determinants of Corporate Borrowing," *Journal of Financial Economics* (1977). For a more detailed examination of these sources of shareholder/debtholder conflict, see Clifford W. Smith and Jerold B. Warner, "On Financial Contracting: An Analysis of Bond Convenants," *Journal of Financial Economics*, 7 (1979): 117–161.

15. Extendible notes also provide bondholders with an option on the firm's credit standing. But, unlike puttable debt, they represent the opportunity to benefit from increases in the firm's credit standing, or decreases in the spread. In the case of extendible notes, if the credit spread of the issuer decreases, the right to extend the maturity of the note (at the old credit spread) has value.

16. More technically, the underinvestment problem arises from the fact that, in financially troubled firms, an outsized portion of the returns from new investments must go to help restore the value of the bondholders' claims before the shareholders receive any payoff at all. This has also been dubbed the "debt overhang" problem.

17. For an exposition of this argument, see Michael Brennan and Eduardo Schwartz, "The Case for Convertibles," *Chase Financial Quar-*

terly (Fall 1981). Reprinted in *Journal of Applied Corporate Finance* (Summer 1988).

18. The put feature also enabled Merrill Lynch to tailor the security for its network of retail investors.

19. John Finnerty, "An Overview of Corporate Securities Innovation," *Journal of Applied Corporate Finance* Vol. 4, No. 4, (Winter 1992): 23–39.

20. See J. Matthew Singleton, "Hedge Accounting: A State-of-the-Art Review," *Journal of Banking and Finance,* 5 (Fall 1991): 26–32.

Chapter 19

Cross Border Federal Income Tax Issues in Financings and Investment Products

Gary J. Gartner, Esq.
Penny Mavridis, Esq.
Goodman Freeman Phillips & Vineberg, New York, NY

This chapter is divided into two parts. The first part discusses the U.S. federal income tax issues that may arise in financing the acquisition or operation of a domestic business. The second part discusses the U.S. federal income tax issues that relate to a domestic entity's issuance of financial products in foreign capital markets.

It is increasingly apparent that a corporation must have access to global capital markets to compete effectively. Further, with the proliferation of foreign-owned U.S. businesses, the issues relating to the financing of U.S. businesses by foreign-related or unrelated parties have become important.

Although not an exhaustive survey, this chapter is intended to provide the reader with a broad overview of the U.S. federal income tax issues affecting some of the forms of financing and financial products issued either in the foreign marketplace or to foreign-related parties. Also, the emergence of new products requires a complete analysis of their consequences based on the principles discussed herein. Finally, one cannot deal comprehensively with the tax issues relating to the described transactions without considering the income tax issues arising in the acquiror's or investor's home country jurisdiction.

Part 1: Financing a U.S. Business

Background

To determine the most tax-effective means of financing an acquisition of a U.S. business and its ongoing operations, a foreign acquiror should consider 1) the effective tax rates applicable to the acquired and acquiror corporations in their resident countries; 2) the deductibility of interest payments; and 3) the U.S. income tax withholding rates on interest paid or accrued to foreign persons.

Effective Tax Rates

Determining the effective tax rates applicable to the parties to an acquisition is significant in identifying the borrower in the acquisition. If the U.S. effective corporate income tax rate exceeds a foreign purchaser's (FP) effective corporate income tax rate in its country of residence, an interest deduction would be more valuable in the United States, (assuming that any interest paid to FP is subject to reduced or zero U.S. withholding tax). Therefore, if FP desires to acquire the stock of a domestic corporation (DC), FP could acquire DC by means of a newly-created or existing domestic subsidiary (A) in other words, FP would make a loan to A equal to the purchase price of DC. A would then acquire the DC stock with the loan proceeds. Following the purchase of DC, A and DC could elect to file a U.S. consolidated return, thereby offsetting A's interest deductions with DC's income. Alternatively, in the above example, if FP wants DC to be the borrower, FP would merge A into DC. DC would then distribute the loan proceeds to DC's former shareholders in redemption of their DC shares. The above lending structures may not be advisable, however, if the U.S. withholding tax on any interest paid by A or DC to FP is subject to a high U.S. withholding tax (e.g., 30% maximum) in which case, FP may want to use a lender resident in a favorable treaty country. The use of offshore lenders is discussed below.

Limitation of U.S. Interest Deductions

A foreign purchaser's decision to use a U.S. borrower, may be severely restricted under the Code. In the case of an acquisition of a U.S. business, the following interest limitation rules may apply: 1) earnings stripping; 2) original issue discount (OID) payments to related persons; 3) matching of income and expense with respect to payments to foreign persons; 4) interest on certain corporate acquisition indebtedness; 5) non-arm's length interest payments between commonly controlled corporations; 6) debt-equity issues; and 7) branch interest allocation rules.

Earnings Stripping Rule. Code §163(j) limits certain thinly capitalized corporations, including foreign corporations with U.S. effectively connected income, from deducting "disqualified interest" payments (the "earnings stripping rule"). A disallowed interest expense, however, is carried forward to succeeding taxable years. The term "disqualified interest" means any interest paid or accrued by a U.S. taxpayer, directly or indirectly, to a related person (within the meaning of Code §§267(b) and 707(b)(1)), to the extent a zero or reduced U.S. income tax is imposed on such interest. The underlying theory is that interest paid by a domestic corporation to its foreign-related party, which is exempt from U.S. income tax under a treaty, erodes the U.S. tax base.

The earnings stripping rule applies to a corporation for any taxable year if 1) such corporation has "excess interest expense" for such taxable year; and 2) such corporation's debt to equity ratio, generally as of the close of such taxable year, exceeds 1.5 to 1.0. A corporation's debt to equity ratio is the ratio of a corporation's total indebtedness to the sum of its money and all other assets (adjusted basis) reduced (but not below zero) by its total indebtedness.

The term "excess interest expense" means the excess of a corporation's net interest expense for a taxable year (interest expense less interest income) over the sum of 1) 50% of such corporation's "adjusted taxable income" (ATI); and 2) any "excess limitation carryforward" (ELC) attributable to such corporation's three preceding taxable years. ATI generally is a cash flow concept defined as a corporation's taxable income computed without net interest expense, depreciation, amortization, and depletion expenses, or net operating loss ("NOL") carryovers. ELC consists of a corporation's unabsorbed "excess limitation" for its three preceding taxable years, not to exceed such corporation's excess interest expense for the taxable year to which the ELC is carried forward. The "excess limitation"

for any taxable year is computed as follows: [(50% ATI)—net interest expense]. In applying the earnings stripping rule, all members of an affiliated group (e.g., U.S. consolidated group) are treated as one taxpayer.

Original Issue Discount Deductions. Code §163(e)(3) provides that if a debt instrument having original issue discount (OID) (i.e., excess of the stated redemption price at maturity over the issue price), is held by a related foreign person (within the meaning of Code §267(b), e.g., a member of the same controlled group of corporations as the debt issuer), any portion of the OID that accrues on the debt instrument is not deductible until paid to the foreign payee. Correspondingly, U.S. withholding tax on the accrued OID is deferred until such OID is paid. The above rule does not apply, however, if the OID income is effectively connected with the lender's U.S. trade or business, unless the OID income is subject to zero or reduced U.S. tax (e.g., the U.S. trade or business does not constitute a permanent establishment under an applicable treaty). The above rule also does not apply if the OID is with respect to a loan between natural persons.

OID that otherwise is deductible under Code §163(e)(3), may be disallowed, however, under the earnings stripping rules discussed above. Therefore, to the extent OID constitutes disqualified interest when paid, Code §163(j) would deny its deduction.

Matching Income and Expense. Code §267(a)(3) authorizes the Internal Revenue Service (the "Service") to issue regulations applying the matching of income and deductions principle contained in Code §267 (the "matching rule"). Pursuant to such authorization, the Service issued proposed regulations which provide that an amount (other than an amount which constitutes U.S. effectively connected income("ECI")) owed to a "related" (within the meaning of Code §§267(b) or (e)) foreign person may not be deducted until such amount is paid to such foreign person, thereby effectively converting an accrual-basis taxpayer to a cash-basis taxpayer with respect to payments made to a related foreign person (the "deductible when paid rule"). For this purpose, the parties' relationship is tested at the close of the taxpayer's taxable year in which such amount otherwise would be deductible. In the case of amounts owed to a related foreign person which constitute U.S. ECI of such foreign person (other than amounts subject to a zero or reduced U.S. income tax pursuant to a treaty), the regulations under Code §267 provide that such amounts are deductible as of the day on which such amounts are includable in the foreign person's gross income or, if later, on the day on which such amounts otherwise would be deductible (the "matching rule"). In the case of amounts which constitute U.S. effectively connected income which is subject to a zero or reduced U.S. tax pursuant to a treaty, the deductible when paid rule applies. Any interest deductible under Code §267, however, may be disallowed under Code §163(j).

The Code §267 deferral rules play an equally important role in the context of payments to foreign-related persons of items other than interest which otherwise would have been deductible to the payor, such as service fees or royalties.

Corporate Acquisition Indebtedness. Code §279 denies a deduction for any interest (stated or imputed) incurred by a corporation on its "corporate acquisition indebtedness" to the extent such interest exceeds, in general, $5 million. The denial of an interest deduction presumably is based on the treatment of certain acquisition indebtedness of thinly capitalized corporations as equity. The term "corporate acquisition indebtedness" means indebtedness that is 1) issued for the acquisition of generally domestic stock or two-thirds of a corporation's trade or business assets; 2) subordinated to creditors' claims or a substantial amount of unsecured debt; 3) convertible into the issuing corporation's stock; and 4) issued by a corporation with a debt to equity ratio exceeding two to one or whose projected earnings, together with the acquired corporation's projected earnings in the case of a reorganization, do not exceed three times the annual interest incurred by such corporation. Projected earnings generally are the average annual earnings for any three-year period ending with the last day of an issuer's taxable year that includes the acquisition. If the issuer is a member of an affiliated group, all members of the affiliated group, including foreign member corporations, are treated as a single issuer.

Interest Payments Between Commonly Controlled Persons. Code §482 provides that in the case of payments between two or more organizations, trades, or businesses (whether or not incorporated, organized in the United States, or affiliated) that are owned or controlled directly or indirectly by the same interests, the Service may distribute, apportion, or allocate income and loss items among such corporations if the Service determines such adjustment is necessary 1) to prevent evasion of taxes; or 2) to clearly reflect the income of any of such related persons. For example, if a domestic borrower pays a related lender interest at a rate in excess of the arm's length rate, the Service may adjust the domestic borrower's interest to deny the domestic borrower its excess interest deductions.

Debt-Equity Characterization. Interest deductions also may be denied if the Service determines the purported debt more aptly resembles equity. The characterization of debt as equity depends, in large part, on whether the corporate borrower is adequately capitalized to finance the debt and interest payments. For example, in the case of a third-party loan to a U.S. borrower that is guaranteed by such borrower's parent, the Service may characterize the transaction as a loan from the third-party lender to such borrower's parent, followed by a capital contribution of the loaned amount to the nominal U.S. borrower, thereby denying such borrower any interest deductions, and treating any payments made on the loan as distributions (taxable to the extent of such borrower's earnings and profits) to its parent. When placing related party debt in a U.S. borrower, one must be satisfied, based on the existing facts, that the borrower has sufficient cash flow and asset base to warrant such a level of debt financing.

Branch Interest Allocation Rules. Code §882 taxes a foreign corporation on its taxable income that is effectively connected with a U.S. trade or business. To determine the interest deduction allocable to a U.S. business, for purposes of determining a foreign corporation's U.S. ECI, Code §882 provides interest apportionment rules based on a foreign corporation's U.S. and worldwide assets and liabilities. Specifically, the proposed regulations, under Code §882, provide that the amount of interest expense of a foreign corporation that is allocable to U.S. ECI is determined under the following three-step process. The amount determined may not exceed, however, the amount of interest on debt paid or accrued by the foreign corporation within its taxable year.

Step One: Determine total value (generally adjusted basis, unless fair market value is elected and determined under certain specialized valuation formulas) of U.S. assets (e.g., depreciable and amortizable property to the extent any related depreciation or amortization is included in determining U.S. ECI; inventory, to the extent the amount of gross sales from such inventory is included in U.S. ECI; and U.S. real property interests ("USRPIs") but only in the year such property is disposed of in a taxable transaction) for the taxable year. The total value of U.S. assets must be determined no less frequently than quarterly.

Step Two: Determine total amount of U.S. liabilities for the taxable year by multiplying the total value of the U.S. assets for the taxable year by the actual ratio of a foreign corporation's worldwide liabilities to worldwide assets ("actual ratio") or alternatively, by a fixed generally 50% ratio ("fixed ratio"). For this purpose, the amount of a liability is determined under U.S. tax principles. The ratios may be computed either in U.S. dollars or the functional currency of a foreign corporation, translated at the spot rate on the applicable valuation date. Also, in determining the actual ratio, the adjusted basis of any stock in a 20% (by vote) owned corporation must be adjusted upward or downward (but not below zero) for any earnings and profits of the corporation (and lower-tier 20% corporations) or deficit earnings and profits, respectively. For this purpose, earnings and profits may be based on the earnings and profits reported by the corporation on its financial records. In addition, the value of a partner's share of partnership's assets is the partner's adjusted basis in its partnership interest, reduced by the partner's share of partnership liabilities, as computed under Code §752, and increased by the partner's share of partnership liabilities based on such partner's share of the partnership's interest expense attributable to a partnership liability.

Step Three: Determine amount of interest expense allocable to U.S. ECI. This amount varies depending on whether a foreign corporation's booked liabilities (BL) (i.e., generally reflected on the books of a U.S. trade or business) equal or exceed such corporation's U.S. liabilities (USL), as determined under step two above. If BL ≥ USL, the amount of interest expense allocable to U.S. ECI is the total amount of interest paid or accrued within the taxable year by the U.S. business, reduced by the following ratio [(BL – USL) / BL]. Alternatively, if USL>BL, the amount of interest expense allocable to U.S. ECI is the total amount of interest paid or accrued within the taxable year by the U.S. business on BL, plus the following amount: [(USL – BL) × an applicable interest rate generally based on 110% of London Interbank Offered Rate (LIBOR)].

The interest expense limitation rule under Code §882 penalizes the excessive leveraging of U.S. operations by apportioning interest expense based on a foreign corporation's U.S. and worldwide asset values. Conversely, such limitation rule favors underleveraged U.S. operations by apportioning a higher interest expense to the U.S. operations than would otherwise be deductible by the U.S. trade or business, subject to the excess interest rule under Code §884(f).

Code §884(f) provides that to the extent the amount of interest apportioned, under Code §882, to a foreign corporation's (FC) U.S. ECI exceeds the sum of 1) FC's "branch interest" for the taxable year; and 2) if FC is a partner in a partnership that is engaged in a U.S. trade or business, FC's distributive share of interest paid or accrued by such partnership (but not to reduce the apportioned interest below zero), such foreign corporation is liable for 30% U.S.

withholding tax, absent a treaty reduction or exemption, as if such excess interest were U.S. non-effectively connected income paid to such foreign corporation by a wholly owned domestic corporation on the last day of such foreign corporation's taxable year. For this purpose, "branch interest" generally means interest paid by a foreign corporation with respect to a liability 1) shown on the books of its U.S. trade or business; or 2) predominantly secured by a U.S. asset of such foreign corporation.

Income Tax Withholding

U.S.-source income that is effectively connected with a U.S. trade or business is subject to the U.S. graduated income tax rates that otherwise apply to corporations or individuals. However, U.S.-source interest, dividends, rents, royalties, or other similar income that is not U.S. ECI, referred to as fixed or determinable annual or periodic income (FDAP), received by a foreign person, is subject to a flat 30% withholding tax, absent either a Code exemption or treaty exemption or reduction. A treaty exemption or reduction generally applies, however, to FDAP income.

Interest (including OID) paid by a U.S. borrower to a foreign lender is exempt from U.S. withholding tax under the Code if such interest constitutes "portfolio interest." Portfolio interest is U.S.-source interest, not effectively connected with a U.S. trade or business, paid on an obligation issued after July 18, 1984, that is registered, (or not registered, and with respect to which a foreign holder satisfies certain certification requirements, including assurances that such obligation will be sold only to foreign persons and the interest on such obligation will be payable outside the United States).

The portfolio interest exemption does not apply, however, to interest paid to a 10% (with attribution) owner (e.g., shareholder or partner). In the case of a corporate recipient, portfolio interest also does not include interest 1) received by a bank on an extension of credit made in its ordinary course of business; or 2) received by a controlled foreign corporation from a related person. Consequently, loans from shareholders or third-party banks generally do not qualify for the portfolio interest exemption. The Service has indicated that it will provide some guidance as to what is meant by a "bank" for this purpose.

If the lender is a resident of a country that has an income tax treaty with the United States (hereinafter referred to as a "treaty lender") any interest paid to such lender may be reduced or exempt from U.S. taxation under the treaty. Ordinarily, interest paid by a U.S. obligor to a treaty lender is subject to a treaty-reduced withholding rate ranging from 0% to 15%. For example, any interest paid by a U.S. borrower to its

U.K. parent, or other U.K. lender, is exempt from U.S. taxation under Article 11 of the Income Tax Treaty between the United Kingdom and the United States.

The availability of treaty reductions or exemptions from U.S. withholding tax spurred the use of offshore finance vehicles located in favorable treaty countries with low income tax and zero or reduced U.S. withholding (e.g., Netherlands and Netherlands Antilles). The use of such offshore finance vehicles may be attacked by the Service. For example, in the case of certain back-to-back loans from a parent to a U.S. borrower, involving the use of an intermediary offshore finance company (e.g., Netherlands Antilles subsidiary), the Service may treat the transaction as a direct loan by such parent to such U.S. borrower thereby precluding such foreign parent from benefitting from the zero or reduced U.S. withholding rate available to the treaty lender. A back-to-back loan transaction generally is subject to recharacterization if 1) the primary purpose for involving the offshore finance company in the borrowing transaction is an attempt to obtain the benefits of the zero or reduced treaty rate; and 2) the offshore finance company lacks dominion and control over the interest received in the borrowing transaction (e.g., such interest ultimately is remitted to the foreign parent as interest on its loan to the offshore finance company).

The Service recently expanded its back-to-back loan analysis to cover a transaction involving a capital contribution by a foreign parent to an offshore finance company for the purpose of lending the amount contributed to a U.S. borrower. The Service treated the transaction as a direct loan from the parent to the U.S. borrower despite the fact that the offshore company was not obligated to remit interest payments to the parent. There does not appear to be any direct authority for such an expanded position; nevertheless, such a position may reflect the Service's desire to litigate this issue.

Anti-treaty shopping provisions also are contained in several U.S. income tax treaties, including those with Barbados, Cyprus, France, Germany, India, and Spain, and most recently in the signed but not yet ratified Netherlands treaty. For example, the recently approved Income Tax Treaty between Germany and the United States (the "German Treaty") limits treaty benefits, under Article 28, generally to 1) resident individuals; 2) a resident corporation whose principal class of shares is substantially and regularly traded on a recognized stock exchange; 3) a person more than 50% of the beneficial interest in which, or the number of shares of each class of which, is owned, directly or indirectly, by persons entitled to German Treaty benefits or U.S. citizens;

or 4) a person more than 50% of the gross income of which is not used, directly or indirectly, to meet liabilities to persons not entitled to German Treaty benefits or who are not U.S. citizens.

The Service's aggressive attack on offshore financing transactions, coupled with the limitation of benefit provisions contained in recently approved treaties, greatly diminishes the ability of taxpayers to reduce U.S. income tax withholding through treaty shopping. Nonetheless, in certain circumstances, taxpayers still may be able to use existing offshore operating subsidiaries, with working capital surplus, to finance U.S. operations without running afoul of the anti-treaty shopping rules.

Part 2: Portfolio Investment in the United States and Financial Products

Background

To appreciate the subtleties of certain financial products developed for domestic issuers, one must first understand the basic pattern of U.S. taxation of portfolio (non-business) investments. Among the portfolio investments available to a foreign person are dividend-paying investments (e.g., common and preferred stocks and mutual funds), and interest-paying investments (e.g., bank deposits, corporate or government securities, and convertible debentures).

As discussed above, absent any Code or treaty protection, dividends and interest (other than income effectively connected with a U.S. trade or business) paid to foreign persons are subject to a 30% U.S. withholding tax. Therefore, a foreign person, resident in a non-treaty country, may want to invest in corporate bonds or securities of domestic corporations by means of an offshore holding company to reduce its U.S. withholding taxes, and in the case of a nonresident alien individual, to avoid U.S. estate tax. For example, the U.S. estate tax applies to shares of domestic corporations held by nonresident aliens at the time of their death. However, U.S. estate tax does not apply to shares of foreign corporations held by nonresident aliens.

The Code exempts dividends paid by certain 80/20 domestic corporations to foreign persons from U.S. tax but only in proportion to such domestic corporation's foreign-source income. A corporation qualifies as an 80/20 corporation if at least 80% of its gross income for the three-year period ending with the close of the taxable year preceding the dividend payment is "active foreign business income." The term "active foreign business income" means gross income 1) derived from foreign sources;

and 2) attributable to a corporation's active conduct of a trade or business in a foreign country or U.S. possession. Dividends not exempt under the Code may be subject to reduced U.S. withholding under an applicable treaty. As noted above, dividends paid to foreign persons generally are subject to a treaty-reduced U.S. withholding tax ranging from 5% to 30%.

In the case of interest (not effectively connected with a U.S. trade or business) paid to foreign persons, the Code provides exemptions from U.S. withholding tax for: 1) interest on bank deposits; 2) portfolio interest; and 3) short-term (i.e., payable 183 days or less from date of original issue) OID income, including OID income on Treasury bills payable in 6 months or less from the date of issue. The exemption for interest on bank deposits includes interest paid on: 1) certificates of deposits, open account time deposits, multiple maturity time deposits; 2) interest paid by a credit union; 3) interest on deposits with insurance companies; 4) deposits on withdrawable accounts with savings institutions such as mutual savings banks and savings and loan associations. Qualified portfolio interest may be paid on nonregistered or registered bonds. However, if the obligation is nonregistered (i.e., in bearer form), the issuer must certify that such obligation 1) is sold under procedures reasonably designed to prevent its sale or resale to U.S. persons; 2) interest on such obligation is payable only outside the United States; and 3) such obligation contains a legend that any U.S. person who holds such obligation is subject to limitations under the U.S. income tax laws. The exemption for portfolio interest is not available, however, to interest paid to a 10% (by vote, in the case of a shareholder, and capital or profits interest, in the case of a partnership) owner.

The Code also exempts from U.S. income tax interest paid to an unrelated foreign person by an 80/20 domestic corporation or resident alien individual (the 80/20 test is discussed above.) In the case of interest paid by an 80/20 corporation or individual to a related foreign person, the exemption only applies to a percentage of the interest based on the ratio of the payor's gross income from sources outside the United States to the payor's total gross income. In addition, interest paid on state and local bonds is tax-free when paid to a foreign person since such interest is excluded from the definition of U.S. gross income. Interest not exempt under the Code may be subject to reduced U.S. withholding under an applicable treaty. Accordingly, interest paid to foreign persons is subject to a treaty-reduced U.S. withholding tax ranging from 0% to 30%, depending on the recipient's country of residence.

Gains or losses recognized by foreign persons on the disposition of their U.S. portfolio investments ordinarily are sourced, under Code §865, based on the seller's residency and therefore are exempt from U.S. income tax. However, gains and losses from dispositions of stock in U.S. real property holding corporations are not exempt from U.S. income tax. Instead, such gains and losses are treated as U.S. ECI. Also, in the case of a sale or exchange of an OID obligation (i.e., any bond or other evidence of indebtedness having OID), the amount of any previously accrued but unrecognized OID constitutes U.S.-source income subject to U.S. withholding tax at the time of the sale or exchange.

Financial Products

The modern financial products issued by domestic corporations in foreign capital markets all have one thing in common. The issuer identifies a specific form of financial engineering that accomplishes certain accounting or tax goals and identifies a purchaser group which could most efficiently absorb the product. Accordingly, in assessing a product's marketability, any product sold to a foreign purchaser must not only consider the proper characterization of the product in the purchaser's country of residence, but also must consider the U.S. taxation of payments on the product. Therefore, every financial product must be analyzed within the framework of the U.S. portfolio investment rules either to fit within an available exemption from tax, or avoid the scope of the tax altogether. The following is a brief summary of some types of products (some specific and other generic) which raise several issues in the cross-border context.

Types of Investment Products

Debt-Equity Hybrid Instruments. A debt-equity hybrid instrument generally provides a holder with typical unsecured creditor's rights, a guaranteed minimum income stream or redemption price, and a variable income stream or redemption price keyed to the issuer's dividend payments or value of stock at maturity. The issues with respect to debt-equity hybrid instruments are whether such instruments constitute debt or equity, or part debt and part equity; whether the payments earned on such instruments constitute deductible interest expense or nondeductible dividend distributions; and whether payments are taxable to the holder.

Code §385 authorizes the Treasury to issue regulations to determine whether an interest in a corporation constitutes debt or equity for U.S. federal income tax purposes. Although proposed regulations were issued in 1980 and 1981, such regulations were withdrawn in 1983. To date, no additional regulations have been issued. Code §385 lists the following nonexclusive factors for determining whether an instrument constitutes debt or equity: 1) whether there is a written unconditional promise to pay on demand or on a specified date a sum certain in money in return for an adequate consideration in money or money's worth, and to pay a fixed rate of interest; 2) whether there is a subordination to or preference over any indebtedness of the corporation; 3) the ratio of debt to equity of the corporation; 4) whether there is convertibility into the stock of the corporation; and 5) the relationship between holdings of stock in the corporation and holdings of the interest in question.

The above factors are not intended to be exclusive or mandatory. Therefore, in the absence of additional guidance from Treasury, taxpayers ordinarily must rely on existing case law to determine the characterization of a hybrid instrument unless a specific Code provision otherwise applies. Among the principal factors used by the courts to distinguish debt from equity are: 1) the source of the interest payments; 2) the presence or absence of a fixed maturity date; 3) the intent of the parties to enter into a debtor-creditor relationship; 4) the right to enforce payment of principal and interest; 5) management participation rights; and 6) whether there is a reasonable expectation of repayment.

Applying these factors, the Service ruled that an adjustable rate convertible note (ARCN) constituted equity, and the periodic payments thereon constituted nondeductible dividend distributions. The terms of the tested ARCN were as follows: 1) 20-year maturity; 2) $1,000 issue price (payable in cash or 50 shares of the issuer); 3) convertible into stock of the issuer; 4) callable 2 years after its issuance at $600 (upon call, a holder has the right to exercise its conversion right); 5) interest payable quarterly at a rate based on dividends paid on 50 shares of the issuer plus 2% of issue price (such payments not to be less than $60 or more than $175); and 6) at maturity, the holder may receive either $600 or 50 shares of the issuer. At the time the ARCN was issued, the yield for noncontingent corporate debt instruments was 12%.

The Service ruled the ARCN was equity since 1) the ARCN favored conversion (i.e., redemption on maturity only would occur if the issuer's stock dropped more than 40% in value); 2) the guaranteed annual return of at least $60 was unreasonably low in comparison to the annual return on comparable debt instruments at the time of issue; 3) up to 65% of the annual yield was based on the level of discretionary dividends paid by the issuer; and 4) the ARCN was subordinated to the issuer's general creditors. The Service distinguished the ARCN from similar instruments the Service earlier ruled were debt, based on their nonconvertibility feature, and fixed interest rates, which although dependent in part on the issuer's net profits, were not discretionary with the issuer as in the case of dividends.

Under the withdrawn Code §385 regulations, a hybrid instrument was treated as either debt or equity, without any provision for bifurcating such instrument into its equity and debt components. However, present Code §385 allows a single instrument to be treated as part debt and part equity. In addition, proposed OID regulations adopt a bifurcation analysis to treat each element of certain contingent payment obligations in accordance with their economic substance.

Taxpayer uncertainty with respect to the treatment of hybrid instruments may result in the inconsistent treatment of such instruments by issuers and holders. To prevent inconsistent treatment, Code §385(c) requires that the U.S. tax characterization (as of the time of issuance) of a corporate instrument as stock or debt by the issuer be binding on the issuer and all holders.

Subsidiary Tracking Stock. Subsidiary tracking stock ordinarily is stock, the market value and dividends of which are based on the earnings of a subsidiary of an issuing corporation. Subsidiary tracking stock may be used by a U.S. parent of an affiliated group to acquire the stock of a foreign-owned domestic corporation. For example, a foreign person may not be willing to dispose of its profitable domestic corporation for stock of an unprofitable U.S. corporation. Therefore, to encourage the sale, the U.S. acquiror may offer the foreign seller cash and an equity interest that tracks the earnings of the foreign person's subsidiary. Although the use of subsidiary tracking stock provides an acquiror with an alternative financing arrangement, as discussed below, the use of such stock raises several U.S. income tax concerns.

Subsidiary tracking stock issued by a parent (P) corporation generally 1) tracks the earnings of its subsidiary (S); 2) has no rights to receive or be converted into S stock; 3) has no voting rights in S, other than indirectly through its voting rights in P; 4) shares *pro rata* in P's assets upon the liquidation or dissolution of P with the common shareholders of P; 5) is subordinated to P's debts regardless of the separate earnings of S; and 6) can be converted into P stock, at fair market value, at P's option.

The issuance of subsidiary tracking stock raises an issue as to the proper classification of such stock as 1) stock of the issuing corporation; 2) stock of the tracked corporation; 3) a joint venture interest in the assets of the tracked corporation; or 4) an option under the proposed option attribution rules under Code §1504. Although the Service initially recognized subsidiary tracking stock as stock of the issuing corporation, the Service later revoked its ruling on tracking stock and announced a no-ruling position with respect to the proper classification of an instrument that has certain voting and liquidation rights in an issuing corporation but dividend rights determined by reference to the earnings of a segregated portion of the issuing corporation's assets, including assets held by a subsidiary. Despite the Service's no ruling policy, the subsidiary tracking stock described above should be treated as stock of P since it 1) is subordinated to P's creditors; 2) participates in P's management; 3) is paid from P's earnings and profits; and 4) is not entitled to any liquidation rights with respect to S.

Although the Service maintains its no-ruling policy with respect to subsidiary tracking stock, classification of subsidiary tracking stock is currently under extensive study by the Service. Nonetheless, in the absence of further guidance on the classification of subsidiary tracking stock, such investment vehicles should be used with extreme caution since a misclassification of tracking stock could produce adverse U.S. tax results. For example, if tracking stock is treated as S stock, P would be treated as distributing S stock to its shareholders in a taxable distribution under Code §311. Also, if S is a member of a U.S. consolidated group, the issuance of more than a 20% interest (vote and value) in S would cause a deconsolidation of S and trigger any related intercompany gains, losses, and excess loss accounts (gains with respect to negative stock basis). Moreover, a deconsolidation of S may result in a basis reduction with respect to S's stock, and the stock of any lower-tier subsidiaries, under the consolidated loss disallowance rules.

High-Yield Obligations. In response to highly leveraged buyouts with insufficient earnings capacity to make current interest payments and, possibly, future interest payments, Congress enacted Code §163(e)(5) to defer or disallow OID on certain significant discount obligations. Specifically, Code §163(e)(5) provides that in the case of an "applicable high yield discount obligation" (AHYDO) issued by a corporation: 1) no deduction is allowed for the "disqualified portion" of the OID on such obligation; and 2) the remainder of such OID is not allowable as a deduction until paid.

An AHYDO is defined as any debt instrument if 1) the instrument's maturity date is more than five years from the date of issue; 2) the yield to maturity on such instrument equals or exceeds the sum of (a) the applicable federal rate for the month in which the instrument is issued, plus (b) five percentage points; and 3) such instrument has "significant OI discount." A debt instrument is treated as havin significant OID discount if the aggregate amoun which would be includible in gross income wit respect to such instrument (both OID and state interest) for periods before the close of any accru period ending after the date five years after suc instrument's issuance exceeds the sum of (i) th aggregate amount of interest to be paid under th instrument before the close of such accrual perioc and (ii) the product of such instrument's issue pric and its yield to maturity. The effect of the above ru is to minimize the unpaid interest to a 12-mont period.

The "disqualified portion" of the OID (not t exceed the amount of OID) is the yield to maturi in excess of the sum of 1) the applicable federal rat plus 2) six percentage points. The "disqualified po tion" is treated as a dividend distribution for pu poses of qualifying such distribution for th dividends received deduction in the case of a corp rate distributee. However, the "disqualified portion is not treated as a dividend for other purpose including the determination of the applicable U.! withholding tax on distributions to foreign person

An OID or paid-in-kind (PIK) bond with a mor than five-year maturity date ordinarily qualifies as a AHYDO. A PIK bond is a bond, interest on which payable, at the issuer's discretion, in cash or i additional securities having the identical terms to th bond on which paid (baby bonds). Alternatively, instead of paying interest with baby bonds, the issue pays interest with stock, interest is treated as pai when the stock is required to be redeemed (fc property other than the issuer's stock or debt.) Sinc the PIK bonds are not payable until maturity of th underlying PIK debt, the PIK bonds generally hav significant OID.

Premium Preferred Stock. Under Code §305(c the entire redemption premium on preferred stoc that is mandatorily redeemable by the issuer at specified time, or is puttable at any time, is treate' as accruing over the shareholder's holding period i the stock as a series of taxable stock dividends (th "economic accrual rule"). The economic accrua rule does not apply if the redemption premium doe not exceed one quarter of one percent of the redemr tion price at maturity multiplied by the number c complete years to maturity (the *"de minimis* rule" For example, if puttable preferred shares are issue at $100, and are redeemable in five years at $11C the preferred shares are treated as having an unrea sonable redemption premium equal to $10 since th redemption premium exceeds $1.37, computed a follows: [(1/4 × 1%) × ($110 × 5 years)].

Preferred stock is subject to the above rules, irrespective of whether it also is callable by the issuer. If preferred stock is callable solely at the issuer's option, and is not otherwise puttable or subject to mandatory redemption at a specified time, the *de minimis* rule does not apply. Instead, the entire call premium is subject to the economic accrual rule if the premium is unreasonable under regulations otherwise in effect. In this case, the premium is treated as accruing over the period during which the preferred stock cannot be called for redemption. At present, it is unclear whether preferred stock that is immediately callable is subject to the economic accrual rule.

For purposes of the above rule, a premium is unreasonable if it is in the nature of a penalty for a premature redemption of the preferred stock, and if it does not exceed the amount the corporation would be required to pay for the right to make such premature redemption under market conditions existing at the time of issuance. The regulations provide the following example: A redemption premium that does not exceed 10% of a stock's issue price, where such stock is not redeemable for five years from the date of issue, is considered reasonable.

If premium preferred shares are held by a foreign person, an issue arises as to whether the issuer of the preferred shares is obligated to withhold U.S. federal income tax on the deemed distributions on the preferred shares as such distributions accrue or whether, as in the case of OID income, no withholding is required until the redemption premium actually is paid. Although the actual payment of an income item generally triggers the payor's withholding obligation under the withholding regulations, the Service has argued successfully, in the case of constructive dividend distributions (e.g., resulting from Code §482 adjustments), that the withholding obligation also is triggered at the time of the deemed distribution since the payee is in constructive receipt of the income item.

The Service's position, however, raises the additional issue as to the means of payment since the withholding agent, in this case, neither possesses the premiums nor the underlying preferred shares. Therefore, to satisfy its withholding obligation, a payor either must pay the withholding tax itself, and seek reimbursement from the payee, or alternatively, retain a portion of the issued preferred shares as security for any future U.S. withholding tax. In the absence of additional guidance on the above withholding tax issues, a foreign payee may be liable for U.S. withholding tax on deemed dividend distributions. Moreover, a foreign payee resident in a treaty country may not be exempt from U.S. withholding tax on such deemed distributions from a U.S. issuer

corporation if the applicable treaty defines a dividend distribution based on the local laws of the payor's Contracting State which would include Code §305(c).

Notional Principal Contracts. A "notional principal contract" is defined, under Code §863, as a financial instrument that provides for the payment of amounts by one party to another at specified intervals calculated by reference to a specified index (e.g., LIBOR or Treasury rates) upon a notional principal amount in exchange for a specified consideration or promise to pay similar amounts. The notional principal amount serves only as a reference for determining the amount of payments to be made under the contract and is not actually borrowed or loaned between the parties. Notional principal contracts include equity swaps, interest rate swaps, commodity swaps, basis swaps, caps, interest rate caps, floors, interest rate floors, and collars.

Equity Swap. In a standard equity swap, an equity holder (e.g., a domestic financial institution) swaps the amount of any appreciation and dividends on shares it owns for a return (e.g., payable by a foreign person) equal to, for example, the LIBOR rate plus the amount of any decrease in the value of the shares. The argument against dividend equivalency with respect to income from equity swaps is that the recipient of the dividends and appreciation is not the beneficial owner of the indexed shares since it does not enjoy voting or liquidation rights.

Interest Rate Swap. An "interest rate swap" is a swap in which the notional principal amount is expressed in dollars and the specified index is an interest rate or interest rate index. Income earned on an interest rate swap does not constitute interest income since there is no underlying debt. Therefore, such income is not subject to U.S. federal income tax unless, as indicated above, such income constitutes U.S. ECI attributable to a foreign person's U.S. permanent establishment. For example, if a foreign bank enters into a U.S. dollar interest rate swap with a domestic corporation for the purpose of effecting asset/liability management with respect to its foreign banking activities, any income paid to the foreign bank on the interest rate swap would constitute U.S. ECI and be subject to U.S. federal income tax. If the foreign bank were resident in a treaty country then it would be taxable on such income only to the extent such income is attributable to the foreign bank's U.S. permanent establishment.

Source of Income. Regulations under Code §863 provide that the source of notional principal contract income generally is determined by the residence of the taxpayer. For this purpose, the term "residence" means a person's tax home (i.e., abode), in the case of an individual, and the place an entity is created or organized, in the case of a corporation or partnership.

The above residence sourcing rule is subject to the following two exceptions, however. First, notional principal contract income is sourced in the United States, and treated as U.S. ECI, if the notional principal contract is attributable to a foreign person's U.S. trade or business. Second, notional principal contract income is sourced based on the residence of a qualified business unit of a taxpayer if 1) the taxpayer's residence is the U.S.; 2) the qualified business unit's residence is outside the U.S.; 3) the qualified business unit is engaged in the conduct of a trade or business where it is resident; and 4) the notional principal contract is properly reflected on the qualified business unit's books. Therefore, payments made to a foreign person resident in a treaty country on a notional principal contract generally are not subject to U.S. federal income tax unless such payments constitute U.S. ECI and are attributable to such foreign person's U.S. permanent establishment.

Conclusion

In the case of financing transactions, the parties' primary concerns in shaping the form of a financial product generally relate to the U.S. federal income tax consequences arising from the use of such financial product. Issuers should proceed with caution when formulating financial products to be issued in foreign markets since the incidence of U.S. income taxation on any payments made thereon may render the financial products uneconomical.

Part IX:
Trends in Structuring Complex Financings

Chapter 20

Asset Securitization: Critical Issues and Trends

David W. Halstead
Managing Director, Securitized Products Group
Continental Bank, Chicago, IL

A Brief Look Back

In less than a decade, securitized financing has evolved from a tool used mainly by major, financially sophisticated corporations, to an indispensable business-financing resource, as much a part of the capital markets landscape as traditional debt or equity financing.

With what, in retrospect, is astonishing speed, securitization has advanced from a market in commercial paper and mortgage-backed securities, to one that covers a wide range of consumer receivables, trade and corporate receivables, commercial bank loans, and other assets. Traditional liquidating securitization programs, which unwind as the assets underlying the security are paid off, in many cases have been replaced by revolving asset-backed commercial paper programs, in which a special-purpose vehicle (SPV) continually funds the purchase of new assets by rolling over outstanding commercial paper.

The litany of factors driving the market's rapid development—the benefits securitization provides to issuers and investors—is by now familiar. In broad terms, properly structured securitized transactions provide asset sellers with a low-cost source of financing which allows them to take assets off their books, diversify their funding sources, and reshape their balance sheets to meet competitive requirements (which, in the case of bank sellers, include market and regulatory demands for strong capital ratios).

Because asset-backed securities are rated on their own merits, independent of the issuing company's credit rating, securitization can provide a crucial source of funding for companies with limited access to other forms of credit.

Likewise, in determining a seller's overall weighted average cost of capital, the all-in cost of securitized financing compares favorably with that of many other kinds of capital raising, even when upfront analysis, structuring, and credit-enhancement costs are factored in. While those costs may seem high to a first-time issuer, they often look extremely attractive on an all-in basis relative to other financing alternatives.

Similarly, investors earn attractive returns from securities backed by asset pools with predictable cash flows and armored in credit enhancements strong enough, typically, to achieve double-A or triple-A long-term ratings or A1/P1/D1 short-term ratings (Figure 20.1).

Given those benefits, it is not surprising that the market for securitized assets has grown dramatically over the last decade. For example, between 1983 and 1992 the outstanding volume of the commercial paper market—an important funding source of securitized assets—quadrupled from about $125 billion to more than $540 billion, while the issuance of other types of asset-backed securities ballooned from less than $1 billion a year in 1983 to more than $50 billion annually at present. And from the time Standard & Poor's rated its first commercial-paper program backed by pooled receivables in 1983, more than 110 additional programs have been rated, representing an issuing capacity totaling at least $85 billion.

The Commercial Paper Market

Where did that growth and the process we now refer to as securitization originate? While the market's roots can be traced to the first commercial paper

219

Figure 20.1   The Changing Mix of Securities

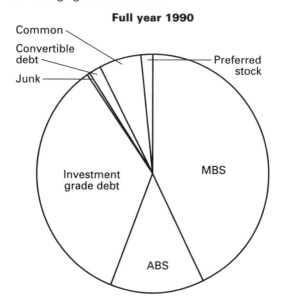

Full year 1990

Total: $312.1 billion

Full year 1991

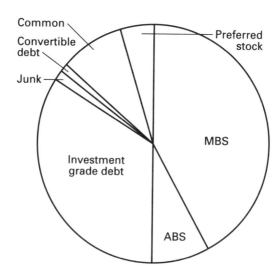

Total: $586.0 billion

Source: *Investment Dealers Digest,* Copyright 1992 by IDD.

issues in the late 19th century, securitization in its current sense really began in the 1950s.

At that time, a significant number of institutional investors with short-term portfolio requirements first began to look beyond the "safe" investments offered by traditional financial intermediaries and purchase paper directly from strong corporate issuers. In the process, they eliminated the need for intermediation by banks, which both boosted borrowing costs for businesses and held down investment returns.

After a period of gradual evolution, the commercial paper market took off in the 1970s, driven not only by a series of shocks to the U.S. system of banking and finance which reduced traditional credit availability, but also by advances in technology that made collecting timely, reliable financial information on business borrowers much easier.

By way of illustration, in the early 1970s commercial paper outstanding nationwide totaled about $34 billion, representing roughly a third of the volume of business loans on the books of commercial banks. By the end of the 1980s, the ratio had been roughly reversed; the traditional players in the financing markets—borrowers and lenders—had been replaced by issuers and investors.

As the commercial paper market expanded, so did interest in other forms of securitized assets. Figure 20.2 is an outline of the structure and cash flows of an asset-backed commercial paper program.

Mortgage-Backed Securities and CMOs

Not surprisingly, residential mortgages were the next asset portfolio to be converted into public securities. The supply of one- to four-family residential mortgages was large and by definition diversified by lender, borrower, and geographic region. Home mortgages were written to highly homogeneous standards, payment patterns on the underlying loans were predictable, and mortgage maturities matched the preferences of a wide range of institutional investors. In short, all the characteristics needed to create a new security were present, and the market in mortgage-backed securities took off. Between the first mortgage-backed issue in 1973 and the beginning of 1980, investors purchased more than $114 billion in mortgage-backed securities, representing 13% of outstanding residential mortgage obligations.

Investor interest in mortgage-backed securities took another quantum leap in 1983, when the Federal Home Loan Mortgage Corporation (the FHLMC, better known as "Freddie Mac") issued $1 billion in Collateralized Mortgage Obligations (CMOs), divided into three maturity classes or tranches, with differing claims on interest and principal and different risk and return characteristics to meet differing investor demands. Since then, the

growth of the market in mortgage-backed securities has been nothing short of spectacular; today, nearly half of all U.S. home mortgages are permanently funded by the issuance of mortgage-backed securities.

Auto Paper

The next logical asset class to be packaged as a security was auto loans. After mortgages, auto paper represented the nation's second-largest pool of financial assets, but appealed to investors with shorter investment horizons. As with mortgages, payment patterns on portfolios of auto loans were diversified by borrower, region, and other criteria. Payment patterns on auto loans likewise were highly predictable, but the maturity of the loans tended to run from 24 to 60 months, instead of the 15- to 30-year maturities in the mortgage-backed market.

The securitization of auto loans—notably by captive finance companies such as GMAC—dramatically altered the auto financing landscape. Once a private market dominated by banks, the auto paper securitization market today is supported largely by investors in the public market. Where banks booked nearly two-thirds of all auto loans in the United States in 1970, today they have about a quarter of the market.

Credit Cards

The mid-1980s witnessed a major shift in the move toward securitization with the creation of large, liquid private markets, driven mainly by the sale of charge-card receivables. In a sense, the securitization of credit-card debt had been around for many years. Continental Bank arranged the private sale of $1 billion in credit-card balances as early as 1961, while a number of retailers regularly sold receivables to banks, before the 1986 change in the federal tax code.

That tax reform is one of two developments that changed the character of this market dramatically. The Tax Reform Act of 1986 brought an end to the installment-accounting treatment of charge-card sales, meaning that such sales no longer resulted in the acceleration of previously deferred income. With the revision in the tax law, tax motivations ceased to be a significant factor in charge-card sales.

Second, and more important, banks had to contend with tougher regulatory treatment of asset sales. A driving factor in asset securitization is the removal of assets from the balance sheet, which, all things being equal, will produce a higher ROA and reduce the amount of capital needed to support assets. In a famous 1986 ruling (the so-called Chatsworth ruling, involving a Citibank transaction)

**Figure 20.2   An Asset–Backed Commercial Paper Program:
Structure and Cash Flows**

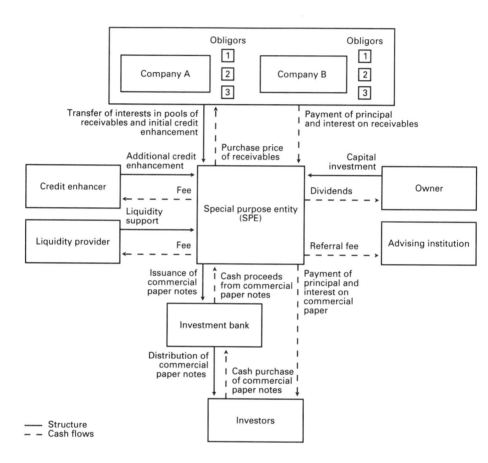

the Comptroller of the Currency decided that a portfolio of assets could not be removed from the balance sheet of the regulated originator if the purchaser had even minimal recourse to this institution.

One predictable response to regulatory barriers is an intensified search for ways around them. A path was found in 1986 when Salomon Brothers underwrote a $50 million securitized issue for Banc One backed by charge-card outstandings. The securities offered a yield high enough not only to meet investors' return expectations, but also to fund a so-called spread account to which investors could look for recourse if portfolio losses built beyond projected levels.

That pioneering transaction led to a surge of bank-card deals and a major shift in the role of banks in the securitization market. Where once banks served primarily as funders of credit-card transactions, by the late 1980s they had come to serve mainly as issuers of transactions funded by other, largely private institutional investors.

Trade and Corporate Receivables

Banks' success in securitizing charge-card and other installment portfolios led to the next step: the search for ways to securitize other types of asset portfolios. Developments in this area come at a much slower pace than in other market sectors. For example, attempts to securitize traditional commercial loans have met with only limited success to date, due to the difficulties of accommodating nonhomogeneous asset portfolios with complex payment patterns, cash flows, and documentation standards; covenant restrictions; and loss experiences. One area has done reasonably well, however: corporate and trade receivables which are funded in a large and growing private market.

In some ways, that success is surprising. These assets are unlike others discussed earlier in that they 1) do not bear interest; and 2) have much shorter maturities, typically 30 to 90 days, in contrast to the average life of a charge-card or auto-loan portfolio, which is generally measured in months. Unlike other securitized assets which have specific maturity characteristics, the timing of payments on trade receivables is nearly always uncertain, although there is an expected payment date. Trade receivables tend to be concentrated among relatively few specific customers, making it difficult to achieve the obligor diversification inherent in other portfolios. Finally, where few credit-card holders or auto buyers know or care if their loan is sold to another institution, sellers of trade and corporate receivables tend to be extremely concerned with protecting customer lists and competitive information.

For these reasons, sales of corporate receivables have until recently been structured as private transactions, originated by commercial banks and effected through one of two general structures: special-purpose vehicles funded by the continuous issuance of commercial paper, or purchases by bank syndicates.

With that review of the development of the securitized markets over the last several years, let us turn to a review of recent developments and trends, and the issues they raise.

Recent Developments

All financial markets (especially those that have come of age quickly) are subject to periods of retrenchment. That was certainly the case in 1991 when several factors combined to produce a marked slowdown in the growth of the market for securitized products from the pace of previous years.

Credit Quality

By far the most significant development during the period is the impact of the lingering recession. The immediate effect of the downturn was a widening of spreads, as issuers rushed to raise funds and investors pulled back, worried about the impact of the recession on the performance of the underlying asset portfolios.

As it turned out, investor concerns over the credit quality of asset-backed securities were largely misplaced. Despite the three-year economic downturn and the painfully slow recovery, no public issues defaulted or suffered downgrades due to losses or delinquencies on the underlying assets. Those concerns were not altogether wrong, however. Losses on many underlying portfolios rose by 30–40%; for example, average losses on some charge-card portfolios rose from 4.5% to nearly 6%, while defaults on auto loans climbed from 0.6% to 1%. As a result, several issues bumped into what are politely termed "payout events." Yields on some portfolios fell below target yields, triggering the prospect of early paybacks of principal.

While such payback provisions were designed to protect investors from unexpected losses, early repayment of principal in a low-rate environment did raise awareness of reinvestment risk. That risk was seen most dramatically in two areas: 1) credit cards, already shaken in 1991 by the threat of a congressionally mandated cap on charge-card rates (a threat that is currently dormant); and 2) the mortgage-backed market, where falling rates triggered a wave of refinancings, thus accelerating prepayments. The result has been a serious reevaluation of pricing and structural issues for mortgage-backeds.

These may sound like fundamental events, but, in fact, the results were less than earthshaking, for a simple reason: many other debt securities were subject to similar pressures. With interest rates falling to their lowest levels in nearly two decades, yields on asset-backed securities have remained highly attractive. The experience in the charge-card sector is particularly telling. While two credit-card trusts did, in fact, begin payouts, investors in four others that were approaching their trigger points elected to stay in the trusts, effectively exchanging a lower payout for an attractive current yield.

Credit Enhancement

While portfolio performance for the most part held up well through the recession, other developments were taking place behind the scenes. Although few issues were downgraded, a large number of banks and financial institutions responsible for credit enhancement were. True to its reputation for innovation, however, the market responded by developing alternatives to the traditional letter-of-credit enhancements, which both reduced administrative and issuance costs and removed the event risk of a downgrade.

One approach involved the use of senior/subordinated structures, which segregate portfolios into two parts. The subordinated piece, which bears the first risk of default, is typically retained by the issuer or sold at a higher yield. The senior piece, on the other hand, is insulated from loss to the extent of the subordinated piece. This widely used structure may remove the need for third-party enhancement from a transaction entirely.

Other forms of credit enhancement also came into vogue, notably the cash-collateral method in which an issuer, directly or through a third party, puts up its own or borrowed cash to support a transaction. Another common form of credit enhancement involves a combination of portfolio retention through a subordinated tranche and cash collateral to cover potential losses. This approach to enhancement was used in several credit-card transactions in 1990 and 1991.

Investor Base

In another major development, the investor base for asset-backed securities has broadened substantially, to the point that demand is running well ahead of supply in some sectors, particularly auto-loan and charge-card securities, and pushing down pricing almost across the board. Securitized transactions are no longer viewed as innovations but as investment staples in the United States. The decline of double-A and triple-A corporates has put similarly-rated asset-backs, in terms of volume, in place as the benchmark for investors.

This pricing improvement likely results in large part from wider investor acceptance of securitized issues. Insurance companies, once the main buyers of public and private securitized issues, have been joined in the market by money managers of all descriptions in the United States and, to some extent worldwide, especially in Europe and Japan.

Of course, the market for securitized assets remains relatively small outside the United States, but it is growing. At this writing, the largest offshore market is in Great Britain, where banks and other lenders have issued some $21 billion in securities backed by mortgages. Likewise, the Basle Accords on bank capital standards and other constraints on credit availability worldwide are driving banks and corporations to consider securitization. For example, Daimler Benz issued Germany's first asset-backed commercial paper in 1991, while a Japanese finance company announced early in 1992 that it would raise cash by securitizing $23 million in yen-denominated equipment leases. In both cases, investors snapped up the offerings, suggesting that the move to securitization will rapidly gain global ground.

Individuals have joined the ranks of investors in securitized issues as well. In an innovative move, Sears sold $1 billion in securities backed by consumer receivables in denominations as low as $1,000 to the retail market last year through its brokerage subsidiary, Dean Witter.

Asset Types

The early 1990s also have seen a broadening in the types of assets securitized. There was, for example, renewed interest in securitization among equipment lessors, including transactions collateralized by office equipment, a wide range of lease receivables, and in a significant development, given the specialized analysis required, sophisticated medical equipment. Innovative issuers here include Comdisco, Concord Leasing, and World Omni Leasing.

Other intriguing transactions in recent history include the securitization of more unconventional cash flows such as in the Stop & Shop, Kroger, and Mesa deals.

Structures

While much of the structuring activity of 1991 involved the application of traditional structures to new situations, three developments stand out.

The first is the introduction of master trust structures in the credit-card arena, which allow issuers to move on market windows without the need for time-consuming trust creation and document preparation.

By creating a trust capable of accommodating a growing number of charge-card accounts, the issuer can streamline the issuance of several series of securities, collateralized by a common pool of accounts. The advantages to investors are just as significant. The master trust structure reduces the risk of a shortfall on a given payment date, both because of the broad diversification of the asset pool and because most available principal payments are allocated to an amortizing series, swiftly repaying principal. Risk of a trigger event is also lessened, since no series is allocated a higher percentage of losses in the pool than any other series.

Moreover, the master trust structure ensures uniform credit quality among offerings from the same issuer. Because pool selection is established at the outset and diversification is substantial, the potential negative effects of poor selections are minimized.

Finally, there is little risk to investors that later series issued by the master trust will impair their claims to principal and cash flow. The reason is that before issuing subsequent series, the master trust usually must obtain confirmation from a rating agency that the new series will not result in a change of rating for the outstanding series.

A second structuring innovation involves the introduction of special-purpose vehicles funded by a combination of commercial paper and medium-term notes. These structures take the traditional benefits of asset-backed commercial paper programs several steps further, by 1) providing committed, medium-term funding with no repricing risk; 2) allowing issuers to better manage their asset and liability structures by providing maturities of up to eight to ten years; and 3) eliminating the need for third-party credit enhancers or liquidity providers.

The third development of note is the continued expansion of the private market. Commercial-paper-funded trade-receivables programs remain an important source of corporate liquidity at very competitive prices. At the same time, growth in securitized private placements, with both banks and institutional investors, is accelerating, particularly for "story" portfolios of assets. This trend resulted partly from demand for more highly structured transactions. Where the market recorded few bank-funded deals in 1989 and 1990, a significant number of transactions were completed in 1991 and 1992.

At present, the asset-backed commercial paper market shows evidence of a natural consolidation. Of course, some reduction in the number of players in the field was inevitable. In general, an asset-backed commercial paper program requires about $1 billion in outstandings to be profitable and at least $750 million to break even. Of the 119 (including single-seller) rated asset-backed commercial paper SPVs in existence at this writing, nearly two-thirds are thought to fall short of that mark. In today's profit-sensitive marketplace, few financial institutions are likely to be willing to withstand losses indefinitely as they attempt to establish market share in a product purely as an accommodation to clients.

Additional pressures have recently arisen from interest shown by the Federal Reserve and other regulators in asset-backed commercial paper programs, specifically the implications for banks regarding risk-based capital. Banks are now being required to provide adequate levels of capital behind facilities that serve to support asset-backed commercial paper programs.

The regulators also have focused more closely on banks' internal policies, procedures, controls, and management information systems. Requiring standards that ensure adequate compliance with these measures, while sound and sensible, also raises costs for less established players in the asset securitization field and, combined with the other factors at work, likely will impair the ability of some players to compete.

The Future

What does the future hold for securitization? The trends in place today point to some general conclusions.

Most important, the move toward securitization will continue to gain ground in the United States and in other parts of the world as well. The evolution outside the United States is liable to be less spectacular than that experienced domestically where securitization has been favored strongly by motivated issuers and an established investor base. But if the offshore markets for securitized assets seem to have a lot of catching up to do, the same could have been said for the eurobond markets of the 1960s. The fact is that the global need for efficient access to capital—the shift in capital markets' roles from borrowers and lenders to issuers and investors—is likely to result in coming years in truly global public and private markets for securitized assets.

At the same time, it does not seem likely that the move toward securitization will, as some have predicted, make commercial banks obsolete anytime soon. Securitization is, of course, likely to continue its march down the balance sheet, touching fewer and fewer "standard" asset portfolios. However, as that march continues, opportunities for banks to intermediate the process as originators, sellers, structurers, and agents are likely to expand, rather than contract.

The march may not be as fast as in the past, but an increasing number of asset pools today meet the requirements for sale into the public markets, the institutional private markets, or both. Banks are in an excellent position to evaluate the credit risks that accompany those assets. Given the trends in place today, as markets evolve, banks will remain a primary force driving the asset-backed marketplace.

Chapter 21

Private Placements: Critical Issues and Trends*

Diane Rausa Maurice
Vice President
Generale Bank, New York, NY

Companies raising long-term capital in the United States can access a wide range of sources including private placements, the public markets, and syndicated bank debt. In this discussion of the private placement debt market, the focus will be on its dynamics, characteristics and factors influencing future development. During the period of the eighties the private markets grew and became an increasingly important source of long-term funding. During this decade, while growth has slowed, the private market sized at $121.8 billion in 1991 according to the *Investment Dealers Digest*, is still a considerable and important source of capital which shows signs of broadening its appeal internationally.

Private Market Defined

Private placements are defined as securities, not registered with the Securities and Exchange Commission, which are distributed to a limited group of institutional investors who hold them to maturity. Investors have traditionally included insurance companies and to a lesser extent funds, as well as banks. Recently, because of regulatory pressures and new legislative directives, the private placement market is undergoing systemic changes with wide-ranging future implications for the investors, deal structures, and borrowers.

Structural Characteristics

Private placements may differ structurally from the registered public deals because, among other reasons, they are highly negotiated with respect to

covenants and pricing. Private transactions are also not subject to the "take or leave it" conditions of public transactions, and are not as widely distributed or "underwritten" by an intermediary such as an investment bank. Privates more closely resemble the syndicated bank market in that they do entail detailed covenant packages and are sold to a smaller number of sophisticated investors. Differences between the private and bank market, however include the following:

♦ Privates traditionally offer fixed-rate coupons based on spread over U.S. Treasuries, although in some cases floating rates may be available;

♦ Private markets typically lend for longer terms (7–30 years) although they can, by definition, include transactions with maturities greater than one year[1];

♦ Unlike bank debt, the penalties for prepaying the private placement earlier than the stated maturity are often onerous, because the lending institutions, insurance companies for example, often match-fund their assets with their liabilities.

Bank debt, involves shorter term maturities (up to 7–10 years) with greater prepayment flexibility and floating rather than fixed rates.[2] It is not uncommon for bank debt to have pricing mechanisms across a range of indices, i.e., spreads based off of LIBOR (London Interbank Borrowing Rate), banks' certificates of deposit or prime rate. Further, unlike private placements, bank debt may have pricing

*Special thanks to Michael Wadler, Vice President, UBS Securities; Alain Verschueren, Senior Vice President, Generale Bank; and also to Yves Chartier, Generale Bank, for his assistance in preparing the graphics.

227

based on performance. For example, a structural feature, which has been built into syndicated bank loans for companies with the prospects for a change in credit quality, includes provisions for the loan rate to adjust with the credit rating. Recent examples of this include widely syndicated loans to Union Carbide and Johnson Controls. Privates are priced according to a credit weighting and maturity matrix which typically remain stable throughout the life of the transaction.

Issuing costs for straight corporate debt, in both the private and the syndicated loan markets are essentially similar. Privates offer distinct cost advantages over a public issue, however. A private issue can save substantial amounts in issuing costs i.e. legal and registration expenses, against a comparable public issue. For first-time issuers, these transaction expenses can range from $400,000 to $750,000 prior to underwriters' discounts and commissions.[3] The SEC registration fee alone amounts to $62,500 on a $200 million issue.[4] This will vary depending on the issuer's credit quality and the complexity of the transaction.

Legislative Directives

One development which purported to make the private placement option increasingly attractive was the advent of a new Securities and Exchange Commission rule in April, 1990- Rule 144A. Restrictions were removed on the trading of unregistered securities with 144A and it was expected to reduce the "liquidity" premium that issuers are expected to pay in the private market. The ruling was to make it easier for both domestic and non-U.S. companies to place debt in the private markets with minimal financial disclosure. Trading in these securities to be allowed among qualified investment institutions.[5] The desired impact was to provide a "nonexclusive safe harbor exemption from the registration requirements of the Securities Act for resales by investors to eligible institutions of privately placed securities."[6]

Currently, many private transactions increasingly have *quasi*public and private characteristics appealing to investors in both markets. This may have been fostered in part by the passage of the 144A. Merrill Lynch, for example, is credited in the Fall of 1991 with a 144A issue for Schering-Plough which raised $575 million. The issue was "underwritten" in the form of initial purchase by the underwriter, similar to a public issue, but had some characteristics of a negotiated private.[7]

One pervasive market view is that 144A is a disappointment, and has not allowed issuers any broader or less expensive access to the private markets. From an investor's standpoint, 144A is not as attractive as a straight private issue because higher rewards may be gained by structuring negotiated transactions.[8] Furthermore, two constructional problems have been cited with 144A. The first suggests that with institutions having to meet certain asset size and other requirements to qualify as purchasers, 144A-qualified investors are limited in number. Secondly, a "user friendly" system to foster secondary trading and thus enhance liquidity has not been established.[9] On the whole, while this new ruling may not have resulted in improving liquidity in the private markets nor eliminated the pricing premium, it is seen as a potential new growth area.

Market Characteristics—Segment Growth Spurts and Contractions

Historical market volume trends and characteristics are highlighted in Figures 21.1 and 21.2. While statistics demonstrate the private market size has continued its decline, there have been significant new areas of opportunity—most notably the new entries associated with 144A deal volume and the growth of securitized transactions. Overall private placements in 1991 reached the $121.1 billion mark, the lowest level in five years and significantly below the 1989 peak of $170.4 billion.[10] It would also appear that the privates have lost some market share to the public bond market. This can be attributed in part to a shift to the public markets in 1991 by corporate issuers seeking the most attractive spreads and the least restrictive covenants.

Ironically, for the first half of 1992, with public volume continuing to surge, spurred in part by lower interest rates, the low supply of private transactions has led many investors to become "less demanding about covenants in the private markets."[11] This trend may continue as volume lags, with growth aspects limited to 144A transactions, securitized asset-backed issues and lease transactions. Many large investors, in anticipation of this trend, have set up special units to focus on the diversification strengths, credit quality, and attractive pricing offered by securitized financing. Except for these specialized market segments, the prospects for a banner year for the 1992 private markets are not promising. Based on six-month results reported on June 26, 1992, private volume has not reached even 10% of 1991 year-end levels, while the public market continues to accelerate.

Figure 21.1   Private Placements—Public Market

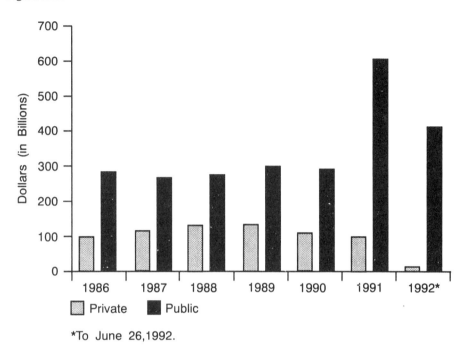

*To June 26,1992.

Source: IDD Information Services

Investor Demand— Dampened by Regulations and Economic Declines

Contributing to volume declines were various regulatory and economic pressures faced by the insurance industry. As the prime institutional investors in privates, insurers found 1991 a year of transition. As described below, regulatory pressures to improve capital positions, forced some insurers in 1991 to follow the path of many banks seeking compliance with the BIS (Bank for International Settlements) capital guidelines—each seeking new mechanisms to raise capital or shed assets.

For example, in the first half of 1991, ten insurers, each with assets of over $4 billion were forced to reduce their exposure to high-yield corporate bonds by an average of 26%.[12] Relatedly, the areas demonstrating the biggest declines were acquisition related placements and issuance of noninvestment grade related debt following general market downturns. The impact on the industry was dramatic as

illustrated in Table 21.1. Transactions rated below investment grade declined substantially between 1990 and 1991 for most of the major insurers.

Insurance companies continued in 1991 as the major purchasers of private placements with four major investors accounting for a substantial share of private market volume (Table 21.2).

In spite of the substantial investment positions, another factor reflecting the private market slowdown may have been related to the recessionary outlook. "Slow credit growth and uneven economic performance led many observers to suggest a prolonged and intensifying "credit crunch" according to the 1991 Annual Report of the Federal Reserve.[13] Perhaps spurred by the outlook for a weak economic recovery and increased regulatory pressures, the insurance industry slowed their involvement in the 1991 private market but were still strongly present as the lead investor class. A pervasive conservative posture however, has created additional opportunities for a more diversified investor base, i.e., public and private pension funds.

Figure 21.2   1991 Private Market—Segments Overview

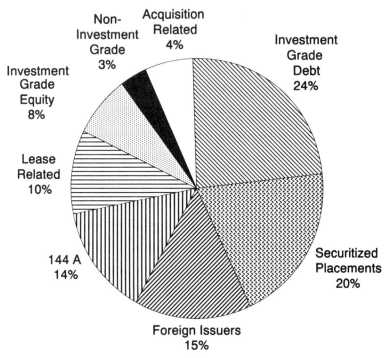

Note: The sum may not equal 100% due to rounding
Source: IDD Information Services

Pension Funds—New Entrants

With an estimated $3 trillion available for investment, pension funds represent an important source of capital for the private markets to tap. Some ana-lysts suggest that "so long as insurance companies, the banks and the finance companies remain focused on credit quality, the pension funds are going to own the market."[14] Seeking higher yields, pension funds are seen as the one investor class best positioned to

Table 21.1   Noninvestment Grade Holdings

Company	Admitted Assets ($million)	Noninvestment 12/91	Grade 12/90
Prudential	114.7	7.8%	9.6%
Metropolitan	96.2	2.2%	2.8%
New York Life	41.8	3.3%	3.4%
Aetna Life	37.7	2.5%	2.7%
Equitable	34.3	6.8%	7.4%
John Hancock	30.9	6.0%	6.1%
Massachusetts Mutual	26.4	5.8%	6.4%
Lincoln National	18.0	3.5%	3.8%
Allstate Life	17.8	6.8%	9.9%

Source: IDD Information Services, Conning & Co.

Table 21.2   Private Placements by Major Institutions (1991) ($Billions)

Insurer	Volume Size
Prudential	$ 7.5
Cigna	$ 3.7
Metropolitan	$ 2.7
New York Life	$ 2.3
Massachusetts Mutual	$ 1.9
Principal Financial	$ 1.7
John Hancock	$ 1.7
Allstate Life	$ 1.6
Equitable	$ 1.0
Travelers	$ 1.0

Source: IDD Information Services

fill the void left by the insurers and take advantage of the "inefficiencies" that may exist in the private markets. For example, lower quality transactions with debt linked equity, may provide these funds opportunities for higher returns than the stock or bond markets.

Listed in Table 21.3 are the top ten pension funds in the United States and the amounts invested in privates over the past two years.

The potential for pension funds to inject capital into the private markets is enormous both for domestic issuers and non-U.S. borrowers as well. The nation's largest public-employee fund, the $67 billion California Public Employees Retirement System (Calpers) recently hired two specialists firms to manage $2 billion in foreign equities including currency exposure.[15] This new source of funds may be attrac-

tive to borrowers but may also not be without some hidden cost. The trend by some of these pension fund investors, particularly those with high investment stakes in certain companies, has been to try to take an active policy role in influencing corporate governance. Calpers, for example, had a five-year campaign of using shareholder proxy resolutions to try to gain a voice in corporate affairs. This strategy has reportedly been softened somewhat in recent months to a more focused approach.[16]

Co-Investment Strategies

Because pension funds, particularly those outside of the top twenty, may be new to the private placement arena, their investment managers serve an important role in providing broader exposure. Insurers, often acting as investment advisors, are seeing coinvest-

Table 21.3   Top Pension Fund Investments in Private Placements ($ Billions)

Pension Fund	September 1991	September 1990
Defined Contribution Plans		
TIAA-CREF (Teachers)	$12.13	$11.20
Defined Benefit Plans		
Wisconsin State	$ 2.59	$ 2.87
AT&T	$ 1.81	$ 1.51
General Electric	$ 1.58	$ 1.40
Alabama Retirement	$ 1.01	$ 1.06
New York State Teachers	$ .52	$ .30
State of Michigan	$ .46	$ .56
Colorado Employees	$ .30	$ .31
Total Top 200 Pension Funds		
Defined Contribution and Benefit	$22.83	$21.76

Source: Reprinted with permission Pension & Investments Jan. 20, 1991/1992
Copyright Crain Communications Inc.

Figure 21.3   1990 Private Market—Segments Overview

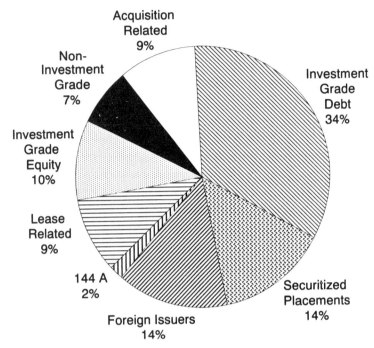

Note: the sum may not equal 100% due to rounding
Source: IDD Information Services

ment opportunities in private placements as they team up with pension funds and other institutional investors. The State of Colorado pension fund hired John Hancock Financial Services to manage a separate account to be invested in national and international direct private investments.[17]

Prudential, for example, as one of the lead investors in privates not only purchases for its own account but has also created a sales and distribution team to sell private placements to other insurers as well as a broader spectrum of institutional investors. They have taken a lead role in specifically designating resources to actively place new and secondary private placement issues. On the whole, the trend toward coinvesting opportunities may increase as institutional investors, insurers included, push toward greater portfolio diversification techniques as

Table 21.4   NAIC: New Credit Rating and Reserve Requirements

Ratings		Reserves		Annual Accumulation	
S&P	NAIC	New	Old	New	Old
AAA to A−	1	1%	2%	.1%	.1%
BBB+ to BBB−	2	2%	2%	.2%	.1%
BB+ to BB−	3	5%	2%	.5%	.5%
B+ to B−	4	10%	2-10%	2.0%	.5%
CCC+ to D	5	20%	20%	5.0%	2.0%
In/Near Default	6	20%	20%	5.0%	2.0%

Note: Certain states have proposed maximum limits per rating category. LBOs are included in the CCC+ rating category.[18]

one hedge against what may be an erratic economic recovery.

Systemic Changes

In 1991, while opportunities may have been created to allow pension funds a larger investor role in the private market, insurance company demand fell for privates as a direct result of regulatory changes implemented by the National Association of Insurance Commissioners (NAIC) These revised guidelines were being considered in the high growth period in the last decade but only implemented recently.

Briefly, the NAIC Securities Valuation Office (SVO) was created in the 1930s for the purpose of providing insurers with a source for uniform prices and quality ratings for their securities holding. Insurers are required by the NAIC to use SVO prices and ratings in preparing the Annual Statements to be filed with state regulatory authorities and the NAIC. The SVO is charged with the herculean task of analyzing all investments made by insurance companies using a credit rating system developed for this purpose.

In the mid-1980s with the volume of private placements soaring, it became evident that the ratings system and methodology then being used to evaluate investments made by insurance companies was not sufficiently comprehensive. The ratings system is also used to determine reserve requirements which were to be a function of the credit quality of the insurer's investment portfolio. The old system did not address the inherent risk imbedded in the real estate and "high-yield" portfolios of some insurers. In response to these and other issues, the SVO developed and gradually implemented a new ratings system. These new guidelines increased the reserve requirements insurers, as the major investors in privates, have to allocate to the various risk categories. Simply put, this served to increase the cost to insurers of capital to be allocated against lower quality transactions (below investment grade or NAIC 3-6).

As illustrated in Table 21.4, these requirements are more exact than the previous guidelines. Under the former NAIC system, private placement and other securities were classified into only two basic categories, "yes" or "no." The new rating system was to provide a clear presentation of the quality distribution of an insurer's portfolio.

Another result of the new guidelines was also to significantly enhance the NAIC's flexibility while improving and modernizing the methodology previously used to develop quality ratings. In addition, not only were reserves increased, but the time permitted to accumulate the reserves was shortened.

By some accounts, there were severe short-term implications to the NAIC rule changes. Insurance industry participation in the below investment grade private market was virtually eliminated in 1991. Little or no appetite exists for "NAIC 3"-rated transactions. Those insurance companies with some interest in NAIC 3-rated private placements are now demanding premium spreads. In general, bidding for an NAIC 3-rated transaction (BB-rated quality) began at 300–350 basis points over comparable treasuries in 1991 versus spreads of 110–150 basis points for higher quality transactions. In what is seen as a concerted effort to increase volume during the second half of 1992, at least two major insurers have eased their return requirements for transactions demonstrating marginal credit quality.

In summary, the premium pricing for noninvestment grade transactions may be expected to continue for the near term. This will create additional opportunities for more nontraditional investors like pension funds and mutual funds to step into the below investment grade arena as the more risk-adverse insurers vacate this market. Given the substantial cashflows of the insurance companies, coupled with an inability to achieve premium yield hurdles, a bigger move may be made back to noninvestment grade transactions. This would mean that the insurers would sacrifice credit quality and higher reserve requirements for yield.

Outlook for the 1990s

The advent of Rule 144A coupled with increased regulatory purview of insurance companies are among the recent structural changes impacting the private markets. This has partially given rise to three trends which will have a longer term structural impact on the industry. The first, as suggested by the statistical overview, is the continued growth of securitization. Secondly, in an effort to accommodate the increase in reserve requirements and the insurer's resultant need for portfolio management, secondary trading in private placements will broaden. And third, we will continue to witness the internationalization of the private markets and the broadening of the investor base.

Demand for Securitized Product

Securitized transactions form an investment class which will continue to expand, following the trend which began in the mid-1980s. Private placements secured by pools or portfolios of assets, are highly rated, well diversified, and offer attractive yields. Traditionally, securitized transactions in the public and private markets trade at premiums to comparably rated industrial credits. They provide an opportunity to buy, for example, a "AAA" rated piece of paper at comparable "A" spreads. For sophisticated investors like insurers and pension funds, securitization offers an investment mechanism to achieve attractive spreads as well as added portfolio diversification.

Highly rated securitized investments maximize the use of limited capital without sacrificing yield. Going forward, as long as the economic incentives are available for financial and other credit institutions to generate securitized product, demand for this investment class will continue its exponential growth. Some insurers have taken steps to purchase asset-backed transactions generated outside the United States. Further, even pension funds are seeking diversity not always offered in the private markets. For example, the director of private placements at the Wisconsin State Investment Board has stated that there are few suitable plain vanilla private placement vehicles that invest in investment grade companies and have a longer term focus. One suggestion to rectify this situation is to fashion securitized private placements which would include a portfolio of diversified companies and receive an investment grade rating.[19]

It is not coincidental that this financial tool which provides such attractive investment opportunities, has also been used on at least two occasions by insurers to liquify their own portfolios. Equitable and Connecticut Mutual approached securitization as a means to divest substantial assets. While some industry observers questioned whether this strategy was accomplished for "economic or cosmetic" reasons,[20] the collateralized bond obligations provided these insurers with a viable balance sheet reduction tool. This move also signaled a stronger move from the traditional buy and hold philosophy which characterized insurers as private placement investors.

Secondary Trading

With balance sheet and regulatory pressures, many insurers curtailed new investments and several institutions sold portfolios to reduce asset size and bolster capital positions. Secondary market trading of privates accelerated, reportedly resulting in trades in excess of $1 billion as insurers refocused their portfolio mix.[21] Secondary trading is expected to become an important part of the market as insurers seek to diversify risk and balance investment needs in a continuing flight to quality.

Internationalization

While 144A has met with slow success, for foreign issuers, the United States private markets are seen as one of the few sources of long term committed finance. United States institutional investors are prepared to buy corporate bonds of up to 30-years, while the Eurobond and syndicated loan markets have a shorter time horizon of up to 7–10 years.[22] It is quite clear, given the low interest rates in the United States market presently, and the pent-up demand for privates which has been building over the past few years, that European-based issuers will find the private markets increasingly attractive.

Among the most notable issuers achieving favorable rates in the private market are Solvay USA (Belgian parent); Saab Scania (Sweden); and Rank PLC (United Kingdom). Future expansion will be seen in cross-border privates. For example, British Bio-Technology Group PLC completed an international private placement with buyers in the United States, Japan and the United Kingdom.[23] The investor base for this product will continue to develop with pension funds and other institutions; they will take a larger market share as they broaden their interest in the investment opportunities in this market. To potentially assist in this development, the SEC is planning to expand the provisions for Rule 144A to allow qualified buyers to include bank collective trust funds and master trusts for pension funds to buy these unregistered securities.[24]

Intermediaries, such as foreign commercial banks with lending relationships with non-U.S. companies and a presence in the United States and Europe for example, are seen as playing a larger role in this development of internationalization. In many cases, both traditional private placements and the 144A qualified transactions, are seen as a bridge to the U.S. capital markets, with relatively low costs of entry.

Endnotes

1. Bavaria, S., "Slipping Away," *Investment Dealers Digest*, (March 9, 1992): 25.

2. Miller, S., "Private Placement Arena," *Loan Pricing Report*, Vol. VI No.3, (March 1991): 4.

3. Major United States law firm price quotations, 1992.

4. Cooper, S., "Placements Under Rule 144A, A Rose by Another Name," *New York Law Journal*, (January 27, 1992).

5. London, S. "Cash from Across the Sea," *Financial Times*, April 10, 1992.

6. Securities and Exchange Commission Rule, Sec 17, CFR, Parts 200 and 230, Release #336862, re: Rule 144A Effective April 30, 1990.

7. "Public or Private—New Hybrid Issues Blur the Distinction," *Wall Street Journal*, March 10, 1992.

8. Star, Marlene G., "A hushed private market," *Pension and Investments*, (July 6, 1992): 30.

9. Cooper, S. *op.cit.*

10. Bavaria, S., *op.cit.* p. 19.

11. Star, Marlene G., *op.cit.*

12. "Insurers Unload Junk Bonds," *New York Times*, September 19, 1991.

13. Frydll, Edward J., "Overhangs and Hangovers: Coping with the Imbalances of the 1980's," *Federal Reserve Annual Report* 1991.

14. "Pension Funds Fill Void in Private-Placement Market," *Wall Street Journal*, January 1992.

15. *Pension and Investment Age*, March 30, 1992.

16. White, J., "Giant California Pension Fund Softens Approach to Influencing Corporations," *Wall Street Journal*, October 7, 1991.

17. Parker, M., Star, M. "Private Deals Lure More Pension Funds," *Pension and Investments*, February 4, 1991): 1.

18. "Insurance Companies Face New Reserve Requirements," *Investment Dealers Digest*, (April 16, 1990): 5.

19. Parker, M., Star, M., *op. cit.* p.31.

20. "Economics, Not Cosmetics Drove Connecticut Mutual's CBO," Private Placement Letter Vol. 10. No. 2.

21. "MONY Sells up to $1 Billion of Private Placement Portfolio," *Corporate Financing Week*, (August 26, 1991): 9–10.

22. London, S., *op. cit.*

23. Private Placement Market Talk Volume 3, Number 68, July 17, 1991.

24. Salwen, Kevin G., "SEC Proposes Rules Making it Easier for Large Companies to Raise Money," *Wall Street Journal*, July 17, 1992.

Chapter 22

The ESOP Advantage—Tax, Legal and Financial Issues*

Jared Kaplan and *Marsha Matthews*
Keck, Mahin & Cate, New York, NY
John Spears and *Lindy Spears*
Kidder, Peabody & Co. Incorporated, Houston, TX

The concept of employee ownership is unique to capitalism. No other form of economic system can permit such ownership if that system is functioning in its purest form. While forms of employee ownership existed in other countries, the concept developed and flourished in the United States, making employee ownership somewhat unique to the American experience.

Employee ownership is not so much revolutionary as evolutionary. In its infant stages, "share the wealth" was not a creation of tax incentives or other legislation, but rather a means of providing incentive and motivation to employees. Although "sweat equity" is not a phrase indigenous to the twentieth century, it was not until the early 1900s that formalized programs designed to encourage employee ownership began. For example, in 1916, Sears, Roebuck and Co. instituted a profit sharing plan invested primarily in employer securities.

The modern concept of employee ownership is most frequently attributed to Louis Kelso, an economist and lawyer who recognized the merits of employee ownership as a vehicle of corporate finance as well. In the mid-1900s, he began to develop employee stock ownership plans (ESOPs) in an environment of uncharted waters. He implemented the plans on virtually a case-by-case basis, primarily without specific guidelines from the Internal Revenue Service (IRS) or Congress.

The employee ownership trend has taken hold in corporate America due largely to Congressional support in the form of tax incentives. Certain kinds of stock bonus trusts and profit sharing trusts were first granted tax exemptions in the Revenue Act of 1921. In 1953, the IRS issued Revenue Ruling 46, which sanctioned the use of qualified plans for debt financing of the purchase of employer securities. In recent years, Congress has fostered the use of ESOP financing in at least 21 different pieces of legislation. Because of such pro-ESOP legislation, the ESOP is a powerful means by which working class Americans can share in the wealth of capitalism and own a piece of America.

Background and General Description

An ESOP is an employee benefit plan which is qualified for tax-favored treatment under the Internal Revenue Code of 1986, as amended (the Code). It falls in the broad category of employee benefit plans known as defined contribution plans. An ESOP is a special kind of defined contribution plan that invests primarily in stock of the employer corporation.

As with all defined contribution plans, there is no fixed or defined schedule of benefits guaranteed to employees. A separate account for each employee is set up in the plan, and each participant's account is credited with the appropriate number of shares of employer stock over the period of his or her employment. Upon the occurrence of death, disability or other termination of service, the participant's account is distributed to him or her in shares of stock or in cash, the amount determined by valuing the

*John Spears and Lindy Spears prepared the following portions of this chapter: 1) introduction; 2) uses of ESOPs; and 3) case studies. Neither John Spears and Lindy Spears nor Kidder, Peabody & Co. Incorporated are engaged in the business of rendering tax or legal advice, and therefore make no representations with respect to the views of Keck, Mahin & Cate regarding the legal and tax aspects of ESOPs.

shares of stock in his or her account. A participant's benefit is thus not defined, but is dependent upon the value of the stock.

As a qualified plan, the ESOP must comply with various coverage, vesting, distribution and other rules established by the Code. These must be set out in a written document and all assets of the ESOP must be held in a trust established under a written trust agreement. The trust is administered by a trustee and/or administrative committee responsible for protecting the interests of employees and their beneficiaries. The ESOP and its fiduciaries must comply with various reporting and disclosure requirements and fiduciary responsibility rules of the Employee Retirement Income Security Act of 1974 (ERISA).

Like other employee benefit plans, employer contributions to the ESOP are tax-deductible with certain limits, and the trust is generally exempt from taxation on the income and gains generated by the assets. Participants in the ESOP are not taxed on contributions to their ESOP accounts (or income earned in those accounts), until the benefits are actually received. Even then, rollovers (into an IRA) or special averaging methods can reduce or defer the tax consequences of distributions.

An ESOP must be established by a regular C corporation. An S corporation can establish an ESOP, but will then lose its S status. Except in limited circumstances, a trust may not hold shares of an S corporation. Since a trust established under an ESOP must hold the shares of the employer corporation, an S corporation would lose its S status upon funding an ESOP.

Uses of ESOP

Employee Benefit

An ESOP is, of course, an employee benefit plan. Unlike other benefit plans, however, which usually diversify their assets, an ESOP *must* invest primarily in the stock of the employer, thereby giving employees an ownership stake in the company where they work. As part-owners in their company, they may become more motivated workers because they benefit directly from increased profits of the company.

A company's annual contribution to a leveraged ESOP can be up to the lesser of 25 percent of each employee's annual compensation or $30,000, and normally this is *in addition* to regular wages and other benefits which are otherwise received. Thus, the benefit is a substantial one.

According to the ESOP Association, an internationally recognized nonprofit advocate, "While there are believed to be a variety of benefits to working in

a well-run employee-owned company, such as pride in a sense of ownership, bonuses, etc., one additional benefit marker is the rate of return . . . The returns on plan investments are closely tied to the performance of the sponsor's stock . . . The mean rate of return on investment for public company ESOPs in 1988 was 15.2%. The top 25% of ESOP public companies averaged a return of 18.2% in 1988. The mean return on investment for private company ESOPs that year was 10.3%."

The ESOP Association also reports the following results from a January, 1991, survey: "A poll of 500 ESOP companies has revealed that ESOP companies appear to have weathered the recession better than their nonESOP counterparts. Moreover, 56% believe that their ESOP has improved their employees' productivity. Furthermore, 80% of those surveyed say that establishing an ESOP was a good idea that has helped their company."

While past performance is not necessarily an indication of future results, the reports from the ESOP Association are encouraging for ESOPs.

Other Uses

ESOPs serve a variety of corporate objectives above and beyond the primary one of providing an employee benefit. It is this attribute that makes an ESOP so attractive and flexible.

The fiduciary rules applicable to tax-qualified plans generally prohibit sponsoring employers from lending money to a qualified plan, guaranteeing loans, or providing collateral for such a loan. A special exemption is provided, however, for loans to ESOPs where the loan proceeds are used to acquire stock of the sponsoring employer. The ESOP is the only type of qualified plan which is permitted to borrow funds on employer credit to acquire employer stock.

A simple leveraged ESOP transaction is illustrated as follows:

1. The ESOP borrows funds from a commercial lender and uses the loan proceeds to purchase shares of the sponsoring corporation, either from the corporation or from existing shareholders. The loan is secured by a pledge of the stock the ESOP purchases. The company, shareholders, or both, may guarantee the loan. If no guarantee is provided, the lender generally will require an agreement that the company will make contributions to the ESOP in amounts sufficient to repay the loan.

2. Alternatively, the sponsoring company, rather than the ESOP, borrows the money and makes a back-to-back loan to the ESOP. The company

then makes annual cash contributions to the ESOP in amounts sufficient to amortize the loan and takes deductions for the amounts contributed.

With a leveraged ESOP, contributions used to pay interest are fully deductible. Contributions used to pay principal are deductible up to 25% of covered payroll. Under Section 415 of the Code, the "annual additions" which may be allocated to the account of an individual ESOP participant each year normally may not exceed the lesser of 1) 25% of his annual compensation; or 2) $30,000. The Section 415 limitations do not apply to contributions used to repay interest on an ESOP loan or to forfeitures if no more than one-third of the employer contributions applied to payment of the principal amount of an ESOP loan is allocated to highly compensated employees. See Section 415(c)(6) of the Code.

Under the Tax Reform Act of 1986, dividends on shares held by an ESOP which are used to repay debt attributable to those shares may also be deducted. See the Dividends Section later in this chapter). The only limitation on amount is that the dividends must be reasonable.

This ability of the ESOP to serve as a technique of corporate finance enables it to be used for a variety of purposes, including:

♦ Capital formation;

♦ Low-cost borrowing;

♦ Refinancing;

♦ Financing an acquisition; and

♦ Creating a market for existing shareholders' stock.

Capital Formation. When the ESOP purchases the stock from the employer company with the borrowed funds, the company is able to finance new capital formation and corporate growth with pre-tax dollars being used to repay the debt. With a conventional loan, principal payments are paid with after-tax dollars. With an ESOP loan, the company can deduct principal of up to 25% of covered payroll, thus enabling the company to service the debt with pre-tax dollars. The result is greater cash flow to the company.

Lower Borrowing Costs—Section 133 Loan. If the ESOP is acquiring 50% or more of the stock of the company, then the ESOP (or the company, if a mirror loan is done) may be able to obtain a below-market interest rate.

Requirements for Section 133 Loan. To encourage lenders to make loans at below-market rates to

finance the acquisition of employer stock by ESOPs, Section 133 of the Code allows banks and other commercial lenders to exclude from income 50% of the interest received with respect to certain ESOP loans. Because of this ability to exclude half of interest received from income, the bank will pass along the savings by lending the money at a below-market rate.

In order to qualify for the 50% lender exclusion, the ESOP loan must satisfy the following conditions:

1. Commercial Lender. The loan must be made by an independent bank, insurance company, mutual fund or other qualified commercial corporate lender.

2. Securities Acquisition Loan. The ESOP loan must meet the requirements of a "securities acquisition" loan, which is defined as either

   2a. A loan to an ESOP or to a company in which the proceeds are used to acquire employer securities for the ESOP; or

   2b. Certain loans to companies with nonleveraged ESOPs—a so-called "immediate allocation" loan to an employer in which: the employer contributes stock to an ESOP equal in value to the amount of the loan within 30 days of the loan and the stock is allocated to participants within one year; and the commitment period does not exceed seven years.

3. 50% Ownership. The ESOP must, following the use of the loan proceeds to purchase shares, own 50% or more of the total value of all outstanding stock of the corporation or 50% of each class of outstanding stock. It is important to note that the 50% ownership requirement does not require the ESOP to hold more than 50% of the voting power of the company, so long as it has more than 50% of the value.

4. Pass-Through Voting. The ESOP must pass through to participants full voting rights on shares acquired with the proceeds of the loan allocated to participants' accounts, and any preferred stock must have voting rights equivalent to the common stock into which it is convertible. There is no requirement for pass-through of voting rights on unallocated stock.

5. Term of Loan. The term of the loan must not exceed 15 years.

Excise Tax Upon Sale Within Three Years. With certain exceptions, a 10% excise tax may be imposed on the employer under Section 4978B of the Code if the ESOP sells or exchanges shares within three years following the loan; or if the ESOP sells or exchanges unallocated shares prior to the time the loan is fully repaid to the extent that sales proceeds are not allocated to participants' accounts. There are exceptions for certain ESOP benefit distributions, certain tax-free reorganizations under Section 368(a)(1) and for dispositions subject to the similar excise tax under Section 4978 of the Code (applicable to stock required in a tax-deferred sale under Section 1042).

Consequence of Falling Below 50%. The interest exclusion is unavailable during any period in which the ESOP's ownership proportion fails to meet the more-than-50% rule, regardless of the reason. For example, if an ESOP acquires 51% of the company's stock, distributes shares, which are then either held by the participants or redeemed by the company, thus causing the ESOP's ownership percentage to fail to meet the more-than-50% rule, the exclusion will be unavailable until the ESOP in some manner exceeds the 50% level again. However, the IRS is authorized to issue regulations that would allow for after-the-fact compliance if the ESOP acquires sufficient stock to meet the more-than-50% rule within 90 days of the failure (or a longer period not exceeding 180 days).

Refinancing. An ESOP may be used to refinance existing corporate debt and to repay it with pre-tax dollars, thereby lowering the borrowing costs. Besides cash contributions, the company could issue new shares of stock to the ESOP equal in value to the amount of debt assumed by the ESOP, thus helping cash flow. This will effectively make the repayment of debt tax deductible within the limits described above.

Financing of an Acquisition. An acquiring corporation's ESOP may borrow funds from a lender in amounts sufficient to enable the acquiring corporation to make an acquisition. For example, the ESOP uses the loan proceeds to purchase stock directly from the acquiring corporation. The acquiring corporation then uses the proceeds of the sale of its stock to the ESOP to acquire target and makes tax-deductible contributions to the ESOP which, in turn, uses the contributions to repay the loan. The acquiring corporation is thus able to amortize acquisition debt with tax-deductible contributions to the ESOP.

Creation of Market for Existing Shareholders' Shares in Tax-Free Transaction—Section 1042. Under Section 1042 of the Code, a shareholder of a "closely-held" corporation may sell employer stock to an ESOP and defer the taxation of gain to the extent that the shareholder reinvests in securities or other corporations.

To qualify for this extremely favorable treatment the following requirements must be met:

30% Ownership. Immediately after the sale, the ESOP must own at least 30% of the fully diluted common equity of the company and at least 30% of each class of stock of the company on a fully diluted basis (other than certain nonvoting, nonconvertible preferred stock).

Long-Term Capital Gain. The sale must be one that would otherwise result in long-term capital gain to the seller. The seller's holding period must be at least three years (for sales after July 10, 1989).

Shares Not Received Through Options. The shares sold to the ESOP must not have been received by the selling shareholder from a qualified employee plan (such as an ESOP) or through certain employee stock options or stock purchase arrangements subject to Section 83 of the Code.

Reinvestment in Qualified Replacement Securities. The nonrecognition of gain applies only to the extent that the sale proceeds are reinvested in replacement securities within a 15-month period that begins three months before and ends 12 months after the sale of employer stock to the ESOP. The replacement securities must be securities of U.S. operating companies whose passive investment income does not exceed 25% of gross receipts and more than 50% of whose assets are used in active conduct of a trade or business. The seller thus has a broad choice of investments. Special forms of securities have been designed for Section 1042 reinvestments.

Tax on the sale is then deferred until the replacement securities are sold. If the replacement securities are held until the seller's death, capital gains tax is never paid. The replacement securities become a part of the seller's estate and will enjoy the advantage of a step-up in basis at the seller's death.

Filing of Statement of Purchase. A notarized "statement of purchase" must be obtained within 30 days after any replacement security is purchased and filed with the IRS with the federal income tax return. The corporation which established the ESOP must consent to the seller's election of tax-deferred treatment under Section 1042. The consent statement must be filed with the statement of election which is required to be filed with the seller's federal tax return.

Excise Tax if ESOP Sells Within Three Years. An excise tax is imposed on the employer corporation for certain dispositions of the stock acquired by the ESOP in a Section 1042 transaction within three years after the sale.

Prohibited Allocation Rule. Under the prohibited allocation rule, no portion of the shares of employer securities purchased by the ESOP to which a Section 1042 election has been made may be allocated to any of the following:

♦ the seller making the Section 1042 election;

♦ members of his or her family (brothers, sisters, spouse, ancestors and lineal descendants and anyone related to the seller within the meaning of Section 267(b) of the Code); or

♦ any shareholder who owns more than 25% of either 1) any class of outstanding stock of either the corporation that issued the qualified securities or any controlled group member; or 2) the total value of any class of stock of such corporation. See Section 409(a) of the Code.

There is a *de minimis* exception to the prohibited allocation rule. Individuals who would be ineligible to receive an allocation of stock just because they are lineal descendants of a selling shareholder may receive an allocation of employer securities to which Section 1042 applies, as long as the total amount of the shares allocated to the lineal descendants of the seller is not more than 5% of all securities to which Section 1042 applies.

A prohibited allocation may not be replaced by benefits under any qualified employee plan. If a prohibited allocation is made, a 50% excise tax is imposed on the employer, and the participant who receives a prohibited allocation incurs a current income tax.

Financial Planning Considerations in Choosing Qualified Replacement Securities. The reinvestment of the selling shareholder's proceeds into qualified replacement securities must not only meet the requirements of the Code, but should also meet the personal financial objectives of the selling shareholder. Once the selling shareholder has sold his shares in his company, he must now reinvest in a business over which he generally has no control.

The portfolio of qualified replacement securities in which the selling shareholder invests must be one with which he is comfortable and which can meet his long-term financial objectives. The selling shareholder must consider, among other things, his risk tolerance, age, and income needs.

The selling shareholder's risk tolerance is especially important to consider. Most sellers assume that they will hold the qualified replacement securities they purchase until their death, thereby forever avoiding income tax liability on the sale of their stock. However, many risky investments which might be tolerated for a short-term investment are inappropriate for such long-term holding.

Common stocks, for example, historically have generated the highest returns of any asset class. However, the selling shareholder should also remember that they are the most volatile. Generally, a sale of the securities for any reason triggers the recognition of capital gain. Thus, if the shares are sold or exchanged in a merger (except in certain tax-free reorganizations), capital gains tax liability would be incurred regardless of the fact that the occurrence of the merger was beyond the selling shareholder's control.

One type of qualified replacement securities which has become popular for Section 1042 sellers are floating rate bonds. Because the interest rate varies with market interest rates, the risk of being locked into an unfavorable interest rate is minimized. Another advantage of bonds is that they may be margined easily, thereby permitting the selling shareholder to obtain cash for any purpose he desires, using the bonds as collateral, without triggering any tax liability.

Any selling shareholder should select his portfolio only after careful consideration of his objectives and consultation with experienced financial advisors.

ESOP Loan Requirements

Both the Internal Revenue Service and the Department of Labor have issued regulations which provide for a prohibited transaction exemption for an ESOP loan (§408(b)(3) of ERISA and Section 4975(d)(3) of the Code). The exemption is available for a loan to an ESOP by the sponsoring employer or by any other "party in interest" (including a fiduciary), as well as a loan to an ESOP from an unrelated lender supported by a guarantee (or pledge of assets) by the sponsoring employer or other party in interest.

As noted above, many ESOP loans are structured as back-to-back loans. That is, the bank lends to the employer corporation and the employer lends the borrowed funds to the ESOP. The regulations apply only to the employer's loan to the ESOP.

The proceeds of the loan must be used *only* to acquire employer securities, as defined in Section 409(l) of the Code, or to refinance a prior ESOP loan [See Type of Stock Held by ESOP Section below for definition of "employer securities"]. The ESOP loan must be "primarily for the benefit of ESOP participants." Regulations set forth "arm's-length standard" test, but independent fiduciary approval is not required.

The only ESOP assets which may be pledged as collateral for the loan are the shares acquired with the loan proceeds. There is no restriction on assets of the employer which may be pledged as collateral. The pledged securities are held in a suspense account pending loan repayments. As loan payments are made, shares of the pledged stock are released from the suspense account and allocated to participants.

There are two formulas used to govern the release of stock from a suspense account. Under the first formula, shares must be released based on the total number of shares in the suspense account immediately prior to the release, multiplied by a fraction, the numerator of which is the amount of principal and interest paid on the loan during the year, and the denominator of which is the total principal and interest expected to be paid in future years plus the numerator. If the interest rate is variable, the interest is computed, for purposes of the fraction, by using the interest rate applicable at the end of the plan year in which the fraction is applied.

The second method involves releasing securities based on the payment of principal alone. This method allows for smaller releases of shares during the early years of the loan repayment schedule. If this formula is used, the term loan must provide for annual payments of principal and interest that are not cumulatively less rapid than level annual payments of principal and interest over 10 years. Interest is disregarded only to the extent it would be disregarded under standard loan amortization tables.

The shares released from the suspense account are then allocated to individual accounts of participants by the end of the year, and these allocations must be made in a nondiscriminatory manner. Allocations are usually based on each participant's annual compensation, subject to limitations imposed by the Code.

The ESOP loan generally may be repaid only from future cash contributions made by the employer to the ESOP to repay the loan and cash dividends on stock purchased with the proceeds of that loan. The loan must be nonrecourse against other ESOP assets except for stock purchased with the loan proceeds.

The interest rate on the loan must be reasonable (and may be variable). The loan must be for a specific term and not payable on demand. If the lender is a party in interest, no acceleration against the pledged shares or other ESOP assets is permitted on default.

Dividends

Although corporations usually are not permitted to deduct dividends paid to shareholders, an exception is provided for dividends paid on shares held by an ESOP if:

1. The dividends are used to repay a loan that was incurred to purchase the company stock with respect to which the dividends are paid;

2. The dividends are paid in cash to plan participants; or

3. The dividends are paid to the ESOP and passed through to the participants within 90 days after the end of the plan year.

The dividends paid to an ESOP must be "reasonable" and the IRS has the authority to disallow deductions for dividends deemed to constitute tax evasion.

The dividends paid on both allocated and unallocated ESOP shares may be used to make deductible ESOP loan payments on shares leveraged with that loan. If dividends are paid on unallocated shares and used for debt repayment, a proportionate amount of stock must be released from the suspense account. All shares released from the suspense account as a result of these dividend payments must then be allocated to individual participant accounts by the year's end. Dividends on allocated shares can be used only for loan repayment if stock of an equivalent value to the amount of the dividends is allocated to the account of such participants.

The Omnibus Budget Reconciliation Act of 1989 restricted the deductibility of dividends paid on ESOP stock by providing that dividends used to repay an ESOP loan will be deductible only where those dividends were earned on shares that were purchased with the proceeds of the loan.

It is important to emphasize that ESOP dividends used for debt repayment may be paid *in addition to* the 25% payroll (subject to $30,000 annual compensation) limit for principal payments. Thus, the dividends-paid deduction can provide a useful mechanism for increasing the amount of stock that may be sold to an ESOP. Where a business has a relatively small payroll, the dividends-paid deduction can be used to deal with the limited payroll problem. The deduction is available without regard to the general limitations on deductions for contributions to ESOPs and without regard to the limitations on annual allocations to individual participants' accounts. The dividends used to repay an ESOP loan are not considered annual deductions for Section 415 purposes.

Type of Stock Held by ESOP— Definition of Employer Securities

Section 409(l) of the Code limits the type of employer stock which may be used in connection with most ESOP transactions. In general, the ESOP must hold common stock or convertible preferred stock. Preferred stock purchased by an ESOP should ideally possess the following characteristics:

♦ a fixed, cumulative dividend rate higher than that paid on common stock;

♦ the right to be converted, at any time, into any class of publicly-traded common stock in a publicly-traded corporation or into the common stock with the highest combination of voting and dividend rights in a closely held company; and

♦ a reasonable conversion price relative to the fair market value of common stock when the ESOP acquires the preferred stock.

Convertible preferred stock acquired with the proceeds of an ESOP loan (after July 10, 1989) must have voting rights in order for the loan to qualify for tax treatment under Section 133 of the Code (See "Lower Borrowing Costs" discussed earlier in this chapter).

The dividends-paid deduction makes the use of convertible preferred stock particularly attractive. The corporation can create a special class of preferred stock to be held by the ESOP. Then, dividend declarations can be limited to ESOP shares and nondeductible dividends do not have to be paid on other outstanding shares. The preferred stock must be noncallable and must be convertible into common stock of the company at a reasonable conversion ratio.

Voting

Because the securities held in an ESOP may constitute a significant block of stock, how voting rights are to be handled is very important.

If the ESOP is maintained by an employer whose stock is not publicly traded, participants are entitled to exercise voting rights on shares allocated to their accounts only with respect to certain major corporate events—merger, consolidation, sale of all or most of the corporation's assets, recapitalization, reclassification, liquidation and dissolution. On all other matters, the ESOP shares are voted by the ESOP trustee or administrative committee which has been appointed by the company's board of directors.

In order for the lender's 50% interest exclusion under Section 133 to be available with respect to an ESOP loan, however, the ESOP must pass through to participants full voting rights on shares acquired with the proceeds of the loan which have been allocated to the participants' accounts. There is no requirement of pass-through of voting rights on unallocated stock.

When voting pass-through is required by law, but not all of the shares held by the ESOP have been allocated to participants, the unallocated shares are voted in the manner prescribed by the ESOP document. The plan document may provide that the unallocated shares will be voted in the same proportion as participants direct the voting of allocated shares. In most cases, however, any unallocated shares are voted by the ESOP administrative committee or ESOP trustee and must be voted in the best interests of participants and beneficiaries.

When voting pass-through is not required by law, the shares usually are voted by the fiduciary. However, voting rights may be provided to participants in excess of what is required by law, from full pass-through on all allocated shares on all issues requiring a shareholder vote, to limiting the vote to certain specific issues (such as the election of one or more corporate directors or limiting the vote to vested shares only).

Distribution of Benefits

The ESOP may provide for distribution of benefits in the form of cash and/or company stock, but participants must have the right to demand benefits in shares of the employer stock. If, however, the corporate charter or by-laws state that only active employees may own stock, the plan may require that departing participants will not receive stock but instead receive the cash value of the stock in the participant's account.

The ESOP must begin to distribute vested benefits to a participant not later than the plan year after the plan year in which the participant 1) retires, 2) becomes disabled, or 3) dies, or the fifth plan year following the participant's separation from service for other reasons.

The plan must also provide that, unless a participant elects otherwise, the participant's account balance will be paid in substantially equal periodic payments over a period not longer than five years. If, however, a participant's account includes employer securities that were acquired in connection with a loan that has not been fully repaid, distribution of stock may be delayed until after the loan is repaid. If a participant's account balance exceeds $500,000, the distribution period will be extended one year for each $100,000 (or fraction thereof) by which the account balance exceeds $500,000, but no longer than five additional years.

Repurchase Liability

If the stock of an employer is not publicly traded, the participants have a "put option" on the stock distributed from the ESOP. The participants have the right to require the sponsoring employer (not the ESOP) to repurchase any shares distributed to them. The put option must give the following benefits:

♦ the trustee of the participant's IRA must be able to exercise the same option;

♦ the participant must have at least 60 days after receipt of the stock to require the employer to repurchase the stock at its fair market value and make payment within 30 days if the shares were distributed as part of an installment distribution;

♦ the ESOP *may* be permitted to take the employer's role and repurchase the stock in lieu of the employer;

♦ the participant must have an additional 60-day period in which to exercise the put option in the following plan year after he has been advised of the updated fair market value; and

♦ if the shares were distributed as part of a lump-sum distribution, payment for the shares must begin within 30 days after the exercise of the put on a schedule at least as rapid as substantially equal payments over a period not exceeding five years.

This requirement of giving participants a right to put the shares to the company creates a future liability for closely-held ESOP companies. This future liability is further compounded by the diversification requirements of Section 401(a)(28)(B) of the Code. It requires the ESOP to provide "qualified participants" an opportunity to diversify their account balances. A qualified participant is one who is at least 55 years old and who has at least 10 years of participation in the plan. Each qualified participant has the option to elect within 90 days after the close of each plan year to direct the plan as to the investment of at least 25% of the participant's account for the first five plan years after being a qualified participant. In the sixth and final plan year, the plan must give the participant the opportunity to diversify at least 50% of the balance of his or her account, less any amounts previously diversified.

The diversification requirements apply only to shares acquired after December 31, 1986. Participants with an account balance of $500 or less need not be given the diversification election. See IRS Notice 88-56.

An ESOP may satisfy the diversification requirement in three ways:

1. The portion of the participant's account eligible to be diversified may be distributed within 90 days after the period during which the election may be made. The distribution may be rolled over tax-free into an Individual Retirement Account.

2. The plan may offer at least three investment options (other than employer stock) to qualified employees and transfer the amounts to such investments within 90 days after the expiration of the election period.

3. The plan may offer rollover into another qualified plan which permits employee-directed investments.

Although the repurchase liability arising from the diversification requirement and the put option initially may be modest, it will grow, perhaps rapidly, as the ESOP matures and as more shares of stock are allocated to accounts of employees. Moreover, if the company is successful, the value of the shares themselves should increase. Even with modest growth in the value of the shares, the repurchase liability can become a significant obligation over time.

Thus, it is extremely important for a closely held company considering an ESOP to prepare for repurchase liability. Otherwise, serious cash flow problems may result.

The first thing a privately held company considering an ESOP must do to confront the repurchase liability problem is to prepare a forecast of the expected extent of the future repurchase obligation. Valuation and actuarial firms can assist in preparing the repurchase liability study. Frequently, a lender may require a repurchase liability study as a condition to the ESOP loan. The factors that such a study will consider are employee turnover and retirement rates, dividend payments, contribution levels and the market value of the company.

Once the future liability is estimated, the company can establish cash reserves, either within the ESOP or in a sinking fund controlled by the company, to be used to fund the repurchase liability.

Valuation of Employer Securities

Proper valuation of employer securities contributed or sold to the ESOP is an important and difficult aspect of an ESOP transaction.

ERISA and the Code prohibit transactions between qualified benefit plans and parties in interest, who include major shareholders of the company and plan fiduciaries. An exemption for ESOPs is provided from the prohibited transaction rules. The exemption, however, is conditioned upon the ESOP not paying more than "adequate consideration" for the stock it receives.

If the stock is publicly traded, "adequate consideration" is the prevailing market price. For the shares of a closely held company, adequate consideration is the fair market value of the company's shares as determined by fiduciaries named by the plan and acting in good faith. These fiduciaries must hire an independent appraiser. Section 401(a)(28)(C) of the Code.

IRS regulations issued under Section 170(a) of the Code may establish standards for determining what constitutes an independent appraiser; otherwise, the proposed Department of Labor regulations on adequate consideration now address the issue. In general, the appraiser must be independent of the company issuing the employer securities and of the other parties to the ESOP transaction.

The shares of a closely held company must also be appraised by an independent appraiser at least once a year. Regulations proposed by the Department of Labor contain specific guidelines that should be followed in determining the fair market value of closely held stock.

The "fair market value" is defined as the price at which the stock would change hands between an informed, willing seller not under any compulsion to sell and an informed, willing buyer not under any compulsion to buy. The valuation report must assess the nature of the business, the outlook for the industry, the earning and dividend-paying capacity of the company, the book value of the company, and the market price of securities in a comparable business. It must also include a summary of the appraiser's qualifications and the methods used to value the stock. Care should be taken to choose an appraiser who regularly performs valuations of businesses.

Case Studies*

Having discussed the rules applicable to ESOPs, let's look at some composite case studies to determine when an ESOP might be appropriate for a company and when it might not.

For each of the composite case studies that follow, a common thread ties them together. Most owners of privately held companies share the common dilemma of how to effectively access equity from their successful businesses. Quite often a ma-

jority of their net worth (as much as 80–90%) is tied up in the value of the company. The paradox is that due to their hard work and successful efforts, they have created substantial wealth, but accessing this wealth is often both a difficult and costly undertaking.

The reasons owners want to access a portion of their equity are as varied as are the owners. The most frequently noted are to 1) obtain liquidity; 2) achieve diversification; and 3) create an exit plan.

Obtaining liquidity refers to accessing cash for any number of needs, i.e., estate planning, funding childrens' or grandchildrens' educations, vacation, retirement home, etc.

Diversification refers to having one's eggs in more than a single basket. As the company grows in size, and the owner grows older, many will desire to diversify their assets outside the company, in order to preserve capital and minimize their risk.

An exit plan refers to the fact that at some point, the owner will be leaving the company, and will want to review the somewhat limited strategies available for selling shares of privately held companies. The time horizon for such an exit plan may be immediate, due to health or personal problems, or possibly longer (5–20 years) for an owner who wishes to gradually phase out his involvement.

Although there are many reasons for a business owner to wish to access equity, there are limited methods available to do so, each with its own tax consequences and complexities. How do you access cash in a privately held business? Seven methods follow:

Salary. Subject to a maximum 31% ordinary income tax (in addition to other taxes, i.e., state and local income tax where applicable, etc.), and a reasonableness standard for deductibility by the corporation.

Dividends or Distributions. Corporate earnings for C corporations are taxed at the corporate level (federal maximum 34%) and at the individual level (31% federal maximum). S corporation distributions are taxed only at the individual level for federal tax purposes; however S corporations in certain states may be subject to state taxes as well.

Qualified Plans. Profit-sharing, pension plans, 401(k) plans all allow contributions with pre-tax dollars and tax-deferred growth. Eventual distributions are taxed at the individual level. Plan contributions are capped at 15% of eligible payroll (25% for leveraged ESOPs). Owners are generally categorized as highly compensated employees, who can restrict their contribution levels even further. Finally, if the

---

*The case studies discussed herein are presented for illustrative purposes only. Business owners should consult their legal or tax advisor to determine the tax and ESOP benefits applicable to their particular situation.

eligible employee base continues to grow in size, the percentage of annual contributions being allocated to the owner will shrink further.

Non-Qualified Plans. These plans are commonly referred to as deferred compensation, or Supplemental Executive Retirement Plans (SERPS), salary continuation plans, or Executive Bonus Plans. They are not subject to the qualification requirements of the Code or the rules and regulations of ERISA. They are also not eligible for the tax advantages of qualified plans.

Sales of Shares (Partial or Full). Most shareholders of closely held businesses find it very difficult to sell a minority position in their company through traditional means, at a price that makes sense. Selling all, or at least a control position of 50% or more is not as difficult, but is still a complicated and time-consuming process. Additionally, while most owners would like to access some of their equity, they do not want to relinquish control of their company.

Going Public. The feasibility of going public is a function of the company's size, its growth rate, industry class and other considerations; going public is not a viable alternative for most companies. For the select few that do meet the strict criteria, the owners must be willing to endure the cost, exposure, loss of control, and other side effects of going public.

Stock Redemption. An alternative to selling shares to outsiders in either public or private transactions is to sell shares back to the company. A partial stock redemption could allow business owners to liquidate their equity while maintaining control of their company. However, the tax ramifications may be less than attractive. Let's assume this company, a C corporation, earns $1,500,000 pretax, and the sole stockholder wishes to access all of these earnings.

Example:

	$1,500,000	Pre-tax earnings
	–510,000	Federal corporate Tax (34%)
	$ 990,000	Net Available for Redemption

If the owner sells his shares back to the company, he will face a capital gains tax (currently 28%) on the difference between his sale price and his basis in his shares. For example, assume the owner wants to sell all of his shares—10,000 shares with a basis of $10 per share at a price of $99 per share.

Example:

	$ 990,000	Gross proceeds (10,000 shares @ $99 per share)
–	100,000	Cost basis (10,000 shares @ $10 per share)
	$ 890,000	Amount Subject to Capital Gains Tax

At the current rate of 28% capital gains tax, the $890,000 would result in federal tax liability of $249,200. ($890,000 × .28 = $249,200). In addition, there may be a state and local tax liability.

Therefore:

	$ 990,000	Gross proceeds
	–249,200	Capital Gains Tax
	$ 740,800	Net proceeds

Of our original pre-tax earnings of $1,500,000, the owner has netted $740,800, or less than 50%!

If the owner sells less than all of his stock and the sale fails to qualify as a redemption under Section 302(b) of the Code, the sale proceeds could be treated as a dividend taxable at ordinary income rates.

Each of the options for accessing equity in a company discussed above has varying degrees of negative tax ramifications, loss of control, or other complexities.

Now let's look at the ESOP alternative.

Case Study 1

Scenario: Assume the same facts as outlined above in the discussion of stock redemptions. Now, however, rather than selling his shares back to the company, the owner sells his 10,000 shares (constituting 100% of the outstanding stock of the company) to an ESOP, at the same sales price of $99 per share. Net proceeds to the seller are $990,000 (10,000 shares @ $99 per share).

Consider: Because the ESOP is purchasing more than 30% of the outstanding stock of the company, the transaction will qualify for Section 1042 treatment. As long as the owner reinvests the $990,000 of sale proceeds in qualified replacement securities, he will pay no capital gains tax on the sale. Thus, by selling his stock to the ESOP, rather than back to the company, the selling shareholder receives $990,000, compared to $740,800, a savings of $249,200.

Case Study 2

Scenario #1: XYZ Company currently does not have a retirement plan. The company is profitable, and is in a tax-paying mode, but cash is tight. The company is comparing alternative retirement plans. Could an ESOP work?

Consider: The company could institute an ESOP as its retirement plan. By funding the plan with company stock, there is no cash outlay. In addition, the contribution is deductible, possibly at the 34% level.

Scenario #2: XYZ Company currently has a 401(k) plan with an average annual matching contribution of $200,000. The company is profitable and growing, but inadequate cash is hampering growth. The objective is to enhance cash flow, but not at the expense of employee well-being. By contributing stock to an ESOP, the company receives the same tax benefit with no cash outlay.

Consider:

Cash Match		ESOP Match
($200,000)	Cash Flow out	$ -0-
68,000	Tax Benefit @ 34%	68,000
($132,000)	Cash flow	+$ 68,000

Difference: Increase in cash flow of $200,000.

Case Study 3

Scenario #1: XYZ Company has multiple owners, one of which is a minority stockholder (40%) who would like to cash out of the business.

Consider: The ESOP could buy 30% of the value of the company, making the stockholder eligible for Section 1042 treatment. The additional 10% could be purchased by the ESOP or remaining stockholders.

Scenario #2: What if the owner is a majority stockholder, not a minority stockholder?

Consider: The ESOP could buy all of the owner's stock. If the stock purchase is financed with borrowed funds, the ESOP might obtain a below-market interest rate, provided the requirements of IRC §133 are met. The selling stockholder would be eligible for Section 1042 treatment as well.

These are just a few simple examples of when an ESOP might be advantageous. There are circumstances where the ESOP is clearly not appropriate, i.e., if the company will not be an ongoing concern, if the balance sheet cannot justify the transaction, etc. The successful design and implementation of an ESOP will require highly competent and experienced advisors. If structured properly, the ESOP will benefit everyone—the selling shareholders, the company, and, of course, the employees.

Part X:
The High Yield and Below Investment Grade Markets

Chapter 23

Defaults and Returns on High Yield Bonds*

Edward I. Altman
The Max L. Heine Professor of Finance, Stern School of Business
New York University, New York, NY

At the end of 1990, there was considerable concern about both the near-term and long-term future of the high yield debt, market. Most analysts and other knowledgeable commentators expected continued high default rates. With additional pressure exerted by liquidity concerns, the market's "average" yield spread over ten-year U.S. Treasury bonds reached the rarefied level of 1,200 basis points.[1] One could interpret these record yield spreads as indications of extremely high estimates of future defaults in 1991 and beyond. These expectations will be discussed at a later point.

The purpose of this chapter is to report on defaults and returns for the full year 1991. It will bring up to date the statistics reported in Altman (1991). The differences in default rates and losses that manifest themselves when prior defaults are subtracted from the base population will be highlighted.[2]

Default Rates and Losses

For the full year 1991, $18.9 billion of high yield debt defaulted or was exchanged under distressed circumstances.[3] (A list of 1991 defaulting issues appears in Appendix A at the end of this chapter.) The record-high volume of defaults resulted in a default rate of 9.01%, as measured by the "traditional" method (Table 23.1).[4] The par value outstanding in Table 23.1 consists of all public, nonconvertible high yield bonds tracked by Merrill Lynch & Co., including issues already in default, but still trading. The 9.01% rate is slightly higher than

the comparable rate for 1990. It also exceeds the weighted (by amount outstanding each year) average annual rates for various historical periods through 1991 (bottom of Table 23.1).

A breakdown of 1991 defaults by quarter is shown in Appendix B at the end of this chapter. Note the sizable quarter-to-quarter fluctuations in rate. In addition, Appendix C at the end of this chapter lists defaults by industry for 1991 and for the entire period 1970–1991. The two most "prolific" industries in terms of the number of defaults in 1991 were retailing and financial services.

Table 23.2 shows that the default rate, calculated *without* including in the population base prior defaulted issues that are still trading, was 10.27%. This was slightly above the 10.14% 1990 figure and considerably higher than either the 5.46% weighted (by amount outstanding each year) average annual rate over the last 22 years or the 5.59% annual rate of 1978–1991. The differential between default rates calculated with and without prior defaults in the base was 1.26 percentage points, slightly less than 1.40-percentage-point difference of 1990 (Table 23.1 and Table 23.2). Note, however, that this differential was much smaller in the years prior to 1990, when the amount of bonds in default was considerably lower.

Table 23.3 shows the *default loss rate* in 1991, calculated on a weighted average (by amount outstanding) per defaulting issue for both default rate methods, as discussed above. We observe that the average recovery rate (price just after default) was about 36% of par value, indicating a 64% loss of

The author acknowledges the data assistance of both Standard & Poor's and Moody's as well as the computation support from Kenneth Zekavat, Vellore Kishore and Stig Hansen of the NYU Salomon Center.
*Copyright, 1992 Merrill Lynch, Pierce, Fenner & Smith Inc.

249

Table 23.1   Historical Default Rates—Straight Debt Only, 1970-1991
Defaulted Issues Included in Par Value Outstanding ($ Millions)

Year	Par Value Outstanding	Par Value Defaults	Default Rates
1991	$209,400	$18,862	9.008%
1990	210,000	18,354	8.740%
1989	201,000	8,110	4.035%
1988	159,223	3,944	2.477%
1987	136,952	7,486*	5.466%
1986	92,985	3,156	3.394%
1985	59,078	992	1.679%
1984	41,700	344	0.825%
1983	28,233	301	1.066%
1982	18,536	577	3.115%
1981	17,362	27	0.156%
1980	15,126	224	1.482%
1979	10,675	20	0.187%
1978	9,401	119	1.265%
1977	8,479	381	4.488%
1976	8,015	30	0.368%
1975	7.720	204	2.644%
1974	11,101	123	1.106%
1973	8,082	49	0.607%
1972	7,106	193	2.720%
1971	6,643	82	1.234%
1970	6,996	797	11.388%

Arithmetic Average Default Rate	1970 to 1991		3.066%
	1978 to 1991		3.064%
	1983 to 1991		4.077%
Weighted Average Default Rate	1970 to 1991		5.054%
	1978 to 1991		5.168%
	1983 to 1991		5.406%

Weighted by par value of amount outstanding for each year.

*$1,841.7 million without Texaco, Inc., Texaco Capital, and Texaco N.V.
The default rate with these is 1.345%.

principal for investors who bought at par. This is based on 124 issues for which confirmed prices (from market makers and the *Standard & Poor's Bond Guide*) were available. The weighted average coupon rate on those issues was 11.59%, resulting in default loss calculations of 6.29% and 7.16%, respectively, for the two above-described methods.

Table 23.4 and Table 23.5 show the default loss rates measured on both population bases for the most recent seven-year period, 1985-1991. Note that despite considerable year-to-year fluctuation, the average recovery rate, weighted by the amount outstanding of each defaulting issue, was very close to the venerable 40% figure. The 1991 default loss rates were somewhat *lower* than the 1990 rates since recoveries averaged considerably higher in 1991. For example, the 7.16% 1991 default loss rate was significantly less than the comparable 1990 rate of 8.42%, which was affected by a historically very low average recovery rate of 23.4% (Table 23.5). We

now turn to a more detailed analysis of recovery rates.

Recovery Rate by Seniority Statistics

As noted above, we calculate the average "recovery" rate[5] in 1991 was about 36% of par value. The average, however, includes securities of very different seniorities. Accordingly, in Table 23.6 we break down default recoveries by seniority of issue. Note that the average recovery varied from a high of 58.2% for senior bonds (62 issues) to a low of 20.3% for cash-pay subordinated issues (35 issues). The fact that senior unsecured issues recovered somewhat more than secured bonds (58.2% versus 54.5%) was a statistical aberration attributable to the high recovery rate on the 23 Columbia Gas System senior

Table 23.2   Historical Default Rates—Straight Debt Only, 1970–1991
Defaulted Issues Excluded in Par Value Outstanding ($ Millions)

Year	Par Value Outstanding	Par Value Defaults	Default Rates
1991	$183,600	$18,862	10.273%
1990	181,000	18,354	10.140%
1989	189,258	8,110	4.285%
1988	148,187	3,944	2.662%
1987	129,557	7,486 *	5.778% *
1986	90,243	3,156	3.497%
1985	58,088	992	1.708%
1984	40,939	344	0.840%
1983	27,492	301	1.095%
1982	18,109	577	3.186%
1981	17,115	27	0.158%
1980	14,935	224	1.500%
1979	10,356	20	0.193%
1978	8,946	119	1.330%
1977	8,157	381	4.671%
1976	7,735	30	0.388%
1975	7,471	204	2.731%
1974	10,894	123	1.129%
1973	7,824	49	0.626%
1972	6,529	193	2.956%
1971	5,805	82	1.413%
1970	6,598	797	12.080%

Arithmetic Average Default Rate	1970 to 1991	3.302%
	1978 to 1991	3.332%
	1983 to 1991	4.475%

Weighted Average Default Rate	1970 to 1991	5.461%
	1978 to 1991	5.593%
	1983 to 1991	5.871%

Weighted by par value of amount outstanding for each year.

*$1,841.7 million without Texaco, Inc., Texaco Capital, and Texaco N.V.
The default rate with these is 1.345%.

Table 23.3   1991 Default Loss Rate

Background Data	Weighted Calculation Including Defaults	Excluding Defaults
Average Default Rate 1991	9.01%	10.27%
Average End of Month Price After Default	36.04%	36.04%
Average Loss of Principal	63.96%	63.96%
Average Coupon Payment*	11.59%	11.59%

Default Loss Computation

Default Rate	9.01%	10.27%
X Loss of Principal	63.96%	63.96%
Default Loss of Principal	5.763%	6.569%
Default Rate	9.01%	10.27%
X Loss of 1/2 Coupon	5.795%	5.795%
Default Loss of Coupon	0.522%	0.595%
Default Loss of Principal and Coupon	6.285%	7.164%

*For issues with prices only; including all issues, the average coupon was 10.49%.

Table 23.4   Default Rates and Losses, 1985–1991
             Defaulted Issues Included in Par Value Outstanding

Year	Par Value Outstanding ($ Millions)	Par Value of Default ($ Millions)	Default Rate (%)	Weighted Price After Default	Weighted Coupon (%)	Default Loss (%)
1991	$209,400	$18,862.0	9.01%	36.0	11.59%	6.29%
1990	210,000	18,354.0	8.74%	23.4	12.94%	7.26%
1989	201,000	8,110.3	4.03%	38.3	13.40%	2.76%
1988	159,223	3,944.2	2.48%	43.6	11.91%	1.54%
1987*	136,952	7,485.7	5.47%	75.9	12.07%	1.65%
1986	92,985	3,155.8	3.39%	34.5	10.61%	2.40%
1985	59,078	992.1	1.68%	45.9	13.69%	1.02%
Weighted Average 1985–1991			5.70%	40.6	12.34%	3.88%

*Includes Texaco.

Table 23.5   Default Rates and Losses, 1985–1991
             Defaulted Issues Excluded in Par Value Outstanding

Year	Par Value Outstanding ($ Millions)	Par Value of Default ($ Millions)	Default Rate (%)	Weighted Price After Default	Weighted Coupon (%)	Default Loss (%)
1991	$183,600	$18,862.0	10.27%	36.0	11.59%	7.16%
1990	181,000	18,354.0	10.14%	23.4	12.94%	8.42%
1989	189,258	8,110.3	4.29%	38.3	13.40%	2.93%
1988	148,187	3,944.2	2.66%	43.6	11.91%	1.66%
1987*	129,557	7,485.7	5.78%	75.9	12.07%	1.74%
1986	90,243	3,155.8	3.50%	34.5	10.61%	2.48%
1985	58,088	992.1	1.71%	45.9	13.69%	1.04%
Weighted Average 1985–1991			6.22%	40.6	12.34%	4.24%

*Includes Texaco

Table 23.6   Average Recovery Prices on Defaulted Debt by Seniority
             Per $100 Face Amount; 1985–1991[a]

Year	Secured	Senior	Senior Subordinated	Cash Pay	Subordinated Non-cash Pay
1991	$54.50 (02)	$58.15 (62) (b)	$34.62 (21)	$20.28 (35)	$21.06 (04)
1990	35.04 (07)	32.02 (27)	24.04 (28)	17.93 (17)	18.99 (12)
1989	82.69 (09)	53.70 (16)	19.60 (21)	23.95 (30)	NONE
1988	67.96 (13)	41.99 (19)	30.70 (10)	35.27 (20)	NONE
1987	12.00 (01)	70.52 (29) (c)	53.50 (10)	40.54 (07)	NONE
1986	48.32 (07)	37.09 (08)	37.74 (10)	31.58 (34)	NONE
1985	74.25 (02)	34.81 (03)	36.18 (07)	41.45 (15)	NONE
Average 1985–1991	$60.51 (41)	$ 52.28 (164)	$30.70 (107)	$27.96 (158)	$19.51 (16)
Average of All Issues	$39.24 (486)				

Notes: Number of Issues in parentheses.
[a] Prices at end of default month.
[b] Includes 23 issues of Columbia Gas; without these issues the recovery rate was $43.30.
[c] Without Texaco, 1987 recovery rate was $29.77.

bonds.[6] Without Columbia Gas, the recovery rate on senior issues would have been 43.3%.

Over the last seven years (1985–1991), weighted average recovery rates have fluctuated between 23% and 78%. (The latter figure was attributable to unusually high recoveries on Texaco issues.[7]) We had noticed a drop in recoveries from the 1987 high to the 1990 low, but this seems to have been reversed in 1991 (Table 23.5)). Furthermore, the reversal was evident in every seniority layer (Table 23.6)

Average Recovery by Original Issuance

We have also compiled post default prices by original bond rating and by number of years after issuance. These figures cover defaulting issues over the two-decade period 1971–1991 and for subperiods 1971–1987 and 1978–1991. The latter four-year period was typified by heightened default activity, with prices available on 268 issues compared to 196 issues for the previous 17-year period.

For the entire sample period, and especially for the initial 17 years, some significant relationship appears to exist between an issue's original rating and its postdefault price (Table 23.7). This is particularly true for investment grade issues, many of which were either secured or senior. Also, as noted above, a large number of Texaco bonds traded at about 80% of par after default. Noninvestment grade, original-issue high yield bonds did not display any correlation at all between original rating and postdefault price.

There does not appear to be any connection between price after default and the number of years between issuance and default (Table 23.8). This is reasonable, since the price just after default is a function of several future-oriented variables, i.e., the potential for successful emergence from bankruptcy, the estimated time required for reorganization, the expected costs of reorganization (also related to time), and the going-concern value of the firm. The length of time that bonds had existed prior to default would seem to be irrelevant.

Finally, we note that the postdefault prices in the later four-year period of our sample (1988–1991) show lower averages in most rating categories and in most recent years after issuance than in the earlier segment (1971–1987).

Rating Drift of Defaulted Bonds

Duen Li Kao and I (1991, 1992) have explored the phenomenon that we call "rating drift," or credit quality changes over time. We have observed the ten-year post-issuance bond rating change experience of all new issues from 1971 through 1988. In this report, I deal only with defaulted issues and observe their Standard & Poor's bond ratings on three dates: 1) at issuance, 2) one year prior to default, and 3) six months prior to default.

Table 23.9 shows that of the 556 issues that defaulted during 1970–1991, 26.3% were "fallen angels" that were investment grade at birth and subsequently dropped to noninvestment grade before defaulting. The remainder, 73.7%, were original issue high yield bonds.

In 1991, 40 of the 182 issues (22%) were originally rated investment grade, representing $2.97 billion or about 16% of the $18.4 billion of defaults for which we found original ratings.

The proportions of defaulting issues that were still investment grade one year and six months prior to default were 9.7% and 7.7%, respectively.[8] These rates may appear surprisingly high to those who believe that a failing firm's deterioration can usually be detected (with a downgrade resulting) long before default. Manville's surprise 1982 bankruptcy, in this view, would be regarded as a rare exception. On the other hand, the proportion of defaulting issues that remain investment grade declines as default approaches, and almost none are still in this category at the time of default. The rating agencies can, with some justification, point to these facts as vindicating the overall accuracy of their ratings.

Mortality Rates

My original mortality study reported rates and losses through 1986[9] and I have continued to update these results. The latest mortality rates on data through 1991 update these results and consider the large default years of 1990 and 1991. Table 23.10 compares marginal (yearly) and cumulative mortality rates.[10] We find that there was a very substantial increase in 1990 especially in years 2, 3, and 5 and again in 1991 for Single-B issues. The five-year cumulative mortality rate for Single-B issues now registers exactly 25.0%. While this number is the highest it has been since we began computing mortality rates, on an average annual basis, the result (over 5.0% per year) is very close to the weighted average annual rate for the period 1970–1991, measured in the traditional way in Table 23.2 (5.46%).

Table 23.7 Average Price After Default by Original Bond Rating (Per $100)

Original Rating	1971–1991			1971–1987			1988–1991		
	Average (Weighted) Price After Default	Average (Arithmetic) Price After Default	Number of Observations	Average (Weighted) Price After Default	Average (Arithmetic) Price After Default	Number of Observations	Average (Weighted) Price After Default	Average (Arithmetic) Price After Default	Number of Observations
AAA	79.44	78.68	5	79.44	78.68	5	NA	NA	0
AA	82.11	69.24	20	87.19	79.30	13	52.69	50.57	7
A	60.63	60.84	49	71.55	46.40	19	50.11	69.98	30
BBB	45.52	44.07	51	39.82	43.27	21	46.85	44.64	30
BB	29.68	28.92	38	33.01	29.27	23	28.22	28.38	15
B	33.29	35.85	233	44.51	37.90	86	31.01	34.66	147
CCC	22.76	31.57	64	32.03	30.57	25	19.44	32.21	39
C	13.27	13.13	4	13.27	13.13	4	NA	NA	0
Average	45.84	45.29		50.10	44.81		38.05	43.40	
Total			464			196			268

Table 23.8   Average Price After Default by Number of Years After Issuance (Per $100)

Number of Years After Issuance	1971–1991			1971–1987			1988–1991		
	Average (Weighted) Price After Default	Average (Arithmetic) Price After Default	Number of Observations	Average (Weighted) Price After Default	Average (Arithmetic) Price After Default	Number of Observations	Average (Weighted) Price After Default	Average (Arithmetic) Price After Default	Number of Observations
<1	52.83	40.26	16	61.57	42.41	10	41.41	36.67	6
1-2	38.62	39.24	48	58.54	42.84	14	34.60	37.76	34
2-3	40.57	37.26	83	78.31	51.17	30	26.04	29.39	53
3-4	37.45	37.23	60	41.84	36.78	23	35.37	37.50	37
4-5	33.96	37.21	54	47.50	40.95	16	31.80	35.63	38
5-6	37.49	38.78	34	53.76	46.55	18	22.88	30.04	16
6-7	31.12	34.81	26	41.03	40.27	11	28.28	30.81	15
7-8	43.01	48.22	12	43.02	36.79	6	43.00	59.65	6
8-9	43.52	39.13	13	31.29	28.33	6	57.23	48.38	7
9-10	35.64	38.18	14	34.77	38.00	9	36.60	38.50	5
>10	47.21	46.38	104	41.60	35.66	53	56.57	57.53	51
Average	40.13	39.70		48.47	39.98		37.62	40.17	
Total			464			196			268

Table 23.9 Rating Distribution of Defaulted Issues at Various Points Prior to Default (1970–1991)*

	Original Rating		Rating One Year Prior To Default		Rating Six Months Prior To Default	
	Number	Percentage	Number	Percentage	Number	Percentage
AAA	5	0.9%	0	0.0%	0	0.0%
AA	19	3.4%	0	0.0%	0	0.0%
A	60	10.8%	2	0.4%	2	0.4%
BBB	62	11.2%	45	9.3%	36	7.3%
Total Investment Grade	146	26.3%	47	9.7%	38	7.7%
BB	59	10.6%	47	9.8%	29	5.9%
B	266	47.8%	238	49.4%	199	40.4%
CCC	81	14.6%	137	28.4%	198	40.2%
CC	4	0.7%	10	2.1%	25	5.1%
C	0	0.0%	3	0.6%	3	0.6%
Total Noninvestment Grade	410	73.7%	435	90.3%	454	92.3%
Total	556	100.0%	482	100.0%	492	100.0%

*Based on Standard & Poor's Bond Rating.

Table 23.10 Mortality Rates by Original Rating (Years After Issuance)

Rating		1		2		3		4		5		6		7		8		9		10	
		1990	1991	1990	1991	1990	1991	1990	1991	1990	1991	1990	1991	1990	1991	1990	1991	1990	1991	1990	1991
AAA	Yearly	0.00%	0.00%	0.00%	0.00%	0.00%	0.00%	0.00%	0.00%	0.00%	0.00%	0.14%	0.12%	0.05%	0.05%	0.00%	0.00%	0.00%	0.00%	0.00%	0.00%
	Cumulative	0.00%	0.00%	0.00%	0.00%	0.00%	0.00%	0.00%	0.00%	0.00%	0.00%	0.14%	0.12%	0.19%	0.17%	0.19%	0.17%	0.19%	0.17%	0.19%	0.17%
AA	Yearly	0.00%	0.00%	0.00%	0.00%	1.19%	1.09%	0.35%	0.32%	0.13%	0.11%	0.00%	0.00%	0.22%	0.19%	0.00%	0.00%	0.09%	0.08%	0.10%	0.09%
	Cumulative	0.00%	0.00%	0.00%	0.00%	1.19%	1.09%	1.54%	1.41%	1.67%	1.52%	1.67%	1.52%	1.89%	1.71%	1.89%	1.71%	1.97%	1.79%	2.07%	1.87%
A	Yearly	0.00%	0.00%	0.21%	0.19%	0.30%	0.25%	0.36%	0.31%	0.19%	0.17%	0.05%	0.04%	0.14%	0.12%	0.27%	0.24%	0.11%	0.17%	0.00%	0.00%
	Cumulative	0.00%	0.00%	0.21%	0.19%	0.51%	0.45%	0.87%	0.76%	1.06%	0.93%	1.10%	0.97%	1.24%	1.08%	1.51%	1.32%	1.61%	1.49%	1.61%	1.49%
BBB	Yearly	0.10%	0.10%	0.90%	1.00%	0.37%	0.42%	0.64%	0.52%	0.54%	0.70%	0.28%	0.19%	1.45%	1.09%	0.00%	0.00%	0.16%	0.13%	0.89%	0.75%
	Cumulative	0.10%	0.10%	1.00%	1.10%	1.37%	1.51%	2.00%	2.03%	2.56%	2.72%	2.83%	2.90%	4.24%	3.96%	4.24%	3.96%	4.40%	4.09%	5.25%	4.81%
BB	Yearly	0.00%	0.00%	0.93%	0.91%	4.25%	3.66%	2.05%	1.93%	2.84%	2.78%	1.91%	1.27%	4.76%	4.33%	0.00%	0.00%	0.00%	0.00%	3.09%	2.66%
	Cumulative	0.00%	0.00%	0.93%	0.91%	5.14%	4.53%	7.08%	6.37%	9.72%	8.97%	11.44%	10.13%	15.65%	14.02%	15.65%	14.02%	15.65%	14.02%	18.26%	16.31%
B	Yearly	1.72%	1.72%	4.69%	4.67%	9.83%	9.16%	5.60%	5.61%	7.01%	6.64%	4.54%	2.65%	5.80%	4.24%	4.25%	2.88%	10.36%	5.07%	2.27%	3.58%
	Cumulative	1.72%	1.72%	6.33%	6.31%	15.54%	14.90%	20.27%	19.67%	25.86%	25.00%	29.22%	26.99%	33.33%	30.09%	36.16%	32.10%	42.77%	35.54%	44.07%	37.85%
CCC	Yearly	1.55%	1.55%	14.84%	14.84%	12.47%	11.74%	11.67%	9.23%	5.36%	3.82%	9.24%	3.86%	NA	1.54%	NA	NA	NA	NA	NA	NA
	Cumulative	1.55%	1.55%	16.16%	16.16%	26.62%	26.01%	35.18%	32.84%	38.65%	35.40%	44.32%	37.90%	NA	38.85%	NA	NA	NA	NA	NA	NA

Table 23.11 Mortality Losses by Original Rating (Years After Issuance)

Rating		1		2		3		4		5		6		7		8		9		10	
		1990	1991	1990	1991	1990	1991	1990	1991	1990	1991	1990	1991	1990	1991	1990	1991	1990	1991	1990	1991
AAA	Yearly	0.00%	0.00%	0.00%	0.00%	0.00%	0.00%	0.00%	0.00%	0.00%	0.01%	0.01%	0.04%	0.04%	0.03%	0.00%	0.00%	0.00%	0.00%	0.00%	0.00%
	Cumulative	0.00%	0.00%	0.00%	0.00%	0.00%	0.00%	0.00%	0.00%	0.00%	0.00%	0.01%	0.01%	0.05%	0.05%	0.05%	0.05%	0.05%	0.05%	0.05%	0.05%
AA	Yearly	0.00%	0.00%	0.00%	0.00%	0.22%	0.20%	0.13%	0.12%	0.02%	0.02%	0.00%	0.00%	0.12%	0.10%	0.00%	0.00%	0.05%	0.05%	0.05%	0.05%
	Cumulative	0.00%	0.00%	0.00%	0.00%	0.22%	0.20%	0.35%	0.32%	0.37%	0.34%	0.37%	0.34%	0.48%	0.43%	0.48%	0.43%	0.54%	0.48%	0.59%	0.53%
A	Yearly	0.00%	0.00%	0.04%	0.03%	0.05%	0.05%	0.22%	0.19%	0.14%	0.13%	0.03%	0.02%	0.06%	0.05%	0.16%	0.15%	0.08%	0.12%	0.00%	0.00%
	Cumulative	0.00%	0.00%	0.04%	0.03%	0.09%	0.08%	0.31%	0.27%	0.46%	0.40%	0.49%	0.42%	0.54%	0.47%	0.71%	0.62%	0.78%	0.74%	0.78%	0.74%
BBB	Yearly	0.07%	0.07%	0.55%	0.61%	0.21%	0.24%	0.44%	0.36%	0.17%	0.21%	0.15%	0.11%	0.12%	0.84%	0.00%	0.00%	0.09%	0.07%	0.59%	0.50%
	Cumulative	0.07%	0.07%	0.62%	0.68%	0.83%	0.92%	1.27%	1.27%	1.44%	1.48%	1.59%	1.59%	2.69%	2.41%	2.69%	2.41%	2.78%	2.48%	3.36%	2.98%
BB	Yearly	0.00%	0.00%	0.63%	0.61%	3.43%	2.95%	1.58%	1.48%	1.89%	1.85%	1.26%	0.84%	4.48%	4.08%	0.00%	0.00%	0.00%	0.00%	2.44%	2.10%
	Cumulative	0.00%	0.00%	0.63%	0.61%	4.03%	3.54%	5.54%	4.97%	7.33%	6.73%	8.49%	7.51%	12.58%	11.29%	12.59%	11.29%	12.59%	11.29%	14.73%	13.15%
B	Yearly	0.79%	0.79%	2.82%	2.81%	8.04%	7.50%	4.11%	4.12%	5.90%	5.59%	3.53%	2.06%	4.39%	3.21%	3.25%	2.20%	6.15%	3.01%	1.62%	2.55%
	Cumulative	0.79%	0.79%	3.59%	3.58%	11.35%	10.81%	14.99%	14.48%	20.00%	19.26%	22.83%	20.92%	26.21%	23.46%	28.61%	25.15%	33.00%	27.49%	34.08%	29.25%
CCC	Yearly	1.24%	1.24%	13.67%	13.67%	10.19%	9.60%	9.57%	7.57%	4.22%	3.01%	6.91%	2.88%	NA	1.38%	NA	NA	NA	NA	NA	NA
	Cumulative	1.24%	1.24%	14.74%	14.74%	23.43%	22.92%	30.76%	28.76%	33.68%	30.90%	38.26%	32.89%	NA	33.82%	NA	NA	NA	NA	NA	NA

**Table 23.12   Annual Returns, Yields and Spreads
on Ten-Year Treasury (Treas), and High Yield (HY) Bonds**

	Return (%)			*Promised Yield (%)*		
YEAR	HY	TREAS	SPREAD	HY	TREAS	SPREAD
1991	34.58	17.18	17.40	13.11	6.70	6.41
1990	(4.35)	6.88	(11.24)	17.58	8.83	8.75
1989	1.62	15.99	(14.37)	15.41	7.93	7.48
1988	13.47	9.20	4.27	13.95	9.00	4.95
1987	4.67	(2.67)	7.34	12.66	8.75	3.91
1986	16.09	24.08	(7.99)	14.45	9.55	4.90
1985	22.51	31.54	(9.03)	15.40	11.65	3.75
1984	8.50	14.82	(6.32)	14.97	11.87	3.10
1983	21.80	2.23	19.57	15.74	10.70	5.04
1982	32.45	42.08	(9.63)	17.84	13.86	3.98
1981	7.56	0.48	7.08	15.97	12.08	3.89
1980	(1.00)	(2.96)	1.96	13.46	10.23	3.23
1979	3.69	(0.86)	4.55	12.07	9.13	2.94
1978	7.57	(1.11)	8.68	10.92	8.11	2.81
Arithmetic Average:						
1978–1991	12.08	11.21	0.88	14.54	9.89	4.65
Compound Averages:						
1978–1991	11.50	10.44	1.06			

It is also notable that while the early years' marginal rates increased substantially in 1990 and 1991, the later years' rates dropped in some cases. For example, the sixth year's Single-B rate fell to 2.65% in 1991 from 4.54% for data through 1990 and compared to a 6.24% marginal fifth-year rate. These later year drops more than balanced the earlier year increases so that the ten-year cumulative rate actually fell to 37.9%.

Mortality Losses

We can measure mortality losses in a manner similar to the earlier default loss calculation. By considering recovery rates and lost coupon payments on all defaults in our mortality rate date base, we can calculate mortality losses in Table 23.11. As in Table 23.10, the results are listed for data through 1990 and then updated for 1991. The five-year Single-B cumulative mortality loss fell slightly to 19.3%, reflecting higher recovery rates, while the ten-year loss decreased to 29.3%. The average annual loss calculated from the five-year cumulative rate is very similar to the average rate on all high yield bonds of 4.24% per year that we saw earlier in Table 23.7.

Returns on High Yield Bonds

Let us now address returns. In a year in which high yield bonds experienced a record volume of defaults, one might surmise that returns to investors in such bonds suffered in a commensurate way. As it turned out, this was decidedly not the case. Indeed, returns were higher in 1991 than in any other year that our data base covers, going back to 1978! The Merrill Lynch High Yield Master Index returned 34.58%[11] compared to −4.35% in 1990 (Table 23.12). The previous high in total return was 32.45% in 1982. For the entire 14-year period 1978–1991, the compound average annual return was 11.50% and the arithmetic average was 12.08%.

In terms of spreads, the high yield index in 1991 outperformed Treasuries by 1,740 basis points (Table 23.12). This was the second largest spread in our data sample period. The high yield market's superior return was especially notable in light of the fact that interest rates fell dramatically in 1991, especially during the second half of the year. Normally, longer-duration U.S. Treasuries outperform the shorter-duration high yield bonds in periods of sharply falling interest rates.

The compound average annual return spread favors high yield bonds by 106 basis points per year

Table 23.13 Compound Average Annual Returns of High Yield Bonds (1978–1991)

Base Period (January 1)	Terminal Period (December 31)													
	1978	1979	1980	1981	1982	1983	1984	1985	1986	1987	1988	1989	1990	1991
1978	7.57	5.61	3.36	4.39	9.48	11.45	11.02	12.40	12.80	11.96	12.10	11.18	9.90	11.50
1979		3.69	1.32	3.36	9.97	12.24	11.61	13.10	13.47	12.46	12.56	11.52	10.10	11.81
1980			(1.00)	3.19	12.14	14.48	13.26	14.75	14.94	13.61	13.59	12.33	10.70	12.52
1981				7.56	19.36	20.17	17.14	18.19	17.84	15.86	15.56	13.92	11.95	13.84
1982					32.45	27.01	20.52	21.01	20.01	17.31	16.75	14.74	12.44	14.48
1983						21.80	14.96	17.42	17.09	14.49	14.32	12.41	10.17	10.17
1984							8.50	15.29	15.56	12.73	12.88	10.92	8.60	11.55
1985								22.51	19.26	14.18	14.00	11.41	8.61	11.99
1986									16.09	10.23	11.30	8.80	6.03	10.33
1987										4.67	8.98	6.47	3.65	9.21
1988											13.47	7.38	3.32	10.37
1989												1.62	(1.42)	9.36
1990													(4.36)	13.45
1991														34.58

Note: All figures are percentages.
Source: Merrill Lynch High Yield Master Index and Author's Compilation.

Table 23.14 Compound Annual Return Spreads Between High Yield and Long-Term Government Bonds (1978–1991)

Base Period (January 1)	Terminal Period (December 31)													
	1978	1979	1980	1981	1982	1983	1984	1985	1986	1987	1988	1989	1990	1991
1978	8.68	6.60	5.01	5.51	3.17	5.82	4.13	2.70	1.59	2.22	2.41	0.98	(0.04)	1.06
1979		4.55	3.23	4.48	1.71	5.22	3.32	1.77	0.62	1.44	1.73	0.23	(0.82)	0.43
1980			1.96	4.45	0.67	5.39	3.05	1.24	(0.02)	1.01	1.38	(0.25)	(1.35)	0.05
1981				7.08	(0.13)	6.74	3.36	1.07	(0.42)	0.85	1.29	(0.54)	(1.73)	(0.16)
1982					(9.63)	6.49	1.93	(0.69)	(2.16)	(0.33)	0.36	(1.60)	(2.80)	(0.96)
1983						19.57	6.62	1.84	(0.56)	1.22	1.74	(0.65)	(2.11)	(0.16)
1984							(6.32)	(7.60)	(7.73)	(3.48)	(1.89)	(4.06)	(5.19)	(2.65)
1985								(9.03)	(8.50)	(2.50)	(0.76)	(3.60)	(5.00)	(2.12)
1986									(7.99)	0.34	1.64	2.41	(4.30)	(1.12)
1987										7.34	5.89	0.76	(3.49)	0.13
1988											4.27	5.16	(7.31)	(1.85)
1989												(14.37)	(12.76)	(3.89)
1990													(11.24)	1.54
1991														17.40

Note: All figures are in terms of percentage points.

Table 23.15 Breakeven Conditions for Total Returns on High Yield Bonds Versus U.S. Treasury Bonds*

Default Rate (%)	Default Loss Recovery Rates			Required Yield on High Yield Debt** Recovery Rates		
	20%	30%	40%	20%	30%	40%
2.0	1.72	1.52	1.32	9.9	9.7	9.5
4.0	3.44	3.04	2.64	11.9	11.5	11.1
6.0	5.16	4.56	3.96	14.0	13.4	12.7
8.0	6.88	6.08	5.28	16.2	15.3	14.4
10.0	8.60	7.60	6.60	18.4	17.3	16.2
12.0	10.32	9.12	7.96	20.8	19.5	18.1
14.0	12.04	10.64	9.24	23.3	21.7	20.0

*Assuming a 12% high yield coupon, 8% risk-free rate, and various default recovery rates.

$$** \quad BEY = \frac{R_f + D_f(1-Rec) + (D_f \times {}^{HYC}/2)}{1-D_f}$$

over the period 1978–1991. This compares with a spread of −4 basis points per year through year-end 1990. Tables 23.13 and 23.14 give the matrices of compound average annual returns and spreads, respectively, for all January 1 starting and December 31 ending periods for 1978 through 1991. These matrices should prove useful to investors and analysts with interest in specific measurement periods.

How Can We Explain 1991's Return?

How can we explain the paradox of exceptionally high default rates combined with record high total returns? The most common explanations for 1991's strong performance include the following:

1. Prices on a broad cross section of high yield bonds were beaten down so badly in 1990 that many individual issues represented bargains.

2. The limited supply of new high yield debt, especially at the beginning of 1991, caused prices to rise sharply in response to increasing demand as the year progressed.

3. Interest rates dropped significantly.

At the start of the year, the market was clearly anticipating a high default loss rate for 1991 and beyond. Perhaps we can add another reason for the excellent returns by referring to this expectation. Table 23.15 illustrates a rather simplistic but instructive analysis for linking expected default rates, and the consequent default losses, with required yields on high yield bond portfolios. As discussed earlier, the default rate expectation is modified to arrive at

a default loss by considering expected recovery rates just after default and the loss of one-half of the annual coupon on the high yield bonds. Since the breakeven yield is earned only on that part of the portfolio which does not default (1-D$_f$), the formula for calculating breakeven yields (BEY) is:

$$BEY = \frac{R_f + D_f(1-Rec) + (D_f \times {}^{HYC}/2)}{1-D_f}$$

BEY = Breakeven yield-to-maturity on portfolio of high yield bonds
R$_f$ = Risk-free yield
D$_f$ = Expected default rate on high yield bonds
Rec = Expected recovery rate on high yield bond defaults
HYC = Annual high yield coupon rate

So, at the start of 1991, the risk-free rate on ten-year U.S. Treasury bonds was about 8%. Assuming an expected default rate in 1991 of 10% and a 30% recovery rate (both reasonable assumptions), and a coupon rate of 12% on high yield bonds, the breakeven yield would have been 17.33% (Table 12.15). But, average yields on high yield bonds were 20%, i.e., a 12% yield spread. Hence, prices were exceptionally low (spreads high) and although the actual default rate was about 10% in 1991, returns on high yield bonds soared to record levels.

These default rate and loss relationships may help to explain why the market rose so dramatically despite record defaults. Looking ahead into 1992, we note that yield spreads fell to about 650 basis points at the start of the year. This implies an expected breakeven default rate of about 8% for the year (assuming a 30% recovery rate) or 9% assuming a 40% recovery (Table 23.15). Since investors hope to do better than merely earning breakeven returns, the consensus could very well be for lower expected default rates.[12]

To apply this analysis to their portfolios, investors must examine their own risk profiles. Again, break-even analysis is just one, perhaps over-simplistic, explanation of market expectations and subsequent movement.

Endnotes

1. The Merrill Lynch High Yield 175 Index had a yield spread of about 1,200 basis points in October and over 1,200 in December. Fridson (1990) has commented on the fact that the "average is not very meaningful since the distribution around the average is enormous. Still, prices were at extremely low levels for a large number of securities that comprised the index.

2. A number of other possible combinations of assumptions about the numerator and denominator in the default rate calculation were pointed out by Fridson in *Extra Credit,* July/August 1991.

3. We include defaults only if they have passed the 30-day grace period without being cured.

4. For a discussion of the default rate calculation by number of issuers, see Moody's Special Report *Corporate Bond Defaults and Default Rates: 1970-1991,* January 1992. Moody's, which includes convertibles in its sample, found a speculative grade issuer default rate of 9.5% in 1991, up from 8.8% in 1990. These rates are quite comparable to ours, which are based on a par value weighting of all issuers, rather than on issuers.

5. We use the phrase "recovery rate" loosely, since it assumes that the investor sold the bond just after default. An alternative calculation would observe the recovery at the time the bond emerged from Chapter 11 reorganization proceedings (if indeed the firm filed). We are currently researching this experience and will report on it shortly.

6. Moreover, there were only two secured issues in our sample.

7. Without Texaco, the 1987 overall average recovery rate was just 30%. On this basis, the peak years were 1985 (45.9%) and 1988 (43.6%).

8. The six-month 7.7% percentage would drop to 3.2% (15 of 469) if we exclude the 23 Columbia Gas System issues (see Table 23.9).

9. See Edward Altman, "Measuring Corporate Bond Mortality and Performance, Working Paper, NYU Salomon Center, February 1988 and *The Journal of Finance,* September 1989.

10. The 1990 figures shown are revisions of earlier data presented in our study in *Extra Credit,* July/August 1991.

11. This index is less volatile than certain other high yield metrics, both in up and down markets. Because it contains all outstanding issues that meet defined criteria, the Master Index weights the Double–B sector more heavily than indexes designed specifically as mutual fund benchmarks and which are therefore deliberately skewed toward Single–Bs. As an indication of the impact of this difference, the Merrill Lynch 175 Index returned 40.22% in 1991. The average high current yield mutual fund, as reported by *Lipper's Fixed Income Performance,* had a 36.6% total return.

12. Indeed, in 1992 the default rate was only 3.4%, considerably below the implied breakeven rate. Returns exceeded Treasury returns by almost 12% in 1992!

References

Altman, Edward I. "Defaults and Returns on High Yield Bonds: An Update through the First Half of 1991." *Extra Credit,* July/August 1991 and *Financial Analysts Journal,* November/December 1991.

Altman, Edward I. and Duen Li Kao. *Corporate Bond Rating Drift: An Examination of Rating Agency Credit Quality Changes.* Charlottesville: Association for Investment Management Research, 1991.

Altman, Edward I. and Duen Li Kao. "Rating Drift in High Yield Bonds." NYU Salomon Center Working Paper #92-5, February 1992 and *The Journal of Fixed Income,* March 1992.

Fons, Jerome S., Andrew E. Kimball and Dennis Girault. "Corporate Bond Defaults and Default Rates 1970–1991." *Moody's Special Report,* January 1992.

Fridson, Martin S. "Inspect That Index, Probe That Proxy." *Extra Credit,* May 1990.

Fridson, Martin S. "Everything You Always Wanted to Know about Default Rates." *Extra Credit,* July/August 1991.

Fridson, Martin S. and Michael A. Cherry. "A Critique of the Spread-versus-Treasuries Concept." *Extra Credit,* July/August 1991.

Appendix 23–A

1991 Defaulting Straight Debt

(Through December 31, 1991)

Company	Bond Issue	Coupon (%)	Outstanding Amount ($ MM)	Default/Exchange Date
Bank of New England	SF Deb '99	8.85	15.9	Jan-91
Bank of New England	Deposit Nts '92	9.00	100.0	Jan-91
Bank of New England	F/R Sub Nts '96	8.38	75.0	Jan-91
Bank of New England	Deposit Nts '93	9.00	100.0	Jan-91
Bank of New England	Nts '96	9.50	150.0	Jan-91
Bank of New England	Sub Nts '99	9.88	250.0	Jan-91
Bank of New England	Sub Cap Nts '99	8.75	200.0	Jan-91
Best Products	Deb '94	9.00	10.4	Jan-91
Best Products	Sr Sub Nts '96	12.63	2.4	Jan-91
Eagle Picher Industries	SF Deb '17	9.50	50.0	Jan-91
Insilco	Sr Sub Nts '99	15.00	270.0	Jan-91
Insilco	Sub Disc Deb '01	0.00	185.0	Jan-91
Insilco	Sr Nts '97	9.50	75.0	Jan-91
Pan American World Airways	Eq SF Ctfs B '94	11.50	15.0	Jan-91
Pan American World Airways	Sr Deb '03	13.50	100.0	Jan-91
Pan American World Airways	Sr Deb '04	15.00	130.0	Jan-91
Peebles	Sr Sub Nts '99	14.75	80.0	Jan-91
Price Communications	Sub Nts '95	11.75	62.0	Jan-91
Price Communications	Sub Deb '00	14.63	73.0	Jan-91
Price Communications	Sub Nts '96	13.00	96.0	Jan-91
Trans World Airlines	Sr Nts '92	16.00	87.5	Jan-91
Trans World Airlines	Jr Sub Deb '01	12.00	328.0	Jan-91
Trans World Airlines	Sr Nts '93	17.25	266.0	Jan-91
Trans World Airlines	ETC's: '94 to '96	12.00	191.0	Jan-91
Trans World Airlines	Sr Sec Nts '94	15.00	239.0	Jan-91
Trans World Airlines	Jr Sub Deb '08	12.00	212.0	Jan-91
USG	Sr Sub Deb '00	13.25	600.0	Jan-91
USG	Jr Sub PIK Deb '08	16.00	150.0	Jan-91
USG	Deb '17 (a)	8.75	200.0	Jan-91
USG	Sr Nts '91 (a)	7.38	100.0	Jan-91
USG	Sr Nts '96 (a)	8.00	100.0	Jan-91
USG	Sr Nts '97 (a)	8.00	100.0	Jan-91
USG	Sub SF Deb '91	4.88	3.0	Jan-91
USG	SF Deb '04 (a)	7.88	42.0	Jan-91
WTD Industries	Sr Sub Deb '97	12.50	23.0	Jan-91
Carter Hawley Hale	Sr Sub Deb '02	12.50	225.0	Feb-91
Carter Hawley Hale	Sr Sub Nts '96	12.25	125.0	Feb-91
Charter Medical	Sr Sub Debs '00	14.00	355.0	Feb-91
Charter Medical	Sub Deb '02	14.25	200.0	Feb-91
Charter Medical	Jr Sub Deb '08	15.85	260.0	Feb-91
Charter Medical	Sr Disc Nts '98	0.00	240.0	Feb-91
CR Anthony	Sr Sub Deb '02	12.13	25.0	Feb-91
EUA Power	Series B Sec Nts '91	17.50	180.0	Feb-91
EUA Power	Series C Sec Nts '91	17.50	100.0	Feb-91
Hills Department Stores	Sr Sub Deb '95	14.13	95.0	Feb-91
Hills Department Stores	Sub Deb '97	14.63	51.0	Feb-91
Hills Department Stores	Sr Nts '92	13.50	87.0	Feb-91
JPS Textile Group	Sr VR Nts '96	12.00	100.0	Feb-91

Company	Bond Issue	Coupon (%)	Outstanding Amount ($ MM)	Default/Exchange Date
JPS Textile Group	Sr Sub Disc Nts '99	0.00	160.0	Feb-91
JPS Textile Group	Sr Sub Nts '99	15.25	125.0	Feb-91
JPS Textile Group	Sr Sub '00	14.25	75.0	Feb-91
Lexington Precision	Sub Nts '97	12.75	27.8	Feb-91
McCrory Parent (E-II Hdlgs)	SF Deb '09	11.75	12.0	Feb-91
McCrory Parent (E-II Hdlgs)	Sub SF Deb '99	12.00	12.0	Feb-91
McCrory Parent (E-II Hdlgs)	Sr Sub Nts '94	14.50	105.0	Feb-91
McCrory Parent (E-II Hdlgs)	Sub SF Deb '04	10.75	5.5	Feb-91
McCrory Parent (E-II Hdlgs)	Sub Deb '94	7.00	66.0	Feb-91
McCrory Parent (E-II Hdlgs)	Sub Deb '94	7.00	50.0	Feb-91
McCrory Parent (E-II Hdlgs)	Sub SF Deb '06	10.00	265.0	Feb-91
McCrory Parent (E-II Hdlgs)	SF Deb '08	15.00	123.0	Feb-91
McCrory Parent (E-II Hdlgs)	Disc Deb '07	0.00	92.0	Feb-91
McCrory Parent (E-II Hdlgs)	Sub SF Deb '05	11.00	11.0	Feb-91
McCrory Parent (E-II Hdlgs)	Sub SF Deb '03	10.75	144.0	Feb-91
CNC Holding	Sr Sub Nts	13.00	187.0	Mar-91
CNC Holding	Sub Deb	13.25	100.0	Mar-91
Continental Health Affiliates	Sub Deb '96	14.13	13.4	Mar-91
Homestead Savings	Sub Deb '95	15.00	41.5	Mar-91
Homestead Savings	Sub Deb '96	13.38	36.2	Mar-91
Meritor Savings	Sub Cap Nts '98	12.00	115.0	Mar-91
Triangle Pacific	Sr Sub Split Resets '98	7.83	180.3	Mar-91
US Home	Nts '94	13.25	34.9	Mar-91
US Home	Sr Sub Nts '96	12.38	63.5	Mar-91
US Home	Resets '97	17.5	7.7	Mar-91
US Home	Resets '00	13.50	0.1	Mar-91
Enstar	Swiss Eurobonds '95	5.75	23.3	Apr-91
Enstar	Sub Swiss Eurobonds '95	6.00	38.6	Apr-91
Executive Life Insurance	Nebraska Inv Fin '93	8.34	100.0	Apr-91
Executive Life Insurance	Louisiana Agr Fin '96	8.25	150.0	Apr-91
Executive Life Insurance	Louisiana Agr Fin '96		150.0	Apr-91
Executive Life Insurance	Louisiana Agr Fin '96	8.80	150.0	Apr-91
Executive Life Insurance	El Pas TX Housing '96		200.0	Apr-91
Executive Life Insurance	Adam County CO IDA '96	9.00	300.0	Apr-91
Executive Life Insurance	Nebraska Inv Fin '96	9.50	100.0	Apr-91
Executive Life Insurance	SE Tx Housing Fin '96	8.60	300.0	Apr-91
Executive Life Insurance	Memphis TN Health '96	8.86	400.0	Apr-91
Marcade Group	Sr Sub Nts '95	13.75	12.1	Apr-91
Sudbury	Sub Nts '93	10.50	25.0	Apr-91
Sunshine Precious Metals	Silver Index '95	8.00	8.0	Apr-91
Sunshine Precious Metals	Silver Index '95	9.50	19.2	Apr-91
Sunshine Precious Metals	Silver Index '95	10.75	9.1	Apr-91
Sunshine Precious Metals	Silver Index '95	8.50	4.3	Apr-91
Sunshine Precious Metals	Silver Index '94	9.00	20.1	Apr-91
Sunshine Precious Metals	Silver Index '95	8.50	5.9	Apr-91
Sunshine Precious Metals	Silver Index '04	9.75	1.3	Apr-91
Sunshine Precious Metals	Silver Index '94	9.50	16.8	Apr-91
Appletree Markets	Sr Sub Deb '00	13.75	85.0	May-91
Barry's Jewelers	Sub Nts '01	12.63	46.5	May-91
First Capital Holdings	Sr Sub Deb '99	13.00	115.0	May-91
First City Industries	Sr Sub Nts '91	9.42	97.0	May-91
Gaylord Container	Sub Nts '96	13.50	250.0	May-91
NACO Finance	Sr Nts '94	12.00	127.0	May-91
Nortek	Sub Fixed Nts '91	8.92	31.0	May-91
Damson Oil	Sub Deb '03	12.00	5.5	Jun-91

Company	Bond Issue	Coupon (%)	Outstanding Amount ($ MM)	Default/Exchange Date
Damson Oil	Sub Deb '00	13.20	6.1	Jun-91
Lionel	Sub Nts '96	12.38	24.6	Jun-91
Mayflower	Sr Sub Deb '96	12.63	160.0	Jun-91
Orion Pictures	Sr Sub Reset Nts '98		199.8	Jun-91
Orion Pictures	Class A Sr Sub Nts '92	6.00	1.8	Jun-91
Orion Pictures	Class B Sr Sub Nts '92	12.00	2.0	Jun-91
Orion Pictures	Sub Deb '94	10.00	44.9	Jun-91
Orion Pictures	Sub SF Deb '98	11.00	16.1	Jun-91
Orion Pictures	Sub SF Deb '99	10.00	5.1	Jun-91
Pay N'Pack	Sub Deb '98	13.25	110.0	Jun-91
Sterling Optical	Sub Deb '01	11.25	13.3	Jun-91
Sun Carrier	Sr Sub Nts '96	13.25	90	Jun-91
Columbia Gas Systems	Med Term Nts '00-20		50.0	Jul-91
Columbia Gas Systems	Deb '99	9.88	32.5	Jul-91
Columbia Gas Systems	SF Deb '94	9.00	18.5	Jul-91
Columbia Gas Systems	Deb '99	10.25	21.8	Jul-91
Columbia Gas Systems	SF Deb'97	7.50	23.7	Jul-91
Columbia Gas Systems	Deb '11	10.25	100.0	Jul-91
Columbia Gas Systems	SF Deb '96	9.13	18.6	Jul-91
Columbia Gas Systems	Deb' 13	10.15	100.0	Jul-91
Columbia Gas Systems	SF Deb '96	8.25	26.4	Jul-91
Columbia Gas Systems	Deb '12	10.50	200.0	Jul-91
Columbia Gas Systems	SF Deb '97	7.50	28.4	Jul-91
Columbia Gas Systems	Med Term Nts '98-19		200.0	Jul-91
Columbia Gas Systems	SF Deb '95	8.75	16.2	Jul-91
Columbia Gas Systems	Med Term Nts '98-20		200.0	Jul-91
Columbia Gas Systems	SF Deb '93	7.00	12.0	Jul-91
Columbia Gas Systems	SF Deb '95	10.13	13.9	Jul-91
Columbia Gas Systems	Deb '93	9.00	150.0	Jul-91
Columbia Gas Systems	SF Deb '93	7.25	15.0	Jul-91
Columbia Gas Systems	SF Deb '95	9.13	20.3	Jul-91
Columbia Gas Systems	SF Deb '98	7.50	23.7	Jul-91
Columbia Gas Systems	SF Deb '97	7.50	26.5	Jul-91
Columbia Gas Systems	SF Deb '96	8.38	33.0	Jul-91
Columbia Gas Systems	SF Deb '92	6.63	7.4	Jul-91
Diversified Industries	Sr Sub Deb '91	10.50	3.1	Jul-91
Diversified Industries	Var Rate IRB '09		14.0	Jul-91
Great American Industries	Sr Sub '94	12.75	22.0	Jul-91
Koger Properties	Sr Nts '97	8.40	66.6	Jul-91
Memorex Telex NV	Sr Nts '96	13.25	418.9	Jul-91
Memorex Telex NV	Sr Var Rate Nts '96		155.0	Jul-91
Memorex Telex NV	Sr Sub Nts '98	14.50	200.0	Jul-91
Memorex Telex NV	Sub Deb '99	15.00	225.0	Jul-91
Mutual Benefit Life	IDRs		638.8	Jul-91
Great American Bank	Sub Var Rate Nts '91		60.0	Aug-91
Great American Bank	Sr Sub Nts '95	13.25	33.0	Aug-91
Burnham Broadcasting	Sub Deb '99	13.88	32.0	Sep-91
Lavalin Industries	Deb '92	12.75	15.6	Sep-91
Petrolane Gas Service	Sr Sub Deb '99-01	13.75	375.0	Sep-91
Southeast Banking	Sub Nts '01	10.25	99.2	Sep-91
Southeast Banking	Float Rate Sub Nts '97		75.0	Sep-91
Southeast Banking	Sr Nts '93	11.25	57.1	Sep-91
Southeast Banking	Float Rate Sub Nts '96		44.8	Sep-91
Alleco	Sr Sub Deb '95	13.50	11.7	Oct-91
Alleco	Sr Sub Deb '95	13.50	11.7	Oct-91
Alleco	Sr Sub Deb '95	14.50	4.5	Oct-91

Company	Bond Issue	Coupon (%)	Outstanding Amount ($ MM)	Default/Exchange Date
Community National Bankcorp	Sub Nts '99	11.00	6.7	Oct-91
Rexene	Sr Inc Rate Nts '92	16.69	253.0	Oct-91
Rexene	Sr Sub Inc Rate Nts '92	17.81	150.0	Oct-91
Thermadyne Holdings	Sr Sub Def Reset '00	18.00	238.0	Oct-91
Thermadyne Holdings	Sub Reset '01	15.00	150.0	Oct-91
Work Wear	Sr Sub Nts '97	13.00	100	Oct-91
Amalgamated Investment	Jr Sub Deb '00	15.00	98.5	Nov-91
Gilbert/Robinson	Sr Sub Nts '99	15.00	85.0	Nov-91
Gordon Jewelry	Sr Nts '96	13.75	149.3	Dec-91
Maxwell Communication	Bearer Bonds	8.38	78.6	Dec-91
Maxwell Communication	Bearer Bonds	5.00	76.7	Dec-91
Maxwell Communication	Bearer Bonds	6.00	73.8	Dec-91
Maxwell Com Finance Canada	Deb '94	11.25	90.4	Dec-91
National Convenience Stores	Sr Sub '96	12.50	39.6	Dec-91
Zale	Sr Sub Deb '07	13.13	200.0	Dec-91
Zale	Sr Deb '01	13.25	100.0	Dec-91
Zale	Sr Deb '97	12.50	99.9	Dec-91
Zale	Sr Deb '95	11.90	75.0	Dec-91
Zale	Sr Deb '92	11.50	36.9	Dec-91
Zale Credit	Sr Nts '97	11.90	75.0	Dec-91
Zale Credit	Sr Nts '94	11.70	70.0	Dec-91
Zale Credit	Sr Nts' 92	11.30	71.4	Dec-91

Source: Merrill Lynch High Yield Master Index and Author's Compilation.

Appendix 23–B

Quarterly Default Rates
High Yield Debt Market
(1989–1991)

Quarter	Par Value of Debt Outstanding ($Billions)*	Amount of Debt Defaulted By Quarter ($Billions)	Quarterly Default Rates (%)
1989 1Q	$183.72 (est.)	$1.03	0.56%
2Q	191.19 (est.)	1.13	0.59
3Q	201.00	3.54	1.76
4Q	204.33 (est.)	2.41	1.18
		$8.11	4.09%
1990 1Q	$209.23 (est.)	$4.16	1.99%
2Q	209.62 (est.)	2.51	1.20
3Q	210.00	6.01	2.86
4Q	210.00 (est.)	5.67	2.70
		$18.35	8.75%
1991 1Q	$210.00 (est.)	$8.74	4.16%
2Q	210.00 (est.)	2.75	1.31
3Q	210.00	5.01	2.41
4Q	210.00	2.36	1.13
		$18.86	9.01%

Includes defaulted issues, par value at beginning of quarter.

Source: Edward I. Altman, New York University Compilation.

Appendix 23-C Corporate Bond Defaults by Industry

Industry	Number of Defaults																	
	1970–75	1976	1977	1978	1979	1980	1981	1982	1983	1984	1985	1986	1987	1988	1989	1990	1991	Total
Airlines/Air Cargo	3						1	2							1	1	2	10
Auto/Motor Carrier						1		2							3	3		9
Conglomerates						1						1	1	3	1	1	1	9
Consumer Goods													1			1	2	4
Energy	1						1	2	3	5	7	12	2	4			4	41
Financial Services	3			1	1		1	1	1	1	1			4	11	7	14	46
Leisure/Entertainment											2			4	4	8	2	20
General Manufacturing	5	1						7	1	1	2	6	2	3	1	4	6	39
Health Care											1	1	1			2	1	6
Miscellaneous Industries	5	1			1		1			2	6	3		2		4	4	29
Ocean Carriers	1				1					1	1							4
Railroads	9	1																10
Real Estate/Construction	5			1		1		2		1	1	1	1	1	3	7	5	29
REIT	1	3	5	1		2												12
Retailing	9		2					1	1	1				1	2	6	15	38
Telecom/Technology	9	1	1			2		2	2	2	1	1	3	1		3	4	32
Utilities													1	1				2
Total	51	7	8	5	3	5	4	17	12	12	19	23	15	24	26	47	62	340

Chapter 24

Rating Drift in High Yield Bonds*

Edward I. Altman
The Max L. Heine Professor of Finance
Stern School of Business, New York University, New York, NY
Duen Li Kao
Director of Investment Research
General Motors Investment Management Corporation, New York, NY

Much of the literature on high yield, low-rated, or junk bonds has concentrated on default rates and losses to investors within a total return context. For example, Altman and Nammacher (1987) examine defaults and performance using the traditional average annual rate approach. Altman (1989) and Asquith et al. (1989) utilize mortality/aging approaches to assess default risk and return (the former study only) on a cumulative basis. In virtually all of these studies, the general assumption is that a bond will either survive to maturity, be called prior to maturity, or default at some point after issuance. The last scenario involves the extreme rating "drift" of an issue from its original rating to its final default status (a D rating by Standard & Poor's).

Two recent studies enable us to analyze bond performance for less dramatic, but still important, credit quality changes. Changes across the full spectrum of original Moody's ratings are described by Lucas and Lonski (1991). Altman and Kao (1991) analyze both the descriptive and predictive aspects of rating changes on the population of 1970–1988 new issues rated by Standard & Poor's. The latter study utilizes a Markov chain approach to model future rating changes based on past experience.

Our 1991 monograph concentrates on original ratings from AAA to CCC, for up to ten years after issuance. The present note focuses primarily on the high yield debt population, with a careful analysis of differences in experience between original issue high yield and those that declined from investment grade ("fallen angels"). In addition, we analyze the serial correlation of high yield bond rating changes with respect to credit quality changes subsequent to initial

rating changes. We concentrate on these subsequent rating changes, rather than total return.

Sample Characteristics

This study analyzes a subsample from the over 7,000 rating changes reported on in our original study.[1] We concentrate on 1,548 issues, of which 1,112 (72%) were originally issued as below investment grade securities and 436 (28%) obtained this status via the fallen angel route.

Our analysis covers the entire 19-year new issue period, 1970–1988. The results, however, are virtually identical to the experience of high yield bonds for the shorter period 1977–1989 in which new low-grade issuance increased dramatically. Indeed, of the 1,112 new low-grade bonds issued during 1970–1988, more than 94% were issued from 1977 onward, while an even greater proportion of fallen angels (96%) entered the noninvestment grade universe during or after 1977. We utilize the entire observation period in our analysis in order to maximize the sample size.

The number of observations diminishes as the post-issuance observation period lengthens. This is partly attributable to redemptions of debt prior to maturity and capital restructurings during bankruptcy. In addition, bonds issued in the 1980s could not be tracked beyond 1989, the last year of our analysis.

While our analysis concentrates on low-grade issues, we also present some comparative statistics for investment grade bonds, particularly noting the

*This is a reprint of the same article which appeared in *The Journal of Fixed Income*, March 1992.

differences between the BBB and higher quality (AAA, AA and A) categories. Finally, we distinguish between utility and nonutility fallen angels in our analysis. This distinction proves to be extremely significant. After describing our empirical findings, we discuss a number of practical conclusions.

Empirical Results

The one-, three-, five- and ten-year post-issuance rating transition results for our original issue low-grade bond population are listed in Table 24.1. In Table 24.2, we observe aggregate upgrade and downgrade experience and we further distinguish between public utilities (mainly electric power companies) and nonutilities (industrials and finance companies) in our breakdown of fallen angels (Table 24.3). We have stratified the sample in this manner based on our earlier observation (Altman, 1991) that public utilities outperformed nonutilities on a total return basis in the period following downgrading to below investment grade. We conjectured that this superior performance resulted from a general improvement in credit quality of utilities. Note that the 1991 study covered the 1984–1988 period only.

Original Issue Low-Grade Bonds

We observe that original issue high yield bonds have essentially an equal incidence of upgrades and downgrades after issuance. Upgrades were slightly greater (4.1%) than downgrades (3.8%) after one year and were identical after ten years (28.1%). Downgrades were slightly greater than upgrades for the three- and five-year horizons, although the differences were not statistically significant.

At every noninvestment grade rating level and for all observation periods, the majority of issues held steady or improved in quality. As an example, of bonds initially rated B, 59.9% remained in that category after five years and another 16.2% were upgraded. At the same time, however, downgrades exceeded upgrades for the five-year horizon and 9% of the Bs dropped all the way to D (default).

Table 24.1   Rating Transitions for Original Issue Low-Grade Bonds (1970–1989)

Rating After One Year (%)

Number of bonds	Original Rating	AAA	AA	A	BBB	BB	B	CCC	CC	C	D
237	BB	0.0	0.0	0.0	6.8	86.1	6.3	0.8	0.0	0.0	0.0
702	B	0.0	0.0	0.1	1.6	1.7	94.0	1.7	0.3	0.0	0.0
173	CCC	0.0	0.0	0.0	0.0	0.0	2.9	92.5	0.0	2.3	2.3
13	CC	0.0	0.0	0.0	0.0	0.0	0.0	0.0	84.6	15.4	0.0

Rating After Three Years (%)

Number of bonds	Original Rating	AAA	AA	A	BBB	BB	B	CCC	CC	C	D
170	BB	0.6	0.6	1.8	17.1	62.9	11.8	2.9	0.6	0.0	1.8
431	B	0.2	0.2	1.2	1.9	4.2	75.4	10.7	1.2	1.4	3.7
77	CCC	0.0	0.0	1.3	0.0	2.6	14.3	66.2	1.3	2.6	11.7
9	CC	0.0	0.0	0.0	0.0	0.0	11.1	11.1	44.4	0.0	33.3

Rating After Five Years (%)

Number of bonds	Original Rating	AAA	AA	A	BBB	BB	B	CCC	CC	C	D
103	BB	0.0	0.0	7.8	20.4	40.8	16.5	6.8	1.0	0.0	6.8
222	B	0.5	0.0	2.7	4.5	8.6	59.9	13.5	0.5	0.9	9.0
28	CCC	0.0	0.0	3.6	3.6	0.0	35.7	28.6	7.1	0.0	21.4

Rating After Ten Years (%)

Number of bonds	Original Rating	AAA	AA	A	BBB	BB	B	CCC	CC	C	D
37	BB	0.0	0.0	10.8	27.0	21.6	13.5	18.9	2.7	0.0	5.4
52	B	1.9	0.0	7.7	9.6	5.8	53.8	9.6	0.0	0.0	11.5
7	CCC	0.0	0.0	0.0	0.0	0.0	0.0	85.7	0.0	0.0	14.3

Note: Boxed numbers are percentages for which ratings did not change following issuance.

Table 24.2   Aggregate Rating Transitions for Original Issue Low-Grade Bonds
(1970–1989)

		Unchanged		Upgrades		Downgrades	
Year(s) After Issuance	Total Issues	Number	Percent	Number	Percent	Number	Percent
1	1,112	1,024	92.1%	46	4.1%	43	3.8%
3	678	678	71.2	82	12.1	113	16.7
5	353	353	51.8	77	21.8	93	26.4
10	96	96	45.1	27	28.1	27	28.1

Table 24.3   Rating Transitions for Fallen Angel Low-Grade Bonds (1970–1989)

			Unchanged		Upgrades		Downgrades	
Year (s) After F.A. *	Type of Bond	Total Issues	Number	Percent	Number	Percent	Number	Percent
1	Utilities	186	122	65.5%	58	31.2%	6	3.2%
	Nonutilities	250	199	79.6	6	3.6	42	16.8
3	Utilities	161	83	51.6	60	37.3	18	11.1
	Nonutilities	159	64	40.2	49	30.8	46	29.0
5	Utilities	89	9	10.1	76	85.4	4	4.5
	Nonutilities	59	14	23.8	18	30.5	27	45.7
10	Utilities	8	0	0.0	7	87.5	1	12.5
	Nonutilities	16	2	12.5	7	43.8	7	43.8

* Year (s) after becoming fallen angel.

Fallen Angels

The aggregate fallen angel population demonstrated a greater propensity for upgrades than for downgrades for every horizon. This result, however, was wholly attributable to the exceptional performance of the public utility segment. For utilities, upgrades dominated downgrades by 31.2% versus 3.2% after one year, by 85.4% versus 4.5% for five years, and by 87.5% versus 12.5% for ten years. Meaningful rate relief was accorded the vast majority of low-grade utilities. More recently, there has been a greater incidence of further deterioration by utilities following their demotion to the fall angel category. For example, Columbia Gas System and El Paso Electric defaulted during 1991. Nevertheless, the experience of fallen angel utilities in the 1970s and 1980s is, in our opinion, an important indicator for the future.

Nonutility fallen angels had a different experience, ranging from virtually equivalent numbers of upgrades and downgrades among their subsequent rating changes (i.e., in years 3 and 10 after the drop to low-grade status) to a greater incidence of further downgrades in year 1 and 5 after the initial downgrade (Table 24.3). And, while the aggregate experience was balanced or slightly favoring future downgrades, the magnitude of the subsequent rating change was dramatic. Defaults occurred in at least 23 cases (out of 320) within three years after the initial downgrade. These dramatic cases no doubt resulted in significant losses to investors, far greater than the small gains from upgrades.

Investment Grade Bond Results

Unlike low-grade issues, investment grade bonds as a whole experienced considerably more downgrades than upgrades. Table 24.4 lists the initial rating change results for investment grade issues, with a further breakdown between the AAA/AA/A categories and the BBB category. While the AAA/AA/A original issues had a predominantly negative first rating change performance for all horizons, the BBB category posted a definite propensity toward upgrades vis-a-vis downgrades. This phenomenon was discussed in Altman and Kao (1991) and is consistent with the superior performance of BBB bonds during the 1980s (Altman, 1990).

Serial Correlation Tests

One of the more intriguing questions regarding bond rating changes is whether an investor can learn anything from past changes. In our earlier mono-

Table 24.4   Aggregate First Rating Change Experience Original Issue Investment
Grade Bonds 1970–1989

		AAA/AA/A Bonds					
Year (s) After	Total	Unchanged		Upgrades		Downgrades	
Issuance	Issues	Number	Percent	Number	Percent	Number	Percent
1	4,976	4,607	97.6%	76	1.5%	293	5.9%
3	3,989	3,142	78.8	170	4.3	677	17.0
5	2,927	2,061	70.4	163	5.6	703	24.0
10	1,645	904	55.0	131	8.0	610	37.1
		BBB Bonds					
Year (s) After	Total	Unchanged		Upgrades		Downgrades	
Issuance	Issues	Number	Percent	Number	Percent	Number	Percent
1	1,090	982	90.1%	60	5.5%	48	4.4%
3	807	592	93.4	126	15.6	89	11.0
5	514	388	65.7	111	21.6	65	12.7
10	217	94	43.3	86	39.6	37	17.1

graph, we constructed several Markov chain models to assist us in modeling future changes, with considerable success. In this study, we ask two questions:

1. After the original issue low-grade bonds experience a rating change, does the next change (if any) tend to be in the same direction?
2. For our fallen angel population, do subsequent changes tend to continue in the downgrade direction?

We can also examine whether two changes in the same direction are an accurate predictor of any further changes. Note that in all of these rating change serial correlation tests, a change can be as small as a single "notch" within a major letter rating, e.g., BB to BB–. Finally, in addition to our tests on

the low-grade, high yield population, we will again split the investment grade issues into the AAA/AA/A and BBB categories.

Table 24.5 lists the first rating change for our three major categories as well as breaking down the fallen angels by utilities and nonutilities and the investment grades by AAA/AA/As and BBBs. It should be noted that with respect to the fallen angel population, the first rating change after becoming a fallen angel is really a second change and can therefore be tested for serial correlation. Our observations are for new issues covering the period 1970–1985 rather than through the entire period ending 1989. This is necessitated by the fact that the vast majority of issues took up to four years to experience their first rating changes.

Table 24.5   First Rating Change Experience for New Issues 1970–1985

Type of Bond	Total	Unchanged	Downgrade (D)	Upgrade (U)	D/U
Original Issue High Yield	620	142	239	239	1.00
Investment Grade					
AAA,AA,A	3733	1139	1859	735	2.53[2]
BBB	732	157	252	323	0.78
	Total	Unchanged	DD	DU	DU/DD
Fallen Angels[1]					
Utilities	193	20	32	141	4.40[2]
Nonutilities	155	15	86	50	0.58[2]

[1]Based on first rating change after becoming fallen angel.
[2]Significant at 0.01 level.

Our first result concerns original issue low-grade bonds. We find that the first rating change after issue has an equivalent probability of being an upgrade (U) as it has of being a downgrade (D). Expressing the same point in the notation we have developed for this research, the D/U ratio = 1.00. We will not comment upon the result for the aggregate fallen angel population, since it will be misleading until it is broken down by utilities and nonutilities. For investment grade original issues, the AAA/AA/A categories experienced a far greater proportion of downgrades than upgrades: D/U = 2.53. BBB bonds experienced a greater proportion of upgrades (323 versus 252, D/U=0.78), again showing the group's distinctively attractive characteristics vis-a-vis the rest of the higher rated issues.

The figures for fallen angels in Table 24.5 actually reflect a subsequent rating change after each downgrade. Results show that public utility fallen angels demonstrate strong negative serial correlation, i.e., reversal of direction. For issues that do experience a second change, the proportion of upgrades following the original downgrade (DU) is 81.5% (141/173), compared to only 18.5% for two consecutive downgrades (DD). The ratio of DU/DD is therefore 4.40, easily significant at the 0.01 level.

The opposite result is realized for the nonutility fallen angels. That is, the number of subsequent downgrades after dropping to fallen angel status (DD) far exceeds the number of subsequent upgrades. The ratio of DU/DD for nonutilities is only 0.58 (50/86). Again the test is significant at the 0.01 level but this time it indicates significant *positive* serial correlation.

In Table 24.6, we proceed to the next level of rating changes. In order to be tested for serial correlation, an original issue low-grade bond must have a second rating change. Recall that the initial changes for these issues indicated equivalent proportions of upgrades and downgrades (Table 24.5). If the initial change is a downgrade, though, the second change is usually in the same direction, i.e., DD. Indeed, the ratio of DD/DU, assuming a second change does take place, is 2.58. This results in a sign-test of 10.5, easily significant at the 0.01 level. On the other hand, if the initial change is an upgrade, the next change is also more often than not in the same direction (UU/UD=1.33, with a sign-test of 3.5). Positive serial correlation in upgrades is not nearly as significant as the downgrade positive serial correlation, however.

Investment grade AAA/AA/A downgrades are also usually followed by subsequent downgrades, with a DD/DU ratio of 2.86 and a very significant sign-test of 35.9. Initial upgrades of these groups show subsequent rating changes that favor a reversal of direction (UU/UD=0.78). If we observe the BB investment grades, however, we again find positive performance (UU/UD=1.47).

Our final tests involve fallen angels with at least three rating changes. We find that the limited number of utilities that experienced two consecutive downgrades had a very small chance of experiencing a third downgrade (DDD) rather than a reversal (DDU). On the other hand, utility fallen angels that had reversals (i.e., that were upgraded) just after falling to "junk" status had a strong likelihood of continuing to be upgraded (DDU), if further rating changes took place.

Conclusions

A number of practical investment conclusions emerge from our results. One finding that is partic-

Table 24.6   Subsequent Rating Change Experience

Type of Bond	First Change: Downgrade				First Change: Upgrade			
	DD	DU	DD/DU	Sign-Test	UU	UD	UU/UD	Sign-Test
Original Issue High Yield	103	40	2.58	10.5	84	63	1.33	3.5
Investment Grade								
AAA, AA, A	1,028	360	2.86	35.9	193	247	0.78	5.1
BBB	101	85	1.19	2.3	125	85	1.47	5.5
Fallen Angels[1]								
Utilities	5	25	0.20	7.3	23	6	3.83	6.3
Nonutilities	40	27	1.48	3.2	74	41	1.80	6.2

[1] Based on second rating change after becoming fallen angel.

ularly pertinent for high yield investors is that original issue speculative grade companies display no tendency either to rise or to decline in quality over time. This result contrasts with pronouncements made by both advocates and critics of high yield bonds. Boosters of such debt sometimes claim these securities represent borrowings by "rising stars" of American industry, headed for inevitable upgrading. Detractors argue, quite the contrary, that overleveraged "junk bond" companies are ticking time bombs for which credit deterioration is preordained. While this may have been the case for certain corporate restructuring bonds issued in 1986–1989, our results show it was decidedly not true for the average low-grade bond issued prior to 1986. Moreover, we expect it will generally not be the case for new issues after 1990.

For original issue low-grade bonds that do experience an initial downgrade, however, the outlook is much bleaker. Our results indicate that the credit prospects of these issues should be very carefully assessed before a decision is made to retain them in one's portfolio. The opposite outlook pertains to issues experiencing an initial upgrade.

Another instructive finding is the contrast between the public utility and the nonutility fallen angels. The numbers say that for nonutilities, investors' better course is generally to cut their losses at the point of downgrading to speculative grade. Further deterioration occurs in the vast majority of cases. Utility fallen angels show a decidedly more positive outlook, however, with as much as an 80% frequency of subsequent upgrading.

Finally, AAA/AA/A original issues that are downgraded display continued downgrading in the great majority of cases. BBB original issues, however, not only show a greater likelihood of being initially upgraded than downgraded, but their upgrade bias continues for subsequent changes.

Endnotes

1. In Altman and Kao (1991), we analyzed 7,195 rating changes for all new issues of 1970–1988, where only major letter changes, e.g., AA to A, B to BB, etc., were covered. We thank the Association of Investment Management Research, Charlotte, VA, for its financial support and the Standard and Poor's Corporation for supplying the raw data.

2. The test for significance is the sign-test, whereby we assess whether the initial rating change (in this case D) is followed by one in the same direction. The test is of the form:

$$Z = \frac{N_{SD} - N_{RD}}{\frac{1}{2}\sqrt{N}}$$

where:

N_{SD} = Number of rating changes in same direction

N_{RD} = Number of rating changes in the reverse direction

N = Total number of observations

References

Altman, Edward I. *Default Risk, Mortality Rates and the Performance of Corporate Bonds.* Charlottesville: The Research Foundation of the Institute of Chartered Financial Analysts, 1989, and *The Journal of Finance,* September 1989.

Altman, Edward I. *Distressed Securities: Analyzing and Evaluating Market Potential and Investment Risk.* Chicago: Probus Publishing, 1991.

Altman, Edward I. "How 1989 Changed the Hierarchy of Fixed Income Security Performance." *Financial Analysts Journal,* May/June 1990.

Altman, Edward I. and Duen Li Kao. *Corporate Bond Rating Drift: An Examination of Rating Agency Credit Quality Changes.* Charlottesville: Association for Investment Management Research, 1991.

Altman, Edward I. and Scott A. Nammacher. *Investing in Junk Bonds.* New York: John Wiley & Sons, 1987.

Asquith, Paul, David W. Mullins, Jr. and Eric D. Wolff. "Original Issue High Yield Bonds: Aging Analysis of Defaults, Exchanges and Calls." *The Journal of Finance,* September 1989.

Lucas, Douglas J. and John G. Lonski. "Changes in Corporate Credit Quality 1970–1990." *Moody's Special Report,* February 1991, and *The Journal of Fixed Income,* March 1992.

Chapter 25

Separating the Jewels From the Junk

Neil D. Dabney
Co-founder and Senior Portfolio Manager
Dabney/Resnick and Wagner, Inc., Beverly Hills, CA
Darryl L. Schall
Senior Researcher
Dabney/Resnick and Wagner, Inc., Beverly Hills, CA

> Speculative excess, referred to concisely as a mania, and revulsion from such excess in the form of a crisis, crash or panic can be shown to be, if not inevitable, at least historically common.
>
> (Charles P. Kindelberger – *Manias, Panics and Crashes*)

Many leveraged buyouts, recapitalizations, mergers, and acquisitions executed in the late 1980s appear, with the help of hindsight, to have been speculative folly. In their time, these transactions appeared attractively priced and were based upon seemingly solid fundamentals: good management, steady earnings track records, recession resistant businesses, commanding market shares, and significant barriers to entry. During this period, the U.S. economy was experiencing its longest run of growth and prosperity in the post-World War II era. Increased interest in the market for high-yield securities pushed underwritings to over $200 billion during the 1980s. To many market participants, it seemed as though the appetite for high-yield securities had no limits.

Businesses that had displayed strong earnings momentum throughout the expansion incurred heavy debt loads at their cyclical peaks with increasing frequency. Financial projections were based upon sustaining annual sales and earnings growth rates of 15% to 20%, which for many companies proved too aggressive to achieve. The success of many transactions relied on subsequent asset sales at record multiples. Accelerated debt amortization schedules left little room for error. Capital structures, which included pay-in-kind or discount/zero coupon bonds, were created to allow companies to defer current cash interest payments, so that they could "grow" into their debt burdens. Unfortunately for some companies, these securities turned out to be time-bombs when envisioned growth did not materialize.

The high-yield market crashed in 1990, closing the doors to easy credit. In December 1989, the high-yield index traded at 625 basis points over treasuries. Within one year that spread had widened to over 1,325 basis points. What was thought of as a rational, functioning market for high-yield securities evaporated. Drexel Burnham Lambert, Inc., the principal high-yield market maker, filed for Chapter 11 protection. Mounting negative economic pressures caused a cash flow squeeze among weaker, more leveraged borrowers. Bank and insurance companies tightened their lending standards. An ensuing credit crunch caused liquidity to dissipate. Motivated by political scapegoating, government regulators promulgated new rules that exacerbated the recessionary drift. The once buoyant high-yield market succumbed to gravity. Selling induced more selling. The market's deterioration was due as much to a supply/demand imbalance as it was to a decline in credit quality.

If one could step out of this quagmire and take an impartial view, what could be learned? Did value just vanish? Was the high-yield market based solely on hype and accounting puffery, or did the pendulum swing too far? Could solid keystones of earnings and asset quality be found, given sufficient examination and analysis?

In markets driven by panic, there are techniques and methods by which one can ascertain relative value and make calculated judgments that are conservative relative to apparent risk. What follows is a brief explanation of our methodology, introducing

277

concepts of enterprise value, valuation of debt at "market" value versus face value, and calculation of asset and interest coverage ratios. We incorporate these analytic techniques into recent case study illustrations. After gaining a basic understanding of valuation techniques, we then discuss how the restructuring process impacts upon investing in distressed companies. We conclude by describing strategy considerations in purchasing and selling securities.

Basic Valuation Methods

Many times an investment opportunity is brought to our attention in the following manner: "The bonds are trading at 10 cents on the dollar, how much lower can they get?" Our reflexive response is "they can be worthless!" A severe discount might signal an investment opportunity, but without an understanding of intrinsic value, one would be merely gambling. The first step in the investment analysis is to measure the market value of debt against the underlying value of assets. The next procedure is to assess how the restructuring process may affect estimated asset values.

In distressed situations, investment decisions based upon face value of debt can be likened to valuing assets based upon book value. Both may have had significance in the past, but today's market prices for assets and liabilities provide a better proxy for current and future value. By gauging the market value of debt against the market value of assets, one can measure downside risk. In other words, an investor can determine the extent to which the principal value of an investment is covered by company assets. The first example analyzes JPS Textile Group, Inc.

JPS Textile Group, Inc.

JPS Textile Group, Inc. (JPS), an industrial textile manufacturer, was an LBO organized in 1988 by Odyssey Partners, a New York investment firm. JPS acquired the assets of five operating divisions of J.P. Stevens & Co. at a cost of $563 million, a multiple of 8.0 times earnings before interest, taxes, and depreciation (EBITD). The five divisions were organized into three segments by JPS: 1) apparel fabrics (31% of sales and 73% of operating profits)—a leading manufacturer of woven fabrics, yarn, and elastic products; 2) industrial fabrics (46% of sales and 11% of operating profits)—a producer of automotive carpets and liner fabrics; and 3) home fashion textiles (23% of sales and 16% of operating profits)—a manufacturer of home and commercial carpeting.

This transaction exhibited many of the symptoms of what has been described as speculative folly. The

capital structure—composed of 88% debt, including $160 million of high-coupon 16.25% discount notes—was feasible only if the company could sustain then current growth. Although the predecessor divisions indicated strong sales growth since 1986, gross margins had declined over 22.2% from 16.2% in 1986 to 12.6% in 1988. Many of the company's customers (automobile makers, construction companies, and apparel manufacturers) were susceptible to a recession. JPS managed to make its cash interest payments and maintain certain capital expenditures. However, it faced an onerous increase in interest expense when the discount notes required cash coupon payments in 1992, as well as a tough bank debt amortization schedule. Anticipating a cash flow shortfall, the company tried in vain to execute an exchange offer for the various outstanding issues of debt. Eventually, JPS was able to negotiate a prepackaged bankruptcy restructuring with a bondholder steering committee. At the restructuring's effective date, March 31, 1991, the company's capital structure was as shown in Table 25.1.

Table 25.1 shows that the "market" value of JPS's total debt was significantly discounted from its face value ($273.5 million versus $524.3 million, or 52% of face value). Since one would invest based upon prevailing market prices, we calculated the company's ratio of asset value to the market value of debt (a "coverage ratio"). These calculations are shown in Table 25.2. Using readily available prices, one can simply calculate the market value of each class of debt. However, estimating asset value is a more involved and subjective process. Businesses such as these are not commodities. Additionally, there is not necessarily a liquid market for the assets, even if broken up and sold piecemeal.

As a start, to determine the company's value, we applied a valuation multiple to projected EBITD for the coming year. We estimated EBITD, incorporating the following variables:

♦ historic operating performance;

♦ comparable industrial performance;

♦ the company's current business plan;

♦ detailed analysis of financial statement accounts;

♦ conversations with company executives, industry experts, and market analysts; and

♦ macroeconomic variables, such as employment data, interest rates, money supply, consumer savings and spending, etc.

To arrive at a valuation multiple, our analysis included an examination of the following factors:

Table 25.1   JPS Textiles, Inc. Mark–to–Mark Capitalization Table ($ millions)

	Face Value as of 3/31/91	Market Price as of 3/31/91	Market Value as of 3/31/91
Senior debt:			
Bank debt	$ 92.0	100.0%	$ 92.0
Senior notes	100.0	70.0	70.0
Total senior debt	$192.0		$162.0
Subordinated debt:			
16.25% Discount notes	133.7	28.0	37.4
15.25% Senior subordinated notes	123.6	43.0	53.1
14.25% Subordinated debentures	75.0	28.0	21.0
Total subordinated debt	322.2		111.5
Total debt	524.3		273.5
Senior preferred stock	37.7	10.0	3.77
Junior preferred stock	23.0	0.0	0.0
Common stock	5.0	0.0	0.0
Deficit	(150.8)		N / M
Total equity	$(122.8)		N / M
Total capitalization	$ 439.2		N / M

♦ estimating a range of comparable industry multiples;

♦ examining at what values companies with similar capital structures were trading in the public and, if available, private markets; and

♦ valuing multiples of other timely restructuring transactions.

The resultant asset coverage ratio and valuation analysis is shown in Table 25.2.

Table 25.2 designated the "enterprise value" as the market value of company assets. The enterprise value was estimated on three levels—"low," "mid" and "high"—which incorporated three estimates of projected EBITD and three estimated valuation multiples. We performed this analysis on a global level (total company EBITD) and on a segment basis (applying different valuation multiples to the various business segments). We then measured the enterprise value against the debt claims to calculate an asset coverage ratio. Traditional financial analysis would suggest that we utilize the face value of debt as a proxy; however, in distressed situations, we believe that the market value of debt is a more relevant measure because: 1) investment decisions are based upon market value today, not par value; and 2) negotiations that resolve claims in distressed situations are based upon the current recoveries not historical values. The above analysis suggested that total enterprise value (range: $300–$435 million) provided asset coverage of 1.1 times to 1.6 times,

and using a segment valuation (range: $328–$529 million), provided asset coverage of 1.2 times to 1.9 times. In other words, "market" debt claims appeared to be covered by asset values by 110% to 190%. Additionally, strict priority ratios (which allocate asset value to creditors in claim seniority) indicated that, even after assuming par recovery to bank debt and senior variable notes, each class of debt would be satisfied by company asset values. This analysis demonstrated that JPS's going concern value exceeded the market value of its debt claims. Barring a significant drop in operating cash flow, an investment in JPS debt appeared to have limited downside risk.

After determining asset coverage estimates, the following assumptions are layered as applicable: capital expenditures, working capital requirements, demands of parties in interest, and economic cycles.

Capital Expenditures. What is the current quality of assets—do they need repairs, upgrades, replacements? If applicable, what then is a normalized level of capital expenditures to maintain the current asset base or to expand that base if management's business plan calls for such expansion? These estimates are made in context of historical experience and industry standards.

Working Capital Requirements. Does management's business plan require an increase or decrease of working capital accounts (inventory, accounts receivable, accounts payable, current maturities of debt, etc.)? This analysis is again performed in the

Chapter 25

Table 25.2 JPS Textiles, Inc.
Coverage Ratios and Valuation Analysis ($ million)

Valuation as a whole:	Low	Mid	High
Projected 1991 EBITD	$ 75.0	$ 82.5	$ 87.0
Valuation multiple	4.0	4.5	5.0
Enterprise value (EV)	$300.0	$371.3	$435.0
Asset coverage			
EV/Face value of debt	0.6x	0.7x	0.8x
EV/ Market Value of debt	1.1x	1.4x	1.6x
Strict priority			
Bank Debt and Senior variable notes[1]	1.6x	1.9x	2.3x
Senior subordinated discount notes[2]	1.1x	1.3x	1.5x
Senior subordinated discount notes[2]	1.1x	1.3x	1.5x
Subordinated debentures	1.0x	1.2x	1.4x
Valuation segment by segment			
Apparel Fabric			
Projected 1991 EBITD	$ 43.9	$ 48.3	$ 51.0
Valuation multiple	5.0	6.0	7.0
Segment EV	$219.5	$289.8	$357.0
Industrial Fabric			
Projected 1991 EBITD	29.3	32.2	33.9
Valuation multiple	3.0	3.5	4.0
Segment EV	$ 87.8	$112.6	$135.6
Home Fashion			
Projected 1991 EBITD	10.4	11.4	12.1
Valuation multiple	2.0	2.5	3.0
Segment EV	$ 20.8	$ 28.5	$ 36.3
Total segment EV	$328.1	$430.9	$528.9
Asset coverage			
Segment EV/ Face value of debt	0.6x	0.8x	1.0x
Segment EV/Market value of debt	1.2x	1.6x	1.9x

[1]Recoveries for Bank Debt and Senior variable notes are assumed at par.
[2]Senior subordinated notes and Senior subordinated discount notes are *pari passu*.

context of industry standards, the current economic climate, and historical performance.

The impact of both the working capital and capital expenditure analyses will determine the level of cash flow available to amortize debt or to provide a cushion for future business needs. EBITD less capital expenditures and working capital requirements is defined as "free cash flow."

Demands of Parties in Interest. Different claimants to the company's assets have different agendas each with their own impact upon the restructuring process. Senior secured claimants (i.e., bank debt) might place certain demands upon the company that

significantly impact its earnings capacity. For instance, they may insist that certain businesses be sold to pay down debt, or that cash generated from operations be applied exclusively to amortization, letters of credit, or capital improvements.

Economic cycles. JPS's operations are cyclical. To understand recovery value, one must estimate whether the business is in its peak, mid, or trough phase. It is necessary to perform several variations of sensitivity analysis to test assumptions against varying degrees of risk.

Our preliminary analysis allowed us to conclude that based on a restructured balance sheet, JPS would have sufficient latitude to weather a protracted downturn and provide bondholders with significant risk-adjusted returns. Before an investment decision was made, we needed to assess the possibility of a successful restructuring and its impact on recovery values. Therefore, before completing the JPS case study, we incorporate a discussion of the financial restructuring process.

The Restructuring Process

We extend our analysis to focus on the *process* of restructuring the company's finances. Emphasis is added to the word *process* because a restructuring, in or out of court, is an extended negotiation with multiple parties, each with varied interests and motivations. Understanding the legal, accounting, and economic characteristics of a financial restructuring is critical to gauging recovery values and the timing of payoffs. A seemingly simple negotiation can deteriorate into a long drawn-out battle, reducing value for all parties. One must learn as much as possible about the economic motivations and legal leverage that each party brings to the negotiating table.

Secured Lenders

Secured lenders (usually banks, credit corporations, and insurance companies) focus much of their attention on maintaining their legal claim to collateral and on insuring that the value of this collateral does not diminish. Since they hold a collateral claim on the company's assets, they usually have a large degree of economic and legal leverage. In analyzing a credit with significant secured claims, it is important to determine that the secured lenders are comfortable with their collateral position and will work with the company to help satisfy parties with subordinate claims. We have seen many situations in which a rapid and significant reduction in asset value has caused secured lenders to exercise their foreclosure rights. This often results in chaos and, subsequently, reduces recovery values for other claimants. In the Eastern Airlines Chapter 11 proceedings, secured creditors eventually prevailed in bankruptcy court. The company was liquidated over the protestations of management and subordinated creditors as business operations consistently consumed cash and the market value of assets (principally jet aircraft, spare parts, and landing rights and gates at various airports) deteriorated. Eastern's unsecured creditors were virtually wiped out.

In order to consider investing in subordinated securities, our analysis allows for secured lenders' claims to be satisfied in full or bear the least degree of discount in either principal value or interest rate. We measure the relationship between the value of underlying collateral and the secured lender's claim using a strict priority analysis, where we allocate asset value to creditors in order of their seniority in the capital structure. This is important in determining recovery values as well as in measuring additional claims secured lenders can assert (specifically post-petition interest claims in Chapter 11 cases). We examine the extent to which security interests have been granted and whether or not these interests have been properly perfected. If there is asset value in excess of secured claims, or if security agreements have not been properly maintained, then there may be additional value available to subordinated claimants. An exchange offer made by Journal Company, Inc. (JCI) (formerly Ingersoll Newspapers) in mid-1991 allowed holders of senior subordinated and subordinated debt to exchange their securities for new senior secured debt guaranteed by and secured with pledges of the common stock of the operating subsidiaries of JCI. Investors choosing to participate in this offer essentially leap-frogged claims senior to them and, thus, improved their standing in JCI's capital structure. Had security interests been granted previously, this inventive exchange offer could not have been executed.

Additionally, there may be instances where secured lenders have overreached to protect their interests and, therefore, have helped to contribute to the company's financial distress. Issues of equitable subordination (a legal doctrine which allows for the subordination of claims of senior creditors because their adverse actions injured junior creditors) and fraudulent conveyance (a legal doctrine that requires the unwinding of a transaction found to have been constructively fraudulent) are being raised more frequently in examining unraveled LBOs. Interjecting these issues may improve the value of a subordinated claim.

In the case of Interco, a manufacturer of furniture and footwear currently in Chapter 11 reorganization, the holders of Medium Term Notes (MTNs), a senior unsecured claim, apparently have a good chance of full recovery by pressing fraudulent conveyance actions against the secured bank group. On face, the MTNs are *pari passu* with the bank claims and, thus, should be entitled to share equally with bank group recoveries. However, the MTN holders allege that the bank group helped structure the LBO transaction to their advantage and to the detriment of the MTNs. According to a court-appointed examiner, the MTN holders apparently have a strong argument. By using this legal leverage, these holders may gain a superior recovery vis-à-vis the secured bank group.

Subordinated Lenders

Most high-yield securities issued in the 1980s were unsecured and subordinated. Institutional holders, particularly insurance companies and mutual funds, are motivated by different accounting and economic conventions which shape their attitudes toward a restructuring. For instance, insurance companies historically do not mark their holdings to market and are resistant to reductions in their claims' principal value which would, in turn, penalize their capital position. Insurance companies often posture for outcomes that maintain relatively high face amounts, while accepting lower coupon rates.

In contrast, mutual funds, which do mark their holdings to market, are more flexible in accepting haircuts in par value. They tend to focus more on economic, rather than accounting-driven outcomes. Additionally, tensions arise between original issue holders and holders who purchased at a discount. Discount purchasers achieve their return objectives at lower thresholds; thus, tend to be more flexible in negotiations.

In the mid-1980s, there were hundreds of financial restructurings (e.g., exchange offers), in which bondholders would exchange one package of securities for another package. The exchange offer typically would contain a combination of the following: reduced coupon; reduced principal; enhanced or reduced security; changes in amortization schedules; company equity; and cutbacks in covenant protection. In many cases, interest rates were reduced and amortization schedules were extended to assist the distressed investor, while principal values remained at or near par; thus, obviating the dilemmas of marking to market. With the severe downturn in economic conditions and changes in state and federal regulations, original institutional holders have become more aggressive and tend not to accept exchange offers that are not heavily negotiated.

In today's financial markets, subordinated bondholders have become increasingly proactive because they are more knowledgeable, better organized, and have better access to professional advice. Additionally, more professional investors have entered the market for distressed securities. Institutions, investment funds, and entrepreneurial investors purchase distressed securities at significant discounts and are willing to test management's nerves by threatening foreclosure or involuntary bankruptcy. The mounting aggressiveness of original holders and the entry of professional investors are changing the expectations and recoveries of subordinated bondholders. Understanding the attitudes, skill, and resolve of these sophisticated participants is an essential step in the investment process.

Management and Sponsors

In most leveraged recapitalization and LBO transactions, the management and institutional investors that invested equity into these deals (sponsors) are important constituencies in the process. Managements, in almost all instances, have complete control over all business information and will use this information to their best advantage in maintaining their job status. Usually, only fraud or malfeasance enable creditor groups to act to successfully effect a change in management. Therefore, for better or worse, the management team in place may be the team that leads the company forward, post-restructuring. Assessment of management capabilities is critical to determining enterprise value.

Sponsors, like Odyssey Partners, guide management through the leveraging process and, with capital and reputation, stand behind the transaction to ensure its success. If a transaction is on the brink of collapse (as JPS was), the sponsor may be there to invest more equity to shore up finances and to lend expertise in restructuring negotiations. A financially strong sponsor may have as much to do with the ultimate outcome of a restructuring as would improving business or market conditions. A committed sponsor, in addition to investing new capital, may be the only party capable of quickly replacing a management team (sometimes a critical and always a difficult action).

Other Parties

As each situation of financial distress is different, there can be a multitude of other parties in interest that can impact upon the process. Tax agencies, pension guarantee agencies, governmental regulatory bodies, unions, organized equity-holders, and trade creditors may all have their say in negotiations. Again, one must identify each constituent group and understand what degree of leverage it holds. Successful investing in distressed situations requires constant evaluation of each party's demands.

Forums of Negotiation

In today's market we have primarily focused on three distinct forums of negotiation: out-of-court restructurings, Chapter 11 reorganizations, and "prepackaged" Chapter 11 reorganizations. There is a wide body of literature explaining the characteristics of each. The following is a brief outline of their advantages and disadvantages from an investor's perspective.

Out-of-Court Restructurings

A negotiation conducted between the company and select creditor groups is an out-of-court restructuring. It may not impact upon all claimants and is conducted with the advice of professionals (attorneys, accountants, investment bankers) representing informally designated creditor groups. In many circumstances, out of court restructurings require a super-majority of claimants (sometimes over 90% of a creditor group) to approve the transaction. Often this allows a small minority of claimants to "hold out" for better treatment than the majority received.

Advantages

1. Can be completed quickly and requires less attention from management. The business is less susceptible to managerial instability.

2. Less costly in terms of professional and court-related fees charged to the business.

3. Less uncertain in terms of business outcome. This process is more controlled by business interests. Economic recoveries have a greater chance of maximization.

Disadvantages

1. Outcome may provide only a temporary solution. Negotiations may be continued to a later date based upon the future outcome of business plans.

2. May not comprehensively address all parties in interest.

3. Subject to "holdouts."

4. Management is less compelled to provide complete access to financial and business plans.

Chapter 11 Reorganizations

A company files for protection under Chapter 11 of the U.S. Bankruptcy Code to stay actions of creditors and allow for the comprehensive reorganization of claims under the supervision of the federal courts. In Chapter 11 cases, claim-holders are organized into classes where they eventually vote for a plan of reorganization. This plan outlines the future business plan as well as contractually provides for the satisfaction of claims. For a plan to be accepted, 67% of the dollar value of each class as well as 50% of claimants in that class must approve the plan. Additionally, the plan must be approved by the bank-

ruptcy court and must demonstrate that the probability of future reorganization is low.

Advantages

1. Comprehensively addresses all categories of claims.

2. Compels a greater degree of disclosure of business and financial plans.

3. Eliminates holdouts and potential of preferred treatment of certain creditors.

4. Provides easier access for credit (e.g., debtor-in-possession financing).

Disadvantages

1. Expensive in terms of court costs and professional fees.

2. May damage business relationships with trade credit and customers.

3. Consumes more management time.

4. Outcomes are not as easy to predict.

"Pre-packaged" Chapter 11 Reorganizations

This negotiation is pre-negotiated, pre-approved plan of reorganization structured under the U.S. Bankruptcy Code. The plan binds all parties as in traditional Chapter 11 cases; however, the plan is filed concurrently with the opening of the case. The plan and its disclosure statement document are subject to approval by the bankruptcy court.

Advantages

1. Faster and cheaper than the traditional Chapter 11 process.

2. Binds holdouts.

Disadvantages

1. Risk that a pre-packaged plan is not approved by the court or claim-holders and so becomes subject to normal Chapter 11 uncertainties.

Application of Restructuring Process

Taking into consideration an understanding of basic valuation methods and the restructuring process, we now apply our analysis to the JPS situation. After negotiating with an informal bondholder committee, JPS forwarded a restructuring plan to be executed through a pre-packaged bankruptcy. As previously noted, in order for the plan to be approved it had to have been supported by a majority of bondholders representing at least two-thirds of the face value of each class of debt. The JPS plan disclosed that the bondholder committee controlled 62% of the face amount of JPS debt; thus, the probability of significant opposition was reduced. Table 25.3 summarizes the salient terms of the pre-packaged plan for bondholders.

Table 25.3 denotes that while principal amounts remained the same, interest rates were reduced in exchange for shares of common stock or, in the case of the senior notes, liens on capital stock. Interest on all of the above issues was to accrue (or, in the case

of the discount notes, accrete) at their original contracted rates until the earlier of the confirmation of the plan or 120 days after the bankruptcy filing. (Interest accruals at the old coupon rates produced current yields of 19% to 51% depending upon the issue.) The common stock distributed to bondholders was not to be transferable (without prior approval of the board of directors) for two years after confirmation of the plan.

Concurrently with the confirmation of the plan, Odyssey Partners and the management group was to contribute $7.5 million to retain 51% of the common equity. Additionally, an amended credit agreement with the senior lenders would be executed. The interest rate on borrowings under the agreement

---

Table 25.3   JPS Textiles, Inc.
Summary of Terms Under Prepackaged Bankruptcy Plan

	Old Senior Notes	*New Senior Notes*
Principal Amount:	$100 million	$100 million
Interest:	Variable/No less than 13.5%	11.75%
Mandatory Redemption:	$50 million on 6/1/95	$50 million on 6/1/94
Collateral:	General unsecured	Secured by second lien on subsidiaries' capital stock
Maturity:	6/1/96	6/1/95
Shares of Common Stock	none	none

	Old Discount Notes:	*New Discount Notes*
Principal Amount:	$160 million	To be determined on plan date
Interest:	16.25%	10.85%
Mandatory Redemption:	$40 million on 6/1/97 and 6/1/98	25% of issue on 6/1/97 and 6/1/98
Collateral:	General unsecured	General unsecured
Maturity:	6/1/99	6/1/99
Shares of Common Stock	none	150,000 shares (15% of common equity)

	Old Subordinated Notes	*New Subordinated Notes*
Principal Amount:	$125 million	$125 million
Interest:	15.50%	9.25%
Mandatory Redemption:	$31.25 million on 6/1/97 and 6/1/98	$31.25 million on 6/1/97 and 6/1/98
Collateral:	General unsecured	General unsecured
Maturity:	6/1/99	6/1/99
Shares of Common Stock	none	150,000 shares (15% of common equity)

	Old Debentures	*New Debentures*
Principal Amount:	$75 million	$75 million
Interest:	14.25%	7.00%
Mandatory Redemption:	$37.5 million on 5/15/99	$37.5 million on 5/15/99
Collateral:	General unsecured	General unsecured
Maturity:	5/15/00	5/15/00
Shares of Common Stock	none	190,000 shares (19% of common equity)

would be at prime plus 200 basis points. The amended credit agreement would include a new $25 million subfacility for purchase of the company's bonds. In addition, new covenants in the restructured bonds contained a $50 million carve-out for debt repurchase. These two provisions would allow the company to repurchase high-cost debt at a significant discount, thus improving overall credit quality.

Improved Credit Quality

Given the plan provisions, as summarized in Table 25.3, the restructuring would enhance credit quality. In particular, the reduced interest expense would translate into better interest coverage ratios and additional funds for capital expenditures and debt amortization. In the plan disclosure statement, JPS indicated that it posted EBITD of $82.7 million in fiscal 1990. Based on its existing debt structure, with cash interest at $60 million and total interest at $80 million, cash interest coverage was 1.4x and total interest coverage was 1.0x. The restructuring plan would reduce cash interest expense to $41 million and total interest expense to $56 million, which would give the company pro forma coverages of 2.0x and 1.5x for cash interest expense and total interest expense, respectively. We estimated that pro forma coverages would remain at those levels during the 12 months following plan approval, since JPS projected that fiscal 1991 EBITD would be flat at $82.5 million. JPS planned to increase annual outlays on capital expenditures ("CapX") from less than $15 million to $20 million. Given pro forma results for a higher level of CapX and lower interest, free cash flow would cover cash interest 1.5x in 1991.

Beyond 1991, we believed that coverages could improve when the apparel, auto, and residential construction markets recovered and company cash flow increased. Company projections through 1995 were as shown in Table 25.4.

Table 25.4 indicates that the proposed restructuring improved the credit quality by strengthening "interest coverages" (the ratio of EBITD to interest); however, projected free cash flow (while improved) remained minimal and certainly could not effectively amortize a large amount of debt. Since projected free cash flow was weak, this restructuring faced the possibility of a significant future adjustment in the form of a refinancing or asset sale.

Valuation of Securities

The combination of improved cash flow, ability to repurchase discounted debt, better amortization terms, and reduced cash and total interest expense led us to conclude that JPS bonds would trade at prices substantially higher than were quoted at the time of the plan announcement. Table 25.5 shows the price levels at which the new bonds would trade given various returns (with and without the previously mentioned equity allocation), taking into account the new rates and assuming a March 31, 1991, effective date for the plan.

From this analysis one could make judgments as to trading ranges of the prospective issues given an estimate of relative risk versus other restructured securities offered in the market at that time. Using Table 25.5, we made our own appraisal of bond value and calculated the expected returns given those estimates. Without taking into account the

---

Table 25.4   JPS Textiles, Inc.
Historical and Projected Cash Flow and Interest Coverages ($ million)

	1990[1]	1991[2]	1992	1993	1994	1995
Sales	$821.4	$792.7	$810.2	$825.5	$842.6	$860.0
EBITD	82.7	82.5	90.5	95.4	100.2	104.6
Total Interest	80.0	56.0	57.6	55.3	53.7	51.3
Cash Interest	60.0	41.0	46.1	52.1	50.2	47.4
CapX	Na	Na	20.0	20.0	20.0	20.0
Free Cash Flow	Na	Na	12.9	20.1	26.5	33.3
EBITD/Total Interest	1.0x	1.5x	1.6x	1.7x	1.9x	2.0x
EBITD/Cash Interest	1.4x	2.0x	2.0x	1.8x	2.0x	2.2x
EBITD–CapX/Cash Interest	Na	Na	1.5x	1.4x	1.6x	1.8x

[1]Interest expense for 1990 is estimated based on current debt structure.
[2]Interest expense for 1991 is pro forma for the proposed restructured debt load.

Table 25.5   JPS Textiles, Inc.
Expected Trading Ranges

Yield:	15.0%	17.5%	20.0%	22.5%	25.0%	27.5%	30.0%
Senior Notes	90.1	83.4	77.3	71.8			
Discount Notes		67.8	60.0	53.5	47.9	43.1	39.0
Plus Equity		68.4	60.6	54.1	48.5	43.7	39.6
Subordinated Notes		56.7	49.4	43.3	38.1	33.6	29.8
Plus Equity		57.2	49.9	43.8	38.6	34.1	30.3
Subordinated Debentures			46.4	40.9	36.4	32.5	29.3
Plus Equity			47.6	42.1	37.6	33.7	30.5

value of the equity to be received, the bonds offered 14%–29% capital appreciation potential from the then-quoted levels. To calculate the equity value, we used a five-year valuation model based on company projections of EBITD, the company's projected capital structure in 1995, an enterprise multiple of 5 times EBITD, and a 25% discount factor for determination of present value. Based upon these assumptions, we calculated that the equity was worth $4.9 million in total, or about half of a point of value per bond for the senior subordinated and discount notes, and 1.2 points for the subordinated debentures. If JPS used its $50 million carve-out to buy debt at a discount, these values could increase considerably. We assumed that if the company purchased $100mm of senior subordinated debt at approximately $50 per bond, equity value per bond would increase to 2.5 points for the senior subordinated notes, more than 3 points for the discount notes, and nearly 17 points for the subordinated debentures.

Table 25.6 summarizes the expected investment returns we estimated at the time of the restructuring offer.

Table 25.6 denotes that the combination of accrued interest and expected capital gains on price appreciation produced very attractive returns.

Asset Coverage and Downside Risk

In preparing our analysis to assess downside risk, we estimated expected and worse case asset coverages as shown in Table 25.7. The expected case was based upon the company's estimated EBITD for 1991 of $82.5 million, while the worst case assumed a 9% decline to $75 million.

Table 25.7 shows that on a worst case basis, the enterprise value covered the senior notes at 1.4 times the market price, senior subordinated notes at 1.7 times, discount notes at 2.7 times and subordinated debentures at 0.78 times. Over the near term, on a worst case basis, it was only the subordinated debentures—the most junior security in the capital structure—that did not appear to be fully covered by our estimate of enterprise value.

Market Strategy Considerations

Understanding when to enter and exit the market for a particular security is just as important as assessing its underlying worth. With respect to JPS, the

Table 25.6   JPS Textiles, Inc.
Calculation of Expected Investment Returns

	Market Price	Expected Price	Expected Capital Gain	Interest Return	Expected Total Return	Annualized Return
Senior Notes	70	80	14.3%	3.7%	18.0%	72.0%
Senior Subordinated Notes	43	51	18.6%	6.8%	25.4%	101.6%
Discount Notes	28	36	28.6%	0	28.6%	114.4%
Subordinated Debentures	28	35	25.0%	9.8%	31.8%	127.2%

Table 25.7   JPS Textiles, Inc. Evaluation of Expected Enterprise Values ($ millions)

	Expected Case	Worst Case
EBITD	$ 82.5	$ 75.0
EV Multiple	5	5
Enterprise Value	$412.5	$375.0

		Expected Case		Worst Case		
	Principal	Coverage	Percentage	Coverage	Percentage	Market Price
Bank Debt	$104	$104	100%	$104	100%	NA
Senior notes	100	100	100	100	100	70
Senior subordinated notes	125	88	75	72	57	43
Discount notes	134	94	75	77	57	28
Subordinated debentures	75	26	35	22	29	28
	$538	$412		$375		

bonds were trading at significant discounts to our estimates of ultimate value at the time of the restructuring announcement. Given the uncertainty associated with executing the transaction, the limited level of quality research available, and the generally weak market conditions, we were not surprised that the bonds were trading at these "fire sale" prices.

Buying smart is only one side of the equation. It is important to make an informed judgment as to when there is more market risk in holding a security than in realizing a gain or loss through a sale. For JPS, we questioned whether or not the restructuring addressed the longer-term considerations of debt amortization, since the face value of debt was not reduced. With pro forma total debt of $538 million and a current enterprise value of $412 million (using an EBITD multiple of 5), EBITD would have to grow by about $25 million (30%) for JPS to be considered solvent.

The company's financial position would have to show significant improvement before a subsequent refinancing could take place. Given this uncertainty, one should expect a premium yield on all outstanding JPS securities. Notwithstanding these concerns, JPS appeared to have sufficient liquidity to survive with its new capital structure through June 1994. Clearly, the opportunity to purchase the old securities at a steep discount to their apparent values was justified on a risk-adjusted basis. However, maintaining positions in the restructured JPS issues would require close monitoring on an ongoing basis.

Another example of profiting from proper investment timing was seen in Eastern Airlines. As previously mentioned, Eastern Airlines filed for Chapter 11 protection and was liquidated. Notwithstanding the outcome, in May 1990 we identified an investment opportunity in the second secured equipment notes (17.25%, due 3/1/93). These securities had

a second priority lien on a pool of jet aircraft, spare engines and parts, and cash. Due to concerns over the creditworthiness of Eastern and its parent, Texas Air (which guaranteed two future semi-annual coupon payments on these notes), the bond prices dropped from 107 to the 93–95 range.

Our analysis focused on the value of the underlying collateral and the likely disruption of coupon payments. At 93–95, the notes yielded between 18% to 31% to maturity, depending on the timing and form of the ultimate resolution. Table 25.8 illustrates the collateral pool values.

As shown in Table 25.8, assuming that the first lien was paid out of the cash in escrow, there would be $173.5 million in cash remaining (or 86.7% of the $200 million face value) to satisfy the second priority notes. In addition, even after applying a 50% haircut on the appraised value of the remaining equipment, the notes were collateralized 1.4 times. The excess collateral value allowed us to conclude that future principal and interest payments would be covered.

On September 1, 1990, the company defaulted on interest payments after Texas Air refused to back its guarantee (Texas Air subsequently filed for Chapter 11 protection in December 1990). The company began to make principal prepayments as well as accrued interest payments at the 17.25% contract rate in April 1991. To date, approximately $777 in principal (plus accrued interest) has been prepaid. If one purchased the bonds in May 1990, at a price of 95, the annualized total return would have been approximately 20%.

As the Eastern Airlines case denotes, perceived risk often exceeds actual risk. This implies undervaluation and opportunity. If one were to rank the distressed securities universe according to real risk versus potential return, Journal Company, Inc. (JCI)

Table 25.8 Eastern Airlines
Description of Collateralized Assets ($ millions)

Asset Description	Appraised Value[1]	Discounted by 30%	Discounted by 50%
Various Jet Aircraft	$187,305	$131,114	$93,653
Spare Engines	29,000	20,300	14,500
Total Equipment	$216,305	$151,414	$108,153
Cash in Escrow	387,000	387,000	387,000
Total Collateral	$603,305	$538,414	$495,153
LESS: First Lien	213,500	213,500	213,500
Available to Second Secured Equipment Notes	$389,805	$324,914	$281,653
Second Secured Equipment Notes	$200,000	$200,000	$200,000
Collateral Coverage	1.9x	1.6x	1.4x
Cash Coverage	86.7%	86.7%	86.7%

1 Lowest value taken from appraisals performed by Avmark in January 1990.

deserves top-tier status. Rarely does one credit exhibit so many attractive qualities.

Journal Company, Inc.

JCI's assets consist of a group of daily newspapers located in several states with a total circulation of 275,000, and a St. Louis free weekly with a circulation of 850,000. The company's bonds had steadily dropped in early 1990 due to concerns over a weak industry operating environment and losses from an ill-conceived start-up operation that was subsequently abandoned. Cash flow margins declined over approximately 55% from 20.4% in 1988 to 9.2% in 1989. Notwithstanding then current operating results, JCI possessed considerable intrinsic value principally based upon strong equity sponsorship, solid asset coverage, and high current yield and yield to maturity.

Strong Equity Sponsorship. Warburg Pincus & Co., an investment firm with $3 billion under management, controlled 100% of JCI's equity. Warburg had publicly stated that it would use its resources to

improve and to expand JCI's operations, implying that it would support the credit, if needed.

Solid Asset Coverage. JCI's estimated enterprise value greatly exceeded the market value of debt. Company assets were readily separable and reasonably liquid. JCI had recently sold assets for $120 million, representing multiples of 4.3 times revenues and 15.5 times cash flow. Proceeds were used to reduce senior debt. After the asset sale, face value of debt was $266 million, comprised of $28 million in senior debt and $238 million of subordinated debt. Market value of debt was approximately $120 million (45% of face value). We estimated that company assets were worth at least 2 times pro forma revenues of $178 million or $356 million (11 times pro forma 1989 EBITD). Conservatively valued relative to recent asset sales, enterprise value covered market value of debt by at least 2.9 times.

High Current Yield and Yield to Maturity. On May 1, 1990, JCI debt traded as shown in Table 25.9.

Table 25.9 Journal Company, Inc.
Publicly Traded Debt Issues

Amount Outstanding	Description	Coupon	Maturity	Price	Current Yield	Yield to Maturity
$ 73 million	Senior Subordinated Debentures	14.625%	5/01/00	51	28.7%	30.5%
65	Senior Subordinated Debentures	11.875	9/01/99	49	24.2	27.1
50	Subordinated Debentures	12.125	9/01/00	35	34.6	36.7
50	Subordinated Debentures	14.825	5/01/00	35	42.4	43.9

Even in the unlikely event of a Chapter 11 filing, these securities were still attractive based upon their discounted trading levels. Unlike JPS, Journal Company, Inc. had relatively very little senior debt and higher asset coverage ratios. Assuming a 24-month bankruptcy proceeding where bondholders would recover 100% face value, yields on these securities would have been: 36.67% for the 14.625s of 5/01/00; 39.05% for the 11.875s of 9/01/99; 60.02% for the 12.125s of 9/01/00; and 60.02% for the 14.825s of 5/01/00. Again, the recurring investment theme of committed sponsorship, strong asset coverage relative to market adjusted debt values, and high current yields made JCI an outstanding investment candidate.

An emerging strategic trend has been to invest in subordinated debt where reorganization value is distributed to claimants entirely in the form of new equity. These instances have arisen when there is insufficient asset value or earnings capacity to support high degrees of leverage. In the previously mentioned Interco Chapter 11 case, there are several tranches of subordinated debt which are currently trading at cents on the dollar. Interco was a leveraged recapitalization that failed due to a dramatic drop in cash flow and asset values. While the core businesses appear viable, they could not support a heavily leveraged capital structure. Therefore, an investor in the senior subordinated debentures, subordinated discount notes, and junior subordinated pay-in-kind debentures should expect to receive value in the form of equity. To value this equity, traditional techniques based upon projected earnings multiples should be used to augment cash flow valuations. Allocation of value among various classes is another critical issue. In recent reorganizations where equity distributions have satisfied the bulk of subordinated claims (Southland Corporation, Memorex-Telex, and Allied-Federated Stores), the allocation of value has more or less been dependent upon two factors: 1) the seniority and subordination provisions of bond indentures; and 2) the representation each security class at the negotiating table. Although there appears

to be an emerging pattern of equity distribution in these types of cases, we believe that each instance is unique and requires individual attention.

Conclusion

Over the past two years, upheavals in the market for high-yield securities produced unprecedented opportunities for investors who could remove themselves from the panic of the moment. Successful investing in distressed securities requires application of fundamental financial analysis to quantify "real" risk versus "perceived" risk so that one can distinguish the jewels from the junk. In the distressed arena, it is preferable to invest in "good" companies with "bad" balance sheets, a restructuring is generally more profitable when underlying problems are related to capital structure, not continuing operations. Determining enterprise value using various case scenarios; marking debt to market and calculating asset coverages at each claim level; assessing sources of liquidity available to meet scheduled interest and principal payments; comparing yields relative to other similarly distressed situations; and anticipating the form of a financial restructuring and its implications for each class of debt are all part of this "bottom up" credit analysis. Moreover, understanding the legal, accounting and economic characteristics of financial restructurings enhances this fundamental approach.

In the future there will be more financial restructurings as companies confront the excesses of the past. Since the inception of orderly financial markets, investors have experienced disappointment and pain caused by market crashes and panics. Often these situations cause an imbalance between perceived risk and real risk. Preparing to step into the fire to take advantage of these market opportunities requires the above-mentioned skill sets and the tenacity and resolve to act upon one's judgment.

Part XI:
Financial Distress

Chapter 26

Financial Distress
Tax and Financial Accounting Issues

Edward J. Abahoonie
Partner
Coopers and Lybrand, New York, NY
Robert H. Herz
Partner
Coopers and Lybrand, New York, NY

Legions of companies imperiled by declining growth and overleveraging are trying to restore financial health, or avoid collapse, by restructuring their debt. Some are in formal bankruptcy proceedings, where restructuring is mandated, while others are seeking to renegotiate financing with banks, bondholders, or trade creditors. Basically healthy firms should have good prospects, since a deliverable business plan based on operational streamlining, cost controls, and other cash maximization techniques are the heart of a well-crafted financial restructuring. Yet, the difference between success and failure can be the tax planning and financial accounting utilized to maximize the value of a restructured company.

As companies attempt major capital structure adjustments, investors seeking to profit from such situations have adopted a variety of strategies for securities of distressed companies. New terms such as "reverse LBO," "prepackaged bankruptcy," and "fulcrum security" have entered the business lexicon. (See Appendix A at the end of this chapter.)

Tax and accounting issues challenge the financial engineers on all sides of a restructuring transaction. The magnitude of these technical issues can intensify the typically protracted negotiations required to reach a restructuring accord. There are alternate approaches to handling tax and accounting questions which can produce widely divergent effects on different players. An ultimate choice balances the different objectives and captures numerous tradeoffs. Minimizing tax liabilities for the troubled company, for example, might have the opposite effect on creditors. The company may have to choose an approach that sacrifices some coveted post-restructuring income and cash flow to meet creditor demands for liquidity and security.

Tax Loss Carryforwards

One of the first tax issues examined is net operating loss (NOL) carryforwards, an area highly regulated by U.S. tax law. Troubled companies—including highly leveraged firms incurring huge interest expense—often have suffered losses for a number of years, and their NOLs may be a major element of value. Careful planning is required to maximize the dollar value and minimize limitations on the utilization of the NOLs to shelter earnings of the revamped entity.

Before considering how to use tax NOLs, it is necessary to carefully evaluate the *quality* of the losses. In general, the closer the losses are to actual operating (and financial reporting) results, the more likely the firm will be able to preserve allowable tax shelter. Restructuring is a wasted exercise if NOLs are based on highly aggressive tax reporting positions that are unlikely to withstand scrutiny by the Internal Revenue Service. Common techniques vulnerable to disallowance include writeoffs of intangible assets obtained through acquisition, covenants not-to-compete, and past deductions for investment banking, legal, and financing fees. Potential liability for unpaid taxes of former affiliated companies and potential claims against affiliates for the uncompensated use of prior losses should also be evaluated.

A change in control of the debtor's stock is a potential trap because it can trigger severe limitations on the use of NOLs. Avoidance is especially challenging in a restructuring that involves an exchange of stock for debt instruments or infusions of fresh equity. Nonetheless, dexterous restructuring can prevent the limitations if other business and legal factors permit.

The test for a change in control is mechanical. It applies if, within three years while losses exist, there is an increase of more than 50 percentage points in the direct or indirect ownership of a corporation. The increase is measured by the value of the holdings, as opposed to proportional or voting interest.

The rules can lead to some surprising results, including situations in which a change in control occurs even though a single shareholder does not obtain a majority position. Table 26.1 shows an increase in ownership as the result of a restructuring.

Although no shareholder has gained absolute control, the increase in ownership is 55 percentage points for this purpose, thus triggering a limitation on the NOLs.

A change is measured by reference to the value of all classes of stock owned, with only nonparticipating, nonvoting preferred stock excluded from the calculation. In addition, certain options to acquire stock and other executory contracts can be deemed exercised, but only in cases in which actual exercise would trigger ownership changes.

Planning opportunities can also be found. Since the rules focus only on value, it is possible to provide a new investor with voting control or common equity and still not trigger a defined change in control. This can be achieved by having old shareholders retain a preferred stock interest.

If a change in control occurs, the annual limitation on the use of NOLs thereafter equals the fair market value of all classes of equity at the date of the transaction (value of debt is excluded), multiplied by a prescribed interest rate, which currently is about 6½%. Thus, if ABC Co. acquires Loss Co. for $2 million in cash and assumes $8 million in liabilities, only $130,000 worth of NOLs can be used in any year. Any amount not used in one year, however, can be added to the following year's limit.

Depending on the overall fair value of the company's assets relative to their tax basis when an ownership change occurs, there may be further adjustments going forward. For example, accrued expenses and "built-in" losses on assets that are recognized after the ownership change can be sub-ject to the NOL limitation as well. On the other hand, accrued income and built-in gains recognized after the ownership change may be sheltered by inherited NOLs without limitation. It is critical, both in measuring overall equity value (especially for private companies) and adjusting for accrued/built-in items, to have an accurate tax valuation performed.

Distress Sales

Failing businesses often consider selling some assets in order to raise funds for debt retirement. Careful tax planning can enhance the value realized on the sale of assets or divestitures by troubled companies.

A key benefit results if the sale is consummated at a gain prior to a change in the seller/debtor's ownership, because it can be sheltered from tax by existing NOLs which otherwise will be limited going forward.

In addition, structuring divestitures as asset sales offers buyers the opportunity to increase ("step-up") the tax basis of acquired assets and thereby obtain future tax write-offs for purchase premiums. Purchases of assets, rather than the stock, of a company being sold by a restructuring debtor, also insulate a buyer from contingent liabilities, including potential joint liability for prior-period taxes of the selling group.

Asset sale structures also are useful for sales of subsidiaries at a loss. Recently issued IRS regulations disallow, or severely limit, the deduction of a loss incurred on the sale of the stock of a subsidiary.

State and local taxes should also be evaluated. Many states do not allow tax loss carryforwards, despite the existence of federal tax NOLs. In addition, sales tax and real estate transfer taxes, potentially applicable both to isolated asset sales and business divestitures, must be weighed in pricing disposals.

Bankruptcy and Insolvency

There are no immediate tax costs or effects from filing for protection under Chapter 11 of the U.S.

Table 26.1   Percentages of Ownership

Shareholder	Before Restructuring	After Restructuring	Increase in Percentage Points
A	30%	10%	0%
B	40%	5%	0%
C	30%	45%	15%
D	0%	40%	40%
	100%	100%	55%

Bankruptcy Code. Generally, a company reorganizing either under a bankruptcy proceeding or, alternatively, one that is insolvent, will receive more favorable tax treatment to assist in its rehabilitation. Indeed, tax factors have caused many companies to pursue a "strategic," or "prepackaged," bankruptcy.

The NOL limitation is imposed somewhat less stringently on companies that undergo an ownership change during Chapter 11 proceedings. In such cases, the limitation is based on the company's equity value as *increased* to reflect any debt forgiven as a result of the reorganization plan. In addition, special rules may apply if control of the reorganized company is awarded to "historic" creditors (i.e., original trade creditors or creditors whose claims arose at least 18 months before the filing). Then, the firm can elect to reduce its NOLs for a portion of the debt forgiveness, plus interest expense of certain previous periods, in lieu of any limitation on NOLs. The IRS recently announced that the historic creditor requirement will be relaxed so as to permit this route for deals with public bondholders as well. However, if this option is taken and another change in ownership occurs within two years of the reorganization, the NOLs are lost entirely thereafter. Creditor liquidity concerns must be carefully considered against this backdrop.

Although preserving value through tax NOLs is important, the structure of many deals is driven by the debtor's need to avoid recognizing taxable income on the restructuring itself. One key source of taxable income is through cancellation of indebtedness (COD) which results when debt is retired at less than its carrying value.

For solvent companies not in bankruptcy, there is no general relief from recognition of taxable income on debt restructurings. Recently issued regulations cause taxable income to arise even when the debt of a company is reduced as part of a buyout or takeover by another company. However, the tax law provides several benefits for insolvent and bankrupt corporations, including partial or full exclusion of COD income from taxable income. The exclusion is applicable to an insolvent company only to the extent of its insolvency, but a bankrupt corporation can omit all COD income.

For debt restructuring purposes, a company not operating in Chapter 11 (bankruptcy) is considered insolvent if its liabilities exceed the fair market value of its assets immediately before the cancellation of indebtedness. The amount that may be excluded from income is the difference between those values. Because a troubled company's equity has some speculative value should not necessarily prevent a determination of insolvency for this purpose. In measuring insolvency, key questions include whether contingent liabilities may be taken into account and, if so, what liabilities qualify. A claim of insolvency is not only a difficult tax valuation matter, but might provide nonparticipating creditors with a basis for trying to force the debtor into bankruptcy. This particular tax relief generally operates only as a deferral. A corporation excluding COD income is required to reduce its "tax attributes"—NOLs, business tax credits, capital loss carryovers, net tax basis of property and foreign tax credit carryovers—by the amount of COD income that is excluded. A permanent benefit results, however, to the extent that excludable income exceeds these attributes. Current law does not appear to require the reduction of attributes of other corporations affiliated with the debtor, even though they may join in filing a consolidated federal tax return.

Debt-for-Debt Exchanges

To determine the amount of COD income in a debt-for-debt exchange, the "adjusted issue price" (essentially carrying value) of the old debt is compared with the "issue price" of the new debt. When publicly traded securities are involved, the issue price of new debt is its market value. For example, a solvent debtor corporation not under Chapter 11 issues a new publicly traded bond having a face and market value of $700 in exchange for $1,000 principal outstanding bonds that were issued at par. There is immediate recognition of $300 in COD income by the debtor. If the company is a Chapter 11 corporation or to the extent it is insolvent, the income is excluded from tax, but the company must reduce its tax attributes.

In swaps in which neither bond is defined as "publicly traded" for tax purposes—possibly including certain "junk bond" restructurings—the issue price of the new debt is its face value discounted at prescribed statutory interest rates. Since those rates are quite low, an artificially high "issue price" often results, thereby reducing or eliminating COD income on bank debt and other private refinancings.

A debt-for-debt exchange also may create an original issue discount (OID) if the issue price of the new debt is less than its principal amount. Let us vary the previous example to assume that the newly issued bonds, despite a $700 face value, were actually worth only $600. In that case, there would be $400 of COD income and $100 of OID. Similarly, if the bonds had a face value of $1,000 but were worth only $600, there would be $400 of COD income and $400 of OID. If in either case none of the bonds exchanged were defined as publicly traded, there could be little or no COD income or OID.

Original issue discount is a two-edged sword. It is deducted by the debtor company and included in the creditor/holder's taxable income over the term of the new debt. The IRS recently announced that a creditor will be entitled to shield its subsequent OID income with a proportionate amount of any loss realized (but generally not allowed) on the debt exchange.

From an issuer's viewpoint, the market discount thus becomes deductible. If the debtor shelters the COD income with NOLs, the discount deductions might operate to freshen expiring NOLs or make use of NOLs that would have been curtailed by a change in ownership. OID deductions may be limited, however, by special "high-yield obligation" rules, which currently apply to yields exceeding roughly 12%.

Deemed Exchanges

It is important to note that the debt-for-debt exchange rules may apply to any significant modification of a company's obligation, on the theory that there has been a "deemed exchange." A reduction in the principal amount, a change in the interest rate, or the waiver of an automatic interest rate reset provision may be treated as a deemed exchange. Because market values are used, a reduction in principal of a publicly traded bond can trigger COD income of a far greater amount.

Stock-for-Debt Exchanges

A second key exception to the rules on recognizing COD income applies to exchanges of stock for outstanding debt. An insolvent or bankrupt company may get full or partial relief from recognition of COD income if the value of the stock is less than the carrying amount of the debt—but only if the newly issued shares are common or perpetual (nonredeemable) preferred. Most importantly, this "stock-for-debt" benefit is permanent—with no reduction of future tax benefits required.

Preferred stock with puts, calls, or mandatory redemption features do not qualify for the exception. The issuer has to recognize as income the amount by which the debt exceeds the value of these types of shares. The theory is that there is no "substitution of liability" since there is no upside potential on redeemable preferred; i.e., creditors can't recover their loan through stock appreciation.

This factor can create tension between the restructuring company and its creditors. Redeemable preferred, featuring both guaranteed dividends and a mandatory cash-out, is the equity security that most resembles debt and, in theory, would be most

acceptable to creditors. But given the tax disadvantages, it can prove difficult for the debtor to offer that kind of stock in an exchange.

When cash and/or new securities also are packaged with stock in an exchange, more than a "nominal or token" amount of stock must be used in order to qualify for stock-for-debt tax relief. If applicable, the tax relief applies to the entire transaction rather than just the portion of the debt forgiveness attributed to the stock. There is uncertainty as to whether parent company stock issued for a subsidiary's debt qualifies for this relief.

Financial Accounting

The financial accounting treatment of a restructuring also varies depending on whether the restructuring results from a formal Chapter 11 bankruptcy settlement or occurs outside of bankruptcy, and on whether there is a change in control of the company.

Bankruptcy

New rules issued in late 1990 govern the accounting for companies emerging from a Chapter 11 proceeding. If no change in control is involved, the accounting is straightforward. Assets generally are carried over at the existing book amounts. Liabilities compromised by the court-confirmed reorganization plan, however, are adjusted to the present value of future principal and interest payments, discounted at appropriate current market interest rates.

If the bankruptcy settlement includes a change in control of the company (e.g., through an equity infusion by a new investor or because a large creditor ends up with more than 50% of the voting equity in the reorganized company), "fresh-start" accounting applies. Under this approach the combination of the change in control and court-approved reorganization is viewed as creating a new reporting entity, for which a complete change in accounting basis is appropriate. Accordingly, any retained earnings deficit (or surplus) is eliminated and the assets and liabilities of the going-forward entity are restated to current fair values in a manner similar to purchase accounting.

Quasi-Reorganizations

For a restructuring outside of Chapter 11 (bankruptcy), the debtor company has greater flexibility as to the accounting treatment.

The first alternative available to a company experiencing continued book losses resulting in a retained earnings deficit is to reorganize on its own, in what is termed a "quasi-reorganization." Under this mechanism—essentially, another variation of fresh-start accounting—the company eliminates its retained earnings deficit and revalues its assets and liabilities to fair market value. This produces a complete readjustment of the balance sheet as though the company was recreated at the reorganization date. While the application of quasi-reorganization accounting generally requires shareholder approval, it is essentially an accounting readjustment, not a legal reorganization.

There are a number of benefits to a quasi-reorganization. Less money and time are required than for a legal reorganization. If the company is generating positive income, dividends may be paid immediately, rather than delayed until the negative retained earnings balance has been eliminated.

An important drawback, however, relates to the accounting treatment afforded the post-reorganization utilization of NOLs. The tax benefit must be credited directly to equity and not earnings, as would be the normal case for a "troubled" company that restructures debt.

Troubled Debt Restructuring

If the company instead chooses troubled debt restructuring treatment, accounting results also vary, depending on whether there is "full settlement" of the debt, a modification of the debt terms, or a combination of modification and partial settlement.

When debt is fully paid off in cash, the company recognizes an extraordinary gain (net of any related tax effect) for the difference between the carrying amount of the debt and the cash payment. Similarly, if equity is issued to extinguish the debt, the extraordinary gain is the difference between the fair value of the stock and the carrying value of the debt. For example, if XYZ Co. retires $100 million of debt for $50 million of cash or equity worth $50 million, it will, ignoring any tax effects, recognize an extraordinary gain of $50 million.

If a company negotiates a modification of the terms of existing debt, the accounting effects depend on whether the "gross flows" (total undiscounted future interest and principal payments) under the new modified debt exceed the carrying amount of the old debt, or vice versa. When the new gross flows exceed the carrying amount of the old debt, the carrying amount is not adjusted; instead, future interest expense is recalculated to an "effective" rate which equates the present value of the future gross payments with the existing book amount of the old debt.

For example, assume XYZ Co. had $100 million of outstanding debt, carrying a 12% annual interest rate, and modified the debt terms to $80 million principal due in five years with annual interest at 6%. This would provide total interest plus principal payments of $104 million. XYZ Co. would not change the carrying value of the debt, as the gross flows of $104 million are greater than the original principal of $100 million. Instead, an effective interest rate would be calculated that would equate the $100 million existing carrying value with the $104 million future cash interest and principal payments. This effective interest rate (under 1% per annum) would then be used to calculate the company's periodic interest expense.

If the gross flows are less than the book value of the debt, the carrying value of debt is reduced to the total gross flow value and extraordinary gain is carried at the amount of all future cash payments, these are all accounted for a reduction in principal, and no future interest expense is recognized.

Often, a restructuring will not involve either an exchange or a modification of terms, but some combination of them. In these cases, the exchange is handled first, with the carrying value of the debt reduced by the fair market value of the assets or equity exchanged. The residual carrying value of the debt is then compared with the gross cash payments under the modified terms. As previously described, either the interest rate is recalculated, or a gain on restructuring results, depending on whether the gross cash payments are greater or less than the carrying value of the debt.

Changes in Control

Many of the recently completed restructurings can be characterized as complete corporate restructurings, involving an infusion of equity that results in a change in control, together with a major debt restructuring.

Another format that can result in a change in control is a variation on the so-called "trading-in-claims" strategy practiced by investors interested in acquiring companies in bankruptcy. The investor buys debt securities and creditor claims and tries to convert them into more than 50% of the firm's equity in a restructuring.

Such transactions raise questions concerning appropriate accounting treatment for the company. As noted earlier, for entities emerging from Chapter 11, the rules now are clear and the choices are limited. In other cases, questions remain and choices exist. Is the deal a restructuring? Or are the changes so profound that it is more appropriate to either use a fresh-start type of accounting along the lines of a quasi-reorganization or apply purchase accounting treatment? Further, if the change in control is viewed as a purchase of the company by a new investor group, a question arises as to whether the acquired company should continue to present its books on a historical basis for separate financial statement reporting. Or should the acquirer's cost in purchasing the troubled company result in a restatement known as "push-down" accounting, as the acquirer's cost is pushed down to the target level?

While push-down accounting is not required for companies not registered with the Securities and Exchange Commission (primarily privately owned firms), the SEC generally requires push-down treatment in an acquisition in which the equity becomes "substantially wholly owned"—usually 80% ownership or greater. This is clearly relevant when the new or modified debt of the target is publicly traded and the company must register with the SEC.

When push-down accounting is applied, the usual purchase accounting method is used. All assets and liabilities are recorded at fair market value, with the amount paid over the fair value of the net assets assigned to goodwill. The choice between this type of fair-value accounting—be it quasi-reorganization or push-down—and troubled debt restructuring accounting can significantly impact the company's balance sheet and future earnings.

Debtor/Creditor Negotiations

Creditors must be considered in view of their make-or-break powers. They are unlikely to agree to proposals with highly adverse tax or accounting results. They will be especially sensitive to proposals that trigger immediate recognition of taxable gain or preclude recognition, for tax purposes, of real economic losses. If the creditor is financially healthy, taxes may be payable immediately.

Since debtor and creditor reporting for both tax and accounting purposes are not mirror images, negotiation to minimize tax exposure and enhance financial reporting can become complex modeling assignments. Tax liabilities, in particular, can vary enormously.

The ability of creditors to recognize losses is often an area in which creditor and debtor interests diverge. A debtor may wish to structure a tax-free transaction to avoid COD income, and the creditor, in cases in which the transaction would generate a loss, will desire taxable treatment on the exchange.

Generally, the receipt of new securities or stock, or the modification of existing obligations, will not allow the creditor to recognize a tax loss. Creditors essentially need to be cashed out, either by the debtor or through a secondary sale, in order to claim a loss for tax purposes. To the extent that principal is reduced in a debt-for-debt exchange, however, creditors with a loss will recognize it for tax purposes in the form of premium amortization over the term of the new debt. Creditors that realize gains in exchange offers (e.g., secondary market investors) will not recognize taxable income except to the extent cash is received or principal is increased. Although unclear, it may be possible for the debtor company to claim a retirement premium deduction for any increased principal amount on a swap.

For financial accounting purposes, the difference between the fair value of an asset or equity ceded to settle debt is an extraordinary gain or loss to the debtor. This is generally an ordinary gain or loss to the creditor when troubled debt accounting is applied. Under the alternate scenarios described earlier, if terms are modified, the creditor will recognize an ordinary loss compared with the debtor's extraordinary treatment when the new gross cash payments are less than the carrying value of the old debt. If the new gross cash flows are greater, the creditor's treatment mirrors that of the debtor; the principal is not restated and an effective interest method is applied prospectively. These rules could change, as renewed consideration is now being given to the subject of accounting by creditors for loan impairments, as well as to the whole subject of fair value accounting for investments in debt and equity securities.

Conclusion

In the increasingly adverse debtor/creditor environment, an understanding of the real cash and financial reporting impact of tax and accounting structuring is critical. That is true both for the one-time impact to income, as recognized for tax or accounting purposes, as well as for the financial statement presentation and tax status of the entity going forward.

Appendix 26
Glossary of Restructuring Terms

COD Income. Taxable income that can arise when debt is restructured or retired at less than its carrying value. Special relief is available, however, for companies that are either insolvent or in bankruptcy.

Fulcrum Security. Subordinated debt or preferred stock of a troubled company which the investor expects to convert into equity once the company restructures or reorganizes.

Grace Period. Obligations providing for little or no cash due for the first few years, allowing the company a "grace period." This includes zero coupon bonds and "pay-in-kind" debt (where interest is paid with additional bonds), as well as "reset" provisions to increase interest rates some years after original issuance. Many companies now undergoing or facing restructuring were leveraged buyouts (LBOs) of the late 1980s having securities with a grace period that has ended.

Prepackaged Bankruptcy. A prearranged bankruptcy settlement under Chapter 11 of the Bankruptcy Code, wherein the key terms of the exchange offer and plan of reorganization are agreed on by company creditors and stockholders in advance of the bankruptcy filing. Nontendering bondholders can be compelled to acquiesce, thereby expediting the bankruptcy settlement.

Reverse LBO. Direct equity investment in a troubled company, wherein the additional capital infusion allows existing debt to be reduced to a more acceptable level. The source of capital can be existing shareholders, creditors, or entirely new investors, including initial public offerings.

Trading in Claims. A way of maximizing yield, or returns, by trading in the securities or trade payables of troubled companies. Similarly, a number of so-called "fallen angel" bonds, originally issued as investment grade, have attracted the interest of investors expecting a turnaround or restructuring by the company.

Wrap Plan. A method of restructuring and refinancing a troubled company that involves "wrapping" the restructuring plan around an SEC S-4 exchange offer. The S-4 describes the restructuring terms and stipulates that unless these terms are accepted, the company will file for Chapter 11 bankruptcy.

Chapter 27

Emerging Trends in Bankruptcy-Reorganization*

Edward I. Altman
The Max L. Heine Professor of Finance
Leonard N. Stern School of Business
New York University, New York, NY

The bankruptcy "game" is a big, complex business as the United States progresses into the 1990s. As the legal-political-economic system concentrates more resources into the rehabilitation of ailing firms, it is not surprising to observe increased creativity and innovation within the evolving confines of bankruptcy law and its practice. This chapter examines several major trends in the distressed firm arena which have either evolved into high-stakes issues and/or have been created to deal with the complexities of the multi-stakeholder Chapter 11 process. It explores three major evolving trends: fraudulent conveyance, debtor-in-possession (D-I-P) financing, and prepackaged Chapter 11 reorganizations.

Fraudulent conveyance and debtor-in-possession financing are not new but have found new dimensions and importance in the aftermath of the leverage restructuring movement of the late 1980s and the attendant bankruptcies of very large entities. Prepackaged Chapter 11 reorganizations are the direct result of attempts to expedite the rehabilitation of entities in the face of complex capital structures and contentious negotiation.

Fraudulent Conveyance

The risk of increased corporate distress and possibly bankruptcy was always apparent in the high-stakes efforts to "buy out" companies by borrowing large amounts of funds in the private (bank-debt primarily) and public markets (high yield "junk" bonds primarily). These corporate restructurings involved small and medium-sized firms in the 1970s and early

1980s and were motivated by managements' efforts to become owners (management buyouts or MBOs). As the target firms grew and the prices paid to buy out the entities increased in the mid- and late-1980s, management usually teamed up with third-party "investment" or LBO (leverage-buyout) firms in order to purchase all of the public firm's stock, retire the stock, and bring the firm to "private" status. In some cases, the bidding to buy the large firm was so competitive that senior management found itself locked in a battle with an essentially outside-the-firm bidder; e.g., the $25 billion RJR Nabisco buyout won by the LBO firm Kohlberg, Kravis and Roberts over the existing senior management's bid.

All of this competition lead to extremely high buyout prices or costly defensive strategies to thwart the takeover, and higher prices meant larger and more costly borrowings to pay for the transaction. What was not anticipated by the parties involved is that the transaction itself could result in a situation where a "fraudulent conveyance" (FC) is created with huge potential liabilities for a number of the key players involved. This was labeled the "LBO Nightmare" by Michel and Shaked (1990) and has become increasingly a major issue in several court cases in the early 1990s.

FC: Roots and Central Concepts

The Bankruptcy Code clearly deals with the power to recover preferential transfers and to redistribute a bankrupt debtor's proceeds from one class of creditor to another. It does not solve the problem of some or

* This is reprinted with permission from Edward Altman, *Corporate Financial Distress and Bankruptcy*, 2nd ed., John Wiley & Sons, New York, 1993, Chapter 4.

299

all creditors' being prejudiced by a transfer of the debtor's property to a noncreditor. Transfers that are ruled fraudulent, however, are recoverable based on a law that was passed in England in 1571 under the statute of Elizabeth (13 Eliz.,c.5). This law carried over to the United States and held that transfers of property (e.g., a firm's assets) with the "intent" to hinder, delay, or defraud creditors are avoidable. Since the individuals that transfer their property (e.g., the old owners) will not admit that their actual intent was to defraud others, the courts must establish this event.

Either of the two types of relevant fraud, intentional or constructive, must be demonstrated in a fraudulent conveyance case. *Intentional* fraud involves the Elizabethan law where willful intent is clearly shown. A modern day example of this occurs when an insolvent corporation transfers assets to other parties, (e.g., old shareholders) prior to defaulting on its obligations and declaring bankruptcy, in order to hinder, delay, or defraud creditors. The transaction can then be considered void.

The second type of fraud involves *constructive* actions and applies to transfers of assets that unfairly harm creditors, regardless of whether the debtor intended to delay, hinder, or defraud. An unfair transfer will result if shareholders receive compensation prior to and to the detriment of creditors when a firm becomes insolvent. That is precisely the case if the LBO transaction results in an "insolvent entity" and the old shareholders (and other parties) are paid off but certain debt holders lose all or part of their investment. (A particularly lucid discussion of fraudulent conveyance law in highly leveraged transactions can be found in Luehrman and Hirt (1991).) Losses may be incurred by the existing creditors from prior to the buyout or by the new creditors, particularly those that are unsecured. Indeed, one class of new creditor often is a plaintiff in a fraudulent conveyance case, e.g., unsecured public debtholder, and another class is one of the defendants, e.g., the senior bank creditor. The latter is involved based on funds it provided as a "bridge-loan," enabling the transaction to take place between the time (the bridge) of the acceptance of the buyout offer and the raising of sufficient long-term capital, usually from the public debt markets. The argument against the banks is that the bridge loan was made to earn interest and fees in the months following the buyout without concern for the long-term viability of the new entity.

Was There a Fraudulent Conveyance?

In order to rule that an FC took place under a constructive fraud ruling, the courts must establish both that 1) there was not "equivalent value" or "fair

consideration" given to the firm when the LBO took place; and 2) the LBO transaction resulted either in the firm's "insolvency," and its resulting "inadequate capitalization" to survive, or where the transfer was made with the belief that it would incur debt beyond its ability to pay. These conditions are specified under section 548 (a) (2) of the Bankruptcy Code. "Equivalent Value" terminology is found under the Code, as well as most state laws which have adopted the Uniform Transfers Act (UFTA) or the Uniform Fraudulent Conveyance Act (UFCA). While all three Acts are similar in content, one important difference is the statute of limitations. The Bankruptcy Code requires that a Chapter 11 filing be made within one year of the highly leveraged transaction (e.g., the LBO) in order for an FC action to be brought, while the UFTA has a four year limit under the UFCA, states establish their own time limitation. For example, in New York the limit is six years. In addition, section 544 of the Bankruptcy Code enables a plaintiff to bring an FC action under applicable state law, effectively lengthening the Code's statute of limitations to the longer state law period.

First, the question of whether the debtor received "reasonably equivalent value" is addressed. Both Luehrman and Hirt (1991) and Michel and Shaked (1990) persuasively argue that almost all LBOs will fail the equivalent value test since the law is interested only how existing creditors fare from the transaction compared to what they would have realized if the LBO had not taken place. Since most of the FC suits involve defaults to these creditors, it is obvious the leveraged transaction worsened their position. The courts are not interested in whether intangible values were created by the LBO; i.e. situations where more efficient firm operation created values greater than the out-of-pocket LBO fees incurred. While these values created by the LBO may be important, as long as they do not go to the debtor they are not considered relevant in an LBO FC defense. Indeed, in a typical LBO, the only tangible value received by the debtor relates to the repayment of any prior existing debt or an increase in cash. Since these amounts are almost always less than the increase in debt incurred after the LBO, the transaction will fail the "equivalent value" test.

The more difficult test relates to the firm's post LBO financial condition. Insolvency or inadequate capitalization requires a valuation of assets and liabilities at the time of the LBO. While the various statutes give some guidance as to what is an insolvent condition, valid methodologies of valuation are not established. Under the UFCA, solvency is defined as when the present value of assets received in a "reasonably prompt sale" is greater than the amount required to pay its probable liability on all existing debts. These debts include all liabilities, not just those found on the balance sheet, i.e., contingent claims, off-balance sheet liabilities, etc.

Courts have differed on whether assets should be valued on a liquidation or a going concern basis. While the proceeds from a hypothetical distressed sale of assets at the time of the LBO has generally been deemed inappropriate, the adoption of a single valuation standard has not emerged. As is well known, valuation is an art and not a science, and apparently "true art" is in the eyes of the beholder (the court). Various authors have pointed out that valuations done in a number of related FC cases have utilized different criteria. For example, in the Gleneagles case (*United States v. Gleneagles Investment Company, 565 F.Supp. 556 [Pa, 1983]*), the court ruled that an FC did take place based on fraudulent intent and value was based on the amount that can be received from a reasonably prompt liquidation based on an arms-length transaction in an existing and not a theoretical market. On the other hand, in *Vadnais Lumber Supply v. Byrne, No. 88-4056 [Bankruptcy D. Mass., 1989]*, the court held that going concern value is proper unless the business is very close to being discontinued. In other cases, the question of liquid v. illiquid assets has been debated. Luehrman & Hirt conclude that what may emerge is the use of several different approaches in order to make a decision. They cite the Revco case examiner's use of three different approaches to estimate going concern value (see *In Re Revco D.S. Inc. et. al. Final Report of Examiner Professor Barry Zaretsky, 3, [Dec. 17, 1990]* and *In Re. Revco D.S. Inc. 118 B.R. 468 [Bankr. W.D. Ohio, 1990]*).

Most academics and many consulting practitioners work on valuation (e.g., Copeland, et.al., [1990] and Stewart, [1991]) recommend the use of a discounted present value approach. If the plaintiff-litigant, e.g., unsecured creditors, can prove that the secured lender or other defendants should have recognized the firm's insolvent condition, an FC will have occurred. The asset values will then be deemed as inadequate to cover all the claims, including that of the unsecured creditors. In the event of a subsequent failure, a typical argument will be that appropriate financial analysis was not applied at the time of the LBO. It has been and will be alleged that a prudent or responsible analysis would have shown that the enormous new debt burden was not supportable.

Who Is at Risk in a Fraudulent Conveyance?

As MacEwen and Wilkens (1991) discuss, from a social viewpoint, there are two primary goals in assessing penalties to those found at fault in an FC case—restitution and deterrence. Restitution transfers wealth from the initial beneficiaries of the highly leveraged transaction to the relevant losing-creditor classes and deterrence seeks to provide adequate disincentives for abusive behavior. The primary parties potentially at risk in an FC proceeding are: banks and other secured or senior lenders, pre HLT insiders, e.g., management and directors, selling shareholders, and professional advisors.

The unsecured creditors can seek reparation from the senior and secured creditor and an "equitable-subordination" could be the result, whereby the court rules that unsecured creditors are given priority to collect their debts. In a case involving the Meritor Savings Bank of Philadelphia, a U.S. Bankruptcy Judge ruled in Boston on May 21, 1991, that $8 million in bank loans, which provided funding for the 1987 buyout of O'Day Corporation, a manufacturer of fiberglass sailboats, constituted a fraudulent conveyance because the bank had reason to know that the transaction would leave the company insolvent. The case is now under appeal. O'Day, a subsidiary of Lear Siegler, went into bankruptcy less than two years after the buyout via an involuntary petition of the same unsecured creditors. The involuntary petition came after the bank sought to foreclose on the company's assets.

It is interesting to note that in the O'Day case, the judge ruled that the bank knew that the financial projections for O'Day's performance were inaccurate and that while fraud was not the bank's intention, the course of action taken by the bank was to improve its own position at the cost of other creditors.

Advisor Liability

Another interesting facet of the O'Day decision is the examination of the role and liability of the financial advisor to the debtor/seller of the firm at the time of a highly leveraged transaction, like an LBO or leveraged recapitalization. Two current FC or potential FC cases involve the direct role of the advisor. In the Interco Corp. bankruptcy, the court-appointed examiner found that the advisor, Wasserstein-Perrella, despite its poor performance in the ill-fated leveraged recapitalization, was not at fault since it was given inaccurate information to make forecasts of asset sales and earnings by the firm's management and thereby should not be held accountable. The Mayerson finding in the matter of Interco Inc., et al.,

Case # 91-4-00442-172, U.S. Bankruptcy Court, Eastern District of Missouri, Report of Examiner Sandra E. Mayerson, October 23, 1991, although not legally binding, specifically addresses advisor liability.

In the case of the Revco D.S. Inc., 1986 LBO and subsequent bankruptcy, the advisor, Salomon Brothers, agreed on October 20, 1991, to pay nearly $30 million to settle a class action suit on the part of unsecured bond holders and a preferred stock issue. Salomon had been accused of failing to use "due diligence" in assessing the overly optimistic projections of management. Salomon denied these allegations but settled to avoid the expense of further litigation.

The Interco and O'Day cases vary somewhat in their implications for advisor liability. The advisor is now deemed to be clearly subject to claims in a resulting bankruptcy. But while the Interco case seems to exonerate the advisor for basing its judgment and forecasts on faulty data supplied by insiders, the O'Day case did not exonerate the defendant bank although the data supplied to it also was inaccurate. Perhaps there is a distinction between a bank and an outside advisor, but both should have the resources to evaluate the firm's prospects and not solely rely on management. The Interco case had the added ingredient that an asset appraisal firm was used by the advisor to assist in its determination of the fair value of the assets at the time of the transaction. This examiner did find that the appraiser was indeed at fault and eventually the advisor did pay a $16 million settlement.

FC: Conclusions and the Future

It is clear that some, perhaps many, highly leveraged transactions will be attacked on the basis of an FC, where the operative fraud basis will be "constructive" rather than "with intent." The most important result will be liabilities to certain parties, primarily the selling shareholders and senior lenders and, to a lesser extent, the various advisors to the transaction. As these transactions become more costly, fewer will be completed which in the long run, will reduce the bankruptcy rate due to excessive leverage. However, one cannot conclude that the economy will be better off, since fewer value-creating deals will also take place.

The short-term outlook is for increased FC claims materializing as a result of the ill-fated deals of the late 1980s. Once the system is flushed of these events, the longer-term outlook is for fewer FC claims. This will be the result of fewer and more soundly financial leveraged deals and the more careful analysis prepared at transaction time by those

parties at risk. Luehrman & Hirt (1991) made the point that the senior creditors are in the best position to see that the unsecured creditors do not find themselves in a position where they must sue to reclaim part or all of their investment. By withholding their financing resources in the case of questionable analysis done by the other principals in a leveraged deal, the senior lender will act as an "enforcer" to ensure careful, conservative analysis.

While we agree with this observation, note that the pendulum may swing, in the short run, too far to the side of ultra-careful and conservative criteria—thereby stifling legitimate economic activities and national growth.

Debtor-In-Possession Lending

The second emerging trend involves a recently enlarged financing mechanism whereby loans are made to companies that have become debtors-in-possession (DIP) under Chapter 11 of the Bankruptcy Code. DIP loans are generally made to provide working capital to companies which became distressed due to capital structures that are overleveraged relative to the firm's earning power and resulting cash flow coverage. Firms which qualify for such loans are judged to be operationally sound but find it necessary to reorganize under the protective provisions of the Bankruptcy Code. This DIP financing is covered under section 364 of the code and is usually secured by the firm's inventories. This section simply provides a framework for financing firms in bankruptcy but does not guarantee repayment. In its desire to rehabilitate ailing companies, the courts give preferential treatment to lenders who are willing to provide post-petition funds. These funds are critical for the company to continue to operate during reorganization. This has never been clearer and more important than for the recent spate of large, retail bankruptcies where the ability to continually stock shelves is imperative to continuing operation.

The history of DIP financing is not as long or steeped in legal precedent as the FC event, discussed earlier, but it has been in existence for several decades. A few banks, as well as some insurance and finance companies, such as Sterling National Bank in New York, have included DIP loans as an important part of its business strategy for many years. Only recently, with the proliferation of bankruptcy filings of large, highly leveraged companies, has the DIP market expanded with lending institutions such as Chemical, General Electric Credit (GECC), Wells Fargo, Bankers Trust, and Citicorp now proudly trumpeting their activity and expertise. The reason for this new-found enthusiasm is simple, although not new. It is the ability to be granted a super-priority status in the hierarchy of creditors while simultaneously realizing large interest margins over the banks' cost of funds and other fee-generating activities. The DIP market has grown to such an extent, and with demonstrated attractive features to all parties involved, that several of the nation's rating agencies are now providing investment grade ratings to these mainly private financings. Both Fitch (March 25, 1991) and Standard & Poor's (May, 1991) have published special reports on DIP financing and designated personnel and resources to cover the emerging market.

Since DIP financing is another form of a private placement, no comprehensive data base exists. Estimates of the size of the market are over $2 billion in 1990 and over $3 billion in 1991 (see Table 27-1 for a partial list of recent DIP financings). The market has grown to include syndicated DIP loans as well as single lender-borrower relationship. In addition to the obvious loan-spread profit potential, banks attempt to acquire DIP clients who will be a source of lending activity after emerging from bankruptcy-reorganization, and to obtain entry for its restructuring group to assist the firm and earn fees while in reorganization. These attractions have made the market far more competitive and margins are already beginning to fall. Demand also fell in 1992.

Fees and Spreads

The DIP business not only has attractive risk priority aspects, it also involves considerable profit potential. The following list of items constitute revenues to the lender:

♦ Upfront fee - usually 2%–4% of the amount borrowed.

♦ Interest on loan - 1%–3% over the prime rate on the amount borrowed except lower where the borrower was also a pre-petition debtor of the same lender.

♦ Unused line fee - 50 basis points (0.5%) on unused part of the DIP line of credit.

Table 27.1   DIP Financings for Major Chapter 11 Companies

Debtor	Date Filed	Amount ($ Million)	Agent
Allied Stores Corp.	1/90	$ 300	Chemical
Allied Stores Credit Corp.	1/90	721	Chemical
Allegheny International	2/88	175	Chemical
Ames Department Stores Inc.	4/90	250	Chemical
Best Products Co.	1/91	250	Chemical
CHH Receivables Inc.	2/91	550	Chemical
C.R. Anthony	2/91	50	GECC
Carter Hawley Hale, Inc.	2/91	800	Chemical
Channel Home Centers Inc.	1/91	145	GECC
Columbia Gas System	/91	275	Chemical
Columbia Transmission	/91	80	Chemical
Federated Department Stores	1/90	400	Citibank
Greyhound Lines Inc.	6/90	10	Toronto-Dominion
Hills Stores Co.	2/91	250	Chemical
Insilco Corp.	1/91	57	Wells Fargo
Interco Inc.	1/91	185	Bank of NY
L.J. Hooker	8/89	50	GECC
Macy's	1/92	600	Chemical/Bankers
National Gypsum Co.	10/90	105	GECC
P.A. Bagner	/91	425	Chemical
Pan Am World Airways	1/91	150	Bankers Trust
Paul Harris Stores	/91	10	Chemical
Revco D.S. Inc.	7/88	145	Wells Fargo
Rexene Chemical	11/91	25	GECC
Seaman's Furniture	1/92	25	GECC
Southland	10/90	400	Bankers Trust
Tracor Inc.	2/91	25	Continental
U.S. Home	4/91	75	GECC
Zale Corp.	1/92	510	Chemical

Sources: Fitch Investors Service, Inc., N.Y.C., Special Debtor-in-Possession Loans Report, March 25, 1991, and discussions with market participants.

♦ Administrative fee - $12,000-$20,000 per month to monitor the collateral, etc. on the loan.

♦ Letter of credit fee - 2%-3% on the LC (if applicable).

Most DIP loans are made for one or two years. If only for one year, the lender may also collect points (upfront fee) for an extension. Due to these relatively high profit opportunities, competition amongst lenders is likely to increase and there were already signs to this effect as the early growing stage of the market stabilized at the end of 1991.

Rating Criteria

The three most important factors in determining whether a DIP issue receives a relatively high investment grade rating are: 1) the super-priority status of the loan, 2) the assessment as to whether the firm will emerge as a going concern from the Chapter 11 process, and 3) the lien over tangible property should the firm have to liquidate. The automatic-stay provision on pre-petition borrowings and the priority status accorded post-petition DIP loans over the earlier creditors, as well as a super-priority status over other post-petition financings, are keys to the market's presence and attractiveness. Since the main purposes of the DIP loan are to both finance operations and to demonstrate a company's viability, the success of the Chapter 11 process is fundamental. Finally, should there be a liquidation, the fact that the lender can look to specific assets for repayment reduces the overall risk even further.

The court can provide DIP loan priorities over the post-petition priority administrative expenses, tax authorities, pre-petition unsecured creditors, and even secured creditors (as long as the latter is adequately protected). It is no wonder then that a properly constructed DIP loan with the appropriate court sanctions can and does receive an investment grade rating from the rating agencies.

Almost all ratings have heretofore been given to nonpublic issues although the firm (debtor) pays for the rating just like a public issue. The fees charged by the rating agencies vary, but have been in the $35,000-$50,000 range. A high grade rating not only facilitates the DIP loan's acquisition but also sends a strong signal to suppliers, customers, and the economy in general that the borrower is a viable entity.

The first *rated* public DIP financing was a $250 million loan to Hills Department Stores from Chemical Bank in February 1991. The issue received an A rating from *Fitch Investors Service*. One of the primary reasons for the public rating was to demonstrate that Hills was a viable entity. An additional reason for a public rating is to help syndicate loans, particularly to foreign investors who rely on the rating services. It is somewhat surprising that there have not been more publicly rated DIP loan issues, since debtors are always looking for credibility and the ratings will likely be investment grade. Perhaps the private DIP market is reasonably well-promoted and the public rating is not valued as an important marginal benefit.

Most of the other credit criteria used to determine a rating are fairly standard and similar to those of public bond issues. They include an assessment of 1) business analysis, 2) industry position, 3) financial structure, and 4) management. In addition, specialized legal and loan-servicing criteria are blended into the rating process. Once a rating is given and the loan made, a periodic review process is carried out. *Fitch* claims this review is done at a minimum on a semiannual basis and also when some important event occurs that affects the Chapter 11 process for the borrower.

Prepackaged Bankruptcies

In the last few years a new type of bankruptcy has emerged that attempts to combine the time and cost-saving attributes of an out-of-court distressed restructuring with the more lenient voting conditions of a formal Chapter 11 proceeding. The key element in the process is the elimination of the minority holdout problem in that only 2/3 of the voting creditors in amount and more than 50% in number need to sanction a reorganization plan, while a successful distressed restructuring prior to bankruptcy requires at least 85%-90% and possibly more of the creditors to vote for amendments to the indenture and other important charges. This is not to minimize the necessity in a prepackaged Chapter 11 to still reach an informal consensus from a reasonable amount of creditors.

Section 11 U.S.C. 1126(b) of the Bankruptcy Code permits a debtor to negotiate with creditors prior to a filing and accepts pre-petition votes with proper disclosure. If no such law applies, then a plan can still be sanctioned as accepted or rejected if "adequate information" to all creditors and owners was disclosed under 11 U.S.C. 1125(a). The latter section now includes a substantial body of law as to what constitutes "adequate information." These include requirements of the SEC Act of 1934 for public securities and the receipt by all impaired stakeholders of the information in a reasonable timeframe for analysis, discussion, and vote. In substantial asset cases, confirmation orders usually take at least 60 days, and as long as 180 days, so reasonable time is not usually an issue. The confirmation period also ensures selection of a representative creditors' committee before the Chapter 11 commences, although appeals for additional members are still possible. While it may not be possible to assemble all creditors in a prebankruptcy meeting, it is often possible to locate the major creditors or their trustees to work up a plan and submit a disclosure statement.

A debtor who negotiates a prepackaged Chapter 11 has the advantage of a clearly defined exit strategy from the bankruptcy and has dramatically increased its chances of emerging as a going concern. We observed, that a recent study estimated that only 10%–12% of all Chapter 11 bankruptcies between 1979–1986, actually successfully emerged from Chapter 11. And, while it still may take many months to emerge even after a prefiling plan is agreed upon, the average time in bankruptcy of these cases is far less than the two years plus average of all Chapter 11s under the new Bankruptcy Code.

Necessary Ingredients

According to Salerno and Hansen (1991), the four essential ingredients of a successful prepackaged reorganization are: 1) foresight of the debtor to realistically assess the magnitude of its financial problems, 2) willingness and ability to incur professional fees necessary to implement the prepackaged strategy, 3) formulation of a viable exit strategy and a going forward business plan, and 4) a creditor group that is willing to negotiate the prepackaged plan and which finds the business plan and exit strategy, i.e., new capital structure, acceptable.

While the last ingredient is necessary, the first three are prerequisites to the plan's acceptance. In our opinion, an additional key ingredient to a successful large firm prepackaged deal reflects the debtor's ability to raise new equity capital. New equity is important even when there is a viable core business and the main problem appears to be too much debt. This was critical in the Southland Corporation case. (This case involved an unsuccessful first effort to prepackage a deal and it took six months to finally conclude a plan. Its final confirmation was mainly based on the new equity's role.) New equity infusion by existing or new investors signals the market that real economic value exists in the firm's assets. While capital can also be raised via DIP financings, the super-priority status of these investors is not as clear a signal as the willingness for investors to contribute equity—the lowest priority type of capital.

Prepackaged Plan Risks and Costs

A prepackaged plan is not without its disadvantages and costs. Again, Salerno and Hansen list these as:

1. requiring cash to pay the necessary fees,

2. informing the business community of the firm's problems, and

3. providing creditors time to undertake collection efforts in anticipation of a bankruptcy.

The first requirement is obvious since there is little chance that an advisor will work toward a prepackaged filing unless there is sufficient cash set aside to cover the newly incurred costs. The second item is not too important since the debtor's problems are probably already known to the industry. While the third item is likely refutable through voidable preference payments, the process of dealing with panicked and difficult creditors is unpleasant at best and certainly costly in time as well as resources spent.

In addition, there is always the possibility that what was thought to be a successfully negotiated pre-petition plan will prove to be rejected once the Chapter 11 confirmation process begins. This can be caused by a change in the business outlook for the debtor and/or a recalcitrant major creditor who changes its mind. A prominent example of a misfired prepackage that took much longer to accomplish in Chapter 11 than planned is Resorts International.

Other Legal and Tax Issues Motivating Prepackaged Deals

Changes in the tax laws now favor Chapter 11 filings over out-of-court distressed restructurings. The Tax Reform Act of 1986 changed the tax treatment of net-operating-loss (NOL) carryovers and the circumstances when they can be used. In rewriting section 382 of the Internal Revenue Code, the new provisions established limitations where there have been ownership changes of more than 50% of the company's stock within a specified period. If the ownership change is more than 50% over the previous three years, the availability of NOLs to offset income will be reduced to an annual limitation. If the company is in bankruptcy, however, section 352 may not apply if the pre-petition stockholders *and* creditors own at least 50% of the vote and value of the new, restructured company. The key point is that the old creditors are included. While the technical facts in preserving NOLs are quite complex, the essence is that a prepackaged Chapter 11 has the ability to save the restructured firm substantial tax payments and the private out-of-court distressed exchange does not.

The Budget and Reconciliation Act of 1990 discourages an exchange of one type of debt for another if the value of the new package is considerably less than the par value of the old, as is typical in most distressed situations. The debtor is liable for the difference in value and must report it as income. This is also true of debt for preferred stock exchanges. The benchmark for the amount of income reported is the trading value of both the new and old securities, or just the old security if the original one is publicly traded and the new package is not. This increased "income" is not taxable under a formal Chapter 11.

In addition, the recent LTV decision by the U.S. Southern District Court in New York required that investor-creditors who accept a distress restructuring plan retain a claim, if and when a bankruptcy occurs in the future, of only the trading value of the old securities at the time of the plan's acceptance and not the par value of the old securities. In essence, the difference in values is treated as an original-issue discount. Hence, a distressed investor who purchases a debt issue at 50% of par value is not likely to be favorably disposed to accept an out-of-court plan when these securities are trading at a lower or even slightly higher value.

The so-called LTV decision has been vigorously opposed by many investors, bankruptcy analysts, and lawyers, but appears to be the "de facto" doctrine although not yet enshrined in law. Since creditors who do not accept the pre-petition restructuring are not bound by it, there is now little incentive for most creditors to accept and the likelihood of a Chapter 11 filing is considerably heightened. In a Chapter 11, however, dissenting minority creditors will, in many cases, have the plan "crammed-down" and made binding to all classes of creditors and owners. Still, it is likely that a heavily impaired class, e.g., common stockholders, will be better-off in a plan crafted out-of-court than one that is based on a long, drawn-out bankruptcy proceeding. Indeed, Gilson, John & Lang (1990) provide evidence that stockholders fare better when debt is restructured privately and we hypothesize that they will also do better in a prepackaged deal.

Since not one creditor can ever be forced to give up its rights to cash interest or principal repayment, outside of a Chapter 11 case or similar state proceeding, this has caused many large company voluntary exchange offers to fail, e.g., Coleco, Petro-Lewis, Public Service of New Hampshire, and Western Union to name a few prominent ones.

Successful Prepackaged Deals

Since the October, 1986 Crystal Oil bankruptcy which was concluded in less than three months prepackaged plans have emerged and continue to grow in number. Still, the incidence of even this seemingly new optimal setup has not been as prominent as one might think.

In addition to Crystal Oil's (1986-three months) and Southland's (1989-six months) results, successful prepackaged Chapter 11s include Republic Health (1989-four months), La Salle Energy (1990-three months), Circle Express (1990-two months), TIE Communications (1991-two and a half months), Edgell Communications (1991-one month), Kroy Inc. (1990-three months), Arizona Biltmore Hotel (1990-one month), Anglo Energy (1990-three months), and 14 Wall Street Associates (1990-two months).

Most prepackaged plans in major cases involve highly leveraged debtors whose primary creditors include publicly held subordinate bonds, as well as some senior bank debt and trade debt. The latter tend to be relatively small but sufficiently crucial to the going forward business plan that the proposal usually leaves them unimpaired. Sophisticated distressed investors know this likelihood and may seek trade debt purchases from creditors who are unwilling to wait even for a relatively quick Chapter 11 confirmation.

Conclusion

A number of economists, including Jensen's (1991) privatization of bankruptcy discussion, have argued for the benefits of out-of-court restructurings, especially their ability to significantly reduce certain bankruptcy costs. While distressed costs can still be sizeable even for the firm that successfully avoids long, drawn-out formal bankruptcy proceedings, it is undeniable that time and cost savings occur if the firm's problems are addressed earlier in the "deterioration chain." The prepackaged Chapter 11 phenomenon is a variation on the privatization theme and as such retains much of the same benefits of the private agreements that seemed to be gaining acceptance prior to recent court decisions and tax enactments.

References

Baird, J. and T. Jackson, "Fraudulent Conveyance Law and Its Proper Domain," 38 *Vanderbilt Law Review*, 829 (1985).

Cook, M.L., et al., "Fraudulent Transfers," *Skadden, Arps, Slate, Meagher & Flom*, New York, February 1991.

Fitch Research, "Debtor-in-Possession Loan Rating Criteria," *Fitch Investor Services, Inc.*, New York, March 25, 1991.

Jensen, Michael, "Corporate Control and the Politics of Finance," *Journal of Applied Corporate Finance*, Summer 1991.

Leeb, Fred and Robert Scheuring, "Pre-packaged Plans: A Useful Tool for Management," Surveyor Crisis Management, *Turnaround & Workouts*, July 15, 1991.

Liss, K.J., "Fraudulent Conveyance Law and Leveraged Buyouts," 87 *Columbia Law Review*, 1491 (1987).

Luehrman, Timothy and Lance Hirt, "Highly Leveraged Transactions and Fraudulent Conveyance Law," *Harvard Business School Working Paper*, July 1991.

McConnell, John & Henri Servaes, "The Economics of Pre-Packaged Bankruptcy," *Journal of Applied Corporate Finance*.

Michel, Allen and Israel Shaked, "The LBO Nightmare: Fraudulent Conveyance Risk," *Financial Analysts Journal*, March/April 1990.

Murdoch, D., L. Sartin and R. Zudek, "Fraudulent Conveyances and Leveraged Buyouts," *The Business Lawyer*, November 1987.

Salerno, Thomas and Craig Hansen, "A Pre-packaged Bankruptcy Strategy," *Journal of Business Strategy*, January/February 1991.

Standard & Poor's Creditweek, "Criteria for Debtor-in-Possession Loans," *Standard & Poor's Corp.*, New York, May 13, 1991.

Wilkens, Odette and Bruce MacEwen, "LBO's & Fraudulent Conveyance Doctrine: Threat or Menace," *NYU Thesis*, May 1991.

Chapter 28
Bankruptcy Investing

Peter M. Faulkner
Head, Distressed Securities Group
Alex. Brown and Sons Inc., New York, NY

For the patient investor with a long-term view, purchasing the secured securities of companies reorganizing under the Bankruptcy Code can be profitable. With disciplined buying and thorough analysis, these assets can be bought below their workout values. The complexity and uncertainty of the bankruptcy process makes for a very fragmented market where bonds can trade at substantial discounts to their liquidation value. When a company begins to formulate a plan to emerge from bankruptcy, this process focuses public attention and encourages the market to fall in line with the new realities. This method of inevesting has provided above average returns with below average risk.

Bankruptcy: The Law

Credit must be given to the British for planting the seed of modern bankruptcy law in the sixteenth century. However, it is in the United States that bankruptcy laws have reached their highest level of development. Since passage of the Bankruptcy Act of 1898, the United States business community has been the beneficiary of a set of unique and helpful reorganization laws. Although the act was reformed in 1978 and amended to its current form in 1984, its spirit has not changed. Simply stated, the act seeks to provide: 1) temporary relief from obligations to creditors in order to gain time to formulate a plan of reorganization; 2) rehabilitation of debtors that have potential to be productive; and 3) distribution of the reorganized debtor's assets to its creditors (and stockholders if possible).

Chapter 7 and Chapter 11 are the two most commonly used sections of the Bankruptcy Code. In Chapter 7, the debtor sells all its assets through a total liquidation and distributes the proceeds to its creditors. This usually takes place when there is no hope of revitalizing the business. Chapter 11 is more akin to the spirit of the Bankruptcy Code. A debtor is protected from the claims of creditors while attempting to restructure its debts. By no means, however, is the debtor discharged from its obligations. The bankrupt company must have all its actions approved by the court. The temporary stay of creditor claims is accompanied by a judicial system aimed at preventing the debtor from dissipating (or intentionally removing) assets of the estate.

The Participants

The interaction in a bankruptcy proceeding occurs among the following parties: the bankruptcy judge, the managers of the debtor's business, and members of the various creditor committees.

The Judge

The judge's role is one of overseer and advisor. A judge that discourages litigation and encourages negotiation speeds up the process considerably. Such a judge can see that the parties avoid legal skirmishes that could bring the case to a standstill. For example, the Allegheny International case made no real progress in 1989 because the court provided no direction to the squabbling factions.

The judge receives assistance from the United States Trustee's Office. Appointed by the Attorney General for each federal judicial district, the trustees' duties are: 1) to supervise the administration of bankruptcy cases; 2) to supervise the appointment

309

of trustees in bankruptcy (the individual who, in some instances, runs the company); and 3) to supervise the formation of creditor and equity committees.

Management

The bankruptcy system offers management a chance for redemption after a corporate failure. The law grants the debtor the exclusive right to formulate a plan of reorganization for the first few months, and then the debtor must ask the court to extend this right every 120 days. Management must show that it is making genuine efforts to emerge from Chapter 11, or exclusivity is withdrawn. If management demonstrates incompetence or lack of cooperation, creditors may seek the appointment of a private trustee to run the company on a day-to-day basis. Eastern Airlines creditors ousted Mr. Bakes as CEO and had Mr. Shugrue appointed as trustee. Often managers find the protection of bankruptcy intoxicating and are in no hurry to leave it. Management is most effective when it realizes that compromise, cooperation, and diplomacy have become part of their job descriptions.

Creditors

Those who have the most at stake are, of course, the creditors/investors. Each class of claimant is entitled to representation on a committee. The U.S. Trustee's office oversees the establishment of the committees. The determination of which committees are formed and who sits on them is crucial. The amount a class of creditors recovers in bankruptcy is not only a function of the rank of its claims but also of the committee's competence.

The choice of a bankruptcy attorney is crucial and this applies equally to all the participants. In a bankruptcy, the attorney must provide more than impartial advice. He or she must be both conciliatory and aggressive as the situation demands. Constant confrontation provides a disservice and usually results in unwarranted and excessive fees.

Bankruptcy investing requires an understanding of the positions and objectives of the participants, which go well beyond straight numerical analysis. An investor in any bankruptcy must be aware of the players. The character of each person, their egos, and secret agendas must be understood. Good bankruptcy analysis rests heavily on considerations involving human values. Investors do well to establish relationships early so as to keep current and also to obtain crutial information on a timely basis. Identifying personality attributes and determining how they mesh or conflict is useful because these can have an effect on how long a company remains in bankruptcy.

Value Investing

A company in bankruptcy must answer to its creditors. The rights that normally belong to equity holders are now shifted to debtholders. Equity holders have rights, but they are considered after debtholders. Value investing means different things to different people, but for the purposes of this chapter, it means buying the assets of a company at a discount from liquidation workout value. A bankruptcy investor can usually accomplish this by buying the debt of bankrupt companies at a meaningful discount from this workout value.

An investor should undertake this analysis based on four considerations: 1) reasons for bankruptcy; 2) basic financial research; 3) legal implications; and 4) management's attitude.

Reasons for Bankruptcy

Companies seek bankruptcy protection for three reasons: management errors, overwhelming legal problems, and industry-wide restructuring problems.

Management errors include an overleveraged buyout, overpayment for another company, promiscuous spending, or perhaps a combination of these. Federated Department Stores was essentially a solid company, but not solid enough to sustain the huge debt piled on by Mr. Campeau. Ames would not be bankrupt today if it had not purchased Zayre Discount Stores for $800 million at the end of 1988. If the error can be isolated then one can account for it and evaluate everything else accordingly.

Huge liabilities resulting from product lawsuits or governmental claims also may force a company into bankruptcy. Johns Manville is a good example. It was flooded with product-related lawsuits that were so overwhelming that bankruptcy was the only way to address them and protect the assets of the company at the same time. As the Manville bonds collapsed in price, profitable assets were overlooked. Investors who bought at these low prices profited handsomely when the assets were considered. LTV was nudged into bankruptcy by the government because it could not meet its mounting pension obligations. The government was involved because it insures the retirement pay of workers through the Pension Benefit Guaranty Corporation (PBGC).

Industry-wide problems include prolonged business downturns and industry restructurings. A company may experience an extended period of severe losses due to a general decline in its core business as the American steel companies did in the early 1980s. In such a case, bankruptcy enables the company to attempt a self-restructuring to reduce its debt in anticipation of an upturn in its cycle. Global Marine, an oil-drilling business, is an excellent example. When oil prices collapsed in the 1980s and drilling came to a virtual standstill, the company found itself unable to sustain its debt load. Global Marine notes traded as low as 4 cents on the dollar at the end of 1988. By mid-1989 holders received equity and warrants in a much less leveraged new company. Oil drilling came out of its down cycle and the stock and warrants have since traded at a level equivalent to 15 cents on the dollar for the old notes.

Financial Research

A simple tally of assets and liabilities is required. These can quickly be found listed in the bankruptcy filing document. Unfortunately there is no magic formula, solid investigative financial analysis is required.

Discussions with management, other analysts and industry consultants, as well as a study of the financial statements are needed to form an opinion of the value placed on the assets by the company. The value will always be a matter of debate since it is a function of future assumptions. Nevertheless, an estimate is crucial.

Close attention must be given to subsidiaries. Many times, subsidiaries report their financials separately and they do not become part of the bankruptcy. These entities can be quite solvent and fully protect any direct debt. Ralph's Grocery was a perfectly viable subsidiary of Federated Department Stores not in bankruptcy and current on its interest payments. It had a 14% senior note outstanding that traded around 65 when Federated went bankrupt. As soon as investors who had done their homework realized the mistake, the notes traded back up to 86.

The liabilities arise primarily from bank debt, public and private bonds, trade payables, taxes due, PBGC claims, environmental clean-up costs, and so on. Initially, the number may seem overwhelming because the debt is stated at its face value and government agencies always assert claims considerably higher than they hope to receive. Establishing

a hierarchy of the debt is the first step. Next, the price at which the securities trade in the market is used to adjust the face amount of the liability. Trade payables are usually treated as unsecured debt. Table 28.1 is an example.

(*Note*: Stockholders are not addressed. Unless all debt claims are paid in full, equity holders theoretically will receive nothing. However, they do retain a certain holdout value and may receive a small distribution. This holdout value is the threat of litigation and the subsequent delay in emerging from bankruptcy. An investor should avoid the purchase of common or preferred stock of a company in bankruptcy.)

In Table 28.1, let's say our financial analysis leads us to the conclusion that Widget Co., Inc. has a workout value of $380–$400 million. The market values the company at $292 million. This "discount" creates a buying opportunity for investors. This is a very simple model and additional factors such as the potential cost of environmental liabilities, pension obligations, unpaid taxes, terminating employment contracts, and the liability of unexpired leases must be considered before investing.

Legal Implications

A multitude of legal questions must also be addressed. For example, fraudulent conveyance of assets is often cited. This occurs when a company disposes of assets without receiving fair payment, thereby eventually making it bankrupt. Fraud is very difficult to prove, but if the case has certain merits, then note holders may be able to improve their standing. Hunt International's 9⅞% subordinated notes were granted a senior claim on top of their subordinated claim of $3.5 million by threatening to sue for fraudulent conveyance and then settling. There could also be a case where money is returned to the company, thereby increasing its value.

Breach of fiduciary duty is another legal question. This is typically a preference payment made to an entity that had a conflicting fiduciary responsibility. Mellon Bank's loan of $28 million to Sharon Steel

---

Table 28.1   Widget Co. Inc. (In Millions)

Assets	Liabilities	Market Price (Cents on the $)	Total Market Value
Workout value: $380–$400	$ 40, Bank Debt	80	$ 32
	100, 1st Mortgage	65	65
	200, Senior Unsecured	30	60
	300, Junior Subordinated	15	45
	$640*		$202

*Does not include pre- and post-petition interest.

was paid off before the company went bankrupt in 1987. Mellon was also the trustee for the Sharon Steel subordinated bonds, so the bond holders sued. The case was settled for $7 million.

Any cash payment made to an insider or controlling party within 12 months of the bankruptcy filing should be scrutinized. If such a payment reduced the value of the estate to the detriment of other creditors, then it must be repaid.

Although not a consideration affecting a buy/sell decision, the buying of trade creditor claims should be addressed here. An investor must be satisfied that the claim is not disputed by the debtor and that the seller is knowledgeable. A trade creditor is usually not considered knowledgeable about investment practices in Chapter 11. Judge Lifland of the Bankruptcy Court for the Southern District of New York has indicated an uneasiness with sophisticated investors buying the claims of unwary trade creditors at large discounts. A judge could disallow the transfer of a claim on the belief that inadequate disclosure was made to the seller. This applies to the sale of a claim by an original creditor; after that a secondary market exists and there is rarely a problem of transfer.

Management's Attitude

Management relates in particular to our observations on human nature. Managers see bankruptcy as a chance to clean up their companies and make substantial capital expenditures with the large cash build up resulting from avoidance of interest payments on debt. While relieved of the obligations their competitors must face (mainly interest payments), they are free to modernize and increase their market share, possibly by underpricing. While all this is good for the company, management may become too comfortable with the edge afforded by bankruptcy. This translates into a prolonged bankruptcy period with erosion of an investor's return.

What to Buy

If the situation holds hidden value, the next question is which securities should be purchased? The following should be considered:

1. *Seniority.* Where to invest in the hierarchy of debt securities depends on an investor's attitude toward risk the more senior the debt, the lower the risk and the return.

2. *Liquidity.* A listed security provides an investor with easy pricing as well as marginability. Listing, however, does not insure liquidity.

The vast majority of trading in bankrupt securities is over-the-counter. A smaller bankruptcy will have fewer securities to buy and fewer interested investors; illiquidity is greater, but so are the margins. For the investor with minimal liquidity requirements and large capital to invest, bank debt and trade claims are usually the choice.

3. *Additional Guarantees.* There may be instances when a bond issue has received pledges of additional guarantees. This might occur if the assurances were granted in order to consummate an exchange offer after which the company filed for bankruptcy. The Republic Steel 11's ½% Senior Notes in the LTV bankruptcy are just such an issue. Aside from its normal claim, the issue has pledged to it a $124 million senior unsecured note, making an added $2.4 of senior unsecured claim for every $1 of note.

4. *Coupon Rate.* A claim in bankruptcy is set by adding the principal to the unpaid pre-petition interest before the bankruptcy filing. The higher the coupon and the longer the unpaid pre-petition interest, the larger the claim. If the collateral behind a bond is larger than the bond issue itself (overcollateralization), then an investor is entitled to principal, unpaid interest during the bankruptcy, *and* interest on that interest as well. However, if the coupon rate is very low, the debt may be reinstated as long as all interest is paid off.

5. *Original Issue Discount (OID).* The principal claim of a bond can be substantially reduced by OID. This means that at original issue, a bond was priced lower than its face value, or par value of $1,000. Therefore, an investor's principal claim is not $1,000 but some lower number. The question of the amount of OID resulting from exchange offers, as opposed to original issuance, is still before the courts. The arguments are complex. Suffice it to say that an investor must be aware of OID and account for it.

The Investor

The bankruptcy process is long and tortuous. It takes time for events to unravel and the pieces to fall into place. Creditors take their place in line according to seniority and stake their claims. This results in confrontation because the problems of bankruptcies are not black and white and do not present easy solutions. The claims are fixed while asset values are not. Furthermore, management frequently wants to distribute as little as possible to the creditors so as not to be stripped of resources. To this end, management almost always attempts to present a scenario that is bleaker than reality.

Discipline is required in choosing the right bankruptcy, deciding when to buy, and having the patience to hold on. A great deal of publicity surrounding a case means it is time to wait because there are too many people chasing too few securities, pushing prices too high. But once the investor is committed, he or she should become accustomed to bearing the vicissitudes of the bankruptcy. Little, if any, price appreciation and possibly a loss on paper for a year or two is not uncommon. Of course this does not mean one must stay with an investment until the very end of a bankruptcy. What is required is the steadfastness to wait for events to take a favorable turn.

Active versus Passive and Big versus Small

A large investment requires a substantial amount of capital not only to purchase the position but also to pay professional fees. An active role means sitting in committee meetings and attending meetings with management—all requiring many hours and exposure to insider information. An investor is made illiquid due to his or her insider status and because the position is so large that any movement significantly alters the market price. Furthermore, the choice of securities is limited. The interests of senior and subordinated creditors are different, hence having large illiquid stakes in both may create irreconcilable conflicts of interest.

The smaller investment requires less commitment of time and money once the purchase is made. One can afford to buy an array of different securities while also being price selective. Of course, a small investor cannot influence the process and may sometimes lack information. What is best is a reasonable position and a network of similar investors who form a large block.

The Four Stage Bankruptcy Cycle

The first stage is the period immediately following the bankruptcy filing. It is the time of greatest uncertainty and risk. Purchases made during this time are not made after consideration of all the facts, since all the facts are not yet available. It is advisable to purchase only if there is a meltdown in prices. In the past, pension funds and certain institutional holders could not hold debt securities that did not pay interest. When a company filed for Chapter 11, these entities would dump their securities on the market. The meltdown occurred and the astute investor could make purchases at very low prices. Along with a host of new investors, these institutions have changed their policies and such opportunities rarely present themselves any more. This period lasts a few weeks to a month.

In the second stage all the potential liabilities are public and a *general* idea of the value of the assets is known. This period lasts two to six months. If there is little publicity involved and prices have not increased materially from the filing date, this is the time to start buying.

The third stage is the longest and consists of many levels. In it, the committees have been formed and stances assumed. Negotiations can now begin for the formulation of a plan of reorganization. A new level is gained every time a compromise is reached. This is the time when most investors make their purchases. The more compromises needed, the more selective an investor can be in purchasing. Eventually a plan of reorganization is filed. This stage can last anywhere from one to five years, although the average life of an entire bankruptcy is three years. The closer one gets to the end of this period, the lower the risk and, consequently, the higher the price of the security.

In the fourth and final stage the arbitrageur steps in. The plan is final and the distributions to creditors set. Margins and spreads are tight as time becomes the greatest risk at this point. This period lasts 3 to 5 months, but there are exceptions such as Johns Manville. In this case the plan was approved and distributions were set to be made, but they were held up on appeal for two years.

Return on Investment

The increase in the popularity of bankruptcy investing has resulted in a decrease of the phenomenal returns enjoyed in the past. Increased competition has caused higher prices. An investor's return will depend upon when the securities were purchased and which type they were.

The most appealing argument for purchasing certain bankrupt securities is the *limited downside risk* in the long run. If assets are bought below their workout value, then the bankruptcy process will work as a catalyst to bring the market price of the securities in line with this value. The real risk is that the bankrupt company's business is not viable and the financial situation , consequently, worsens. The investment should be evaluated over a three to five-year horizon and not at the end of each year. Over time, an annualized return of 20%–30% may be anticipated. Returns of 50%–70% are not uncommon.

Conclusion

Bankruptcy is a unique form of value investing. Absent market fluctuations, the downside risk is far less than the potential rewards. The risk is low because, theoretically, an investor is buying assets at a discount from workout values. The bankruptcy process will eventually coalesce these values with greater efficacy than if events were allowed to run their normal course. With patience, discipline, and a long-term view, an investor can experience handsome returns on investments that have little inherent risk.

Part XII:
The Valuation Process

Chapter 29

The Valuation Process and Trends Affecting Valuations

Patrick F. Dolan
Senior Manager, Valuation and Appraisal Group
KPMG Peat Marwick, New York, NY

This chapter describes commonly used approaches for valuing public and private companies, and divisions and subsidiaries of public companies, that are being considered for sale, acquisition, or for any other business reason. Every attempt was made to be as practical as possible in providing guidelines for performing a valuation analysis and penetrating the mystique of the valuation process. All of the discussion and examples are based on our work and the theories, concepts, and ideas presented are ones we commonly use. Accordingly, you may wish to refer to this chapter when presented with a valuation challenge or when critiquing the work performed by others.

Reasons for Performing a Valuation Analysis

The price at which property (tangible and intangible) is exchanged determines, in many instances, whether a deal is successful. An unsatisfactory price and terms are the reasons most often behind discontinued negotiations. Once an owner decides to sell his or her business, or a potential buyer becomes genuinely interested in buying a business, price becomes particularly important.

A thorough valuation analysis can help sellers:

♦ determine a range of possible values based on today's market conditions;

♦ ensure that they do not underprice or overprice the business;

♦ establish reasonable price expectations and build consensus among owners;

♦ provide feedback for decisions to sell, hold, go public, or liquidate the company; and

♦ strengthen sale negotiations by using information developed during the valuation.

A thorough valuation analysis can help buyers:

♦ determine a range of possible values based on today's market conditions;

♦ ensure that they do not overpay;

♦ evaluate available methods of financing, based on expected purchase price and internal cash flows;

♦ consider the impact that alternative growth scenarios may have on the attractiveness of a deal;

♦ strengthen their negotiating position by using information developed during the valuation analysis;

♦ evaluate the tax ramifications of the transaction (with the assistance of tax counsel and/or tax accountant); and

♦ improve their knowledge of the competitive position of the target company and its industry.

In addition, a valuation analysis can help the boards of both the selling and buying companies fulfill their fiduciary duty to their respective shareholders.

315

Trends Affecting Valuation

Recent Trends in Transaction Activity

During the years 1985 to 1991, mergers, tender offers, and leveraged buyouts represented approximately 90% of transaction activity in terms of dollar volume in both mid-sized and large companies. (Mid-sized companies are defined as those having an enterprise value of between $5 million and $50 million and large companies as those with an enterprise value greater than $50 million.) Based on data provided by Securities Data Company, Inc., total transaction volume during the years 1985 to 1991 was approximately $20 billion in mid-sized companies and $1,636 billion in large companies. As Table 29.1 indicates, mergers alone accounted for approximately half the transaction activity. In addition, Table 29.2 shows that for completed merger transactions from 1985 to 1991, the target company was mostly public.

During 1990 and 1991, dollar volume in mergers, tender offers, and leveraged buyouts decreased dramatically, as shown in the year-by-year comparison in Table 29.3. In 1991, merger volume declined to 44% of peak 1988 volume for mid-sized companies, and to 31% of peak 1989 volume for large companies. The biggest decline in transaction volume was seen in 1991, when leveraged buyouts of large companies dropped to 10% of 1989 highs.

Overall in 1991, the dollar value of transactions in mid-sized companies declined by approximately 55% from 1988 peaks, and by approximately 70% from 1989 peaks for large companies. Possible reasons for this decline in dollar value include:

1. Higher stock market prices and multiples than in 1988 and 1989, particularly for large industrial companies, made transactions such as tender offers and leveraged buyouts less financially feasible. For example, in 1991, the price/earnings ratio paid for all transactions recorded by *Mergerstat*^{SM} *Review* was slightly higher (7.5% higher) than the S&P 500 price/earnings ratio. From 1977 to 1990, this differential was much greater, averaging 57% higher. In 1987 alone, it was 20.7% higher.

2. More conservative lending practices limited the number and prices of completed transactions. As Table 29.3 shows, the 1991 leveraged buyout volume of large companies was 10% of peak 1989 volume.

3. Acquiring firms and target companies may have had less debt capacity in 1991 than in 1988 and 1989 because of reduced cash flows in the recession.

4. The collapse of the junk bond market.

Table 29.1 Dollar Volume of Completed Transactions From 1985 to 1991

	Mid-Sized Companies			Large Companies		
Type of Transaction	Dollar Value in Billions	Number of Deals	Percentage of Total Dollar Volume	Dollar Value in Billions	Number of Deals	Percentage of Total Dollar Volume
Mergers/Acquisitions	9.65	642	49	756.5	2,232	46
Tender Offers	2.49	96	13	384.7	505	23
Leveraged Buyouts	0.87	42	4	141.6	170	9
Nonclassified Transactions	5.12	217	26	168.6	481	10
Subtotal			92			88
Spin-Offs	0.14	8	1	17.1	35	1
Recapitalizations	0.16	2	1	45.4	33	3
Self Tender Offers	0.25	32	1	42.0	124	3
Repurchases	0.18	50	1	25.4	207	2
Minority Stake Purchases	0.62	197	3	33.7	729	2
Acquisition of Remaining Interests	0.16	20	1	19.1	86	1
Exchange Offers				1.4	6	
Total	19.64		100	1,635.5		100

Source: Securities Data Company, Inc.

Table 29.2 Merger Transactions Completed from 1985 to 1991

	Mid-Sized Companies Percentage Based on		Large Companies Percentage Based on	
Target Company	Dollar Volume	Number of Deals	Dollar Volume	Number of Deals
Public	88	93	97	95
Private	8	5	1	3
Subsidiary	4	2	2	2

Source: Securities Data Company, Inc.

During 1991, outside advisors were involved in 28% of the total number of mid-sized and 33% of large merger transactions. However, in terms of dollars, Table 29.4 shows that advisors participated in 80% of mid-sized and 90% of large merger deals.[1]

Trends Affecting Valuation Approaches

The following trends have influenced the application of accepted valuation approaches, and, hence, resulting values:

1. In the past few years, the high valuations of publicly traded securities, particularly within the S&P Industrials (S&P 400), have placed financial restrictions on the number of deals and their prices, especially for large firms. As of July 1992, buyers could not justify paying the historical average premium over market of 35%–50% because the current public market, particularly for large firms, was not priced at average historical levels. Accordingly, relying on current prices in some markets may overstate value.

2. Strategic buyers (such as customers, competitors, and suppliers) accounted for a greater proportion of transactions in 1991 than in earlier years and this trend may continue. Strategic buyers may wish to determine both the stand-alone value of a target company and the potential dollar-added value to the buyer of a combination.

3. Recently, leveraged-buyout lenders have required "real" equity (instead of the 9:1 debt-to-equity levels of the mid-1980s). More conservative lending practices, by lenders who

Table 29.3 Completed Transactions from 1985 to 1991: Comparison of Dollar Volume by Year

	Mid-Sized Companies				Large Companies			
Years	Mergers (%)	Tender Offers (%)	LBOs[1] (%)	NCTs[2] (%)	Mergers (%)	Tender Offers (%)	LBOs (%)	NCTs (%)
1985	26	17	25	27	34	40	9	16
1986	48	41	2	67	61	47	42	87
1987	46	63	38	38	58	56	32	63
1988	100	100	100	100	83	88	50	48
1989	88	77	41	94	100	100	100	100
1990	77	22	42	87	49	52	13	47
1991	44	36	36	53	31	14	10	71
Total Activity[3]	49	13	4	26	46	23	9	10

[1]Leveraged buyouts.
[2]Nonclassified Transactions.
[3]See Table 29.1 for details.
Note: Expressed as a percentage, the best year is 100%
Source: Securities Data Company, Inc.

Table 29.4   Merger Transactions Completed in 1991

	Mid-Sized Companies Percentage Based on		Large Companies Percentage Based on	
	Dollar Volume	Number of Deals	Dollar Volume	Number of Deals
Deals with Advisors	80	28	90	33
Deals without Advisors	20	72	10	67

Source: Securities Data Company, Inc.

are still willing to participate, have resulted in a smaller universe of buyers paying decreasing multiples.

4. A mature market for older industries within the S&P 400 may also justify lower multiples.

Focus of a Valuation Study

The first and most important step in determining the value of a company is to analyze and understand its operations, finances, and markets. It is most helpful to perform a thorough study of the company and its competitive position within its industry before performing other steps of a valuation analysis.

The initial study of a business enables the analyst to form an opinion of the company's viability and its future prospects, which, in turn, influence every aspect of the subsequent valuation analysis. The analyst can then begin to answer the question, "Does the company deserve to be valued at, above, or below current industry valuation benchmarks?" The study may also uncover special factors that may alter the analyst's valuation approaches. A side benefit of this study may be that the structure of a proposed deal can be improved in a manner that is mutually beneficial to both parties.

A Company and its Competitive Position

In analyzing a company and its competitive position, an analyst may focus on all or some of the following factors:

Company Characteristics. Company characteristics include: recent operating history, ownership history, current owners and ownership interests, owner's compensation and management philosophy, recent and historical changes in business, current lines of business, main products or services, customers, suppliers, financial performance (historical and prospective), nonrecurring and discretionary items on the income statement, management and personnel, facilities, business plans and objectives,

organizational structure, and past and ongoing investment requirements.

Industry Characteristics. Industry characteristics include: a definition of the company's industry and market, the size and nature of its market, market growth (historical and prospective), market and submarket trends, barriers to entry, factors influencing demand (such as sensitivity to general business cycles and foreign competition), competitive features (such as price, quality, service, or reputation), competitors, recent acquisitions of competitors, demographics, and regulatory environment. The analyst should assess how industry conditions affect the company and its prospects.

Company's Competitive Position. The analyst should identify: the company's market share, its competitive advantage(s) and disadvantage(s), growth strategy, geographic concentration, methods of distribution and sale, latent or unaccommodated opportunities, and current and prospective industry ranking.

Sources of Information

On the Company. Some of the most important sources of information on a company are: its audited financial statements,[2] internal business plans, management personnel and advisors, articles in trade journals and newspapers, and the analyst's review of the company's major facilities. The analyst may use a standard checklist to identify and obtain all relevant information.

On the Industry. The following sources provide useful information on a variety of industries and identify the major companies in each: *Standard & Poor's Industry Surveys, The Value Line Investment Survey, The Wall Street Transcript, U.S. Industrial Outlook,*[3] research reports by Wall Street investment firms,[4] and reports and information from industry and trade groups.

In practice, it is not always possible to obtain all relevant information, but, because valuations depend on a mixture of judgment and hard facts, a lack of company and industry information need not prevent an analyst from approximating the value of a company.

Adjustments to a Company's Financial Statements

In the process of studying a company, an analyst may deem it necessary to adjust the historical financial statements that will be used in the valuation analysis. Normally, financial statements are adjusted to better reflect the ongoing or recurring profitability of a business or to place a firm on a more even level of comparison with selected public companies.

In essence, an analyst will strip away whatever nonoperating layers exist to get to the core businesses, and attempt to eliminate distortions to earnings performance caused by nonrecurring events and circumstances. The analyst will typically make these adjustments at the beginning of the financial analysis of the company and before applying specific valuation approaches.

Fundamental Factors Affecting Value

A company's historical and expected financial performance affect its value. Useful financial performance indicators include:

Size	sales and total assets
Growth	sales growth and growth in EBIT[5]
Margins	profit margins
Returns	return on equity, return on invested capital, or return on assets
Leverage	stockholders' equity relative to total assets
Market Share	larger is better than smaller

All other factors being equal, larger firms with high growth rates, good margins and returns, and low leverage are priced much more attractively than operationally similar firms with a less impressive financial performance. Most likely though, the good financial performer will have an advantage in a nonfinancial area, such as management, operations, location, products, or markets.

Major Valuation Approaches

To determine a range of values for a private or public company, a valuation analyst typically considers three standard approaches (and variations thereof). They include: 1) the income approach (of which a discounted cash flow method is one of the most common) 2) the market approach, and 3) the asset-based approach. A more detailed description of each approach follows.

Discounted Cash Flow Method

The primary focus of the discounted cash flow (DCF) method is on a company's future financial performance. The DCF method, a form of the income approach, bases value on a company's forecasted surplus cash flows. This approach is frequently used to value both public and private companies in countries with stable economic environments and developed capital markets because these qualities facilitate better forecasting.

Market Approach

The market approach bases value on transactions that have recently taken place in the public marketplace. Analysts use publicly available prices and financial information as a basis for determining the value of private and thinly traded public companies in countries with highly developed equity capital markets. In the United States, three different markets provide reported prices: the public stock, acquisitions, and initial public offerings markets. The market approach is the most commonly used valuation approach in the United States for private firms.

Asset-Based Approach

The asset-based approach bases a company's total value on the current values of its individual assets (tangible and intangible) and liabilities. This approach is frequently used in developed economies to value companies whose primary source of income is derived from investments (for instance, a portfolio of marketable securities, a venture capital fund, or a real estate partnership), and, in developing economies, such as the newly privatized economies of Eastern Europe, to value a broader spectrum of companies. This approach is often referred to as the restated-balance-sheet method or the adjusted-book-value method.

Performing a Valuation Study

We have described the DCF approach in somewhat more detail than the market and asset-based approaches because it is more technical. In addition, as of the autumn of 1992, the public market appeared to be out of line with the private market, thereby requiring the application of additional judgment in the use of the market approach. Finally, the asset-based approach is only useful in a limited number of industries and for a limited number of purposes.

Discounted Cash Flow Method

The DCF method views a business purely in terms of cash and risk. The more cash flow a company is expected to generate over time, the more valuable it is, holding risk equal, and the lower the risk of achieving a given level of cash flow, the more valuable the company is. (It is assumed that all surplus cash will be paid to stockholders during the year the surplus is achieved.) To apply the DCF method, the analyst must have an understanding of the business, its past performance, and a good sense of the company's growth and earnings prospects.

In applying the DCF method, an analyst uses assumptions (based on his or her analysis of the company, current and historical economic factors, trends within the company's industry, and management's estimates of future performance) to forecast the surplus cash *(cash flow)* a business will produce over a certain period of time (the *forecast horizon* or *forecast period)*.

Expected cash flow for all future years in the horizon is then discounted back to the present by the risk-adjusted cost of capital to obtain the *net present value* of future cash flows.

Next, the value of the company at the end of the projection period *(terminal value)* is estimated and discounted to the present by a risk-adjusted discount rate.

Finally, the fair market value of the company is calculated by summing the net present value of its cash flows over the forecast period and the net present value of its terminal value at the end of the period.

Mechanics of the DCF Method

To review, the DCF method consists of the following steps:

1. Select a forecast horizon (often five to ten years).

2. Develop a forecast of the company's expected financial performance and condition for the horizon period. For the DCF method to be useful, the balance sheet and income statement should be projected.

3. Identify the cash flow to stockholders or to stakeholders (equity plus debt) for each year in the forecast horizon. Cash flow may be negative or positive.

4. Estimate the company's cost of capital.

5. Estimate the value of the company at the end of the forecast period (terminal value).

6. Discount the cash flow and the terminal value back to the present by the cost of capital.

7. In the case of the debt-free method, subtract recurring borrowings, whether recorded as long-term or short-term, as of the valuation date, to estimate the value of the business to its equity owners.

The DCF approach can be applied using the *debt-free method* (identify cash flow as if the firm had no debt) or the *leveraged method* (identify cash flow after deducting interest expense and net change in financing). The debt-free method is more commonly used to value controlling ownership interests.

1. Select a Forecast Horizon

In order to determine a current DCF value, the valuation analyst must estimate internal cash flows and the terminal value of the company for some period of time, most commonly for five to ten years in the future. (It is assumed that, at the end of the forecast period, there will still be an operating business.) A forecast period of five years is probably the most common, but the number of years in the forecast horizon should be a rational decision. The length of the forecast period can be influenced by any of the following considerations:

a. Expected market conditions, the company's rate of growth, and its competition.

b. The firm's market share and its competitive strategy and investment.

c. The number of years of expected rapid or uneven growth. (One should forecast one year past the first year of the normal growth rate.)

d. The number of years of expected improving (or declining) margins (gross profit, operating profit, or pretax profits).

e. The number of years in which capital expenditures can be reasonably estimated.

f. The valuer's degree of confidence in forecasting the firm's financial performance and condition for each year in the forecast period (as well as his or her degree of confidence in the reasonableness of the terminal value).

2. Develop a Financial Forecast

Ideally, a simple forecast model, which lets a valuation analyst test assumptions and perform a sensitivity analysis, becomes the basis on which to develop the financial forecast. Good DCF valuation models provide a list of assumptions and will reveal the impact on value that changes in key assumptions will have. To develop a realistic financial forecast, a study of the company, as outlined earlier, should have already been performed. An analyst must have a good understanding of the company, its industry, its position within its industry, the current phase of its business cycle, and its prospects for growth.

To forecast the operating part of the business, the balance sheet and income statement must be stripped of nonoperating assets and nonoperating income. For DCF valuation purposes, investments are typically considered nonoperating assets.

Both statements—income statement and balance sheet—should be developed. If only the income statement is projected, the assumed incremental changes in the balance sheet may appear reasonable in isolation; however, in aggregate, they may not be.

Projecting the balance sheet allows the analyst to assess his or her assumptions based on:

a. the actual individual assets and liabilities and their relative percentage to total assets, and

b. the actual historical amounts and rates of growth.

3. Identify the Cash Flow

Cash flow is the surplus cash that a business generates from operations. In theory, surplus cash represents cash that could be taken out of a business each year without impairing current performance or growth potential. Once a forecast of the financial statements has been prepared, calculating cash flow is a mechanical process using certain items that were already forecasted.

The mechanics of the DCF can be carried out using either of two methods, each using a different type of cash flow, to determine value: a debt-free method and a leveraged method. In the debt-free method, *free cash flow* is forecasted as if the company had no debt during the forecast period. In financial terms, free cash flow is defined as operating cash receipts minus all operating cash disbursements, whether recorded on the income statement or balance sheet. The costs of debt financing, such as interest expense, debt repayments, and new debt financing are excluded, and a pro forma income tax is imputed on earnings before interest and taxes (EBIT) instead of using actual interest expenses and income taxes.

In the leveraged method, *net cash flow* is forecasted starting with the current capital structure and by deducting interest expense, income taxes, and net changes in debt financing (among other variables).

In this chapter, the term *net cash flow* is used to denote cash flow detrimental in the leveraged method, as opposed to the term free cash flow, which applies to the debt-free method.

Following is a step-by-step look at each method:

Debt-Free Method. The calculation of free cash flow is as follows:

Operating profit (excluding nonoperating income (expense)), defined as EBIT after depreciation and amortization.

Less: Imputed income taxes on EBIT
Add: Noncash charges itemized on statement of cash flows, such as depreciation and amortization and deferred taxes
Add: Income from sale of business segment or property, plant, and equipment
Less: Capital expenditures
Less: Changes in noncash working capital (common elements are listed below)
= Free cash flow

Leveraged Method. The calculation of net cash flow is as follows:

Net income
Add: Noncash charges itemized on the statement of cash flows, such as depreciation and amortization, extraordinary items and discontinued operations and deferred taxes
Add: Income from sale of a business segment or property, plant, and equipment
Less: Capital expenditures
Less: Changes in noncash working capital, including receivables, inventory, accounts payable and accrued liabilities, income taxes accrued, and net change in other assets and liabilities
Add: Net new debt (minus existing debt paid down, plus new debt incurred)
= Net cash flow

Common assumptions used in the leveraged method:

♦ Interest rates will remain at current levels.

♦ The company will maintain a constant debt-to-equity ratio.

Depreciation and capital expenditures can be obtained directly from the statement of cash flows, along with changes in working capital.[6]

Note that, with positive growth over time, capital expenditures will typically exceed depreciation, using either method. Table 29.5 is an example of a calculation of free cash flow.

4. Estimate the Company's Cost of Capital

At this point in the DCF analysis we have identified the cash flows for each year of the forecast period. We may also have estimated the value of the company at the end of the forecast period (See step 5). We must now combine these separate pieces of value to arrive at one total current value. To do so, discount the forecasted amounts back to the present using a discount rate.

The discount rate should incorporate both the business and financial risks associated with investing in a company. Investors' perceptions of these risks, and, the estimation of the discount rate will affect the value of a business. In addition to reflecting general business and financial risk, the discount rate might be adjusted upward to reflect the likelihood that the forecasted cash flows may not be achieved. A higher discount rate means a lower value; con-. versely, a lower discount rate means a higher value.

The discount rate most often used for DCF analysis is the company's cost of capital(COEC). In the leveraged method, the applicable discount rate is the company's cost of equity capital. In the debt-free method, the applicable discount rate is the

company's weighted average cost of capital (WACC) i.e., the blended cost of both equity and debt capital. In this method, even if a company has no debt in its capital structure, the analysis may indicate that the company has the ability to borrow, thereby changing its overall blended cost of capital and its DCF value.

Cost of Equity Capital. The cost of equity capital represents the expected after-tax return to investors in a company, to compensate them for inherent business and financial risks. Among many methods used to calculate the COEC, the Capital Asset Pricing Model (CAPM) is perhaps most commonly used in analyzing public companies. One variation of the CAPM shown, is commonly used in analyzing closely held companies. In this variation, the cost of equity capital of a public or private company can be expressed by the formula:

$$COEC = R_f + B(R_p) + Sp \pm$$
Subject Company Adjustment

Where $COEC$ is the cost of equity capital, R_f is the "riskless" rate of return, B s the beta of the stock, R_p is the equity risk premium, and Sp is the small stock premium.

Table 29.5   Discounted Cash Flow Approach: Calculation of Free Cash Flow[1] (Debt Free Method)

	Years									
	1	2	3	4	5	6	7	8	9	10
Sales ($)	21,000	22,000	23,000	24,000	26,000	28,000	30,000	33,000	36,000	39,000
Earnings Before Interest and Taxes (EBIT)[2]	1,400	1,500	1,600	1,700	1,900	2,100	2,300	2,600	2,900	3,200
Income Taxes and Taxes (EBIT)[3]	(600)	(500)	(600)	(600)	(600)	(700)	(800)	(900)	(1,000)	(1,000)
Debt-Free Earnings After Taxes[4]	800	1,000	1,000	1,100	1,300	1,400	1,500	1,700	1,900	2,100
Add: Depreciation[5]	300	300	300	400	400	400	500	500	500	600
Less: Capital Expenditures[5]	(400)	(400)	(400)	(500)	(500)	(500)	(600)	(600)	(600)	(700)
Less: Increase in Working Capital[5,6]	(200)	(200)	(200)	(200)	(400)	(400)	(400)	(600)	(600)	(600)
Free Cash Flow[7]	500	700	700	800	800	900	1,000	1,000	(1,200)	(1,400)

[1]Free Cash Flow can be approximated from accounting data as follows:
   Operating earnings before interest and taxes (EBIT) and other nonoperating, noncash expenses, such as amortization of goodwill (adjusted EBIT)
   Less: Provision for income taxes on EBIT or adjusted EBIT
   Add: Depreciation
   Less: Capital expenditures
   Less: Changes in noncash working capital
[2]Represents the operating profits of the company.
[3]Income tax is calculated based on EBIT even if the company has debt and interest expense.
[4]Represents after-tax profits of a debt-free company.
[5]From statement of cash flows.
[6]Represents the additional cash investment in items such as receivables and inventories, net of current payables and accruals, required by the expanding level of business.
[7]See Table 29.6 for use in determining the DCF value.

The *"riskless" rate of return* is the yield on an investment considered to be risk free, such as a government security. *Beta* measures the price volatility of the stock relative to the overall stock market and is often calculated based on the Betas of similar public companies when valuing a closely held firm. The *equity risk premium* is the additional total return that an investment in the stock market would have provided over and above the yield of a "riskless" security such as a government bond. The *small stock premium* is the additional return that, historically, would have been earned by an investment in a group of New York Stock Exchange companies ranked in the lowest quintile in terms of equity market capitalization. The subject company adjustment is based on the judgment of the analyst as to whether the subject company's cost of equity capital is above or below the level suggested by these normal public market benchmarks.

For example, the cost of equity capital for a firm in a stable industry would be calculated as follows:

COEC = 5.5% (intermediate-term Treasury rate) plus 1.07 (beta of stock) × 7.0% (equity risk premium) plus 5.0% (small stock premium) plus 0.0% (subject company adjustment)

$$= \ 5.5\% + 1.07\ (7.0\%) + 5.0\%$$

$$= \ 18.0\%$$

In this example, we used a five-year treasury note as the basis for the "riskless" rate of return. A beta of 1.07 was based on the betas of a group of comparable public companies. The equity risk premium[8] was the difference between common stock total returns and intermediate-term government bond yields. The small stock premium was the difference between total small stock returns and total common stock returns, using a recognized source.[9] The subject company adjustment was a judgmental determination of risk associated with ownership of the company.

The cost of equity capital as determined earlier would be the applicable discount rate in a leveraged method. In a debt-free method, it would be one of two main factors used in determining the weighted average cost of capital.

Cost of Debt Capital. The cost of debt capital represents the after-tax cost of borrowing longer-term funds. The cost of debt capital can be expressed by the formula:

$$CODC = i\,(1 - TD)$$

Where *CODC* is the cost of debt capital, *i* is the borrowing rate, and *TD* is the corporate income tax rate. In this valuation we estimated the after-tax cost of debt capital at 6.0%. The benefit of debt financing is offset by the additional financial risk that a company assumes as it increases its debt as a percentage of total capital. Such financial risk drives up marginal borrowings costs.

Weighted Average Cost of Capital. The WACC is a company's blended cost of equity and debt capital. The weighting is based on the expected capital structure of equity and debt at market—not book—value. The WACC is usually used as the discount rate in a DCF analysis because it represents the average cost of debt and equity funds. When using the WACC, the analyst assumes that the company's capital structure includes debt and that the proportion of debt relative to equity at market value can be determined.

In the valuation mentioned earlier, we calculated the WACC as follows:

	Cost (%)	Weight (%)	Weighted Amounts
Equity capital	18.0	60.0	10.8
Debt capital	6.0	40.0	2.4
Weighted average cost of capital			__13.2__

We assumed that the acquired company would have a debt/equity ratio of 1/1, and estimated that the market value of the equity would be 1.5 times book (based on a market approach), whereas the market value of the debt would be its stated balance sheet value.

5. Estimate the Value of the Company at the End of the Forecast Period (Terminal Value)

Most DCF valuation models contain at least five years of forecasted data, but there is nothing inherently incorrect in using a shorter forecast period. In practice, analysts try to forecast as many years as it takes until the company is operating in a mature marketplace, so that no further value can be created for shareholders. In a leveraged method, the equity of a firm is most commonly valued at the end of the forecast period. In a debt-free method, the enterprise (equity and debt of the firm) is valued at the end of the forecast period.

To estimate what a company's value will be five to ten years in the future, an analyst makes a terminal value assumption. The most common method is known as the perpetuity method, which assumes that the operating cash flows in the final forecasted year will remain constant forever. The perpetuity method (an important variable of the DCF approach) is based on the concept that competitors will enter the business and drive down a company's returns until the value of the company cannot be increased by additional investment. Since, in this method, there is no growth and no reinvestment assumed beyond an amount to maintain the existing size of the fixed asset base, the terminal year cash flow will be equal to the company's after tax operating income, on a debt-free basis, and equal to the net income, on a leveraged basis. There are also variations on the perpetuity method, such as assuming that the expected cash flows in the last forecasted year will grow at a certain rate forever. But, if a perpetuity growth assumption is used, an analyst must be mindful that perpetual real (or volume) growth (as opposed to inflationary or price growth) is theoretically impossible.

Another way to estimate the terminal value is to apply multiples (such as current or adjusted multiples of EBIT, and/or EBIT plus depreciation, and/or earnings, and/or book value) to relevant financial attributes estimated for the final year of the forecast period.

When using this method, the analyst should recognize that the multiples used with the leveraged and debt-free methods differ. The following multiples are only relevant when using a leveraged method:

♦ Equity price/net income

♦ Equity price/three-year (four-year, etc.) average net income

♦ Equity price/book value of stockholder's equity

The following multiples are relevant when using a debt-free method:

♦ Total capital/EBIT

♦ Total capital/EBITDA[7]

♦ Total capital/book value plus debt

♦ Price/earnings

♦ Price/three-year (four-year, etc.) average earnings

It is wise to calculate the terminal value in more ways than one, especially if two or more assumptions result in similar values. Even if a book value multiple is not used, the reasonableness of the estimated terminal value might be assessed by comparing it to the forecasted book value of the company at the end of the forecast period. It is important to calculate a realistic terminal value because this amount can often contribute 50% or more to the final DCF value when a five-year forecast period is used.

6. Discount the Free Cash Flow and the Terminal Value

Discounting the net cash flow or free cash flow for each forecasted year and the terminal value at the end of the forecast period is a mechanical process. The important elements of the DCF approach are the assumptions used to determine either the net cash flow or the free cash flow, the terminal value, and the discount rate.

In a leveraged method, the net cash flows and the terminal value are discounted by the cost of equity capital. In a debt-free method, the free cash flows and the terminal value are discounted by the weighted average cost of capital.

7. Subtract Borrowing as of the Valuation Date (Only in the Case of the Debt-Free Method)

In the debt-free method, the net present value of the free cash flows and the terminal value represent the market value of a company's total capital (debt and equity). Since most businesses have some level of debt, it should be subtracted to arrive at the value of the company to its equity owners. This is necessary because the claims of debtholders represent a stake in the value of the company that must be settled, in theory, before the owners can obtain value. Recorded borrowings may approximate market value if the interest rate on debt represents current market rates. If interest is not at market, the market value of the debt may differ from the recorded amount. Table 29.6 is an example of a determination of DCF value.

Nonoperating Assets. The DCF approach estimates the value of an operating company based on its expected cash generating performance. It values only the operating entity and ignores assets that are not used in operations. However, such assets provide additional value to the company above the DCF value. (Conversely, nonoperating liabilities detract from value.) Therefore, all nonoperating assets, such as excess cash, marketable securities, unused land, buildings, plant and machinery, or an investment in another business not generating income, should be identified, appraised, and valued. Their cumulative value is added to the DCF value to arrive at the value of the operating entity plus its nonoperating assets.

Market Approach

The market approach bases value on current prices of similar businesses. Depending on the source of

Table 29.6   Discounted Cash Flow Approach: Determination of DCF Value (Assuming a 13% Discount Rate)[1] (Debt Free Method)

Years	Free Cash Flow[2]	Discount Factor[3]	Present Value[4]	Cumulative Present Value
1	$ 500	0.885	$ 442	$ 442
2	700	0.783	548	990
3	700	0.693	485	1,475
4	800	0.613	491	1,966
5	800	0.543	434	2,400
6	900	0.480	432	2,832
7	1,000	0.425	425	3,257
8	1,000	0.376	376	3,633
9	1,200	0.333	399	4,032
10	1,400	0.295	412	4,444
Residual Value	16,200[5]	0.295	4,779	9,223[6]
Less: Present Value of Debt Assumed[7]				(1,000)
Add: Assets Not Required for Operations[8]				1,100
Value of Equity				$9,323

[1]Based on weighted average cost of capital. See text for explanation.
[2]See Table 29.5 for calculation of free cash flow.
[3]Based on the discount rate in the year the cash flow is received.
[4]The present value is the free cash flow multiplied by the discount factor.
[5]We assume that the Year 10 debt-free earnings after taxes of $2,100 (see Table 29.5) would be the free cash flow in perpetuity. (See discussion on Terminal Value for Rationale.) The present value of a perpetuity is the cash flow divided by the discount rate. In our example, the perpetuity is calculated as follows:
$$\frac{\$2,100}{.13} = 16,200 \text{ (rounded)}$$
This amount represents the value of the business at the year end of Year 10. We then discounted this amount by the Year 10 discount factor to obtain its present value as of the valuation date.
[6]This amount represents the value of the firm's total capital (equity and debt) based on its operating cash flows.
[7]See text for explanation.
[8]Additional value in business entity not reflected by the DCF value.

these comparable prices, one of three possible sub-sets to the market approach can be applied:

♦ The *comparable company method* is applied when value is based on prices paid for publicly traded shares (prices paid by investors in the secondary market for minority ownership interests in publicly traded companies).

♦ The *comparable acquisitions method* is applied when value is based on prices paid in reported acquisitions (prices paid by purchasers of ownership interests in reported acquisitions).

♦ The *comparable IPO (initial public offerings) method* is applied when value is based on prices paid in initial public offerings (prices

paid by investors for minority ownership interests in companies whose common stock is issued to the public for the first time).

The remainder of this discussion will focus on the first two methods. The comparable company and comparable acquisitions methods derive value through analogy, by comparing the performance of a firm with similar public and acquired firms. The comparable company method is used to value private firms and thinly traded public firms, and the comparable acquisitions method is used to value private and public firms.

Comparable Company Method. Many medium to large private firms in the United States are valued using the public market as a benchmark. There are more than 13,000 publicly traded companies in the United States that make information available to the public. Standard & Poor's maintains current information on approximately 5,000 of the most actively traded public companies. Some of these data, including recent stock prices, are published monthly in the S&P *Stock Guide*. In addition, publicly traded companies file with the SEC annually and quarterly. These public documents provide detailed descriptive and financial information.

Comparable Acquisitions Method. A lack of detailed financial information and a lack of confidence in published data may prevent an analyst from using the comparable acquisitions method. However, there are many reported acquisitions per year in the United States that provide some financial history on the seller, and an analyst can use financial information from these transactions to develop appropriate acquisition price multiples. Relevant transactions may be identified through secondary sources that specialize in collecting merger and acquisition transaction data. But, to develop acquisition price multiples, an analyst should rely only on original source documents.

Most reported acquisitions include transactions involving public companies or their divisions. Transaction details involving two private companies tend not to be reported. And even if a private transaction price were reported, an analyst could not compute the acquisition price multiples without financial information on the seller.

Mechanics of the Market Approach. The mechanics of the comparable company and the comparable acquisitions methods are similar:

1. Select publicly traded firms and/or reported acquisitions.

2. Calculate relevant market/price multiples.

3. Apply selected market/price multiples to company data.

4. Weight resulting indicated values to obtain one overall value.

5. Apply discounts and/or premiums.

1. Select Publicly Traded Firms and/or Reported Acquisitions

As a group, comparable companies and comparable acquisitions should have characteristics that are similar to the subject company. Ideally, these should include operational and financial (including growth) characteristics. In practice, it is rare to find companies that are both operationally and financially sim-

ilar to the company being valued. Sometimes an analyst is forced to select a mixture of companies, of which some are financially comparable and the rest are operationally comparable. For example, we recently valued a small lease advisory/brokerage firm and found no similar public companies. Therefore, we used two groups of companies—larger brokerage firms in industries different from the subject company's and small service firms of size and performance similar to the subject company's. This is a valid procedure because comparable companies seldom exist.

The first step in searching for comparable companies or acquisitions is to define the business of the subject company in general economic terms, such as a metals processor, a professional services firm, or a wholesaler of consumer nondurables. Next, the company's main line of business is identified by a four-digit (primary) Standard Industrial Classification (SIC) Code, found in the *Standard Industrial Classification Manual 1987* (most recent edition), a government publication prepared by the Office of Management and Budget. Primary SIC Codes, under which public companies or acquisitions similar to the subject company may be classified, are also identified. The analyst then conducts a search for comparable companies or acquisitions using secondary sources of data.

Comparable Companies. Although there are more than 13,000 public companies in the United States, it is seldom possible to identify one that is comparable to the subject company. Realizing that finding an exact match is unlikely, analysts define comparability in broad terms. The public companies selected should have characteristics similar to the subject company, but not necessarily *operationally* similar. The goal is to find companies which, *as a group*, can be viewed by rational investors as having similar investment characteristics.

Comparable Acquisitions. Although, in the United States, public information on thousands of acquisitions provide some financial history on sellers, seldom does an analyst find a recent acquisition of a firm that is operationally and financially similar to the subject company. Therefore, comparability may be defined in terms that are at least as broad as those for comparable companies.

2. Calculate Relevant Market/Price Multiples

Market/price multiples show the relationships between value and financial performance. Market/price multiples are obtained by dividing the market value of a company's equity, or its enterprise value, by financial performance characteristics that the analyst believes contribute to its market value, such as earnings, cash flow, and book value.

Market/price multiples can be developed based on:

a. The market value of the equity (equity multiples). These multiples are calculated by multiplying the per-share price of the common shares by the total number of common shares outstanding. Commonly used equity multiples include price/earnings (latest 12 months, latest fiscal year, three-year average, current fiscal year estimate, next fiscal year estimate); price/net cash flow (latest fiscal year, three-year average net cash flow), and price/tangible book value.

b. The market value of the equity and the book value of debt, commonly referred to as total capital or invested capital. Total capital multiples are calculated by adding the long-term and short-term outstanding debt (obtained from a recent balance sheet) to the market value of the equity. Long-term debt includes capitalized lease obligations and normal borrowings. Short-term debt includes notes payable to financial institutions and current portion of long-term debt. Commonly used total capital multiples include total capital/EBIT (latest 12 months, latest fiscal year, three-year average, current fiscal year estimate, next fiscal year estimate); total capital/net cash flow before income taxes and interest expenses; and total capital/tangible book value plus debt.

c. The market value of the equity and book value of the debt *minus* excess cash. This multiple is calculated by subtracting available excess cash from the total capital amount previously determined.

Market price multiples should be calculated on a per-share basis, particularly when dealing with multiyear periods of earnings or cash flow. As discussed earlier, either equity multiples or total capital multiples can be used. The total capital method is preferable because it allows consideration of the effect of debt on the value of the company.

The actual multiples used depend on the industry and on the financial characteristics of the subject company. For example, price/revenues may be a more important indicator of the value of a service business, such as an insurance brokerage or investment management firm, than of a manufacturing company because the buyer (and, indeed, the seller) may often have the ability to adjust the reported cost structure and profits to some industry norm. Conversely, a price/tangible book value multiple may be a better indicator of the value of a manufacturing

Table 29.7 Market Approach: Calculation of Total Capital Multiples[1] of Selected Specialty Chemical Firms (Comparable Company Method)

Public Companies	Total Capital/ Current 12 Months' EBIT	Total Capital/ Recent Fiscal Year EBIT	Total Capital/ 3-Years Average EBIT	Total Capital/ 5-Years Average EBIT	Total Capital/ Current 12 Months' EBITDA	Total Capital/ Recent Fiscal Year EBITDA	Total Capital/ 3-Years Average EBITDA	Total Capital/ 5-Years Average EBITDA	Total Capital/ Total Assets
Lawyer International, Inc.	8.9	9.7	11.9	11.4	7.9	8.5	10.3	10.0	2.0
Valspar Corporation	8.4	8.5	10.1	11.7	6.4	6.5	8.0	9.5	1.3
Guardsman Products, Inc.	7.2	7.5	8.1	9.7	5.8	6.0	6.5	7.7	1.2
Aceto Corporation	7.0	7.3	6.0	6.2	6.6	6.8	5.7	5.9	0.8
Lilly Industrial Coatings, Inc.	8.0	8.1	9.0	9.2	6.9	7.1	7.9	8.2	1.7
MacDermid, Inc.	8.6	9.6	11.5	10.1	6.3	6.9	8.5	8.1	1.2
Crompton and Knowles Corporation	9.6	11.0	13.4	14.2	3.2	9.3	11.1	11.6	1.2
Stepan Company	7.2	7.8	9.9	11.6	4.6	4.9	6.0	6.8	1.0
Selected Multiples[2]	8.2	8.3	10.0	10.8	6.5	6.9	8.0	8.2	1.2

[1]See text for definition of total capital multiples.
[2]See Table 29.8 for determination of market value. In this example, selected multiples are the medians of each group.

business than of an insurance brokerage company because the book value of a manufacturing firm often sets the range of potential profitability, while revenues may set this range for certain service firms. Table 29.7 displays total capital multiples of selected public companies used for the valuation of a hypothetical specialty chemicals manufacturer. Using another example, if a manufacturing company has a history of recent losses, an investor would place greater emphasis on the price/tangible book value multiple than if the company had been profitable because a company's liquidation value typically sets a price floor.

3. Apply Selected Market/Price Multiples

Market/price multiples are then applied to the adjusted financial data of the company, resulting in a separate estimate of fair market value for each multiple applied. For example, application of a price/earnings multiple, a price/cash flow multiple, and a price/book value multiple would result in three separate estimates of value. The closer together these values are, the more confidence an analyst may have in them. In Table 29.8, a determination of market value for the hypothetical chemical company is shown. Notice that of the nine multiples used, five resulted in very similar values (column four).

Applying equity multiples gives the estimated fair market value of the stockholders' equity in a company. Applying total capital multiples (either before or after considering available cash) gives the estimated fair market value of the total capital (equity plus debt) of a company. The long-term and short-term debt should be subtracted from the estimated value of total capital to determine the value of the equity alone.

The total capital multiples tend to provide more consistent estimates of value when either the subject company or the selected public companies are highly leveraged, or the capital structures of the selected public companies and the subject company vary significantly. The application of total capital multiples in the valuation of the hypothetical specialty chemicals manufacturer is visible in Table 29.8.

It is wise to rely on audited financial information obtained from original sources, such as 10Ks, 10Qs, or annual reports, when calculating market/price multiples. The value derived is especially sensitive to price multiples, so it is extremely important to use correct information and to calculate the multiples carefully.

Selection of Multiples. If the subject company's financial performance or size is significantly different from those of the comparable group of public firms,

an analyst may consider selecting market/price multiples above or below the median or average multiple of the public firms. The analyst's judgment will be influenced by the relative financial performance of the subject company and the public firms in at least the following areas: profitability, growth, leverage, and size.

4. Weight Resulting Indicated Values

An overall estimate of value is calculated by weighting the individual estimates obtained by applying market/price multiples. The weights are normally judgmental, based on the performance characteristics the analyst considers most important in driving market value, but they can also be influenced by any consistency in the multiples derived from the public companies' performance.

5. Apply Discounts, Premiums, and Other Adjustments

Finally, discounts, premiums, or other adjustments may be made to the estimated value of a company to reflect differences between it and the group of comparable firms.

Comparable Companies. After applying the appropriate market/price multiples and weighting the resulting values to obtain one overall estimate of value, the analyst considers adjusting the value to reflect the differences between owning 100% (or at least a large holding) of a private company and a minority position in a public company. Remember, by using multiples at which investors value publicly traded firms, we are actually relying on prices paid for shares, not for the whole firm. Consequently, the following two adjustments are often necessary when valuing a controlling interest in a private company.

Control Premium. A control premium is the difference between the per-share price paid for ownership of 100% of a company's common stock (or at least a controlling interest) and ownership of a minority (noncontrolling) interest in the company. The control premium represents the additional price one must pay to have significant influence over or control of the company. An investor with control of a company has the power to change the nature of its business, cost structure, management, policies on dividends, capital investments, and capital structure. An investor with control also has the power to sell or liquidate the company or any part of it, or to bring the company public. Generally, a holder of a minority interest has none of these powers.

Table 29.8   Market Approach: Determination of Market Value of
              "A Specialty Chemical Company" (Comparable Company Method)

Type of Multiple[1]	Market Multiple[2]	Subject Company Component of Value Value[3]	Value of Equity and Debt[4]	Weight[5]	Weighted Amount[6]
Total Capital/Current 12 Months' EBIT	8.2	$ 15,220,000	$ 124,804,000	15%	$ 17,700,000
Total Capital/Recent Fiscal Year EBIT	8.3	14,758,000	122,491,400	15%	18,400,000
Total Capital/3-Year Average EBIT	10.0	11,739,000	107,390,000	8%	9,400,000
Total Capital/5-Year Average EBIT	10.8	9,948,000	107,438,400	8%	8,600,000
Total Capital/Current 12 Months' EBITDA	6.5	18,435,000	119,827,500	15%	18,000,000
Total Capital/Recent Fiscal Year EBITDA	6.9	17,722,000	122,281,800	15%	18,300,000
Total Capital/3-Year Average EBITDA	8.0	12,958,000	103,664,000	8%	8,300,000
Total Capital/5-Year Average EBITDA	8.2	10,746,000	88,117,200	8%	7,000,000
Total Capital/Total Assets	1.2	65,886,000	79,063,200	8%	6,300,000
Total Value of Equity and Debt				100%	$113,000,000

Less: Outstanding Debt at June 30,19xx[7]	(29,900,000)
Estimated Value of Equity If Publicly Traded	83,100,000
Less: 10% Illiquidity Discount	(8,300,000)
	74,800,000
Add: 20% Control Premium	15,000,000
Estimated Value of Equity	$ 89,800,000

[1] See text for description of multiples
[2] See Table 29.7 for market multiples of selected companies.
[3] From adjusted figures of the subject company.
[4] The value of equity and debt is the product of the market multiple and the component of value.
[5] These weights are examples only. In an actual valuation, weights are based on the analyst's judgment of the relative importance of each component of value.
[6] The weighted amount is the product of the value of equity and debt and the corresponding weight.
[7] From the subject company's June 30,19xx balance sheet.

The W.T. Grimm & Co.'s MergerStat[SM] Review[10] is a good source of data on control premiums paid in recent transactions.

Illiquidity Discount. Prices paid for publicly traded shares represent a liquid investment that can be sold at any time and exchanged for cash at current prices. Ownership of a private company, however, represents an illiquid investment. Since the value of a privately held company, as determined by the market approach, is based on prices paid for publicly traded shares, it should be reduced by an appropriate discount, known as an illiquidity or nonmarketability discount. An illiquidity discount for a minority block of stock is normally computed as the difference in price per share between ownership of a marketable security and an otherwise identical restricted security of the same company. An illiquidity discount for a control block of stock is normally based on the private or public companies. However, in the comparable acquisitions method, an analyst may have to consider applying an illiquidity discount as well as other premiums and discounts. In a recent valuation of a privately held firm, an illiquidity discount was not applied because three of four acquisitions of privately held firms were used to estimate the value of the private company. Accordingly, the prices paid in these acquisitions already reflected both a control premium and an illiquidity discount.

Other Premiums and Discounts. An analyst should consider adjusting the value obtained from both the comparable company and comparable acquisitions methods if differences between the subject company and the group of public companies (or acquired firms) affect the value of the subject company. For example, the subject company may have a performance history and prospects better than the group of public companies (or acquired firms). Accordingly, the value of the subject company may have to be adjusted upward (if its superior prospects were not already reflected through an adjustment in the market multiples). Such upward adjustments are usually referred to as premiums.

Frequently, however, the value of a company is adjusted downward because of its weaker position in relation to the selected public companies and/or acquisitions. Such adjustments are referred to as discounts. Commonly applied discounts include: key person discount, key customer discount, and (infrequently) key supplier discount. These discounts are applied because the subject company may depend on one or a few key managers, or on a few customers or suppliers to provide a significant percentage of business, while the selected public companies or acquisitions are not similarly dependent. Discounts may also be appropriate if a company depends on one product or service or one geographic region for its business and the selected public companies or acquisitions do not.

Asset-Based Approach. The asset-based approach is also referred to as the restated-balance-sheet method or the adjusted-book-value approach. According to this approach, the value of an operating business depends on its assets, less its liabilities, when each asset and liability is appraised at fair market value. The value of a company is assumed to be the sum of the individual assets restated to fair market value, less the sum of the individual liabilities restated to fair market value.

The asset-based approach is particularly relevant for businesses where the market or replacement values of significant assets differ from stated balance-sheet values. For example, a holding company with only a portfolio of marketable securities, a real estate

partnership or S corporation, or a fleet of tugs anᵈ barges. Also, companies which rely on resources iⁿ the ground, or which have liquid, fast-turning assets are often valued by using this approach.

The asset-based approach can be applied on a going-concern premise or a liquidation premise. Iⁿ the going-concern premise, each asset is valued aˢ part of a going concern in continuous use. In a liquidation premise, each asset is valued as if it werᵉ to be sold today or in an orderly manner over a shoᵣ period of time. The earning performance and viability of a company may determine which premisᵉ makes more sense. For example, if a company iˢ consistently unprofitable, a liquidation premise iˢ more relevant in most cases. The following discussion focuses on the going-concern premise.

The asset-based approach is important in manʸ acquisitions because future depreciation expenseˢ are estimated using the market values of tangible anᵈ intangible assets as of the transaction date, and theseᵉ expenses may then be used in the DCF approach.

Mechanics of the Asset-Based Approach. Theᵉ asset-based approach is simple in theory. The analysᵗ values each tangible and intangible asset and eacʰ liability separately. The difference between the assets (restated to market value) and liabilities (restateᵈ to market value) is deemed to be the value of theᵉ company. Valuing each asset and liability, howeveʳ can be cumbersome. Fair market value for individuaˡ assets and liabilities is determined by using theᵉ appropriate approach(es). A comprehensive exampleᵉ using a ready-mix concrete company is shown iⁿ Table 29.9. Assets are grouped under current assetˢ noncurrent assets, and property, plant, and equipᵐ ment. Liabilities are grouped under current liabilitieˢ and long-term liabilities.

Combining Valuation Approaches and Results

As indicated earlier, it is a good idea to estimate theᵉ fair market value of a company in more than oneᵉ way, and, frequently, all available valuation approaches and combinations should be used. It woulᵈ be nice if all valuation methods resulted in similaʳ values, but this does not usually happen. The resultᵗ ing indicated values may differ substantially becauseᵉ each analyst applies his or her own experience anᵈ judgment throughout the process. Hence, the oftᵗ used phrase, "valuation is an art, not a science."

Therefore, after applying all relevant valuatioⁿ approaches (and variations), an analyst must decideᵉ which approaches and submethods provide the mosᵗ reliable estimate(s) of value. By doing so, the analysᵗ may be able to determine why disparate values haveᵉ

Table 29.9   Asset-Based Approach:
Restatement of Assets and Liabilities to Fair Market Value

	Balance Sheet at December 31, 19xx[1]	Adjusted Balance Sheet at December 31, 19xx[2]
Assets		
Current Assets		
Cash and marketable securities	$ 1,150,000	$ 1,100,000
Accounts and notes receivable	4,070,000	3,600,000
Inventories	400,000	400,000
Prepaid expenses	200,000	200,000
Total current assets	5,820,000	5,300,000
Cash surrender value of life insurance policy	310,000	310,000
Notes receivable, net of current portion	200,000	200,000
Property, plant, and equipment		
Land	170,000	2,900,000
Buildings	570,000	1,400,000
Machinery and equipment	2,640,000	1,700,000
Transportation equipment	3,950,000	1,800,000
Furniture and fixtures	390,000	340,000
Laboratory equipment	20,000	20,000
Fence	30,000	30,000
	7,770,000	
Less: Accumulated depreciation and amortization	5,000,000	—
Total property, plant, and equipment	2,770,000	8,190,000
Total assets	$ 9,100,000	$ 14,000,000
Liabilities and Stockholders' Equity		
Current liabilities:		
Notes payable	$ 700,000	$ 700,000
Current installments of long-term debt	300,000	300,000
Accounts payable	3,240,000	3,240,000
Accrued expenses	570,000	570,000
Total current liabilities	4,810,000	4,810,000
Long-term debt, excluding current installments	2,250,000	2,000,000
Deferred income taxes	1,040,000	700,000
Total long-term liabilities	3,290,000	2,700,000
Stockholders' equity	1,000,000	6,490,000[3]
Total liabilities and stockholders' equity	$ 9,100,000	$ 14,000,000

[1]From audited financial statements of a ready mix concrete company.
[2]All assets and liabilities were appraised at fair market value.
[3]Adjusted stockholders' equity increased by $5,490,000 due to a $520,000 reduction in current assets, a $5,420,000 increase in property, plant, and equipment, a $250,000 reduction in long-term debt, and a $340,000 reduction in deferred income taxes.

Table 29.10 Determining Value from Results of More Than One Method or Approach[1] "A Specialty Chemical Company" (Summary of Values at September 23, 19xx)

Estimated value based on selected public companies[2]	$ 89,800,000
Estimated value based on selected acquisitions	$ 85,000,000
Estimated value based on most comparable acquisition	$ 101,100,000
Estimated value based on pending acquisition	$ 93,800,000
Estimated range of value[3]	$ 85,000,000 to 95,000,000

[1]Based on results of various market methods.
[2]See Table 29.8 for determination of value.
[3]In developing our overall opinion of value, we have placed most emphasis on the value derived from the selected public companies because: a) we relied on eight public companies, as a group, to develop value, b) we applied nine different capital multiples which resulted in very similar values, c) we used public market prices as of September 23, 19xx to calculate capital multiples (not prices in prior years as in the case of the comparable acquisitions method), d) we selected public companies in the specialty chemical business with consistent profitability, and e) we applied a control premium lower than the industry average which reflected our opinion that Specialty Chemicals, Inc. had fewer value enhancement opportunities than the average public company being acquired in its industry.

been obtained. In the process, the more reliable approach may become apparent. Table 29.10 shows an example of a rational approach to selecting one valuation method over another.

Basically, the market approach provides a range of values based on comparable publicly traded equity and on recent transactions. The range of values indicated by the market approach drives the thinking of buyers and sellers. For buyers, it is the range within which a serious offer should be made. For sellers, it is the range in which to expect a fair offer.

In many instances, the range of values developed using the DCF approach may be lower than that obtained with the market approach because the DCF approach bases value on the expected future performance of the specific company and not on fluctuations in the equity market. In such instances, principals and their advisors should reconcile the gap in their own minds so that buyers and their lenders don't overpay, particularly in a cash transaction, and sellers set realistic expectations.

The asset-based approach is most often used to value businesses that derive most or all of their income from investments (such as investment companies, venture capital funds, and real estate partnerships) and for companies in extraction industries, such as mining. However, it is also frequently used for tax and accounting purposes to allocate an actual or hypothetical acquisition price (determined by using both the market and DCF approaches) to the tangible and intangible assets of a company.

Conclusion

Determining realistic values for a business is crucial. Sellers do not want to give away value that may have

taken a generation to build and buyers do not want to pay for value that does not currently exist. Therefore, the importance of an analyst's judgment, experience, and assessment of the current market cannot be underestimated.

Endnotes

1. This commentary is based on data provided by Securities Data Company, Inc. These data probably do not include all transactions, particularly transactions between two private firms, certain transactions between a public buyer and a private seller, and a foreign buyer and a private seller. Nevertheless, the data probably account for the majority of transactions (in terms of dollar volume), and the historical trends developed from these data would be indicative of the overall transaction market in the United States.

2. Audited financial statements are crucial to both prospective buyers and sellers. Without them, a buyer will not be confident about the performance of a company as presented in the financial statements and the seller will have difficulty reassuring the buyer that "the numbers are good." Accordingly, many valuation experts will not express a valuation opinion for companies with no audited financial statements.

3. *U.S. Industrial Outlook* is published by the U.S. Department of Commerce, International Trade Administration, and is available from the U.S. Government Printing Office, Washington, DC 20402.

4. *Nelson's Directory of Investment Research,* Rye, New York, provides a list of firms and analysts by industry. Research reports can also be obtained on line from the *NEXIS* database.

5. Earnings before interest and taxes.

6. These numbers are the same for both methods.

7. Earnings before interest, taxes, depreciation and amortization.

8. A client wondered if the arithmetic or geometric mean should be used in the determination of the equity risk premium. Implicit in the arithmetic mean provided by Ibbotson Associates is a one-year holding period. But, owners and prospective owners of companies are looking at a longer time horizon than one year, which suggests that the equity risk premium should more correctly

fall between the geometric mean and the arithmetic mean: between 5.1% and 7.0% for large firms. Likewise, the small stock premium should more correctly fall between the geometric mean and the arithmetic mean: between 1.5% and 5.0%. Based on the writer's research, a five-year holding period suggests an equity risk premium (and a small stock premium) in the lower half of these ranges.

We note that even a one percent change in the discount rate can result in a meaningful change in the DCF value.

9. *Stocks, Bonds, Bills and Inflation, 1991 Year Book Market Results 1926-1990,* Ibbotson Associates, Chicago, Illinois.

10. *MergerStat*^SM *Review.* The W.T. Grimm & Co., 135 South LaSalle Street, Chicago, IL 60603.

Chapter 30

Real Estate Valuation: Current Issues and Trends

Lawrence R. Nicholson, MAI
Vice President and Managing Director, Real Estate Advisory Group
American Appraisal Associates, Inc., Milwaukee, WI
Duncan O. Douglas
Director of Research, Real Estate Advisory Group
American Appraisal Associates, Inc., Milwaukee, WI

The real estate appraisal industry is experiencing one of the most dynamic periods ever. Commercial real estate values are plummeting. Banks, thrifts and savings and loans that have loans on commercial real estate have become insolvent, and as a result, the appraisal industry has become a highly regulated profession. The savings and loan crisis has been the catalyst for significant governmental regulation within the industry and has brought about the realization that the role of the appraiser has definitely changed.

Current issues are many and multifaceted. Issues as basic as the definition of value are under scrutiny. Environmental issues, including hazardous wastes, asbestos, and indoor air quality, must be addressed in every report. The Americans with Disabilities Act (ADA) went into effect January 26, 1992, and mandates new requirements for all public and commercial facilities. New valuation techniques must consider the often ignored element of market demand by including a demand side analysis. And because commercial real estate values are being devastated, new techniques have emerged for valuing properties in soft markets.

What Is Market Value?

The recipients of most appraisal reports often request them only because they were instructed, or obliged to do so. When appraisals are ordered, it is important for the client to specify precisely what the purpose and function of the appraisal is to be, for this has an impact on what interests are appraised and what

value is to be determined. Among the most often confused definitions are the following:

Market Value Defined

As defined by the Appraisal Institute (The Appraisal of Real Estate, 9th edition, page 19):

> Market Value is the most probable price, as of a specified date, in cash, terms equivalent to cash, or in other precisely revealed terms, for which the specified property rights should sell after reasonable exposure in a competitive market under all conditions requisite to fair sale, with the buyer and seller each acting prudently, knowledgeably, and for self-interest, and assuming that neither is under undue duress.

As defined by the Federal Home Loan Bank Board:

> Market Value is the most probable price which a property should bring in a competitive and open market under all conditions requisite to a fair sale, with the buyer and seller each acting prudently and knowledgeably, and assuming the price is not affected by undue stimulus. Implicit in this definition is the consummation of a sale as of a specified date and the passing of title from seller to buyer under conditions whereby:
>
> a. Buyer and seller are typically motivated.

335

b. Both parties are well-informed or well-advised, and each acting in what he considers his own best interest.

c. A reasonable time is allowed for exposure in the open market.

d. Payment is made in terms of cash in U.S. dollars or in terms of financial arrangements comparable thereto.

e. The price represents the normal consideration for the property sold, unaffected by special or creative financing or sales concessions granted by anyone associated with the sale.

Fair Value Defined

As defined by the "Rules and Regulations," *Federal Register*, Vol. 55. No. 129, page 2771:

Fair value is the cash price that might reasonably be anticipated in a current sale under all conditions requisite to a fair sale. A fair sale means that the buyer and seller are each acting prudently, knowledgeably, and under no necessity to buy or sell—i.e., other than in a forced or liquidation sale. The appraiser should estimate the cash price that might be received upon exposure to the open market for a reasonable time, considering the property type and local conditions. When a current sale is unlikely—i.e., when it is unlikely that a sale can be completed within twelve months—the appraiser must discount all cash flows generated to the property to obtain the estimate of Fair Value. These cash flows include but are not limited to those arising from ownership, development operation and the sale of the property. The discount applied shall reflect the appraiser's judgment of what a prudent, knowledgeable purchaser under no necessity to buy would be willing to pay to purchase the property in a current sale.

While an accountant or financial analyst would consider market value and fair value to be synonymous, to a real estate professional, there is a significant difference. Appraisers generally consider fair value as the net cash proceeds to the vendor. Market value is the gross sale price to the purchaser.

Liquidation Value

As defined by the Appraisal Institute (*The Dictionary of Real Estate Appraisal*, 2nd edition, page 184):

The price that an owner is compelled to accept when a property must be sold without reasonable market exposure.

The Resolution Trust Corporation (RTC) currently manages the largest portfolio of real estate in the United States. This property is predominantly foreclosed collateral from failed banking institutions, thrifts, and savings and loans. Each of the properties owned are required to be appraised on a regular basis in order to effectively market the properties. Similar to foreclosed properties owned by banking institutions, the RTC looks at a 60 to 90 day period to "unload" the property. When contracting for appraisal services, the RTC requests the market value of the property, not the liquidation value. To an appraiser, the marketing period of a property is assumed to have already occurred, in many cases this can be six to nine months, and the opinion of value is valid only on the date specified. Economic changes or physical changes to the property itself that occur after the appraisal date would substantially alter the value conclusions. This particular assignment really requires an opinion of the liquidation value.

Investment Value

As defined by the Appraisal Institute (*The Dictionary of Real Estate Appraisal*, 2nd edition, page 164):

The specific value of an investment to a particular investor or class of investors based on individual investment requirements, as distinguished from market value, which is impersonal and detached.

There are real estate investors whose appraisal requirements are completely different. They may own property which is subject to favorable financing, or require an analysis for buy/sell or hold/sell decisions. When contracting for appraisal services, the emphasis should be on investment value.

Use Value

As defined by the Appraisal Institute (*The Dictionary of Real Estate Appraisal*, 2nd edition, page 316):

The value of a specific property for a specific use.

For large corporations, the values reported could differ once again. A large industrial complex which covers hundreds of acres of land, on which are constructed a variety of building styles would be a prime example. To an investor, the value of the property without the manufacturer would be minimal. To the manufacturer, the value is in the use of the property as a factor of production. If the two parties were to consider a sale-leaseback situation, what value should be used as a basis? Obviously, if both parties are not fully informed before entering into the agreement, their negotiations may be less than equitable.

Prospective Value Estimate

As defined by the Appraisal Institute (*The Dictionary of Real Estate Appraisal*, 2nd edition, page 239):

> A forecast of value expected to occur at a specified future date. A prospective value estimate is most frequently utilized in connection with real estate projects that are proposed, under construction, under conversion to a new use, or that have otherwise not achieved sellout or a stabilized level of long-term occupancy at the time the appraisal report is written.

Traditionally, real estate appraisers have avoided providing estimates of value that hinge upon future events. This has changed slowly with the inception of discounted cash flow analysis and the use of personal computers. There are very few methods available to appraise subdivisions, proposed buildings, or estimate the value of properties which are subject to conversion without the use of discounting a future cash flow. There are several econometric services available (DRI/McGraw-Hill) which aid appraisers in providing more reliable lease-up scenarios, etc.; a term referred to as Demand-Side Analysis.

The Impact of Appraisal Regulation

After the stock market crash of 1929, the federal government turned to regulations to ensure that such a financial disaster did not reoccur. In a similar manner, after the failure of hundreds of savings and loans and banks in the late 1980s and early 1990s that resulted primarily from troubled real estate loans, the federal government has stepped in with regulations to prevent such a situation from happening again.

The Financial Institutions Reform, Recovery, and Enforcement Act of 1989, commonly referred to as FIRREA, was passed in the aftermath of the savings and loan crisis. In addition to creating the Resolution Trust Corporation (RTC) to liquidate assets of failed savings and loans, FIRREA set minimum real estate appraisal standards and certification requirements for real estate appraisers. No other regulatory change has made such an impact upon the appraisal industry as FIRREA.

During the late 1970s and early 1980s, the Federal Home Loan Bank Board (FHLBB) made some attempts at setting minimum appraisal standards with its Memorandums R-41(b) and R-41(c). However, from a practical standpoint, few lending institutions enforced the consistent application of these standards upon real estate appraisers. If the R-41(b) and R-41(c) standards were universally adhered to, the real estate crisis that we are experiencing today would either not have occurred or would have been much less severe. FIRREA has now been set forth with the legal teeth mandating that any and all real estate appraisals for federally regulated lending institutions must conform to the minimum standards.

Biased and overly optimistic appraisals contributed substantially to the savings and loan crisis. FIRREA has made some long strides in ensuring the independence and quality of the appraisal process by addressing three major areas: identifying which transactions require the use of state certified appraisers; providing minimum appraisal standards for federally related transactions; and, the independence of the appraisal function.

Beginning January 1, 1993, and even earlier based upon individual state mandates, appraisers will be required to complete certification procedures before being allowed to conduct appraisals for any federally related transactions worth more than $50,000. Appraisers will have to meet educational experience in the appraisal industry and pass a state-licensed examination. Furthermore, there are continuing educational requirements necessary to keep the appraisal certification. Some states have taken this certification requirement one step further, requiring that an appropriately certified state appraiser be required to conduct any real estate appraisal within their state, not just for appraisals for financing through federally regulated entities. Each state has both licensed and certified residential appraisers and commercial appraisers with clear rules on when either are required.

Whether the appraisal is to be conducted for federally regulated financing or not, every appraisal in every state must now conform to the Uniform Standards of Professional Appraisal Practice (USPAP). Much like the certified public accountants have a professional code of standards, the Appraisal Standards Board of The Appraisal Foundation have created USPAP to help ensure improved reliability and eliminate biases, resulting in more accurate and sound values for real estate properties and developments, which will ultimately lead to more prudent underwriting decisions.

In order to ensure the independence of the appraisal function, FIRREA has effectively removed the potential borrower from the appraisal process by requiring that the bank independently retain the appraiser rather than the historically typical practice of the borrower commissioning the appraisal service. This action has had the impact of focusing the underwriting concern away from the magnitude of the appraisal numbers, and more appropriately upon the quality of the appraisal and the supportability of the specific assumptions and conclusions the appraiser utilized in reaching the value opinion. Furthermore, the appraiser must attest to the integrity of the appraisal process by stating within every report that:

My compensation is not contingent upon the reporting of a predetermined value or direction in value that favors the cause of the client, the amount of the value estimate, the attainment of a stipulated result, or the occurrence of a subsequent event.

The choice of an appraiser should not be based upon where state borders fall. An appraisal is only as good as the appraiser who writes it, and a good appraiser is one who is qualified and experienced in the specific property type and market—whether the assignment involves a national, regional, or local market. Therefore, the federal government has mandated that states provide for reciprocity between themselves regarding the certification of appraisers. These reciprocal agreements allow a certified appraiser to cross state boundaries to value a property. Users of appraisal services now need to not only determine that the appraiser hired is properly certified for the property type being appraised, but as importantly, that the individual appraiser has had appropriate experience.

FIRREA has impacted the appraisal industry significantly and these impacts will continue to be positively felt throughout the entire real estate industry. Investors will return to the real estate markets once the long-term, positive effects of FIRREA work to correct the current real estate environment. FIRREA has already lead to an upgrading of the appraisal profession by recognizing the quality-oriented, trustworthy appraiser. Appraisals have become more than just a "file-stuffer" or checklist item; they are now appropriately an important informative factor driving real estate underwriting and investment decision-making processes.

Value Trends

When institutional investors began allocating funds to real estate there was no index to measure the performance of real estate as an asset class. There was a need for better understanding of the performance of real estate by region and by property. Analysts also needed to know how real estate compared with other asset classes, stocks, bonds, etc. On December 31, 1977, a pool of 234 properties valued at $587 million became the basis for the index of institutional grade properties. Voting members of the National Council of Real Estate Investment Fiduciaries (NCREIF), and the Frank Russell Company aggregate data on institutional grade properties. The property types are segmented into the following classifications: office, retail, R&D office, warehouse, and apartment. Data on the income and appreciation returns for each property type are submitted on a quarterly basis and the aggregate data is known as the Russell-NCREIF Property Index. This is not a transactional database, but represents the appraised value of the portfolios combined with the changes in income. The index measures the historical performance of income-producing properties owned by commingled funds on behalf of qualified pension and profit-sharing trusts.

As of March 31, 1992, the index contained almost 1700 properties valued at $22.7 billion. As Figures 30.1 and 30.2 illustrate, for the first quarter of 1992, institutional investors wrote down the value of their real estate portfolios by 12.1%, the largest in the history of the index. It is the first time in the history of the index that there was a negative index value, −5.8%, and the first time that every property class endured write downs. If it were not for the 7% income appreciation return to offset the negative appreciation, write downs would have been significantly higher.

The office market, with write downs of 16.2%, represents an asset class valued at almost $7.4 billion; the write down would be in the neighborhood of $1.2 billion. The R&D office market was devalued by over 14%, a $320 million dollar loss on an asset class valued at almost $2.3 billion. Retail product, valued at $6.1 billion, was devalued by 9.1%, over $550 million. Apartments, valued at almost $2.6 billion, were written down by 9%, or $234 million. Warehouse properties, once considered the backbone of the asset classes, were written down for the second time in history; a loss of 8.9% on nearly $4.0 billion. The index reported value reductions of almost $2.7 billion in the first quarter of 1992. Due to the fact that this is an appraisal based index, it is likely that the spate of write downs is not over and

Figure 30.1   Russell-NCREIF Index Property Appreciation Returns

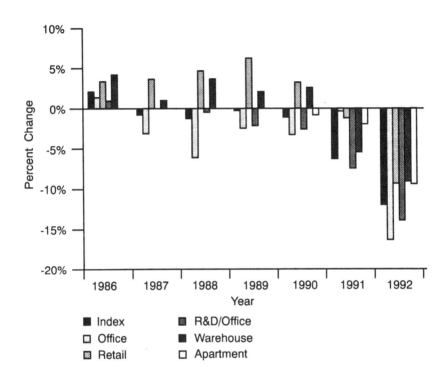

Source: Frank Russell Company
1st quarter 1992 results

that the lag is a function of appraisers using an historic perspective.

In July 1992, *The Wall Street Journal* announced that JMB Realty Corp. has written down the value of the Cadillac Fairview portfolio to $3.4 billion from $4.2 billion, a loss of 19%. Investors are anticipating that the appraisal value of the portfolio will be down an additional $500 million, 15%, in 1992. Institutional investors recently lost their entire $424 million equity position in Randsworth Acquisition, Ltd. when creditors forced the company into the British equivalent of Chapter 11 Bankruptcy.

Figure 30.2   Russell-NCREIF Property Index

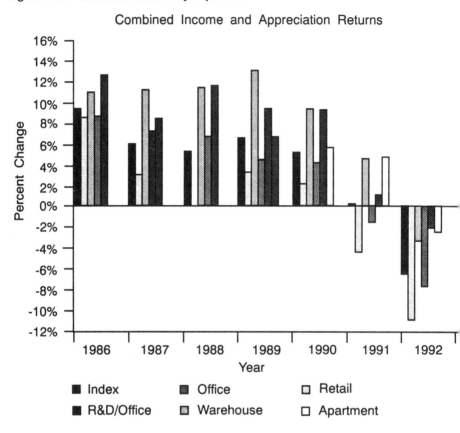

Combined Income and Appreciation Returns

Source: Frank Russell Company

Valuation Techniques For Soft Markets

Utilization of the sales comparison approach in the valuation process is highly reliable when recent sales of comparable properties exist in the market. This approach consists of comparing recent sales of similar properties to the appraised property and making adjustments for specific factors that affect value. When recent comparable sales are lacking in the market, very typical of most real estate markets today, the sales comparison approach is less reliable. However, it can still be used with careful consideration given to market demand factors and the concept of the time value of money.

Using the sales comparison approach in a down or inactive market presents the appraiser with a real dilemma. The key to a proper sales analysis is to have recent, arm's length transactions of comparable properties within the market. In a soft or inactive market, it is clear that since sales do not exist, using the sales comparison approach for improved properties and particularly for vacant land might be a futile exercise. Typically the sales that do exist do not reflect the actions of willing sellers in arm's length transactions.

The concept of market value includes the fundamental assumption of a willing buyer and willing seller. A property sale involving a developer fending off bankruptcy or sold by the Resolution Trust Corporation (RTC) or FDIC clearly do not constitute arm's length transactions. An abundance of these types of transactions in a market makes the search for truly comparable sales a very tenuous task and the resulting market value estimation is highly unreliable.

Applying the present value of money concept as the driving economic investment criteria along with an understanding of market demand and supply, the sales comparison approach can be used in a soft market by answering two questions: First, what would the value of the property be *if* the market were under normal conditions; and, second, how long will it be until there is a market or until market conditions become normal again?

When markets act rationally, buyers and sellers of properties act for their best self-interest. By searching back several years in most markets, and several more in others, the appraiser can find comparable arm's length sales. Let's say that using the typical sales comparison approach adjustment process, sales occurring four to five years ago, when market conditions were more normal, indicate a value for a land parcel being appraised of $5.00 per square foot. In other words, a willing buyer would pay a willing seller $5.00 per square foot for the subject land parcel.

The difficult question now arises, when will the market ever be able to support this land value of $5.00? Stated differently, when will the development of the subject land be economically justifiable? The appraiser must thoroughly research and understand the market balance of demand and supply in order to answer this question. Demand generators for developmental commercial land such as population, employment, and other demographic factors creating demand for space must be researched and analyzed.

For example purposes, assume that based upon a thorough demand side analysis, it is projected that the market will cure; that is, supply and demand will be in normal balance, in a period of five to seven years from now. What this means is that in the next five to seven years, the subject property will be worth $5.00 per square foot. Applying the present value concept to this projection results in a range of values for the subject property as presented below.

Cure Period	Discount Rate	Present Value
5 years	17%	$2.28
6 years	15%	$2.16
7 years	13%	$2.13

The discount rate selected should be property and market specific, reflecting the confidence in and the quality of the data used in projecting the market cure period. The discount rate range should be different for each of the different projected cure periods. In the preceding example, a five-year cure period is more aggressive than a seven-year cure period, and therefore, the discount rate used should reflect this difference in uncertainty and risk. A 400 basis point range was considered a reasonable spread for this property and market risk.

To arrive at the final indicated value, the present value of holding and carrying costs must be deducted. For a land parcel, these costs will consist primarily of real estate taxes. If real estate taxes are 2% of market value, then the appropriate deductions are summarized as follows:

Present Value	Taxes		Indicated Value
$2.28	$0.17	=	$2.11
$2.16	$0.20	=	$1.96
$2.13	$0.22	=	$1.91

The indicated present market value range for this property is $1.91 to $2.11 per square foot, or approximately $2.00 per square foot.

This present value application to the traditional sales comparison approach can result in a reliable value conclusion in current inactive markets; that is, when recent, arm's length transactions do not exist in the market.

Appraiser or Economist: Using Demand Side Analysis and the Changing Role of the Appraiser

While appraisers and economists aren't traditionally mentioned in the same sentence, if real estate investors, pension fund managers, and developers have their way, this will change. Appraisal clients are asking for insights as to what is driving demand and where the anticipated demand is coming from. Some appraisers are responding.

During the recent real estate boom period, the focus of many within the real estate industry was not on rationally anticipated demand, but on historical trends—relative rental and absorption rates—and the reliance that history would repeat itself. This technique of basing value estimates *solely* on historic sale prices is comparable at best to operating with blinders on, and at worst to looking over your shoulder to predict what's ahead.

Demand-Side Analysis (DSA) is a little-used appraisal method that enables appraisers to provide answers to many of the questions investors are asking. The process involves an in-depth look at the demographic and economic trends in the region, state, metropolitan area, and the subject property's neighborhood. The result is a better qualified value estimate, along with trend information that could be vital to future plans for the property.

One method appraisers use to determine the value of investment real estate is the income approach. The income approach bases value on the principal of anticipation; value is measured by the expectation of future benefits; the property's future earnings. A large factor in the income approach equation is the occupancy rates at the subject property.

A traditional appraisal projects future space demand based on historic absorption rates. DSA estimates what the demand for the property will actually be in the future, resulting in realistic vacancy rates and more accurate pro forma income analysis.

DSA relies on employment growth projections combined with historic absorption rates and historic employment trends to determine future demand. These, coupled with an analysis of the existing and projected future supply of competitive space, determine the future strength of the market.

In fundamental terms, the process involves seven steps, identified as follows. Each is considered in respect to the entire Demand-Side Analysis and is weighted according to its impact on the subject property. This outline pertains to an office property; although changes in economic and social variables allows for applications to other property uses.

1. *Identify the Market.* The appraiser identifies the broader market according to geographic area; homogeneity of economic, demographic, and political factors; and the complementary nature of existing real estate. The same is also done for a definitive competitive submarket. The market is usually a large area, such as a specific suburb of a city, while the submarket consists of directly competitive properties in the subject property's neighborhood.

2. *Correlate Historic Employment Growth and Leasing Activity.* The appraiser seeks a correlation between historic employment growth and historic leasing activity or absorption rates. Upon developing a meaningful correlation of the two sets of variables, the appraiser can use future employment calculations to project market absorption rates, rental concessions, and rental rates.

3. *Divide Employment into Source Classifications.* The appraiser must divide employment into several major classifications, including, but not limited to, the following: financial, insurance, real estate (FIRE); services; wholesale and retail trade; and manufacturing. Growth in a classification reveals what type of real estate will be in demand. For instance, if FIRE and service industries are booming, there is a strong indication that more office space will be needed or absorbed in the market.

4. *Develope Employment Growth Projections.* Employment growth projections are developed through a careful synthesis of relatable demographic and economic data sources from available local level origins, and also from leading national firms such as DRI/McGraw-Hill, Sales & Market, and Woods & Poole Economics MSA Profile. Forecasts are currently available for every region, state, major metropolitan area, and county across the country through the year 2005.

5. *Determine Space Needs per Employee.* The appraiser estimates the average amount of space each employee will require. This number, mul-

tiplied by the growth in employment, results in the total increase in future space demanded of a specific property type within the submarket.

6. *Determine Existing Supply and New Develop- ments.* The appraiser researches how many square feet of competitive developments cur- rently exist in construction and that are being planned. The appraiser must also project, based on historical development trends and conversa- tions with local experts, how many more square feet of unknown competitive space might be added to the submarket in the future.

7. *Calculate the Demand-Based Real Estate Mar- ket Model.* The utilization of meaningful demo- graphic factors relating to existing and anticipated supply produces the basis of the future demand-based economic model. This model sets forth the conditions that the ap- praiser projects for the property. Specific charac- teristics of the property—location, condition, and functional adequacy—allows the appraiser to assign a penetration rate singularly applicable to the subject property. Average penetration— 100%—allows the property to participate fully in demand-based changes in the market, and receive its proportionate size share of the overall market. Less than 100% penetration, due to an unfavorable position relative to the market, will produce a lower than proportionate share of the potential market improvement; more than 100% penetration will indicate a series of prop- erty characteristics generating an above propor- tionate share of market improvements.

Once equilibrium is met for the property, other value-determining variables will be impacted for a growth market, including: increased rental rates; fewer rental concessions; stabilized occu- pancy levels; and the "cure period," or the time frame in which new construction is economi- cally justified.

A major result of the fallout of the 1980s and current real estate recession is greater emphasis on evaluating property based on *future* economic and market demand. To view future economic and mar- ket demand objectively, the appraiser must study sound market information, and projected trends within the market.

The Real Estate Advisory Group, a division of American Appraisal Associates, Inc., utilizes market information from sources such as DRI/McGraw-Hill, Sales & Market, and Woods & Poole Economics MSA Profile. This economic data allows an appraiser to base property valuation on independent, empirical

market information and incorporates a macroeco- nomic aspect to the analysis. In addition, state and local government information on trends within a market are assimilated into the overall study.

As with any form of valuation, subjectivity does play a role in the makeup of the final appraisal analysis. However, in employing objective market information in the manner summarized earlier, the appraisal will be supported by an unbiased founda- tion.

If an appraiser were to utilize an income analysis based on historical trends only, or not using any market analysis support, the results will differ with the demand-side analysis conclusions. If two de- mand-side appraisals were conducted at the same time, on the same property, utilizing the steps pre- viously discussed, the property valuations should tend to be consistent.

Utilizing demand-side analysis—especially in dy- namic real estate markets—will produce a truer valuation not only for today, but for future value as well.

Americans with Disabilities Act

The Americans with Disabilities Act (ADA) is having a decided influence over how many firms conduct business. For commercial real estate, concerns have arisen from investors and financiers because of its potential impact upon property value.

In July, 1991, the Department of Justice released the act's final guidelines. In essence, the ADA re- quires that building owners must remove architec- tural and communication barriers if such removal is readily achievable. The act's guidelines are struc- tured to ensure that future renovation or remodeling plans are made to comply. By January 26, 1992, new construction of commercial properties must be de- signed to meet the act's requirements.

The law is affecting all existing public access facilities within restaurants, hotels/motels, enter- tainment and recreational facilities, office buildings, and shopping centers. Typical areas needing various amounts of adaptation include rest rooms, elevators, stairways, doorways, drinking fountains, and com- mon areas.

Those property developers that had the foresight to make their new developments "friendly" to the physically disabled will not suffer any further value erosion due to the necessity for ADA compliance. For building owners that do not comply, the impact upon value may be more than simply the construc- tion cost of compliance. In soft real estate markets with owners battling over tenants, those buildings not in compliance will not be as appealing to prospective tenants that have ADA concerns for their employees or clientele.

The owners of buildings that would need to undergo substantial expense to comply with ADA's requirements are pleading that such improvements are not "readily achievable" as the costs are excessive and not economically feasible. However, these buildings automatically become less desirable from a market standpoint and surely value is negatively impacted.

Some real estate professionals believe that capital expenditures necessary to bring a tenant's space into compliance can be passed on to the tenants as a reimbursable expense. However, in today's "tenant's market," it is likely that these added costs will deter prospective tenants from leasing space and existing tenants from releasing space or exercising renewal options.

The ADA regulations have a compounded effect on older buildings, as the compliance costs are just one more financial blow added to environmental (asbestos) impacts, increased functional obsolescence from physical and technological factors, as well as the impact of soft real estate markets and financial capital illiquidity.

Environmental Impacts Upon Appraisers and Market Value

One of the most significant trends affecting appraisers and their opinions of value relates to the potential environmental problems that a property might have. Some of these environmental concerns clouding the real estate market include asbestos, PCB's (polychlorinated biphenyls), lead in paint, pipes and gasoline, indoor air quality, underground storage tanks, radon gas, soil and groundwater contamination, and hazardous waste.

An appraiser is a specialist in the valuation of property, not an environmental engineer expert. However, appraisers are becoming more frequently asked to identify and report on the existence of environmental problems as part of the appraisal process. For instance, the federal government has developed environmental checklists that the appraiser is required to complete for FDIC and RTC engagements. Many leading institutions also have similar forms and requirements of the appraiser.

Appraisers need to become educated regarding environmental concerns of their clientele. Lack of education will no longer excuse the appraiser from not noticing obvious environmental problems. During the appraiser's property inspection process, evidence of contamination must be investigated. Evidence such as a building's age being pre-1975 is

a strong clue as to the possible existence of asbestos. Soil discoloration should send up a red flag that some sort of contamination caused it. The existence of an old gasoline pump strongly suggests that an underground tank exists.

The appraiser is professionally obligated to call to the attention within the appraisal report any and all potential environmental problems that were noticed, and the existence of environmental contamination should be clearly stated near the valuation conclusion. As most appraisers are not trained environmental engineers, they should avoid attempting to quantify the amount of contamination and related cleanup costs. The appraiser's recommendation should be for the client to seek consultation from a professional environmental engineer and have at least a phase one, environmental site assessment done.

Environmental firms generally conduct three levels of site assessments, known as phases. A phase one site assessment essentially consists of a site inspection without any drilling or tests being conducted. As a minimum, the phase one site assessments consist of the following:

1. A physical site description.

2. A 60-year chain-of-title review.

3. Interviews of past owners and/or employees to gather information concerning historical site uses and hazardous materials.

4. A review of all reasonably available historical aerial photographs.

5. Identify all sites within the immediate subject area that are listed on the Environmental Protection Agency's (EPA) contaminated site database.

6. Document inquiries made to state regulatory agencies, the local health department, and the local fire marshall.

7. Document a site visit, visually looking for signs of hazardous waste indications.

8. Document all the above activities in a written report which states the professional's conclusion as to the likelihood of the presence of hazardous substances on the site.

Phase two environmental assessments are conducted based upon the outcome of the phase one report. A phase two analysis involves the actual sampling, testing, and monitoring necessary to professionally assess the extent of all environmental problems. Oftentimes soil samples are collected and analyzed. Temporary and/or permanent groundwater monitoring wells may be placed and chemical analyses conducted for on-site and off-site (i.e., adjacent properties) water samples. As part of the phase two report, a professional assessment of the cost to cleanup all environmental problems is provided. It is this cost that the appraiser can then use in estimating the value of a contaminated property.

Environmental liability impairs the value of real estate, as contaminated property is worth less (or even worthless) as a result of the expense of having to clean it up. However, the impact upon value can be much more than just the associated cleanup costs. In addition, the appraiser must consider the added expenses and loss in operating income that may occur due to the contamination. Furthermore, the appraiser must consider the impact that the contamination "stigma" has and will have upon value. Income loss is fairly straightforward to estimate, but the stigma effect is much less quantifiable.

The decrease in value due to income loss is directly tied to the extent the cost to cure encumbers the property's income stream. For example, asbestos abatement for an income producing property must consist of a coordinated effort with lease expiration dates. When a floor becomes vacant, then the abatement process can be safely completed. However, this floor will not be able to be leased during the abatement process, reducing the rental income that the building generates and thereby directly reducing the property's market value. Oftentimes a building owner will incur the costs of moving tenants to other available space within the building so that the asbestos abatement can be started earlier.

Another common expense is the cost of operating a monitoring system to measure the re-emergence of an environmental problem. Examples of these include groundwater well monitors and indoor air quality monitoring. A property's value can be permanently impaired due to this added expense of monitoring.

The final impact upon value is referred to as stigma. Stigma, an intangible factor, impacts a property's value due to the negative perception that the market has towards a property previously contaminated. The stigma effect is greater with manufacturing-related properties than income-producing properties because the environmental contamination is generally of greater magnitude for industrial properties.

Stigma impacts the rent that a property can command versus a competitive property that was never contaminated. Stabilized occupancy may also be lower and due to uncertainty and risk, mortgage rates and investor yield rates will be higher, thereby reducing a property's value. The most significant negative impact that stigma has is on the marketability of a property. Potential buyers will not be interested in buying any property with historical contamination problems. Furthermore, lenders hesitate in providing debt capital on a contaminated property. In the work case, stigma may make a property worthless in the marketplace. In any case, a property's unencumbered market value will be decreased due to the additional marketing time that a property will experience before it sells. Given the importance of the time value of money, dollars received further in the future are simply worth less on a present value basis.

One emerging trend is the need for environmental liability insurance. Virtually all real estate transactions and loan commitments require at lease a phase one audit, and a clean phase one audit does not guarantee that a property is clean. Environmental insurance can now be purchased that will transfer the contamination cleanup risk away from buyers and lenders. It is likely that environmental insurance will become very similar to title insurance that a lender requires with every loan.

Environmental contamination issues are now with the real estate industry forever. Real estate investors and appraisers need to familiarize themselves with the types of potential contaminants. Importantly, appraisers need to understand how to measure the three different impacts upon a property's market value: cost to cure, loss in operating income, and stigma.

Chapter 31

Valuation of Thinly Traded Fixed Income Securities*

Donald C. Wiss
Principal
BondCalc Corporation, New York, NY

In recent years investors have shown increasing concern about the valuation of the financial assets under their care. The volatile noninvestment grade markets have raised doubts about the value of some of these assets. Moreover, the valuation of thinly traded fixed income securities is made difficult due to the lack of any posted prices. But appropriate valuations of these securities can be achieved using a matrix pricing system.

Are Matrix Pricing Systems Accurate?

The purpose of a pricing system is to determine the market value, or the price that the secondary trading community thinks the bond is worth at that point, even if there is no buyer present at the time. It is not an exercise in determining some theoretical value. A theoretical value, using spot curve pricing or option adjusting, may be able to tell whether a security is priced fairly, but such techniques are not used by the majority of the private placement trading community to price and trade issues. Issues are priced in this market using yields derived by taking some spread to treasuries, using an average life, either to maturity or to one of the call dates, to interpolate from the Treasury base. Since the Treasury yield curve is widely available, the problem left is to determine what spread and what average life to use. A few of the larger market participants have developed proprietary trading systems and may be using more sophisticated techniques.

In addition to the private placement community there are other thinly-traded markets that focus more on price than yield. The higher yield markets, for example, do not necessarily trade on a spread over treasuries.

The pricing process should use the same methods used by the secondary market traders. Many private placement issues have pro rata sinking funds. The holder of such an issue knows with some certainty the sinking funds, as opposed to a public issue where the issuer has the option of purchasing bonds in the open market, or if the bond is selling at a premium it most likely will be called. But if not, a lottery will be held to pick the bonds that will be sunk out. Knowing the future sinking funds requires using discounted cash flow techniques to do precise yield to price calculations. All traders in this market use DCF to price the securities. Pretending that the bond is a straight bond to the average life of a sinking fund bond, will get a similar result when the bond is trading near par, but the result gets increasingly inaccurate the further one gets from par.

While this is true for the private placement community, the group trading the debt of Less Developed Countries (or Emerging Market Debt) trades by price and not all participants use DCF to calculate their yields.

Average Life

What average life should one use to determine the Treasury yield base and to use when interpolating from the spread matrix? Traders frequently price privates on a yield-to-worst. For a given price they look at the yield to each of the call dates and then assume that the worst yield will be the one that will happen.

*Originally given at the Fixed Income Technology conference (FITECH '92) in New York City on June 23, 1992.

Further refinements on this can also include the following:

1. If the bond is currently callable, add a phantom call date in 30 days.

2. Look at the worst/worst alternatives. Many sinking fund issues have a provision where the issuer has the option of doubling up the sinking funds. The worst/worst case would then be when the issuer sinks double the amount and also calls the issue at one of the call dates.

A pricing system should look at all of these alternatives before selecting which call date and average life to use. It is quite possible that the lowest yield is the first worst/worst case or the first par call date.

Spread over Treasuries

One then has to determine what spread over Treasuries to use. This is the most difficult part of the process as it is highly subjective. In addition to credit quality it includes collateral value. I am not aware of any system that includes collateral value as part of a mechanical pricing method. Spread matrices must be derived for various market sectors (for example, industrial, financial, and utility). These matrices assume spreads for issues with a coupon that is relatively current, or in other words, for an issue which has a price near par. One can derive the matrices by either of the following methods:

1. Contact a few dealers in the secondary market and average their responses. One very large trust organization gets seven responses and then averages them.

2. Use a public debt matrix and create a spread differential matrix for each average life and quality. A public matrix can be derived by getting some real prices, knowing the associated ratings, and then filling in the gaps using regression. But, when using this methodology one also has to build matrices of the premium between the public and private markets. This extra premium is currently 20-50 basis points but it varies over time and is a function of each piece of paper. In the past it has been at a discount and is not necessarily the same between the new issue market and the secondary one.

One then has to determine the credit quality of each issue held in the portfolio. The problem here is that a BBB type private may trade like a BBB++ or BBB or BBB– and only three categories are not

enough for pricing purposes. If you will settle for accuracy to the nearest 25 basis points for each quality level (BBB+, BBB, BBB–), then a matrix may come close. Presumably, however, with a portfolio of many issues the errors will net out against each other and the total portfolio value will be acceptable.

Noncurrent Coupon Adjustment

A further refinement to the process is an adjustment for issues with a noncurrent coupon. Issues with a high coupon, and selling at a premium, presumably will be called and the yield-to-worst analytics will adjust for this. However, issues with a low coupon, and selling at a discount, presumably will remain outstanding until maturity. To compensate, a thorough pricing system will include an adjustment factor that will add a yield differential for low coupons. The differential should change the more noncurrent the coupon is. Again, to get this information one can contact a secondary trader.

Are There Cost Effective Alternatives?

The available alternatives fall into two main categories: using an outside service bureau and running a program in-house. In addition to these alternatives, one can contact a secondary trader and ask them to directly price each issue, but this alternative is not matrix pricing and will only work if you hold few issues and have a good relationship with a trader.

Determining which alternative is more cost-effective will depend on the number of issues being priced and the frequency of pricing. The service bureau will charge for each issue priced and the in-house alternative will have a high upfront cost but minimal cost to run. The in-house alternative will also require more effort as you have to construct your own spread matrices. In choosing which alternative to use one must also take into consideration the wishes of company management, who may desire that the pricing be done by an independent party. Interactive Data and Merrill Lynch Securities Pricing Service are two service bureaus that will price private placements.

Interactive Data

Interactive Data will price thinly traded securities in their Fund Services division which deals with evaluations on a customer by customer basis. The evaluators in this group will contact brokers and dealers to obtain round lot prices for selected issues held in the special fund database. However, because of the practical limits of obtaining daily quotations from market sources, Interactive Data additionally utilizes various other techniques to determine the market values. For illiquid securities those techniques include several matrices, which are fine-tuned daily by their senior evaluators and spread relationships between government notes/bonds and public corporate bonds. As noted earlier there are two ways to get the spread over Treasuries. Interactive Data appears to use the second method and maintains matrices for the spread differentials between the public and private markets. Once the current values have been established by their staff they are subjected to supervised edits prior to release. Based on comparisons to the previous day's evaluations, discrepancies or large fluctuations are identified and reviewed. This is a service with a premium price, but, as Interactive Data does not sell securities, it does provide for unbiased evaluations from an independent vendor.

Merrill Lynch Pricing Service

The Merrill Lynch Pricing Service produces values for private placements using a model and a methodology based upon Merrill Lynch trader provided yields. The model values the issues using seven industry sectors: Industrial, Financial, Utility, Canadian, Government guaranteed, Yankee/Euro, and Pipeline. Alternative and customized methodologies are used to handle the nonstandard issues such as ESOPs. The model calculates price and duration on a DCF basis using all remaining cash flows. For callable bonds, the crossover yield is used to determine which yield will be lower between the DCF to maturity and the yield to the next call. The price corresponding to the lower yield is then reported to the client.

In-house Alternatives

The in-house alternative can be broken down into two subgroups. One can develop a system in-house or one can license an already written system. An example of each follows.

The large trust organization noted earlier has an in-house system that prices the portfolio daily. They update the spread matrices every two weeks. They maintain the three basic matrices, industrial, financial, and utility. In their database they maintain a separate pricing rating in addition to the quality rating. For example, an A rated airline may trade like a Baa. They are working on Option Adjusted Pricing to automate some of the adjustments that a trader now does by the seat of his or her pants. For example, they are working on pricing adjustments on bonds

that are currently callable. Through actual trading they are able to verify the system.

BondCalc, the PC-based system that I developed, has matrix pricing, utilizes DCF techniques, has full worst/worst logic, has noncurrent coupon adjustment, and can handle the quirks of any private placement or high yield security structure, including all issues with tax preferences.

How Often Should Private Placements Be Valued?

The frequency of pricing depends on management's desires. Private placements are usually matched against long-term liabilities that were bought with the intention of holding them until they mature (or are called). Annual pricing could therefore be adequate. Valuing monthly or quarterly makes the most sense to be in compliance with management reporting and financial statements. Daily valuation could be done with a well-thought-out matrix. The valuation frequency would also be more frequent if the portfolio manager has to report any performance numbers, such as the total return of the portfolio. The recently released AIMR Performance Standards (Association for Investment Management and Research at 804-980-3647) require the use of time-weighted returns. A time-weighted rate of return requires valuing the portfolio at each cash flow as well as at the end of the measurement period. The subperiod returns are then linked together.

NAIC

The National Association of Insurance Commissioners, or NAIC, maintains a Securities Valuation Office in New York City. Valuations are required by the regulators annually with the year-end statement, but if there have been material changes then the insurance companies have to file more often. However, in many instances insurance companies need only report the amortized cost. But when a market value is required then the value must come from the NAIC. The life insurance companies need to report market value. But when the company is in default, then value must be mark-to-market. A property and casualty insurance company must report the lower of market or amortized cost only when the NAIC rating of the security is three or below. On a scale of one to five these would be the issues that are below investment grade. As for deriving the values, the NY office calls brokers, gets comparable yields, and uses matrix pricing.

Part XIII:
The Mergers and Acquisitions and Buyouts Markets

Chapter 32

Mergers and Acquisitions in the 1990s

Martin Sikora
Editor, Mergers and Acquisitions
IDD Enterprises, Philadelphia, PA

Clearly, the mergers and acquisitions (M&A) boom of the 1980s has run its course. Measured in breadth, diversity, and the breakneck pace of activity, it was a phenomenon that may not be replicated for decades, if ever again. But unlike the cyclically abbreviated bursts of merger activity that preceded it, M&A activity of the 1980s has left important legacies for dealmakers of the 1990s. While down substantially, the deal flow continues at a respectable clip because the acquisition has entrenched itself as a viable mechanism for businesses to pursue value, thus creating growth.

Comparing the 1990s and 1980s

Certainly, contrasts between the 1990s and the 1980s are inescapable. Deals of epic size—ranging upwards to the $24.7 billion leveraged buyout of RJR Nabisco Inc.—seemed to be put together effortlessly in the last decade. There is, however, considerable scratching to do transactions in the 1990s. Push-the-envelope financing has been replaced by tightfisted lending and ultraconservative deal structures. Intense competition for coveted target businesses that catapulted purchase prices to stratospheric levels has given way to one-on-one negotiations dominated by hard bargaining. Deals are smaller, subject to rigorous due diligence that can lead to purchase price adjustments, and take longer to complete. Risk management issues such as environmental and product liabilities more frequently loom as deal breakers.

Yet, companies of all sizes and stripes continue to look for suitable acquisitions and continue to maintain them as important weapons in their long-range game plans. The acquisitions add critical stra-

tegic advantages at a time when no well-managed company can leave any stone unturned in meeting the difficult challenges in remaining competitive.

Strip away the mythical veneer of the 1980s—the headlines that featured high-rolling financial engineers, megabuck hostile takeover bids, excessive fees, the overpriced acquisitions that didn't pay out, and the ebbs and flows of junk bonds. What emerges is that the vast majority of deals were based on highly strategic rationales. Most deals were either straightforward acquisitions of operating business by other operating businesses or strategic divestitures of subsidiaries and divisions by companies forced to restructure. Sell-offs actually accounted for nearly a third of all deals.

The lesson handed down to dealmakers of the 1990s is that the judicious acquisition can be an exquisite response to the problems of doing business in an era pervaded by globalization of industries, advancing technologies, and increasing economic pressures that have generated industrial consolidations.

Actually, M&A is no stranger to adversity. Even the lushest days of the 1980s had their nervous moments, when a confirmed total of nearly $1.4 trillion was expended on at least 31,000 transactions. There were fears of an early demise when a 1986 overhaul of U.S. tax laws wiped out some important M&A tax benefits, insider trading scandals broke wide open, the stock market plunged in October 1987, some LBOs started to go sour, and Congress made noise about possible regulations. All passed without lasting effect, again because of the strategic objectives underscoring most buying and selling.

351

The Impact of an Eroding Economy

What finally caught up with M&A activity was the series of drags that started developing in late 1989 and cascaded the following year. The resilience that dealmakers had demonstrated in overcoming the setbacks of the 1980s could not stand up to pummeling from myriad directions.

The most pervasive pounding was delivered by the battered economy, exacerbated by the sometimes bizarre confusion over whether the country was or was not in recession. It was not an environment that persuaded corporate buyers to make large capital commitments even if they promised benefits over the long pull. Instead, many turned inward, streamlining operations, slashing costs, trimming work forces, and shoring up core businesses. And if the company had succumbed to the lure of leverage during the 1980s, it was likely to zero in on reducing an increasingly uncomfortable debt load.

Even before the eroding economy had been acknowledged, acquirers—both corporate and leveraged—started to experience a credit crunch. Once-accommodative bankers and other lenders, who had aggressively reached for risk in the 1980s, suddenly all but shut their M&A lending windows, except for an occasional sure-shot proposition. The crisis-riddled savings and loan industry, which was a major funding source for middle-market deals in the western U.S., dropped out of the M&A market completely. And while the importance of junk bonds to M&A financing has been greatly exaggerated—their principal role was to refinance a relative handful of high-profile leveraged transactions—the collapse of the high yield market removed still another financing tool.

Lender Retrenchment

Probably no force was as potent as lender retrenchment in bringing M&A activity to its knees.

Now it is easy to strike a causal connection between the lender skittishness and the well-publicized unraveling of scores of leveraged transactions that often led to the bankruptcy courts. The casualty list runs from the Southlands, the TWAs, the Federated Department Stores, the Best Products in the leveraged buyout area to the Intercos and Carter Hawley Hales in the leveraged recapitalization sector. Once-burned, lenders hardly were willing to bet huge sums on debt-funded transactions again.

However, the problems related purely to dealmaking take up but a corner of the full picture. The degree of the lender retrenchment outstripped the actual losses from M&A lending. It is far more traceable to the entire panoply of ailments that shook the American banking and financial systems. The difficult economy that flagged many of the aforementioned leveraged companies was one. The massive portfolios of nonperforming real estate loans was another. And while trying to sort out these problems, bankers faced such long-term generic pressures as overall capital adequacy and the growing demands for industry consolidation that have been manifested by such megamergers as BankAmerica and Security Pacific and Chemical Banking and Manufacturers Hanover.

At the very time that bankers were clamping down on M&A lending of their own volition, a new federal regulatory directive created another complication. It was the definition of highly leveraged transactions, or HLTs, created by the Federal Reserve Board, the Federal Deposit Insurance Corp., and the Comptroller of the Currency in late 1990. The directive imposed no new regulations on leveraged-deal lending, but it did require banks to isolate these types of loans for examination and supervisory purposes. Nervous about being stigmatized as high-risk lenders, many banks seized on the definition as another excuse to intensify tight lending policies. The HLT definition finally was scrapped, effective July 1, 1992. Although the move was expected to free up some additional credit for M&A, there was a question of how loose lenders would become in the face of the other impediments to doing business as usual.

Corporate acquirers have not escaped the credit axe. Large companies with huge, long-established credit lines have been relatively unscathed. But small and middle-sized companies have come up short. Their problems tend to run across the board, with rationed credit affecting the financing of all types of operations, functions and projects, not just acquisitions. But the fact remains that the smaller and mid-sized firms' difficulties in obtaining credit have sidelined the largest segment of the business buying population for the last few years.

However, the largest impact has been on the financial or leveraged buyer who once had been the preferred customer for yield-minded banks and other financial institutions. Risk aversion rules the financier's roost. Bridge lending is a rarity. To pry scarce credit loose, the leveraged deal must pass a tight screen. Asset-based lending has returned in force, consigning cash flow lending to virtual limbo. The target company must be solid as a rock, clean as a whistle, and able to weather any economic cyclicality. Coverage ratios have been ratcheted upward. Where the financiers once willingly backed deal structures with as little as 5% to 10% in equity, they now demand at least a 30% equity input and often more.

Leveraged Deals

Conditions have tightened in the peripheries of that leveraged deal market as well. Mezzanine funding—the strip that fills the gap between senior debt and equity—is harder to come by. And its principal suppliers, insurance companies, are shouldering many of the same financial problems as banks and pension funds and have jacked up their prices. Meanwhile, junk bonds, which principally were used in their heyday to take down bank loans, are virtually unavailable to the M&A dealmaker.

The numbers dramatize the erosion of the LBO segment. At its peak, leveraged dealmaking included 378 deals (valued at a minimum of $5 million each) worth $47.1 billion in 1988, according to the M&A Data Base ADP/MLR. In the following year, there were 371 transactions collectively worth $66.8 billion, including the $24.7 billion buyout of RJR engineered by Kohlberg Kravis Roberts. By 1991, the number of deals had fallen to 112 and the dollar value to $5.5 billion.

Contrary to myth, the LBO did not pack the awesome dominance that was commonly ascribed to it during the 1980s. For example, in 1988, only 11.4% of all mergers and acquisitions were leveraged deals and they accounted for only 20.2% of the money that changed hands in all M&A activity. In 1989, LBOs comprised 12.1% of total deals. Even with the inclusion of RJR's jumbo deal, the dollar value share was just 27.4%.

But the qualitative influence of the LBO player went far beyond the numbers. With plentiful credit at their fingertips and their sophistication growing geometrically, the financial buyers helped drive the fierce competition—epitomized by hotly contested auctions—for desirable targets during the 1980s. The corporate buyer with a walkaway price based on financial and operating fundamentals and keyed to the ability to earn back purchase price premiums and generate shareholder value, was a frequent also-ran. By contrast, the leveraged bidder was largely interested in whether the going-in price would leave enough of a cash flow margin to service the debt. Playing by different rules, the leveraged buyer often could ante up the highest price and win the competitions. Hence, the mere presence of a leveraged player could propel purchase prices to astronomical levels.

A classic case was the KKR acquisition of the Duracell battery business for $1.8 billion in 1988. Duracell was put up for sale by Kraft Inc. as part of its restructuring program. The sale triggered spirited bidding by a small army of both strategic and financial buyers. At the end of the day, KKR not only won the deal but paid a price that some knowledgeable observers described as at least 50% more than Kraft expected.

By contrast, in the 1990s the leveraged buyer, stripped of much of its financial strength, is unable to mount the competitive threat of a decade earlier.

Foreign Buyers

There is, however, one additional dimension to the measurement of competition—the foreign buyer. During the 1980s, foreign companies spiced the U.S. M&A scene with some of the largest and most eye-catching deals of the era. A sampling would include the entertainment field acquisitions of MCA Inc. by Matsushita Electric (Japan) and the Columbia Pictures acquisition by Sony Corp. (also Japan), the merger of SmithKline Beckman into the U.K.'s Beecham Group in health care, the hostile acquisition of Pillsbury Co. by Grand Metropolitan of the U.K. in foods, and B.A.T Industries' acquisition of Farmers Group in insurance in still another Anglo-American tie up.

As with the U.S. companies, the foreign firms were playing a highly strategic game. Many required outposts in the huge North American market to compete in globalizing industries—food, health care, financial services, industrial equipment, chemicals, oil and gas, etc.—while others, constrained by limited growth prospects at home, sought new geographical outlets. Regardless of the purpose, their competitive entry put additional upward pressure on pricing. Overseas companies were often willing to pay high premiums for franchises in the United States, and in many cases lower costs of capital and less ambitious horizons on profitability enabled them to outbid American counterparts.

Yet, by the early 1990s, the tables had turned on the buy side of the M&A market. Each of three primary bidding elements were tiptoeing rather than moving aggressively. U.S. corporate buyers were eschewing big bets in the face of the troubled economy. Leveraged buyers had been defanged financially. And the overseas bidders were toning down U.S. acquisitions to either face up to recessions at home or to concentrate on deals in continental Europe that would deliver increased market share and scale as economic harmonization of the Common Market drew closer to its December 31, 1992 deadline. Even the privatization of eastern Europe diverted some western European companies and caused them to look east rather than west across the Atlantic for acquisitions.

The Sell Side

Restrained buying ardor generated a unique fallout on the sell side. Initially, this took the form of a seller's revolt. Reduced competition meant reduced offering prices from the slimmer rolls of willing buyers. And many potential sellers, who had warmed to the pricey 1980s, simply balked—often taking their businesses off the market rather than accept what they considered fire-sale prices. In the 1980s, the seller could fetch purchase prices equaling eight to 12 times earnings before interest and taxes (EBIT). In the 1990s, the more likely multiple obtainable in tough bargaining was four to six. The shrinkage in the ranks of willing buyers was matched by a contraction in the supply of willing sellers. This psychology was manifested principally by reduced activity in two sectors. One was in the middle market where most targets are entrepreneurially or family-owned businesses. The other was in the divestiture segment where diversified companies, such as Kraft, had come to expect rich price tags for their unwanted businesses.

Another factor exacerbated the buy-sell gridlock. Given their ultracautious mindset, many corporate buyers also refused to bite immediately for the lowest selling prices. Their belief was that prices would come down still further if they held back.

The IPO Market

All of this proved to be a boon for initial public offerings. Many of the companies taken public during the prolonged IPO boom of the early 1990s were firms that would have been logical M&A targets in the 1980s. But the red-hot IPO market, in tandem with the lofty levels of the overall stock market, provided a vehicle for company owners to sell partial interests at multiples far greater than those available through M&A channels.

Moreover, an increasing number of diversified companies used the IPO as a divestiture vehicle. Citicorp took the IPO route to dispose of its AMBAC municipal bond insurance unit, Henley Group to sell off Fischer Scientific International and Primerica to shed Margaretten Financial.

The correlation between the M&A slowdown and the IPO surge is not coincidental. It has been one of the major responses by investment banks to the slippage in their M&A businesses. Some bankers have candidly noted that when they call on a potential client with a sale proposal, they also come armed with a pitch for an IPO should prevailing acquisition prices prove unpalatable.

Changes at Investment Banking Houses

Besides trying to manufacture silk purses from IPOs, the investment banks have also shuffled their ranks to offset the loss of M&A business. Layoffs of excess personnel have been extensive and many former M&A kingpins at marquee-named Wall Street houses have been, willingly or unwillingly, left to set up their own M&A boutiques. Internal reorganizations at some banks have folded once discrete M&A units into general corporate finance services. And some banks have opted for industry spins. A newly created unit may serve a specific industry, i.e., health care or technology, with a menu of services that include public offerings, private placements, strategic alliance formations, and valuations as well as M&A.

Some observers unsympathetically regard these overhauls as overreactions. The cynics charge that the big investment banks had grown too used to the high-flying leveraged transactions that produced multiple fees, ranging to many millions of dollars and principal positions in some deals. With fewer lucrative opportunities to financially engineer, the critics say, many banks have simply pulled the plug on the standard M&A business.

By contrast, the smaller regional investment banks still like M&A business. Although many are willing to steer potential sellers into IPOs, they remain active in M&A and sometimes pick up deals that don't interest the larger houses. But the regionals have not been hit as much by the radical changes. After all, they did not wax rich on multi-fee deals and merchant banking was anathema to them. As in the 1980s, their focus remains on the smaller to mid-sized deal with the key payoff in the form of a flat fee for getting the deal done.

However, both the larger and the smaller banks profess to be positioned for an upturn in M&A activity. They see an upturn as an encore to the slump that was in its third year in 1992.

What is the basis for this silver lining? Besides the placement of mergers and acquisitions as viable and well-established strategic initiatives, a significant inheritance from the 1980s was the creation of a systematic market for M&A. This includes the identification of benchmarks for pricing—based on multiples of, or premiums over, stock prices, earnings, cash flow, asset, or book values. It includes state-of-the-art techniques for valuing operating businesses, such as discounted cash flow modeling. And of course, it also includes the people who comprise the M&A service infrastructure—investment and commercial banks, accounting firms, lawyers, valuation experts, tax specialists, risk management consultants, and postmerger integration mavens to name some.

In sum, M&A has become a business with a lineup of people dedicated to doing M&A business. That alone should be a stimulus. To remain in business, they must go after business. But the fact is that they have a product to sell. While many of the conditions in the M&A marketplace have changed, the primary triggers for the 1980s dealmaking remain in place during the 1990s, and if anything, the trends have accelerated.

Industries Consolidate and Go Global in Scope

Industries continue to consolidate under relentless cost pressures. Mass and scale are critical to meeting the mounting costs in such industries as pharmaceuticals, computers, and technology. Acquisitions provide the means for the buyers to expand quickly and cost effectively and for smaller players that can't stand the gaff to be propitiously rescued. Consolidation also is axiomatic in the mature industries, for example industrial equipment, food, steel, and chemicals, where market share is a key to survival. And of course there are "special situations" such as banking and insurance where efficiency demands that the ranks have to be slimmed through absorption of smaller players.

Many industries, of both the mature and growth variety, are globalizing. The survivors will be those that can spread their wings the fastest to far-flung regions of the world. The Philip Morris acquisition of Swiss-based Jacobs Suchard, for example, enabled the American firm to greatly expand its food business in Europe. The acquisition of Firestone Tire & Rubber by Bridgestone Tire of Japan was emblematic of the need for major tire makers to fight their competitive battles on a worldwide basis. The merger of Time Inc. and Warner Communications created a media-entertainment giant with the prowess to compete worldwide in a variety of related fields.

Acquisitions provide a means for adding value to a core business, such as the American Telephone & Telegraph acquisition of NCR. The Proctor & Gamble acquisitions of Noxell and Max Factor in cosmetics provided for a move into a new but compatible product line. The Borland International acquisition of Ashton-Tate in software widened a customer base in a primary business. The variations are endless.

One of the greatest ironies is that despite the building of economic pressures and the versatility of acquisitions in countering them, the M&A market had yet to break out of its relative lethargy by late 1992.

A Buyers Market

Taking the purely marketplace view, the big change in the M&A arena from the 1980s to the early 1990s was a shift from a seller's market to a buyer's market. Presumably, that would give well-heeled strategic buyers enormous clout to pick up good businesses at very attractive prices. They have exercised that power gingerly, even though M&A professionals report that many sellers have adjusted to the pricing decline. These would include sellers who have limited options, such as entrepreneurs facing retirement age, owners of basically good businesses that lack the size or resources to continue as stand-alone companies, companies with mundane or commodity businesses that have little appeal in the IPO market, and even firms that have been battered by the recession and need bailing out.

The major remaining impediment seems to be the overhang of the ragged economy. Companies that might otherwise be beating the bushes for good deals that will add long-term value stay on the sidelines because of the general problems in navigating the tough times.

Yet, activity in early and mid-1992 suggested that in some quarters the itch to buy and sell is returning. The market was dominated in this period by a significant number of deals aimed at getting strategic advantage or honing competitive edge. And several involved stock-swaps that were in virtual oblivion during the cash-is-king 1980s, further indicating there are ways to ease the sting of up-front cash commitments.

Few of the deals were blockbusters, such as Sprint's stock-swap acquisition of Centel in the telephone industry for more than a billion dollars. But others were notable. In the gold mining industry, Homestake Mining and International Corona created one of the largest firms in the field. Duty Free International expanded its duty-free store operations that had been concentrated on the Canadian border to the Mexican border by absorbing UETA. And Microsoft widened its premier position in software by acquiring Fox Software. Banking acquisitions remained on the active side with deals that included Bank One's agreement to buy Valley National and Society Corp.'s absorption of Ameritrust.

Occasional auctions for especially desirable properties still could be done. Colgate-Palmolive bought Mennen Co. and its prized personal products franchise by beating back a host of competitors. Even the LBO market showed sporadic signs of life—and the ability to get financing—when KKR bought the American Re-Insurance operation of Aetna Life & Casualty in a megadeal. And many diversified companies decided to get on with their restructurings even if they had to bite the price bullet. General Dynamics sold its Cessna private airplane unit to Textron while Pfizer Inc. sold Coty Perfumes to Joh. A. Benckiser of Germany in two of the notable dispositions.

A number of key factors have to be in place before a stronger pace of M&A activity resumes. American corporate buyers want a stronger handle on the economy. Leveraged buyers need further loosening in credit. Foreign buyers must rev up their acquisi-tion engines again. Still more sellers, both corporate divestors and private company owners, must adjust to pricing realities. To a lesser extent, the IPO boom, with its alternatives to M&A, must wind down a bit.

But these are generally cyclical factors. The key stimuli of optimism on the future of M&A are the omnipresent strategic and economic pressures that, over the long haul, make it conducive to buy and sell businesses.

Appendix 32

Mergers and Acquisitions in the Marketplace

The data was supplied by the M&A Data Base, ADP/MLR Publishing and is designed to statistically measure dealmaking activity and provide empirical information on merger, acquisition, and divestiture trends of the recent past. All information covers deals valued at a minimum of $5 million, acquisitions of majority or substantial interests in companies, and acquisitions of lesser interests with values of at least $100 million. These are new criteria that were adopted in 1991, and all previously published data have been revised to bring them into conformity.

The data are restricted to deals involving American companies. For crossborder transactions, a U.S. firm must be either the buyer or the seller.

The dynamics of the marketplace from 1982–1991 can clearly be seen in Figures 32.A2 and 32.A3.

Table 32-A.1 Mergers and Acquisitions Completions (1991 versus 1990)

	1991				1990			
All M&A Activity	No. of Deals	% of Total	Value ($mil1)	% of Total	No. of Deals	% of Deals	Value ($mil2)	% of Total
U.S. acq. U.S.	1,711	80.8%	$69,583.5	71.0%	2,445	77.5%	$101,067.1	61.5%
Non-U.S. acq. U.S.	217	10.3	21,348.7	21.8	446	14.2	46,159.3	28.1
U.S. acq. Non-U.S.	189	8.9	7,076.7	7.2	263	8.3	17,066.8	10.4
Total	2,117	100.0	98,008.7	100.0	3,154	100.0	164,293.3	100.0
Divestitures Only*	1,007	47.6	32,629.0	33.3	1,306	41.4	59,276.7	36.1
LBOs Only*	112	5.3	5,457.6	5.6	241	7.6	15,927.2	9.7

*Divestitures and LBOs are included in all M&A Activity Data
[1]Based on 642 deals for which price data were revealed (includes 315 divestitures and 36 LBOs).
[2]Based on 1,048 deals for which price data were revealed (includes 455 divestitures and 83 LBOs).
Note: 1990 figures were revised to eliminate deals valued at less than $5 million and acquisitions of interest valued at less than $100

Table 32-A.2 Ten Year History of Mergers by Total Number and Dollar Volume (1982 to 1991*)

Year	Number of Deals	% Change	Value ($ bil)	% Change
1982	1,617	—	$55.7	—
1983	1,812	12.1%	48.9	-12.2%
1984	2,416	33.3	121.1	147.7
1985	2,773	14.8	141.3	16.7
1986	3,803	37.1	200.7	42.0
1987	3,150	17.2	171.5	-14.6
1988	3,310	5.1	232.4	35.5
1989	3,061	-7.5	244.1	5.0
1990	3,154	3.0	164.3	-32.7
1991	2,117	-32.9	98.0	-40.3

*Data from 1982 to 1990 have been revised to eliminate deals priced at less than $5 million and acquisitions of interest valued at less than $100 million.

357

Figure 32-A.1 Ten Year Merger Completion Record (1982 to 1991)

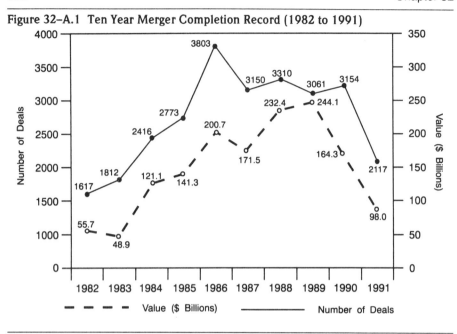

Figure 32-A.2 Annual Average and Median Purchase Prices in
Mergers and Acquisitions (1982 to 1991)

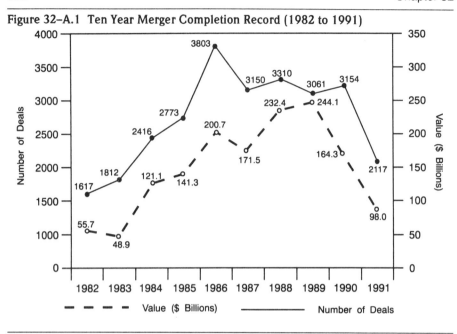

*Prices reported in $millions. Data are based on deals with reported prices. Figures for 1982 to 1990 have been revised to eliminate deals
valued at less than $5 million and acquisitions of interest valued at less than $100 million.

Figure 32–A.3 Annual Average Premiums over Stock Prices (1987 to 1991)

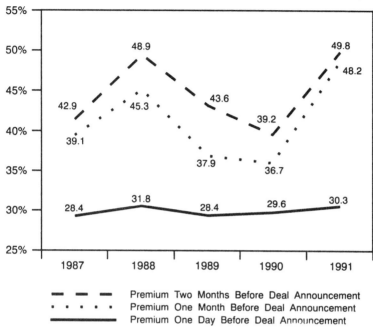

```
— — —     Premium Two Months Before Deal Announcement
· · · · · ·   Premium One Month Before Deal Announcement
————       Premium One Day Before Deal Announcement
```

Source: Mergers and Acquisitions Philadelphia

Snapshot Analysis of Divestiture Activity

The breakdown of activity in the Top 100 deals disclosed that 48 of them were divestitures. Additionally, nearly 48% of all M&A transactions in 1991 were sell offs. The hefty share of divestitures in total activity is further amplified in the industry breakdowns. Divestitures drove much of the activity that landed industries on the most active list for all types of M&A. Banking, which duplicated its firstplace finish on the divestiture list, logged 136 selloffs out of a total of 298 deals. Around a third of all deals in both business and professional services were selloffs and for media the proportion approached two-thirds. The three industrial segments that made the most active list—electrical and electronic equipment, machinery, and energy—did so on the strength of selloffs. And 80% of the value of all deals in energy, No. 1 in divestiture dollar volume, stemmed from selloffs. And 80% of the value of all deals in energy, No. 1 in divestiture dollar volume, stemmed from selloffs.

Table 32–A.3 Completed Divestitures (1982 to 1991)

Year	Number of Deals	Percentage of All Deals	Value ($billion)	Percentage of Total M&A Value
1982	508	31.4	$ 8.2	14.7%
1983	600	33.1	12.8	26.1
1984	753	31.2	30.5	25.2
1985	1,000	36.1	44.5	31.5
1986	1,414	37.2	72.7	36.2
1987	1,228	39.0	58.1	33.9
1988	1,260	38.1	83.8	36.0
1989	1,260	41.2	66.5	27.2
1990	1,306	41.4	59.3	36.1
1991	1,007	47.6	32.6	33.3

Figure 32–A.4 Completed Divestitures (1982 to 1991)

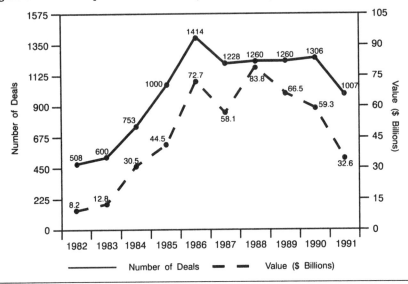

Table 32–A.4 Ten Most Active Divesting Industries by Number of Transactions (1991)

Industry	Number of Deals	Value ($ billion)
Banking	136	$0.4
Business and Professional Services	67	1.0
Health Care	65	1.0
Media	61	1.6
Electrical and Electronic Equipment	58	1.2
Energy	51	5.7
Wholesale Trade	45	1.0
Retailing	41	1.6
Nonbank Financial	41	2.1
Computer and Data Processing Services	39	.28
Machinery	34	.28

*Industries are determined by target companies.

Table 32–A.5 Ten Most Active Divesting Industries by Dollar Value (1991)

Industry*	Value ($billion)	Number of Deals
Energy	$5.7	51
Insurance	3.0	33
Transportation	1.9	19
Computer and Office Equipment	1.8	16
Consumer Products	1.8	12
Food and Tobacco	1.7	24
Media	1.6	61
Banking	1.4	136
Electrical and Electronic Equipment	1.2	58
Retailing	1.2	41

*Industries are determined by target companies.

Snapshot Analysis of Crossborder M&A Activity

While the sizes of inbound acquisitions continued to dwarf American acquisitions overseas, U.S. buyers showed signs of limbering up. Note that outbound acquisitions, although down in number from 1990, actually increased their share of the total dealmaking base. U.S. acquisitions overseas still tend to be much smaller than crossborder deals for U.S. targets, but the Common Market unification and market trends could drive American firms to seek bigger game. While Japanese buyers have put restraints on overseas M&A activity, European buyers could be back in stronger numbers once they have secured their flanks on the Continent.

Table 32–A.6 Foreign Acquisitions of U.S. Companies (1982 to 1991)

Year	Number of Deals	% of All Deals	Value ($ bil)	% of Total M&A Value
1982	126	7.8%	$4.2	7.6%
1983	80	4.4	1.7	3.4
1984	130	54.0	7.9	6.5
1985	160	5.8	18.7	13.3
1986	281	7.4	24.7	12.3
1987	274	8.7	43.9	25.6
1988	432	13.1	61.5	26.5
1989	473	15.5	54.1	22.2
1990	446	14.1	46.2	28.1
1991	218	10.3	21.3	21.8

Figure 32–A.5 Foreign Acquisitions of U.S. Companies (1982 to 1991)

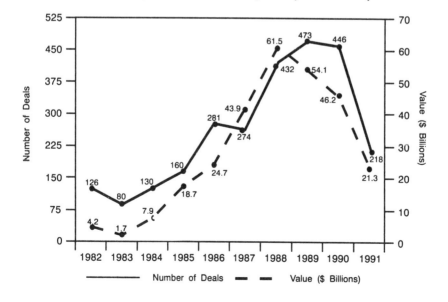

Table 32–A.7 U.S. Acquisitions Overseas (1982 to 1991)

Year	Number of Deals	% of All Deals	Value ($ bil)	% of Total M&A Value
1982	82	5.071%	$0.7	1.3%
1983	102	5.6	1.2	2.5
1984	130	5.4	2.1	1.7
1985	162	5.8	1.0	0.7
1986	166	4.4	2.4	1.2
1987	181	5.7	7.0	4.1
1988	157	4.7	7.1	3.1
1989	245	8.0	15.9	6.5
1990	263	8.3	17.1	10.4
1991	218	8.9	7.1	7.2

Figure 32–A.6 U.S. Acquisitions Overseas (1982 to 1991)

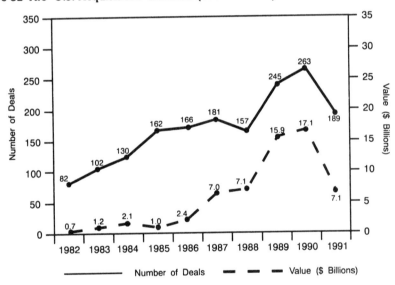

Snapshot Analysis of the LBO Market

Need a more graphic illustration of the swan dive of the LBO market than Figure 32.7? It may be subtitled the rise and fall of the LBO market. Note that the number of deals in 1991 was actually less than the level of 1982 which often is cited as ground zero for the modern LBO movement.

Leveraged dealmaking is suffering from a drought in financing which is said to be temporary. However, Figure 32.8 suggests how this has exerted pressures across the board. The mere handful of going-private transactions may not be surprising since these usually involve rather large deals—and large financings. But note the plunge in divestitures done through LBOs. That indicates that in many cases leveraged dealmakers, whether LBO packagers or managements, have not been viable bidders for corporate selloffs because of difficulties in squeezing out the financing. The drop in private market deals also may be attributable to reluctance of owners to sell at reduced pricing in the general M&A market.

Table 32–A.8 The Leveraged Buyout Market (1982 to 1991)

Year	Number of Deals	% of All Deals	Value ($ bil)	% of Total M&A Value
1982	148	9.2%	$3.4	6.1%
1983	210	11.6	4.5	9.1
1984	237	9.8	18.7	15.4
1985	238	8.6	19.7	14.0
1986	330	8.7	45.2	22.5
1987	270	8.6	36.2	21.1
1988	378	11.4	47.1	20.2
1989	371	12.1	66.8	27.4
1990	241	7.6	15.9	9.7
1991	112	5.3	5.5	5.6

Figure 32–A.7 The Leveraged Buyout Market (1982 to 1991)

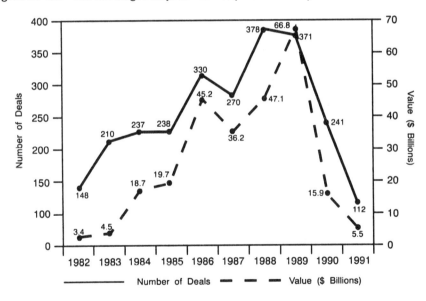

Number of Deals ———   Value ($ Billions) — — —

Figure 32–A.8 Types of Leveraged Buyouts (1991 versus 1990)

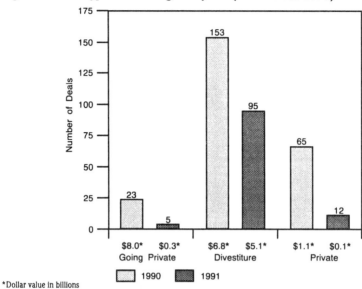

*Dollar value in billions

Chapter 33

Middle Market Buyouts*

Scott H. Lang
Executive Vice President, Head of Investment Banking
Rodman and Renshaw, Inc., Chicago, IL

This chapter provides a summary of leveraged buyout activity in the middle market over the past five years. The chapter starts by providing a broad definition and description of middle market companies including approximate size parameters and operating characteristics. Motivations for buying and selling middle market companies are discussed to the extent that they differ from those involved in larger leveraged buyout transactions. A brief history of middle market leveraged buyouts follows, focusing on the use of leverage, proliferation of financial buyers, and trends in valuation multiples which have occurred over the past five years. This history is best summarized by a comparison of typical deal structures used in the late 1980s versus the early 1990s, as illustrated in the text. Finally, the investment banking infrastructure available to facilitate middle market buyouts is discussed. The past five years have been marked by tremendous changes in the way middle market leveraged buyouts are financed, and this chapter summarizes both those changes and the factors which are motivating them.

Definition and Description of "Middle Market" Companies

In attempting to define the middle market, it becomes readily apparent that no common definition is widely accepted by practitioners. Each practitioner uses its own size parameters to characterize a middle market company. Rodman and Renshaw identifies middle market companies by their estimated total enterprise value (value of debt plus value of equity)

rather than sales volume. This eliminates the problems caused when comparing different industries with vastly different operating margins and, instead, focuses on the total financing required to fund an acquisition. We characterize middle market companies as those with a total enterprise value in the $15 million to $300 million range. This broad category can be further separated into two categories: those companies with valuations less than $50 million (referred to as smaller middle market companies) and companies in the $50 million to $300 million range.

In addition to size, there are a number of operating characteristics common to middle market companies. These characteristics are generally more pronounced in companies of less than $50 million in value. First, middle market companies are often privately owned or family owned businesses compared to their larger, public counterparts, and they tend to be involved in basic manufacturing, distribution, or retailing businesses. Middle market companies tend to be financed by secured, asset-based commercial lenders rather than unsecured lenders who may be more relationship-oriented. Finally, the internal systems utilized by middle market companies, particularly the smaller companies, tend to be less sophisticated than in larger corporations, reflecting the more entrepreneurial culture and relaxed management typical of middle market companies. Although from a size standpoint, many high technology firms may fall into the middle market category, they are generally excluded from discussions about middle market buyout activity because most such companies are inherently unleverageable. Industries

*Mr. Lang was assisted in the preparation of this chapter by Susan W. Wilson, formerly an Associate in the Investment Banking Department at Rodman and Renshaw, Inc.

with a high degree of regulatory oversight such as banks are also often excluded because, like high technology companies, they comprise a separate niche of their own.

Motivations for Buying and Selling Middle Market Companies

While some of the motivations for buying and selling middle market companies are the same as those for buying and selling larger, public companies, some distinct differences do exist. For larger companies, many of the classic motivations have centered on potential operating synergies that may exist between companies. The opportunity to consolidate a sales force or distribution network, to leverage R&D or advertising expenditures, to eliminate duplicate administrative overhead, or to utilize excess manufacturing capacity have motivated much of the merger and acquisition activity among larger corporations. While these motivations can be equally compelling for middle market companies, several additional motivations, which may be characterized as more personal on the part of middle market private business owners, are equally important.

Financial and estate liquidity are often the reasons that middle market business owners decide to sell their companies. After years of building and developing their businesses, many owners find that a significant portion of their personal net worth is tied up in the equity value of their companies. A sale of the business to a strategic or financial buyer provides financial liquidity to the business owner. While an IPO helps to value an owner's equity for estate purposes and provides a good measure of liquidity, an IPO rarely will provide an owner with as much cash liquidity as an outright sale, because an owner is usually unable to sell more than 20%-30% of his shares in an IPO. Moreover, the initial public offering market is frequently unavailable to smaller middle market business owners and a private sale may be their only means of achieving liquidity. Similarly, estate planning may motivate a business sale, as owners strive to plan for the next generation which may not be expected to join the family business.

A sale of the business may also be a way to effectuate the transition to a more professional management team. As a company grows and eventually requires a change in management style from its entrepreneurial founder to more professional business managers, equity incentives are frequently used to facilitate the transition and attract capable, new managers. A sale of the business to a financially strong entity or individual that can provide growth capital for the business is also a common motivation. Small business owners often realize that a successful,

growing business can require a significant amount o growth capital that must be sought from outside sources with deeper pockets.

Finally, an important motivation for buying and selling middle market companies is the potentia investment returns available with small, private companies. As will be discussed, expected invest ment returns for equity sponsors are typically 30% 40%, even in the early 1990s with equity capita requirements substantially larger than in the late 1980s. These returns are particularly attractive when compared to investment returns typicall achieved with investments in public stocks or the S&P 500. As long as investment returns for middle market buyouts remain attractive, investors will con tinue to pursue such transactions.

The Early Buyouts

Buyouts in the middle market are not a recen phenomenon. While media attention has high lighted buyout activity which occurred during the 1980s, middle market buyout activity commenced during the 1960s and increased during the 1970s These early buyouts, known as "bootstrap" acquisi tions, were notable in terms of the financing struc tures they employed and the purchase price multiples involved. Bootstraps required minimal eq uity capital and relied heavily, if not exclusively, or asset-based financing. These early buyouts involved smaller companies with predictable, steady cash flow histories, minimal to moderate capital expendi ture requirements, and heavy asset concentrations which supported formula-based lending. In essence these transactions followed classic corporate finance theory in terms of the types of companies able tc sustain a high degree of leverage in their capital structure. Bootstraps provided private business own ers the opportunity to liquify their personal balance sheets through the sale of their companies. Since the initial public offering market was often unavailable to middle market companies during that time, boot straps provided an important vehicle for ownership transfer and liquidity in the middle market.

Purchase price multiples in bootstrap buyouts were low by today's standards and generally fell in the two to three times cash flow range. These early buyouts were usually sponsored by entrepreneurs who intended to operate the companies in a "hands on" manner. Multiples increased in late 1970s and early 1980s as more sophisticated equity sponsors entered the market, and by the mid-1980s senior financing began to move away from a strictly asset based approach to one which relied increasingly on projected cash flow.

Middle Market Buyouts in the 1980s

Middle market buyout transactions during the middle to late 1980s were marked by rising purchase price multiples, the increasing availability of senior financing, the advent of "mezzanine" financing, and a less than proportionate increase in equity commitments. Purchase price multiples peaked in 1989 at approximately five to seven times cash flow for smaller middle market companies (i.e., less than $50 million in total enterprise value) and seven to nine times for middle market companies valued above $50 million. The additional financing required to fund these aggressive purchase price multiples came from "cash flow" (i.e., unsecured) senior lenders and from "mezzanine" lenders who were willing to bridge the gap between senior financing and equity capital in return for a higher rate of interest and usually an equity participation (or "kicker") in the ownership of the company. A number of new institutional sources of senior unsecured and mezzanine financing entered the market, anxious to participate in the buyout activity and attracted by the particularly high investment returns projected by middle market buyout sponsors compared to alternative portfolio investments. In particular, large insurance companies entered the mezzanine financing market, and several commercial finance companies and large money center banks began to advertise themselves as "one stop shops" that provided senior secured, senior unsecured, mezzanine, and even common equity financing in one financing package, often taking the lion's share of risk in return for a disproportionately small share of the potential rewards. These new institutional sources of capital played a critical role in accelerating the pace and the price of middle market buyouts during the 1980s.

Higher purchase price multiples reflected the fact that middle market companies were being purchased at valuations based more on projected than on historical earnings. Almost invariably, the repayment of unsecured senior financing and mezzanine debt depended on ever-improving operating results from an acquired company. Projections used to support middle market buyouts during this time were almost universally upward trending. Uninterrupted sales growth, increasing gross profit margins, improving working capital management, and nominal capital expenditure requirements were often used as "base case projections" for determining a repayment schedule of senior and mezzanine financing. This left little room for error in management's projections, which, in most cases, also relied on the assumption of economic expansion in the United States continuing for the foreseeable future.

Proliferation of "Financial Buyers"

The second half of the 1980s also witnessed a fundamental change in the types of sponsors of middle market acquisitions. By the mid-1980s, there had developed a dramatic proliferation of "financial buyers"—i.e., wealthy individuals and investment firms backed by blind pools of capital that were devoted to the aggressive accumulation of portfolios of middle market companies through the use of financial leverage. Unlike most bootstrap acquirors of the 1960s and 1970s who might acquire and manage one or two companies at a time, the financial buyers of the 1980s often had little operational experience but possessed more sophisticated financing, administrative, and computer forecasting techniques than bootstrappers. They also brought far greater acquisitiveness and larger professional staffs to middle market acquisitions and, in doing so, they "institutionalized" the leveraged buyouts business. Many of these financial buyers had experience and backgrounds in the venture capital business where they provided seed capital to start-up companies with a high degree of operating and business risk. These investors were attracted to the leveraged buyouts business because it offered the opportunity to invest in more mature, stable businesses and, through the use of financial leverage, achieve potential investment returns on par with those experienced with venture capital investments.

Two key reasons for the proliferation of financial buyers were, first, it appeared that many American corporations, especially entrepreneurially owned middle market businesses, could be run more efficiently and, hence, more profitably than their current owners were running them; and second, the equity capital required to complete middle market buyouts continued to be nominal, even though purchase price multiples were increasing, because financial institutions were competing for this business by taking on increasing portions of the risk. Given such a favorable risk/reward environment, competition among financial buyers intensified as professionals from the commercial lending, investment banking, accounting, and legal professions entered the field. These investors often lacked the operating and management experience which the previous business owners had when they were cashed out of their businesses by financial buyers in the 1980s.

The End of the 1980s Buyout Craze

The upward trend in valuations peaked in 1989, as the economy slowed and loan portfolio problems began to accelerate among those institutions that most heavily supported leveraged buyouts. As mentioned, many of the leveraged buyout transactions financed during the late 1980s relied on projections which included escalating increases in sales growth and profitability. These projections simply could not be achieved during an economic recession. An increasing number of companies involved in leveraged buyout transactions began having difficulty making scheduled repayments. Rather than devoting resources to new transactions, the lending community became focused on managing existing portfolio problems which were highlighted during this recessionary period.

In particular, federal regulators required banks to maintain additional capital reserves against loans classified as "highly leveraged transactions" based on specific parameters regarding the capital structure, interest coverage ratios, and other financial and operating aspects of the borrower. Insurance regulators and rating agencies began placing similar constraints on insurance companies that had taken on significant volumes of loans rated below investment grade. In effect, such loans became more costly to provide. In addition, problems faced by the savings and loan industry sensitized the lending community to the pitfalls of lending during a deflationary period to both real estate and highly leveraged transactions. Thus, senior and mezzanine financing sources began to curtail sharply their new business activities with regard to leveraged buyouts and real estate, and the aggressive financing available earlier in the decade all but disappeared.

Two transactions in particular, both involving buyouts of very large public companies, signaled a rapid change in the financing environment for all LBO's. The first was the rejection by financial institutions of the management-led leveraged buyout of United Airlines in October, 1989. The second was the rapid failure of Robert Campeau's leveraged acquisitions of Allied Stores and Federated Department Stores. Although many other leveraged transactions began showing signs of failure around the same time, these two highly publicized transactions, perhaps more than any others, brought the leveraged buyout markets at almost all levels to a standstill by early 1990.

Buyouts in the Early 1990s

The profound effect that changes in the senior debt financing market had on leveraged buyout activity is perhaps best illustrated by statistics. Figures 33.1, 33.2, and 33.3 show the dollar volume, average transaction size, and number of buyout transactions completed from 1986 through the second quarter of

1992. Buyout activity, in terms of dollar volume, showed a dramatic peak in 1988, declining significantly in 1989 and even further in 1990. In 1991, activity began to increase and continued at approximately the same pace through the first half of 1992. Interestingly, the data also demonstrate how the average size of completed buyout transactions dropped dramatically over this time period. (*Note:* These data do not tell the entire story of activity during this period, because they do not include the many restructuring, refinancing, and recapitalization transactions that occurred from 1990 through the present, many of which involved a change of control but did not qualify as leveraged buyouts for statistical purposes.)

Again, much of the decline in buyout activity between 1988 and 1991 was due to the lack of financing after 1989. In addition, the purchase price multiples achieved in the late 1980s had raised the expectations of sellers regarding the value of their companies, and these expectations did not fall correspondingly as senior financing dried up and buyers could not finance acquisitions at such high multiples. Such disparity between the expectations of buyers and sellers contributed to the rapid decline in buyout activity in the early 1990s.

This disparity was even more pronounced by the resurgence in 1991 of the initial public offering (IPO) equity market, which afforded many middle market business owners, including many financial buyers that owned portfolios of middle market companies, a window of opportunity to sell equity to the public at pricing multiples that were often double what they could achieve in a private sale. The IPO market, which as of this writing has slowed somewhat but is still vibrant, was stimulated by the combination of enormous pent-up demand from highly liquid pension funds and mutual funds for new equity issues, coupled with the Federal Reserve Board's dramatic lowering of interest rates, which made equity investments appear more attractive than debt. Whatever the cause, the overheated IPO market of 1991 and early 1992 certainly contributed to the significant reduction of middle market buyout activity.

It is important to mention that the preceding charts and statistics do not tell the entire story regarding activity in the middle market during the late 1980s and early 1990s. While leverage buyout activity dropped off significantly in 1989 and 1990, merger and acquisition activity overall was less volatile. Merger and acquisition activity, of which leveraged buyout activity is only a subset, did decline during the late 1980s but was more stable and appears to be returning to historical levels more quickly than leveraged buyout activity. As Figures 33.4 and 33.5 demonstrate, on a broader scale, the

Figure 33.1 Dollar Volume of Middle Market Buyouts

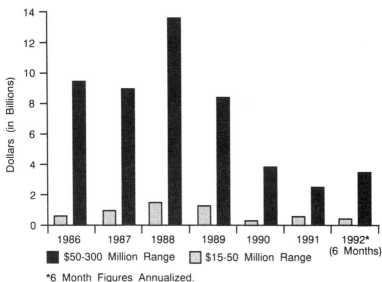

$50-300 Million Range $15-50 Million Range

*6 Month Figures Annualized.

*6 month figures annualized
Source: Securities Data Company, Inc.

middle market continues to be a very active arena for transactions.

While middle market leveraged buyout activity slowed considerably during the early 1990s, it did not end altogether. Instead, transactions completed during the early 1990s began to be financed on very different terms compared to transactions completed during the mid-to-late 1980s. Significant changes occurred at all levels of the capital structure, from senior debt to mezzanine financing and equity. The changes that occurred translated into lower pricing multiples (four to six times operating cash flow for most smaller middle market companies, and five to seven times for larger ones) and much more conservative capital structures for those buyout transactions that have been successfully completed.

Senior financing for buyouts completed during 1990 and 1991 returned to almost a strictly asset-based and collateral-oriented environment, much like in the bootstrap era. Over-advance or cash flow (i.e., unsecured) senior loan facilities became the exception rather than the rule. Instead, the amount of senior financing that could be obtained for a transaction generally would be no more than 50% of the total capital structure compared to 60%–70% in the late 1980s. Although the total amount of senior financing was still based on the customary borrowing

base formulas, loan advance rates were lowered, asset eligibility requirements became much stricter and borrowers' projections were viewed more skeptically, all of which resulted in substantially reduced borrowing bases compared to the 1980s. (It is worth mentioning that the recession and the savings and loan crisis drove down the appraised value of most fixed assets, especially real estate; indeed many asset-based lenders refused to assign any significant value to real estate for lending purposes because of the very poor liquidity of real estate assets during the recession, and this continues to be the case today.) By thus curtailing the amount of senior financing available to finance leveraged buyout transactions, senior lenders forced purchase price multiples of middle market companies down and equity commitments from transaction sponsors up to represent a larger percentage of the overall capital structure.

Two notable changes have also taken place with respect to mezzanine financing. The first has been the virtual exit from the market of the two most important sources of mezzanine debt—insurance companies and commercial finance companies. Plagued by portfolio problems of their own and sensitive to the threat of rating downgrades caused by portfolio problems and concentrations in real estate and leveraged transactions, these two institutional

Figure 33.2   Average Middle Market Buyout Size

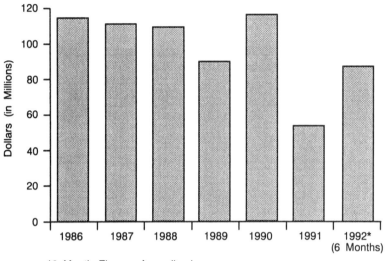

*6 Month Figures Annualized.

Source: Securities Data Company, Inc.

sources of mezzanine financing left the market almost entirely during 1990. Today, however, the mezzanine markets are in the process of being partially replenished, this time by special mezzanine funds, backed by limited partnership investments supplied primarily from large pension funds, as well as a few insurance companies and banks that survived the late 1980s without significant losses. The second change in mezzanine financing has been the return of seller financing or "seller paper" representing deferred payments to sellers, often based on "earn-out" formulas. As the institutional sources of mezzanine capital continue to grow, however, seller paper is becoming a diminishing factor.

With less competition among sources of mezzanine financing, pricing of mezzanine debt increased. In the late 1980s, mezzanine investors typically required projected internal rates of return ranging from 20%–25%, often based on aggressive growth assumptions and high exit pricing multiples. In contrast, mezzanine investors in the early 1990s began seeking projected returns in the 25%–30% range, and sometimes higher, and these increased return hurdles would be based on more conservative operating projections and exit pricing multiples. The ability to pay mezzanine interest by issuing more mezzanine debt (PIK or payment in kind interest) virtually disappeared. All of these factors contributed

to the rising cost of mezzanine debt in 1990 and 1991. However, as new players began to enter the mezzanine market in 1992, and as bond rates in the United States continued to fall, mezzanine pricing has begun to moderate again.

Mezzanine investors have also become more focused on the strength of the equity sponsor and the amount of equity contributed by the sponsor in leveraged transactions. Sponsor strength is often viewed as critically important, because a sponsor with deep pockets is more able and likely to provide additional equity support if a company runs into operating problems. Without a strong sponsor, the mezzanine lender is more likely to be required to invest additional funds in distressed situations or suffer a substantial principal loss.

Middle market buyouts completed during the early 1990s have required financial sponsors to bear a significant amount of financial risk as compared to the level of risk they typically faced in transactions completed during the 1980s. Equity contributions in the early 1990s have usually equaled 20%–30% of total capitalization versus 5%–10% in the late 1980s, forcing sponsors to make a meaningful financial contribution to the total financing requirement of a transaction. The amount of fees that sponsors can expect to receive at the closing of a transaction as well as in the form of annual management fees

Figure 33.3   Middle Market Leveraged Buyouts

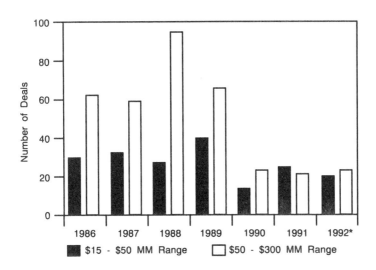

*6 month figures annualized
Source: Securities Data Company, Inc.

has also been curtailed. Although purchase price multiples have come down, the increased equity requirements have translated into lower return expectations for equity investors. During the 1980s it was not uncommon for an equity investor to expect returns on a buyout investment to be in the 50%–70% range; however, the lower degree of leverage involved in more recent transactions has resulted in lower return expectations in the 30%–40% range for middle market acquisitions, and even lower for very large leveraged buyouts.

Larger equity requirements have also led to more corporate partnering and a greater emphasis on synergistic buyers, including financial buyers making add-on acquisitions to existing portfolio company investments. It has also become more common to see two or three equity sponsors each contributing part of a total equity requirement of a transaction thereby allowing them to limit their individual exposures in any single investment and increase the degree of diversification within their investment portfolios. In order to maximize return expectations in the face of increasing equity requirements, the identification of any and all possible operating synergies resulting from a buyout have also become more important. "Synergistic" buyers (i.e., corporate buyers from the same or a related industry as the seller)

who can effectuate distribution improvements, cost savings, administrative consolidation and the like are more likely to achieve favorable investment returns on their now larger and more significant equity investments. Synergistic buyers are also usually able to justify (and finance) a higher purchase price than a "stand alone" acquiror, which gives them a distinct advantage in what has become a far more expensive, time-consuming, and unpredictable acquisition environment. Many financial buyers have attempted to become synergistic buyers through acquisition strategies known as "consolidation plays" which involve the purchase and consolidation of multiple businesses in a fragmented industry in order to achieve favorable operating synergies. In general, the larger equity requirements have forced equity investors to rethink the ways they formerly did business and form new alliances within the investment community. They have also forced numerous financial buyers to exit the business altogether.

Perhaps the best way to summarize the different financing structures involved in middle market buyouts completed during the late 1980s versus buyouts completed during the early 1990s is by using an example. Table 33.1 is a breakdown of the typical capital structure utilized for a $50 million

Figure 33.4   Dollar Volume of Mergers and Acquisitions Transactions

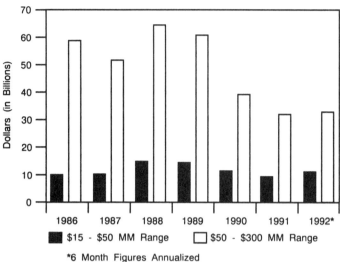

■ $15 - $50 MM Range   □ $50 - $300 MM Range

*6 Month Figures Annualized

*6 month figures annualized
Source: Securities Data Company, Inc.

leveraged buyout completed in the late 1980s versus the early 1990s.

As Table 33.1 demonstrates, buyouts completed during the late 1980s typically employed a much higher level of senior debt financing and lower amount of equity capital compared to buyouts completed during the early 1990s. These changes in financing structures were motivated by regulatory changes in the banking industry and portfolio problems that were exacerbated by the U.S. recession. In response to these issues, the financing of middle market leveraged buyouts has become more conservative, providing buyers lower projected returns but also lower risk, because the companies involved in such transactions should have a greater ability to withstand any unexpected downturns in operating performance or the economy.

Investment Banking Services for Middle Market Companies

Relatively few investment banking firms in America provide a full range of services oriented to the needs of middle market businesses. While most bulge bracket and major bracket Wall Street firms do offer a full range of services, their primary focus continues

to be the Fortune 1000 companies. Therefore, a frequent complaint among middle market business owners—particularly those in the bottom half of the middle market—is that large investment banks rarely assign experienced bankers to middle market transactions.

Many regional brokerage firms, on the other hand, have limited investment banking staffs and tend to focus more on public equity offerings of companies within their regions or within discreet industries followed by their research staffs. Unlike Rodman and Renshaw, relatively few established firms have invested in staffing and the expertise to handle middle market buyouts and merger and acquisition transactions in a systematic, sophisticated manner. Consequently, it is often difficult for middle market companies—especially those in the bottom half of the middle market—to obtain competent buyout-related or merger and acquisition investment banking services from "name brand" firms.

A number of new investment banking operations have sprung up since the mid-1980s to fill this void. These include "boutique" firms organized by investment bankers that left or were let go by larger investment banking concerns, as well as large accounting firms and banks that have hired investment banking staffs primarily to provide buyout-related

Figure 33.5   Merger and Acquisition Activity

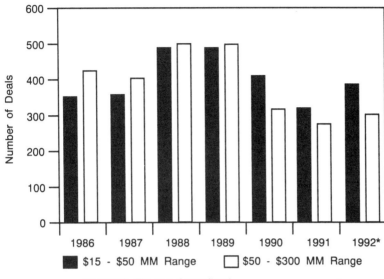

6 Month Figures Annualized

Source: Securities Data Company, Inc.

and merger and acquisition investment banking services to their middle market customers. Relatively few boutiques, however, have managed to sustain sufficient business flow. And accounting firms and banks have not faired much better. The latter have been particularly hampered by their inability to attract and retain highly qualified investment bankers, because their compensation systems and cultures are less entrepreneurial than investment banks. As a result, the turnover among investment bankers at

Table 33.1 $50 Million Leveraged Buyout
Capital Structure in Late 1980 Versus Early 1990
(Dollars in Millions)

Late 1980	Amount	Percentage	Returns	Collateral
Sources of Funds:				
Senior Debt	$32.5	65%	N/A	50%–100%
Mezzanine Capital	15.0	30%	20%–25%	0%
Equity	2.5	5%	50%–70%	N/A
	$50.0	100%		
Purchase/Exit Multiples	5-7x EBIT			

Early 1990	Amount	Percentage	Returns	Collateral
Sources of Funds:				
Senior Debt	$25.0	50%	N/A	80%–100%
Mezzanine Capital	15.0	30%	25%–30%	Sometimes
Equity	10.0	20%	30%-40%	N/A
	$50.0	100%		
Purchase/Exit Multiples	4-6x EBIT			

such firms has been substantial and is likely to remain so.

There are exceptions to the foregoing generalizations, i.e., Wall Street investment banks and regional brokerage firms that have dedicated substantial resources to the middle market niche, as well as boutiques, banks, and accounting firms that have established the right culture in which to grow their investment banking business—but these are still relatively few in number. As a result, a number of would-be investment banking clients in the middle market—again, particularly in the lower half of the middle market—choose to handle their own transactions directly without investment banking assistance, which continues to make this one of the least efficient sectors of the U.S. investment banking market.

The Future of Middle Market Buyouts

The middle market remains the most active market for leveraged buyouts today. Even though middle market buyout volume has not returned to the level observed during the 1980s, activity is beginning to increase. As previously mentioned, one of the major factors affecting this activity has been the IPO market, which historically has been countercyclical with merger and acquisition activity and private leveraged buyouts. During the mid to late 1980s, valuation multiples in the public market were frequently low compared to replacement values, sparking activity in the leveraged buyout market whereby many public companies were taken private. As the IPO market heated up in late 1991 and early 1992, private business owners who were contemplating a sale of their businesses began turning increasingly to the public market where they were able to realize very attractive pricing multiples. More recently, however, activity in the IPO market has began to level off (particularly for nontechnology companies) and, in turn, valuations available to business owners through private sale transactions have begun to improve; hence, private leveraged buyout activity has begun to increase.

Another encouraging sign for the buyouts marketplace is that many financing sources and institutional investors that left the leveraged buyout market in early 1990 are returning, and fund raising activity on the part of mezzanine and equity leveraged buyout pools has picked up. Several commercial banks and commercial finance companies have cautiously begun financing leveraged transactions, not merely on asset-based terms but with a cautious return to cash flow lending. To be sure, senior financing continues to be primarily asset-based; but it is becoming more common for some component of a total senior financing package to be advanced on a cash flow basis. Pension fund interest in middle market buyouts continues to grow, as evidenced by the number of new mezzanine and equity buyout funds that have been raised with pension money in the past year. This is significant because these investors clearly have the greatest liquidity to provide to the market.

Another recent trend, which Rodman and Renshaw expects to continue, is the convergence of buyer and seller expectations regarding valuations in the private market. The high purchase price multiples realized in middle market buyouts in the late 1980s coupled with the even higher IPO market valuations achieved since 1991, kept seller expectations high throughout this period. However, many business owners have been unable or unwilling to utilize the public market as an exit mechanism and are more likely than at any time in the past few years to turn to the private market, including the LBO market, to sell their companies.

In general, Rodman and Renshaw anticipates that the market will continue to develop capacity for high quality middle market leveraged buyouts. Although the experience of many institutional players who participated in the buyouts binge of the late 1980s was very negative, the potential returns available to lenders and investors—particularly in the more conservative pricing and financing environment that exists today—will continue to attract responsible institutional players to middle market buyouts.

Part XIV:
Crossborder Transactions

Chapter 34

Crossborder Deals Are Different

Emanuele Costa and Peter G. Gould
Principals
Overseas Partners, Inc., New York, NY

Stepping beyond the borders of the United States takes corporate acquirors not just into other countries, but into a deal-making environment that, for an American, can occasionally seem otherworldly. For several years, Overseas Partners has been active as a financial buyer of middle-market companies in Europe and in the United States. That experience shapes the comments made here, which seek to characterize the voyage of discovery an experienced American acquiror will make when venturing into Europe.

Overseas Partners began, in fact, as an exercise in cross-border investing. Founded in 1984 by Europeans arranging investments in the United States for their clients on the continent, Overseas Partners has managed 17 acquisitions in the United States since 1985. Through this experience, the principals of the firm acquired the skills and approach of American-style deal making.

The European principals of Overseas Partners are all Italian with extensive business and personal contacts throughout Europe. Italy, where the firm made six acquisitions, was a natural starting point for Overseas Partners. In 1989, the firm turned homeward and initiated an active acquisition program in Europe. Recent major acquisitions in France and Scandinavia have extended the firm's activities throughout the continent.

With feet planted firmly on both sides of the Atlantic Ocean, and with roots both in the tightly knit business culture of Europe and the aggressive deal market of the United States, Overseas Partners has a unique perspective on the differences between acquisitions in the United States and those in Europe. These comments will be focused on the situa-

tion in Europe in general, and in particular on the challenges that financial buyers face in Europe.

Three Observations

Acquirors venturing for the first time beyond the United States are frequently surprised at the complexity and impenetrability of foreign markets. To the rest of the world, the United States is an extraordinary environment. There is no equivalent to the huge, integrated, nationwide U.S. market for consumer and industrial products. Few markets, if any, feature the competitiveness that results from U.S. anti-trust laws, the sheer size of the market, and America's historic commitment to free trade. The first thing any American contemplating an overseas acquisition must do is drop preconceived notions based on experience in the United States and recognize some basic differences abroad.

First, each country is unique. While this may seem obvious, Americans in particular are noted for failing to recognize or accommodate the many differences among even small, contiguous states. In Europe, much of the dynamism and excitement for acquirors stems from the persistent, if sometimes perilous, progress being made toward integration of the European Community's trade, tax, and industrial structures. Even European economic integration will not, and is not intended, to eliminate the very real differences among the countries of Europe.

As minor examples, one Italian company in the Overseas Partners portfolio produces regional specialty dessert products. While well-known and important in the Italian market, none of these products would find a ready market in neighboring Spain, let

375

alone in Sweden, where Overseas Partners has acquired Scandinavia's leading outdoor advertising company. By the same token, the outdoor market in Sweden, where TV advertising is sharply curtailed and cigarette ads were banned years ago, is distinctly different from Italy, France, and other Southern European countries. Environmental regulations vary enormously in Europe, ranging from German rules that can be tighter than those in the United States to very limited environmental regulation in Italy and other countries just awakening to these issues.

In short, tastes, laws, and business customs will differ even among neighboring nations in Europe. Although American companies are adept at detailed market segmentation and target marketing in their home market, many move offshore without realizing that a similar, detailed understanding of each overseas market is essential to successful acquisitions. Ingrained differences in national cultures and legal history will not be cast aside merely by the elimination of transborder barriers in Europe.

Second, European businesses have grown up within what are, by American standards, small and protected national markets. As a consequence, Europe has a dual industrial structure—extremely large, world-class multinational companies and much smaller businesses that serve local markets or tightly defined international niches. There are far fewer firms of the sort known in the United States as "middle market" companies—$100 million or larger multiproduct, often multidivisional companies.

The smaller European companies, the likely targets for most foreign acquirors, are typically owned by the founding families. Their managements are entrepreneurial, with strong technical capabilities, and focused marketing efforts. In their home markets, these companies are preeminent, and frequently they are superb exporters with state-of-the-art manufacturing capabilities. Equity is tightly held among the family owners and almost never spread to employees. These companies are run by the owners, for the owners. They are not experienced in the ways of big-company management.

These smaller firms very often face limited competition in their home markets. For example, there are only two outdoor advertising companies in Sweden. It is not unusual to find national monopolies or duopolies throughout Europe. This is expected to change significantly as Europe's integration continues, but for the moment the unique entrée these companies offer to their home markets is one of their most important attractions to an acquiror. However, by their very nature, smaller family-owned businesses are difficult to acquire and integrate into foreign parent-company operations.

The third general observation is that European acquisition markets are highly personal. Europe's business culture is centuries old, and in most countries, business leaders are personally close to one another and close to their governments and banks. These relationships extend even to areas that in the United States would be problematic, such as interlocking directorships. In one Overseas Partners acquisition, for example, an instrumental player in the financing package was a key director of the seller who also was a senior director of one of the lead banks in the transaction.

For a foreign acquiror entering a new country, there is no substitute for developing close relationships with individuals who have access to these personal networks. For Overseas Partners, that route has been through the business contacts of our principals in Southern and Central Europe and, in the case of our Swedish transaction, through an intermediary with extensive Swedish contacts who became our partner in the transaction. As a practical matter, it is difficult for all but the largest U.S. companies to make middle-market acquisitions in Europe without direct contacts of this sort.

Europe's Acquisition Market

Europe's acquisition environment naturally segments into two distinct markets: the United Kingdom and everywhere else. In the United Kingdom, there is a highly developed system of merchant bankers, intermediaries, and venture capital groups that source and provide capital for acquisitions. It is in most critical respects similar to the United States market; that is, transactions are analyzed, structured, and marketed very similarly by professionals who are fully conversant in U.S.-style deal making. Lending institutions are familiar with the various forms of buyout transactions and operate easily in that arena. The market for businesses is competitive, well-organized, and professional.

Overseas Partners does not actively pursue acquisitions in the United Kingdom, in part, precisely because the market is so well-developed and thoroughly populated with local competitors. On the continent, conditions are very different. The opportunities for foreign buyers are greater, but so are the challenges.

First among the issues a foreign acquiror faces outside the United Kingdom is access to transaction opportunities. For the most part, networks of acquisition intermediaries—investment banks, business brokers, and so forth—are highly underdeveloped in Europe compared to those in the United States. Acquisition markets are primarily local, with bankers, lawyers, accountants, and other business advisors often acting as the intermediary for a seller. Negotiated transactions between the principals predominate, with few, if any, competitors to the buyer. Sales in U.S.-style auctions, although increasing in number, are unusual.

Several American networks of intermediaries are attempting to offer European transaction opportunities to American buyers. In those countries or industries, such as Italy or the European food industry, where our firm is well-established, Overseas Partners ordinarily learns of opportunities first in Europe. The transactions that reach us through American brokers are often shopworn or mispriced. While we occasionally encounter attractive opportunities in this manner, particularly in countries where we are not yet active, there is no substitute for direct relationships in Europe.

Once a target company is identified, it is harder in Europe than in the United States to develop cogent market information. The United States, with its numerous trade associations, government agency reports, and computerized data banks, is a cornucopia of market data, compared to Europe, where industry data is often country-specific, if it exists at all. Studies by marketing consulting firms are often limited in number and scope. Reliable background financial data on competitors is frequently impossible to obtain. Even where intermediaries are directing the sale, the voluminous memoranda typically prepared by U.S. investment bankers are not often provided in Europe. An acquiror must expect that the assessment of markets and competitors that is integral to the decision to buy a company will be more difficult, less precise, and more expensive than in the United States.

Once the decision to acquire has been made, negotiations are the next challenge. Personal relationships and chemistry can be vital to this process. In the case of Overseas Partners' most recent European acquisition, the relationships among principals of our firm, the seller (a French/Italian company), and its financial advisor were essential. All the key individuals had known one another for years and were able to build on that relationship to complete, in perfect confidence and without real competition, a complex and quite viable transaction. That is typical in Europe.

Once negotiations commence, acquirors with U.S. experience will quickly discover that they are negotiating in a new context. Concepts of valuation—multiples of earnings, cash flow, or of revenues, for example—are inconsistently interpreted and applied in Europe. There is no sense of a "market" for companies in which "standard multiples" would apply. Rather, the value of a company in Europe often has a subjective element—the value it

has to the owner in personal, not merely financial terms—that can be a serious obstacle to successful transactions. It also can be an advantage. Sellers may be as concerned about whom they allow to buy, or prevent from buying, their companies as they are about the final price. Europeans frequently consider family heritage, pride, and obligations to employees—not merely maximum financial gain—when they sell a company.

Prices for quality companies in Europe tend to be higher than in the United States. Good companies in Europe typically have very strong profit histories, strong market positions, and good operations. Their quality, combined with the fact that owner/managers tend to be excellent negotiators in no hurry to sell, leads to a prevailing level of pricing—compared with U.S. benchmarks—that will appear high to the U.S. buyer. If the buyer has done the proper homework, however, these companies offer market access and product capabilities unrivaled by equivalently sized companies in the United States. They are worth the price.

Due Diligence and Transaction Structures

It is customary in the United States, once a transaction has been negotiated, to inundate a target company with lawyers, accountants, and operating personnel who comb through every agreement, policy, accounting record, and factory. This due diligence process is intimately related to the legal framework of detailed contracts and loan documentation that prevails in the United States. America is unique in the intrusiveness of its pre-acquisition investigations, however. Even among the most sophisticated European companies, procedures such as these are uncomfortable. For midsize and small company owners managers, they are unheard of and, when they occur, come as a distinct shock and often a personal affront to the owners and managers.

There is no easy way to prepare a seller for the due diligence process. Acquirors must be sensitive to the intrusive nature of an American-style exercise and, to the extent possible, control the process to minimize disrupting either the operations or the seller's willingness to complete the transaction. That said, however, due diligence takes on particular importance in smaller European companies because they can be full of surprises.

The first due diligence problem to face is the prospect that there are multiple sets of books. In much of Europe, this is a near-certainty among smaller companies. In one acquisition, after several weeks of probing, Overseas Partners unearthed three sets of financial records. One set was for bankers and other outsiders, one set for the owner, and one set for the internal revenue service. Deciphering the financial reality of a business and conveying it to lenders can be a trial under such circumstances.

The difficulty is compounded by the tendency of privately owned companies in Europe to be operated and even organized with tax minimization, not profit maximization, in mind. As an example, a Dutch company analyzed by Overseas Partners had a holding company and 12 financing and operating subsidiaries (many headquartered in Dutch tax havens)—all for a company with only $60 million in revenues. The complexities of unraveling such a structure and evaluating the performance of the company in a more conventional corporate structure and tax environment are daunting.

The tendency toward tax minimization is abetted by the differences in accounting rules in some European countries. Germany and Belgium, for example, support very aggressive depreciation policies. If a piece of equipment is purchased in Belgium close to year-end, it is possible to write off most of the cost within one year. Swedish tax laws authorize the write-off of goodwill over five years, a benefit unknown in the United States. At a minimum, it is important for buyers to recognize such differences exist and to factor their effects carefully into financial models. In the extreme, as encountered at a company in Belgium, capital investment incentives were so lucrative that owners had been incentivized to overcapitalize their operations rather than pay taxes.

Unfortunately for acquirors, the professionals on whom they typically rely in completing due diligence and structuring acquisitions often are quite inexperienced in modern corporate transactions, particularly leveraged acquisitions. In some cases, even the overseas affiliates of large U.S. law or accounting firms are very weak in this area.

At an early stage in our Swedish acquisition, for example, we were conferring with the Stockholm affiliate of a recognized New York law firm. Our principals asked for guidance on the legal distinctions between a "Heads of Agreement," or letter of intent, in the United Kingdom and a similarly labeled document in Sweden. After a moment's hesitation, one partner of the Swedish firm asked: "What is a Heads of Agreement?" So began a lengthy education process for our lawyers. The good news is that European legal documentation is substantially shorter and simpler than U.S. acquisition documents. Indeed, Europeans typically recoil from American legal documentation, which is wildly excessive in the context of most European legal systems.

Financial buyers will also have a very different experience with lenders in Europe. To begin, capital structures are more conservative. Senior debt in a leveraged transaction rarely exceeds 50% of permanent capital. Mezzanine debt is still a very new concept in Europe, with few investors in the market outside of London. Equity required will be in the range of 25–50% of the transaction value, depending on the degree of asset coverage for loans.

In general, bank fees will be lower in Europe than in the United States and approval processes will tend to be somewhat less bureaucratic. Indeed, frequently in Europe the lender is familiar with the target company or its industry and makes its lending decisions on that historical base of knowledge rather than on presentations by buyers. It has been Overseas Partners' experience that, in such a circumstance, lenders may require minimal background information, by American standards, to complete the approval process. Loan documentation also tends to be less voluminous and difficult to negotiate than in the United States.

As in all such matters, of course, generalizations can be risky. Lenders in the United Kingdom, for example, are noted for extremely careful approval processes and documentation that easily parallels that required by their U.S. counterparts. British financial partners can be as difficult to come to terms with as their Italian counterparts can be cooperative. European countries differ markedly in the degree of sophistication of their lending processes and documentation requirements. A great deal depends on the degree to which the borrower is familiar to the lender. Thus, once again, personal contacts and longstanding relationships in a country can be critical to completing a transaction on reasonable terms.

After the Acquisition

Just as the process of completing a transaction in Europe can be difficult for the acquiror, the experience of operating under U.S.-style investor ownership will mean major changes for company managements. Particularly if companies are operating under the strictures of a leveraged transaction in which debt covenants and repayment schedules become important for the first time, managements will be operating in unfamiliar terrain.

Management's disorientation is likely to be due to the limited focus on management systems and financial controls in many midsize European companies. Entrepreneurial managers, unused to the fetters of banks, tend to develop highly personalized management styles and frequently operate without sophisticated financial support staffs. Even in the case of companies that had been subsidiaries of large

European groups, managers frequently have not had to submit to the sort of budgeting and financial control disciplines American counterparts consider routine. One Italian company, a subsidiary of a large U.K. group before being acquired by our investors is an extreme example. The Italian managing director of that company spoke no English; his direct superior at the London home office spoke no Italian. Where there is no communication on this most basic level, one can imagine the very limited degree to which the managers of that business had any experience with close corporate oversight. Our experience has consistently been that preexisting managements in Europe often simply fail to recognize the importance of bank strictures, and often rebel at what they perceive to be a loss of independence, either financial or strategic, that comes with acquisition by an American-style buyer.

In one half of the acquisitions Overseas Partners has completed in Europe, we have elected to face these issues early and have replaced the chief executive officers at those companies as soon as the acquisitions were completed. Chief financial officers, individuals with broad experience in accounting, control and treasury functions, are extremely rare in midsize European companies. It is almost always necessary to add a senior financial executive to the corporate staff soon after an acquisition is closed.

Once the key management personnel have been identified, shoring up the internal management systems is urgent. Frequently, budgeting procedures are minimal, accounting systems weak, and computerization well behind equivalent companies in the United States. Managements frequently lack the skills, the data base, and the computer tools required to satisfy the demand for accurate and timely financial data that accompanies acquisition by a crossborder buyer. Acquirors should inspect these systems closely prior to acquisition and expect to make investments in information systems.

Post-acquisition issues involving senior executives and information systems can be resolved in typically American ways—by changing people and investing money. Many other matters affecting the performance of European acquisitions are not so easily resolved in the accustomed U.S. manner. In particular, acquirors should expect that labor-management relations and the prerogatives of managers will be distinctly different in many countries of Europe.

First, from the cost perspective, European labor is quite expensive. Direct wage and salary rates are high. Even higher are benefit and social security programs, most of which are funded partially or wholly through payroll taxes or through customary,

and by U.S. standards rich, employer-paid benefit programs. These programs are protected through a virtually universal presence of labor unions, many of them considerably more assertive than their American counterparts. Very few benefits or wages can be easily reduced; the labor "give backs" increasingly prevalent even in unionized U.S. operations are not easily achieved in Europe and should not be the basis for justifying an acquisition.

Corporate governance itself is affected by the unionization of European labor. Company managements deal directly with unions on matters that are the sole province of management in the United States. Plant rationalization—closings, restructuring of layouts and work forces, and so forth—can be severely impeded by legal restrictions and union resistance. In many countries with strong socialist political legacies, the barriers to plant closings and restructuring of companies can be extreme—very high severance costs, long notice requirements, union bargaining, and so forth.

In countries such as Germany, union representation on Boards of Directors is mandatory. Some form of worker participation in management is common in many parts of Europe. Although day-to-day operations of the company remain in the hands of management, labor has a stronger voice in operating matters in Europe than elsewhere, and these limitations need to be carefully understood, in the context of each particular country's legal, union and customary restraints on the exercise of management prerogatives.

For financial buyers, another important matter to evaluate carefully from a post-acquisition standpoint is the ultimate exit from the business. The characterization of the European M&A marketplace above should make clear that this is not a matter to be taken lightly. Intermediaries are underdeveloped; buyers are unsophisticated; and local entrepreneurial buyers scarce. Public market exits are much more difficult than in the United States. Certain countries, such as France, have improving public stock markets, and the U.K. market is extremely highly developed. In most of Europe, though, sale of shares through public offerings is limited and thus, a doubtful primary exit strategy.

It is critical to the success of an investment that there be a clear exit strategy at the time of acquisition. In general, particularly for smaller and midsize companies, this probably will entail sale to strategic buyers located either in Europe or in other parts of the world. As Europe draws closer economically and politically, demand will continue to strengthen for well-managed companies with strong market positions. These will be natural acquisition targets for larger strategic buyers seeking footholds in particular countries or in Europe generally.

For financial buyers and acquirors of smaller companies that ultimately will be sold, it is critical to take care during the period of ownership to place those businesses in the proper condition to eventually be acquired by larger companies. Part of the opportunity in Europe today is to buy smaller businesses and to add value through the sorts of changes described in this article. In so doing, an undermanaged small business that a larger company could not or would not own can be converted into a highly attractive investment for a disciplined corporate buyer. Acquirors should be targeting candidates for exit from the start. Priority should go to ensuring that acquired companies develop the management teams, financial systems, and operating controls necessary to assure the exit buyer that past performance can be replicated and that the organization can be melded into the structured operations of large multinational organizations.

Conclusions

In the broadest terms, Overseas Partners believes there are three key factors to successful acquisitions in Europe.

First, acquirors need to develop the strongest possible local contacts and pay great attention to the multitude of differences among countries in Europe. In all likelihood, this will mean moving into one country at a time—developing contacts and understanding in one market before beginning to explore the next. A local presence, involving individuals or organizations that are well established in the local business culture, is essential to ensure access to transactions and to financing.

Second, whenever possible, acquirors should buy in industries they understand. For financial buyers, this means targeting industries in which their principals have worked or in which they have previously held investments. The challenges of due diligence and post-acquisition operations will be more manageable for a buyer who is familiar with the industry involved, even if the culture and practices of a European country are new.

Third, acquirors must recognize the strengths and limitations of midsize European businesses and plan to build on one while correcting the other. Attractive companies frequently exhibit substantial technical and product strengths, have powerful positions in their local market shares, and are far more sophisticated exporters than their American acquirors. These and other compelling values offered by European companies must be retained and built upon. When companies are introduced into a leveraged environment, these strengths can be undermined severely if an acquiror fails to shore up controls, systems, and financial management.

Investments across borders, and particularly across the Atlantic Ocean, are different. The challenges of such investments are many and are not for acquirors without the patience and hands-on approach required to assist their companies to make the transition required. Excellent European companies, however, also possess technical, market, and human resource assets that make the effort highly rewarding in the long run.

Chapter 35

Case Study of a Successful Middle-Market Crossborder Buyout

Harvey Mallement
Managing General Partner
Harvest Ventures Inc., New York, NY
Michael Druckman
Former CFO
Wallace & Tiernan Group, Inc., Belleville, NJ

On May 25, 1989, an investment group led by Harvest Ventures, Inc. of New York and Allsop Venture Partners of Overland Park, Kansas, and management, completed the $44 million acquisition of the Wallace & Tiernan family of companies from the Pennwalt Corporation. This transaction utilized $11 million of equity and a $50 million senior debt facility. The transaction was described by one publication as "one of the most complex middle-market leveraged buyouts on record." The following discussion will provide a case history of the many factors involved in completing this buyout. The key elements of the buyout that will be discussed include the background of Wallace & Tiernan, the reasons for its sale, the nature of the investment group that bought the company, the debt financing required, the tax and regulatory issues dealt with, and the foreign exchange issues that affected the transaction.

Background

Wallace & Tiernan was founded in 1913 when Charles F. Wallace & Martin F. Tiernan combined to develop the first successful commercial gas chlorinator, which was installed in Boonton, New Jersey. At a time when waterborne diseases such as typhoid fever claimed many lives, Wallace & Tiernan devised a better water purification method than liquid hypochlorite, an alternative method used by a few cities.

The Wallace & Tiernan device immediately gained market acceptance. In the ensuing years, the startup venture established subsidiaries in Germany, the United Kingdom, Canada, Australia, Brazil and Mexico, as well as its base of operations in the United States. In the process, Wallace and Tiernan became the world leader in the treatment of drinking water and wastewater.

During its history, the company entered into and abandoned various additional business ventures, such as aids to navigation, marine lanterns and buoys, and sundry other businesses. However, the core business remained the treatment of drinking water and wastewater. In 1969, the company was acquired by a leading producer of chlorine, the Pennsalt Chemicals Corporation, which later changed its name to Pennwalt Corporation. During the last ten years of ownership under Pennwalt, the company's performance deteriorated, particularly in the United States. In the summer of 1988, Pennwalt placed Wallace & Tiernan on the market as part of a defensive program to thwart a hostile tender offer from Centaur Partners to acquire Pennwalt.

Once Pennwalt placed the company on the market, the general managers of Wallace & Tiernan's U.S. and German operations independently proposed management buyouts. The German manager contacted Deutsche Beteiligungsgesellschaft mbH (DBG), a subsidiary of the Deutsche Bank and a Limited Partner of Harvest Ventures. Meanwhile, the U.S. manager contacted Allsop Venture Partners. Rather than compete for Wallace & Tiernan, Harvest and Allsop joined forces, along with the DBG, ECI Ventures, an experienced London-based venture capital group affiliated with Harvest and DBG, and Davis Ventures Partners, introduced by Allsop. This group of investors was based in each of the major countries in which Wallace & Tiernan operated (the United States, Germany and England). In this fashion, investor/ownership involvement was maintained throughout the painstaking and expensive process of negotiating the acquisition with the seller, performing due diligence, working with bank financing sources, as well as post-acquisition serving on the Boards of Directors of the parent company and the local operating subsidiaries.

In February 1989, when the investors and management signed a definitive agreement, subject to financing, to acquire Wallace & Tiernan, the company had sales of approximately $110 million and Earnings Before Interest and Taxes (EBIT) of about $3.5 million. However, the U.S. operation, with sales of $60 million, was performing poorly and losing approximately $3.5 million annually.

Fortunately for the investor group, these operational problems created a buying opportunity by weeding out those potential acquirors, particularly foreign entities, concerned with the risks of turning around the U.S. operation.

Bank Financing

The investor group, after initial discussions with a variety of potential asset-based lenders, began final negotiations with Bank X (name deliberately omitted) and the Chicago office of StanChart Business Credit, the asset-based lending arm of Standard Chartered Bank of the United Kingdom.

In arriving at their pricing strategy, the banks had to wrestle with the most difficult aspect of the transaction—namely, matching the amount of borrowing per country with the underlying asset base. It was decided early on that for tax and collateral reasons, debt would be placed in four countries: United States, the United Kingdom, Germany, and Canada. These allocations were not necessarily in line with the wishes of the investor group, which needed to ensure adequate working capital subsequent to the transaction under a "worst-case" scenario.

Specifically, the German subsidiary had the strongest cash flow and highest income tax rate; however, the German assets did not warrant the largest individual loan in the borrowing arrangement. By contrast, the U.S. operations were underwater with negative cash flow, but required the largest borrowing facility to support its manufacturing turnaround strategy and to finance its receivables. (For tax purposes, the U.S. and Canadian accounts receivable were retained by the sellers.)

The final decision to proceed with StanChart, as compared to Bank X, was primarily based on the maximum amount of borrowing facility proposed by each lender. Bank X proposed a maximum facility of approximately $42.0 million. StanChart, on the other hand, was willing to provide a maximum facility of $50.5 million. In addition, although the fees negotiated with StanChart were higher than

those proposed by Bank X, Bank X's final proposal required a warrant for the purchase of 7% of Wallace & Tiernan's common stock. StanChart's deal included no such equity "kicker."

Once the decision to proceed with StanChart was made, the bank and investor group, and their respective attorneys, met in Chicago, Germany, the United Kingdom and Canada to hammer out the definitive loan agreement.

As both sides continued their negotiations around the world, various unanticipated issues surfaced, which required attention.

Regulatory Compliance Issues

Under the Financial Assistance Provision of the Companies Act of the United Kingdom, before a change in control could be consummated, an independent auditor's certification was required. This states that the company would not be rendered insolvent within 12 months of the transaction as a result of the additional debt incurred in the change in control. Since the U.K. Directors had personal liability in the event of bankruptcy, the investor group agreed not to declare any dividends, impose management fees, increase royalties or change intercompany pricing for a 12-month period.

New Jersey has some of the toughest environmental laws in the United States. Under certain circumstances, the transfer of real property under the New Jersey ECRA process requires an onsite evaluation and remediation process and the posting of some sort of security to ensure compliance. Fortunately, Pennwalt had contractually undertaken to finance any cleanup and posted a bond.

Perfecting the bank's lien on assets in Australia posed a difficult problem. In Australia, a minimum publication period is required to notify the public of a lien on assets to ensure that unsecured creditors have received notice. Ultimately, this issue resulted in a limitation of the amount of upstream debt which the Australian operation could guarantee to the fair market value of the assets in Australia.

Tax Issues

The financing of Wallace & Tiernan also carried with it some significant and perhaps unusual U.S. tax implications. The necessity of having Wallace & Tiernan's foreign affiliates guarantee the acquisition debt was treated as an investment in U.S. "property" under U.S. tax law. To the extent these affiliates had earnings and profits (not previously subject to U.S. tax on Pennwalt's income tax returns), the "investment" was treated as a taxable dividend to Wallace

& Tiernan, even though cash may or may not have been available or allowed under the Loan Agreement for repatriation. (Ultimately Mexico and Brazil were carved out of the upstream guarantee because of perceived difficulties in repatriation.)

Due primarily to tax strategies employed by Pennwalt, the German subsidiary was the main source of earnings and profits not previously subject to U.S. tax. Given the significant German trade and income tax rates, which, combined, approach 50% even on distributed earnings, Wallace & Tiernan, as of December 31, 1989, had significant excess foreign tax credits, which were due to expire in five years if unused.

To make matters worse, under U.S. tax law, the acquisition interest had to be allocated to both U.S. and foreign sources. Since the interest expense in the early years was significant, every $1.0 million of interest allocated to foreign source income would prevent the use of $340,000 of foreign tax credits to otherwise offset our U.S. income tax liability.

The excess foreign tax credit was not, however, an asset we intended to let expire without realizing a benefit. Our assault on the problem ultimately involved three actions.

First, we felt that the royalty income generated from U.S.-owned intangibles, based on rates determined years before the acquisition, was likely to be less than could be justified under the new "commensurate with income" standard embodied in the U.S. Internal Revenue Code. Ultimately, an independent pricing study confirmed this assumption, and we were able to increase our foreign source royalty income significantly. The effects were increased royalty expense deductions among our foreign affiliates (other than the United Kingdom, which already complied with the new U.S. tax code standard), and the ability to shelter the accompanying U.S. royalty income for U.S. tax purposes with excess foreign tax credits.

Second, we had to take steps to lower the high German effective tax rate. To do this, we established a "dual resident corporation" (i.e., a corporation incorporated in the United States, but managed and controlled in Germany, which in effect is treated as a resident corporation in both the United States and Germany), called Eurocon. Wallace & Tiernan GmbH was then sold to Eurocon for an interest-bearing promissory note. The effects of this sale were as follows:

♦ For U.S. tax purposes, Eurocon's interest expense was offset by Wallace & Tiernan's corresponding interest income on the consolidated U.S. tax return. (This offset, however, required that Eurocon's income from dividends, or deemed dividends, ex-

ceeded Eurocon's interest expense under the so-called "dual consolidated loss" rules.)

♦ For German tax purposes, Eurocon's interest expense offset the earnings of German operations, effectively lowering the tax liability from operations.

♦ Dividends paid by Wallace & Tiernan GmbH to Eurocon were not subject to withholding tax (or at least not subject to a nonrecoverable withholding tax), since the dividends were treated as remaining within Germany. When the dividends were subsequently remitted to Wallace & Tiernan, Inc. in the form of interest, no German withholding tax was imposed pursuant to the U.S.-Germany income tax treaty.

Finally, we converted some of our export profits to foreign source income by transferring title of goods shipped overseas to F.O.B. destination. The profit allocated to our marketing and sales effort (as opposed to manufacturing), was treated as untaxed foreign source income, absorbing excess foreign tax credits.

Once these strategies were implemented, we were able to use our foreign tax credits, which would otherwise have expired, to reduce our U.S. taxes.

Solvency Opinion

StanChart requested the investor groups to provide a "solvency opinion" which would essentially state the following:

♦ The fair salable values of the companies' assets exceeded the stated value of their respective liabilities, including all contingent liabilities;

♦ The companies would have adequate capital for the operation of their businesses; and

♦ The companies would be able to pay their respective stated liabilities including identified contingent liabilities, as they matured.

A major Financial Valuation Co. (FVC) was retained to provide the solvency opinion. Their review entailed a painstakingly detailed analysis of historical financial statements, various appraisal reports, and Coopers & Lybrand's Wallace & Tiernan Financial Model, on which the entire transaction was based.

Initially, relations between FVC and the company's Chief Financial Officer were not good. The enormous pressure of negotiating the Loan Agreement and dealing with FVC's numerous requests, including daily changes in the Financial Model, rendered all sides somewhat antagonistic to one another. Ultimately, when it appeared the transaction was going to close, the company used FVC for leverage in negotiating looser terms on StanChart's two financial covenants: Profit Before Tax and Interest Coverage. Eventually a financial model was prepared satisfying everyone's requirements.

Foreign Exchange Issues

With all significant legal, tax, and solvency issues resolved, things were proceeding smoothly, except for the foreign currency markets. In the few weeks preceding the anticipated closing, the U.S. dollar strengthened significantly against the British Pound and German Deutschemark, essentially rendering the Agreement, as approved by StandChart's parent company, partially obsolete through a mismatch between the borrowing facilities and the underlying assets. Therefore the pounds and deutschemarks being borrowed were being converted into fewer dollars than originally planned, thereby causing a dollar shortage for the purchase of the company. In addition, transaction-related fees, which were originally estimated at $3.0 million, now were approximately $5.0 million. The investor group considered hedging the currency risk, but purchasing options would have added approximately $500,000 in fees to the already very expensive transaction.

At around 9:00 P.M. on the day prior to the expected closing, we received a call from StanChart stating the deal was in peril due to the foreign currency movements. Six hours later, with 10 months of work hanging in the balance, both sides reached an accommodation to get the transaction back on track.

The investors agreed to increase the amount of their equity investment from $10 million to $12 million within 90 days after the closing and defer receipt of certain deal-related fees and expenses. (Fortunately, we eventually needed to provide only an extra $1 million due to stronger than expected results in the United States.)

In exchange, the bank rewrote certain aspects of the Agreement to ensure that the borrowing availability matched the value of the underlying assets and needs of the borrowing countries.

Senior Debt Loan Agreement

The five-year Loan Agreement, as finally approved by all parties, contained the following items:

◆ an advisory fee and closing fee totalling $505,000 paid at closing;

◆ a monthly management fee of $10,000;

◆ an unused line fee of .5% per year on the unborrowed amount of the revolving credit facility;

◆ a deferred transaction fee equal to 3% of profit before taxes, with a minimum of $900,000. (In a subsequent amendment, this open-ended obligation was fixed at $1,100,000.)

◆ a term-loan premium fee of $500,000, payable on June 1, 1991, if the Term Loan collateralized by certain real property in the United Kingdom was not repaid;

◆ a prepayment fee of up to 3% if the Agreement was terminated within five years;

◆ advance rates for the revolving credit facilities in the United States, Germany, England and Canada of 70–85% of eligible accounts receivable and 30% of eligible inventories; cash receipts continuously applied against outstanding balances; interest at rates ranging from prime plus 2% in the United States to LIBOR plus 3 1/2% in the United Kingdom.

◆ term loans providing a one-time advance based upon a percentage of the estimated fair market value of the company's property, plant, and equipment; interest at rates ranging from prime plus 2 1/2% in the United States to LIBOR plus 4% in the United Kingdom; mandatory prepayments commencing with the calendar quarter ending December 31, 1991, based upon 35% of the company's excess cash flow; and

◆ covenants which required the attainment of specified profit levels and interest coverage ratios and which prohibited the redemption of capital stock; substantially all of the company's assets pledged as collateral under the Agreement.

The Closing

The acquisition was consummated on May 25, 1989, by a coordinated purchase of the seven independent Wallace & Tiernan companies from Pennwalt, concurrent with the execution of a Master Loan Agreement, along with separate loan agreements with each of the major subsidiaries. Simultaneous closings took place in the United States, England, Germany, Canada, Australia, Mexico, and Brazil.

Post-Purchase Footnotes

Subsequent to the closing of the transaction, the other half of the Wallace & Tiernan story began: the turnaround. The German operation, which was the strongest profit contributor with sales of approximately $18 million and pre-tax margins of 20%, maintained its strong position and its historic growth rate. The dramatic change in Wallace & Tiernan was in the U.S. and U.K. facilities. The U.S. operation was transformed from a money-losing operation to a $4 million plus profit contributor within two years of acquisition. This was accomplished with the help of several new members of management recruited to Wallace & Tiernan to effect the manufacturing turnaround.

This team, coupled with existing management and supported by the investment group, changed manufacturing methodology, cut lead time for delivery dates, introduced Just-In-Time (JIT) manufacturing techniques and provided an overall rationalization of the manufacturing operation. In addition, the U.K. operation, a marginally profitable business at the time of acquisition, increased operating income from approximately $1 million to $3 million plus within two years. Similarly, operations in Mexico, Canada, Brazil, and Australia all experienced increases in earnings during the period of ownership. As a result of the above, overall EBIT increased from $3.5 million at the time of acquisition to $13 million within two years.

Given the company's position as the leading water treatment company in the world, the initial investor strategy for the company was to build value over the long term, with a view toward an initial public offering. However, in early 1991, the company received an unsolicited offer from Northwest Water Group plc, of Manchester, England. The company, an important customer of Wallace & Tiernan in the United Kingdom, had a fundamental strategic interest in expanding their water utility business into the water treatment business. The offer was considered by the investor group to be preemptive at $130 million plus. On July 16, 1991, the company was sold for a total consideration of $132.6 million. With bank debt down to $19.6 million, the stockholders received approximately $113 million. Management received approximately 22% of the total, with the balance distributed to the investor group that had provided the $11 million of original equity capital.

Clearly, the Wallace & Tiernan acquisition was a successful investment for both the investor group and management. Among the most important reasons for this success was that we involved experienced local investment people from the outset of the transaction to its ultimate disposition. The investor group had common attitudes about the financing of the company, the business operations and strategy, the relationship with management, and the need for sensitivity to local and global issues. The attitudes and expertise brought by each of the groups enabled Wallace & Tiernan to function most effectively in each of its own local environments while contributing to the overall prosperity of a multinational, medium-sized business employing a total of approximately 1,500 people worldwide.

Part XV:
Private Equity and Venture Capital Investors

Chapter 36

The Institutional Investor's View:
Effect on Venture Capital and Private Equity Funds

Katherine M. Todd
Partner
Testa, Hurwitz & Thibeault, Boston, MA

The public equity markets are increasingly affected by the attitudes and actions of the largest institutional investors. Similarly, the venture capital industry is changing in response to the pressures of growing participation by and the greater sophistication of these large institutional investors.

The venture capital industry has been instrumental in building and growing new businesses. In order to understand where the venture capital industry is going and the effect this will have on companies seeking capital, it is important to look at where it came from.

A Brief History

The professional venture capital industry—a group of professionally managed venture capital firms investing other people's money—first developed on a large scale in the 1970s and 1980s. In the early 1970s, venture capitalists had approximately $3 billion under management. In 1990, this number was approximately $70 billion. The earliest venture capitalists primarily managed money for wealthy individuals, university endowments and foundations; and many venture funds formed in the early 1970s had a capitalization in the range of $10–$20 million. These venture groups almost universally had an investment focus on small, often early-stage, technology companies.

In the late 1970s, a major new source of capital for venture funds appeared when the U.S. Department of Labor clarified that the high risk/return investment in a venture fund could be prudent for a private pension plan. In addition, through the mid-1980s insurance companies were significant sources of capital for venture funds. The traditional investors—individuals, foundations and endowments—also continued to be active. As shown in Figure 36.1, the investment in venture capital, particularly by private pension plans, accelerated through the 1970s and 1980s and reached a peak in 1987.

The major reason for the enormous increase in funding for the venture industry in the mid- to late-1980s was the hot market for initial public offerings in 1983 and then again in 1987. Many venture-backed companies went public in those two waves, and some returned the investment of their venture capital investors over 100-fold. Capital flooded to the industry, which apparently could achieve spectacular returns with almost no loss of overall investor capital. Many new investors, who had not previously participated in the venture industry, came in on an opportunistic basis. The number of venture firms exploded from 1970 to 1987.

Many new venture capitalists joined the industry, some of whom probably did not have the fundamental skills to succeed at venture investing across the investment cycle. In addition, many of the new investors attracted to the industry in the mid-1980s forgot, or never understood, the basic character of venture investing—that it is both a high-reward and a high-risk area, and that the returns of 1983 were atypical of the industry's average performance across the cycle. In addition, due to the explosion of dollars, in certain investment areas, too many dollars were chasing too few good deals. The result has been that venture returns in the mid- to late-1980s in many cases seriously disappointed investors.

In the late-1980s, the leveraged buyout industry also expanded rapidly. Returns to investors were generally high, but a trend developed toward large

387

Figure 36.1   Net New Capital Committed to Venture Capital Firms (1980–1991)

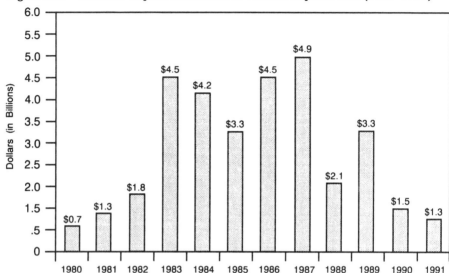

Source: Venture Economics Publishing

fees to sponsors and the use of excessive leverage. The explosive growth of the junk-bond market and the subsequent collapse of Drexel led to a serious reexamination of the use of leverage, with the result that buyouts must now be conducted on a more sound economic footing. The effect has been that buyout funds now are more frequently directed toward equity participation in deals and toward management buyouts. Distressed situation funds, focused on correcting the excesses of the late 1980s, also present to investors the opportunity for attractive returns.

Industry Crisis?

The failure of venture capital to continue to produce returns comparable to that of the early 1980s and the shift away from leveraged buyouts, have resulted in an overall decline in available funding from all classes of investors (Figure 36.2).

Secondary transfers of fund interests are becoming more common, and transfers of large packages of interests held by investors exiting the industry are occurring. Many investors who came in on an opportunistic basis in the mid- to late-1980s have now exited. The insurance industry has experienced its own crisis, and as a result, insurance company investors are now rare.

Due to the fact that most venture funds are closed-end and have a finite life of from eight to twelve years, venture fund managers have to seek new capital every three to five years. The groups with poor performance are not receiving funding and are exiting the industry. Other groups are merging forces in a continuing process of industry consolidation. The IPO market of 1991–1992 has again improved returns for many groups and improved fundraising prospects. Funding levels showed significant improvement in the first half of 1992.

Definition of the Industry- Pension Investors and the Asset Allocation Process

The result of the "industry crisis" described above is that the role of major institutional investors has increased. Sophisticated private pension plan investors with an understanding of the industry cycle have continued to invest, albeit more selectively, and state and local pension plans are playing an increasing role. In particular, state plans represent a large potential source of capital, since many state plans are very large and often have a very small percentage of their assets allocated to venture activities. In addition, many state plans did not participate in the investment glut of the mid- to late-1980s, and therefore do not have to overcome the poor returns

**Figure 36.2   Limiteds Scale Back Commitments
(Capital Commitments by Type of Investor)**

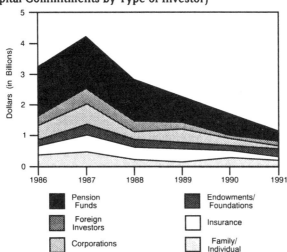

Source: Venture Economics Publishing

experienced then. Due to the reduction in available funding from investors, funds have to be more competitive on terms. Due to the dynamics of the asset allocation process within pension plans, the shape of the industry is changing.

Pension plan managers must first decide how to allocate their investment dollars among broad classes of investments. It has been estimated that 80% of a pension plan's returns are determined by its asset allocations, rather than by the performance of the investments within any asset class. Asset classes include: public equity, bonds, foreign investments, real estate and private equity. Venture capital funds fall within the private equity asset class.

Pension plan managers generally target allocations of up to 5% of their funds for private equity. Some allocate more than 5% to private equity. This class provides a high risk/reward component of pension plan portfolios. Within the private equity class itself, plan managers seek additional diversification through the selection of funds that make different types of investments. Using portfolio modeling techniques, plan managers try to invest in each sector of the private equity market: early-stage venture, later-stage venture, mezzanine, buyout, distressed company and foreign venture funds.

The *Venture Capital Journal* reported that in 1991 approximately $1.3 billion in new capital was committed to venture capital funds. This represented a decline of 30% from 1990. By way of comparison, private equity funds of all kinds, includ-

ing venture, mezzanine, and buyout funds, raised $6.4 billion in 1991, according to *The Private Equity Analyst.* New funding appears to be rebounding in 1992. Any increase in funding, however, will probably not translate into a proportionally larger number of venture groups receiving new capital commitments. In 1991, only 30 venture groups received new capital commitments, compared to 78 in 1986. With three-quarters of new funding being committed to venture groups in existence for ten or more years, the lion's share of private equity allocations is clearly going to the larger, more experienced venture groups.

As successful venture groups continue to attract larger pools of capital, they will continue to broaden their investment focus, often by the addition of qualified general partners with experience in segments outside traditional venture capital. As the scope of the industry has expanded beyond its traditional base of seed and start-up financings, the lines have blurred between early-stage, later-stage, mezzanine, buyout, and distressed company investing; and more groups are investing across a large part of this spectrum. In addition, those quality venture groups whose core experience and success is in the area of early-stage investing will continue to prosper and attract investment dollars, either as stand-alone groups or as part of larger organizations.

The Investor's Objectives

As the venture industry (broadly defined to include all the categories mentioned above) matures, investors are holding venture capitalists more accountable for results. Venture capitalists must now justify venture capital's place in future asset allocations versus other investment classes. Increasingly, investors are focused on IRR and cash flow. These pressures encourage venture capitalists to make later-stage investments and to look for the quick turn.

Since the venture area must compete in the asset allocation process with other asset classes and with other components of the private equity class, pension managers must be able to justify investments as providing opportunities for higher returns, to offset perceived higher risk and volatility. The major pension plan investors generally expect the private equity class, including venture, to achieve returns which are 5–6% above the expected returns of their marketable stock portfolio. Since those plans may be using a figure of 10% for their stock portfolios, this produces a target for venture of 15–16%. This number is relatively modest when compared with the extremely high rates of return (25%+) being promised by venture funds in the mid-1980s, whose returns in most cases have not been delivered.

These return targets represent returns to the investor, not returns to the venture fund. The expected investor returns represent cash flow net of all expenses and the general partners' carried interest. It is beyond the scope of this chapter to discuss the process underway in the venture industry to develop standard methods of valuation of investment portfolios and standard methods of presenting investment returns. The industry is in the earliest stages of developing standards, largely under pressure from the institutional investors.

The investors, in particular the largest pension plans, are having other effects on the shape of the industry. As noted above, groups with poor performance are exiting the industry. Other groups are combining forces to compete more effectively. As noted above, many successful groups are broadening their investment focus to include more segments of the industry, from seed to buyouts and restructuring. Despite the dearth of dollars available to the industry, the best groups continue to be able to raise money with relative ease and are often oversubscribed.

The influence of the largest investors has caused the following effects:

♦ the successful venture organizations continue to get larger, both in terms of numbers of people and assets under management;

♦ the effect of larger amounts of capital under management is the investment of larger dollars in each deal, with a resulting shift up the spectrum toward later-stage deals. This reduces risk and volatility but may also reduce returns;

♦ pressure to produce quicker cash returns to the investor has resulted in an increased tendency toward later-stage deals and increased pressures for liquidity of investments;

♦ the investor's desire to avoid poor or mediocre returns has affected funds' allocation and distribution policies;

♦ pressure on management fees;

♦ investors are more sophisticated about conflicts of interest;

♦ certain investors have special issues: ERISA, tax- exempt and state benefit plans; and

♦ the industry is increasingly international in nature.

Preferred Returns

In the typical venture fund, the managers receive an allocation of 20% of the realized net gains of the fund (the "carried interest"). During the period of the mid- to late-1980s, when many venture funds produced poor performance for their investors relative to returns of the early 1980s, the managers continued to receive their 20% carried interest, which even further reduced the returns to investors. Investors, as a result, began to think about whether the venture managers' carried interest should be dependent upon the investors achieving a certain base rate of return.

In the earlier days of venture funds (e.g., pre-1980), it was common for fund agreements to provide that all distributions went to the investors before the managers were entitled to receive anything. Furthermore, many buyout funds of the mid- to late-1980s had requirements that the investors earn a preferred return (analogous to a cumulative dividend on preferred stock) on their capital, plus often return of their capital, before the managers received their carried interest. As a result, there has been an ongoing debate between investors and fund managers about the concept of so-called hurdle rates.

The basic problem with any discussion of the concept of hurdle rate arises out of confusion about its definition. To some, a hurdle rate implies a restriction on a distribution of profits (even if accrued currently—in partnerships an allocation of gains to a partner's account within the partnership may be made even if no current distribution is permitted). For others, the concept of hurdle rates implies a cumulative preferred return payable before the manager can earn, much less receive, its profits. In the case of a so-called vanishing preference, any interim deprivation of a manager's profit allocation is made up later out of subsequent profits (caveat—these subsequent profits may not be large enough) before the deal reverts to its basic economics (e.g., 80–20%).

Since the industry is now composed of many overlapping segments, from seed and early-stage investing through large buyouts, the question is what variant of a preferred return or hurdle rate most effectively addresses the concerns of investors in each situation. Where funding is tight, each group raising money must also present an attractive, competitive package to prospective investors. In the pure venture end of the spectrum, a true compounding preferred return is inadvisable, since it would be difficult to achieve in an environment where investments are not producing current cash flow and where the timing of realizations is unpredictable. A requirement that all distributions be made to investors until their capital is returned (or capital plus some premium) before distributions to the managers may be made would not have the same problems. Many venture funds, even if they permit interim distributions to the managers, often restrict these distributions if the managers would thereby receive more than 20% of cumulative net gains to date, or if the net asset value of the fund were to fall below some percentage (e.g., 125%) of unreturned investor capital.

Conversely, in the case of mezzanine, debt or buyout funds, a requirement for an annual preferred return distribution presents less of a risk to the managers. Certain buyout funds also have included a special incentive to the managers if they achieve unusually good returns—an increase of the carried interest to a number greater than 20%.

Other Profit Allocation Issues

Almost all funds of whatever type now calculate overall profit-splitting based on cumulative net gains over all periods. All investments are treated as part of a single pool. This cumulative gain and loss concept is reinforced by the requirement that the managers return distributions that they receive which turn out to be excessive, based on overall cumulative fund performance. This is the so-called "make-up" or "claw-back."

In contrast to the agreements of the early to mid-1980s, where the investors typically bore all expenses out of capital, it is now generally the case that all expenses, including the management fee paid to the service company or general partner (see below), are counted in the cumulative net gain or loss determination of profit sharing, so that the managers must effectively earn back their expenses before creating a profit share for themselves.

Occasionally, funds have attempted to require investors to return distributions to allow the fund to meet unexpected liabilities (the reverse "make-up" or reverse "claw-back"). As can be imagined, this has met with a less than enthusiastic response from investors. Sophisticated investors will usually refuse to invest in funds with this feature. The state laws under which investment funds are organized usually provide for a very limited right to recover distributions, generally only if the distribution made the fund insolvent. The result, when coupled with the pressure to make prompt distributions to investors (discussed in detail later) has been to put the general partners (most investment partnerships are organized as limited partnerships) at increased risk in the later years of a fund if unexpected liabilities arise. Investors express sympathy with this problem, but are not willing to have distributions at risk for even a limited period of time.

Management Fees

Through the mid-1980s, venture fund managers generally received an annual fee to cover overhead and administrative expenses. This fee was 2.5% of capital committed (not capital actually under management or net asset value). Cost-of-living adjustments were standard. When funds were small (under $30 million), this number approximated the costs to manage the fund—to pay healthy but not outrageous salaries to the number of people needed. As funds got larger and the most successful groups had even larger amounts under management (often with several funds in existence at once), investors began to see these fees as excessive.

The result of this has been steady downward pressure on management fees. Cost-of-living adjustments are now rarely found; fees rarely reach a full 2.5% except in the middle of a fund's life; and fees are generally tapered, starting out low, building to a maximum in mid-life, and then trailing off in later years. Although the fee is generally still computed as a percentage of committed capital, there is often a cap on it, which is expressed as a percentage of assets. The purpose of the cap is to deal with later years when the fund may have sold or distributed most of its investments.

If the managers receive fees from portfolio companies, whether minimal directors' fees or large transaction or break-up fees, investors are pressing for these fees to either offset the management fee or be paid directly to the fund. In certain cases, this sort of arrangement causes tax problems for otherwise tax-exempt investors.

Distributions

Investors increasingly desire liquidity from investments in the private equity class, including venture, as soon as possible. For pension plans, this arises in part from the need to meet pensioners' claims, but also from the need to maximize the rate of return for the asset class. This rate of return is extremely time-dependent, and has led to just-in-time capital calls from funds, together with requirements that funds distribute the cash proceeds of sales of investments as soon as possible.

The question of reinvestment of the cash basis of sold investments does not have an easy answer. Many investors would prefer no reinvestment—e.g., all proceeds are to be distributed promptly. Fund managers, on the other hand, have an interest in 1) continuing to invest (at least through the early mid-life of a fund, because after that, disposition of the investment before the end of the 10- to 12-year life of the fund may be difficult); and 2) being able to make follow-up investments in existing portfolio companies. There are arguments pro and con about why reinvestment should either increase or reduce returns to investors. A common compromise permits reinvestment through a fund's mid-life, and follow-up investment thereafter.

An even more controversial subject relates to distribution of securities in kind to investors. After a portfolio company goes public, and after any underwriters' lock-up expires (generally after 180 days), if the portfolio company's stock has been held by the venture fund for at least three years, the stock, if distributed to investors, will be freely tradeable in their hands. This, of course, does not mean that the stock will be easy to sell at the current market price; the venture fund often holds a significant position; the other potential sellers who were subject to the underwriters' lock-up may also be trying to sell; and the stock may be thinly traded. Investors who have the ability to effectively manage post-venture small-capitalization stocks strongly prefer to receive distributions in kind at the earliest possible moment; this cuts off the managers' profit participation in subsequent gains, and gives the investor the ability to hold the stock until an appropriate point to sell.

The investors with this ability to effectively manage venture distributions are also likely to be those with the greatest influence on the terms of the fund agreement. On the other hand, investors who would

likely sell immediately after a distribution might very well prefer that a fund hold the stock and continue to manage it, perhaps at a reduced carried interest.

Other Issues

Other issues of fund structure and terms are heavily affected by the nature of the major investors, almost all of whom are tax-exempt and many of whom are pension plans regulated under the Employee Retirement Income Security Act of 1974 (ERISA) or state law. State plans, in particular, usually have their own specific issues related to state law or requirements. Certain aspects of fund structure are influenced by the desire of many tax-exempt investors to avoid "unrelated business taxable income," including "unrelated debt-financed income." Since taxable investors do not care about this, there is an obvious conflict between taxable and tax-exempt investors on this issue. Venture and other private equity funds with significant (generally 25%) participation by benefit plans must meet a specific set of requirements (the "venture capital operating company," or VCOC, exemption) to avoid having their assets treated as plan assets under ERISA, which would require fund managers to register under the Investment Advisers Act of 1940 and would also subject the Fund to complicated and difficult ERISA requirements.

Another area of increasing investor scrutiny relates to conflicts of interest. Sophisticated investors want to avoid having fund managers invest in portfolio companies for their own account (unless such investment is mandatory in each case to prevent "cherry-picking"). In addition, investments by a fund in a company when a fund manager has a pre-existing investment interest present obvious conflicts of interest. Finally, when a group of venture managers have multiple funds, investments by later funds in the portfolio companies of earlier funds must be done in such a way as to prevent the fund managers from using later investors' money to bail out a poorly performing investment of an earlier fund, which probably does not have identical investors. Strict prohibition of such co-investment is not the best solution, but investors and fund managers have developed a variety of strategies to prevent real problems in this area.

Conclusion

The venture industry is rapidly maturing after its explosive growth of the 1980s. The investment focus of the industry is shifting; the industry is undergoing consolidation; and it is increasingly responsive to investor concerns.

Chapter 37

Future Directions of Private Equity Investing

Steven P. Galante
Editor and Publisher
The Private Equity Analyst Newsletter, West Newton, MA

Seed-stage venture capital isn't usually mentioned in the same breath as leveraged buyouts. But, increasingly, the two investment strategies are being viewed as the two end-points of a continuous investment spectrum.

Both the seed investor and the buyout specialist make long-term investments in private companies. Both place big bets (relative to their assets) on the entrepreneurial managers of those companies. Both are attracted to the private market by its inefficiency. And both use value-added skills to turn that inefficiency into above-average returns.

The traits shared by seed and LBO investors are the essence of private equity investing. Those six traits are outlined in Table 37.1, and elaborated on later. They can be summarized with a single phrase: "value-added investing."

Private-equity investors of all stripes provide portfolio companies with more than capital. And, when successful, they achieve more than a financial return. They create, grow, or revitalize businesses, leaving them healthier and more competitive in the end than at the outset.

Viewed this way, it is easy to recognize that the private equity arena is a single market in which firms practice a myriad of investment subspecialties. It isn't going too far to say that the private equity market embraces seed, start-up, growth, mezzanine, buyout, spinout, influence-block, post-venture, turnaround and special situation investing. There's even a good argument to be made that it includes distressed-security investing, too.

Along this broad spectrum of private equity investing, the shifts from one strategy to the next are so subtle as to be almost imperceptible. It's a natural step, of course, to move from seed to start-up investing, and just as natural to proceed from there to expansion financing.

At some point in a company's growth phase, an add-on acquisition opportunity is likely to present itself. If the synergies are there and the capital structure can be properly built, then why not? It hastens growth and perhaps achieves other goals, such as elimination of a competitor.

Well, if a single add-on acquisition works, why not a series of them? For that matter, why not an entire strategy based on buying similar businesses to build one larger one? In fact, a number of private equity investment firms have established successful franchises based on just such a strategy.

In no time at all, we've arrived in the kingdom of the financial buyer, or LBO investor. It turns out that some of the financial buyer's tools can be put to work, not only for buy-and-build consolidation plays, but for other value-added acquisition strategies as well. Indeed, the buyout, whether moderately leveraged or not, has an important place in value-added investing. It can be used to liberate a neglected corporate division, transform the undermanaged family-owned business, or take an undervalued public company off the market.

If acquisition-oriented investors belong in the private equity arena, turnaround investors certainly do, too. They may "buy trouble," but if the pricing is right, the prospects for adding value to the investment are enhanced as well. Turnaround investing can be done at any point along the spectrum where a business has run into operational or financial difficulty.

These similarities are compelling enough on their own to define the private equity market as a single entity. But there is a practical reason for doing so as

393

Table 37.1   The Essence of Private Equity

♦ Privately negotiated investments

♦ Participation in strategic vision

♦ Investors/management in partnership

♦ Board-level control or influence

♦ Long-term, illiquid commitments

♦ Above-average returns

well: Institutional investors already view the market that way. These institutions primarily include public and corporate pension funds, educational endowments, nonprofit foundations, insurance companies, banks, and savings and loan associations. Institutions are increasingly determining the shape of the private equity market. They are doing so by conducting asset allocation studies, developing analytical tools for tracking private limited partnership performance, negotiating the terms and conditions of partnership agreements, and committing or withholding capital when private equity managers come calling.

The capital committed to private equity investing grew rapidly in the late 1980s, both in the venture capital and LBO segments. Money entered this market through specialized holding companies, bank subsidiaries, and a variety of other investment vehicles. But the most common vehicle was the institutionally funded, private limited partnership.

As Table 37.2 shows, the money committed to such partnerships grew from less than $1 billion in 1980, to more than $18 billion in 1987. But commitments grew too quickly for the market to absorb. Cash-rich partnership managers, competing for a limited number of transactions, bid prices too high for both venture capital and LBO transactions. As a result, investment returns suffered. Some companies that were acquired in LBOs eventually were forced into financial restructurings that wiped out their equity holders; some were liquidated.

As a result of these excesses, institutions have sharply slowed their funding of private limited partnerships. Today, the pace of funding has stabilized at around $10 billion annually, where it is likely to remain for the foreseeable future.

Institutions invest in private equity partnerships for two compelling reasons:

1. Over time, the investment returns from such partnerships have exceeded the returns from the public stock and bond markets. Over a 20-year period, the annualized return on venture capital has been around 15%, according to a number of studies. LBOs are still too new a phenomenon to have an established track record of returns. But early indications are that buyout investments have a return somewhat higher than venture returns. By comparison, the long-term annualized return on the S&P 500 stock index has been under 12%.

2. The returns from private equity investments have a low correlation with returns from public market securities. Again, private equity as an asset category is too new to make any definitive statments. But studies indicate that the returns on private securities may move in the same direction as returns on public stocks as rarely as three times out of ten. This low correlation is very important to the investment manager of an institution, such as a pension fund, who is trying to make the returns on his portfolio as consistent and predictable as possible. By bundling into the portfolio a variety of investments whose returns have low correlations with one another, he can get closer to his goal of predictability.

The proliferation of creative private investment strategies in the late 1980s has given institutional investors a wide range of opportunities to choose from. In general, an institutional manager doesn't care if a private limited partnership invests in venture capial, buyouts, or some other private investment opportunity. He is more concerned about whether he can put a meaningful amount of money to work with private-investment fund managers who will produce an exceptional return.

The following are likely to be the dominant segments of the private equity market in the future.

Table 37.2 Commitments to Private Equity Partnerships
($ in millions)

1980	$ 780
1981	1,081
1982	1,753
1983	4,336
1984	5,165
1985	4,000
1986	8,423
1987	18,025
1988	12,671
1989	14,051
1990	6,347
1991	7,013
1992	10,142

Venture Capital

Emerging growth companies continue to be a major focus of the private equity investment community. The technologies of interest today tend to be computer software, medical devices, and biotechnology. Computer hardware and electronic components are less popular among venture investors today because these markets have become capital-intensive and highly competitive. Also, venture capitalists today are favoring later-stage investments over early-stage opportunities for several reasons:

The earlier a technology is in its development, the greater the likelihood that it won't be successful. Similarly, the younger a business is, the greater its chance of failure.

Theoretically, early-stage investors should be rewarded for taking those higher risks by obtaining a higher return on their investment. In the real world, though, they actually wind up being "penalized" for their decisions. As new investors put additional capital into a company in later-stage rounds, the original investor's holdings become diluted. Often, a company's first investors earn a lower return than its last investors.

The performance of venture capital firms is measured by the internal rate of return, or IRR, that they earn on the capital they manage. In the calculation of IRR, the length of time it takes to sell an investment is as important as the absolute profit ultimately earned. The shorter the investment, the higher the IRR. Thus, venture capitalists increasingly choose to invest in later-stage companies rather than early-stage businesses. The sooner they can cash out of the company through a public offering or sale to a

corporate buyer, the higher their IRR (and the better their measured performance) will be.

Management Buyouts

The LBO wave crested in 1989 with the purchase of RJR Nabisco Inc. for more than $25 billion. Since then, buyout activity has contracted sharply. Lately, it has shown signs of recovering. But the new wave in acquisition activity should be more sensible and sustainable than the frenzy that preceded the market's near-total shutdown in early 1990.

In the future, transactions promise to be much smaller. Acquisitions of closely held companies and corporate subsidiaries will dominate the new wave. Taking public companies private will be difficult because of high stock market prices and more conservative lending practices of banks, insurance companies and other debt providers. For that reason, mega-deals and mega-funds will be scarce. The same caution will help to keep prices more sensible and capital structures of buyouts more conservative. Management buyouts typically will be financed with 30% equity and 70% debt, instead of the 10%–90% ratio that prevailed in the late 1980s.

Mezzanine Finance

One of the most promising private investment opportunities to emerge from the 1980s has been the use of subordinated debt financing to help mature, medium-sized companies accelerate their growth rates. This mezzanine financing, as it is called, is filling a gap that banks are creating as they pare their lending.

Institutional investors find mezzanine partnerships to be especially attractive investment vehicles because they obtain their return in two ways: from an annual interest (or "coupon") payment, collected quarterly, and from detachable warrants that are convertible into equity at some point in the future.

Prime candidates for this kind of financing are middle-market companies that are adding or enlarging facilities, expanding sales geographically, or extending existing product lines. Mezzanine lenders generally won't back expansions that require leaps of faith about a company's future prospects. They tend to look for consistent and predictable cash flow that can support a coupon payment.

Distressed Securities

Because the explanation is intuitive, it may not be immediately evident how distressed securities (both senior and subordinated debt) fit into the private equity picture. By the time a debt instrument has become distressed, it has lost its fixed-income character. Its value and payoff are no longer certain; they depend on the course of a company's bankruptcy proceedings and economic prospects. That is, the security effectively has become equity. Accordingly, investors in distressed debt expect equity-like returns.

Other Opportunities

In the broadly defined private equity market, the number of viable investment strategies continues to proliferate. Several investment firms, for example, now concentrate on making privately negotiated equity investments in publicly traded companies. Others provide equity-based project financing for the construction of industrial plants. Still others inject equity into heavily indebted companies that are otherwise healthy, helping to strengthen their balance sheets.

These and all other private-equity investment strategies boil down to six essential elements: privately negotiated investments, participation in strategic vision, investors/management in partnership, board-level control or influence, long-term, illiquid commitments, and above-average returns.

Privately Negotiated Investments

Unlike the public market, where the auction process, at least in theory, wrings out excess profit, the private market generally is a negotiated and inefficient market. Private equity investors of all types aim to capitalize on that inefficiency by obtaining non-

auction pricing and favorable terms to achieve above-average returns.

Of course, market inefficiency has its downside too. While it can produce enhanced returns, it car just as easily magnify losses. That's because mistakes in an illiquid market aren't quickly reversible. If a bad investment is to be unloaded, it must again be through a negotiated sale. The buyer will set the price low enough to discount the portfolio company's problems and provide an above-average return for *his* investors.

Participation in Strategic Vision

As we said at the outset, private equity investmen firms provide more than money. By contributing their own skills to a portfolio company's strategic vision, they add value to the investment. Though it begins with a strategic review, it is (or should be) much more than armchair input.

The precise nature of the value they add depend on several things: which private equity specialty the investment firm practices, the investment firm' own internal skill set, and the portfolio company' needs. It can range from assistance in marketing o manufacturing, to the identification of add-on acqui sitions.

Investors/Management in Partnership

Private equity investors will wait several years t achieve returns only if a portfolio company's manag ers have earned their confidence. The flip-side of tha relationship gives management the opportunity t earn a significant stake in the equity.

The ability to assess management, therefore, i the private equity investor's most important skil That is why private investing is so frequently referre to as a "people business."

Board-Level Control or Influence

Board-level control, or at least significant influence is usually a condition for a private equity investor' long-term commitment. Board control permits th investor not only to protect the investment, but als to provide consistent and effective input.

Long-Term, Illiquid Commitments

Private equity fund managers invest with the recog nition that the portfolio company is likely to tak years to achieve its strategic vision. They're willin to take that gamble in expectation of above-averag gains.

But the illiquid nature of the investment serve to instill discipline in the investment process, partic ularly in the pricing. That's because illiquidity assures that the same individuals who make investments will be around when it is time to reap the consequences, whatever they may be.

Above-Average Returns

The prospect of a superior profit, of course, is the investor's main incentive. The anticipated enhanced return is the culmination of four factors that are unique to the private equity market: negotiating the investment in an inefficient marketplace; adding value to the portfolio company; compensation for the investment's illiquid nature; and taking a greater-than-average business and/or financial risk.

In the end, defining the private equity market broadly is intensely liberating. It gives the institutional investor a broader spectrum of private equity-oriented strategies to choose from. And it offers the private equity fund manager greater flexibility in defining a strategy.

The trick for both is to keep their investment decision-making crisp even while strategy distinctions blur within the more broadly defined market. That can be accomplished by ensuring that a private equity investment firm has spelled out a strategy clearly and has the skills aboard to support it.

Chapter 38

Venture Capital Transformed*

David G. Schutt
Editor-in-Chief
Venture Economics Publishing Company, New York, NY

The Venture Capital Industry in Transition

The venture capital market, after nearly five years of painful consolidation, appears to be in the early stages of a gradual recovery that should see more money raised and invested by the industry, better returns for limited partners and, most importantly, more money directed toward both new and established businesses in need of financing.

In this transition, however, the very nature of the business is likely to be redefined as a greater part of the industry's financial and intellectual resources is directed toward later-stage investments, buyouts and special situations cutting across a more diverse array of industries and, increasingly, across national borders as well. Venture capital needs this diversity if, in the future, it is to adapt to shifting economic environments and changes in investor preferences without undue suffering for prolonged periods.

Ironically, while the range and types of venture capital investment may multiply in coming years, the funding for the industry is likely to come increasingly from just a single source: the pension fund. Both of these trends—a broader range of investment choices and a narrower base of investors—can be expected to exert powerful influences reshaping the industry's make-up. In effect, they are a reversal of the early 1980s when the range of investments seemed limited to a narrow menu of options—primarily at an early stage in high technology—and the investor base included, in more equal parts, wealthy individuals and families, banks, insurance companies, cor-

porations, pension funds, endowments, and a handful of other funding sources.

To be sure, all of the traditional elements of venture capital, such as seed and early-stage investments in high technology companies, will continue to play an important role in the business, but they are more likely to become discrete elements in a much wider spectrum of activities. These changes result, in part, from a difficult transition period, from which venture capital is just now beginning to extricate itself. Here are just a few examples of the recent troubles:

In 1987, which represented the near-term peak in activity, venture capitalists disbursed nearly $4.0 billion to mostly fledgling businesses. By 1991, the dollar amount of disbursements had plunged to just $1.36 billion, a drop of roughly 66%. (See Figure 38.1.)

Fund Raising by Venture Capitalists

♦ Fund raising by venture capitalists, which in 1987 totalled more than $4.0 billion, fell to $1.34 billion in 1991, an approximately 67% decline. (See Figure 38.2.)

♦ While it is difficult to pinpoint venture capital returns, average annual internal rates of return to investors are thought to have remained under 10% in this period while average public market gains easily eclipsed those levels.

*All of the data in this article comes from the Venture Capital Journal, published by Venture Economics, unless otherwise noted in the text.

♦ The number of independent private venture capital firms, which at one point in the late-1980s was above 600, today is closer to 500, or possibly just below that.

Despite these gloomy barometers of the industry's decline since the late 1980s, there are some encouraging signs that the business, in a changed form, is beginning to come back to life:

♦ Fund raising in the first half of 1992 rose to almost $1.2 billion, nearly as much as was raised in all of 1991 and more than twice the level seen in the same period in 1991. Most venture capitalists believe that more than $2 billion will be raised this year, which would bring the industry back near the levels last seen in 1989. (See Figure 38.3.)

♦ The initial public offering market, which is the most favored exit vehicle for venture capital-backed companies and their investors, has surged in the last 18 months. In 1991, 121 venture capital-backed companies, the most since 1983, went public. In the process, these companies raised nearly $4.0 billion, well above the roughly $3 billion raised in 1983. Through the first half of 1992, another 99 venture-backed companies had sold shares to the public, setting the stage for a new record (barring a severe setback in the second

half) of public market activity this year. These figures are not even a full measure of activity since secondary sales of stock were also at record levels in 1991. As a result of this activity, venture capitalists have been able to regain some of the liquidity lost in the previous five years. (See Table 38.4.)

♦ Internal rates of return have also shown signs of improvement triggered by the resurgent IPO market. According to Venture Economics' Investment Benchmarks Report (IBR), the upper quartile of venture capital funds posted a return of 27.4% in 1991 and, among mature funds, the upper quartile return was 31.6%. While not in a league with the 56.8% gain of NASDAQ Index, these returns bested both the S&P 500 and the Wilshire Index performances over the same time period.

Although the process has been painful and the recovery to date very uneven, the industry as a whole has returned to levels of funding close to those from which it first began to expand rapidly in the early 1980s. Given the experience of the last few years, however, growth this time around is more likely to head in a new direction—or more accurately—directions to avoid the mistakes of the previous decade.

Figure 38.1   Disbursements 1982–1991 (Dollars in Billions)

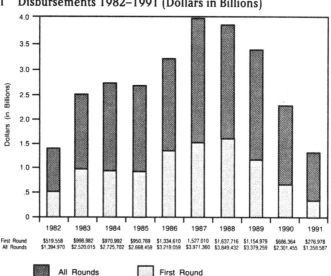

	1982	1983	1984	1985	1986	1987	1988	1989	1990	1991
First Round	$519.558	$998.982	$970.992	$950.769	$1,334.610	1,527.010	$1,637.716	$1,154.979	$686.364	$276.978
All Rounds	$1,394.970	$2,520.015	$2,725.702	$2,668.459	$3,219.059	$3,971.360	$3,849.432	$3,379.259	$2,301.455	$1,358.587

■ All Rounds   □ First Round

Source: Venture Economics Publishing Co.

Figure 38.2   Capital Commitments by Year*

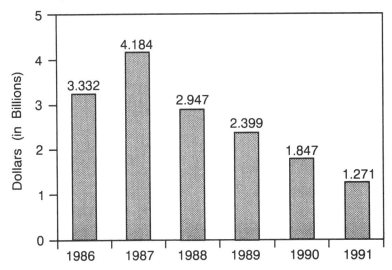

*Excludes funds of funds.
Source: Venture Economics Publishing Co.

The Problems of the Past

Before looking too far ahead, it is important to know what happened in the 1980s and the late-1970s.

Fueled by a substantial capital gains tax cut, an expansion of U.S. Labor Department rules allowing increased pension fund investment, the beginnings of a powerful bull market in equities, and several

Figure 38.3   Full-Year and First-Half Dollar Totals

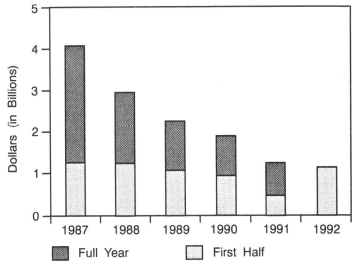

■ Full Year   ☐ First Half

Source: Venture Economics Publishing Co.

Figure 38.4   Number of New Issues 1982–1992*

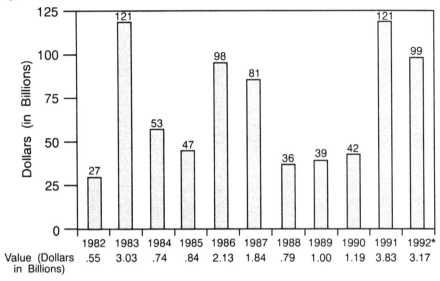

| Value (Dollars in Billions) | .55 | 3.03 | .74 | .84 | 2.13 | 1.84 | .79 | 1.00 | 1.19 | 3.83 | 3.17 |

*First Six Months

high-profile venture-backed success stories, the previous trickle of money into the area became a torrent in the early 1980s. In 1980, the entire venture capital market represented just $3.6 billion in total capital under management. By 1986, that figure had topped $26 billion. And, by the end of the decade, capital under management had risen to almost $36 billion.

The results of this newfound funding, unfortunately, did not meet the expectations of many participants. Venture capitalists, particularly those with little or no previous experience, were badly burned in more than one instance by start-ups and other, early-stage investments that did not pan out. What resulted in many cases was an overconcentration of funds going to relatively narrow industries, particularly the high-technology area that spawned the industry's biggest early successes. As much as 40% of total disbursements in certain years of the early 1980s went to computer companies. In many instances, the industry ended up competing with itself, with several venture capital firms backing a number of fledgling companies in the same business. Such a process doomed the majority of participants to fail since only a handful of companies in a given business were destined to survive.

Often, venture capitalists with money to spend were suddenly paying much higher valuations to participate in new businesses. Because of the competition, small businesses in attractive niches found themselves in a strong bargaining position. The net result was to make it much more difficult to attract new money at later stages of development or to exit the investment at a reasonable level of profit.

In turn, the record IPO market of 1983 turned into a disaster as many lower quality, high-risk companies jumped in to raise money before they were ready. Indeed, in the next two years, the IPO market virtually shut down to all but the highest quality companies. After the 121 venture-backed companies that went public in 1983, just 53 were able to tap the market in 1984 and 47 in 1985.

Similarly, returns fell for all but the most experienced venture capital firms. With the greater institutional backing that began in the late 1970s and early 1980s came more money but closer, more systematic scrutiny of returns. Many institutions found themselves locked into partnerships that were providing single-digit returns at a time when large parts of the public markets were surging to new highs and providing instant liquidity. In some cases, they never returned to the venture capital arena once the partnerships had expired.

At the same time, a number of corporations that had jumped into venture capital in the early 1980s found that it no longer fit with their strategic goals and they pulled back. In the latter part of the 1980s—a trend still in place today—many financial institutions such as banks and insurance companies came under increased regulatory and general economic pressures that argued for cutbacks or elimination of venture capital funding.

A Small Number of Venture Capitalists Succeed

Interestingly, a small number of venture capital firms—largely the most experienced firms, which had been through more than one market cycle—continued to post strong returns to investors throughout this period, validating the fundamental concept of venture capital at the same time the industry was beginning its consolidation. Indeed, the current state of venture capital has been nowhere more evident than in the recent rounds of fund raising. As mentioned above, institutional investors such as pension funds and endowments now comprise more than half of the industry's funding. These investors have clearly decided to favor that small group of firms that have managed to post relatively strong returns through the most recent investment cycle. Of the more than $1.3 billion raised in 1991, nearly 40% went to just three funds: Institutional Venture Partners V, Oak Investment Partners V and Summit Ventures III. Each of these firms had strong returns in its previous fund, a well-defined, time-tested strategy, and the ability to articulate those strengths to its institutional investor base. In the case of one of the firms, Oak Investment Partners, the fund raising took barely a month. In the other two instances, the fund raising required less than five months to meet its target.

Even for those funds that took longer to close their partnership funding, experience was still a key variable. In 1991, funds with senior partners possessing more than 10 years of experience managed to take down nearly 75% of all of the money raised.

In contrast, less experienced firms have often taken more than a year to raise money, when they have been successful at all. In 1991, which may go down as the toughest fund-raising year for venture capitalists ever, less than 5% of the money secured by the entire industry went to firms with senior partners with less than three years of experience in venture investing. In the first half of 1992, just one of the more than 20 venture capital funds that successfully raised money was a first-time fund raiser.

Venture Capital Disbursements By Sector

Even as the fund raising prowess seems to be centering on a smaller group of firms able to raise large amounts of money, in aggregate, the venture capital industry has spread its range of investment options over a much wider field than in the 1980s. Venture capital disbursements are still tilted toward high technology, but that sector is no longer as dominant. For instance, in 1991 computer hardware and systems received 12.4% of the total disbursements from the venture capital industry. That figure, which was well behind the more than 20% that went to software companies, was closely grouped with telephone and data communications companies, which got 12.4%, medical/healthcare-related companies, which received 11.2%, consumer-related businesses, which took 9.9%, and biotechnology companies, which garnered 8.2% of the total dollar figure. (See Table 38.1.)

By comparison, in 1982, computer-related companies received 42% of the total dollars disbursed while the second-most favored category was a related one, other electronics, which received just 14% of the total.

At various times in the last five years, software companies, medical/healthcare and biotechnology have all been at the top of the disbursements recipient lists, suggesting a better balance of investment alternatives spread over a broader array of industries. The diversity of investment is naturally reflected in the types of funds venture capitalists are currently trying to raise. Public power projects, environmental clean-up operations, educational alternatives, and minority-owned businesses, among others, are all the investment targets for these fledgling funds. To be sure, computer hardware and software, medical and healthcare-related, and biotechnology are key foci for fund raisers, but they are far from the only beneficiaries of venture capital at this point.

In addition, the amount of cross-border and country-specific venture capital activity is also taking off. In just one instance, nearly 20 private equity funds overseeing more than $1 billion have been raised just this year for investment in China, according to Russell & Co., a New York-based consulting firm for Asian projects. That compares with just seven investment groups managing less than $270 million a few years ago.

Similar developments are underway for funds targeted specifically at Mexico, the Pacific rim countries, Eastern Europe, the former Soviet Union and Eastern Europe. And the flow is no longer directed from North America outward. European fund raisers now routinely visit U.S. institutions for money to invest back in their own countries; a Mexican fund is aiming at investments in the United States; and Japanese funds increasingly are looking to neighboring Asian countries as investment opportunities rather than to the United States. Both the United

Table 38.1   Industry Breakdown by Dollars Invested in Millions (1991)

Industry	Total Invested	Percent of Dollars	Number of Companies	Number of Financings	Number of Investments
Biotechnology	$ 112	8.2%	60	85	172
Commercial Communications	20	1.5	14	22	35
Computer Hardware and Systems	168	12.4	79	107	280
Consumer-related	135	9.9	68	80	140
Energy-related	3	0.2	4	5	5
Industrial Automation	3	0.3	10	12	23
Industrial Products and Machinery	47	3.4	44	55	90
Medical/Healthcare-related	152	11.2	115	153	294
Other Electronics	129	9.5	69	90	225
Other Products and Services	83	6.2	55	75	105
Software and Services	337	24.8	178	229	534
Telephone and Data Communications	169	12.4	96	126	309
Total	$1,358	100%	792	1,039	2,212

Source: Venture Economics Publishing Co.

Nations and the World Bank have active investment programs in place around the world. And fund raising in Europe has begun to exceed the levels seen in the United States in certain years.

Venture Capitalists in Later Stage Investments

This diversity extends beyond specific targets of investment to the actual methods of investment. It has been said that as venture capital matures, it naturally evolves toward later-stage investments in existing portfolio companies and buyouts and away from new investments in early-stage companies. Certainly, this has proved true in the United States over the last few years. Until 1990, first-round financing, as percentage of all disbursements, had remained relatively constant at more than 33%. In 1990, however, it fell below 30%. In 1991, it dropped further to about 20%. In total dollar amounts, first-round financing has fallen from a peak of more than $1.6 billion in 1988 to just over $275,000 in 1991.

Part of this trend is natural. Many venture capitalists preferred to reinvest in their existing portfolio companies during a difficult economic environment and the lower levels of fund raising made it impossible to consider new investments. In turn, many venture capitalists viewed 1991 and early 1992 as a period in which to "harvest" existing portfolio companies via the IPO market, rather than one in which to seek out new investments.

However, the evidence also suggests that many venture capitalists have turned their attention to later-stage investments as a fundamental investment strategy that requires less intensive monitoring and yields more predictable results. Just 45 companies in 1991 received seed-stage financing, down from 74 in 1990 and 138 in 1989. The total dollars disbursed fell to about $56 million in 1991, down from more than $84 million in 1990 and $131 million in 1989. In a number of recent industry gatherings, some prominent venture capitalists have flatly stated that this area of venture capital activity has effectively run its course, and they have urged colleagues to shift toward later-stage investing and buyouts.

In all likelihood, early-stage investing will continue to attract those firms that are comfortable with it. Because seed-stage financing requires relatively small amounts of money in most cases, it is likely to remain a small percentage of venture capital's annual disbursements, rising and falling as cyclical changes draw in newcomers and push out those who are unsuccessful at it. Certainly firms such as Kleiner Perkins Caufield and Byers and The Mayfield Fund, among others, have proven that it can be a profitable area for those who possess the right skills.

In turn, "angels," or wealthy individuals willing to invest in new businesses, are likely to become even more important in the very early-stage investment area. For many of these investors, financial returns may not be quite as important as they are to venture capitalists and their institutional backers. These angels may have an interest in a particular business or an individual and are willing to take on added risk to see a company get started. In addition, state governments are increasingly taking steps to create small businesses as a means of ensuring employment and economic growth within their boundaries.

Finally, corporations can often justify participation in a fledgling business for reasons other than immediate financial return. They may have an interest in winning the licensing for a new technology or may see a strategic advantage in helping a new venture get off the ground. In several instances in the last year, venture capitalists have declined to participate in start-up businesses, and large corporations have stepped in to provide funding.

As a result, the very early-stage end of the investment spectrum is likely to be divided among a relatively small number of venture capitalists with a demonstrated interest and ability in the area, individual angels, government and corporations willing to take on the added risk inherent in such activities.

The debate over the fate of this area is important because it points to some of the changes currently overtaking the industry. Venture capital today is increasingly being grouped with other investment areas such as turnaround investing, management buyouts and buyings, mezzanine financing, as well as certain special situations keyed to shorter-term opportunities afforded by economic dislocations. As a result, venture capital is being viewed by pension funds and other institutional investors as a subset of what is called "private equity." In each of these areas, investors are purchasing equity in a wide variety of companies spanning the entire gamut of age and economic well-being. These privately negotiated purchases are all done outside the normal public market vehicles.

Many traditional venture capitalists have been naturally drawn to these areas, in part due to their own shrinking marketplace and also because their skills are suitable for them.

The Expanding Role of the Venture Capitalist

Historically, venture capitalists have worked with companies over long time periods, involving themselves in everything from identifying and solving management problems to finding financing and setting day-to-day operational priorities. Indeed, venture capitalists, by the inherent failure rate and volatility of small and mid-sized businesses, have generally been exposed to a great variety of business problems in a relatively short timespan. These types of skills are being transported to other kinds of investments—whether it is a turnaround, a management buyout or an equity investment in a new business.

The shift toward a broader definition of venture capital activities, such as those outlined above, is well underway. In 1991, for instance, nearly $800 million of the more than $1.3 billion disbursed by venture capitalists was directed to expansion financing or acquisition. In contrast, just over $400 million was devoted to seed, start-up or other early-stage financing. While early stage investment is likely to come back as the economic cycle changes, most venture capitalists doubt that it will assume the dominant position it had in the early 1980s.

Many of the largest venture capital firms already reflect internally many of the changes that have taken place by organizing their firms to participate in most, or all, of these niches. In the process, they are seeking access to a steady stream of attractive deals. Smaller, newer firms, generally choose to specialize in particular niches and leave the other areas to the "full-service" firms.

The venture capitalist's skills should be in great demand in the coming decade, which some have dubbed as the "decade of management,"—a period that synthesizes the venture capital skills acquired in the 1970s and early 1980s and the management buyout skills acquired in the 1980s. In some cases, this may entail working closely with a handful of portfolio companies providing the financial and strategic skills needed to build an existing business several-fold. In the early days of venture capital, this growth was expected to come almost exclusively through the marketing of a product line. However, growth in the immediate future may also come from strategic acquisitions or other financial devices created during the rapid growth of the buyout area in an attempt to unlock the value in a relatively small company.

The Venture Capital Investor Base

As mentioned at the outset of this article, the diversity of strategies currently seen in the venture capital, or private equity, market, is not mirrored in its investor base. As banks and insurance companies have left the venture investing process, the industry has become increasingly dependent on pension funds, both public and private, for its funding. In 1991, nearly 40% of the money for venture capital funds came from pension funds. As a result of this concentrated funding power, these pension fund managers are likely to exert increasing influence over the entire venture investing process.

The only other investor category that is expected to grow in the immediate future is the endowment or foundation. Their share of the market has been expanding over the last two years, in part because other investors have been cutting back and also because they have a fundamental interest in locating investments that can provide a 4–5% real return over time for annual distributions, while keeping their capital base constant. By most accounts, the endowments believe that venture capital can meet that objective, particularly now that many of the excesses appear to have been wrung out of the system. Indeed, endowments and foundations accounted for 13% of the new funding for venture capitalists in 1990 and 23% in 1991.

However, their role as investors is likely to remain secondary to pension funds for the foreseeable future. These funds have already changed the entire nature of the fund raising procedure in the last five to ten years and are likely to exert still more influence in the future. They view venture capital as part of an amalgam of "alternative assets" that include buyout funds, real estate, and oil and gas partnerships. Venture capitalists increasingly are treated in the same way as public equity or fixed-income money managers who must be able to demonstrate histori-

cal returns and to articulate a clear investment strategy that differs from competitive plans. (See Figure 38.5.)

We already see certain instances in which these limited partners, particularly in a time of scarce funding, are seeking different types of terms from both buyouts and venture capital general partners. For instance, in some cases an investor will be granted a right of refusal to participate in certain investments that, either for financial or social reasons, do not appeal to him.

The pension fund managers at public and private retirement funds are likely to do everything possible to promote competition among venture capitalists seeking funding. They already are negotiating fees more aggressively, meeting among themselves more frequently to share information about venture capital and generally taking a more proactive approach to

Figure 38.5   The Venture Capital Investor Base 1990 and 1991

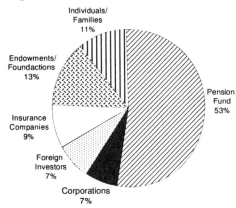

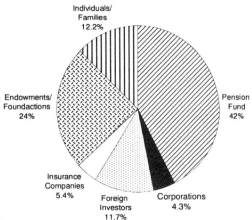

*Excludes funds of funds.
Source: Venture Economics Publishing

the venture capital process. In the cases of the larger funds, they have their own inhouse staffs that are capable of participating in private equity transactions as equals with venture capitalists.

These investors also will put greater demands on venture capitalists and other private equity practitioners to provide regularly updated material on performance and other information about venture capital. The pension funds are also creating additional demand for advisory firms, similar to those already existing in the public markets, which can help sort through all of the competing venture capital plans to isolate those funds that help the pension accomplish its own objectives.

Perhaps nowhere is the power of pension funds more apparent than in the direct investment programs currently in place at some of the largest funds. In these programs, the funds act as full coinvestors alongside venture capitalists in certain transactions. Already, state employee pension funds such as those in Alabama, California, Florida, Wisconsin and Michigan are making direct investments in companies. On the corporate side, IBM, AT&T, and General Electric, among others, are involved in the direct investment game. Although this area is likely to be restricted to the largest, most sophisticated pension funds, the new activism on the part of the pension fund industry indicates that they want to exert more control over how and where their money is invested. They also want to be treated as sophisticated investors who are the equal of anyone else involved in the transaction. Venture capitalists who fail to understand this new power are likely to have difficulty raising money in the future.

Certainly, the concentration of the investor base for venture capital is unlikely to change any time soon. One pension fund manager noted recently that public pensions, which constituted about 16% of the investor base for venture capital funds in 1991, have already earmarked somewhere between $5 billion and $9 billion for investment in venture capital, buyouts, and special situations. That money has been allocated, but has not yet been invested. That dollar figure alone, a multiple of what was raised by private equity funds in 1991, is enough to assure that the pension fund role in the industry is likely to become increasingly important, at least for the next several years.

In turn, there are fundamental reasons for these investors to be interested in venture capital and other forms of private equity in the years ahead. The United States has entered what some believe will be a relatively long period of low yields for securities such as bonds, which are a key investment category for pensions. Pension funds, which need to meet their own annual funding commitments, obviously have begun to eye private equity as an alternative to some of these lowering yielding instruments. In the last year, a number of investment strategists have begun to advise their clients that venture capital seems to be at, or close to, a market bottom and may prove to be an attractive asset class in the years ahead.

If venture capital can provide an attractive alternative to other assets, it may just be able to travel down the right performance path this time around.

Appendix

Investment Banking Firms Rankings

Table A.1 Manager Ranking: Full Credit to Book Manager

Managers	01/01/92, 09/30/92 Proceeds (mils)	Rank	Mkt. Share	# of Issues	01/01/91, 12/31/91 Proceeds (mils)	Rank	Mkt. Share	# of Issues	01/01/90, 12/31/90 Proceeds (mils)	Rank	Mkt. Share	# of Issues
Merrill Lynch & Co.	111,519.7	1	16.6	630	100,897.3	1	17.1	573	54,969.8	1	17.5	373
Goldman, Sachs	84,819.4	2	12.6	408	71,566.3	2	12.1	452	39,536.1	2	12.6	200
Lehman Brothers	79,848.3	3	11.9	374	68,378.9	3	11.6	497	19,863.7	8	6.3	116
First Boston	64,184.3	4	9.6	287	58,735.3	4	10.0	315	33,988.6	3	10.8	167
Kidder, Peabody	61,922.2	5	9.2	210	51,152.8	5	8.7	205	22,157.2	6	7.1	82
Salomon Brothers	58,781.4	6	8.7	202	46,377.9	7	7.9	198	32,774.0	4	10.4	142
Morgan Stanley	47,690.0	7	7.1	251	49,130.8	6	8.3	282	30,501.0	5	9.7	191
Bear, Stearns	42,009.3	8	6.3	132	33,651.6	8	5.7	102	20,345.5	7	6.5	61
Prudential Securities Inc.	21,637.2	9	3.2	82	17,292.7	9	2.9	75	12,612.1	9	4.0	49
Donaldson, Lufkin & Jenrette	16,708.5	10	2.5	90	11,502.1	10	1.9	70	6,369.2	10	2.0	30
PaineWebber	15,387.2	11	2.3	80	10,789.0	11	1.8	75	5,915.8	11	1.9	38
J.P. Morgan & Co. Inc.	14,911.7	12	2.2	72	10,052.0	12	1.7	75	4,170.7	14	1.3	15
Citicorp	7,864.5	13	1.2	73	4,744.5	19	0.8	26	4,178.9	13	1.3	20
Smith Barney, Harris Upham	5,872.4	14	0.9	73	6,252.8	14	1.1	69	3,694.6	15	1.2	44
Nomura Securities Co. Ltd.	5,838.6	15	0.9	20	5,596.9	15	0.9	15	3,093.7	16	1.0	14
First Tennessee Bank, N.A.	3,290.8	16	0.5	25	731.5	25	0.1	6	249.5	26	0.1	1
Daiwa Securities	3,165.5	17	0.5	11	4,769.9	18	0.8	13	36.0	50	0.0	1
Alex. Brown & Sons	2,632.6	18	0.4	44	7,315.1	13	1.2	67	2,933.7	17	0.9	33
Greenwich Capital Markets	2,568.9	19	0.4	9	5,159.3	17	0.9	17	1,496.6	20	0.5	6
Dean Witter Reynolds	1,958.5	20	0.3	22	5,546.0	16	0.9	38	4,956.3	12	1.6	21
Dillon, Read	1,783.2	21	0.3	23	1,656.1	22	0.3	21	528.4	22	0.2	9
Union Bank of Switzerland	1,643.2	22	0.2	7	2,516.9	21	0.4	7	2,812.3	18	0.9	11
Nikko Securities	1,425.4	23	0.2	4	600.6	29	0.1	2	28.2	54	0.0	4
Piper, Jaffray & Hopwood	1,223.0	24	0.2	23	1,053.8	23	0.2	21	488.9	24	0.2	19
Montgomery Securities	1,111.3	25	0.2	27	850.1	24	0.1	30	307.3	25	0.1	6
Top 25 Totals	659,797.0	-	98.2	3179	576,320.2	-	97.7	3251	308,008.2	-	98.0	1653
Industry Totals	671,968.0	-	100.0	3828	589,940.0	-	100.0	3868	314,214.3	-	100.0	1979

Source: Securities Data Corporation

Table A.2 Manager Ranking: Domestic Common: Full Credit to Book Manager

Managers	01/01/92, 09/30/92 Proceeds (mils)	Rank	Mkt. Share	# of Issues	01/01/91, 12/31/91 Proceeds (mils)	Rank	Mkt. Share	# of Issues	01/01/90, 12/31/90 Proceeds (mils)	Rank	Mkt. Share	# of Issues
Merrill Lynch & Co.	9,620.7	1	16.9	75	7,283.0	3	13.0	61	1,989.2	3	10.4	31
Goldman, Sachs	9,116.6	2	16.1	50	10,100.4	1	18.0	59	2,601.2	2	13.6	22
Morgan Stanley	6,628.4	3	11.7	43	4,063.2	5	7.3	35	883.2	8	4.6	13
Lehman Brothers	5,854.1	4	10.3	57	3,893.7	6	7.0	57	1,705.6	4	8.9	20
First Boston	3,995.3	5	7.0	36	4,260.8	4	7.6	42	923.6	7	4.8	13
PaineWebber	2,713.0	6	4.8	34	1,618.7	8	2.9	41	1,213.6	6	6.3	20
Alex. Brown & Sons	2,623.1	7	4.6	42	7,305.8	2	13.0	63	2,891.7	1	15.1	31
Prudential Securities Inc.	2,011.7	8	3.5	13	1,449.8	9	2.6	14	303.2	12	1.6	6
Smith Barney, Harris Upham	1,616.4	9	2.8	27	1,272.4	11	2.3	31	754.3	10	3.9	18
Donaldson, Lufkin & Jenrette	1,604.3	10	2.8	21	1,375.7	10	2.5	18	100.1	24	0.5	3
Dean Witter Reynolds	1,306.3	11	2.3	14	668.9	18	1.2	16	777.1	9	4.1	5
Salomon Brothers	1,217.7	12	2.1	11	3,286.1	7	5.9	32	1,655.4	5	8.6	21
Piper, Jaffray & Hopwood	1,178.7	13	2.1	15	1,027.6	13	1.8	14	231.0	14	1.2	4
Kidder, Peabody	843.6	14	1.5	19	1,221.0	12	2.2	32	400.2	11	2.1	10
Montgomery Securities	746.3	15	1.3	25	850.1	14	1.5	30	237.3	13	1.2	5
Bear, Stearns	646.6	16	1.1	16	676.5	17	1.2	13	189.0	16	1.0	4
Robertson Stephens	627.0	17	1.1	18	678.6	16	1.2	23	186.8	17	1.0	8
Hambrecht & Quist	436.5	18	0.8	16	686.7	15	1.2	21	145.7	19	0.8	7
Oppenheimer	401.0	19	0.7	11	365.9	21	0.7	10	212.5	15	1.1	9
William Blair	313.7	20	0.6	15	257.3	22	0.5	10	114.5	23	0.6	3
Dillon, Read	246.3	21	0.4	7	441.8	19	0.8	9	122.2	22	0.6	4
Kemper Securities	179.9	22	0.3	9	69.7	33	0.1	3	93.6	25	0.5	7
Stephens	150.4	23	0.3	5	59.4	37	0.1	3	91.2	26	0.5	2
Tucker Anthony	141.0	24	0.2	5	68.3	35	0.1	4	31.1	33	0.2	1
J.P. Morgan & Co. Inc.	125.4	25	0.2	1	21.3	55	0.0	1	139.5	20	0.7	3
Top 25 Totals	54,344.0	-	95.7	585	53,002.6	-	94.6	642	17,992.8	-	93.9	270
Industry Totals	56,780.8	-	100.0	810	56,012.6	-	100.0	867	19,153.3	-	100.0	402

Source: Securities Data Corporation

Table A.3 Manager Ranking: Domestic Debt: Full Credit to Book Manager

Managers	01/01/92, 09/30/92 Proceeds (mils)	Rank	Mkt. Share	# of Issues	01/01/91, 12/31/91 Proceeds (mils)	Rank	Mkt. Share	# of Issues	01/01/90, 12/31/90 Proceeds (mils)	Rank	Mkt. Share	# of Issues
Merrill Lynch & Co.	61,515.8	1	25.6	385	51,254.5	1	25.5	330	29,136.3	1	27.1	246
Goldman, Sachs	40,991.5	2	17.1	245	37,465.0	2	18.6	301	17,446.0	3	16.2	101
Lehman Brothers	33,645.6	3	14.0	193	29,685.3	3	14.8	328	6,837.8	6	6.4	38
First Boston	24,352.1	4	10.1	141	19,915.1	5	9.9	168	9,204.2	5	8.6	44
Morgan Stanley	22,505.8	5	9.4	157	24,992.7	4	12.4	174	22,796.5	2	21.2	154
Salomon Brothers	20,037.1	6	8.3	119	16,125.3	6	8.0	90	13,772.4	4	12.8	68
J.P. Morgan & Co. Inc.	7,474.4	7	3.1	48	4,678.5	8	2.3	59	437.8	11	0.4	4
Kidder, Peabody	4,871.8	8	2.0	55	5,830.4	7	2.9	79	2,367.6	7	2.2	12
Bear, Stearns	3,813.9	9	1.6	18	1,950.8	9	1.0	12	1,749.2	8	1.6	8
Donaldson, Lufkin & Jenrette	3,497.9	10	1.5	22	1,246.9	11	0.6	10	483.4	10	0.4	5
First Tennessee Bank, N. A.	3,286.0	11	1.4	23	725.0	13	0.4	3	249.5	16	0.2	1
Citicorp	1,808.0	12	0.8	56	685.7	14	0.3	12	392.4	14	0.4	10
Prudential Securities Inc.	1,669.9	13	0.7	5	544.7	17	0.3	4	323.0	15	0.3	3
PaineWebber	1,601.0	14	0.7	14	1,775.6	10	0.9	7	962.3	9	0.9	5
Smith Barney, Harris Upham	1,574.3	15	0.7	16	453.9	18	0.2	4	399.9	13	0.4	3
Dillon, Read	1,350.3	16	0.6	11	1,003.6	12	0.5	9	406.3	12	0.4	5
Union Bank of Switzerland	947.6	17	0.4	4	599.5	15	0.3	3	70.0	18	0.1	1
Bankers Trust	903.8	18	0.4	6	598.6	16	0.3	4	200.0	17	0.2	1
Industrial Bank of Japan	813.7	19	0.3	3	200.0	21	0.1	1	-	-	-	-
Nomura Securities Co. Ltd.	582.7	20	0.2	3	54.0	23	0.0	1	-	-	-	-
Lazard Houses	397.3	21	0.2	2	373.3	19	0.2	2	50.0	21	0.0	2
ScotiaMcLeod	336.1	22	0.1	2	180.0	22	0.1	1	-	-	-	-
Stephens	297.8	23	0.1	1	299.6	20	0.1	3	-	-	-	-
Dean Witter Reynolds	272.0	24	0.1	4	39.9	26	0.0	1	-	-	-	-
Norwest Investment Services	228.0	25	0.1	2	10.0	32	0.0	1	12.0	25	0.0	2
Top 25 Totals	238,774.4	-	99.5	1535	200,688.0	-	99.9	1607	107,296.6	-	99.8	713
Industry Totals	240,039.4	-	100.0	1568	200,894.7	-	100.0	1619	107,472.1	-	100.0	723

Source: Securities Data Corporation

Table A.4 Manager Ranking: Mortgage: Full Credit to Book Manager

Managers	01/01/92, 09/30/92 Proceeds (mils)	Rank	Mkt. Share	# of Issues	01/01/91, 12/31/91 Proceeds (mils)	Rank	Mkt. Share	# of Issues	01/01/90, 12/31/90 Proceeds (mils)	Rank	Mkt. Share	# of Issues
Kidder, Peabody	55,535.6	1	16.0	124	43,424.5	1	14.5	89	18,900.3	3	10.7	52
Salomon Brothers	37,197.1	2	10.7	65	25,795.3	6	8.6	67	16,816.1	6	9.5	45
Bear, Stearns	36,920.9	3	10.7	82	30,635.4	5	10.2	71	17,983.0	5	10.2	43
Lehman Brothers	36,554.5	4	10.6	90	32,296.8	4	10.7	83	10,586.9	8	6.0	44
First Boston	34,259.3	5	9.9	97	33,983.5	2	11.3	96	21,888.0	1	12.4	82
Merrill Lynch & Co.	31,621.5	6	9.1	97	32,780.7	3	10.9	114	20,322.7	2	11.5	65
Goldman, Sachs	29,846.1	7	8.6	66	19,224.4	7	6.4	61	18,383.6	4	10.4	55
Prudential Securities Inc.	17,788.0	8	5.1	60	14,989.1	8	5.0	48	11,905.4	7	6.8	35
Morgan Stanley	15,757.4	9	4.6	33	12,647.9	9	4.2	42	6,496.3	9	3.7	19
PaineWebber	10,866.2	10	3.1	26	6,927.1	11	2.3	20	3,716.7	14	2.1	10
Donaldson, Lufkin & Jenrette	10,783.8	11	3.1	40	8,841.1	10	2.9	38	5,700.7	10	3.2	20
J.P. Morgan & Co. Inc.	7,007.6	12	2.0	20	5,043.6	14	1.7	13	3,732.9	13	2.1	11
Citicorp	6,056.5	13	1.8	17	4,058.9	17	1.4	14	3,786.5	12	2.1	10
Nomura Securities Co. Ltd.	5,162.5	14	1.5	14	5,596.9	12	1.9	15	2,934.7	15	1.7	11
Daiwa Securities	3,115.5	15	0.9	10	4,769.9	15	1.6	13	595.0	20	0.3	4
Greenwich Capital Markets	2,568.9	16	0.7	9	5,159.3	13	1.7	17	1,496.6	19	0.8	6
Smith Barney, Harris Upham	1,568.7	17	0.5	6	3,520.9	18	1.2	14	1,765.3	17	1.0	9
Nikko Securities	1,425.4	18	0.4	4	600.6	21	0.2	2	187.8	22	0.1	11
The Chase Manhattan Bank, N.A.	749.1	19	0.2	1	3,297.7	19	1.1	5	498.7	21	0.3	1
Union Bank of Switzerland	695.6	20	0.2	3	1,917.5	20	0.6	4	2,812.3	16	1.6	1
Dean Witter Reynolds	183.5	21	0.1	1	4,296.7	16	1.4	15	3,984.2	11	2.3	9
Chemical Banking Corp	159.9	22	0.0	2	179.2	23	0.1	2	1,609.7	18	0.9	7
NationsBank	104.9	23	0.0	1	203.6	22	0.1	1	93.5	23	0.1	1
Inter-Regional Finance Group	75.0	24	0.0	5	55.5	25	0.0	5	62.0	24	0.0	3
Kemper Securities	42.8	25	0.0	3	160.9	24	0.1	10	21.0	27	0.0	1
Top 25 Totals	346,046.3	-	100.0	876	300,407.0	-	100.0	859	176,279.8	-	100.0	565
Industry Totals	346,056.0	-	100.0	879	300,454.7	-	100.0	866	176,362.0	-	100.0	578

Source: Securities Data Corporation

Table A.5   Manager Ranking: Domestic Convertible Debt: Full Credit to Book Manager

Managers	01/01/92, 09/30/92				01/01/91, 12/31/91				01/01/90, 12/31/90			
	Proceeds (mils)	Rank	Mkt. Share	# of Issues	Proceeds (mils)	Rank	Mkt. Share	# of Issues	Proceeds (mils)	Rank	Mkt. Share	# of Issues
First Boston	1,000.0	1	20.1	3	225.0	8	3.0	2	1,341.7	2	28.2	7
Merrill Lynch & Co.	636.7	2	12.8	5	3,418.6	1	45.7	15	2,076.6	1	43.7	8
Goldman, Sachs	490.0	3*	9.8	4	653.4	3	8.7	4	371.5	3	7.8	3
Donaldson, Lufkin & Jenrette	490.0	3*	9.8	4	545.2	4	7.3	4	60.0	11	1.3	1
Lehman Brothers	394.6	5	7.9	2	817.8	2	10.9	4	100.0	6*	2.1	1
Montgomery Securities	365.0	6	7.3	2	140.0	11	1.9	2	70.0	10	1.5	1
J.P. Morgan & Co. Inc.	300.0	7	6.0	1	325.0	6	4.3	2	100.0	6*	2.1	1
Smith Barney, Harris Upham	285.0	8	5.7	4	150.0	9	2.0	2	95.0	8	2.0	2
Bear, Stearns	275.0	9	5.5	3	147.8	10	2.0	1	200.1	4	4.2	1
Salomon Brothers	190.0	10	3.8	3	250.0	7	3.3	2	150.0	5	3.2	1
Kidder, Peabody	136.5	11	2.7	3	431.9	5	5.8	3	78.5	9	1.7	1
Wertheim/Schroder Group	100.0	12*	2.0	1	100.0	13	1.3	1	50.0	12	1.1	1
Prudential Securities Inc.	100.0	12*	2.0	1	110.0	12	1.5	2	25.0	13	0.5	1
National Westminster Bank PLC	65.0	14	1.3	1	60.0	14*	0.8	1	15.0	14	0.3	1
Robertson Stephens	50.0	15	1.0	1	60.0	14*	0.8	1	10.0	15*	0.2	1
Dillon, Read	40.0	16	0.8	1	25.0	16	0.3	1	10.0	15*	0.2	1
Morgan Keegan	30.0	17	0.6	1	15.0	17	0.2	1	1.7	17	0.0	1
American Securities	12.5	18	0.3	1	4.0	18	0.1	1	1.5	18	0.0	1
Ladenburg, Thalmann	10.0	19	0.2	1	-	-	-	-	-	-	-	-
Inter-Regional Finance Group	5.0	20	0.1	1	-	-	-	-	-	-	-	-
Top 25 Totals	4,975.3	-	100.0	43	7,478.6	-	100.0	49	4,756.5	-	100.0	34
Industry Totals	4,975.3	-	100.0	43	7,478.6	-	100.0	49	4,756.5	-	100.0	34

Source: Securities Data Corporation

Table A.6 Manager Ranking: Domestic Preferred: Full Credit to Book Manager

Managers	01/01/92, 09/30/92				01/01/91, 12/31/91				01/01/90, 12/31/90			
	Proceeds (mils)	Rank	Mkt. Share	# of Issues	Proceeds (mils)	Rank	Mkt. Share	# of Issues	Proceeds (mils)	Rank	Mkt. Share	# of Issues
Merrill Lynch & Co.	6,627.4	1	45.5	57	5,202.4	1	49.8	42	1,331.0	1	31.1	19
Lehman Brothers	3,366.1	2	23.1	29	1,293.5	2	12.4	15	585.0	3	13.7	10
Goldman, Sachs	1,758.0	3	12.1	27	875.0	4	8.4	12	510.0	4	11.9	10
Smith Barney, Harris Upham	785.0	4	5.4	12	695.0	5	6.7	13	600.0	2	14.0	9
Morgan Stanley	750.0	5	5.1	9	1,152.5	3	11.0	14	225.0	7	5.3	4
Kidder, Peabody	289.4	6	2.0	5	75.0	10	0.7	1	485.0	5	11.3	7
First Boston	270.0	7	1.9	5	15.0	14	0.1	1	4.9	12	0.1	1
Dean Witter Reynolds	180.0	8	1.2	2	480.0	6	4.6	4	125.0	8	2.9	5
Salomon Brothers	139.5	9	1.0	4	306.3	7	2.9	3	340.0	6	7.9	6
Donaldson, Lufkin & Jenrette	100.0	10	0.7	1	35.0	13	0.3	1	24.0	10	0.6	1
Stifel, Nicolaus	62.0	11	0.4	2	55.0	11*	0.5	1	10.6	11	0.2	1
Kemper Securities	60.0	12	0.4	1	55.0	11*	0.5	1	45.0	9	1.1	1
Prudential Securities Inc.	55.0	13	0.4	1	100.0	8*	1.0	2	-	-	-	-
Dillon, Read	50.0	14	0.3	1	100.0	8*	1.0	1	-	-	-	-
Lazard Houses	30.0	15	0.2	1	-	-	-	-	-	-	-	-
Legg Mason Wood Walker	25.0	16	0.2	1	-	-	-	-	-	-	-	-
Robert W. Baird	18.0	17	0.1	1	-	-	-	-	-	-	-	-
Top 25 Totals	14,565.3	-	100.0	159	10,439.7	-	100.0	111	4,285.5	-	100.0	74
Industry Totals	14,565.3	-	100.0	159	10,439.7	-	100.0	111	4,285.5	-	100.0	74

Source: Securities Data Corporation

Table A.7 Manager Ranking: Domestic Convertible Preferred: Full Credit to Book Manager

Managers	01/01/92, 09/30/92				01/01/91, 12/31/91				01/01/90, 12/31/90			
	Proceeds (mils)	Rank	Mkt. Share	# of Issues	Proceeds (mils)	Rank	Mkt. Share	# of Issues	Proceeds (mils)	Rank	Mkt. Share	# of Issues
Goldman, Sachs	2,402.3	1	37.3	6	1,850.0	2	19.6	1	37.6	5	9.2	1
Morgan Stanley	1,563.6	2	24.3	6	5,206.8	1	55.1	10	3.0	11	0.7	1
Merrill Lynch & Co.	1,400.0	3	21.7	2	738.5	3	7.8	5	40.0	3*	9.7	1
Donaldson, Lufkin & Jenrette	232.5	4	3.6	2	615.0	4	6.5	4	40.0	3*	9.7	1
Kidder, Peabody	224.4	5	3.5	1	170.0	6	1.8	1	147.2	1	35.8	3
Bear, Stearns	200.0	6	3.1	3	150.0	7	1.6	1	7.7	6	1.9	1
Keefe, Bruyette & Woods	140.0	7	2.2	2	55.3	11	0.6	2	5.0	7*	1.2	1
A. G. Edwards & Sons	61.3	8	1.0	1	130.0	8	1.4	2	-	-	-	-
Morgan Keegan	50.0	9	0.8	1	8.0	12*	0.1	1	3.6	9	0.9	1
McDonald & Company Securities	47.5	10	0.7	2	60.0	10	0.6	1	3.0	10	0.7	1
First Boston	25.0	11*	0.4	1	327.0	5	3.5	4	117.1	2	28.5	1
Dillon, Read	25.0	11*	0.4	1	100.0	9	1.1	1	1.8	12	0.4	-
Chicago Corporation	17.5	13	0.3	1	8.0	12*	0.1	1				
Stratton Oakmont Inc.	11.2	14	0.2	1	2.5	18	0.0	1				
Paulson Investment	11.0	15	0.2	1	5.0	15	0.1	1	5.0	7*	1.2	1
Wheat First Butcher & Singer	10.0	16*	0.2	1	3.7	16	0.0	1				
Interstate/Johnson Lane	10.0	16*	0.2	1	3.0	17	0.0	1	-	-	-	-
Thomas James Associates	4.6	18	0.1	1	5.5	14	0.1	1	-	-	-	-
VTR Capital, Inc	1.6	19	0.0	1	2.1	19	0.0	1	-	-	-	-
Top 25 Totals	6,437.4	-	100.0	35	9,442.1	-	100.0	41	410.9	-	100.0	14
Industry Totals	6,437.4	-	100.0	35	9,442.1	-	100.0	41	410.9	-	100.0	14

Source: Securities Data Corporation

Table A.8   Manager Ranking: Taxable Municipals: Full Credit to Book Manager

Managers	01/01/92, 09/30/92 Proceeds (mils)	Rank	Mkt. Share	# of Issues	01/01/91, 12/31/91 Proceeds (mils)	Rank	Mkt. Share	# of Issues	01/01/90, 12/31/90 Proceeds (mils)	Rank	Mkt. Share	# of Issues
Morgan Stanley	484.8	1	15.6	3	522.5	2	10.0	3	3.2	42	0.2	1
Inter-Regional Finance Group	284.0	2	9.1	4	27.5	25	0.5	9	514.0	1	29.0	20
First Boston	282.6	3	9.1	4	23.9	26	0.5	3	186.2	3	10.5	8
Goldman, Sachs	214.8	4	6.9	10	1,398.2	1	26.8	14	23.2	13	1.3	3
PaineWebber	207.0	5	6.6	6	327.6	5	6.3	5	224.2	2	12.6	5
Bear, Stearns	152.9	6	4.9	10	91.1	13	1.7	4	113.9	4	6.4	4
Merrill Lynch & Co.	97.7	7	3.1	9	219.7	6	4.2	6	60.2	8	3.4	1
George K. Baum	81.7	8	2.6	14	172.1	9	3.3	14	1.0	63	0.1	1
McDonald & Company Securities	75.0	9	2.4	1	31.0	24	0.6	1	34.0	10	1.9	1
Dillon, Read	71.7	10	2.3	2	10.6	38	0.2	3	25.0	11*	1.4	1
Whipple, Kinsell & Co Inc	51.5	11	1.7	2	9.3	42	0.2	1	7.9	25	0.4	3
Newman & Associates	43.0	12	1.4	14	147.3	10	2.8	18	80.1	7	4.5	3
Smith Barney, Harris Upham	42.8	13	1.4	8	100.5	11	1.9	4	21.4	14	1.2	3
NBD Bank NA	42.3	14	1.4	2	85.3	14	1.6	2	9.7	22	0.5	3
Miller & Schroeder Municipals	36.1	15	1.2	4	35.0	23	0.7	5	3.8	36	0.2	1
Magnus Securities	35.7	16	1.1	2	58.6	16	1.1	2	11.9	19	0.7	2
A. G. Edwards & Sons	33.9	17	1.1	3	36.0	22	0.7	9	3.5	37	0.2	1
First Midstate	33.7	18	1.1	2	54.4	18	1.0	1	1.2	60	0.1	1
Lehman Brothers	33.4	19	1.1	3	336.4	4	6.4	8	1.4	56	0.1	1
Sutro	27.8	20	0.9	1	4.3	64	0.1	1				
Banc One Capital Corporation	25.3	21	0.8	11	56.6	17	1.1	15				
Dougherty,Dawkins,Strand& Yost	25.0	22	0.8	9		57	0.1	5	0.7	68	0.0	1
Park Investment	24.1	23	0.8	10	13.0	31	0.2	10	9.5	23	0.5	7
First American Municipals Inc	21.9	24	0.7	2	16.3	29	0.3	1	8.0	24	0.5	1
Kidder, Peabody	20.9	25	0.7	3	52.0	19	1.0	1	4.2	35	0.2	1
Top 25 Totals	2,449.5	-	78.7	139	3,834.6	-	73.5	145	1,348.1	-	76.0	73
Industry Totals	3,113.7	-	100.0	334	5,217.7	-	100.0	315	1,773.9	-	100.0	154

INDEX

About the Publisher

PROBUS PUBLISHING COMPANY

Probus Publishing Company fills the informational needs of today's business professional by publishing authoritative, quality books on timely and relevant topics, including:

* Investing
* Futures/Options Trading
* Banking
* Finance
* Marketing and Sales
* Manufacturing and Project Management
* Personal Finance, Real Estate, Insurance and Estate Planning
* Entrepreneurship
* Management

Probus books are available at quantity discounts when purchased for business, educational or sales promotional use. For more information, please call the Director, Corporate/Institutional Sales at 1-800-PROBUS-1, or write:

Director, Corporate/Institutional Sales
Probus Publishing Company
1925 N. Clybourn Avenue
Chicago, Illinois 60614
FAX (312) 868-6250